MODERN MANAGERIAL ECONOMICS

ECONOMIC THEORY FOR BUSINESS DECISIONS

William F. Shughart II

*Professor of Economics
and Holder of the P.M.B. Self, William King Self,
and Henry C. Self Free Enterprise Chair
University of Mississippi*

William F. Chappell

*Associate Professor of Economics
University of Mississippi*

Rex L. Cottle

*President
Lamar University*

COLLEGE DIVISION South-Western Publishing Co.

Cincinnati Ohio

Acquisitions Editor: Jack W. Calhoun
Developmental Editor: Alice C. Denny
Production Editor: Peggy A. Williams
Production House: GEX, Inc.
Cover Design: D. Betz Design
Internal Design: Ellen Pettengell Design
Marketing Manager: Scott D. Person
Sponsoring Representative: Jan McMillan

HT60AA

Copyright © 1994

by South-Western Publishing Co.

Cincinnati, Ohio

All Rights Reserved

Library of Congress Cataloging-in-Publication Data

Shughart, William F.
   Modern managerial economics : economic theory for business decisions / by William F. Shughart II, William F. Chappell, Rex L. Cottle.
      p. cm.
   Includes bibliographical references and index,
   ISBN 0–538–81734–8
      1. Managerial economics. I. Chappell, William F., 1953–
II. Cottle, Rex L. (Rex Lee), 1947–, III. Title.
HD30.22.S53 1993
338.5'024'658—dc20   93–29632
                                                                  CIP

1 2 3 4 5 6 7 8 9 D 1 1 0 9 8 7 6 5 4 3

Printed in the United States of America

I(T)P

International Thomson Publishing
South-Western Publishing Co. is an ITP Company. The ITP trademark is used under license.

This book is printed on acid-free paper that meets Environmental Protection Agency standards for recycled paper.

To Hilary, Willie, and Frank
                        –WFS

To Donna, Heather, and Brooke
                        –WFC

To Carol, Rex, and Kyle
                        –RLC

Preface

Managerial economics is, in our view, not a course in intermediate microeconomic theory, statistics, or operations research. It is a course that applies economic principles to managerial decision-making problems. Our primary goal in writing *Modern Managerial Economics* is to show the wide range of business decisions to which economic theory can fruitfully be applied and to convey the excitement and intellectual challenge of the contemporary work being done by scholars who are actively studying the firm and the role played by managers in guiding its activities.

Over the past two decades, the theory of the firm has expanded beyond its traditional boundaries. The firm is no longer treated as a featureless "black box" characterized solely by equations for demand, production, and cost. The firm is instead defined as a rich set of contractual interrelationships among its owners, managers, customers, and suppliers. Contributions in the areas of property rights, transaction costs, and imperfect information have led to the development of the "modern" theory of the firm that stresses the importance of the organizational structure of the firm in shaping the managerial decision-making process. Although this dimension of economic theory is especially important in the study of managerial economics, it is almost completely neglected by the current stock of managerial economics textbooks. *Modern Managerial Economics* fills this gap by incorporating recent developments and integrating them with the more traditional, neo-classical theory of the firm.

The modern theory of the firm builds on the traditional theory that was initially formalized a century ago in Alfred Marshall's *Principles of Economics* (1890). The objective of profit maximization, the usefulness of marginal analysis, and the linkage between production and cost are important dimensions of the traditional theory of the firm and are equally important in this text's presentation of economic principles for managerial decision making. However, our presentation assigns a lesser role to the structural characteristics of industries than that of both the traditional theory of the firm and conventional managerial economics textbooks. Part of the reason for this is our belief that managerial economics should focus on decisions *within* the boundaries of the firm rather than on performance at the level of the industry. While the two are of course intimately related, the principal purpose of managerial economics is to demonstrate that economic theory can be applied fruitfully by managers to solve business decision-making problems in ways that are consistent with the firm's long-run survival.[1]

The traditional emphasis on market structure and ad hoc appeals to monopoly power has often limited the economic analysis of business practices. For example, advertising and promotional activities are cast in an entirely new light when the analysis is based on the relationships among imperfect information, the cost of search, full product price, and producer signaling. While economists will continue to debate the degree of competitiveness in the economy and antitrust and regulatory agencies will continue to rule on the degree of competitiveness in specific markets, management's chief concern is how the firm can remain viable in today's globally competitive market environment.

Modern Managerial Economics takes a fresh approach which is at the same time both more rigorously analytical and less quantitative than existing textbooks. Traditional topics are not neglected, but are instead presented in a streamlined fashion to allow room for emphasizing issues that managers must actually grapple with on a daily basis. The firm and the market are treated as alternative institutions for directing the allocation of scarce productive resources. The incentives and constraints that each imposes on managerial decision makers are highlighted. Such an approach allows a host of important questions to be addressed that are either ignored or given very little coverage in existing managerial economics texts. The novel topics covered range from the internal organization of the firm to "codetermination," from the financial structure of the firm to transfer pricing, and from profit strategies to managing quality.

This text is designed for upper-level undergraduate and MBA courses. Calculus is used sparingly. Statistics is limited to the working knowledge required to interpret linear regression results. Mathematical examples are developed carefully and supplemented with both verbal and graphical explanations. At the same time, appendices and footnote material are provided for instructors wishing to utilize a more mathematical approach.

"Studies in Managerial Economics" represent another unique feature of the text. These studies, which are based on the theoretical and empirical results of papers published in professional economics journals, apply, extend, and reinforce the theory; they actually teach important lessons. "Studies in Managerial Economics" provide students with a better understanding of how economic research is relevant to managerial decision making

---

1 The modern theory of the firm and its emphasis on the firm's organizational structure are equally important at the industry level. The influence of the modern theory of the firm on the field of industrial organization is presented in William F. Shughart II, *The Organization of Industry* (Homewood, IL: Richard D. Irwin, 1990).

2 A brief review of this topic is provided in the appendix to Chapter 3.

than the business-type vignettes commonly included in managerial texts that are drawn from popular sources like *Business Week*, *Fortune*, and *The Wall Street Journal*. MBA instructors may want to assign some or all of the journal articles used in these studies.

The Plan of the Book

Chapter 1 introduces the study of managerial economics by providing an overview of the historical evolution of the modern business firm. Alternative behavioral theories of the firm are discussed and the power of economic analysis is illustrated by applying it to the ethical responsibilities of business. The remainder of *Modern Managerial Economics* is organized into four parts. Part I covers the theory of the firm and is composed of five chapters. Chapter 2 presents the demand side of the market. The consumer's demand for the firm's product is derived from optimizing behavior and the important relationship between price, marginal revenue, and the elasticity of demand is derived. Neoclassical production and cost analysis are covered in Chapters 3 and 4. The theory of least-cost input combinations is applied to determine the optimal plant size in both the long run and the short run. Building on these foundations of demand and cost, Chapter 5 derives the marginal-cost-equals-marginal-revenue rule for determining the firm's profit-maximizing quantity and price. Chapter 5 then presents various alternative pricing policies for the firm, including cost-plus or markup pricing, and their relationships to marginal-cost pricing and the elasticity of demand. The discussion of marginal-cost pricing sets the stage for the material on price discrimination presented in Chapter 6.

Part II contains five chapters that focus on internal-to-the-firm managerial decisions. Chapter 7 lays out the relevant theory which treats the market and the firm as alternative institutions for guiding the allocation of scarce productive resources. The chapter addresses the basic question of why the firm emerges as an economic entity by discussing such topics as information costs, asset specialization, team production and shirking, and principal-agent problems. Chapter 8 places the firm in the context of its market environment. Chapter 9 covers advanced pricing topics. The three major issues addressed there are multi-plant production, multiple-product pricing, and transfer pricing. The last of these issues, which analyzes the pricing of resources transferred internally between the firm's operating divisions or units, is treated in some detail. A variety of advanced topics in strategic managerial decision making are presented in Chapter 10. The topics include pricing a new product, learning-by-doing, and advertising and promotional strategies. Chapter 11 then examines special issues related to choosing strategies for managing quality.

Part III focuses on the incentives and constraints imposed on managers by the organizational structure of the firm. Chapters 12 and 13 address "make-or-buy" decisions and provide a detailed analysis of the economic determinants of the scale and scope of the firm's operations. Chapter 14 focuses on the links between the firm's internal organization and the managerial decision-making process, the degree of control managers exercise over the activities of the firm, and the ability of the firm to adapt to changing market conditions. The origins of the conglomerate firm and the multinational enterprise are presented. Chapter 15 introduces topics related to the financing of the firm's operations, including debt versus equity and internal versus external financing of investment projects. Chapter 16, which ends Part III, is devoted to the unique problems associated with managing the not-for-profit firm and the labor-managed firm. Emphasis is placed on "gain-sharing" strategies and on the relationship between ownership structure, property rights, and shirking.

The book closes with Part IV, which contains two chapters that consider the politics and economics of public policies toward business. Chapter 17 sets the stage by outlining the public choice approach to analyzing governmental policy, showing how legislative and policy outcomes in a representative democracy are shaped not by the "public interest," but rather emerge through the interplay of special interest groups seeking policy favors. The book's final chapter discusses how various public policies—antitrust, environmental, and health and safety regulations—tend to be designed and implemented in a way that confers differential benefits and costs on the business sector.

Pedagogy is enhanced by organizing each chapter around an introductory application problem. A problem of appropriate difficulty is presented at the beginning of each chapter to motivate the discussion of the theory that follows. Solutions to various parts of the problem are presented as the chapter proceeds. In this way, the student is actively involved in the analysis and should gain a clearer understanding of the theoretical concepts.

We have strived for comprehensive coverage of the traditional and modern approaches to managerial economics. But in order to devote the amount of space required to develop a reasonably thorough understanding of the critical issues we think should be covered in a standard one-semester course, we have made some tradeoffs. We devote an entire chapter to the internal organization of the firm instead of discussing utility surfaces, indifference curves, and marginal rates of substitution. We provide extensive discussions of property rights, managerial shirking, and gain-sharing rather than developing the classical linear regression model from the ground up. We present material on market contracting versus ownership integration as alternative institutions for governing transactions instead of providing an extended introduction to linear programming.

In short, we have written a text aimed at future business men and women, not budding economic theoreticians. The authors are economists, though, and *Modern Managerial Economics* illustrates our belief that the unique insights offered by the economic way of thinking are essential for successful managerial decision making in the global marketplace of the 21st century.

Ancillary Materials

A study guide and an instructor's manual are made available to accompany *Modern Managerial Economics*. The study guide provides the following study aids for each chapter: a list of important terms and names, a series of questions based on the chapter outline, and multiple choice questions. The study guide also includes five empirical case studies (and a data disk) for instructors who want to place greater emphasis on this area. The instructor's manual contains a suggested reading list and three exams. For each text chapter, the manual provides an annotated chapter outline, suggested answers to all of the text end-of-chapter questions and problems, and answers to the worksheet outline questions and multiple choice questions in the study guide. Lastly, the manual provides answers to the case studies found in the study guide.

Acknowledgements

We have accumulated a large number of debts over the more than two years it has taken to make *Modern Managerial Economics* a reality. Jan McMillan, South-Western's local representative, sold us on writing the book and signing with her company. Jim Keefe shepherded the project during its early stages and offered encouragement throughout. Our developmental editor, Alice Denny, was ruthless with long sentences and even longer chapters; she deserves a great deal of credit for the final product.

Two of our colleagues, Jon Moen and Artie Powell, graciously read a number of early chapter drafts. We are especially grateful to the outside reviewers retained by South-Western. Their critical comments were especially helpful. Without holding them responsible for any remaining errors, we thank

Dale G. Bails, Iowa Wesleyan College
Dean Baim, Pepperdine University
Barbara Beliveau, University of Connecticut
David Besanko, Northwestern University
Dianne Betts, Southern Methodist University
Andrew Buck, Temple University
Robert Catlett, Emporia State University
Darius Conger, Le Moyne College
Gary D. Ferrier, Southern Methodist University
Simon Hakim, Temple University
Dean Hiebert, Illinois State University
James Henderson, Baylor University
William H. Hoyt, University of Kentucky
Robert Johnson, University of San Diego
Randall Kesselring, Arkansas State University
Jay Marchand, Westminster College
Craig J. McCann, University of South Carolina
Randy Nelson, Colby College
Robert Parsons, Brigham Young University
Carol Rankin, Xavier University
Margaret A. Ray, Texas Christian University

Steven Rock, Western Illinois University
Richard E. Romano, University of Florida
Charles E. Scott, Loyola College
Paul Seidenstat, Temple University
Steve Shmanske, California State University
William J. Simeone, Providence College
David J. Teece, University of California–Berkeley
Richard Winkelman, Arizona State University

Finally, we are indebted to our students at the University of Mississippi and Wichita State University, who suffered through manuscript chapters containing odd typesetting symbols and misplaced tables and figures. Their feedback was indispensable in helping clarify the exposition. After all, this book was written for them.

William F. Shughart II
William F. Chappell
Rex L. Cottle

Brief Table of Contents

ρ

Table of Contents

PART III THE ORGANIZATIONAL STRUCTURE OF THE FIRM 405

Introduction

OVERVIEW

This chapter introduces the study of managerial economics and the format to be followed throughout the remainder of the text. After a brief overview, each chapter begins with a boxed application problem and then presents the theoretical tools needed to solve the problem. Our goal in adopting this format is to show how useful economic theory can be in promoting profit-maximizing decision making across a wide range of practical business problems.

Chapter 1 takes a broader view than later chapters. It begins with an extended application that summarizes important developments in the evolution of the modern business firm. This historical summary describes how the structure of the modern corporation evolved to streamline information flows within the firm, to decentralize managerial decision-making authority, and to foster profit maximization.

The Introduction then describes the subject matter of managerial economics and defends the choice of profit-maximizing behavior over other behavioral theories of the firm (sales or growth maximization, for example). The chapter closes with a discussion of the optimal amount of ethical business behavior in a market economy.

"In the beginning, so to speak, there were markets."[1]

The large American business firm of the 1990s, with its complex managerial hierarchy directing the activities of thousands of employees in the manufacture, distribution, and sale of scores of products to millions of customers, evolved from modest beginnings over the past 150 years. Alfred Chandler identifies 1840 as the watershed year in this evolutionary process.[2]

Before that time, production was carried out and managed by traditional methods. The few manufacturing facilities in existence (primarily textiles and firearms producers) were small concerns. They rarely employed more than a few dozen workers. They were organized either as **sole proprietorships**, owned and operated by one person, or as closely held **partnerships.** The typical manufacturing enterprise before 1840 was much like the textbook perfectly competitive firm. The owner-manager made all of the important decisions about the production and sale of the firm's product. This individual had the time, expertise, and financial resources to run the entire enterprise. Decisions running from the purchase of raw materials through the consignment of finished goods to an independent agent who marketed the company's output to shopkeepers or to final consumers were within the owner's grasp. In short, "owners managed and managers owned."[3]

The firm took the form it did before 1840 because neither the volume of commerce nor the market's geographic scope was sufficient to warrant the adoption of more complicated business organizations. Owners had little difficulty controlling the daily activities of their firms. A fifteenth century Venetian merchant would have had no trouble understanding the managerial and record-keeping methods used by a Baltimore business in 1790.[4] These same traditional business methods continued to be used widely until well into the nineteenth century.

Emergence of the Great American Railroads

The revolution in American business organization began with the coming of the railroads.[5] The railroads played a double role in the development of the

---

1 Oliver E. Williamson, "The Modern Corporation: Origins, Evolution, Attributes," *Journal of Economic Literature* 19 (December 1981), p. 1547.

2 Alfred D. Chandler, Jr., *Strategy and Structure: Chapters in the History of the American Industrial Enterprise* (Cambridge, MA: MIT Press, 1962). Also see Alfred D. Chandler, Jr., *The Visible Hand: The Managerial Revolution in American Business* (Cambridge, MA: Harvard University Press, 1977) and Alfred D. Chandler, Jr., *Scale and Scope: The Dynamics of Industrial Capitalism* (Cambridge, MA: Harvard University Press, 1990). A concise exposition of the origins of the modern corporation, which relies partly on Chandler's work, can be found in Williamson, "Modern Corporation."

3 Chandler, *Visible Hand*, p. 9.

4 Stuart W. Bruchey, *Robert Oliver, Merchant of Baltimore, 1783-1819* (Baltimore: Johns Hopkins University Press, 1956), cited in Williamson, "Modern Corporation," p. 1551.

5 Chandler, *Visible Hand*, also credits the development of improved means of communication by telegraph and telephone (pp. 195-203), the emergence of new credit instruments and financial

modern firm. First, the westward expansion of railroad track networks that began in the 1840s required managers to adopt new organizational structures. These new organizational structures were needed to solve the complex coordination problems associated with providing "safe, regular, reliable movement of goods and passengers . . . over an extensive geographical area."[6]

Second, the low-cost, "dependable, precisely scheduled, all-weather transportation" that the railroads made widely available spurred important organizational developments in other industries.[7] Manufacturers integrated forward into product distribution to better serve the growing urban markets the railroads brought within reach. They integrated backward into extraction and processing to meet their own demands for reliable supplies of essential raw materials. The railroads promoted these developments by making it increasingly economical to tap more distant supply sources. Similarly, wholesalers acquired ownership interests in manufacturing plants and began operating their own retail outlets as a result of the steady decline in transportation costs that accompanied the expansion of the railroads.

The railroads were also the first modern firms in which it became necessary to separate ownership from control.[8] As Chandler puts it,

the capital required to build a railroad was far more than that required to purchase a plantation, a textile mill, or even a fleet of ships. Therefore, a single entrepreneur, family, or small group of associates was rarely able to own a railroad. Nor could the many stockholders or their representatives manage it. The administrative tasks were too numerous, too varied, and too complex. They required special skills and training which could only be commanded by a full-time salaried manager. Only in the raising and allocating of capital, in the setting of financial policies, and in the selection of top managers did the owners or their representatives have a real say in railroad management. On the other hand, few managers had the financial resources to own even a small percentage of the capital stock of the roads they managed.[9]

Thus, the origins of the salaried, professional manager can be traced to the railroads.

The organizational innovations introduced by the railroads were partly a response to technological demands and partly a response to the need to

---

markets (pp. 89-94 and 211-15), and the invention of continuous process machinery and manufacturing techniques (pp. 240-83) with spurring the organizational changes that began in the middle nineteenth century. In Chandler's view, however, none of these innovations was more critical than the coming of the railroads.

6 *Ibid.*, p. 87.

7 *Ibid.*, p. 86.

8 The invention of limited liability—a feature of the corporate contract that facilitated this separation—can be traced much earlier, perhaps going back as far as the mercantilist era (roughly 1500-1750). See Robert B. Ekelund, Jr. and Robert D. Tollison, *Mercantilism as a Rent-Seeking Society: Economic Regulation in Historical Perspective* (College Station: Texas A&M University Press, 1981)

9 Chandler, *Visible Hand*, p. 87.

solve increasingly complex coordination problems. Before the 1840s, the typical railroad was no more than 50 or 100 miles in length. Traffic patterns were uncomplicated because shipments were normally scheduled in only one direction on the road at a time. With a workforce of at most 50 employees, the railroad's manager—the general superintendent—had little trouble maintaining close, hands-on contact with all aspects of the business of moving passengers and goods by rail.

Expansion of the Railroads. But the promise of the railroads could only be fulfilled by increasing traffic densities and by moving goods and passengers over greater distances. Building a railroad requires large capital outlays to purchase rights of way, to lay track, to erect terminals, and to acquire locomotives and other rolling stock. Once such investments have been made, however, operating costs for fuel, labor, and maintenance of railroad capital are trivial in comparison.[10] Hence, the railroad business is characterized by sharply declining average costs. Average costs per cargo ton or per passenger mile decline substantially with increases in the volume of traffic carried and with increases in distances shipped.

The westward expansion of the railroads would have proceeded much more slowly had it not been for the heavy subsidies they received from federal, state, and local governments. This public aid, which ranged from land grants to secure rights of way to low-interest loans to tax exemptions, enabled the railroads to build new track through sparsely settled territory long before there was enough business to support it.[11]

How was this excess shipping capacity to be utilized? How could the railroads increase traffic densities to take advantage of declining average costs? The obvious answer was for one railroad to coordinate its activities with those of connecting roads to secure a greater and more constant flow of goods and passengers across its own lines. Such coordination required cooperation on three important fronts. The managers of neighboring railroads "had to arrange the physical connections of the many roads; they had to devise uniform operating, accounting, and other organizational procedures; and they had to agree on the use of a standardized technology."[12]

Linking the railroads physically was by no means a small undertaking. It took decades to accomplish and even by the Civil War, American railroads were in no sense fully interconnected: "Roads entering the same city had no direct rail connections. Roads used different gauges and different types of equipment. Therefore, cars of one railroad could not be transferred to the track of another.... [R]ailroad managers were by 1861 only beginning to develop organizational procedures to permit the movement of freight cars over the tracks of several different railroad companies."[13]

---

10 Chandler, *Visible Hand*, p. 134, reports that in the 1880s, fixed costs (i.e., those costs that did not vary with the volume of traffic carried) accounted for two-thirds of total railroad costs.

11 Clair Wilcox, *Public Policies Toward Business*, 3E. (Homewood, IL: Richard D. Irwin, 1966), pp. 386-87.

12 Chandler, *Visible Hand*, p. 124.

13 *Ibid.*, p. 122. Chandler notes that "in the early years this differentiation [in track gauges and

But the railroads eventually made these physical connections and they standardized track gauges and equipment. Much more difficult to overcome were the problems of creating uniform operating and accounting procedures. Agreements had to be reached that would establish common rates and schedules for passengers and goods moving across the lines of several connecting roads. "Ways had to be found to allocate the amount to be paid and to make the payment for that share to each of the roads involved in carrying through shipments or through passengers to their destination."[14] Such arrangements were in fact worked out, but they all soon unraveled.

Informal alliances between connecting roads were plagued by the constant pressure facing each to obtain and increase through traffic on its own lines. Because of the large amount of excess shipping capacity during the 1860s and 1870s, rate wars broke out and threatened the railroads with ruin. Competition between rival rail companies serving the same geographic territory created similar rate-cutting pressures as each sought to utilize more fully its own shipping capacity.[15]

Ownership Integration. To solve these cooperation and competition problems, the railroads turned to **ownership integration**.[16] End-to-end traffic links over heavily travelled routes were joined under common ownership. The ownership of competing rail lines was consolidated. Ownership integration resolved inter-firm conflicts concerning rate structures and shipment schedules. These mergers ushered in a period of rapid growth that, between the depression of the 1870s and the first few years of the twentieth century, established the great national railroad systems as the largest businesses in the world.

Consolidation brought with it, however, coordination problems that were much more complicated than had been faced earlier by companies that operated lines only 50 or 100 miles long. Once a railroad's end-to-end track network had grown to about 500 miles, traditional managerial methods became inadequate. No longer was it possible for one individual to give personal attention to all of the details of the railroad's operations and to make decisions in a timely manner. The larger systems that continued to rely on the same procedures that had proved comparatively successful in simpler times soon found their costs to be unacceptably high.

Managerial innovations were clearly necessary. The railroads needed new administrative structures to schedule the movement of passengers and goods and to maintain and repair their capital equipment. New managerial

---

equipment] had been made purposely so that freight shipped on a railroad sponsored by the merchants of one city could not be syphoned [*sic*] off by those of another."

14 *Ibid.*, p. 125.

15 For a discussion of the role these events played in the imposition of federal railroad rate regulation by the Interstate Commerce Commission in 1887, see William F. Shughart II, *The Organization of Industry* (Homewood, IL: Richard D. Irwin, 1990), pp. 240-42.

16 Williamson, "Modern Corporation," p. 1552. The use of ownership integration to solve problems of opportunistic behavior arising between autonomous contracting parties is discussed in Chapter 7.

hierarchies were required both to decentralize decision-making authority and to coordinate the railroads' activities over an extensive geographic area. And managers at all levels needed new accounting and statistical controls to provide access to timely information. In short, "the operational requirements of the railroads demanded the creation of the first administrative hierarchies in American business."[17]

Organization Structure and Administrative Hierarchy

New administrative structures appeared in two distinct steps. The first of these developments was the functional organization. In many industries, this type of organization subsequently gave way to the modern multidivisional firm.

Functional Organization. The structural innovation adopted and later perfected by the railroads is the line-and-staff concept of organization."[18] This structure is sometimes referred to as the *unitary* (or "U-form") type of organization. Because managerial authority in the U-form firm is divided along functional lines, we call it the **functional firm**.

Under the **line-and-staff** concept, operational ("line") and support ("staff") functions were separated. The transportation department created geographic divisions, each headed by a superintendent, to break the track system down into units of more manageable proportion. The superintendents of these geographic divisions were held accountable for the "day-to-day movement of trains and traffic" on "direct line of authority from the president through the general superintendent" to whom they reported.[19]

The transportation department's geographic divisions included other support or staff managers responsible for functions such as accounting, telegraph, traffic (passenger and freight offices), maintenance of rights of way, and purchasing. These managers reported to their divisional superintendents rather than to functional superiors at the central office. Figure 1.1 shows an organization chart for such a functional firm.

The line-and-staff concept, first put into operation by the Pennsylvania Railroad in 1857, came in time to be used by all of the major American railroad systems. The functional organization structure was successful for the railroads because it "spelled out the lines of communication and authority between the major and ancillary units within the transportation department and also between the transportation and the other major departments."[20] It allowed the general and divisional superintendents to specialize in supervising the day-to-day scheduling and operation of

---

17 Chandler, *Visible Hand*, p. 87.
18 *Ibid.*, p. 106.
19 *Ibid.*, pp. 102 and 106.
20 Chandler, *Strategy and Structure*, p. 22.

trains. Specialization permitted the superintendents to concentrate on the myriad details necessary to assure the safe, regular, and reliable movement of goods and passengers.

Freed from these responsibilities, the other top-level managers in the central office could spend more of their time working with the railroad's president to coordinate, evaluate, and plan the activities of all of the separate departments to promote the interests of the firm as a whole. With clear lines of authority and responsibility, managers at all levels were able to gather and put into use far more detailed information about the particular affairs of the road under their direction than had been possible before.

The functional structure devised by the railroads paved the way for the development of the modern business organization. Other large firms copied, adapted, and refined its principal features. But as the manufacturing giants that emerged in the petroleum, chemical, and automobile industries expanded their operations, defects in the functionally departmentalized structure became increasingly clear. These firms expanded not by supplying more of the same product to more of the same type of customer. They grew by

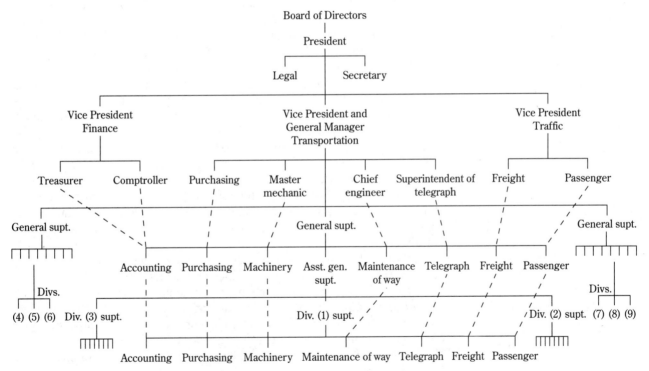

FIGURE 1.1
A Stylized Functional Railroad Organization

developing new products and new uses for existing products and by advancing into new territories. They also grew by integrating backward to acquire larger and more reliable supplies of raw materials, and by integrating forward into distribution and retailing.

These developments, which were in large part made possible by the coming of the railroads, stretched the functional organization to its breaking point. The president and the top-level managers in the central office simply could no longer cope with all of the demands placed on them in supervising such a diverse set of businesses. "The enterprise became too complex and the problems of coordination, appraisal, and policy formulation too intricate for a small number of top officers to handle both long-run, entrepreneurial, and short-run, operational, administrative activities."[21]

Multidivisional Organization. The innovation was to fashion a more decentralized decision-making structure to again free "the executives responsible for the destiny of the entire enterprise from the more operational activities, and so give them the time, information, and even psychological commitment for long-term planning and appraisal."[22] The innovators were Pierre S. du Pont and Alfred P. Sloan, the presidents of E. I. du Pont de Nemours & Company and General Motors Corporation. The organizational innovation they introduced in the early 1920s was the **multidivisional** (or "M-form") **firm.**

Figure 1.2 shows a stylized organizational chart for a multidivisional firm. A central corporate or home office is responsible for allocating resources and for evaluating and coordinating the activities of two or more semi-independent operating divisions. Each operating division (which may be set up along product, brand, or geographic lines) is in turn treated as a "profit center." The multidivisional structure might therefore be thought of as equivalent to creating "firms within the firm." Divisional managers are responsible for all of the functions related to their own products or territories—input purchasing, manufacturing, accounting, marketing, and so on. These managers are judged on the basis of the profitability of divisional operations.

Although the multidivisional structure involves some duplication of functions across divisions, it has a distinct performance-evaluation advantage over the more centralized, functional organization. In particular, it is much easier to calculate the profits of an operating division that sells a product than it is to calculate the profits of a functional division that supplies goods or services to other units of the same company.

Consider a firm that sells two related products. One way of structuring the company's operations is to establish a separate unit for each major business function. There might be a manufacturing division that is respon-

---

21 *Ibid.*, pp. 382-83.
22 *Ibid.*

sible for producing both products, a central purchasing department that acquires raw materials and transfers them to the manufacturing division, a marketing unit that sells the firm's two products, and so on. Alternatively, two separate product divisions could be created, with each division being held responsible for its own manufacturing, purchasing, and marketing.

In the first case (the functional organization), the company's top-level managers cannot easily disentangle the contributions to overall profits made by each of the firm's two products. Doing so requires allocating the common costs incurred by the various functional divisions across product lines. What share of the costs of, say the marketing unit or the accounting department, should be assigned to each product? In the second case (the multidivisional organization), by contrast, product-specific profit figures are generated naturally by each operating division.

The multidivisional firm thus "takes on many of the properties of (and is usefully regarded as) a miniature capital market."[23] By furnishing top-level

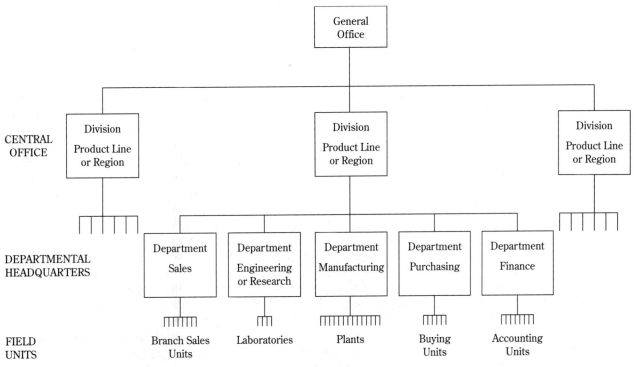

FIGURE 1.2
A Stylized Multidivisional-Form Organization

Source: Alfred D. Chandler, Jr., *Strategy and Structure: Chapters in the History of the American Industrial Enterprise* (Cambridge, MA: MIT Press, 1962), p. 10. Copyright © by Massachusetts Institute of Technology. Used by permission of the MIT Press.

---

23 Williamson, "Modern Corporation," p. 1556. Also see Oliver E. Williamson, *Markets and Hierarchies: Analysis and Antitrust Implications* (New York: Free Press, 1975), pp. 143-48.

managers with access to more and better information about the performances of the company's constituent parts, the multidivisional structure provides superior monitoring and control capabilities. Divisional profits return to the center where top managers can reallocate them to their highest-valued uses. This facilitates managerial decisions concerning which of the firm's activities should be expanded or contracted.[24]

This performance-evaluation advantage, along with the benefit of redefining lines of communication and authority to relieve the firm's top-level managers of operating duties and tactical decisions, was soon exploited. The multidivisional organization was rapidly adopted by firms as they grew in size and diversified into new products and new markets. "The multidivisional type of administrative structure, which hardly existed in 1920, had by 1960 become the accepted form of management for the most complex and diverse of American industrial enterprises."[25]

The multidivisional type of organization was not adopted universally. Growth did not present all firms with the same set of new administrative problems. Successful firms in basic industries like mining, steel, tobacco, meat, and sugar, for example, expanded largely by supplying more of the same type of product to more of the same type of customer. Their operations, though larger in scale, did not become wider in scope. Most of these firms therefore continued to rely on the more traditional, functionally departmentalized structure. But in some industries, growth came through diversification into new products and new markets or through integration into wholly new functions like manufacturing, distribution, and retailing. For those industries, the multidivisional structure offered distinct advantages.

The organizational advantages of the multidivisional firm were not simply cosmetic. They showed up on the bottom line. The multidivisional structure provided clearer lines of authority and streamlined information flows. It enabled top-level managers to specialize in strategic planning while lower-level managers specialized in tactical matters. These features reduced decision-making costs. The new structure also made it easier to evaluate the performances of the major units of the firm and to reallocate the company's cash flows to their most highly valued uses. The multidivisional structure provided managers at all levels of the organization with incentives to use resources more efficiently, that is, to behave in ways compatible with the objective of maximizing overall company profits.[26]

The prediction that adoption of the multidivisional structure should lead to higher profits has been tested using data collected on a sample of

---

24 The conglomerate and the multinational firm, two modern derivatives of the multidivisional structure, can also be usefully thought of in this way. See Williamson, "Modern Corporation," pp. 1557-63. Chapter 14 provides a detailed discussion of the firm's internal organization.

25 Chandler, *Strategy and Structure*, pp. 48-49.

26 Williamson, *Markets and Hierarchies*, p. 150.

U.S. petroleum companies over the period from 1955 to 1973.[27] In 1955, 16 percent of the firms in this sample were organized along multidivisional lines. By 1973, 78 percent of the companies had adopted the multidivisional structure. Armour and Teece found that the multidivisional firms experienced about a 30 percent initial improvement in profit over their counterparts who continued to use the more traditional functional type of organization.

As would also be expected, however, by 1973 there was no significant difference in profit performance between those petroleum companies that adopted the multidivisional structure and the other firms. This is because the earliest adopters of the multidivisional structure were firms for which the benefits of reorganization were greatest relative to the costs. The initial profit improvement experienced by these companies was then competed away over time as other petroleum firms copied the structural innovation and likewise expanded and diversified their operations. By the end of the period, competition had reduced the profits of the multidivisional companies to normal levels. At this point, their profits were equal to those of the firms for whom the costs of reorganizing were greater than the expected benefits. Not all of the petroleum companies in the sample grew at the same rate. Nor did they all integrate backward into oil exploration or forward into retailing to the same extent. The functional organization remained workable for the less diversified firms, allowing them to compete effectively with their multidivisional rivals.

It is certainly true that the functions of the firm are basically the same no matter how it is organized. However, the perspective gained by studying the evolution of the modern business firm suggests that internal organization has a powerful influence on the incentives and constraints managers face. The critical constraint is information; the important incentive is to use resources efficiently. As such, an organizational structure that is appropriate at one stage in a firm's development can prove to be wholly inappropriate at another. Modern theories of the firm increasingly stress this simple point. Innovations in organizational structure are now widely viewed as being every bit as important as technological innovations. Indeed, structural innovations may be of greater importance than technological innovations, as they enable the firm to more effectively use existing technologies and to more proficiently search for new ones.

What is Managerial Economics?

The basic idea of managerial economics is straightforward: Managers must make a wide range of business decisions that are fundamentally grounded in economic theory. Some decisions involve the firm's relations with outsiders—

---

27 Henry O. Armour and David J. Teece, "Organization Structure and Economic Performance: A Test of the Multidivisional Hypothesis," *Bell Journal of Economics* 9 (Spring 1978), pp. 106-22.

customers, suppliers, dealers, and rivals. For example, the manager must determine the combination of selling price and quality performance that best satisfies buyers' demands. He or she must secure timely, reliable deliveries of raw materials. Incentives for retailers to supply optimal sales effort in the firm's behalf must be created. And the manager must stand ready to respond to a competitor's price cut or to a rival's introduction of a new product or a new, aggressive advertising campaign.

Another set of managerial decisions involves the allocation of resources within the firm's existing organization. Which activities of the firm should be expanded and which curtailed? How should the firm's wage and benefit package be tailored to enhance labor productivity? Should a promising investment project be financed by issuing new stock or should the funds be borrowed? What charges should be made against the internal budgets of the manufacturing division and the billing department, both of which use the company's central computing facility?

A third useful classification of business decisions is between **tactical decisions** and **strategic decisions.** Tactical decisions involve matters of shorter-term consequence. Strategic decisions affect the future direction of the entire enterprise. A manager's response to a competitor's aggressive price-cutting campaign is a tactical decision. One option is to match the price cut. A second, less-obvious option is to institute price cuts selectively by issuing cents-off coupons that will be redeemed by some buyers. A longer-term, strategic decision is illustrated by a firm that considers expanding its operations overseas. There are at least three ways that this expansion can be undertaken. First, the firm can simply export goods produced domestically to the foreign market. Second, the firm can license its product or production technology to an existing foreign firm. Third, a new production facility can be built overseas or an established foreign producer can be acquired.

The decisions that affect the firm's external relationships, its internal operations, and its short- and long-term goals must be made alongside the more routine managerial duties of supervising the daily activities of a modern business enterprise. Coordinating the every day activities of people, money, and equipment provides its own set of challenges.

Some managerial decisions can be made with the aid of objective, numerical computations. With the proper information, comparing the profitability effects of a simple price reduction versus selective price cutting with coupons is a straightforward exercise. On the other hand, how will managers evaluate the tradeoffs between licensing a technology transfer versus direct overseas investment? This decision will rely at least as much on theory and intuition as it will on precise measurement and rote computation. Managerial economics equips the manager to handle both types of problems by supplying a collection of concepts and tools—and more importantly, a way of thinking—that can be useful in analyzing and understanding the broad range of problems that shape the manager's role in modern business enterprises.

Managerial economics is more closely related to microeconomic theory than it is to macroeconomic theory. **Macroeconomics** is the study of the economy as a whole. The total output of goods and services produced in the economy, the aggregate level of employment, and the rate of inflation are macroeconomic topics. **Microeconomics** narrows the focus to the individual markets within the larger macroeconomy. The analysis of demand and supply in specific markets—hamburgers, compact discs, and steel, for example—is the central concern of microeconomic theory.

The topical focus is narrowed once again in the transition from microeconomics to **managerial economics.** Microeconomic analysis concentrates on the behavior of all firms in an industry, while managerial economics concentrates on the behavior of a single firm within that industry. Indeed, modern approaches to managerial economics narrow the focus even further by adopting as the unit of analysis each of the separable transactions that comprise the activities of the firm. Each of these transactions—the acquisition of an input, the purchase or lease of capital equipment, the delivery of a customer's order, and so on—becomes an element from which the boundaries of the firm are derived piece by piece.

Managerial economics also differs from microeconomics by dealing with complications typically assumed away or glossed over in studying the pure theory of the firm and the market. Among these complications are imperfect information, product differentiation, transactions costs, ownership integration, innovation, and the separation of ownership from control in the modern corporation. Microeconomic theory also assumes away a whole host of real-world business practices such as advertising, warranties, incentive pay, mergers and acquisitions, franchising, joint ventures, and resale price maintenance. Rather than ignoring these and other rich features of the modern business firm, managerial economics makes them the center of attention.

Obviously, managerial decisions do not take place in a vacuum. The manager's choices are limited at every turn by consumers, by technology, by cost, and by governmental policies of all sorts. A basic understanding of the economic and political environments in which the firm operates is critical to the survival and growth of the business organization. Although it does not replace the valuable insights and experience that successful managers apply to business decision-making problems, managerial economics identifies the critical factors that must be recognized in making these choices.

THE PROFIT-MAXIMIZATION ASSUMPTION

In analyzing a broad range of managerial decision-making problems, this text assumes that the goal of **profit maximization** guides managerial choices. However, a fundamental question must be asked: Do firms in fact strive to maximize profits? There is an important debate about whether the goal of profit maximization adequately describes the basis upon which managerial choices are actually made.

One standard criticism is that profit maximization only considers the short-run rather than the long-run implications of business decisions. The objective of long-run profit maximization is equivalent to maximizing the present value of the firm. The present value of the firm, in turn, is equal to the discounted value of the anticipated future stream of profits generated by the firm's business activities. That is,

$$VALUE = \frac{\pi_1}{(1+i_1)} + \frac{\pi_2}{(1+i_2)^2} + \frac{\pi_3}{(1+i_3)^3} + \dots = \sum_{n=1}^{\infty} \left[\frac{\pi_n}{(1+i_n)^n} \right].$$

π_n is the profit or net cash flow expected to be earned in any future period. It is simply the difference between total revenue and total cost (i.e., $\pi_n = TR_n - TC_n$). The variable i_n is the interest rate chosen for discounting the future net cash flows expected in period n.[28]

The market value of a firm is represented by the price of its publicly traded stock or by the price an investor would be willing to pay for an ownership position in a privately held enterprise. If capital markets are efficient, the market value will fully reflect "the present value of the firm's expected future net cash flows, including expected cash flows from future investment opportunities."[29] In other words, the current market price of a company's stock is equal to the present value of the firm divided by the number of outstanding shares. The present value of the firm, in turn, incorporates all relevant, publicly available information about the firm's expected future net cash flows. As such, the **efficient-markets hypothesis** contends that stock prices adjust quickly to any "news" about the firm's prospects.

The efficient-markets hypothesis has several important implications about the objectives that guide managerial decisions. First, managers need not choose between maximizing long-run profits, maximizing the value of the firm, or maximizing stockholders' (owners') wealth. These three goals are identical.[30] Second, managers have nothing to gain from trying to manipulate earnings per share. Decisions that increase earnings but do not affect profits will have no impact on the value of the firm. Finally,

---

28 The concepts of present values and discounting are discussed more fully in Chapter 15. For our purposes here, it is sufficient to recognize that $1 received in the future is worth less than $1 received today because $1 today can be invested at some rate of interest, say 10%, to yield $1.10 one year hence. Thus, $1 is the present value of $1.10 in profit received one year from today to a firm facing a 10 percent cost of capital.

29 Clifford W. Smith, Jr., "The Theory of Corporate Finance: A Historical Overview," in Clifford W. Smith, Jr., ed., *The Modern Theory of Corporate Finance*, 2E. (New York: McGraw-Hill, 1990), p. 5

30 It is worth stressing that the goal of maximizing owners' wealth is *not* the same as maximizing the market price per share of the firm's stock. The latter depends both on aggregate value and the number of outstanding shares which, of course, is subject to change. For example, other things being the same, a two-for-one stock split cuts the market price per share in half. Neither the total value of the firm nor stockholders' wealth is affected by this transaction, however.

if stock prices provide an unbiased estimate of future net cash flows, managers will *not* have a time horizon that is "too short."[31]

The basis for this last conclusion is that if a manager chooses to invest the firm's resources in a project that promises short-run gains but long-run losses, that decision will cause the market value of the firm to fall. On the other hand, investing in a project that pays off in the long run will increase the market value of the firm even if the project generates losses in the short run.

Consider the two hypothetical investment opportunities shown in Figure 1.3. Investment A generates positive profits in the near term, but at some point in the future the project turns sour and losses are sustained. Investment B, by contrast, entails large costs up front but generates significant profits once the project comes to fruition. Project A might represent the expected net cash flows to the production and sale of a product like the Ford Pinto having a known design defect. Project B might be an investment in basic research and development.[32]

A myopic manager interested only in short-run profits might be tempted to forego investing in project B in favor of project A because A's profits begin

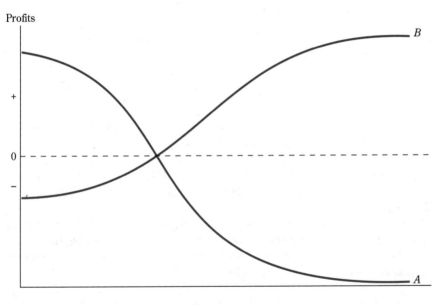

FIGURE 1.3
Expected Future Net Cash Flows to Two Hypothetical Investments

31 Smith, "Theory of Corporate Finance," p.5.
32 The two profit streams in Figure 1.3 are drawn assuming a market interest rate at which investment A has a negative expected present value (the discounted value of the future losses on the project more than offset the short-run gains) and investment B has a positive expected present value (discounted future profits more than offset the short-run losses). Alternative rules for selecting investment projects are discussed in Chapter 15.

accruing earlier and its losses do not show up until later. But the market will penalize such a decision. Regardless of the time shape of cash flows associated with it, investing in project A will cause the value of the firm to fall because the project has a negative expected net present value. According to the efficient-markets hypothesis, this reduction in market value will be reflected in a lower price per share for the company's stock. Investing in project B, on the other hand, will increase the firm's market value (and stock price) because the project has a positive expected net present value. In short, the capital market forces managers to adopt a long-run perspective when making investment decisions for the owners of the firm. Thus, the terms profit maximization, value maximization, and shareholder-wealth maximization are used interchangeably in this text.

NON-VALUE-MAXIMIZING MODELS OF THE FIRM

More serious objections to the profit-maximization assumption come from critics who argue that managerial decision making may be guided by other objectives. Non-value-maximizing behavior might include the objectives of maximizing sales growth or market share. **"Satisficing"** behavior, the pursuit of multiple goals consistent with the long-run survival of the firm, has also been attributed to corporate management.

Maximization of Sales Growth or Market Share

Edith Penrose is one critic of the profit-maximization assumption adopted by economists. She has argued that managers are interested more in growth than value because individuals in managerial positions "gain prestige, personal satisfaction in the successful growth of the firm with which they are connected, more responsible and better paid positions, and wider scope for their ambitions and abilities."[33]

Similarly, William Baumol has proposed a model in which the managers of the firm strive to maximize total revenue subject to the constraint that "profits do not fall short of some minimum level which is just on the borderline of acceptability" (to stockholders). He suggests that

> such a goal may perhaps be explained by the businessman's desire to maintain his competitive position, which is partly dependent on the sheer size of his enterprise, or it may be a matter of the interests of management (as distinguished from shareholders), since management's salaries may be related more

---

[33] Edith Penrose, *The Theory of the Growth of the Firm* (Oxford: Basil Blackwell and Mott, 1959), p. 242. Also see Robert N. Anthony, "The Trouble with Profit Maximization," *Harvard Business Review* 38 (November-December 1960), pp. 126-34.

closely to the size of the firm's operations than to its profits, or it may simply be a matter of prestige.[34]

There is, in fact, some limited empirical evidence supporting these non-value-maximizing models of managerial behavior. One group of researchers investigated the correlations among managers' compensation, sales, and profits. The findings suggested a positive and significant relationship between sales and the pay of top-level managers, but no such relationship was found when profits were used as a performance measure.[35] However, other studies have reported evidence that profits and market values are more important than sales in determining managerial compensation.[36]

The issues raised by the models of sales, growth, or market-share maximization point to the separation of ownership from control that characterizes the modern corporation. It was long ago observed that the owners of large business enterprises are numerous and dispersed. Rarely does any one of them control enough shares or have enough expertise to justify taking an interest in the day-to-day operations of the firm. The stockholders therefore delegate decision-making authority to managers whose specialized business knowledge enables them to make more profitable use of the firm's resources.

---

34 William J. Baumol, *Economic Theory and Operations Analysis*, 4E. (Englewood Cliffs, NJ: Prentice-Hall, 1977), p. 378. These sales-, growth-, and market-share maximization models of the private, for-profit firm are closely related to the objectives that have been attributed to individuals (bureaucrats) who manage public, not-for-profit organizations. See, for example, Anthony Downs, *Inside Bureaucracy* (Boston: Little, Brown, 1967) (bureaucrats have multiple goals, including power, prestige, income, convenience, security, loyalty, pride in excellent work, commitment to a program, and desire to serve the public interest); William A. Niskanen, *Bureaucracy and Representative Government* (Chicago: Aldine, 1971) (bureaucrats attempt to maximize their agency's total budget); Gordon Tullock, *The Politics of Bureaucracy* (Washington, D.C.: Public Affairs Press, 1965) (bureaucrats are motivated by a desire for career advancement); and R. Douglas Arnold, *Congress and the Bureaucracy: A Theory of Influence* (New Haven, CT: Yale University Press, 1979) (bureaucrats seek budgetary security, budgetary growth, and the serving of their own conception of the public interest).

35 Joseph W. McGuire, John Y. S. Chu, and Alvar O. Ebing, "Executive Incomes, Sales, and Profits," *American Economic Review* 52 (September 1962), p. 760. Also see Arch Patton, "Deterioration in Top Executive Pay," *Harvard Business Review* 43 (November-December 1965), pp. 106-18.

36 William G. Lewellen and Blaine Huntsman, "Managerial Pay and Performance," *American Economic Review* 60 (September 1970), pp. 710-20. More recently, Roger L. Faith, Richard S. Higgins, and Robert D. Tollison, "Managerial Rents and Outside Recruitment in the Coasian Firm," *American Economic Review* 74 (September 1984), pp. 660-72, report evidence from a sample of *Forbes'* 500 companies suggesting that while both firm size (sales) and short-run performance (measured as average rates of return on equity) have a positive and statistically significant effect on the pay of chief executive officers, sales have a larger impact on compensation at the margin than does performance. Some additional evidence on this issue is discussed below.

At the same time, however, the managers' superior knowledge (information) gives them some discretion in guiding the firm's resources that they may use to further their own self-interests rather than those of the owners at large. Some managers may fail to maximize stockholder wealth by, for example, neglecting detail, avoiding risk, and excessively consuming on-the-job amenities and perquisites of office.[37]

One may well ask, then, why do millions of stockholders willingly turn over a portion of their wealth to small groups of managers who have so little regard for the owners' welfare?[38] One answer is that the discretionary behavior of managers is disciplined by market forces. Another answer is that the corporate form of ownership provides advantages to stockholders that more than offset the costs associated with their diminished control. Without denying that managers have discretion to pursue goals other than value maximization, modern theories of the firm increasingly focus on the actions that both parties can take to bring managers' objectives more in line with those of stockholders.[39]

Satisficing Behavior

Another challenge to the value-maximization hypothesis of managerial behavior is the possibility of satisficing behavior. Because managers operate in a world of imperfect information, they may not always explicitly try to find the optimal solution to any particular objective function.[40] Without the precise knowledge of demand and cost that is required for profit maximization, managers may "satisfice" rather than maximize. They may seek acceptable levels of performance, or minimal standards of achievement, that are consistent with the firm's long-run survival.

In this theory, managers have multiple goals and use a variety of decision-making rules. The firm

> solves problems in each of its decision areas more or less independently; it searches for solutions in a manner learned from experience; it adjusts its decision rules on the basis of feedback or experience. Decisions on price, output,

---

37 Adolf A. Berle and Gardiner C. Means, *The Modern Corporation and Private Property* (New York: Macmillan, 1932). Berle and Means' basic criticism of the corporation was restated recently in Gardiner C. Means, "Corporate Power in the Marketplace," *Journal of Law and Economics* 26 (June 1983), pp. 467-85.

38 Armen A. Alchian, "Corporate Management and Property Rights," in Henry Manne, ed., *Economic Policy and the Regulation of Corporate Securities* (Washington, D.C.: American Enterprise Institute, 1969), p. 337.

39 See Michael C. Jensen and William H. Meckling, "Theory of the Firm: Managerial Behavior, Agency Costs, and Ownership Structure," *Journal of Financial Economics* 3 (1976), pp. 305-60. The theory of principal-agent relationships is discussed in Chapter 7.

40 Kalman J. Cohen and Richard M. Cyert, *Theory of the Firm*, 2E. (Englewood Cliffs, NJ: Prentice-Hall, 1975). Also see Richard M. Cyert and James G. March, *A Behavioral Theory of the Firm* (Englewood Cliffs, NJ: Prentice-Hall, 1963).

and sales strategy are made on the basis of profit, inventory, production-smoothing, sales, market share and competitive position goals.[41]

Economist Richard Day provided an important insight into this issue by formulating a simple learning model. In his model, the traditional profit-maximization result generated by equating marginal revenue and marginal cost emerges from managerial satisficing behavior.[42] The significance of Day's point is that the harsh information requirements usually associated with finding optimal solutions to managerial decision-making problems are not necessary. That is, Day argues that the firm's performance will converge toward a profit maximum even in the extreme case where its managers operate in complete ignorance of their revenue and cost functions.

In Day's model, managerial decision making is governed by two simple principles:

1. Successful behavior should be repeated and unsuccessful behavior avoided.
2. If a change in circumstances indicates that previously unsuccessful behavior should be repeated, its use should be approached with caution.

Specifically, given information about changes in output and profit in the past period, Day's satisficing manager chooses the next period's output. The current production decision is one of increasing, decreasing, or leaving unchanged the quantity of output produced last period. The choice is based on the observable profit outcome from the previous decision.

This simple feedback mechanism implies that success is defined by results, not by motivation.[43] It highlights the importance of uncertainty in the firm's economic environment. The managerial decision-making process is treated as partly a matter of adaptation or imitation and partly a matter of trial and error. Day's two behavior principles lead to equally straightforward decision rules. Past expansions or contractions in output that result in increased profit should be repeated. If, however, output was expanded (contracted) in the previous period and profit fell, then output should be contracted (expanded) in the next period. Finally, output changes that lead to decreased profit should induce caution. For example, if output is contracted in response to an unsuccessful expansion in the last period, the next output expansion should be smaller. (These relationships are summarized in Table 1.1.)

---

41 Cyert and March, *Behavioral Theory of the Firm*, p. 182.
42 Richard H. Day, "Profits, Learning, and the Convergence of Satisficing to Marginalism," *Quarterly Journal of Economics* 81 (May 1967), pp. 302-11.
43 See Armen A. Alchian, "Uncertainty, Evolution, and Economic Theory," *Journal of Political Economy* 58 (June 1950), pp. 211-21.

TABLE 1.1 "SATISFICING" FEEDBACK RULES

	Observed Consequence of Past Behavior	
PAST BEHAVIOR	INCREASE IN PROFIT	DECREASE IN PROFIT
Expanded output	Expand output again.	Contract output. Be more cautious in next expansion.
Contracted output	Contract output again.	Expand output. Be more cautious in next contraction.

The trial-and-error strategy does not guarantee that the firm's performance will converge to the global profit maximum. In a later paper, Day and Tinney showed that the effectiveness of behavioral decision rules depend on the values of various parameters in the manager's "learning function." Some types of decision makers (who are too cautious and overreact to losses) may converge to a suboptimum. Others (who are too daring and underreact to losses) may "wander," converging only after an extended period of time and then also possibly to a suboptimal solution.[44]

Based on evidence from computer simulations, however, Day and Tinney concluded that the feedback strategy "will work tolerably well for almost all environments, . . . even though for any given one it may not produce uniformly superior results when compared with alternative models." Thus, an unstable economic environment only delays convergence to profit maximization. So long as the manager contracts output in response to a fall in profit and expands output when profit has risen, satisficing can approach profit maximization in the limit. In fact, managerial decision making will generally involve a search for the location of an ever changing optimum.

The empirical significance of these simple feedback rules has been investigated using a random sample of 107 firms drawn from the 500 largest companies listed by *Forbes Magazine* each year from 1972 through 1982.[45] After calculating year-to-year changes in output and profit, the researchers observed behavior consistent with Day's rules nearly 63 percent of the time. Moreover, the managers in the sample who followed the feedback rules experienced a higher proportion of successful outcomes. In particular, Day-type behavior was successful (led to increased profit) in almost 70 percent of the cases. Managers following other decision rules experienced increased profit only half the time.[46]

---

44 Richard H. Day and E. Herbert Tinney, "How to Co-operate in Business without Really Trying: A Learning Model of Decentralized Decision Making," *Journal of Political Economy* 67 (July-August 1969), pp. 583-600.

45 W. Mark Crain, William F. Shughart II, and Robert D. Tollison, "The Convergence of Satisficing to Marginalism: An Empirical Test," *Journal of Economic Behavior and Organization* 5 (1984), pp. 375-85.

46 *Ibid.*, p. 380. There was also evidence of an asymmetry in managerial "learning functions" in the sense that decision makers seemed to be more daring in the face of unsuccessful output expansions than in the case of unsuccessful contractions.

The researchers also investigated whether managerial compensation was tied to the decision rules they adopted. The empirical results suggested that the chief executive officers were rewarded with salary increases if their decisions led to increased profits. The particular decision rule used by managers did not affect their reward for successful performance, however. That is, while successful satisficers experienced salary increases, managers following other successful strategies also received financial rewards. By contrast, those unsuccessful managers whose output decisions led to lower profit were not rewarded even if they behaved according to Day's feedback rules.[47]

In sum, the evidence drawn from a sample comprised of the largest U.S. firms appears consistent with the idea that managerial decision making can be characterized as adaptive. More importantly, however, such satisficing behavior tends to move firms in the direction of profit maximization. Of course, the question of convergence to the unique marginal-cost-equals-marginal-revenue optimum remains open. But the data generated by actual managerial decision making in the economy leads to the conclusion that satisficing and profit-maximization are more coincident than the critics of the profit-maximization assumption have argued. Thus, the emphasis *Modern Managerial Economics* places on the objectives of profit-, value-, or shareholder-wealth maximization is compatible with how managers actually seem to make a wide range of business decisions.

Economic theory supplies a powerful set of tools for guiding managers to the goal of profit maximization. It does so by developing a set of pricing and output rules that leads to this objective. It provides models for analyzing the behavior of consumers, the costs of production, the reactions of rivals, and government policies that limit managers' choices. And it reveals the weaknesses of some popular business practices (like mark-up pricing) whose use can jeopardize the firm's long-run survival. The manager who understands the lessons of economic theory is better equipped to deal with the ever-changing environment in which he or she is required to operate.

ETHICS AND ECONOMICS

In a market-based economic system, profit-maximizing firms play a fundamental role in the allocation of scarce productive resources. They determine what will be produced and what will not be produced in response to the demands of consumers. The role of profit-driven, self-interest-seeking behavior in promoting effort and efficiency in a market economy is well-known. It is a role whose importance is appreciated by all who have witnessed the collapse of the Soviet Union's economy. The absence of market-based price and profit signals leads to waste, shortages, and corruption on the part of public officials who hold authority to dictate how society's resources will be employed.

---

47 *Ibid.*

The Economics of Snow Shovels

Consider a local hardware store that sells snow shovels for $15 each. The morning after a heavy snowstorm, the store's owner raises the price to $20.[a]

Such behavior would undoubtedly be considered grossly unfair by large numbers of people.[b] Angry charges of "gouging" and "profiteering" are common reactions to price increases announced in the wake of "killer storms" and other natural disasters. While such reactions are certainly understandable, they fail to appreciate the role of prices and profits in a market economy. Charging a higher price for snow shovels helps assure that shovels are purchased only by those customers who value them most highly. This limits the strain on available inventories.

The price increase also represents a signal that snow shovels have become more valuable in the area affected by the storm. The higher price (and higher profit margin) of snow shovels, in turn, provides incentives for the store's owner to obtain rush-order supplies of additional shovels from wholesalers. Hardware store owners in outlying areas unaffected by the storm can likewise take advantage of the situation by shipping additional shovels to the snowbound city. In the process, of course, the number of available snow shovels is increased. This enables the local residents to dig out from under the storm sooner.

Another option is for the hardware store's owner to continue charging the pre-storm price of $15. In this case, the existing stock of snow shovels will be depleted more quickly and there will be less incentive to order more of them. Moreover, the quantity of snow shovels the store's customers wish to buy exceeds the number available for sale at $15. An alternate method of rationing the shovels must therefore be found. Perhaps selling snow shovels on a "first-come-first-served" basis might be considered fair. But this rationing scheme risks violating commonly accepted standards of equity as well. Suppose that an early rising retiree buys the last available shovel and a practicing physician cannot get out of his driveway to treat seriously ill patients that day. Is this outcome more fair than raising the price of snow shovels to a level that the physician is willing to pay but the retiree, who presumably has a less pressing desire to clear his driveway, is not? Is it more unfair for the hardware store's owner to charge the physician $20 for a snow shovel than it would be for the fortunate retiree to buy one for $15 and resell it to someone else at a higher price?

The fable of the snow shovels illustrates that while the market may not always be "fair," it does perform a valuable function, namely helping reallocate resources to their most highly valued uses. The hardware store's owner personally benefits from raising the price of snow shovels. But so do the local residents who in short order will be able to obtain more shovels than would have been available had the price remained at its pre-storm level. This is the "invisible hand" of the market at work. In responding to price and profit signals generated by a freely functioning marketplace, people do well by doing good.

a This scenario is adapted from a survey question administered to a random sample of adults in Toronto and Vancouver by Daniel Kahneman, Jack Knetsch, and Richard Thaler, "Fairness as a Constraint on Profit Seeking," *American Economic Review* 76 (September 1986), pp. 728-41. An analysis of the responses of a random sample of business executives to this and similar questions is reported in Raymond F. Gorman and James B. Kehr, "Fairness as a Constraint on Profit Seeking: Comment," *American Economic Review* 82 (March 1992), pp. 355-58.

b In fact, 82 percent of the Canadian adults and 71 percent of the business executives surveyed considered the action unfair. See Gorman and Kehr, "Fairness as a Constraint on Profit Seeking: Comment," p. 357

On the other hand, unethical and illegal behavior does occur in a market system, as it does in all other economic systems where human beings interact. Managers and stockbrokers occasionally trade on "inside information," thereby profiting at the expense of shareholders. Employees sometimes pilfer company tools and supplies for their own use. Customers shoplift. Plants and offices close with often devastating effects on workers and the local economy. Firms sometimes sell shoddy products or make misleading advertising claims. Does the objective of profit maximization lead firms to ignore their social responsibilities? Is ethical behavior inconsistent with profit maximization?

Although the answers to these important questions might be best left to moral philosophers, economic theory can provide some insights into the ethics of the market. First, limiting undesirable or socially irresponsible behavior consumes resources that could have been used elsewhere. Therefore, there is an optimal amount of unethical behavior that society will tolerate. This optimal amount of unethical behavior is not zero. Rather, the optimal amount of such behavior is the amount at which the marginal benefit and marginal cost of reducing it are in balance.

For example, consider the problem of disposing of the toxic wastes that are the byproducts of many manufacturing processes. Disposed of improperly, these toxic wastes pollute groundwater, harm wildlife, damage crops, and impair the health of the people exposed to them. But proper disposal is costly to the firm and illegal dumping may be economically rational. Whether it is so depends on the chances of being caught, the size of the fine if convicted, and the cost savings realized by disposing toxic wastes improperly.

One lesson of economic theory is that society must make a similar cost-benefit calculation. While improper disposal of toxic wastes is certainly harmful to the environment, it will never pay to stop such behavior completely. Doing so would demand massive expenditures of resources to enforce the relevant environmental protection laws. At the extreme, enforcement personnel would be posted at every potential polluter's back door and at every possible illegal dump site. Resources used for law enforcement would be diverted from other valuable uses. Fewer public resources would accordingly be available for supporting medical research, for training air traffic controllers, for financing public education, for repairing highways, and so on. In short, it is simply not worth spending more than $1 to prevent $1 worth of environmental damage from the improper disposal of toxic wastes.

A second lesson of economic theory is that market forces discipline unethical behavior on the part of profit-maximizing firms. Revelations of socially irresponsible practices like producing defective or harmful products, making misleading or unsubstantiated advertising claims, or maintaining an unsafe workplace damage a firm's most valuable asset—its reputation. Lost goodwill translates into lost customers, smaller profits, and lower market values. The managers of profit-maximizing firms consequently have incentives to limit irresponsible behavior to avoid the penalties the market will impose on them.

Social Responsibility and Corporate Giving

An important issue in the study of managerial economics is the social role played by the profit-maximizing behavior of firms in a competitive economic system. American corporations contribute billions of dollars every year to charitable organizations. Are charitable donations consistent with profit-maximization? Or are they evidence of social goals of firms that transcend the profit-maximizing model of firm behavior?

To answer this question, Peter Navarro developed an empirical model of the determinants of corporate contributions to charity.[a] The variables that explain corporate giving in his model are divided into two categories. One category includes variables that are derived from the profit motive for corporate giving. The other includes variables that reflect managerial discretion that is exercised at the expense of stockholders' interests.

Giving can increase the profits of a firm by either increasing revenue or reducing costs. Charitable contributions can increase revenue if charitable contributions are used as part of the firm's overall advertising strategy for promoting its products or image. Navarro used two variables to capture the effect of charitable giving on the firm's revenues. The first variable, advertising expenditures, is a measure of a firm's reliance on advertising as a marketing tool. Corporate giving will be positively related to advertising intensity if both advertising and giving can be used as marketing tools. The second variable, the firm's price-cost margin, is defined as

$$\text{price-cost margin} = (\text{price} - \text{marginal cost})/\text{price}.$$

Marginal cost represents the cost of the last unit produced.[b] The price-cost margin is therefore a measure of the firm's markup and reflects the sensitivity of sales to price changes. A high price-cost margin characterizes products that are relatively price insensitive. A low price-cost margin characterizes products that are relatively price sensitive.[c] The revenue increasing effect of giving-as-advertising increases as the price-cost margin increases. Hence, corporate giving should be positively related to price-cost margins.

According to Navarro, corporate giving can also reduce costs. For example: Workers consider the social characteristics of a community (crime, pollution, cultural amenities) when they choose among employment opportunities. Therefore, corporate contributions that enhance the community's quality of life can aid the firm in attracting employees. The labor-attracting motive for giving led Navarro to include another variable, labor intensity, as a determinant of corporate giving. Navarro expected a positive relationship between corporate giving and labor intensity.

On the other hand, Navarro noted that corporate charity that improves a community's quality of life will benefit all firms in the community, not just those that do the giving. The more firms there are in a community, the greater the tendency for firms to free ride on the generosity of others. This effect is measured by the number of firms operating in a firm's SMSA.[d] The expected sign is negative.

As a final cost variable, Navarro included a variable that accounts for changes in the federal budget during President Reagan's administration. Navarro argued that decreased spending on social programs during the Reagan years could have caused corporate giving to increase. Why? Because corporate giving would have a larger impact when federal social spending is reduced.

The profit-maximizing motive for giving led Navarro to include advertising expenditure, price-cost margin,

a Peter Navarro, "Why Do Corporations Give to Charity?" *Journal of Business* 61 (1988), pp. 65-93.
b Marginal cost is defined formally in Chapter 3.
c The sensitivity of consumers to a change in price (the price elasticity of demand) is defined in Chapter 2. The use (and misuse) of markup pricing is discussed in Chapter 5.
d Standard Metropolitan Statistical Areas (SMSAs) are population-based urban localities defined by the Department of Commerce for data collection purposes.

labor intensity, number of firms in the community, and federal social spending as determinants of corporate giving. Alternatively, the separation of ownership and management in modern corporations might cause giving to be motivated by managerial discretion rather than profit maximization. Navarro used five proxies for the possible effect that managerial discretion has on corporate giving. The variables and their theoretical signs are as follows.

(1) A variable that separates firms into those that are managerially controlled versus those that are owner controlled. Firms that are managerially controlled are expected to give more to charity.

(2) Managers may be more conservative than owners in using debt. If this is the case then debt-equity ratios will be inversely related to managerial influence and, by extension, inversely related to corporate giving.

(3) A third managerial-discretion variable measures changes in the firm's dividends. Navarro hypothesized that an increase in dividends is associated with increased managerial control and, by extension, increased corporate giving.

(4) The salary of the firm's chief executive officer is a fourth managerial-discretion variable. If large managerial salaries imply managerial control,

then this variable will be positively related to corporate giving.

(5) Navarro demonstrated that a corporation's profit-maximizing level of giving is not affected by its tax rate. But giving that reflects managerial discretion is negatively influenced by taxes. He therefore included a firm's tax rate, expecting a negative sign if managerial discretion explains corporate giving.

Navarro's empirical results indicate that charitable giving by corporations is explained by profit-maximizing motives rather than altruistic behavior on the part of managers. Four of the five profit-maximizing variables have the "right" sign and are statistically significant.[e] Advertising, price-cost margin, labor intensity, and number of firms in the SMSA are statistically significant. Only the variable representing federal social spending is insignificant. On the other hand, none of the five managerial discretion variables was a significant determinant of corporate giving. In other words, altruism does not explain why corporations give to charity. Corporations give to charity because it is in their self interest to do so.

---

e Navarro reported three sets of results: ordinary least squares (OLS), restricted OLS, and weighted least squares (WLS). The results summarized here refer to the unrestricted OLS results in his paper. See Chapter 3 for an introduction to regression techniques.

There is another way of stating this same point: Managers of profit-maximizing firms are motivated to behave responsibly when consumers are willing to pay for such behavior. Biodegradable packaging will be supplied, for example, if the additional value the firm's customers place on it is equal to or greater than the additional costs incurred by the firm in using those materials. Similarly, a financial institution will invest its loanable funds exclusively in local businesses and construction projects if its depositors are willing to forego the higher interest rates the bank may have been able to pay had it invested elsewhere.

A final economic lesson about the ethics of the market: In striving to reduce costs, profit-maximizing firms free resources for use in the pursuit of other social goals. Maximizing profits enhances the wealth available for charitable contributions, for funding the arts, or for establishing day-care centers for employees' children. It is not by accident that only the market-based economies of the industrialized world can afford to be concerned with environmental quality. Where resources are squandered by not-for-profit, state-owned enterprises, less wealth remains to satisfy the nonmaterialistic objectives of society.

In short, ethical behavior is entirely consistent with profit-maximization. This observation does not mean that unethical or socially irresponsible behavior will not occur in a for-profit firm any more than it means that such behavior is absent (or even that it occurs less frequently) in a not-for-profit organization. After all, corruption and scandals involving public officials and the management of the United Way are not unknown. The important point is that markets assist in the production of ethical behavior, as they do in the case of any other scarce economic good, by conserving on the resources devoted to supplying it.

SUMMARY

This chapter has introduced the study of managerial economics. It has described the evolution of the modern business organization and compared and contrasted the assumption of profit maximization with other behavioral theories of the firm. The chapter stressed a basic theme that will recur throughout the remainder of the text: Business strategy is linked to business structure. As it evolved, the modern firm had to adapt to an increasingly complex decision-making environment. Expansions in the firm's scale and scope placed ever greater demands on managers to acquire and utilize information. They needed to know about the firm's activities, to coordinate its resources, to evaluate its performance, and to formulate policies aimed at promoting long-run prosperity.

Successful organizations coped with these demands by adopting structures that enabled decision-making authority to be placed in the hands of those individuals having more ready access to relevant information. Decentralized organization structures delegated routine, operational decisions to lower-level managers. This freed the firm's top-level managers to devote more of their attention to long-run, strategic planning. But decentralized decision-making authority was only half the story. Successful organizations also adopted structures that provided managers having access to relevant information with incentives to use their knowledge in ways that served the organization's overall objectives.

This text assumes that the overall objective of the firm is to maximize profit. In a sense, this assumption is unrealistic. Individuals make decisions for firms on the basis of more than one criterion. The firm's growth rate, the power and prestige of its managers, the welfare of its employees, and the nonmaterialistic social responsibilities of business could all be included in a more realistic theory of firm behavior. But like all choices, this one has a cost. As the list of objectives attributed to the firm expands, the theory becomes more complex and less readily applied to business decisions. Moreover, most alternative behavioral objectives are ultimately subject to the harsh realities of the competitive marketplace. Managers that single-mindedly pursue growth over profits will eventually impair the long-run viability of their firms. On the other hand, "environmentally friendly" packaging is entirely consistent with long-run profit maximization—provided that consumers demand it.

1.1 Discuss the principal differences between the functional and multidivisional types of business organization.

1.2 The traditional division of economic theory is between microeconomics and macroeconomics. Is managerial economics more closely related to microeconomics or to macroeconomics? Defend your answer.

1.3 How does managerial economics differ from microeconomics?

1.4 Classify the following business decisions as tactical or strategic and explain your reasoning.
   a. McDonald's is considering introducing a new product line of healthier, low-fat alternative sandwiches.
   b. Levi's jeans are sold only in major department stores because the company wants consumers to associate its brand name with quality. Management is considering a policy change that would allow Wal-Mart, a major discount store, to carry its product.
   c. A company in Birmingham, Alabama sells tomatos grown in greenhouses to grocery stores year-round. During the months of July and August these grocery stores tend to purchase locally grown produce rather than tomatos grown in greenhouses. The company wants to negotiate long-term contracts with major grocery chains that would guarantee the company a minimum amount of sales.
   d. A marketing vice president believes that his firm should institute a warranty program for its product.

1.5 What effect does each of the following have on the revenue, cost, or discount rate components of the valuation model? What effect does each have on the long-run profitability of the firm?
   a. The government requires textile firms to reduce the amount of cotton dust that workers are exposed to in their plants.
   b. Firms in the beef industry set up a trade organization that will promote beef consumption with a national advertising campaign.
   c. AT&T is a large player in the communications industry. If AT&T provides financial support for basic research (research in theoretical physics, for instance), how does that investment affect AT&T's long-run profitability?
   d. A recession reduces the demand for loans and interest rates decline.

1.6 Discuss the ethical issues raised by the following business practices.
   a. A pharmaceutical manufacturer charges $10,000 for the yearly dosage of a new life-saving drug.
   b. A grocery store's supplier raises the wholesale price of coffee. The store's manager immediately marks up the retail price of coffee purchased at the previously lower wholesale price.
   c. The owner of a small chain of clothing stores charges higher prices at inner city locations than at suburban locations.
   d. In the wake of a devastating hurricane, the owner of a local convenience store raises the price of a bag of ice from $1 to $10.
   e. A college student offers to "scalp" a ticket to a sold-out football game for three times the ticket's face value.

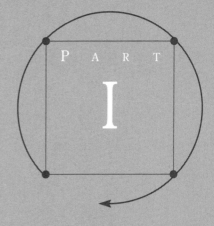

Decision-Making Tools

Demand Theory and Analysis

OVERVIEW

Part I, comprising this chapter and the four to follow it, provides a detailed overview of the basic tools of economic theory that are prerequisites to informed managerial decision making. It does so within the context of a stylized example involving the J. Johnson Clothing Company. In these chapters, the firm's owner, Janet Johnson, evaluates the potential profitability of selling a new product designed by the company's research and development team.

Chapter 2 introduces the demand characteristics of the new product. A summary of the economic theory of consumer behavior provides a starting point for this discussion. We then present an estimated demand curve for the new product and describe its important characteristics. This chapter focuses on the consumer side of the market and lays the groundwork for the subsequent analysis of profit-maximizing pricing strategies.

The remaining chapters in Part I extend Chapter 2's application in a number of directions. Chapters 3 and 4 present the production and cost characteristics of the company's new product. Chapter 3 also begins introducing the statistical techniques needed for estimating the firm's demand and cost relationships empirically. Chapter 5 derives profit-maximizing pricing and production rules, and alternative pricing strategies are discussed in Chapter 6.

The J. Johnson Company produces a line of casual clothing. The company's research and development department has recently designed an ultra-light, waterproof, all-weather coat that is being considered for introduction to the market. The coat is light enough to use as a rain jacket in warm weather and has sufficient insulating features for cool weather. The design team believes that the new product's versatility will appeal to a wide range of consumers.

After the successful development of the product, the company's president, Janet Johnson, engages the services of a consulting firm that specializes in advising clients on the marketing of new product lines. In its initial report on the all-weather coat's prospects, the consulting company notes that sales projections are apt to be affected by two other products. A rival clothing company produces a ski jacket that has some of the same features as Johnson's newly developed coat. The consulting firm believes that the ski jacket, which sells at a price of $50, will be the primary competitor of Johnson's all-weather coat. Another rival clothing company sells a popular all-weather hat that could easily complement Johnson's new coat. This all-weather hat sells for $20.

Revenue projections for the all-weather coat are based on the following demand function which the consulting firm has estimated for the Johnson Company's new product:

$$Q_x^d = 60 - 5P_x + 2.4P_y - 4P_z + 10I. \qquad (2.1)$$

Q_x^d is the quantity of all-weather coats demanded during a one-year period and is measured in units of thousands of coats. The variables on the right-hand side of the equation are defined as follows. P_x is the price that the J. Johnson company charges for its new product, P_y is the price of the competing ski jacket, P_z is the price of the all-weather hat that consumers may match with the all-weather coat, and I is the average annual income of prospective buyers, measured in thousands of dollars. Based on responses to a survey which asked potential buyers to report their household earnings, the consulting firm estimates average annual consumer income to be $40,000.

The consulting firm does not yet have complete information about the costs of producing the new coat and therefore cannot supply a definitive price recommendation. However, it suggests that the Johnson Company anticipate setting a price somewhere between $55 and $65. This pricing recommendation is based on the results of the marketing survey which also asked potential buyers to rate the price and quality features of the ski jacket that is expected to be the new product's closest competitor. Because consumers judged the all-weather coat to be superior on a number of dimensions, the consulting firm thinks that the new product can be sold competitively at a price that is between $5 and $15 higher than the rival ski jacket. However, the consulting firm emphasizes strongly that this is only a tentative recommendation. A final determination of the optimal price can be made only after production cost figures have been finalized by Johnson's manufacturing department.

After receiving the consulting firm's report, the company's president draws up a list of questions to be answered before the all-weather coat project is approved. It is understood that the final decision to undertake the project depends on the manufacturing department's cost estimates. These estimates are not yet ready, but a preliminary analysis of the project's profitability based on the demand information at hand seems warranted. After the preliminary analysis, the company decides to use $60 as an initial estimate of the price of the all-weather coat.

Ms. Johnson hopes to answer the following questions based on the consulting firm's demand analysis.

1. How many all-weather coats can the company expect to sell each year at a price of $60?
2. Because a price of $60 is only tentative, what effect will charging either a higher price or a lower price have on sales and total revenue?
3. There are three variables in the demand function that the firm does not control directly—the price of its rival's ski jacket, the price of the complementary all-weather hat, and consumer income. What impact will changes in these variables have on sales of the company's all-weather coat?
4. Based only on the demand information provided, is it possible to determine whether a price of $60 is within the range of prices that will be consistent with profit maximization?
5. Rather than selling the all-weather coat at a price of $60 initially, might it not pay to set a relatively low price when the product is first introduced in order to quickly establish a dominant market share?[a] While the firm may forego some profits in the short run by adopting this alternative pricing policy, it may be rewarded with larger profits in the future due to a higher-than-otherwise level of demand generated by brand loyalty and customer goodwill. If the firm uses this market penetration strategy, what price should it set?

---

a Market share can be defined either in terms of quantity of sales (physical units) or value of sales (price times quantity). Defining a firm's market share as the ratio of its physical quantity of sales to the market total is a valid and probably preferred market share measure if the firm and its competitors produce largely homogeneous products. However, if the products included in a market differ significantly in terms of quality or other nonprice attributes, then value of sales will be a more logical market share measure. This chapter assumes that the Johnson Company measures its market share in terms of value rather than quantity. A quantity-based market share model is developed in William J. Baumol, *Business Behavior, Value, and Growth* (New York: Harcourt Brace Jovanovich, Inc., 1967).

The following sections show how economic analysis can help answer these important questions. The law of demand is first derived from the economic model of consumer choice. The consulting firm's estimated demand function then provides information which, once distilled, guides managerial pricing and production decisions toward the goal of maximizing the firm's profits.

THE DEMAND FUNCTION

Demand refers to the relationship between price and the quantity of a good that consumers are willing and able to purchase. This relationship is represented by the familiar downward-sloping demand curve which expresses a fundamental observation: Consumers are willing to buy more of a good at lower prices than at higher ones. The inverse (or negative) relationship between price and quantity demanded is the economic **law of demand**.

Market demand refers to the demand for an entire industry's product. Firm demand refers to the demand confronting an individual seller within the industry. Because the firm's own demand curve more directly affects managerial decisions, this chapter focuses on firm demand rather than market demand. Chapter 8 discusses managerial decisions related to market demand characteristics.

The firm's demand curve is the summation of the demands of the individual consumers who are willing and able to make offers to buy its product. These offers to buy, in turn, emerge from the inevitable tradeoffs faced by consumers in the marketplace. Consumers must decide how to allocate their limited incomes across the wide variety of goods and services available for purchase in such a way as to make themselves feel as well off as possible. The model of consumer choice that provides a solution to this decision-making problem is outlined below.

Rational Consumer Choice

Economists assume that consumers choose rationally. Rational choice is a process of sorting through the available alternatives to identify and select the particular combination of goods and services that yields the highest possible level of satisfaction. The consumer must weigh a large number of tradeoffs in this process of choosing. Given that a consumer's money income is limited, when additional units of one good are purchased, the amount that can be spent on other goods is necessarily reduced. It is for this reason that the model of consumer choice stresses the notion of **opportunity cost**. Opportunity cost expresses the idea that the proper measure of the cost of anything is the value of the sacrifice that must be made in selecting one option over another.

The goal of consumer choice is to maximize utility. The term **utility** refers to the amount of pleasure or satisfaction an individual derives from consuming a particular bundle of goods and services. Utility is an entirely artificial concept in the sense that it cannot be observed or measured. Moreover, economists have no theory that describes how consumers form their tastes for various goods. Some people like broccoli and therefore derive a great deal of satisfaction from consuming it. Others would much rather eat pork rinds. Economists simply take these preferences as given and stable. Without making value judgments, economists model behavior *as if* consumers strive to maximize the total utility they derive from consumption.[1]

Consumer choices are assumed to be rational in the following sense. First, consumers are able to *compare* the total utilities of any two bundles of goods and on the basis of this comparison make one of three statements. The consumer either prefers bundle A to bundle B (meaning that bundle A yields a higher level of total utility than bundle B), prefers bundle B to bundle A, or is "indifferent" between bundle A and bundle B (meaning that the two bundles yield the same level of total satisfaction).

Second, economists assume that these preference statements are **transitive** (or **consistent** with one another) when comparisons are made among three or more bundles. For example, suppose a consumer compares bundles A and B and prefers A over B. He or she then compares bundles B and C and prefers B over C. Transitivity requires that the consumer prefer bundle A to bundle C.

Finally, consumers always prefer more to less. A bundle that contains more of at least one good and no less of any other good is always strictly preferred to (*dominates*) another.

Although we cannot measure utility, it is still possible to numerically rank order various bundles of goods in terms of the total utilities they yield to an individual consumer. In this rank ordering, higher numbers are assigned to bundles of goods from which the consumer derives higher levels of total satisfaction.

The magnitudes of the rank ordering numbers are meaningless. That is, if the consumer prefers bundle A to bundle B, the number 100 might be assigned to A and 99 to B. On the other hand, the number 25 can be assigned to A and 1 can be assigned to B. Nothing is thereby implied about the relative amounts of total utility associated with the bundles. In other words, one cannot logically conclude that in the first case the consumer only slightly prefers A to B while in the other case A is 25 times more satisfying than B. The rank ordering is all that matters. Higher numbers are assigned to bundles that stand higher in the consumer's preference ranking.

Consider now a simplified example of the consumer's decision-making process. Suppose that an individual consumer must select the particular combination of two goods, pizzas and compact discs, that maximizes his or

---

1 Although individual tastes and preferences obviously differ considerably, the model of consumer choice loses none of its explanatory power even if the extreme assumption is made that all consumers have identical preferences. See George J. Stigler and Gary S. Becker, "De Gustibus Non Est Disputandum," *American Economic Review* 67 (March 1977), pp. 76-90.

her total utility. These choices are constrained. They are limited by the amount of money income the consumer has to spend and by the prices of the two goods. The consumer's **budget constraint** can be written as

$$I = P_{Pizza}Q_{Pizza} + P_{CD}Q_{CD}.$$

I is the consumer's total money income per time period, say per week. P_{Pizza} and P_{CD} are the unit prices of pizzas and compact discs, and Q_{Pizza} and Q_{CD} are the quantities of the two goods purchased.

Because it is combinations of pizzas and compact discs (and the levels of total utility associated with them) that are of interest, the budget constraint must be rearranged to illustrate the range of choices available to the consumer. In other words, the quantity of one of the goods, say pizza, the consumer is able to buy depends on the amount purchased of the other in the following way:

$$Q_{Pizza} = \left(\frac{I}{P_{Pizza}} \right) - \left(\frac{P_{CD}}{P_{Pizza}} \right) Q_{CD}.$$

This budget line traces out the various combinations of pizzas and compact discs available at a given money income and set of relative prices. Suppose that an individual's weekly income is $100, the price of a pizza is $10, and a compact disc sells for $20. Under these conditions, if the consumer chooses to spend all income on pizzas ($Q_{CD} = 0$), he or she can at most buy $100/$10 = 10 pizzas per week. The term I/P_{Pizza} is consequently the budget line's vertical intercept in a two-dimensional diagram with Q_{Pizza} measured along the vertical axis and Q_{CD} measured along the horizontal axis.

At market-determined prices, the consumer must give up two pizzas in order to buy one compact disc. Notice that this tradeoff is represented by the slope of the budget line, $-(P_{CD}/P_{Pizza}) = -$20/$10 = -2$, which is equal to the ratio of the prices of the two goods. This price ratio determines the rate at which the consumer can substitute pizzas for compact discs while holding total expenditures on the two goods constant. The terms of trade between the two goods are the essence of the opportunity cost concept. The opportunity cost of a compact disc to a consumer is not its price, but rather the utility associated with the two pizzas the consumer must necessarily forego in order to purchase an additional CD.

The consumer's budget line is shown graphically in panel *a* of Figure 2.1. The assumption of dominance ("more is always preferred to less") assures that the consumer will spend all money income on the two available goods. If he or she does not, total utility will not be maximized. The consumer could, by buying more pizzas, more CDs, or more of both goods, increase the total satisfaction derived from consumption. Hence, the various combinations of the two goods that lie on the budget line defined above (i.e., $Q_{Pizza} = 10 - 2Q_{CD}$) represent candidates for the utility-maximizing bundle.

Suppose that the individual considers each alternative and then chooses to purchase bundle *A* consisting of six pizzas and two compact discs per

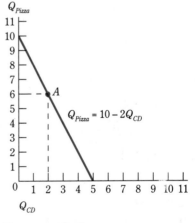

FIGURE 2.1a
The Consumer's Choice Set

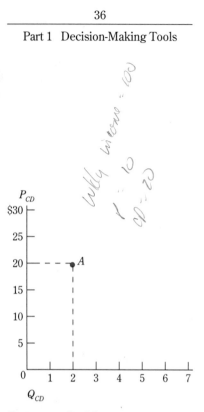

FIGURE 2.1b
Price and Quantity Demanded of
Compact Discs

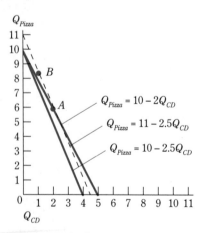

FIGURE 2.2a
Income-Compensated Increase in
the Price of Compact Discs

week. This selection reveals that of all of the various combinations of these two goods available, the consumer feels as well off as possible by allocating money income in this way. Given the same income and relative prices, other individuals might choose differently, of course. The important point is that this consumer prefers bundle A over the others. The information about the consumer's preferences revealed by this choice can be used to derive the demand functions for the two goods.

The Derivation of the Demand Function

An individual's demand function for a good can be derived directly from the utility-maximizing behavior described in the previous section. Given a weekly income of $100 and market-determined prices of pizzas and compact discs of $10 and $20, respectively, the consumer chooses to purchase six pizzas and two CDs (point A in panel a of Figure 2.1). Corresponding to this choice are points on the consumer's demand functions for both goods. For instance, when the price of a compact disc is $20, the consumer is willing and able to purchase two CDs. This price and quantity combination is illustrated by point A in panel b of Figure 2.1. Point A in panel b is one point on the consumer's demand curve for compact discs. (There is also a price-quantity combination on the consumer's demand curve for pizza corresponding to point A in the top panel, but it is not illustrated.)

Now conduct the following experiment. Suppose that the price of CDs increases, all other things being the same. If the consumer continues to choose rationally, he or she must not buy more than two compact discs (and will likely buy less). Transitivity of preferences requires that the consumer reallocate expenditures on the two goods so as to buy more of the now relatively cheaper good (pizzas) and less of the other.

To see how this conclusion is reached, assume that the price of a compact disc rises from $20 to $25. If the price of pizzas and the consumer's money income are held constant, this price increase causes the consumer to face a new, steeper budget line defined by the equation $Q_{Pizza} = 10 - 2.5Q_{CD}$. This new budget line has the same vertical intercept as the old one because the consumer is still able to buy 10 pizzas if all income is spent on that good. The slope of the budget line increases to 2.5 in absolute value, however, because with a CD price of $25 the consumer now must sacrifice 2.5 pizzas in order to purchase an additional CD. The new and old budget lines appear in panel a of Figure 2.2.

The higher price of compact discs has two effects. There is a pure price effect (or **substitution effect**) represented by the steeper slope of the consumer's budget line. This steeper slope indicates that compact discs have become relatively less attractive (and pizzas have become relatively more attractive) per dollar spent than before. The rate at which the consumer can substitute one good for another has changed because the relative prices of the two goods have changed.

There is also an **income effect**. Even though the consumer's money income has not changed, he or she has become poorer in the sense that fewer combinations of pizzas and CDs are now available for purchase. Because compact discs have become more expensive, the consumer can buy at most four per week if all income is spent on that good. Previously, he or she could have purchased as many as five CDs at their lower price. Indeed, the consumer loses the opportunity to consume all of the combinations of pizzas and CDs that lie in the "wedge" between the old and the new budget lines. These lost consumption opportunities represent a reduction in the consumer's **real** (as opposed to money) **income.**

The assumption of dominance implies that such a reduction in real income lowers the consumer's total utility. The consumer's new utility-maximizing choices all lie along a budget line that traces out different bundles of pizzas and compact discs. These bundles contain fewer units of at least one of the goods than had been consumed previously at point A. However, it is the effect of a price change that is of interest in deriving the individual's demand function. Therefore, we must disentangle the substitution and income effects.

The substitution and income effects can be separated if the consumer is compensated for the higher price of compact discs. This compensation experiment provides the consumer with enough additional **money income** to continue purchasing the old combination of pizzas and compact discs under the new set of circumstances.[2] In particular, the consumer's original consumption choices will remain available (his or her purchasing power or real income will remain constant) if he or she can still purchase bundle A. Bundle A can still be purchased at the new price ratio if the consumer has an additional $10 to spend. With a total money income of $110, the consumer can, if he or she chooses, continue to purchase six pizzas and two CDs when a pizza sells for $10 and a compact disc sells for $25.

The required compensation is illustrated graphically by constructing a third, hypothetical budget line that is parallel to (has the same slope as) the new one, but passes through point A in panel a of Figure 2.2. This hypothetical, dashed budget line is defined by the equation $Q_{Pizza} = 11 - 2.5Q_{CD}$.

Given that the price of pizzas and the consumer's real income both remain constant in this experiment, the individual can of course continue to consume the original combination of the two goods. But what happens if the consumer makes a new choice now that compact discs have become more expensive? That new choice must be a bundle which contains fewer CDs and more pizza than the bundle at point A. This conclusion follows because in making the original selection at A, the consumer revealed that he or she preferred A to all of the bundles lying on the dashed budget line to the right (southeast) of A. All of these bundles were available when A was chosen (they lie interior to the consumer's original budget line). When A becomes

---

2 This compensation experiment yields the Slutsky substitution effect, named for the Russian economist Eugene Slutsky. An alternative approach suggested by Nobel laureate Sir John Hicks compensates the consumer by providing enough additional money income to hold total utility (rather than total purchasing power) constant.

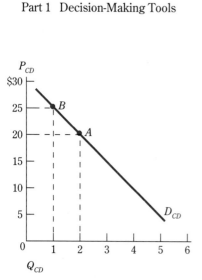

FIGURE 2.2b

The Compensated Demand
Curve for Compact Discs

available again with the appropriate compensation, the consumer cannot reject A in favor of any of these previously attainable combinations without violating the assumption of transitivity.

Consequently, if the consumer chooses a different combination of pizzas and compact discs under the new circumstances, that choice must lie along the segment of the dashed budget line lying to the left (northwest) of point A. The characteristic common to all of these bundles that makes choosing one of them consistent with the assumptions of rational consumer behavior is that they contain fewer CDs (and more pizza) than A. Hence, the compensated demand curve for compact discs is downward-sloping: In response to an increase in the price of CDs, the consumer reduces his or her purchases of this good by moving to a point like B that contains one CD rather than two.

The familiar downward-sloping demand curve shown in panel b of Figure 2.2 thus emerges logically from rational, utility-maximizing behavior on the part of individual consumers.[3] This **compensated demand curve** is derived by holding the consumer's real income constant. It shows only the pure sub-stitution effect of a change in the price of compact discs on the quantity demanded by the consumer.

In the naturally occurring economy, of course, consumers are not com-pensated for changes in the prices of the goods they buy in ways that hold their real incomes constant. The uncompensated, **ordinary demand functions** that can be derived from observations on actual consumer behavior therefore reflect both the substitution effects and the income effects generated by price changes. Although these ordinary demand curves will tend to be less steeply inclined than their compensated counterparts, they will nevertheless be downward-sloping.

Economists derive ordinary demand curves by holding the consumer's money income constant. These demand curves are downward sloping because for most goods—called **income-normal goods**—the impact of a price change on the consumer's real income (the income effect) reinforces the substitution effect. When an increase in the price of one good reduces a consumer's real income, the consumer tends to buy fewer units of all normal goods, including the good whose price has risen. Similarly, when a reduc-tion in the price of one good increases a consumer's real income, the con-sumer tends to buy more of all normal goods, including the good whose price has fallen. In the case of normal goods, then, the income effect moves the consumer in the same direction as the substitution effect, causing quantity demanded to vary inversely with price changes (the law of demand).

For other goods—called **income-inferior goods**—the income effect moves the consumer's purchases in the direction opposite to the substitution

---

3 Indeed, downward-sloping demand curves are likely to be the norm even if consumers choose "irrationally." See Gary S. Becker, "Irrational Behavior and Economic Theory," *Journal of Political Economy* 70 (February 1962), pp. 1-13. For laboratory evidence that downward-sloping demand curves exist for species other than humans, see John H. Kagel, Raymond C. Battalio, Howard C. Rachlin, and Leonard Green, "Demand Curves for Animal Consumers,"*Quarterly Journal of Economics* 96 (February 1981), pp. 1-15.

effect. A rise in real income causes the consumer to buy less of an income-inferior good, and a decline in real income causes the consumer to buy more of it. But because the income effect tends to be small relative to the substitution effect in the case of an inferior good, it can safely be ignored in most cases.[4]

The Determinants of Demand

The foregoing discussion suggests that an individual consumer's demand for any good—the number of units of the good he or she is willing and able to buy—depends on the good's own price, the prices of other goods, the consumer's tastes and preferences, and money income. A **demand function** is a formal mathematical statement of this relationship; it includes all of the variables that affect demand. A representative demand function for a consumer has the following general form:

$$Q_x^d = f(\text{price of } x, \tag{2.2}$$
$$\text{prices of substitute goods,}$$
$$\text{prices of complementary goods,}$$
$$\text{consumer's money income,}$$
$$\text{consumer's tastes and preferences,}$$
$$\text{price expectations, and}$$
$$\text{other relevant variables}).$$

Q_x^d is the quantity of good x demanded during some specified time period.[5]

The demand function in equation 2.2 lists six specific factors that affect demand. Because a two-dimensional graph is limited to the two variables that define the vertical and horizontal axes, the general form of the demand function is not amenable to graphical representation. However, a two-dimensional diagram can represent the demand function if equation 2.2 is converted into a form in which only price and quantity demanded are allowed to vary while all other variables in the equation are temporarily held constant. Specifically, the demand function can be written as

$$Q_x^d = f(P_x), \tag{2.3}$$

where P_x is the price of good x and all other variables affecting demand are held constant.

The graphical representation of the demand function departs from convention by placing the independent variable, price, on the vertical axis. In

---

4 Robert D. Willig, "Consumer's Surplus without Apology," *American Economic Review* 66 (September 1976), pp. 589-97. Income-normal and income-inferior goods are defined more precisely below.

5 The impact of price expectations and the classification of goods into the substitute and complement categories are explored later in the chapter.

other words, the standard graphical representation of the demand curve depicts the **inverse demand function,**

$$P_x = g(Q_x^d), \tag{2.4}$$

where all other variables affecting demand are again held constant.[6]

Graphing the demand function in this way leads to the critical distinction between a **change in quantity demanded** and a **change in demand.** Holding all other variables constant, a change in the price of x leads to a change in the quantity demanded of good x. This change in quantity demanded is represented by a movement along a particular demand curve. By contrast, a change in any of the variables that have been held constant in graphing the relationship between price and quantity demanded causes a change in demand. A change in demand is represented by a shift in the entire demand function.

From an Individual's Demand to the Firm's Demand

The general demand function presented above was derived from the utility-maximizing behavior of a representative consumer. The demand function facing a firm sums the demands of all of the consumers who are willing and able to make offers to buy that seller's product. In other words, the firm's demand curve is determined by adding the various quantities demanded by individual consumers at each possible price. This curve shows the total number of units the firm can expect to sell at each of those possible prices. The experimenter allows price to vary while holding all other variables affecting demand constant. In this way, the firm's demand curve is built piecewise by summing horizontally the demand curves of the individual consumers who are willing and able to buy the firm's product.

Figure 2.3 illustrates the construction of the firm's demand curve. Panels a and b show the quantities of compact discs two individual consumers, Bill and Hilary, are willing to buy per month at various possible prices. The monthly quantities demanded by all of the firm's other customers are shown in panel c. To determine the total number of compact discs the firm can expect to sell at any given price, the quantities demanded by each consumer at that price are simply summed. For example, if the firm charges a

---

6 The convention of graphing the demand curve in inverse form can be traced at least as far back as Alfred Marshall, *Principles of Economics*, 8E. (London: Macmillan, 1930), pp. 96-97. (The first edition was published in 1890.) Marshall viewed the demand curve as representing a list "of the prices at which [the consumer] is willing to buy different amounts" of the good in question. In this sense, the consumer's willingness to pay (price) is a function of the quantity purchased. When the quantity of the good consumed is small, the consumer is willing to pay a relatively high price to acquire a little more of it (i.e., to sacrifice the opportunity to buy a relatively large number of other goods). As the quantity of the good consumed increases, the consumer is willing to sacrifice fewer alternatives to acquire a little more of this good. In Marshall's analysis, then, price is the dependent variable and the convention has stuck.

price of $15, Bill is willing to buy 5 CDs, Hilary is willing to buy 3 CDs, and the firm's other customers are willing to buy 192 CDs. On a monthly basis, then, the firm can expect to sell a total of 5 + 3 + 192 = 200 CDs at a price of $15 per unit. Summing the quantities demanded at other possible prices yields the monthly demand curve for CDs confronting the seller in panel d.

The Demand for All-Weather Coats

The empirical demand function presented in the chapter's opening application (equation 2.1) provides a concrete illustration of the foregoing concepts. The demand curve for all-weather coats produced and sold by the J. Johnson Clothing Company is diagrammed by holding constant all of the variables in the demand function other than price. (Recall that the price of the competing ski jacket, P_y, is $50, the price of the complementary all-weather hat, P_z, is $20, and consumers' average money income, I, is $40,000.) Keeping in mind that quantity demanded and money income are denominated in thousands, the demand curve for all-weather coats is given by the following equation:

$$Q_x^d = 60 - 5P_x + 2.4(50) - 4(20) + 10(40) \qquad (2.5)$$
$$= 60 + 120 - 80 + 400 - 5P_x$$
$$= 500 - 5P_x.$$

The constant term in this linear equation represents the quantity demanded associated with all factors other than price. Because quantity is denominated in thousands, the constant term of 500 represents sales of 500,000 all-weather coats. This is the number of coats the firm would "sell" if it charged a zero price.

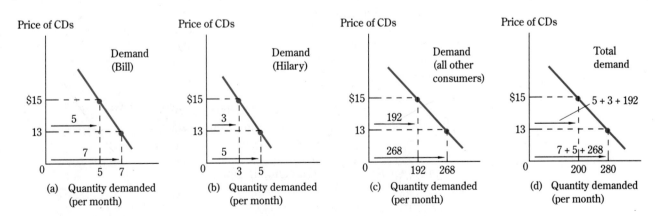

FIGURE 2.3
The Demand Curve Facing a Seller of Compact Discs

The coefficient associated with P_x is the slope of the demand function.[7] In accordance with the law of demand, the slope is always negative, indicating that price and quantity demanded vary inversely. The value of this coefficient, –5, shows the magnitude of the effect of a change in price on anticipated sales of all-weather coats. In particular, holding all other variables constant, the firm can expect to sell 5,000 fewer all-weather coats if price is increased by $1; it can expect sales to increase by 5,000 units if price is reduced by $1.

As mentioned above, demand curves are diagrammed conventionally in inverse form, with P_x on the vertical axis and Q_x^d on the horizontal axis. Rearranging equation 2.5 in this way yields

$$P_x = 100 - .2Q_x^d. \tag{2.6}$$

Equation 2.6 is illustrated graphically in Figure 2.4. The vertical intercept of this inverse demand function is 100, indicating that if the firm charges a price of $100, it cannot expect to sell any all-weather coats. The slope of the inverse demand function is –.2, meaning that if the firm wants to sell an additional 1,000 all-weather coats, price must drop by $.20 per unit.

The demand function in equation 2.5 provides an estimate of the quantity of all-weather coats the J. Johnson Company can expect to sell at various possible prices, holding all other variables affecting demand constant. For example, if the company sets a price of $60 for the all-weather coat, it can expect to sell

$$Q_x^d = 500 - 5(60)$$
$$= 200,$$

or 200,000 coats per year. The concept of a change in quantity demanded is illustrated by the movement from point A to point B in Figure 2.4. If price is increased from $60 to $70, the quantity demanded per year falls from 200,000 all-weather coats to 150,000 all-weather coats.

On the other hand, a change in demand occurs only in response to changes in factors other than price. Of the variables that potentially affect any demand function, price is the *only* variable that does *not* cause a change in demand. In this example, a change in demand can be initiated by a change in any one of the following three variables: P_y, P_z, or I. For example, if average annual consumer income increases from $40,000 to $50,000 the demand function becomes

$$Q_x^d = 60 - 5P_x + 2.4(50) - 4(20) + 10(50) \tag{2.7}$$
$$= 60 + 120 - 80 + 500 - 5P_x$$
$$= 600 - 5P_x$$

and the inverse demand function is now

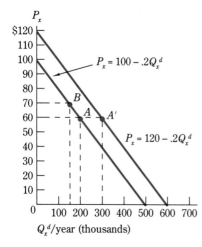

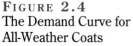

FIGURE 2.4
The Demand Curve for
All-Weather Coats

7 The appendix of this chapter provides a brief introduction to the concepts of derivatives and partial derivatives.

$$P_x = 120 - .2Q_x^d.$$ (2.8)

The new inverse demand curve is also shown in Figure 2.4. Higher consumer incomes translate into an increase in demand that shifts the entire demand curve to the right. This rightward shift in demand indicates that consumers are willing and able to buy a larger quantity of all-weather coats at every possible price. If the firm charges a price of $60, it can now expect to sell 300,000 all-weather coats per year. At the lower income level, it would have sold 200,000 (compare points A' and A).

An increase in demand for all-weather coats would also result from an increase in the price of the ski jacket (P_y) or a reduction in the price of the all-weather hat (P_z). By the same reasoning, a decline in demand—illustrated by a leftward shift of the entire demand curve—would result from a reduction in consumer income, a reduction in the price of the substitute good (the ski jacket), or an increase in the price of the complementary good (the all-weather hat).

The demand curves in Figure 2.4 have two critical features. First, they represent the planned or *ex ante* consumer behavior that is independent of the quantity of the good the firm is willing to supply at various prices. The quantity that will actually be bought and sold depends on the interaction of consumers' willingness and ability to buy a product (as represented by the demand curve) and the willingness of the firm to supply the product at various prices. The willingness of the firm to supply the product, in turn, depends on its costs of production and a host of other factors. Second, quantity demanded is a flow variable that is measured over a specific period of time. A demand curve relating price to annual sales was illustrated above. The relationship between prices and quantities over a shorter or longer period would necessarily yield a different demand curve. The influence of time as well as the other factors held constant in deriving a demand function are explored more fully below.

PRICE ELASTICITY OF DEMAND

One of the first questions the Johnson Company's president asks when presented with the consulting firm's recommendations is, What effect does a change in price have on the sales of all-weather coats? The coefficient of price in the demand equation provides one answer to this question. The price coefficient is –5. The price coefficient is the slope of the two-dimensional demand curve and is also the partial derivative of the demand function with respect to price. That is,

$$\frac{\partial Q_x^d}{\partial P_x} = -5.$$

The interpretation of this coefficient depends on the units in which price and quantity demanded are measured. Price is measured in dollars and quantity demanded is measured in thousands of coats. Therefore, a price

Demand Shifts Caused by Product Improvements

Among the factors that cause a demand curve to shift are prices of related products (substitutes and complements), consumers' money income, consumers' tastes and preferences, and the seller's advertising and promotional expenditures. Improvements in product quality will also increase the demand for a product. Consumers obviously benefit from increased product quality. Susan Vroman and Louise Russell have estimated the benefits of a particular product improvement—the development of freeze-dried coffee in the mid-1960s.[a]

The production of freeze-dried instant coffee uses a technology developed initially by biomedical researchers. Large scale freeze-drying became possible following the discovery, during World War II, of a new process for storing blood plasma. After additional research and development, the technique began producing a "better tasting" instant coffee in 1965. By 1969, freeze-dried coffee accounted for 20 percent of the instant coffee market.

Vroman and Russell estimate the benefits from the introduction of freeze-dried coffee in two steps. First, they estimate the ordinary demand curve for instant coffee and the shift in the curve caused by the availability of the freeze-dried alternative. Next, they use the size of the demand shift to estimate the dollar value of the benefits of this new product to consumers.

The following demand equation is estimated from data covering the years 1962-77:

$$QUANTITY = .992 - 8.115 PRICE - .01 INCOME + .004 FREEZE.$$

QUANTITY is the quantity of instant coffee consumed in a year, PRICE is the corresponding retail price of instant coffee, and FREEZE is the share of instant coffee sales accounted for by freeze-dried coffee. Importantly, PRICE and FREEZE are statistically significant while INCOME is statistically insignificant.

The estimated demand function for instant coffee shows the expected negative relationship between price and quantity demanded (the law of demand). Vroman and Russell report that the price elasticity of demand is somewhere between −.2 and −.3, indicating that the demand for instant coffee is very price inelastic. (The price elasticity of demand is defined in the following section.) Because INCOME is statistically insignificant, the data indicate that income does not affect the demand for coffee. Finally, the availability of freeze-dried coffee increases the overall demand for instant coffee. Vroman and Russell estimate that the demand for instant coffee increased by six percent following the introduction of the freeze-dried alternative.

As a final exercise, Vroman and Russell estimate the dollar value of the increased benefits realized by consumers from the introduction of freeze-dried coffee. Between 1971 and 1977, the estimated benefits from this product improvement varied between $136 million and $198 million annually (in 1967 dollars).

a Susan B. Vroman and Louise B. Russell, "The Net Social Benefits of a Product Improvement: The Case of Freeze-Dried Coffee," *Applied Economics* 19 (1987), pp. 127-142.

coefficient of –5 suggests that, holding all other factors affecting demand constant, 5,000 fewer coats will be purchased by the firm's customers if price is increased by $1. Alternatively, other things being the same, a $1 reduction in price will result in the sale of 5,000 additional coats.

The effect of **ceteris paribus** unit changes in the other three variables can also be gauged with reference to the respective coefficients associated with these variables in the demand equation.[8] These coefficients are also found by taking the partial derivatives of the demand function with respect to the appropriate variable, namely

$$\frac{\partial Q_x^{\ d}}{\partial P_y} = 2.4, \ \ \frac{\partial Q_x^{\ d}}{\partial P_z} = -4, \ \text{and} \ \frac{\partial Q_x^{\ d}}{\partial I} = 10.$$

If the price of the ski jacket increases by $1, for example, and the price of all-weather coats and other factors affecting demand remain the same, the Johnson Company can expect to sell 2,400 additional all-weather coats. Similarly, if the price of the matching all-weather hat increases by $1, the firm can expect to sell 4,000 fewer coats. And if average consumer income increases by $1,000, the firm can expect to sell an additional 10,000 coats.

However, these coefficients provide only one measure of the individual effects of the variables in the demand function on the quantity demanded by consumers. The advantage of using these coefficients is that they are denominated in the units in which the variables are measured. The disadvantage is that these coefficients do not provide a useful measure of the relative sizes of the effects of the variables on expected sales. For instance, suppose that quantity demanded is measured as the number of coats consumers are willing and able to buy (rather than being denominated in thousands of coats). And suppose further that money income is measured in dollars rather than in thousands of dollars. The demand function would then be

$$Q_x^{\ d} = 60,000 - 5,000P_x + 2,400P_y - 4,000P_z + 10I. \tag{2.9}$$

Despite the apparently large change in the values of all but one of the coefficients, equation 2.9 represents the same demand function as equation 2.1. A $1 change in price still causes the number of all-weather coats sold to change by 5,000, and a $1,000 change in money income still causes sales to change by 10,000. But the relative magnitudes of these effects seem to differ across the two demand functions. The coefficient associated with income is the largest coefficient in equation 2.1, but it is the smallest coefficient in equation 2.9. This difference in coefficient sizes materializes even though the effect of income relative to the other variables in the demand equation is exactly the same in both equations 2.1 and 2.9. Hence, a variable's coefficient does not do a good job of measuring the relative effect of one variable vis-a-vis

---

8   *Ceteris paribus* is Latin for "all other things held constant."

another. For this reason we need another measure of the size of the effect of each of these variables. The name of this measure is elasticity.

The **price elasticity of demand** provides a unit-free measure of the responsiveness of the quantity demanded of a good to a change in the good's own price. More specifically, the price elasticity of demand is the percentage change in quantity demanded divided by the percentage change in price:

$$\eta_p = \frac{\%\Delta Q_x^d}{\%\Delta P_x} \quad \text{Price Elasticity of Demand} \quad (2.10)$$

The Greek letter η (pronounced eta) represents the demand elasticity coefficient and, to emphasize the fact that it is the *price* elasticity of demand, a subscript p is also added. The Greek letter Δ (pronounced delta) commonly represents "change in."

The definition in equation 2.10 indicates three important properties of price elasticity. First, the price elasticity of demand is always negative in sign. This is because price and quantity demanded always move in opposite directions along the demand curve (the law of demand). When price increases, quantity demanded declines, and vice-versa. Thus, the numerator and the denominator in equation 2.10 are always of opposite sign and the ratio will consequently always be negative.

Second, the price elasticity of demand is calculated as the ratio of percentage changes in price and quantity demanded. Therefore, the units in which these two variables are measured cancel out. The value of the price elasticity coefficient is thus independent of these units of measurement.

Third, the absolute value of η_p will be greater than, less than, or equal to 1. This depends on whether the absolute value of the percentage change in sales is greater than, less than, or equal to the absolute value of the percentage change in price.[9] This property provides a convenient benchmark for defining elastic and inelastic demand.

Unitary, Elastic, and Inelastic Demand

When the price elasticity of demand is equal to 1, demand is said to have **unitary elasticity** or to be **unit elastic**. Unitary elasticity has special significance because it provides a benchmark that avoids the ambiguities of making statements about "large" and "small" price and quantity changes. If $|\eta_p| = 1$, the percentage change in sales is exactly equal to the percentage change in price.

On the other hand, when the percentage change in sales is greater than the percentage change in price, the absolute value of the price elasticity coefficient will be greater than 1. Consequently, an elasticity measure of 1.1, 2, or 10 means that the percentage change in sales is greater than the percentage change in price. For example, if the elasticity coefficient is 2, a one percent

---

9   The absolute value of a number ignores the algebraic sign and is denoted by | |. Hence, $|+a|$ = $|-a|$ = a for any a.

change in price causes a two percent change in sales (or a ten percent change in price causes a twenty percent change in sales). Whenever the absolute value of the elasticity of demand is greater than one, demand is said to be **elastic**.

There is one last possibility. This final category occurs when the absolute value of the demand elasticity is less than one, that is, when elasticity is a fraction like ½, ⅜, or ¾. Elasticities of these magnitudes indicate that consumers are not very responsive to price changes, because the percentage change in sales is less than the corresponding percentage change in price. An elasticity of .5, for instance, is interpreted to mean that a one percent change in price causes a one-half percent change in sales (or that a ten percent change in price causes a five percent change in sales). Demand is said to be **inelastic** when the absolute value of the elasticity coefficient is less than one.

The price elasticity of demand can be divided into three categories: unitary elasticity of demand, elastic demand, and inelastic demand. Table 2.1 provides a summary of this classification scheme.

The concept of price elasticity is one of the most important and useful concepts in economics. The next section discusses alternative methods for calculating the price elasticity coefficient.

Arc and Point Elasticity

The price elasticity of demand measures the responsiveness of consumers' purchases to a change in price. Holding all other variables affecting demand constant, what percentage change in quantity demanded is expected to follow from a given percentage change in price? Three formulas for calculating the price elasticity coefficient defined in equation 2.10 are stated in the following paragraphs.

TABLE 2.1 INTERPRETING THE ELASTICITY OF DEMAND

I. GUIDE: Elasticity $= \eta_p = \dfrac{\text{percentage change in sales}}{\text{percentage change in price}}$

II. INTERPRETATION[a]

NUMERICAL VALUE	NAME	INTERPRETATION
$\eta_p = 1$	unitary elastic demand	percentage change in sales is equal to percentage change in price
$\eta_p > 1$	elastic demand	percentage change in sales is greater than percentage change in price
$\eta_p < 1$	inelastic demand	percentage change in sales is less than percentage change in price

[a] The negative sign is ignored in interpreting the numerical value of the elasticity coefficient.

Consider the following pairs of observations on price and quantity demanded which are taken from the estimated demand function for the Johnson Clothing Company's all-weather coats:

Price (P)	Quantity Demanded (Q)
	(IN THOUSANDS)
$70	150
$60	200

Using the definition in equation 2.10, the percentage change in quantity demanded can be calculated as the change in quantity demanded relative to the initial level of sales. By using the same method for determining the percentage change in price, the following calculation formula can be stated:

$$\eta_p = \frac{\Delta Q}{Q_1} \div \frac{\Delta P}{P_1} = \frac{(Q_2 - Q_1)}{Q_1} \div \frac{(P_2 - P_1)}{P_1}. \qquad (2.11)$$

The problem with calculating the price elasticity of demand in this way is that one set of price and quantity changes yields two different demand elasticity estimates. The values chosen for P_1 and Q_1 and, hence, the elasticity coefficient itself, depend on whether a price of $60 or a price of $70 is used as the starting point for applying the formula. In particular, a price increase from $60 to $70 represents a ($70 – $60)/$60 = $10/$60 = .167, or a 16.7 percent change. Quantity demanded declines by (150 – 200)/200 = – 50/200 = –.25, or –25 percent. The elasticity of demand is thus |–25/16.7| = 1.5. On the other hand, a reduction in price from $70 to $60 represents a –14.3 percent change. This price reduction leads to a 33.3 percent increase in quantity demanded. The implied elasticity coefficient is |33.3/–14.3| = 2.3. Thus, the formula in equation 2.11 does not provide a unique, one-to-one correspondence between price-quantity changes and the elasticity of demand.

One solution to this problem of nonuniqueness is to use the average values of price and quantity over the relevant range of the demand function as the bases for calculating the percentage changes in these two variables. Adopting this convention leads to the following formula for the **arc elasticity of demand**:

$$\eta_p = \frac{(Q_2 - Q_1)}{\left(\dfrac{Q_2 + Q_1}{2}\right)} \div \frac{(P_2 - P_1)}{\left(\dfrac{P_2 + P_1}{2}\right)},$$

which can be simplified by noting that the 2s in the numerator and denominator cancel one another out. This simplification yields

$$\text{ARC } \eta_p = \frac{Q_2 - Q_1}{Q_2 + Q_1} \div \frac{P_2 - P_1}{P_2 + P_1}. \qquad (2.12)$$

Applying the arc elasticity formula to the price and quantity changes shown in the previous table, it can be seen that the calculated percentage changes are independent of the starting point. That is, because the same base is used in the calculation, the percentage change in price is $10/($60 + $70) = .077, or 7.7 percent whether price is increased or decreased. Similarly, the associated percentage change in quantity demanded is 50/(150 + 200) = .143, or 14.3 percent. Hence, the arc price elasticity of demand is 14.3/7.7 = 1.86. The arc elasticity of 1.86 means that a one percent increase in price causes quantity demanded to fall by 1.86 percent, or that a one percent reduction in price causes quantity demanded to increase by 1.86 percent. Because the absolute value of this arc elasticity coefficient estimate is greater than one, demand is categorized as "elastic."

The arc elasticity of demand measures the average responsiveness of con- sumers' purchases to changes in price over a discrete range of the demand curve. It is only an estimate of the price elasticity of demand because, as the problem encountered with equation 2.11 suggests, demand elasticity differs at every point on the demand curve. Any discrete change in price can be made arbitrarily smaller and smaller until the "arc" over which the price elasticity of demand is calculated corresponds to an infinitely small region around a single point on the demand curve. The formula for calculating the **point elasticity of demand**, or the elasticity of demand at a particular point on a demand curve is:

$$\text{POINT } \eta_p = \frac{\Delta Q}{Q} \div \frac{\Delta P}{P} = \left(\frac{\Delta Q}{\Delta P}\right)\left(\frac{P}{Q}\right).$$

For very small changes in price and quantity, the ratio $\Delta Q/\Delta P$ is the slope of the demand function. We can therefore replace the symbol Δ with the par- tial derivative symbol, ∂,[10] and rewrite the point elasticity formula as

$$\text{POINT } \eta_p = \left(\frac{\partial Q}{\partial P}\right)\left(\frac{P}{Q}\right). \tag{2.13}$$

For example, consider the demand function for the Johnson Company's all-weather coat. Holding consumers' money income and the prices of other goods constant, the demand function for this product is

$$Q_x^d = 500 - 5P_x.$$

What is the point elasticity of demand at, for instance, a price of $60? At this price, quantity demanded is 200,000 units. The slope of the demand curve is –5. Ignoring signs and recalling that quantity demanded is denomi- nated in thousands, the point elasticity of demand is therefore

$$\text{POINT } \eta_p = \left|-5 \times \frac{60}{200}\right| = 1.5.$$

---

10 The partial derivative symbol is used because demand is a function of variables other than price that are held constant when the slope of the demand function is computed.

Price Elasticity and the Linear Demand Function

The formula for the point elasticity of demand in equation 2.13 provides a straightforward way of demonstrating that the price elasticity of demand varies continuously along a linear demand curve. Holding all other variables affecting demand constant, the first term in the equation, $\partial Q/\partial P$, is the slope of the demand *function*. In view of the fact that the demand *curve* is diagrammed two-dimensionally with price on the vertical axis, the term $\partial Q/\partial P$ is the inverse of the demand curve's slope. Because linear functions have a constant slope, the slope of the demand curve, $\partial P/\partial Q$, is also a constant.

The second term in the point elasticity formula—the ratio of price to quantity demanded—is not constant, however. Because this ratio is different at each point on the demand curve, η_p takes on a different value at each of those points. In particular, price falls and quantity demanded rises with movement down a demand curve. The equation for point elasticity therefore implies that demand becomes more inelastic (less elastic) the further one moves down a linear demand curve.

For example, at prices of $70, $60, and $50, the point price elasticity of demand for the Johnson Company's all-weather coats is:

PRICE (P)	QUANTITY DEMANDED (Q) (IN THOUSANDS)	$\eta_p = \left\vert -5 \times \dfrac{P}{Q} \right\vert$
$70	150	2.33
$60	200	1.50
$50	250	1.00

The table illustrates clearly that the point elasticity of demand declines (demand becomes more inelastic) as price falls and as quantity demanded correspondingly rises. As an additional note, recall that the arc elasticity of demand associated with a price change from $70 to $60 was calculated to be 1.86. The value of arc elasticity necessarily lies between the values of the point elasticities at the two prices that bound the discrete price change. This is because it is a measure of the average responsiveness of consumers' purchases to a change in price over a discrete range of the demand curve. In this example, the arc elasticity of 1.86 is greater than the point elasticity of demand at a price of $60 (1.5); it is less than the point elasticity of demand at a price of $70 (2.33).

Because the price elasticity of demand falls continuously along a linear demand curve, it follows that there is an elastic region of demand, a point of unitary elasticity, and an inelastic region of demand. Figure 2.5 illustrates this pattern with the demand curve for the Johnson Company's all-weather coats.

The midpoint quantity on the horizontal axis corresponds to sales of 250,000 coats. Substituting 250 for Q_x^d in the inverse demand function ($P_x = 100 - .2Q_x^d$) generates the associated price of $50. Demand is unit elastic at this price as shown in the previous table. At prices above $50, the absolute value of point price elasticity is greater than one. At prices below

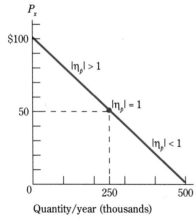

FIGURE 2.5

Elasticity of a Linear Demand Curve

$50, the absolute value of point price elasticity is less than one. For instance, at a price of $40, the point elasticity of demand is $\eta_p = |-5 \times (40/300)| = .67$. In sum, at points to the left of the linear demand curve's midpoint, demand is elastic; at points to the right of the linear demand curve's midpoint, demand is inelastic; and demand is unit elastic at the linear demand curve's midpoint.

A note of caution is warranted at this stage. Students often leap to the conclusion that because the slope of the demand curve enters into the calculation of the elasticity of demand, the relative steepness or flatness of a demand curve can be used to determine its elasticity characteristics. Figure 2.4 (see p. 42) reveals the defect in this reasoning. The two linear demand curves in this figure have exactly the same slope, yet the first is more elastic at every price than the second. At a price of $60 (point A), for example, the elasticity of the first demand curve is $\eta_p = |-5 \times (60/200)| = 1.5$. At that same price (point A') the elasticity of the second demand curve is $\eta_p = |-5 \times (60/300)| = 1.0$. Therefore, we cannot make elasticity comparisons across demand curves solely on the basis of their slopes.[11]

ELASTICITY, TOTAL REVENUE, AND MARGINAL REVENUE

Price elasticity, or the responsiveness of consumers to a change in price, is perhaps the most critical characteristic of demand. A firm rarely, if ever, is able to specify the demand function it confronts precisely. Thus, information about demand and about the sensitivity of sales to price changes must be gathered as the firm searches for the particular price that maximizes profits. This search process is complicated by the fact that the price elasticity of demand varies continuously along a (linear) demand curve. And so there is no one price elasticity at which a firm's profits will be at a maximum. The following discussion shows, however, that the firm can use information about the price elasticity of demand to reduce the cost of searching for the profit-maximizing price by excluding certain prices from consideration. This information is derived from the distinctive relationship between the price elasticity of demand and the firm's total revenue.

---

11 This observation can be generalized for linear demand curves by noting that the value of the elasticity coefficient at any given price can be calculated directly on the diagram's vertical axis. The calculation involves taking the ratio of the distance between the origin and the given price to the distance between the origin and the demand curve's vertical intercept. The elasticity of demand is consequently the same at every price on any two linear demand curves that have the same vertical intercept. Similarly, if two linear demand curves have different vertical intercepts, the demand curve with the lower intercept is more elastic at every price than the other. See Roger L. Miller and Roger E. Meiners, *Intermediate Microeconomics*, 3E. (New York: McGraw-Hill, 1986), pp. 146-51.

Elasticity and Changes in Total Revenue

The total revenue earned by the firm is simply price times quantity sold. Because the quantity the firm expects to sell changes when price changes, a change in price may cause total revenue to increase, to decrease, or to remain the same. For example, when price is reduced, total revenue may fall because each unit is sold at a lower price. On the other hand, total revenue may rise because more units are sold at the lower price. The net effect of reducing price on the firm's total revenue, *TR,* therefore depends on which of these two effects dominates. That is,

$$P(\downarrow) \times Q(\uparrow) = TR(?).$$

If the quantity change is large relative to the price change, total revenue will change in the direction of the quantity change, rising when price is reduced and falling when price is increased. If the quantity change is small relative to the price change, total revenue will change in the direction of the price change, falling when price is reduced and rising when price is increased.

The price elasticity of demand is classified into three categories depending on whether the percentage change in quantity demanded is larger, smaller, or the same as the percentage change in price. The relationship between changes in price and changes in the firm's total revenue is therefore directly related to the elasticity of its demand curve. This relationship is shown in Table 2.2.

If a firm reduces price in order to increase expected sales, what will happen? Total revenue will increase if demand is elastic, remain the same if demand is unitary elastic, and decline if demand is inelastic. In the first case, this relationship holds because the percentage increase in quantity demanded is greater than the percentage reduction in price when demand is elastic. The potential reduction in total revenue associated with the lower price is more than offset by the increase in total revenue associated with additional

TABLE 2.2 THE ELASTICITY OF DEMAND AND TOTAL REVENUE

$\eta_p = \dfrac{\text{percentage change in quantity demanded}}{\text{percentage change in price}}$		
ELASTIC	UNIT ELASTIC	INELASTIC
$\mid\eta_p\mid \underset{\downarrow}{>} 1$	$\mid\eta_p\mid \underset{\downarrow}{=} 1$	$\mid\eta_p\mid \underset{\downarrow}{<} 1$
$\%\Delta Q^d \underset{\downarrow}{>} \%\Delta P$	$\%\Delta Q^d \underset{\downarrow}{=} \%\Delta P$	$\%\Delta Q^d \underset{\downarrow}{<} \%\Delta P$
the change in total revenue follows the change in quantity	total revenue does not change	the change in total revenue follows the change in price

sales. The other two cases follow from similar arguments. By the same reasoning, if price is raised and sales decline, total revenue will fall if demand is elastic, remain the same if demand is unitary elastic, and increase if demand is inelastic.

The upper two panels of Figure 2.6 apply these relationships to the linear demand curve for the Johnson Company's all-weather coats. As established previously, the midpoint of this demand curve—the point at which demand is unit elastic—corresponds to a price of $50 and a quantity of 250,000 coats. Demand is elastic at prices above $50 and demand is inelastic at prices below $50.

Beginning at the demand curve's vertical intercept, total revenue rises initially as price is reduced. This happens because reductions in price cause total revenue to increase when demand is elastic. In the inelastic region of the demand curve, reductions in price cause total revenue to fall. Because total revenue is rising over the elastic portion of the demand curve and falling over the inelastic portion, total revenue must be at a maximum where demand shifts from elastic to inelastic. As the middle panel of the diagram shows, this maximum occurs at the midpoint of the linear demand curve where demand is unit elastic.

Price and Marginal Revenue

The bottom panel of Figure 2.6 introduces the concept of marginal revenue. **Marginal revenue** is defined as the change in total revenue divided by the associated change in quantity. More specifically, marginal revenue, MR, is equal to

$$MR = \frac{\Delta TR}{\Delta Q},$$

where total revenue, TR, is P x Q. For very small changes in sales, marginal revenue is equal to the derivative of total revenue with respect to quantity (i.e., $MR = \partial TR/\partial Q$). Marginal revenue thus measures the rate of change in total revenue accompanying a change in sales. Marginal revenue is the slope of the total revenue function.

If total revenue rises when the firm expands its sales, marginal revenue is positive. That is, total revenue increases if each unit sold adds a positive increment to total revenue. By similar reasoning, if total revenue declines with additional sales, marginal revenue is negative. The particular level of sales at which total revenue stops rising and starts falling is the point at which total revenue is at a maximum. At this point, marginal revenue changes from positive to negative and is equal to zero. Total revenue is consequently highest at the point where marginal revenue is equal to zero.

We can derive an explicit expression for marginal revenue from the Johnson Company's inverse demand function, $P_x = 100 - .2Q_x^d$. Total revenue is price times quantity, or

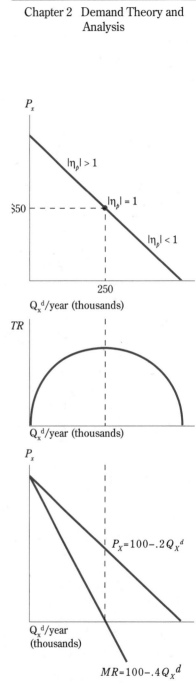

FIGURE 2.6
Elasticity, Total Revenue, and Marginal Revenue

$$TR = P_x \times Q_x^d = (100 - .2Q_x^d) \times Q_x^d$$
$$= 100Q_x^d - .2(Q_x^d)^2.$$

Marginal revenue is the change in total revenue divided by the change in output, or the derivative of total revenue with respect to quantity. Taking this derivative yields

$$MR = \frac{d\,TR}{dQ_x^d} = 100 - .4Q_x^d. \tag{2.14}$$

By comparing the equations for price and marginal revenue we see that price is always greater than marginal revenue. This is a general characteristic of all downward-sloping demand curves.[12] To see this conclusion, suppose the Johnson Company reduces the price of all-weather coats from $70 to $68. On the basis of the estimated demand function for this product, the firm can expect to sell an additional 10,000 coats at this lower price. How much will total revenue increase or, on a per unit basis, how much does each additional coat sold increase total revenue? At first blush, the answer to this question may seem obvious—total revenue increases by $680,000 because 10,000 extra coats are sold at a price of $68 each. Marginal revenue must also be $68.

But these answers are wrong, because they consider only one of the two effects that accompany a price change. Although revenue does indeed increase by $680,000 when 10,000 additional all-weather coats are sold, the firm also loses $2 worth of revenue on each of the coats it could have sold at $70. Thus, the net effect on the firm's total revenue depends on whether the increased revenue associated with additional sales is larger or smaller than the accompanying reduction in revenue associated with the lower price.

The two opposing effects of a change in price on total revenue are disentangled in Table 2.3. The *net* increase in total revenue is $380,000. On a per unit basis, each additional coat sells for $68 but adds only $38 to total revenue ($380,000 in additional revenue divided by 10,000 additional sales). The marginal revenue associated with this discrete change in price, $\Delta TR/\Delta Q$, is thus $38, not $68.

Equation 2.14 can be applied to calculate point estimates of marginal revenue. The point estimates of marginal revenue at prices of $70 and $68 are

$$P = \$70: MR = 100 - .4(150) = 100 - 60 = \$40, \text{ and}$$
$$P = \$68: MR = 100 - .4(160) = 100 - 64 = \$36.$$

Consistent with the discussion of point and arc elasticities of demand, the estimate of marginal revenue over this discrete price range ($38) is an average of the point estimates of marginal revenue at the beginning and ending prices.

---

12 Price is greater than marginal revenue, *provided* that the firm sells all units at the same price. Price will not necessarily be greater than marginal revenue with alternative pricing strategies. The implication of alternative pricing strategies that do not limit the firm to a single-price policy are explored in Chapters 6 and 9.

	PRICE	QUANTITY (THOUSANDS)
initial situation	$70	150
new situation	$68	160
	↓ lowering the price by $2 on 150,000 coats *reduces* total revenue by $300,000	↓ increasing sales by 10,000 coats *increases* total revenue by $680,000

Managerial Decisions Based on Elasticity and Marginal Revenue

As stressed earlier, knowledge of a firm's demand curve (and, hence, information about marginal revenue and price elasticity) is not sufficient for determining the firm's profit-maximizing price. Profit-maximizing pricing decisions also require information on the cost conditions of the firm. However, information about demand alone can provide a useful guide for managerial decisions. Indeed, because demand, elasticity, and marginal revenue have a unique relationship, the word "demand" in the previous sentence can be replaced with either "elasticity" or "marginal revenue."[13]

Suppose the Johnson Company wants to maximize the value of all-weather coat sales (total revenue) during the first year following their introduction. In a single-period model, total revenue maximization and profit maximization are not consistent with one another. However, the two objectives can be compatible from a multi-period perspective. That is, the Johnson Company may have reason to believe that demand, price, and profits will be higher in subsequent periods if the value of sales is maximized in the initial period.

According to Figure 2.6, the value of the Johnson Company's sales (total revenue) is maximized at a price of $50 and sales of 250,000 units. Moreover, the diagram also shows that sales are at a maximum at the point where marginal revenue is equal to zero and demand is unit elastic ($|\eta_p| = 1$). Hence, if short-run sales maximization is a temporary goal of the firm, the firm can achieve its objective by producing and selling the particular quantity of output at which marginal revenue is equal to zero and the price elasticity of demand is equal to 1.[14]

---

13 The exact relationship between demand (price), elasticity, and marginal revenue is developed in the next section.

14 The total-revenue-maximizing level of sales is determined algebraically by calculating the quantity at which marginal revenue is equal to zero. Setting $MR = 100 - .4Q_x^d = 0$ and solving for Q_x^d yields $Q_x^d = 100/.4 = 250$, or 250,000 units. See the appendix for a discussion of the condition that is sufficient for assuring a maximum.

Alternatively, suppose that the firm's objective is to maximize short-run profits rather than sales. Given the information in Figure 2.6, where will the firm want to produce? Although this question cannot be answered definitively without information about costs, we can answer a slightly different question: Where will the firm *never* want to produce? The answer is that the firm will never want to produce in the region of demand where marginal revenue is negative. The justification for this conclusion is that additional sales in this region of the demand curve cause total revenue to decline. It is plainly impossible to increase profit by increasing sales if the additional revenue associated with the sales is negative. Marginal revenue is negative in the region of the demand curve where demand is inelastic ($|\eta_p| < 1$). Hence, if the goal is to maximize profits, the firm will never want to operate on the inelastic portion of its demand curve.

Price, Marginal Revenue, and Elasticity

The demand curve defines a unique marginal revenue curve and set of elasticity characteristics. Price, marginal revenue, and elasticity are related to one another, as the following expression shows:[15]

$$MR = P\left(1 - \frac{1}{|\eta_p|}\right). \tag{2.15}$$

The relationships described in the previous section are summarized by this expression. In particular, when $|\eta_p| = 1$, it follows that $MR = 0$. Moreover, the profit-maximizing firm will never operate in the inelastic region of demand because $MR < 0$ when $|\eta_p| < 1$. Finally, in the elastic region of demand (i.e., where $|\eta_p| > 1$), $MR < P$.

THE DETERMINANTS OF PRICE ELASTICITY

A linear demand curve contains both elastic and inelastic regions; there is also a single point on a linear demand curve—the midpoint—at which demand is unit elastic. This section discusses four factors that influence the relative elasticity characteristics of the demand curve confronting the firm.

Availability of Substitutes. The first determinant of price elasticity is the availability of substitute products. Consumers are more sensitive to an

---

15 Marginal revenue is the derivative of total revenue with respect to quantity, that is $\partial TR/\partial Q$. Total revenue, in turn, is price times quantity, or $P \times Q$. Price itself depends on the quantity sold through the inverse demand function. Taking the required derivative therefore yields $MR = \partial TR/\partial Q = P + Q(\partial P/\partial Q)$. The right-hand side of this expression for marginal revenue can be rewritten in terms of the price elasticity of demand by multiplying through by P/P, factoring out a P, and noting that $(Q/P)(\partial P/\partial Q) = -1/|\eta_p|$. Specifically, $MR = (P/P)\ [P + Q(\partial P/\partial Q)] = P[1 + (Q/P)(\partial P/\partial Q)] = P[1 - (1/|\eta_p|)]$.

Hizzoner Learns About Price Elasticity

The art of taxation consists in so plucking the goose as to obtain the largest amount of feathers with the least amount of hissing."

Jean Baptiste Colbert, 1619-1683

One of the most important lessons of price elasticity is that firms do not have complete freedom to set price. In virtually all circumstances, an increase in price causes a reduction in sales. The revenue effects of price increases, in turn, depend on the price elasticity of demand. If demand is elastic, an increase in price leads to a reduction in total revenue. On the other hand, if demand is inelastic an increase in price leads to an increase in total revenue.

Similarly, if the government taxes a specific product (with a sales or excise tax), the ability of that tax to generate revenue depends on the responses of consumers to the tax-induced price increase. Other things being the same, a tax on a product with inelastic demand will generate more tax revenue for the government than a tax on a product with elastic demand. The following example demonstrates that even politicians can benefit from a basic understanding of managerial economics.

In August 1980, the city government of Washington, D.C., imposed a six percent sales tax on gasoline.[a] City officials predicted that the tax would raise $13 million a year in much needed revenue for the city. The new tax was in effect for only three months when the city's mayor, Marion Barry, abruptly called for an immediate repeal of the tax. In support of this move, Barry was quoted as saying that the tax "caused undue hardships both on the consumers of gas in our city and those who operate retail gas businesses."[b] In fact, Mayor Barry was probably responding to political pressure from both consumers and businesses to repeal the gasoline tax.

Political discontent notwithstanding, Mayor Barry's readiness to repeal the tax was probably also related to its failure to generate the windfall in revenues that the city expected. There were indications that the tax contributed to a 30 percent reduction in gasoline sales in the city during the short period it was in effect. The large reduction in gasoline sales crippled the tax's ability to generate revenues. In fact, if sales of gasoline had declined enough, overall tax revenues could have fallen because of the tax increase.

From the perspective of the city's politicians, what went wrong? They failed to recognize that the elasticity of demand for gasoline sold in the District of Columbia is much greater than the demand for gasoline in general. When the tax increase was translated into a price increase, many consumers were able to easily substitute lower-priced gasoline from nearby retailers in the Maryland and Virginia suburbs. Moreover, because the elasticity of demand tends to be greater in the long run than in the short run, the negative effect of the tax on city sales would probably have increased the longer it was in effect.

Because it did not consider the reaction of consumers to the tax, as reflected by the elasticity of demand for gasoline in the D.C. market, the city government found itself in a worst-case position. In the words of Jean Baptiste Colbert, the city failed to pluck many feathers from the goose and the goose hissed loudly at the effort.

a "Barry Asks Gasoline Tax Repeal," *Washington Post*, 2 November 1980, p. A1.
b *Ibid.*

increase in a product's price if alternative products are available to which they can turn. A firm that sells a product having a number of close substitutes can expect a reduction in the product's price to provoke a relatively large percentage increase in its own sales as consumers shift their purchases away from higher-priced alternatives.

Hence, products that have a number of close substitutes will tend to have more elastic demand curves than products that do not compete with close substitutes. The degree of substitutability among competing products is defined by the effect of changes in the prices of the alternative products on the demand for the good in question. Changes in the prices of competing products affect the demands for products having close substitutes more than they affect the demands for products without close substitutes. The next section's discussion of the cross-price elasticity of demand defines the concept of substitutability more rigorously.

Importance to the Consumer's Budget. A second factor that determines the price elasticity of demand for a product is the relative importance of the product in the consumer's budget. Other things being equal, the demand for products that represent a small fraction of a consumer's total expenditures will tend to be less elastic than the demand for products that represent a large share of the consumer's total expenditures. This conclusion follows because price changes for "big-ticket" items have a larger impact on the consumer's real income than do comparable price changes for less expensive goods. A 10 percent increase in the price of an automobile, for example, is likely to provoke a larger percentage reduction in purchases than a 10 percent increase in the price of salt. The demand for items that represent a significant share of the consumer's budget will tend to be more elastic than the demand for low-budget-share goods. This is because the income effect associated with a given change in price is larger.

Frequency of Purchase. Third, the price elasticity of demand is affected by the frequency with which the product is purchased. Products that are purchased frequently tend to have more elastic demands than products that are purchased infrequently. This increased sensitivity to changes in the prices of frequently purchased items is due to the fact that consumers have the opportunity to acquire more information about prices and the availability of substitutes. Consumers have more information about the prices and qualities of various brands of bread and milk, which are purchased weekly, than they have about exotic spices that are purchased much less often. Because of this superior information, the demand for bread or milk will tend to be more elastic than the demand for spices.

Time. The fourth factor that affects the price elasticity of demand is the length of time over which the demand function is specified. The relationship between price and quantity demanded can be defined for the period of a week, a month, a year, and so on. Demand curves tend to become more elastic as the period of analysis lengthens. As the period over which the demand curve is defined lengthens, consumers have more opportunities to search out alternatives and to rearrange their expenditures in response to a given change in price. The price of gasoline might increase substantially, for example, without provoking much of a reduction in weekly or monthly sales. However, as the time horizon over which this price increase has taken effect becomes longer, consumers will respond to the price change by switching to public transportation, by trading in their gas-guzzlers for more fuel efficient vehicles, and so forth. This response will cause a larger percentage reduction in gasoline purchases as times goes by.

The impact of time on the price elasticity of demand underscores the importance of a fundamental understanding of demand analysis to managerial decision making. Firms operate in dynamic markets where time plays a critical role. Therefore, managers who recognize that market responses depend on the length of time being analyzed are better equipped to compete than managers who take only a static view of demand.

We have now explored the price elasticity of demand extensively. In addition to gauging consumers' sensitivity to changes in a good's own price, the elasticity concept can measure the responsiveness of quantity demanded to other variables in the demand function. The following section introduces one of these alternative elasticity measures, the cross-price elasticity of demand.

CROSS-PRICE ELASTICITIES OF DEMAND

Goods are classified as substitutes or complements on the basis of the cross-price elasticity of demand. The **cross-price elasticity of demand** is defined as the percentage change in the quantity demanded of one good, say good x, associated with a given percentage change in the price of some other good, good y. More specifically, the cross-price elasticity of demand, η_{xy}, is

$$\eta_{xy} = \frac{\%\Delta Q_x^d}{\%\Delta P_y}. \quad \text{CROSS} - \text{PRICE ELASTICITY OF DEMAND} \quad (2.16)$$

The cross-price elasticity of demand measures the responsiveness of the demand for one product to a change in the price of some other product, holding all other variables constant, including the good's own price. If the cross-price elasticity of demand between two goods is positive, the goods are said to be **substitutes**. In this case, an increase in the price of one of the goods causes the demand for the other to increase, and vice-versa. On the other hand, if the cross-price elasticity of demand is negative, the two goods are said to be **complements**—an increase in the price of one of the goods causes the demand for the other to decline.

The cross-price elasticity of demand can be calculated in two ways. For discrete changes in the price of one of the goods, use the arc elasticity formula:

$$\text{ARC } \eta_{xy} = \frac{\left(Q_x^2 - Q_x^1 \right)}{\left(Q_x^2 + Q_x^1 \right)} \div \frac{\left(P_y^2 - P_y^1 \right)}{\left(P_y^2 + P_y^1 \right)}. \quad (2.17)$$

The numerator in this formula, $(Q_x^2 - Q_x^1)/(Q_x^2 + Q_x^1)$, is the average percentage change in consumers' purchases of good x. The denominator, $(P_y^2 - P_y^1)/(P_y^2 + P_y^1)$, is the associated average percentage change in the price of good y. (The superscripts 1 and 2 denote beginning and ending values, respectively.) The formula for the point cross-price elasticity of demand,

$$\text{POINT } \eta_{xy} = \left(\frac{\partial Q_x}{\partial P_y} \right) \left(\frac{P_y}{Q_x} \right), \qquad (2.18)$$

applies when (infinitesimally) small changes in price are being considered.

Equation 2.18 yields numerical measures of the sensitivity of the demand for the Johnson Company's all-weather coat to changes in the prices of the related goods identified by the consulting firm. The demand function for all-weather coats is

$$Q_x^d = 60 - 5P_x + 2.4P_y - 4P_z + 10I,$$

where P_x is the Johnson Company's own price, P_y is the price of a rival firm's ski jacket, P_z is the price of a matching all-weather hat, and I is consumers' average money income.

The value of the cross-price elasticity of demand depends on the particular price and quantity of all-weather coats at which η_{xy} is calculated. Suppose that the Johnson Company selects a price of \$60. Holding all other variables affecting demand constant at previously assumed levels (P_y = \$50, P_z = \$20, and I = \$40), the firm can expect to sell 200,000 coats annually. At this price and quantity, the point cross-price elasticity of demand between the company's all-weather coat and its rival's ski jacket is

$$\text{POINT } \eta_{xy} = 2.4 \times \left(\frac{50}{200} \right) = .6.$$

Hence, if the rival firm increases the price of its ski jacket by one percent, the Johnson Company can expect to increase its sales of all-weather coats by six-tenths of one percent.

Equation 2.18 likewise provides a point estimate of the cross-price elasticity of demand between the Johnson Company's all-weather coat and the matching all-weather hat available to consumers. Once again assuming that all-weather coats are sold at a price of \$60 and that all other variables affecting demand are held constant, the cross-price elasticity of demand between these goods is

$$\text{POINT } \eta_{xy} = -4 \times \left(\frac{50}{200} \right) = -.4.$$

A one percent increase in the price of the all-weather hat leads consumers to reduce their purchases of Johnson's all-weather coat by four-tenths of one percent.

According to the assumptions made in constructing the chapter's stylized example, the ski jacket is a substitute for the Johnson Company's new product (the cross-price elasticity of demand is positive). By the same example the all-weather hat is a complement to it (the cross-price elasticity of demand is negative). It is worth emphasizing, though, that the cross-price elasticity of demand between any two goods is determined by the behavior of consumers. If consumers view two or more goods as capable of satisfying essentially the same demand, these goods will tend to be substitutes in the demand function and individuals will shift their purchases among them in response to a change in relative prices. The level of response in any particular case depends not so much on objective similarities in the goods' attributes, but on individuals' perceptions of these attributes. Buicks and Hondas may be close substitutes in the minds of some consumers, in which case the cross-price elasticity of demand between them will be relatively large. Or in the eyes of other consumers they may be poor substitutes and, hence, have a cross-price elasticity of demand close to zero.

The degree of substitutability among goods also depends on how narrowly or broadly the market for the good in question is defined. Gasoline sold in the United States as a whole, for instance, has few good substitutes. However, there are many good substitutes for gasoline sold at the local service station. "Food" likewise has no good substitutes, but there are many alternatives to steak. Consumers have even more alternatives to steak sold by Safeway. In short, when the market in which the good is sold is defined broadly, there tend to be few other goods which exhibit large, positive cross-price elasticities with it. The opposite is true when the market is defined narrowly.

Complementary goods can be thought of as inputs in the production of household goods or services. Bacon, eggs, toast, and orange juice, for example, are inputs in the production of breakfast. If the price of bacon rises, then a bacon-and-egg breakfast becomes more expensive and egg sales will tend to decrease. Again, however, the magnitude of the quantity response depends on consumers' tastes and preferences. If large numbers of consumers equally enjoy eating either steak or bacon with their eggs, then an increase in the price of bacon may have little or no impact on the demand for eggs.

In short, while many goods can be classified as substitutes or complements on *a priori* grounds, in the final analysis the degree to which the classifications are valid is not arbitrated by the opinions of the managers of firms or those of economists. These judgments are instead made by consumers.

INCOME ELASTICITY OF DEMAND

Like other elasticity measures, the **income elasticity of demand** is defined as the percentage change in quantity demanded divided by the percentage change in consumers' money income. Specifically, the income elasticity of demand, η_I, is equal to

$$\eta_I = \frac{\%\Delta Q_x^{\,d}}{\%\Delta I}. \quad \text{INCOME ELASTICITY OF DEMAND} \quad (2.19)$$

Holding all other variables constant, the income elasticity of demand measures the responsiveness of the demand for a product to a change in income. The income elasticity of demand can be positive or negative. If $\eta_I > 0$, an increase in income causes the demand for the good in question to increase. Because this is the expected relation between demand and income for most products, goods having a positive income elasticity are called *normal goods*. (If $\eta_I > 1$, the good is sometimes called a **superior good.**)

On the other hand, if $\eta_I < 0$, an increase in income causes the demand for the good to decline. Goods having a negative income elasticity are called *inferior goods*. The generic or "house brand" of a product provides a relevant example. An increase in money income might cause consumers to rearrange their spending patterns in favor of a national brand of paper towels, thereby reducing their purchases of generic versions of this product. Similarly, a reduction in money income could lead to an increase in the demand for off-brand products. Generic paper towels are classified as income-inferior (and national brands are classified as income-normal) if these relationships hold.

If the income elasticity of demand is positive, then the demand for the good in question shifts in the same direction as the income change. The opposite is true when the income elasticity of demand is negative. The numerical value of the income elasticity coefficient provides an estimate of the magnitude of this demand response.[16]

Like the own-price and cross-price elasticities of demand, the income elasticity of demand can be calculated in two ways. For discrete income changes, use the arc income-elasticity of demand:

$$\text{ARC } \eta_I = \left(\frac{Q_x^2 - Q_x^1}{Q_x^2 + Q_x^1} \right) \div \left(\frac{I^2 - I^1}{I^2 + I^1} \right), \tag{2.20}$$

where the superscripts again denote the initial and ending values of the two variables. The point income elasticity of demand,

$$\text{POINT } \eta_I = \left(\frac{\partial Q_x}{\partial I} \right)\left(\frac{I}{Q_x} \right), \tag{2.21}$$

is appropriate for gauging the sensitivity of demand to infinitesimally small income changes.

Using equation 2.21, we can estimate the income elasticity of demand for the Johnson Company's all-weather coat. Once again assuming that the new product is sold at a price of $60 and that the prices of all other goods are held constant, the point income elasticity of demand at consumers' average annual income of $40,000 is

$$\text{POINT } \eta_I = 10 \times \left(\frac{40}{200} \right) = 2.$$

16 Goods having an income elasticity between –1 and 1 are sometimes referred to as *noncyclical goods* because the percentage change in demand is smaller than the associated percentage change in income. The demands for such goods are consequently not affected strongly by the business cycle. On the other hand, if the absolute value of income elasticity is greater than 1, the good is said to be a *cyclical good* because variations in income over the business cycle are apt to provoke a relatively large positive or negative demand response depending on whether the good is income-normal or income-inferior.

This point elasticity estimate suggests that a one percent increase in consumers' money income will increase the Johnson Company's sales of all-weather coats by 2 percent. The all-weather coat is a normal good at *current* prices and money income.

The last proviso is necessary because the classification of goods as either normal or inferior has nothing whatsoever to do with their intrinsic qualities or attributes. The same good can be income-normal for one consumer and income-inferior for another. Likewise, a good can be income-inferior for a consumer at one income level and income-normal at another. The characteristics of normality and inferiority are based solely on the direction of the demand response to a change in income. An inferior good is not necessarily a low-quality good; nor is a normal good necessarily a high-quality one.

OTHER DEMAND ELASTICITIES

The foregoing discussion has focused on three important elasticity characteristics of demand: own-price elasticity, cross-price elasticity, and income elasticity. The elasticity concept is not limited to these three definitions, however. An elasticity coefficient can be computed to measure the sensitivity of consumers' purchases to a change in any of the variables in the demand function, holding all other relevant variables constant. For example, we may include the firm's advertising expenditures as a determinant of the demand for a product because advertising informs consumers about prices, locations of sales, and so on. This advertised information reduces the consumer's cost of search and enables the firm to increase its sales at given prices. The responsiveness of consumers to changes in advertising expenditures—an advertising elasticity of demand—could then be measured by calculating the *ceteris paribus* percentage change in demand relative to the corresponding percentage change in advertising.

Similarly, the willingness and ability of consumers to purchase a seller's product at various possible current prices depends in part on their expectations about the product's future price. Other things being the same, if consumers expect price to be higher next period than this period, the current demand for the product will tend to shift outward as consumers rationally buy more units of the good at today's lower price than they would otherwise. On the other hand, if consumers expect next period's prices to be lower than this period's, the current demand for the product will tend to decline as consumers cut back their purchases in anticipation of future savings. The elasticity concept can likewise be applied in estimating the relative magnitude of this demand effect.

In short, elasticity is one of the most useful concepts in the analysis of consumer behavior. It provides a unit-free measure of the responsiveness of purchases to a change in any of the determinants of demand. It can be applied generally to any of these determinants. The own-price elasticity of demand is clearly the most critical to business decision making, however, because the manager exercises most direct control over the firm's own price. The manager must be extremely attentive to the elasticity of demand in searching for the particular price that maximizes profits.

SUMMARY

This chapter has explored the economic theory of demand in detail. Beginning with a model of rational consumer choice, we used utility-maximizing behavior subject to a budget constraint to derive an individual consumer's demand function for a product. We saw that the principal determinants of demand are the consumers' tastes and preferences, his or her money income, and the relative prices of the goods from which consumption choices are made. We saw also that consistency with the assumptions of rational consumer choice requires that the consumer's demand curve be downward-sloping. In other words, *ceteris paribus* (i.e., holding all other variables affecting demand constant), the law of demand states that rational consumers are willing and able to buy more of a good at lower prices than at higher prices.

We then summed the separate demand curves of individual consumers horizontally to obtain the demand curve facing the firm. A hypothetical demand function for the Johnson Company's proposed new all-weather coat was specified. The following equation represents the demand for this product.

$$Q_x^d = 60 - 5P_x + 2.4P_y - 4P_z + 10I.$$

Q_x^d is the quantity of all-weather coats (in thousands per year), P_x is the price of all-weather coats, P_y is the price of a ski jacket that competes with the all-weather coat, P_z is the price of a matching all-weather hat, and I is consumers' average annual money income (denominated in thousands of dollars).

Holding money income and the prices of the other goods constant at predetermined levels, this demand function shows how the *quantity demanded* of all-weather coats varies with changes in that product's own price. For example, if the price of the ski jacket is $50, the price of the all-weather hat is $20, and income is $40,000, the firm can expect to sell 200,000 coats per year if it charges a price of $60 per coat. Given that the slope of the demand function is constant and equal to -5, the firm can expect to sell 5,000 additional coats per year when price is reduced by $1.

This chapter has also analyzed the impacts on the *demand* for all-weather coats caused by changes in variables other than the good's own price. In particular, a $1 increase in the price of the ski jacket increases demand by 2,400 units; a $1 increase in the price of the all-weather hat reduces demand by 4,000 units; and a $1,000 increase in income increases demand by 10,000 units.

The sensitivity of consumers' purchases to *ceteris paribus* changes in the independent demand variables was computed from the formulas for the arc and point elasticities of demand. Given the values of P_x, P_y, P_z, and I assumed above, the absolute value of the own-price elasticity of demand was equal to

1.5 at a price of $60, indicating that the demand for all-weather coats is elastic at this price. Similarly, the cross-price elasticity of demand with respect to the ski jacket is .6, indicating that these two goods are substitutes. The cross-price elasticity of demand with respect to the all-weather hat is –.4, indicating that these two goods are complements. And the income elasticity of demand is 2, suggesting that the all-weather coat is an income-normal good.

An analysis of the relationship between total revenue, marginal revenue, and the own-price elasticity of demand showed that total revenue is at a maximum at the point on the demand curve where demand is unit elastic and marginal revenue is consequently zero. By similar reasoning, we found that a profit-maximizing firm will never choose to produce in the region of its demand curve where demand is inelastic because marginal revenue is negative in this region.

QUESTIONS

2.1 What are four determinants of the price elasticity of demand? Some textbooks list the "necessity" of a good as one of the determinants of the elasticity of demand. Should the authors of *Modern Managerial Economics* have included necessity on the list of the determinants of demand elasticity?

2.2 The income-compensated demand function is more elastic than the ordinary, uncompensated demand function. True, false, or uncertain? Explain.

2.3 The demand curves diagrammed in this chapter are all downward-sloping. Can demand curves be upward sloping? Can demand curves be horizontal lines? If so, under what conditions? If not, why not?

2.4 Define each of the following concepts with both arc and point elasticity formulas.
   a. own-price elasticity of demand
   b. cross-price elasticity of demand
   c. income elasticity of demand
   d. advertising elasticity of demand

2.5 Demand analysis indicates that profit-maximizing firms will never want to produce in the region of demand where demand is inelastic, that is, where the absolute value of the own-price elasticity of demand is less than one. Yet empirical demand studies often report price elasticities of less than one in absolute value. For example, the price elasticities of demand for medical services and gasoline have been found to be around .5, and the price elasticity of demand for food is estimated to be about .2. Is it possible to reconcile the theoretical proscription against operating in the inelastic region of demand with these empirical results? [Note: The answer that firms do not maximize profits is not acceptable.]

2.6 How does the own-price elasticity of demand for an industry compare with the own-price elasticity of demand for an individual firm in that industry? Explain.

2.7 Suppose that a firm is currently producing a single product that has an income elasticity of demand equal to 2. The firm's manager is considering beginning production of a second product. One of the new products being considered has an income elasticity that is also equal to 2; a second product that has an income elasticity of –2 is also being evaluated. If the two products are expected to be equally profitable in the long run, which of the two products might the firm choose to produce based solely on its income elasticity characteristics?

2.8 The demand for VCRs is characterized by the following point elasticities of demand: own-price elasticity = 3 (in absolute value), cross-price elasticity with televisions = –5, and income elasticity = 2. Explain whether each of the following statements is true or false.

a. A reduction in the price of VCRs will lead to an increase in sales of VCRs and an increase in profits.

b. A reduction in the price of VCRs will lead to an increase in sales of VCRs and an increase in total revenue.

c. If the price of VCRs increases by one percent, the firm can anticipate a five percent increase in the sales of television sets.

d. The demand for VCRs is elastic and a VCR is a normal good.

e. If consumers' money income increases by two percent, VCR sales will remain steady if at the same time the price of VCRs is increased by three percent.

2.9 Government plans to increase tax revenues often target tax increases for cigarettes and alcohol. What demand characteristic makes these products attractive targets for tax increases?

2.10 The own-price elasticity of demand and the cross-price elasticity of demand are both used to characterize the degree of competition that a firm faces. What are the relative merits of these two elasticities as measures of competitiveness?

2.11 Suppose that the market for orange juice is dominated by two firms, Tastee Squeeze and Florida Fresh. Florida Fresh has observed that both its cross-price elasticity of demand and its cross-advertising elasticity of demand are positive. What factors might explain these observations?

PROBLEMS

2.1 The Arkadelphia Toy Company sells rubber balls for $2.75. Last year the company sold 3.75 million rubber balls. The company's owner conjectures that the elasticity of demand for rubber balls is 1.5. If the firm faces a linear demand curve, what is the equation of that demand curve?

2.2 Earnest T. Bass is the owner of a franchise pizza restaurant. Because his restaurant is located in a small college town, pizza sales typically decline substantially during the summer months. The months of June, July, and August have historically had about the same volume of business. During the month of June, his restaurant sold 2,600 pizzas at an average price of $12 per pizza. In an effort to attract more customers, Earnest lowered the average price of pizzas to $9 in July and found that sales increased to 3,400 pizzas. Beer sales were bolstered as well. The 1,300 bottles sold in July were 200 units above the previous month's level.

a. What is the arc own-price elasticity of the demand for pizzas?

b. What is the arc cross-price elasticity between pizza and beer?

c. The beer distributor who serves all of the restaurants in town holds a contest in August. The restaurant owner who sells the most beer is awarded a free one-week vacation in Hawaii. The catch is that restaurant owners are not allowed to reduce their beer prices during the contest period. Earnest believes he can win the Hawaii trip if he sells 1,500 bottles of beer in August. If the cross-price elasticity of demand is relatively constant, what price should Earnest charge for pizzas in order to sell 1,500 bottles of beer?

2.3 Frank's Premium Hot Dogs sell well in gourmet food shops in Atlanta. Its primary competitor is the South Fork Beef Wiener. The demand function for Frank's Premium Hot Dogs is

$$Q_x^d = 50{,}000 - 70{,}000P_x + 30{,}000P_y - 30{,}000P_z + 5I + 2A_x - .5A_y.$$

In this function, Q_x^d is the number of packages of hot dogs sold annually, P_x is the price of Frank's Premium Hot Dogs, P_y is the price of South Fork Beef Wieners, P_z is the price of Frank's Gourmet Hot Dog Buns, I is disposable income, A_x is advertising expenditure on Frank's Premium Hot Dogs, and A_y is advertising expenditure on South Fork Beef Wieners. (The last three variables are denominated in thousands.) Frank sells his Premium Hot Dogs at a price of $4.50 per package and Gourmet Hot Dog Buns fetch $2 per package. South Fork Wieners currently sell at a price of $4.00 per package. The average annual disposable income of Atlanta's consumers is $25,000. Finally, Frank spends $125,000 each year promoting his Premium Hot Dogs while his competitor spends $50,000 annually to advertise South Fork Beef Wieners.

a. What is the own-price elasticity of demand for Frank's gourmet franks?
b. What is the cross-price elasticity of demand between Frank's franks and South Fork Beef Wieners?
c. What is the income elasticity of demand for Frank's franks?
d. What response can Frank expect if he raises the price of Gourmet Hot Dog Buns by $.50 per package?
e. What is the cross-advertising elasticity of demand between Frank's franks and the promotional efforts of his competitor?
f. If Frank wants to maximize the total revenue associated with hot dog sales, what price should he set?

2.4 Consider a nonlinear specification of the demand function for the Johnson Company's all-weather coats. In particular, suppose that the demand function is

$$Q_x^d = aP_x^b P_y^c P_z^e I^f.$$

As before, Q_x^d is the quantity demanded per year (in thousands), P_x is the unit price of all-weather coats, P_y is the price of the rival firm's ski jacket, P_z is the price of the matching all-weather hat, and I is consumers' money income (in thousands of dollars).

a. Find an expression for the point elasticity of demand with respect to the good's own price. Provide an economic interpretation of your answer.
b. Find point estimates for the two cross-price elasticities and for the income elasticity of demand. Interpret your results.
c. Derive an expression for the marginal revenue function associated with this nonlinear demand function. Can marginal revenue ever be negative? What does your answer imply about the selection of the firm's profit-maximizing price?

Techniques Of Differentiation

Marginal analysis is perhaps the economist's most important analytical tool. The term *marginal* means "rate of change." For example, marginal revenue, a concept introduced in this chapter, is defined as the change in total revenue associated with a change in quantity sold. Similarly, marginal cost, a concept that will be introduced in Chapter 3, is defined as the change in total cost associated with a change in the quantity of output produced. Marginal revenue and marginal cost are the keys to understanding profit-maximizing pricing decisions. In addition to verbal and graphical reasoning, this text employs a modest amount of elementary differential calculus because it offers an efficient method of working with marginal concepts.

The knowledge of calculus required of the readers of this text is limited to three areas—simple differentiation, the maximization or minimization of an unconstrained objective function, and the Lagrangian technique for solving constrained optimization problems. This appendix is devoted to the topic of simple differentiation. Appendices to subsequent chapters cover optimization techniques.

The following discussion is carried out in the context of the linear and nonlinear functions used as examples in this chapter. The derivative of any one of these functions corresponds to the economist's concept of the margin. "Marginal" refers to the change in value of one variable caused by the change in the value of some other variable. Marginal changes can occur over any arbitrary, discrete range of a function. As the discrete range over which the change occurs is made smaller and smaller, the range becomes confined to an infinitesimally small region around a particular point on the function. The magnitude of this change is measured by taking the derivative of the function at that point. Taking the derivative is equivalent to evaluating the *slope* of the function in the direction of the change under consideration.

More formally, consider the general demand function for a good, $Q = f(P)$, where Q is the quantity demanded by consumers per time period and P is the good's own price. This notation states that Q is some arbitrary function, f, of P, or that Q depends on P. The derivative of this function is defined as

$$\lim_{\Delta P \to 0} \frac{\left[f(P+\Delta P)-f(P)\right]}{\Delta P} = \lim_{\Delta P \to 0} \frac{\Delta Q}{\Delta P}.$$

In other words, the derivative of the demand function measures the difference in the value of the function when it is evaluated at two different points. One of these points is $Q = f(P)$; the other is at some arbitrary distance away from P, that is, $Q = f(P + \Delta P)$. The difference in the function's value at these two points is evaluated relative to the associated change in P, ΔP. As this change in P becomes very small and approaches zero in the limit (lim $\Delta P \to 0$), the derivative measures the corresponding instantaneous change in Q.

The foregoing definition leads to a number of rules for taking the derivatives of particular functional relationships between two or more variables. These rules are stated in the following paragraphs.

Simple Differentiation

Simple differentiation is relevant for functions that contain only two variables. The simple demand function $Q = f(P)$ is such a function. In this function, Q is the *dependent variable* and P is the *independent variable* because the value of Q depends on the value selected for P. The derivative of a simple two-variable function is denoted by dQ/dP.

Derivative of a Constant. Suppose that $Q = f(P) = c$, where c is a constant. More concretely, suppose that $Q = 500$. In this simple case, quantity demanded does not depend on price and so Q does not change when P changes. The derivative of a constant function is therefore identically equal to zero. In other words, if

$$Q = 500, \text{ then}$$
$$\frac{dQ}{dP} = 0.$$

This rule should be geometrically obvious because the graph of a constant function is a horizontal straight line and the slope of this line is consequently zero at every point.

Power Rule. Suppose that $Q = f(P) = P^n$, where n is a positive integer. Then the derivative of Q with respect to P is nP^{n-1}. As a special case of this rule, consider the linear demand function for the Johnson Company's all-weather coat. This demand function is

$$Q_x^d = 500 - 5P_x,$$

where Q_x^d is measured in thousands of coats sold per year and P_x is measured in dollars. According to the power rule,

$$\frac{dQ_x^d}{dP} = \frac{d(500)}{dP} - 5\left[\frac{d(P_x)}{d(P_x)}\right]$$

$$= 0 - 5(1)P_x^{1-1}$$
$$= -5P_x^{0}$$
$$= -5$$

because $P_x^0 = 1$.

The value of the derivative is the slope of this particular demand function. It is a constant, indicating that if price is increased (reduced) by $1, quantity demanded falls (rises) by 5,000 units. Similarly,

$$P_x = 100 - .2Q_x^d$$

is the inverse demand function for all-weather coats. P is now the dependent variable and Q is the independent variable. According to the power rule,

$$\frac{dP_x}{dQ_x^d} = \frac{d(100)}{dQ_x^d} - .2\left(\frac{dQ_x^d}{dQ_x^d}\right)$$
$$= 0 - .2(1)\left(Q_x^d\right)^{1-1}$$
$$= .2\left(Q_x^d\right)^{0}$$
$$= -.2.$$

The intuition behind the power rule may not be as clear as the intuition for taking the derivative of a constant function. The power rule is, however, a fairly straightforward application of the definition of a derivative. Consider the inverse demand function above. If Q changes by a small amount, the new value of P will be

$$P + \Delta P = 100 - .2(Q_x^d + \Delta Q_x^d)$$
$$= 100 - .2Q_x^d - .2\Delta Q_x^d.$$

Subtracting $P = 100 - .2Q_x^d$ from both sides of this expression yields

$$\Delta P = -.2\Delta Q_x^d,$$

and dividing through by ΔQ_x^d results in

$$\frac{\Delta P}{\Delta Q_x^d} = -.2\left(\frac{\Delta Q_x^d}{\Delta Q_x^d}\right) = -.2,$$

which is simply the slope of the inverse demand function.

A slightly more general application of the power rule is provided by the Johnson Company's total revenue function. Total revenue is price times quantity, or

$$TR = P_x \times Q_x^d = (100 - .2Q_x^d)Q_x^d = 100Q_x^d - .2(Q_x^d)^2.$$

The derivative of this equation with respect to Q_x^d is marginal revenue (*MR*) and is computed as follows:

$$\begin{aligned}
MR = dTR/dQ_x^d &= 100(dQ_x^d/dQ_x^d) - .2[d(Q_x^d)^2/dQ_x^d] \\
&= 100(Q_x^d)^{1-1} - .2(2)(Q_x^d)^{2-1} \\
&= 100(Q_x^d)^0 - .4(Q_x^d)^1 \\
&= 100 - .4Q_x^d.
\end{aligned}$$

The derivative of the first term, $100Q_x^d$, applies the definition of the derivative in the same way it was applied in the previous paragraph. The derivative of the second term, $-.2(Q_x^d)^2$, is found by extending this same argument. In particular, when Q changes by a small amount, the new value of *TR* will be

$$TR + \Delta TR = -.2(Q_x^d + \Delta Q_x^d)^2$$

as far as the second term is concerned. Expanding this expression yields

$$TR + \Delta TR = -.2[(Q_x^d)^2 + 2Q_x^d\Delta Q_x^d + (\Delta Q_x^d)^2].$$

Subtracting $TR = -.2(Q_x^d)^2$ from both sides and dividing through by ΔQ_x^d results in

$$\frac{\Delta TR}{\Delta Q_x^d} = -.4Q_x^d - .2\left(\Delta Q_x^d\right)^2.$$

Finally, if the change in quantity demanded is very small (i.e., $\lim \Delta Q_x^d \to 0$), then the second term disappears, leaving

$$\frac{\Delta TR}{\Delta Q_x^d} = -.4Q_x^d.$$

Because the first derivative of a function is the slope of that function, the first derivative can be used to determine the point at which the value of the function is at a maximum or a minimum. At such an extreme point, the slope of the function is zero. For example, total revenue is at a maximum at the point where marginal revenue (the slope of the total revenue function) is zero. Using the linear demand function for the Johnson Company's all-weather coat, we found that

$$MR = 100 - .4Q_x^d.$$

Setting this expression equal to zero:

$$100 - .4Q_x^d = 0,$$

and solving for Q_x^d yields the total-revenue maximizing level of sales $Q_x^d = 250$, or 250,000 coats.

Second Derivatives

The derivatives in the prior examples are called first derivatives. The second derivative, which gauges the rate of change in a function's slope, is found by differentiating the first derivative. The same differentiation rules stated previously apply in calculating the second derivative of a function. If the first derivative of a function is represented by the notation dy/dx, the second derivative is represented by d^2y/dx^2.

For example, the second derivative of the demand function for all-weather coats determines whether the impact of a change in price on quantity demanded varies at various levels of sales. As determined above, the first derivative of the demand function is

$$\frac{dQ_x^{\ d}}{dP_x} = -5.$$

Because the derivative of a constant function is identically equal to zero, the second derivative of the demand function is

$$\frac{d^2Q_x^{\ d}}{dP_x^{\ 2}} = 0.$$

In other words, the slope of this function is constant. The impact of a small change in price on quantity demanded is the same at every point on the function.

Similarly, the second derivative of the Johnson Company's total revenue function is found by taking the derivative of the first derivative. The first derivative of this function is

$$\frac{dTR}{dQ_x^{\ d}} = 100 - .4Q_x^{\ d},$$

and so the second derivative is

$$\frac{d^2TR}{d\left(Q_x^{\ d}\right)^2} = -.4.$$

The first derivative of the total revenue function is marginal revenue. Therefore, the second derivative is interpreted to mean that for this particular function, marginal revenue declines by a constant amount as the firm's sales of all-weather coats increase. Information of this sort is particularly useful in interpreting the optimization problems covered in future chapters.

The second derivative also tells us whether the value of the function is at a maximum or a minimum at the point where the first derivative is equal to zero. This information is provided by the algebraic sign of the second derivative which evaluates the rate of change in the function's slope. If the rate of change is declining (the second derivative is negative), the function reaches a maximum at the point where the first derivative is zero. On the other hand, if the rate of change is increasing (the second derivative is positive), the function reaches a minimum at the point where the first derivative is zero. In the previous paragraph's example, $d^2TR/d(Q_x^d)^2 = -.4$. So total revenue is indeed maximized when the Johnson Company sells 250,000 coats per year.

Partial Derivatives

The techniques of partial differentiation apply when a function contains two or more independent variables. Partial derivatives use the notation ∂ to indicate that in taking the derivative of a function containing two or more independent variables with respect to one of those variables, the other variables are held constant.

For example, the following equation specifies the demand function for all-weather coats.

$$Q_x^d = 60 - 5P_x + 2.4P_y - 4P_z + 10I.$$

This function has four partial derivatives, namely $\partial Q_x^d/\partial P_x$, $\partial Q_x^d/\partial P_y$, $\partial Q_x^d/\partial P_z$, and $\partial Q_x^d/\partial I$. Each measures the change in quantity demanded associated with a change in one of the independent variables, holding all other variables constant. When the partial derivative of this function is taken with respect to, say P_x, the remaining independent variables (P_y, P_z, and I) are treated as constants. The partial derivative $\partial Q_x^d/\partial P_x$ is therefore simply equal to

$$\frac{\partial Q_x^d}{\partial P_x} = -.5.$$

Similarly, the partial derivatives of Q_x^d with respect to P_y, P_z, and I are $\partial Q_x^d/\partial P_y = 2.4$, $\partial Q_x^d/\partial P_z = -4$, and $\partial Q_x^d/\partial I = 10$, respectively.

The multiplicative demand function introduced in problem 2.4 supplies a second example of the techniques of partial differentiation. This multiplicative function was specified as

$$Q_x^d = 18.414429P_x^{-1.5}P_y^{.6}P_z^{-.4}I^2.$$

The partial derivative of this function with respect to P_x is

$$\frac{\partial Q_x^d}{\partial P_x} = (18.414429)(-1.5)P_x^{-1.5-1}P_y^{.6}P_z^{-.4}I^2$$

$$= -27.621644P_x^{-2.5}P_y^{.6}P_z^{-.4}I^2.$$

The linear demand function has a constant slope with respect to each of the independent variables. In contrast, the effect of a change in the price of x on quantity demanded depends on the values of all of the independent variables in the case of the multiplicative function. If the values of these other variables are known, the slope of the function can be computed at any given price. For instance, if $P_y = \$50$, $P_z = \$20$, and $I = \$40,000$, then the slope of the demand function at a price of $60 is equal to

$$\frac{\partial Q_x^{\,d}}{\partial P_x} = -27.621644(60)^{-2.5}(50)^{.6}(20)^{-.4}(40)^2$$

$$= -27.621644(.0000359)(10.456396)(.3017088)(1600)$$

$$= -5.$$

Second partial derivatives are likewise found by taking the derivative of the first partial derivative and treating all other variables in the equation as constants. The second partial derivative of the multiplicative demand function with respect to P_x is accordingly

$$\frac{\partial^2 Q_x^{\,d}}{\partial (P_x)^2} = -27.621644(-2.5)P_x^{-2.5-1}P_y^{.6}P_z^{-.4}I^2$$

$$= 69.05411 P_x^{-3.5} P_y^{.6} P_z^{-.4} I^2.$$

Production and Cost in the Long Run

OVERVIEW

In their pursuit of profits, managers can target a wide array of intermediate objectives. One manager might believe that sales growth is the key to the firm's prosperity; another may think that market share is the most important indicator of success. Other managers can emphasize innovation, diversification, product quality, or any combination of these and many other possible objectives. However, no one of these goals is—or should be—an end in and of itself. Rather, profit maximization is the vital element in determining the firm's long-run survival. The manager's pursuit of sales growth, market share, product quality, or any other performance target must therefore be compatible with the ultimate objective of profit maximization.

Cost plays an obvious and basic role in determining profitability. When the firm chooses the profit-maximizing level of output, it must produce that output at the lowest possible cost. If costs can be reduced without reducing output, then the firm is not producing efficiently. Inefficiency, of course, always reduces a firm's profits.

There are two types of efficiency associated with the production process. **Technical** or **production efficiency** means that a firm produces the maximum possible quantity of output from a given set of inputs. However, the definition of production efficiency does not imply that there is just one, best way of producing a given quantity of output. For example, automobiles can be produced in plants that make extensive use of robotic technology or they can be produced in plants that employ more labor-intensive technologies. The plant that employs robotic technology is not necessarily "more efficient" than the plant that relies on alternative production methods. Rather the robotic plant is technically efficient if it produces the maximum quantity of output possible from the given combination of equipment, labor, and materials employed. Similarly, the non-robotic plant is also technically efficient if it produces the maximum possible quantity of output from the less capital-intensive combination of inputs it employs.

When choosing among alternative, technically efficient production methods, the firm should choose the one that is economically efficient. **Economic efficiency** is associated with cost minimization, or producing a given quantity of output at the lowest possible cost. The least-cost method of production depends both on the substitutability characteristics of inputs in the production process and on the relative prices of those inputs. While technical efficiency can be achieved in a variety of ways, there is a unique, economically efficient way to produce a given level of output.

Production theory and cost theory provide the basic framework for managerial decisions concerning the optimal use of inputs in the production process. Managers make these decisions, like all their decisions, in a dynamic, changing business environment. Firms must adjust to changes in the demands for their products, to changes in the relative prices of inputs, and to changes in technology that affect the productivities of inputs.

The firm's ability to respond to these changes is, in turn, constantly influenced by the constraints of technology and cost. If an unexpected increase in demand warrants a production increase, some inputs are more difficult to adjust than others. Plant size usually is more difficult to adjust than the number of workers employed in the plant, for instance. To address the impact of input constraints on managerial decisions, production and cost theory distinguishes between the short run and the long run. In the **long run**, the firm is free to vary its usage of all inputs. In the **short run**, at least one of its inputs is treated as fixed while all other inputs are variable.

This chapter presents long-run production and cost analysis and, from it, derives the condition for economic efficiency. Economic efficiency in the long run involves the selection of the least-cost combination of inputs when all inputs are variable. The next chapter presents short-run production and cost analysis.

———————————————●———————————————

APPLICATION

Chapter 2 analyzed the demand characteristics of the J. Johnson Company's new product, an all-weather coat. At the request of the company's president, the firm's production department has conducted a preliminary analysis of the new product's materials, labor, and equipment requirements. Each coat requires three yards of fabric, one zipper, and two buttons. Materials usage varies in direct proportion to the number of all-weather coats produced. For example, producing 200,000 coats requires 600,000 yards of material, 200,000 zippers and 400,000 buttons. By contrast, labor and capital equipment can be employed in variable proportions. That is, the same number of coats can be produced with a relatively labor-intensive input combination or with a relatively capital-intensive input combination. Because management has tentatively forecast an annual production run of 200,000 coats, the production department provides a table (reproduced in Table 3.1) that illustrates how labor and capital can be variously combined to produce this quantity of coats.

The table shows that the firm can produce 200,000 coats with a relatively capital-intensive combination of 100,000 machine-hours of capital and 16 production workers. The same quantity of output can be produced with a relatively labor-intensive combination of 20,000 machine-hours of capital and 80 production workers. And so on.

A simple list of various technically efficient combinations of capital and labor, as shown in Table 3.1, has its limitations. It will in general not be practical to specify all possible combinations of two inputs that can produce a given quality of output. If capital and labor are sufficiently divisible, for example, then the firm may be able to choose plant sizes between 100,000 and 80,000 machine-hours of capital or between 80,000 and 60,000 machine-hours of capital. In addition, the production figure of 200,000 coats is only a tentative estimate of sales. A complete production table would also list the input requirements for other possible levels of output.

According to the production department, a more compact way of writing the general relationship among capital, labor, and output for this production process is

$$Q = 5K^{.5}L^{.5}. \tag{3.1}$$

In this *production function*, Q represents output in thousands of coats per year, K represents capital in units of 1,000 machine-hours, and L represents labor in terms of number of production workers.[a] Substitution of alternative quantities of capital and labor into equation 3.1

TABLE 3.1 PRODUCTION OF ALL-WEATHER COATS

QUANTITY OF COATS (THOUSANDS) Q	UNITS OF CAPITAL (THOUSANDS OF MACHINE-HOURS) K	UNITS OF LABOR (NUMBER OF WORKERS) L
200	100	16
200	80	20
200	60	27
200	40	40
200	20	80

a Notice that equation 3.1 has the same general form as the multiplicative demand function introduced in Chapter 2's problem 2.4.

yields different levels of output. For example, if 100,000 machine-hours of capital are combined with 16 production workers, total output is

$$Q = 5K^{.5}L^{.5} = 5(100)^{.5}(16)^{.5} = 5(10)(4) = 200,$$

or 200,000 coats per year. On the other hand, if 100,000 machine-hours of capital are combined with 36 production workers, total annual output increases to 300,000 units. That is,

$$Q = 5K^{.5}L^{.5} = 5(100)^{.5}(36)^{.5} = 5(10)(6) = 300.$$

Equation 3.1 thus shows the various combinations of capital and labor that can be employed to produce a particular quantity of output. The production function also shows how total output varies as input usage varies. In summarizing its findings, the production department also noted that capital can be acquired at a price of $10 per machine-hour per year and that production workers receive a total compensation package (wages plus benefits) valued at $40,000 annually.

After reading the production department's report, the Johnson Company's owner prepares a list of questions about the productivities and prices of the two inputs used to produce all-weather coats. She recognizes the need to approach input usage from two different perspectives. In the planning phase, both capital and labor are variable. The firm's initial decision consequently involves choosing an optimal plant size and an optimal number of employees. This analysis will also provide a framework for future decisions about expansion or contraction of production capacity and associated changes in employment levels. Once the plant is in operation, the firm, in the short run, will be limited to responding to changing market conditions by adjusting the number of workers employed in the plant size chosen at the planning stage.

The owner makes a decision to concentrate on questions about production and cost when both inputs are variable. She composes the following list of questions.

1. The production department prepared a table showing alternative combinations of capital and labor that can produce 200,000 coats. How can the substitutability of capital and labor be measured?
2. If the firm wants to increase production in the future by expanding its plant size and the number of workers it employs, how much will output increase? For example, if both plant size and employment are doubled, will output also double?
3. Capital and labor are measured differently. Capital is measured in units of 1,000 machine-hours and labor is measured in terms of the number of production workers hired. How can the relative prices of these factors of production be compared?

4. What is the optimal combination of plant capacity and employment for any level of output the firm might want to produce over time?
5. How do the production function and the unit prices of inputs determine the total cost of producing different levels of output that the firm can produce when it varies the size of its plant?

The following sections show how the theory of production and cost can be used to answer these questions, given the production function shown in equation 3.1 and the input prices assumed in this application. The theory is then generalized to show the characteristics of alternative production and cost functions.

AN INTRODUCTION TO PRODUCTION FUNCTIONS

Every production process combines inputs to produce a good or service valued by consumers. A **production function** specifies the maximum quantity of output that can be produced with various combinations of inputs given the state of existing technology. Firms in the economy employ a wide array of production technologies. The Ford Motor Company, for example, combines skilled labor, heavy manufacturing equipment, electronic components, steel, glass, fabric, paint, and other materials to produce automobiles and trucks. In addition to the inputs that are directly associated with the assembly of motor vehicles, Ford's production function also includes the inputs associated with all other aspects of the company's operations. Corporate management, accounting, finance, consumer credit, research and development, energy requirements, and so on all involve inputs in Ford's production function.

"Production" is not synonymous with "manufacturing," however. Firms in the agricultural and service sectors of the economy employ very different input mixes than firms in the manufacturing sector. McDonald's Corporation combines unskilled labor, cooking equipment, packaging materials, and a healthy dose of advertising to produce and sell fast-food meals. The local doctor's office combines the physician's medical skills with diagnostic equipment, prescription drugs, and insurance claims processing to produce health care services. Despite the substantial differences across firms in the technologies and the resources they employ and in the outputs they produce, the economic theory of production is built on the premise that all production functions share a number of common characteristics. These regularities can help us fruitfully analyze the production function of any firm.[1]

---

1 The economic theory of production focuses on the technological relationships that govern the transformation of inputs into outputs. In doing so, it suppresses a number of important issues concerning the ownership of productive resources in the economy and the internal organization of the firm. Modern theories of the firm that place these issues at center stage are introduced in Chapter 7 and explored in detail in Part III.

The basic properties of production functions can be illustrated in a simple model that incorporates two inputs and one output. Because the two broad categories of capital and labor are part of virtually all production functions, a general relation between inputs and output can be written as

$$Q = f(K, L). \tag{3.2}$$

Q is the quantity of output produced during a specified time period, and K and L represent the quantities of capital and labor employed in the production process. The functional notation $f(.)$ indicates a general but as yet unspecified mathematical relationship between the quantity of output produced and the quantities of the two types of inputs employed. Equation 3.2 means "Q is a function of K and L." The only restriction we place on the mathematical relationship between the inputs and output at this point is to rule out negative values of Q, K, and L.

Fixed and Variable Inputs

Production and cost theory distinguish between the long run and the short run. In the long run the firm can vary all inputs, while in the short run some inputs are variable and at least one input is fixed. Characterizing an input as "fixed" does not mean that the firm cannot vary its usage of that input under any circumstances. Rather, an input is treated as fixed in the sense that it would be relatively costly for the firm to increase or decrease the quantity of it employed in the short run. A firm could conceivably abandon one of its production facilities on 24 hours notice, for example, but the costs of doing so (canceling contracts with suppliers, laying off workers, finding buyers for equipment and buildings, and so on) would likely swamp any savings expected from the decision.

Hence, in the short run, the firm makes decisions about how much output to produce under the constraint that only some of the inputs employed in the production process are variable while the usage of other, more-costly-to-vary inputs will be held constant at current levels. For the long run, in contrast, the firm can plan to vary its usage of all inputs, including those it treats as being too costly to vary over a shorter time horizon.[2]

---

2 Because of the distinction between the short run and the long run, the two inputs in equation 3.2 typify the productive resources that are either fixed or variable in the short run. From this perspective, capital includes the services of some types of labor as well as physical assets like plant and equipment, land, and buildings. If the firm cannot or does not plan to vary the number of managers, accountants, computer operators, and other staff personnel it employs when the volume of production changes, then these inputs should be included as part of the fixed input, "capital," in the production function. "Labor" typically represents production workers as well as inputs like raw materials and energy whose usage varies directly with the quantity of output produced.

Technology determines two characteristics of a production function. First, technology determines the *maximum* quantity of output that can be produced with any set of inputs and, second, technology determines the degree to which inputs can be *substituted* for one another in the production process.

Fixed proportions technology exists when there is one (and only one) combination of inputs that can produce a specified quantity of output. The input-output ratio is fixed in this case, meaning that total output does not change unless the usage of all inputs changes in the required proportion. Inputs cannot be substituted for one another with fixed-proportions production technology.

For example, producing a bicycle requires two wheels and one frame. These two inputs obviously cannot be substituted for one another. No one can assemble a bicycle with two frames and one wheel or with three wheels and no frame. Hence, wheels and frames must be employed in a two-to-one ratio per unit of output whatever quantity of bicycles the firm chooses to produce. Input combinations do not depend on input prices if production involves fixed proportions technology. Input prices determine the total cost of production and, hence, the total quantity of output produced. However, changes in input prices do not affect the input-output ratio.

The description of the production process for all-weather coats in the chapter's opening application reflects the use of fixed proportions technology for some inputs. Each coat requires a fixed quantity of materials—fabric, zippers, and buttons. These resources do not enter the production function in equation 3.1 explicitly because the economic theory of production and cost is primarily concerned with choices among alternative combinations of inputs which, by definition, do not exist with fixed proportions technology.

Variable proportions technology characterizes production processes which allow substitution of one input for another. That is, the *same* quantity of output can be produced with *different* combinations of inputs. In other words, with variable proportions production technology, output can be varied by varying the usage of one input while all other inputs are held constant.

Two inputs are perfect substitutes if the *rate* at which they can be substituted for one another remains the same as the firm varies the quantities of inputs employed. Suppose, for example, that the production of all-weather coats can employ two different types of cutting machines, brand *A* and brand *B*. Assume that the only difference between the two machines is that brand *A* cuts twice as many patterns per hour as brand *B*. These machines are **perfect substitutes** because the same number of patterns can be cut per hour with either two brand-*B* machines or one brand-*A* machine.

With perfect substitutability, only one of the inputs will be employed. The firm bases its selection solely on relative input prices. If the price of a brand *A* machine is $10,000 and the price of a brand *B* machine is $6,000, then the firm would only buy brand *A*. On the other hand, if the price of a brand *A* machine is $10,000 and the price of a brand *B* machine is $4,000, then the firm would only buy brand *B*. Because the choice between perfect substitutes is an either-or choice, perfect substitutes are typically treated as a single factor of production in production theory. If the production function for all-weather coats explicitly includes cutting machines, no distinction between the two brands is necessary.

The economic theory of production and cost is most concerned with variable proportions technology in which inputs are **imperfect substitutes** for one another. Two inputs are imperfect substitutes if the ability to substitute one input for another depends on the relative quantities of the two inputs in use. Imperfect substitutability characterizes production processes in which the inputs exhibit a diminishing **marginal rate of technical substitution** (*MRTS*). A diminishing *MRTS*, which is explained in more detail below, refers to a particular property of production technologies in which successively larger increases in the usage of one input are required to compensate for a given reduction in the employment of the other if total output is to be held constant.

Consider a farmer who grows 100,000 bushels of corn using labor and fertilizer as inputs. Imperfect substitutability means that the rate at which labor can be substituted for fertilizer depends on the relative quantities of the inputs currently in use. For example, compare a relatively labor-intensive farming method that requires 100 workers and 50 bags of fertilizer with a relatively fertilizer-intensive method that requires 1,000 bags of fertilizer and 10 workers. Assume that both farming methods yield 100,000 bushels of corn per growing season. If one more worker is hired in the first case, that worker will add little to the total harvest, given the contributions of the 100 workers hired previously. Only a small reduction in fertilizer usage would therefore be required to maintain output constant at 100,000 bushels of corn. On the other hand, hiring one more worker in the second case would increase the total harvest substantially. This worker would consequently substitute for a much larger number of bags of fertilizer if 100,000 bushels of corn continue to be produced.

What characterizes the substitution possibilities of capital and labor in the manufacture of the Johnson Company's new product? Table 3.1 (see p. 77) shows various combinations of labor and capital that can produce 200,000 all-weather coats. The input combinations there are reproduced in Table 3.2, which also shows the variation in the substitutability of capital and labor across different input mixes. When 100,000 machine-hours of capital and 16 production workers are combined to produce 200,000 coats, output can be held constant by substituting 4 workers for 20,000 machine-hours of capital. When the production process is more labor-intensive and 20,000 machine-hours of capital and 80 workers produce 200,000 coats, 40 additional workers must be hired to maintain output constant if capital usage decreases by 20,000 machine-hours. Hence, capital and labor are imperfect substitutes in the production of all-weather coats.

It is worth stressing that imperfect substitutability is a technological property of production. Each combination of capital and labor that produces 200,000 all-weather coats is technically efficient in the sense that it yields the maximum total output possible. But only one of these input combinations

TABLE 3.2 IMPERFECT SUBSTITUTES IN PRODUCTION

QUANTITY OF COATS (THOUSANDS) Q	UNITS OF CAPITAL (THOUSANDS OF MACHINE-HOURS) K	UNITS OF LABOR (NUMBER OF WORKERS) L	
200	100	16	
	$-20K$ <	>	$+4L$
200	80	20	
200	60	27	
200	40	40	
	$-20K$ <	>	$+40L$
200	20	80	

will be economically efficient, namely the combination of capital and labor that produces 200,000 coats at the lowest possible total cost. While the least-cost input combination clearly depends on the rate at which technology allows inputs to be substituted for one another, it also depends on the terms at which inputs can be substituted for one another at market-determined prices.

FUNCTIONAL FORM OF THE PRODUCTION FUNCTION

The production function, $Q = f(K, L)$, provides a general statement of the mathematical relationship between the quantity of output produced and the quantities of capital (K) and labor (L) employed. Specific functional forms for this relationship illustrate some important characteristics of the production function.

Consider a linear, additive production function. With two inputs, such a production function can be written as

$$Q = b_1 K + b_2 L. \tag{3.3}$$

The coefficients b_1 and b_2 represent the marginal productivities of the individual inputs. In particular, b_1 is the **marginal product of capital** and b_2 is the **marginal product of labor**. The marginal product of any input is defined as the change in total output (or total product) associated with a small change in the usage of that input, holding all other inputs constant.

An input's marginal product is found by taking the partial derivative of the production function with respect to that input. Applying the power rule explained in the appendix to Chapter 2 to take the partial derivatives of equation 3.3, the marginal product of capital, MP_K, is

$$MP_K = \frac{\partial Q}{\partial K} = b_1,$$

and labor's marginal product, MP_L, is

$$MP_L = \frac{\partial Q}{\partial L} = b_2.$$

In the economic region of production defined more fully below, the marginal products of all inputs are positive. That is, hiring more of any input causes total output to increase and hiring less of any input causes total output to decline. Hence, the coefficients b_1 and b_2 in equation 3.3 are both greater than zero. Because b_1 and b_2 are positive constants, a linear, additive production function is characterized by constant marginal products.

An alternate functional form commonly specified is the cubic production function:

$$Q = b_1 KL + b_2 K^2 L + b_3 KL^2 - b_4 K^3 L - b_5 KL^3. \tag{3.4}$$

The marginal products of capital and labor in the cubic production function vary depending on the quantities of both inputs in use. (See problem 3.4 on p. 111).

Perhaps the most commonly specified production function is a multiplicative power function of the form:

$$Q = aK^{b_1}L^{b_2}. \tag{3.5}$$

This production function is known as the **Cobb-Douglas** production function.[3] Many empirical studies of production functions use the Cobb-Douglas specification because it has many of the properties predicted by the economic theory of production.

For example, as the production function for all-weather coats demonstrated, inputs are imperfect substitutes in a Cobb-Douglas production function. This property follows from observing that the marginal product of one input depends on the quantity of both inputs in use. That is, the impact of a change in capital usage on output depends on the quantities of capital *and* labor employed. The impact of a change in labor usage on output likewise depends on the quantities of capital and labor employed. Specifically, the marginal product of capital is

$$MP_K = \frac{\partial Q}{\partial K} = ab_1 K^{b_1-1}L^{b_2},$$

and the marginal product of labor is

$$MP_L = \frac{\partial Q}{\partial L} = ab_2 K^{b_1}L^{b_2-1}.$$

---

3 See C. W. Cobb and P. H. Douglas, "A Theory of Production," *American Economic Review* 16 (1928), pp. 139-165 and P. H. Douglas, "Are There Laws of Production?" *American Economic Review* 38 (1948), pp. 1-41.

A second property of the Cobb-Douglas production function is that the percentage change in output associated with a one percent change in the usage of an input is equal to that input's exponent. This property can be shown by calculating the elasticity of output with respect to a change in the usage of one input, holding all other inputs constant. For example, the percentage change in total output associated with a one percent change in capital usage is

$$\left(\frac{\partial Q}{\partial K}\right)\left(\frac{K}{Q}\right) = MP_K\left(\frac{K}{Q}\right) = \left(ab_1K^{b_1-1}L^{b_2}\right)\left(\frac{K}{aK^{b_1}L^{b_2}}\right).$$

Simplification of this expression yields

$$\left(\frac{\partial Q}{\partial K}\right)\left(\frac{K}{Q}\right) = b_1.$$

A similar calculation shows that a one percent change in labor usage causes a b_2 percent change in total output.[4] Hence, because $b_1 = b_2 = .5$ in the Cobb-Douglas production function for all-weather coats in equation 3.1 (see p. 77), a one percent change in either capital *or* labor usage causes a one-half percent change in total output.

THE ISOQUANT MAP

The production function $Q = f(K, L)$ shows the maximum quantity of output that given combinations of capital and labor can produce. Table 3.2 (see p. 83) shows, for example, that with production governed by the function $Q = 5K^{.5}L^{.5}$, 40,000 machine-hours of capital and 40 production workers can produce a maximum of 200,000 all-weather coats per year.

A map of the relationship among output, labor, and capital can be constructed on a two-dimensional graph. Such a graphical representation is shown in Figure 3.1 where capital is measured on the vertical axis and labor is measured on the horizontal axis. This figure plots the five combinations of capital and labor (shown in Table 3.2) that can be used to produce a total output of 200,000 all-weather coats per year.

The curve that connects the various input combinations that yield the *same* level of output is called an **isoquant** ("iso" means "equal" and "quant" represents quantity). The convex schedule connecting the five input combinations in Figure 3.1 is the isoquant that represents the production of 200,000 all-weather coats.

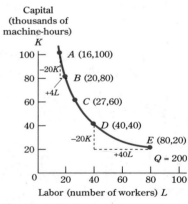

FIGURE 3.1

An Isoquant for All-Weather Coats

4 This property of the Cobb-Douglas function can be see more directly by writing the function in logarithms. Taking the natural logs of both sides of equation 3.5 yields $\ln(Q) = \ln(a) + b_1\ln(K) + b_2\ln(L)$. The impact of a one percent change in capital usage on output is then $(\partial Q/\partial K)(K/Q) = \partial\ln(Q)/\partial\ln(K) = b_1$, and the impact of a one percent change in labor usage is $(\partial Q/\partial L)(L/Q) = \partial\ln(Q)/\partial\ln(L) = b_2$.

Appointments, Waiting Time, and Physicians' Productivity

One of the more annoying aspects of going to the doctor is the time spent sitting in the waiting or examining room. A survey by the American Medical Association found that patients typically must wait 20 minutes beyond their scheduled appointments before seeing their physician.

Doctors use an appointment system for scheduling patient visits that incorporates waiting time as an input in the production process partly because the amount of time the doctor spends with any one patient is both uncertain and highly variable. By making some patients wait, a physician is able to reduce the amount of idle time between patients. In effect, waiting time allows the capacity of the doctor's office to be utilized more fully, thereby increasing the doctor's productivity —and income.

A recent study presented empirical evidence concerning the impact of patient waiting time on the productivity of doctors.[a] The following production function was estimated:

$$\ln(Q) = a + bDELAY + c\ln(ROOM) + dROOM \\ + eNURSE + fNURSE^2 + gCLERK + hCLERK^2 \\ + iEXPERIENCE + jEXPERIENCE^2 + kNEW + lGP \\ + mPED + nCERT + oSELF,$$

where ln indicates that the variable was entered in its natural logarithm.

In this function, the dependent variable, Q, is physician productivity, measured by the average number of patient visits per hour. *DELAY* is the average time patients wait to see each doctor in the sample. The next three variables represent ancillary inputs in the production of patient visits. Specifically, *ROOM* is the number of examining rooms in the doctor's office, *NURSE* is the number of nurses, and *CLERK* is the number of clerical workers. *EXPERIENCE* is the number of years the doctor has been practicing medicine. *NEW* is the proportion of patients being seen for the first time. Finally, *GP*, *PED*, *CERT*, and *SELF* are dummy variables that are set equal to one if the doctor is a general practitioner, a pediatrician, a board-certified specialist, or self-employed, respectively.

The model was estimated with data for 684 physicians' offices.[b] The regression results are presented below.[c]

Determinants of Visits per Hour Worked

VARIABLE	COEFFICIENT (t-RATIO)	VARIABLE	COEFFICIENT (t-RATIO)
DELAY	0.0027 (2.52)	EXPERIENCE	0.024 (3.93)
ln(ROOM)	0.084 (1.83)	EXPERIENCE²	−0.0005 (−4.34)
ROOM	0.020 (1.72)	NEW	−0.373 (−5.81)
NURSE	0.125 (4.16)	GP	0.245 (5.69)
NURSE²	−0.115 (−3.19)	PED	0.298 (5.12)
CLERK	0.112 (3.63)	CERT	0.046 (1.16)
CLERK²	−0.002 (−0.037)	SELF	0.122 (1.95)

The empirical evidence shows that *DELAY* has a positive and statistically significant impact on the average number of patients the physician treats per hour.[d] Other things being the same, the longer the average patient waits before seeing the doctor, the greater is the typical physician's productivity.

a Alvin E. Headen, Jr., "Productivity Enhancing Customer Delay: Estimates from Physician Data Corrected for Measurement Error," *Southern Economic Journal* 58 (October 1991), pp. 445-58.
b The study reported more than one set of results. Only the ordinary least squares (OLS) results are reported here.
c Appendix 2 of this chapter provides a brief review of regression.
d If the absolute value of the t-ratio is greater than 1.96, the estimated coefficient is significantly different from zero at the 5 percent level on a two-tailed test.

Neither ln(*ROOM*) nor *ROOM* is statistically significant at the 5 percent level. An increase in the number of examining rooms apparently does not have an important effect on the doctor's productivity. The statistically significant coefficients associated with *NURSE* and *NURSE²* indicate that additional nurses increase the number of patients the doctor is able to see per hour at a decreasing rate. Because *CLERK* is statistically significant, but *CLERK²* is not, additional clerks appear to have a constant, positive impact on physicians' productivity.

The estimated coefficients associated with *EXPERIENCE* and *EXPERIENCE²* are positive and negative, respectively. These results indicate that a physician's productivity increases at a decreasing rate with experience. The remaining results show that seeing new patients tends to reduce productivity, that general practitioners and pediatricians treat more patients on average than other doctors in the survey, and that board-certification or self-employment do not have a statistically significant effect on physician productivity.

Like the isoquant in Figure 3.1, isoquants are, in general, downward sloping and convex to the origin. The negative slope indicates that if the usage of one input decreases, the usage of the other must increase in order to continue to produce the same level of total output.[5]

An isoquant is convex when the rate at which labor can be substituted for capital declines as production becomes more labor-intensive. In other words, ever-increasing quantities of labor are required to compensate for successively equal reductions in capital as input usage is varied along an isoquant.

Figure 3.1 illustrates this property of a diminishing marginal rate of technical substitution. Different numbers of production workers are needed to compensate for given reductions in capital usage between two different sets of points on the $Q = 200,000$ isoquant. When production is relatively capital-intensive, total output can be held constant by substituting four workers for 20,000 machine-hours of capital. (The movement from point *A* to point *B* illustrates this substitution.) When production is relatively labor-intensive, on the other hand, 40 workers are needed to compensate for the loss of 20,000 machine-hours of capital (points *D* and *E*). Hence, the rate at which labor can be substituted for capital declines as more labor is employed. As discussed previously, a diminishing marginal rate of technical substitution is the characteristic that defines inputs as imperfect substitutes.

The capital-labor space is literally filled with isoquants because there is a unique isoquant associated with each level of output. Figure 3.2 shows four representative isoquants of the Cobb-Douglas production for all-weather coats. Table 3.3 lists the combinations of capital and labor that correspond to the three points referenced by letters on these isoquants. As an additional aid, this table also shows the equation for each isoquant.[6]

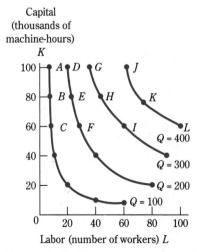

Capital (thousands of machine-hours) *K*

FIGURE 3.2

An Illustration of Four Isoquants

---

5 The isoquant's slope is calculated by totally differentiating the production function, $Q = f(K, L)$. In particular, $dQ = (\partial Q/\partial K)dK + (\partial Q/\partial L)dL$. Setting $dQ = 0$ so as to hold total output constant, $(\partial Q/\partial K)dK + (\partial Q/\partial L)dL = 0$, and solving for the slope, dK/dL, yields $dK/dL = -(\partial Q/\partial L)/(\partial Q/\partial K)$. The negative algebraic sign indicates that the isoquant is downward sloping.

6 The equation for an isoquant is derived from the production function by substituting the numerical value of output for Q and solving for L in terms of K. For example, solving the

TABLE 3.3   POINTS REFERENCED ON THE ISOQUANTS IN FIGURE 3.2

POINT	QUANTITY OF COATS (THOUSANDS) Q	UNITS OF CAPITAL (THOUSANDS OF MACHINE-HOURS) K	UNITS OF LABOR (NUMBER OF WORKERS) L	ISOQUANT EQUATION
A	100	100	4	
B	100	80	5	$L=400/K$
C	100	60	7	
D	200	100	16	
E	200	80	20	$L=1600/K$
F	200	60	27	
G	300	100	36	
H	300	80	45	$L=3600/K$
I	300	60	60	
J	400	100	64	
K	400	80	80	$L=6400/K$
L	400	60	107	

THE MARGINAL RATE OF TECHNICAL SUBSTITUTION

The economic theory of production is primarily concerned with inputs that are imperfect substitutes. The **marginal rate of technical substitution** (*MRTS*) is a measure of the degree of substitutability between two inputs. The *MRTS* is the absolute value of the isoquant's slope.

Imperfect substitutes are characterized by marginal rates of substitution that decline as one input is substituted for another. In terms of the isoquant map, a declining marginal rate of technical substitution produces convex, nonlinear isoquants along which the slope varies continuously.

The slope of an isoquant (and, hence, the marginal rate of technical substitution) at any point can be calculated as the ratio of the marginal products of the two inputs. To see this, let MP_K and MP_L represent the marginal products of capital and labor as before. Now consider the movement along the Q_1 isoquant from point A to point C in Figure 3.3. The slope of the Q_1 isoquant over the range between point A and C is

$$\frac{\Delta K}{\Delta L} = \frac{AB}{BC}.$$

Holding the number of production workers constant, the reduction in capital usage from K_1 to K_2 causes total output to fall by an

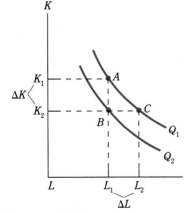

FIGURE 3.3

The Marginal Rate of Technical Substitution

equation $100 = 5K^{.5} L^{.5}$ for L yields the equation for the isoquant corresponding to 100,000 units of output, $L = 400/K$.

amount equal to the change in the number of units of capital employed times capital's marginal product. That is, $AB = -\Delta K \times MP_K$. At the same time, holding the quantity of capital constant, the increase in labor usage from L_1 to L_2 causes total output to rise by an amount equal to the change in employment times labor's marginal product. Hence, $BC = \Delta L \times MP_L$.

Setting $AB = BC = \Delta Q$ so that these two effects exactly offset one another (total output remains constant), we can write

$$\Delta K = \frac{-AB}{MP_K} = \frac{-\Delta Q}{MP_K}$$

and

$$\Delta L = \frac{BC}{MP_L} = \frac{\Delta Q}{MP_L}.$$

The slope of the isoquant Q_1 over the region between points A and C can therefore be rewritten as

$$\frac{\Delta K}{\Delta L} = -\frac{\Delta Q}{MP_K} \div \frac{\Delta Q}{MP_L}$$

$$= -\frac{\Delta Q}{MP_K} \times \frac{MP_L}{\Delta Q}$$ (3.6)

$$\frac{\Delta k}{\Delta l} = -\frac{MP_L}{MP_K}.$$

Finally, multiplying through by -1 to restate the marginal rate of technical substitution as a positive number yields

$$MRTS = \frac{-\Delta K}{\Delta L} = \frac{MP_L}{MP_K}.$$ (3.7)

The marginal rate of technical substitution, or the rate at which one input can be substituted for another while holding total output constant, is thus equal to the ratio of the marginal products of the two inputs.[7]

In the previous section, it was stated that isoquants are generally downward sloping (have a negative slope). It is theoretically possible, however, for one of the inputs to have a negative marginal product, thereby causing the isoquant to be positively sloped. This situation can occur when so much of one input is combined with another that total output starts to decline. The marginal product of a factory's production workers could be negative if so many of them are

---

[7] Alternatively, it is shown in footnote 5 that the slope of an isoquant, dK/dL, is equal to $-(\partial Q/\partial L)/(\partial Q/\partial K)$. The numerator of this expression is labor's marginal product,

K

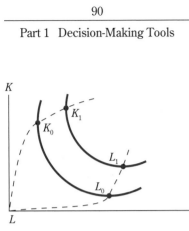

FIGURE 3.4
Ridge Lines and the Economic
Region of Production

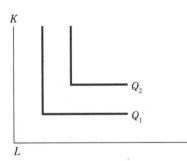

FIGURE 3.5
Isoquants for Fixed-Proportions
Technology

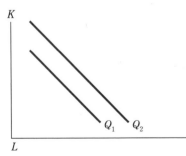

FIGURE 3.6
Isoquants for Perfect Substitutes

employed that they get in each other's way and interfere with the production process. Obviously, no firm would ever want to be in such a situation.

In Figure 3.4, the marginal product of capital becomes negative beyond (to the left of) points K_0 and K_1 and the marginal product of labor becomes negative beyond (to the right of) points L_0 and L_1. The lines that define the boundaries of the economic region of production, thereby excluding the positively sloped areas of the isoquant map, are called **ridge lines**.[8] Ridge lines are shown as the two dashed lines in Figure 3.4. Firms will never want to employ so much capital or so much labor that they cross one of the ridge lines and produce where one of the inputs has a negative marginal product.

The reasoning underlying this conclusion can be seen by comparing a point on an isoquant that lies outside one of the ridge lines with a point within the ridge lines on the same isoquant. By definition, total output is the same at both of these points. Hence, by moving from a point outside one of the ridge lines to a point within the economic region of production, the firm can produce the same total output while using less of *both* inputs. Because using less of both inputs obviously reduces the firm's total costs, production within the ridge lines is economically efficient compared with production outside of them.

The two extreme cases of input substitutability occur when two inputs are used in fixed proportions and when two inputs are perfect substitutes. Production isoquants for fixed proportions technology are L-shaped, as illustrated in Figure 3.5. Production isoquants for inputs that are perfect substitutes are linear, as illustrated in Figure 3.6. Because inputs cannot be substituted for one another in the fixed proportions case, the marginal rate of technical substitution is either zero or infinity.[9] On the other hand, because the slope of a straight line is constant, the marginal rate of technical substitution is constant when inputs are perfect substitutes for one another.

The marginal rate of technical substitution for the Cobb-Douglas production function reduces to a relatively simple expression. As determined earlier, the marginal product of capital is

$$MP_K = ab_1 K^{b_1-1} L^{b_2};$$

and the marginal product of labor is

$\partial Q/\partial L$, and the denominator is the marginal product of capital, $\partial Q/\partial K$. Hence, the marginal rate of technical substitution, $MRTS = -dK/dL = MP_L/MP_K$.

8 The points that define the boundaries of the economic region of production are the points at which a line drawn tangent to the isoquant is either vertical (K_0 and K_1) or horizontal (L_0 and L_1).

9 The slope or marginal rate of technical substitution is equal to zero on the horizontal section of the L-shaped isoquant; the slope is equal to infinity on the vertical section of the L-shaped isoquant.

$$MP_L = ab_2 K^{b_1} L^{b_2-1}.$$

The marginal rate of technical substitution is equal to the ratio of the marginal products of the two inputs (the marginal product of the input measured on the horizontal axis is always the numerator of this ratio). Hence, for the Cobb-Douglas production function,

$$\begin{aligned}
MRTS &= \frac{MP_L}{MP_K} \\[2mm]
&= \frac{ab_2 K^{b_1} L^{b_2-1}}{ab_1 K^{b_1-1} L^{b_2}} \\[2mm]
&= \left(\frac{b_2}{b_1}\right) K^{b_1-(b_1-1)} L^{b_2-1-b_2} \\[2mm]
&= \left(\frac{b_2}{b_1}\right)\left(\frac{K}{L}\right).
\end{aligned}$$

(3.8)

That is, the Cobb-Douglas production function yields isoquants with slopes that depend on the ratio in which capital and labor are combined. In the special case used to describe the production function for all-weather coats, $b_1 = b_2 = .5$, and so $MRTS = K/L$.

Figure 3.7 illustrates the calculation of the marginal rate of technical substitution at different points along the $Q = 200{,}000$ isoquant associated with the Cobb-Douglas production function for all-weather coats. This graph clearly shows that the marginal rate of technical substitution falls with movement down the isoquant. This characteristic is generally true when inputs are imperfect substitutes and the isoquant is consequently convex to the origin.

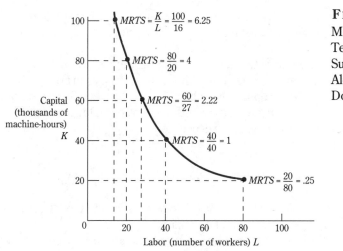

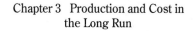

FIGURE 3.7

Marginal Rates of Technical Substitution Along a Cobb-Douglas Isoquant

TABLE 3.4 RETURNS TO SCALE

CASE	DEFINITION
Constant Returns to scale (CRS)	A proportional increase in the usage of all inputs causes output to increase in the same proportion
Increasing Returns to Scale (IRS)	A proportional increase in the usage of all inputs causes output to increase by a greater proportion
Decreasing Returns to Scale (DRS)	A proportional increase in the usage of all inputs causes output to increase by a smaller proportion

RETURNS TO SCALE

One of the most important characteristics of production in the long run is the relationship between proportional changes in the usage of *all* inputs and the corresponding change in output. This relationship, referred to as the concept of **returns to scale**, characterizes production in the long run as follows. It asks whether a given percentage increase in the usage of all inputs causes output to increase by the same percentage, by a larger percentage, or by a smaller percentage.

Table 3.4 shows the three possible cases. If the usage of all inputs doubles, for example, and this increased input usage leads to a doubling of output, then the long-run production function exhibits **constant returns to scale**. On the other hand, a condition of **increasing returns to scale** exists if a doubling of input usage causes output to more than double. If the usage of all inputs doubles and this causes output to less than double, production takes place under conditions of **decreasing returns to scale**.

Long-run production functions are not necessarily limited to just one returns-to-scale characteristic. A long-run production function may well be characterized by increasing returns to scale over some initial range of output and then exhibit a region of constant or decreasing returns to scale at higher levels of output.

The returns-to-scale characteristic of the Cobb-Douglas production function for all-weather coats can be determined directly by summing the exponents associated with capital and labor. To see this conclusion, recall that the power to which an input is raised in the Cobb-Douglas function indicates the elasticity of output with respect to that input. Hence, given the production function

$$Q = 5K^{.5}L^{.5},$$

a one percent change in capital alone or a one percent change in labor alone causes output to change by one-half of one percent.

By extension of this argument, a one percent change in *both* capital and labor causes output to change by one percent. This production function therefore exhibits constant returns to scale.[10] By the same reasoning, if the exponents of K and L sum to a number greater than one, the Cobb-Douglas production function exhibits increasing returns to scale. And if the exponents sum to a number less than one, the Cobb-Douglas production function exhibits decreasing returns to scale.

ECONOMIC EFFICIENCY AND THE COST-MINIMIZATION RULE

An isoquant shows the various combinations of two inputs at which technical efficiency in the production of a given quantity of output is achieved. However, only one of these input combinations is economically efficient. The economically efficient input combination is the one that minimizes the cost of producing the given quantity of output. The determination of the economically efficient input combination requires information on both the characteristics of the firm's production function and on the prices of the inputs employed in the production process.

The Isocost Line

The J. Johnson Company hires capital at a price of $10 per machine-hour per year. A production worker can be hired with an annual compensation package worth $40,000. Given this information, the total cost of producing all-weather coats can be written as

$$TC = \$10K + \$40L. \tag{3.9}$$

Total cost (TC), capital requirements (K), and the value of labor's annual compensation package are denominated in thousands.

Figure 3.8 graphs three alternative budget lines. For instance, if the firm draws up an annual budget of $1,000,000 for the production of all-weather coats, it can hire any combination of capital and labor shown on the line segment "*ab*" in Figure 3.8. Line "*ab*" is drawn by calculating the various combinations of capital and labor the firm can employ by spending $1,000,000 in total, given that one machine-hour of capital services costs $10 and that the annual expense of hiring one production worker is $40,000. For example, if the firm spends its entire budget on capital, it can employ at most 100,000 machine-hours (point *a*). On the other hand, if only production workers are hired, the firm can employ at most 25 workers (point *b*).

---

10 More generally, let both capital and labor usage change by a factor of λ. The new level of output will therefore be equal to $5(\lambda K)^{.5}(\lambda L)^{.5} = \lambda^{.5+.5}(5K^{.5}L^{.5}) = \lambda(5K^{.5}L^{.5}) = \lambda Q$. If $\lambda = 2$, for example, a doubling of both capital and labor usage leads to a doubling of output. The production function therefore exhibits constant returns to scale.

FIGURE 3.8

The Least Cost
Combination
of *K* and *L* for
the Production
of 200,000
Units of Output

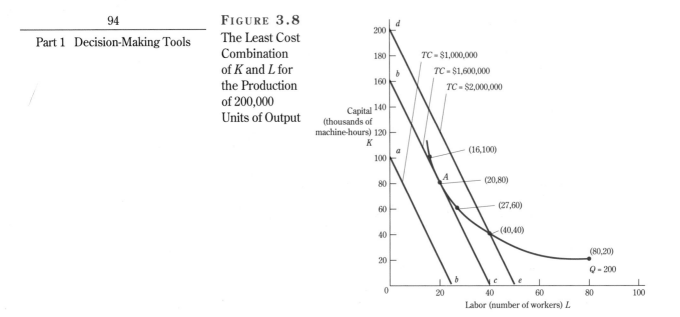

The line "*ab*" is known as an **isocost line** because it represents the various combinations of capital and labor that a given total expenditure will allow. It is derived algebraically by rewriting the total cost function to express *K* as a function of *L*. Doing so yields

$$K = \frac{TC}{\$10} - \frac{\$40}{\$10} L = \frac{TC}{\$10} - 4L. \qquad (3.10)$$

The vertical intercept of this straight line, $TC/\$10$, represents the maximum quantity of capital the firm can employ if it spends its entire budget on capital. As the previous paragraph explains, if the firm budgets $1,000,000 for the production of all-weather coats, it can hire at most ($1,000,000/$10) = 100,000 machine-hours of capital.

The slope of the isocost line is equal to the ratio of the input prices. In this example, the slope is −4, indicating that at the given input prices, four more units of capital (4,000 machine-hours) can be acquired if one less worker is employed. The slope of the isocost line consequently shows the rate at which capital can be substituted for labor while holding the firm's total expenditures constant.

The isoquant for 200,000 all-weather coats is also drawn in Figure 3.8. It should be obvious from the diagram that the firm cannot produce 200,000 units of output if it only spends $1,000,000 on capital and labor. The *Q* = 200,000 isoquant lies everywhere to the right of the isocost line corresponding to a total expenditure of $1,000,000. The feasible input combinations for producing 200,000 all-weather coats are unattainable under this total cost constraint.

Suppose that at the given input prices the firm doubles its budgeted input expenditures to $2,000,000. This level of expenditure is represented by the isocost line "*de*" in Figure 3.8. The isocost line "*de*" has the same slope as the previous isocost schedule because the firm faces the same relative input prices as before. By spending $2,000,000 the firm can hire a maximum of 200,000 machine-hours of capital (point *d*), a maximum of 50 production workers (point *e*), or any other combination of the two inputs that lies on the line "*de*." The relationship between the isocost line "*de*" and the isoquant for 200,000 all-weather coats indicates that the firm can produce this output level with a smaller budget.

Input combinations that yield 200,000 units of output can be obtained at a lower cost because some of the points on the $Q = 200,000$ isoquant lie to the left of isocost line "*de*." As the firm reduces its expenditures below $2,000,000, the isocost curve shifts parallel to the left. The firm can continue to reduce its budgeted expenditures as long as the isocost curve intersects the isoquant. If any point on the $Q = 200,000$ isoquant lies to the left of the isocost schedule, the firm's total expenditures are more than sufficient to produce the targeted output level. Hence, the firm can continue reducing its total input expenditures until the isocost line is tangent to the isoquant for 200,000 all-weather coats.

This tangency occurs at point *A*. At point *A*, the firm employs 80,000 machine-hours of capital and 20 production workers, incurring a total cost of $1,600,000. This is the lowest possible production cost for 200,000 all-weather coats, given the input prices and production technology assumed.

The Cost-Minimizing Input Combination

The foregoing discussion indicates that the firm's total costs are lowest at the point of tangency between an isoquant and the isocost line. When two curves are tangent to one another, their slopes are equal at the point of tangency. Recall that the (negative of the) slope of an isoquant—the marginal rate of technical substitution—is equal to the ratio of the marginal products of the two inputs; that is,

$$MRTS = -\frac{dK}{dL} = \frac{MP_L}{MP_K}.$$

The slope of the isocost line is equal to the ratio of the prices of the two inputs. In general, total cost is

$$TC = (P_K \times K) + (P_L \times L),$$

where P_K is the unit price or rental cost of capital and P_L is the price per unit of labor. Rewriting this expression so that K is a function of L,

$$K = \frac{TC}{P_K} - \frac{P_L}{P_K} L,$$

and taking the derivative, dK/dL, yields

$$\frac{dK}{dL} = \frac{-P_L}{P_K}.$$

Thus, the condition for cost-minimization requires that the marginal rate of technical substitution (the ratio of the marginal products of the two inputs) be equal to the (negative of the) ratio of their prices. Writing this out formally (i.e., setting $-dK/dL = MP_L/MP_K = P_L/P_K$), the condition for economic efficiency or the least-cost input combination is

$$\frac{MP_L}{MP_K} = \frac{P_L}{P_K}. \quad \text{LEAST – COST CONDITION} \quad (3.11)$$

Stated differently, cost minimization requires that the rate at which input substitution is technologically feasible, MP_L/MP_K, must be equal to the rate at which the inputs can be substituted on the market, P_L/P_K.

The cost-minimization condition can be rearranged to provide yet another interpretation. In particular, some algebraic manipulation yields

$$\frac{MP_L}{P_L} = \frac{MP_K}{P_K}. \quad \text{LEAST – COST CONDITION} \quad (3.12)$$

Equation 3.12 states that total costs are at a minimum when the marginal productivity per dollar of expenditure is equal across the last units of capital and labor employed.

In any form, however, the cost-minimization condition is quite general and holds for any arbitrary number of inputs that are imperfect substitutes in production. For example, if the firm employs n inputs designated as 1 through n, the least cost condition requires that the ratio of the marginal product of each input to its own price be equal across the last units employed of all inputs. The algebraic equivalent of this statement is indicated by the following equation:

$$\frac{MP_1}{P_1} = \frac{MP_2}{P_2} = \frac{MP_3}{P_3} = ... = \frac{MP_n}{P_n}. \quad \text{LEAST – COST CONDITION} \quad (3.13)$$

The least-cost condition for economic efficiency applies for all output levels and dictates the optimal combination of inputs when the firm expands or contracts output. Figure 3.9 illustrates the tangencies associated with four isoquants and four isocost lines. The straight line connecting these four points (A, B, C, and D) is called an **expansion path**.[11] The expansion path traces out optimal (least-cost) input combinations at various levels of output, holding relative input prices constant.

Because the slope of an isocost line is equal to the ratio of input prices, a change in this ratio will shift the isocost curves and the expansion path. For

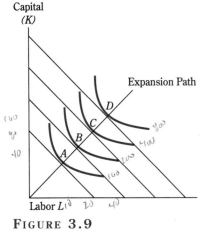

Capital
(K)

Expansion Path

Labor L

FIGURE 3.9

Expansion Path

---

11 The expansion path is a straight line in the special case of constant returns-to-scale production technology. The expansion path will be nonlinear for other production technologies.

example, holding the price of labor constant, an increase in the price of capital will cause the isocost schedules to become flatter and the expansion path would therefore tend to shift to the right. That is, the firm would respond to an increase in the relative price of capital by shifting to a less capital-intensive production process.[12]

LONG-RUN COST CURVES

Production theory provides a framework for analyzing the behavior of cost as inputs and output vary along the firm's expansion path. The derivation of a firm's long-run total cost schedule from its expansion path can be illustrated with the Johnson Company's production function for all-weather coats.

Table 3.5 lists six output levels and the corresponding least-cost combinations of capital and labor that lie on the expansion path for all-weather coats. The output levels chosen to define the expansion path are arbitrary. Table 3.5 is constructed by successively doubling output from one point on the expansion path to the next. The table shows that as output doubles, the total cost of production also doubles. This one-to-one correspondence between changes in output and changes in total cost is due to the constant-returns-to-scale characteristic of this particular production function. With constant returns to scale, a doubling of both inputs causes output to double. With input prices held constant, total cost necessarily also doubles.

A change in relative input prices does not affect this basic relationship between changes in output and changes in total cost. For example, suppose that the price of capital is held constant at $10 per machine-hour per year, but that the value of a production worker's annual compensation is $30,000 rather than $40,000. The firm would then employ a different ratio of capital to labor (least-cost input combinations would tend to be more labor-intensive), the expansion path would rotate clockwise (become flatter), and the total cost figures in Table 3.5 would shrink. However, the constant-returns-to-scale characteristic would not change, and Table 3.5 would therefore con-

TABLE 3.5 DERIVATION OF A LONG-RUN COST SCHEDULE

OUTPUT (THOUSANDS OF COATS)	LEAST COST USAGE OF		*LRTC* TOTAL COST = $10K + $40L (THOUSANDS)
	CAPITAL (THOUSANDS OF MACHINE-HOURS)	LABOR (NUMBERS OF WORKERS)	
100	40	10	$800
200	80	20	1,600
400	160	40	3,200
800	320	80	6,400
1600	640	160	12,800
3200	1280	320	25,600

---

12 Note that if the prices of both inputs change in the same proportion, there would be no effect on the optimal input combination or on the expansion path's slope.

tinue to show that a doubling of inputs causes both output and total cost to double.

Returns to Scale and Long-Run Marginal Costs

The general relationship between changes in output and changes in long-run total cost is determined only by the production function's returns-to-scale characteristics. As has just been shown, total cost changes in the same proportion as the corresponding change in output when production is subject to constant returns to scale. On the other hand, total cost changes less-than-proportionately with output when production is subject to increasing returns to scale. And total cost changes more-than-proportionately with output when production is subject to decreasing returns to scale.

The nature of the returns to scale that characterize production in the long run determines the slope of the total cost function. The slope of the long-run total cost function, in turn, is **long-run marginal cost** (*LRMC*), defined as the change in long-run total cost associated with a change in output. More specifically,

$$LRMC = \frac{\Delta LRTC}{\Delta Q}. \quad \text{Long – Run Marginal Cost} \quad (3.14)$$

The graphs in Figure 3.10 depict the relationships among long-run total cost, long-run marginal cost, and returns to scale. Constant returns to scale are associated with a linear total cost function (panel *a*). Because a linear function has a constant slope, long-run marginal cost is constant in this case. Increasing returns to scale are associated with a total cost function that increases at a decreasing rate (panel *b*). The long-run marginal cost schedule corresponding to this total cost function is falling. Decreasing returns to scale are associated with a total cost function that increases at an increasing rate; long-run marginal cost is consequently rising (panel *c*).

The final graph in Figure 3.10 (panel *d*) illustrates a common composite case in which the long-run total cost curve first increases at a decreasing rate and then increases at an increasing rate. Long-run marginal cost first falls (increasing returns to scale), reaches a minimum at the point of inflection on the long-run total cost schedule, and then rises (decreasing returns to scale).

Economies of Scale and Long-Run Average Costs

Each of Figure 3.10's panels also graphs the **long-run average cost** (*LRAC*) schedule. Long-run average cost is calculated by dividing long-run total cost by the number of units of output produced, or

$$LRAC = \frac{LRTC}{Q}. \quad \text{Long – Run Average Cost} \quad (3.15)$$

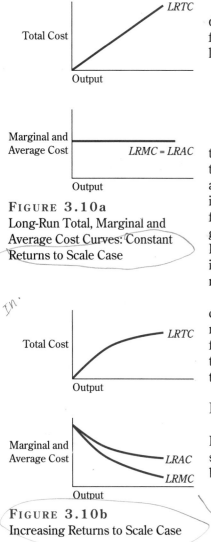

FIGURE 3.10a
Long-Run Total, Marginal and Average Cost Curves: Constant Returns to Scale Case

FIGURE 3.10b
Increasing Returns to Scale Case

The nature of the response of long-run average cost to a change in output provides an alternative way of characterizing production in the long run. In the case of constant returns to scale, long-run marginal cost is constant. Long-run average cost is also constant and equal to long-run marginal cost under these circumstances. This relationship necessarily follows from the definitions of *LRMC* and *LRAC*. *LRMC* measures the change in long-run total cost associated with a given change in output. If LRMC is constant, proportional changes in output lead to proportional changes in total cost.

For example, suppose that each unit of output produced adds $10 to long-run total cost (*LRMC* = $10). To produce one unit of output, total cost is $10; to produce two units of output, total cost is $20; to produce three units of output, total cost is $30; and so on. Long-run average cost is also constant in this case. The long-run average cost of producing one unit of output is $10/1 = $10; the long-run average cost of producing two units is $20/2 = $10; and the long-run average cost of producing three units is $30/3 = $10. Hence, when the change in long-run total cost (*LRMC*) is equal to the previous average, the average does not change.

By similar reasoning, the long-run average cost curve declines when long-run marginal cost is both falling and below *LRAC*. If the increment to long-run total cost is smaller than the previous average—if long-run total cost is rising at a decreasing rate as in panel *b*—the average must fall. (Consider the sequence $10, $10, $10, $8. What is the average of the four numbers?) Lastly, long-run average cost increases when long-run marginal cost is both rising and above *LRAC*. If the increment to long-run total cost is larger than the previous average—if long-run total cost is rising at an increasing rate as in panel *c*—the average must rise. (What is the average of the sequence $10, $10, $10, $12?)

If the *LRAC* schedule is falling when *LRMC* is both falling and below *LRAC*, and if *LRAC* is rising when *LRMC* is both rising and above *LRAC*, it follows that *LRAC* = *LRMC* at *LRAC's* minimum point. The bottom graph of Figure 3.10 (panel *d*) shows this relationship. *LRMC* intersects *LRAC* when *LRAC* is at its minimum.[13]

The term **economies of scale** refers to the declining portion of the long-run average cost curve. **Diseconomies of scale** are encountered on the rising portion of the long-run average cost curve.

Formally, the economies of scale "constitute the relationship between the size of a firm (or plant) and its cost of production in the broadest sense."[14] In the presence of scale economies, unit production costs decline with increases in the *rate* of output. Economies of scale are usually thought of in terms of the physical manufacturing or processing functions of the firm. But the concept

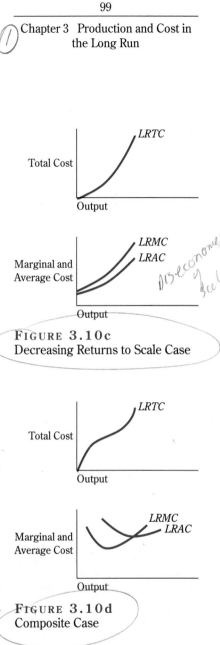

FIGURE 3.10c
Decreasing Returns to Scale Case

FIGURE 3.10d
Composite Case

---

13 This result can be shown mathematically. *LRAC* = *LRTC*/*Q* is at a minimum when the first derivative of the function is equal to zero. Taking this derivative yields $d(LRTC/Q)/dQ = [Q(dLRTC/dQ) - LRTC]/Q^2$. But $dLRTC/dQ = LRMC$. Setting $[(Q \times LRMC) - LRTC]/Q^2 = 0$ and simplifying, the expression states that *LRAC* is at a minimum when *LRAC* = *LRMC*.

14 George J. Stigler, "Barriers to Entry, Economies of Scale, and Firm Size," in George J. Stigler, *The Organization of Industry* (Homewood, IL: Richard D. Irwin, 1968), p. 67.

applies equally to other inputs and activities, including entrepreneurial and managerial talent, purchasing, sales, and finance.

Sources of Economies of Scale

Scale economies can arise from nonpecuniary (technological) or pecuniary factors. Increasing returns to scale are the main technological determinant of economies of scale. In addition, technological economies arise from specialization and the division of labor.[15] Such cost savings derive from the observation that "proficiency is gained by concentration of effort."[16] When, in a small plant, each worker performs a variety of distinct tasks, time is lost moving between jobs, changing tools, and so forth, and each worker's attention is divided among several operations. A larger plant with a larger work force allows each worker to specialize in one task, or in a small number of closely related tasks, and thus to acquire a proficiency that increases output per unit of labor input. This increased proficiency brings about a corresponding reduction in average production costs.[17]

An additional source of technological economies of scale is associated with the indivisibilities that often characterize modern, capital-intensive production processes. Machines differ in their optimal utilization rates, and a proper "meshing" of their functions may require a large rate of output.[18] For example, suppose that finishing machines can turn out 30,000 units per day and that packaging machines can box 45,000 units per day. Total output will then have to be 90,000 units per day in order to utilize fully the capacities of these machines, thereby minimizing downtime and start-up costs.

Larger output rates also enable the firm to acquire specialized capital that would not be economical with shorter production runs. The high degree of mechanization typical of mass production techniques permits automation of many operations, causing labor's productivity to rise and unit production costs to fall. Increasing the rate of output helps smooth inventory fluctuations and allows the firm to take advantage of economies of scale in the distribution and marketing of its product.[19]

Pecuniary economies of scale are a second source of the cost savings associated with producing large rates of output. Larger enterprises are often able to obtain more favorable terms from input suppliers by purchasing raw materials in bulk. They may be able to obtain similar advantages when dealing

---

15 See Chapter 7 for a more detailed discussion of the cost savings due to specialization and the division of labor.

16 Charles E. Ferguson, *Microeconomic Theory,* 3E. (Homewood, IL: Richard D. Irwin, 1972), p. 235.

17 For a further discussion of the economies stemming from the division of labor, see John S. McGee, "Efficiency and the Economies of Size," in Harvey J. Goldschmid, H. Michael Mann, and J. Fred Weston, eds., *Industrial Concentration: The New Learning* (Boston: Little, Brown, 1974), pp. 55-97.

18 Ferguson, *Microeconomic Theory,* p. 236.

19 For additional discussion, see Michael E. McGrath and Richard W. Hoole, "Manufacturing's New Economies of Scale," *Harvard Business Review*, May-June 1992, pp. 94-102.

with shipping companies and advertising agencies. Capital costs per unit of output typically decline with increases in the scale of operation as well. A printing press that can run 200,000 newspapers per day does not cost 10 times as much as one that can only run 20,000 newspapers per day; nor does it take up 10 times as much floor space or require 10 times as many workers to operate it.[20]

Volume Effects, the "Learning Curve," and Economies of Scope

Armen Alchian has identified several other aspects of production that affect the firm's long-run average costs. The most important of these is the total volume of output the firm plans to produce.[21] To illustrate, suppose that a firm contemplates producing 100 units of output at the rate of 100 units per year. At the end of first period, unforeseen events cause the firm to revise its plans and to produce an additional 100 units of output, again at the rate of 100 units per year.

Now compare the total costs of that production plan with the costs of one in which the firm initially contemplates producing 200 units in total at the rate of 100 units per year. Both production plans take two years to complete and result in the same total volume of output, but their total costs are likely to differ substantially. It will in general be cheaper to produce from a production plan that contemplates a two-year volume of 200 units at the rate of 100 units per year than to duplicate the manufacturing techniques that are optimal for a planned volume of only 100 units.

This is because larger planned output volumes make it economical for the firm to adopt large-scale, capital-intensive production methods that would not be cost-effective at lower output volumes. For example, custom workshop techniques will suffice for producing only a small number of automobiles, but assembly line methods become economical when a larger output volume is contemplated, even if the planned output *rate* per unit of time is the same. Mass production methods are not simply large-scale replications of small-scale methods.

The volume effect identified by Alchian is a result of several factors. One is the aforementioned observation that the techniques of production are a function of the planned volume of output. The technological economies of large-scale production cause unit costs to fall with larger contemplated output volumes.

A related source of production cost savings is associated with "learning by doing." A firm that has produced a large volume of output has in many cases encountered and solved a number of practical problems that were not

---

20 Ferguson, *Microeconomic Theory*, p. 236.
21 Armen A. Alchian, "Costs and Output," in Moses Abramovitz, et al., *The Allocation of Economic Resources: Essays in Honor of Bernard F. Haley* (Palo Alto, CA: Stanford University Press, 1959), pp. 23-40.

anticipated when production began. The more times an activity is repeated, the more likely it is that better (more efficient) techniques will be discovered. Both workers and management become more proficient as they gain more experience with a particular production process. This experience, along with the increased proficiency gained by repetition, translates into lower unit production costs.

The **learning curve,** which relates average production costs to accumulated volume,[22] is especially important in industries where production entails intricate workmanship with low tolerance for error, such as aircraft and computer chip manufacture. In cases of this kind, the productivity increases associated with learning-by-doing can be quite dramatic. For example, studies of aircraft production during World War II estimated that labor costs per unit fell by about 20 percent with each doubling of cumulative output.[23]

The economies associated with increases in the scale of operations and with learning-by-doing are product specific. **Economies of scope** are the reductions in average production costs achieved by producing two or more closely related products. That is, economies of scope exist when the total cost of producing two or more products within the same plant or firm is less than the total cost of producing the same products in separate plants or firms.

For example, consider a manufacturing process that involves the use of dies, molds, and other specialized capital equipment. Demand conditions for one product may prevent the firm from exploiting all of the technical economies of larger output rates. But by replacing removable sections of the same basic dies or by interchanging molds, the firm may be able to produce several different products without incurring proportionately higher total costs. Expanding the scope of operations in this way allows fuller employment of the basic stamping or extruding equipment, thereby generating reductions in unit costs that would not be possible if the firm produced only a single product.[24]

---

22 Note that the learning curve is *not* a source of economies of scale. Scale economies are defined with respect to the slope of the firm's long-run average cost curve which relates unit cost to the *rate* of output produced. The learning curve relates unit production costs to the accumulated *volume* of output produced. Learning-by-doing causes a downward shift in the firm's long-run average cost schedule. See Chapter 10 for a more complete discussion.

23 Harold Asher, *Cost-Quantity Relationships in the Airframe Industry* (Santa Monica: RAND Corporation, 1956). For some criticisms of the empirical techniques used in early learning-curve estimates, see Armen A. Alchian, "Reliability of Progress Curves in Airframe Production," *Econometrica* 31 (October 1963), pp. 679-93. For more recent theory and evidence on the subject, see Thomas R. Gulledge, Jr. and Norman K. Womer, *The Economics of Made-to-Order Production: Theory with Applications Related to the Airframe Industry* (Berlin: Springer-Verlag, 1986).

24 For theory and evidence on product diversification as a motive for merger, see Michael T. Maloney and Robert E. McCormick, "Excess Capacity, Cyclical Production, and Merger Motives: Some Evidence from the Capital Markets," *Journal of Law and Economics* 31 (October 1988), pp. 321-50.

Although undoubtedly quite important, economies of scope are not limited to the reductions in average costs associated with the sharing of physical assets. Product diversification more fully exploits managerial skills, sales networks, and the firm's reputational capital.[25] Some organizational resources are "fungible" in the sense that their use in the manufacture or distribution of one good does not reduce their availability for use in the manufacture or distribution of some other good.[26]

This observation implies that the range of products over which scope economies are advantageous is potentially quite broad. In the 1920s, General Electric and Westinghouse, which had previously specialized in the manufacture of light and power equipment, diversified into the production of a wide array of household appliances as well as radios and X-ray equipment. During the Great Depression, General Motors diversified into the production of diesels, household appliances, tractors, and airplanes. In the same period, food companies began producing and marketing an increasing number of products.[27]

As David Teece points out, opportunities for taking advantage of scope economies typically result from the emergence of excess production capacity.[28] Equally important is his observation that such economies need not be exploited within the same plant or firm. In the absence of specialized capital, market contracting offers a feasible arrangement through which two or more firms can share assets and thereby lower their individual unit costs of production.

Consider apple growing and bee keeping. The joint production of apples and honey involves significant technical economies because, on the one hand, the apple blossoms provide a ready source of nectar for the bees and, on the other hand, the bees pollinate the apple blossoms in their search for nectar. Joint production of apples and honey does not require joint ownership of apple trees and bee hives, however. In Washington State, a leading apple-producing area, there is a long history of explicit and implicit contractual arrangements between apple growers and bee keepers that compensate the latter for the marginal contribution their bees make to the apple crop.[29]

This example points to a useful distinction between *internal* and *external* economies of scale and scope, and serves as a reminder that both transaction-cost and production-cost considerations influence the nature of the firm's activities. That is, the economies of scale and scope are exploitable within a

25 Len M. Nichols, "On the Sources of Scope Economies in U.S. Manufacturing Firms," *Review of Industrial Organization* 4 (Spring 1989), pp. 1-22. Nichols concludes from empirical evidence that "perhaps the most important shared assets in manufacturing firms are the skills of various personnel."

26 David J. Teece, "Economies of Scope and the Scope of the Enterprise," *Journal of Economic Behavior and Organization* 1 (September 1980), pp. 223-47.

27 Alfred D. Chandler, Jr., "The Structure of American Industry in the Twentieth Century: A Historical Review," *Review of Business History* 63 (1969), p. 275.

28 David J. Teece, "Towards an Economic Theory of the Multiproduct Firm," *Journal of Economic Behavior and Organization* 3 (March 1982), pp. 39-64. Also see Maloney and McCormick, "Excess Capacity, Cyclical Production, and Merger Motives."

29 Steven N. S. Cheung, "The Fable of the Bees: An Economic Investigation," *Journal of Law and Economics* 16 (April 1973), pp. 11-33. See Chapter 17 for a more complete discussion of these contracts.

plant or firm (through internal expansion or diversification) or across ownership boundaries. The option chosen in any particular case will simply be the one that generates the larger reduction in unit production costs.[30]

Diseconomies of Scale

Beyond some rate of output, economies of scale are exhausted and the firm's long-run average costs of production begin to rise. Diseconomies of scale take over.

Diseconomies of scale can emerge for technological reasons—decreasing returns to scale—or because of other limiting factors. As the firm expands in size and more layers of bureaucracy are added, the daily production routine becomes more remote from the firm's top-level managers. The paperwork burden increases, and managers must coordinate an increasingly diverse set of business activities and functions—transportation, finance, sales, research and development, personnel, and so on.

Managerial decisions become more complex and more costly as the firm expands in scale and scope. Failures to make the best use of the firm's productive resources become more frequent. Errors in assigning tasks, monitoring performance, and scaling rewards to effort become more likely. The loss of control ("control loss") impedes management's ability to hold costs down and unit production costs begin to rise. Diseconomies of scale are the principal factor limiting the sizes of firms.

PRODUCTION AND COST REVISITED

This chapter's opening application asks five questions. This section applies the economic theory of production and cost to answer these questions. Recall that the production function is $Q = 5K^{.5}L^{.5}$, where Q is measured in thousands of all-weather coats, K is measured in units of 1,000 machine-hours of capital, and L is the number of production workers employed. Workers are paid $40,000 annually, and the price of capital is $10 per machine-hour per year.

The production department prepares a table showing alternative combinations of capital and labor that can be used to produce 200,000 coats. How can the substitutability of capital and labor be measured? The marginal rate of technical substitution (*MRTS*) provides a measure of the degree of input substitutability. The *MRTS* is the slope of an isoquant, which is in turn equal to the ratio of the marginal products of the inputs. When two inputs are imperfect substitutes, the *MRTS* varies continuously along a given isoquant, diminishing as one input is substituted for another.

In the special case assumed in the application, the marginal rate of technical substitution is simply equal to the capital-labor ratio, K/L. The *MRTS* tends to be relatively high when the firm employs a relatively capital-intensive production process. Holding total output constant, the *MRTS* falls continuously

---

30 These ideas are explored more fully in Chapter 7 and Part III.

Government Regulation and Production Costs

The extent to which production reflects economies of scale has a direct impact on the number of firms in an industry. For example, if the minimum efficient scale for an industry is 100 units of output and industry demand is 400 units of output, then there is room for, at most, four firms that produce at minimum long-run average cost.[a] In the case of a "natural monopoly," economies of scale exist over the entire relevant range of output. There is room for only one firm of minimum efficient size in this case. Because scale economies can be associated with limited competition in an industry, their existence provides a rationale for government regulation designed to protect the interests of consumers when they are not protected by competition among firms.[b]

Public utilities are often cited as obvious examples of natural monopolies. Even in this case, however, studies have shown that efficient production does not always require extremely large firms. For example, Christensen and Greene estimated the cost characteristics of firms that produce electric power in the United States.[c] They found that in 1955 there were significant scale economies in the generation of electric power. But they concluded that by 1970, most firms were operating on the flat part of their average cost curves and that public policies aimed at fostering competition in the industry by promoting the entry of new firms would not necessarily sacrifice economies of scale.

Another example of a highly regulated industry, at least over the period 1935 to 1980, is the trucking industry. Economies of scale are relatively unimportant in the trucking industry, so why did government regulate the industry for 45 years? One reason is that trucking regulation was an extension of government's efforts to regulate the railroads. Competition from motor carriers made it difficult for regulators to maintain prices high enough to assure the railroads a "reasonable" rate of return. Railroads and trucking were deregulated in 1980 with passage of the Staggers Rail Act and the Motor Carrier Act of 1980.

John Ying has recently estimated the effect of deregulation on the costs of trucking firms.[d] Ying estimates a total cost function (operating expenses plus net capital costs) that incorporates the following explanatory variables: Average length of haul (*HAUL*), average shipment size (*SIZE*), average load per mile driven (*LOAD*), percent of traffic consisting of less-than-full-load shipments (*LESS*), average insurance cost (*INSURANCE*), output as measured by revenue per ton mile (*OUTPUT*), and the prices of fuel (*PFUEL*), rental trucks (*PRENT*), and capital (*PCAP*), respectively. The following table presents the empirical results.

Determinants of Trucking Total Cost

	1975 COEFFICIENT (t-RATIO)	1980 COEFFICIENT (t-RATIO)	1984 COEFFICIENT (t-RATIO)
HAUL	−0.404 (−5.80)	−0.430 (−2.76)	−0.019 (−0.10)
SIZE	−0.114 (−1.27)	−0.563 (−3.62)	−0.530 (−2.14)
LOAD	−0.282 (−2.48)	−0.328 (−1.79)	−0.590 (−2.60)
LESS	0.254 (2.12)	−0.349 (−2.15)	−0.447 (−1.69)
INSURANCE	−0.121 (−1.70)	−0.045 (−0.45)	0.058 (−0.37)
OUTPUT	1.025 (25.86)	1.003 (16.04)	0.890 (11.10)
PFUEL	0.064 (20.39)	0.090 (16.54)	0.084 (11.45)
PRENT	0.092 (6.05)	0.124 (5.35)	0.142 (4.62)
PCAP	0.244 (33.78)	0.248 (21.19)	0.273 (15.87)

a The minimum efficient scale corresponds to the plant size at which long-run average cost first reaches a minimum. See Chapter 4.

b See Part IV for a discussion of public policies toward business.

c Lauritis R. Christensen and William H. Greene, "Economies of Scale in U.S. Electric Power Generation," *Journal of Political Economy* 84 (August 1976) pp. 655-76.

d John S. Ying, "Regulatory Reform and Technical Change: New Evidence of Scale Economies in Trucking," *Southern Economic Journal* 56 (April 1990), pp. 996-1005.

According to Ying, there were no major technological changes during this period. Therefore, changes in costs result from changes in the regulatory environment. Because the dependent variable is a measure of total cost and output is held constant on the right-hand side, we can interpret the effect of the independent variables in terms of their impact on average total cost.

Ying expected the variables HAUL, SIZE, and LOAD to have negative effects on average cost. That is, the average cost of shipping goods by truck will tend to be lower as the length of the average haul increases, as the average shipment size increases, and as the average load per mile increases. Ying argues that the more competitive environment after deregulation should increase the magnitude of these negative effects on average cost.

In 1975, HAUL and LOAD are negatively and significantly related to trucking cost while SIZE is not significantly related to trucking cost. Contrary to Ying's hypothesis, HAUL becomes an insignificant determinant of cost by 1984. However, the changes in SIZE and LOAD are consistent with Ying's expectations. The coefficient associated with SIZE is both negative and significant in 1984, and the coefficient associated with LOAD more than doubles in magnitude after deregulation.

The variables LESS and INSURANCE are hypothesized to have a positive effect on average cost. Ying argues that deregulation should have diminished these effects. In 1975, LESS has a positive, significant effect on cost while INSURANCE is an insignificant determinant of cost. In 1984, both LESS and INSURANCE are insignificant determinants of cost. Thus, consistent with Ying's hypothesis, the variable LESS has a smaller impact following deregulation.

One of the basic hypotheses of the paper was that increased competition will tend to increase the impact of variables that reduce costs and to decrease the impact of variables that increase costs in the trucking industry. With the exception of the variable HAUL, the empirical results tend to support these predictions.

---

as the firm substitutes labor for capital and employs a more labor-intensive production process.

If the firm wants to expand production in the future by expanding its plant size and the number of workers it employs, how much will output increase? For example, if both plant size and employment double, will output also double? The production function $Q = 5K^{.5}L^{.5}$ is characterized by constant returns to scale. A given percentage change in both capital and labor usage causes output to increase by that same percentage. Hence, if capital and labor double, output will also double.

Capital and labor are measured differently. Capital is measured in increments of 1,000 machine-hours and labor is measured in terms of number of production workers employed. How can the relative prices of these factors be measured? Capital is measured in units of 1,000 machine-hours and the price of capital is $10 per machine-hour per year. Workers are paid a total compensation of $40,000 annually. The price of labor relative to capital is therefore $40,000/$10,000 = 4. At these relative prices, the firm can substitute one production worker for 4,000 machine-hours of capital while holding total expenditures constant.

What is the optimal combination of plant size and employment for any level of output the firm might want to produce over time? The optimal combination of capital and labor for producing a given quantity of output is the input combination that minimizes the total cost of producing that quantity of output. Economic efficiency is synonymous with the least-cost input combination. Economic efficiency requires that the ratio of the marginal products of labor and capital be equal to the ratio of their prices, that is, $MP_L/MP_K = P_L/P_K$. Given the assumptions made, the firm minimizes the total cost of producing 200,000 all-weather coats per year by employing 80,000 machine-hours of capital and 20 production workers.

How do the production function and the unit prices of inputs determine the cost of producing different levels of output that the firm can produce when it varies the size of its plant? The firm's long-run cost schedule shows the cost of producing different levels of output when both employment and plant size are variable. When the firm varies output it should vary its input mix by following the least-cost rule. With relative input prices constant, the different combinations of capital and labor that follow least-cost adjustments in output define an expansion path which determines the behavior of total cost in the long run.

Summary

Firms employ a wide array of inputs to produce goods and services valued by consumers. The economic theory of production and cost usually assumes a simple two-input production function that employs capital and labor. This chapter presents the characteristics of production in the long run when both capital and labor are variable.

Production can use inputs in either fixed or variable proportions. Economic theory has limited usefulness in the case of fixed proportions because there is no element of choice. With variable proportions technology, inputs can be either perfect or imperfect substitutes for one another. Perfect substitutes can be treated as a single input in the production function because the firm will employ only one input (the one that is cheaper) from a list of perfect substitutes. When two inputs are imperfect substitutes, the firm can choose among different combinations of inputs to produce the same level of output. The economic theory of production addresses the set of choices faced when inputs are imperfect substitutes.

Graphical analysis is one method for presenting and understanding the economic theory of production and cost. An isoquant traces out the various combinations of capital and labor that can produce a given level of output. The slope of an isoquant, the marginal rate of technical substitution, is a measure of the degree of substitutability of capital and labor. The marginal rate of technical substitution is equal to the ratio of the marginal products of the two inputs. If labor is graphed on the horizontal axis, the marginal product of labor is the numerator of this ratio.

"Returns to scale" characterizes the relationship between proportional changes in input usage and the corresponding proportional change in output. If output changes in the same proportion as the two inputs, production exhibits constant returns to scale; if output changes proportionately more than the two inputs, production exhibits increasing returns to scale; and if output changes proportionately less than the change in the two inputs, production exhibits decreasing returns to scale.

Key Terms
production efficiency
economic efficiency
long run
short run
production function
fixed proportions technology
variable proportions technology
perfect substitutes
imperfect substitutes
marginal rate of technical substitution
marginal product of capital
marginal product of labor
Cobb-Douglas production function
isoquant
ridge lines
returns to scale
constant returns to scale
increasing returns to scale
decreasing returns to scale
isocost line
expansion path
long-run marginal cost
long-run average cost
economies of scale
diseconomies of scale
learning curve
economies of scope
Lagrange multiplier

The least-cost combination of inputs determines economic efficiency. Graphically, the combination of capital and labor that produces a given quantity of output at least cost occurs where that output's isoquant is tangent to an isocost line. This point of tangency is equivalent to requiring that the ratios of the marginal products of the two inputs be equal to the ratio of the input prices. In the two-input case, this condition is written as $MP_L/MP_K = P_L/P_K$. Alternatively, we can write the least-cost input combination in terms of the ratios of marginal products to input prices, $MP_L/P_L = MP_K/P_K$. The condition for economic efficiency applies to any arbitrary number of inputs: $MP_1/P_1 = MP_2/P_2 = MP_3/P_3 = ... = MP_n/P_n$.

The firm's long-run total cost function is derived from the set of input combinations on the firm's expansion path, which traces out the least-cost input combinations as output is varied holding input prices constant. The behavior of long-run total cost responds to its economies of scale properties which, in turn, depend partly on the nature of the production function's returns-to-scale characteristics. Economies of scale dictate that the firm's long-run average costs decline as output expands. Economies of scale may exist when production reflects increasing returns to scale and when other pecuniary and nonpecuniary factors such as specialization and the division of labor are exploitable. Diseconomies of scale exist when the firm's long-run average cost curve is rising. Diseconomies of scale may be encountered when production is characterized by decreasing returns to scale and when control loss by management leads to increases in unit production costs. If production is subject to constant returns to scale, the long-run marginal and average cost curves are horizontal.

QUESTIONS

3.1 Two inputs —capital and labor—define a firm's production function. Describe the adjustments the firm should make in each of the following situations.

$$a.\frac{MP_K}{MP_L} > \frac{P_K}{P_L} \qquad c.\frac{MP_K}{P_K} > \frac{MP_L}{P_L}$$

$$b.\frac{MP_K}{MP_L} < \frac{P_K}{P_L} \qquad d.\frac{MP_K}{P_K} < \frac{MP_L}{P_L}$$

3.2 Evaluate the following statements. If a firm employs the least-cost combination of inputs, it is producing the maximum quantity of output for a given total expenditure. If a firm is producing the maximum quantity of output for given total expenditure, it is employing the least-cost input combination.

3.3 A firm has a monthly operating budget of $100,000. The price of capital is $5 per machine-hour per month and the price of a unit of labor is $2,500 per month.

a. Draw the isocost line for this firm, graphing labor (measured by the number of workers employed) on the horizontal axis and capital (measured in units of 1,000 machine-hours) on the vertical axis. What is the slope of this line?

b. Draw the isocost line if the firm increases its monthly operating budget to $200,000. What is the slope of the new isocost schedule?

c. On a new graph, draw the original isocost schedule from part (a). Holding the price of labor constant, add a new isocost schedule to the graph in which the price of capital falls to $2.50 per machine-hour. What is the slope of this line?

d. On a new graph, draw the original isocost schedule from part (a). Draw a new isocost curve in which the price of labor rises to $3,500 per month, holding the price of capital constant. What is the slope of the new isocost curve?

3.4 Draw an isoquant for a production technology that uses capital and labor in variable proportions. Capital and labor are imperfect substitutes. Explain the effect of the following changes on this isoquant.

a. There is an increase in the marginal productivity of labor.

b. There is an increase in the marginal productivity of capital.

c. Capital and labor both become twice as productive.

3.5 Vegetable farmers in France tend to plant their vegetables closer together and to fertilize their land more intensely than American vegetable farmers. French farmers spend more time and effort keeping weeds out of their land. American farmers often use machines to harvest their crops while French farmers are more likely to harvest by hand. Machines harvest the land more quickly but they tend to leave a larger proportion of the crop in the field than if harvesting is done by hand. Which group of farmers is more efficient, the French farmers or the American farmers?

3.6 Equilibrium in a competitive labor market requires that each input be compensated in proportion to its marginal productivity. If worker A is twice as productive as worker B, then worker A should earn twice as much as worker B. This is consistent with the following condition for economic efficiency: $MP_A/MP_B = W_A/W_B$, where W_A and W_B represent the wages of worker A and worker B respectively. If all the workers in a fast food restaurant are paid the same wage even though some workers are more productive than others, is the restaurant inefficient? Why or why not?

3.7 Discuss the following statement. The production of shoes requires both capital and labor. These inputs are imperfect substitutes for each other. Each input has a constant average product.

3.8 Compare and contrast increasing returns to scale, constant returns to scale, and decreasing returns to scale with economies of scale and diseconomies of scale.

3.9 The Tupelo Table Company currently employs 50 unskilled workers, 30 semi-skilled workers, and 10 skilled workers. The company believes that the last unskilled worker has a marginal product of 75 tables per day, the marginal product of the last semi-skilled worker is 120 tables per day, and the marginal product of the last skilled worker is 150 tables per day. Unskilled workers earn $50 per day, semi-skilled workers earn $75 per day, and skilled workers earn $100 per day. Is the company employing the optimal combination of unskilled workers, semi-skilled workers, and skilled workers to produce its targeted output of tables? If not, what adjustments should be made?

3.10 Suppose that a firm's long-run average cost curve is U-shaped. To what specific technological and economic factors can the U-shape be attributed?

3.11 Is a fixed-proportions production function characterized by constant returns to scale? Explain.

Processed Tax Returns	Accountants with CPAs	Accountants without CPAs
3,000	100	4
3,000	50	8
3,000	25	16
3,000	20	20
3,000	10	40
3,000	8	50
3,000	4	100

PROBLEMS

3.1 Tax Experts Inc. processes tax returns in Santa Fe, New Mexico. The company hires accountants with and without CPAs to process tax returns. Based on its prior experience the company expects to prepare an average of 3,000 individual tax returns per month during the months of January through April. The company believes it can process this number of tax returns with the combinations of accountants with and without CPAs in the chart above. Accountants with CPAs earn $4,800 per month and accountants without CPAs earn $1,200 per month.

   a. What is the economically efficient combination of accountants with and without CPAs?

   b. Draw a graph with "accountants with CPAs" on the horizontal axis and "accountants without CPAs" on the vertical axis. Sketch in the isoquant for 3,000 processed tax returns.

   c. Draw an isocost line on the graph in part (b). This isocost line should represent the minimum cost of producing 3,000 processed tax returns.

   d. What is the slope of the isocost schedule?

   e. Suppose that the marginal rate of technical substitution between accountants without CPAS and accountants with CPAs can be estimated by the ratio of these two inputs. What is the marginal rate of technical substitution of each input combination that can produce 3,000 tax returns?

   f. Compare the marginal rate of technical substitution and the ratio of the input prices for each combination of inputs that can produce 3,000 tax returns. How could this comparison allow us to answer the original question in part (a)?

3.2 The following production functions exhibit the same returns-to-scale characteristic over all output levels. Determine the returns-to-scale characteristic for each function.

a. $Q = 2K + 3L$
b. $Q = 2K + 3L + 100$
c. $Q = 2K + 3L + 5KL$
d. $Q = 2K^2 + 4L^2 - 3KL$
e. $Q = 10K^{.4}L^{.5}$
f. $Q = 15K^{.7}L^{.8}$

3.3 Use the production function $Q = 5K^5L^6$ to complete the production table shown below.
   a. What is the returns-to-scale characteristic of this production function? Base your explanation on the entries in the completed table.
   b. What are the marginal products of capital and labor if the firm employs three units of capital and three units of labor? What are the marginal products of capital and labor if the firm employs three units of labor and six units of capital?

3.4 Consider the cubic production function $Q = b_1KL + b_2K^2L + b_3KL^2 - b_4K^3L - b_5KL^3$.
   a. Calculate the marginal products of capital and labor.
   b. What is the marginal rate of technical substitution between the two inputs?

| | | | | L | | | |
	1	2	3	4	5	6
	$L^6 = 1$	1.516				2.930
K	K^5						
1	1	5	7.6				14.6
2	1.414	7.1	10.7				20.7
3	1.732	8.7	13.1				25.4
4							
5							
6	2.449	12.2	18.6				35.9

APPENDIX 1:

Production and Cost as Constrained Optimization Problems

The condition for the least-cost combination of capital and labor for producing a given quantity of output can be derived using the Lagrange multiplier technique for solving constrained optimization problems. This mathematical technique involves specifying an objective function for the firm and then computing the values of the parameters under its control that satisfy the objective function subject to the constraints imposed on the firm's choices. Two such constrained optimization problems are solved in this appendix—cost minimization and output maximization.

Constrained Cost Minimization

The point of tangency between an isoquant and an isocost schedule is the graphical solution to the firm's problem of selecting the particular input mix that minimizes the total cost of producing some targeted rate of output. The solution to this cost-minimization problem is derived mathematically as follows.

The Johnson Company's objective is to minimize total cost subject to the constraint that yearly output be equal to 200,000 units. The cost function is

$$TC = \$10K + \$40L. \quad \text{OBJECTIVE FUNCTION}$$

Capital is measured in units of 1,000 machine-hours and labor's compensation is denominated in thousands of dollars. The firm must select the values of K and L that minimize its costs, but its choices are limited. It must select from among the technologically feasible combinations of K and L that yield 200,000 units of output This constraint is represented by the production function

$$200 = 5K^{.5}L^{.5}. \quad \text{CONSTRAINT}$$

Output is also denominated in thousands.

In order to solve this constrained cost-minimization problem, a Lagrangian function, $\mathcal{L}$, is constructed from the objective and the constraint in the following manner:

$$\mathcal{L} = \$10K + \$40L + \lambda[200 - 5K^{.5}L^{.5}]. \quad \text{LAGRANGIAN}$$

112

The new and as yet unknown variable λ (pronounced "lambda") is called the **Lagrange multiplier**.

The values of K, L, and λ that minimize the function $\mathcal{L}$ are also the values of K and L that minimize total cost subject to the given constraint. The more difficult constrained optimization problem is transformed by the Lagrangian technique into a simpler unconstrained optimization problem. Minimizing $\mathcal{L}$ is accomplished by setting three partial derivatives equal to zero:

$$\frac{\partial \mathcal{L}}{\partial K} = 10 - \lambda 2.5 L^{.5} K^{-.5} = 0 \tag{3a.1}$$

$$\frac{\partial \mathcal{L}}{\partial L} = 40 - \lambda 2.5 K^{.5} L^{-.5} = 0 \tag{3a.2}$$

$$\frac{\partial \mathcal{L}}{\partial \lambda} = 200 - 5 K^{.5} L^{.5} = 0 \tag{3a.3}$$

These equations specify three conditions that must be satisfied in order to minimize the firm's total costs.[31] Except for the introduction of the new variable λ, equations 3a.1 and 3a.2 should look somewhat familiar. Indeed, if the negative term in each equation is transposed to the other side of the equal sign and equation 3a.1 is divided by equation 3a.2, λ cancels out, leaving

$$\frac{40}{10} = \frac{K}{L}.$$

The left-hand side of this equality is the input-price ratio, or the slope of the isocost schedule, and the right-hand side is the slope of the isoquant, or the ratio of the marginal product of capital to the marginal product of labor (see equation 3.8 on p. 91). Hence, cost minimization requires that the firm select the input combination at which the marginal rate of technical substitution, K/L, is equal to the ratio of the input prices.

Equation 3a.3 restates the constraint that the firm's choice of capital and labor must yield 200,000 units of output. Because the specific form of the production function is known, the three equations can be solved to determine the cost-minimizing input combination. In particular, equation 3a.1 can be rewritten as

$$10 L^{.5} K^{-.5} = \frac{40}{\lambda}, \tag{3a.4}$$

and equation 3a.2 can be rewritten as

$$2.5 K^{.5} L^{-.5} = \frac{40}{\lambda}. \tag{3a.5}$$

---

31 At an extreme point (maximum or minimum) on any function, the slope of the function is equal to zero. Equations 3a.1 through 3a.3 therefore specify the values of K, L and λ at which an extreme point on the Langrangian function exists.

Because both of these conditions must hold simultaneously (that is, the left-hand sides of equations 3a.4 and 3a.5 must both be equal to $40/\lambda$ when costs are at a minimum) the two expressions can be set equal to one another, providing a solution for the relationship between K and L at the optimal point. That is, setting

$$10L^{.5}K^{-.5} = 2.5K^{.5}L^{-.5},$$

and simplifying yields

$$4L = K. \tag{3a.6}$$

In other words, the optimal quantity of capital is four times the optimal quantity of labor. (Alternatively, it is optimal for the firm to combine one unit of labor with four units of capital.) This relationship is then substituted into equation 3a.3 to solve for the cost-minimizing number of production workers. That is, solving

$$200 - 5(4L)^{.5}L^{.5} = 0$$

for L yields $L^* = 20$. The optimal quantity of capital is then determined by substituting $L^* = 20$ into equation 3a.6, which yields $K^* = 80$, or 80,000 machine-hours.

The Lagrangian function, $\mathcal{L}$, is constructed by adding the objective function, TC, to the product of the undetermined Lagrange multiplier, λ, and the constraint, Q. The Lagrange multiplier is interpreted as representing the change in the objective function brought about by a change in the constraint. When total cost is minimized subject to an output constraint, the Lagrange multiplier has a straightforward meaning. In particular, if

$$\lambda = \frac{\Delta \text{ objective}}{\Delta \text{ constraint}} = \frac{\Delta TC}{\Delta Q},$$

then λ is marginal cost. Indeed, once the cost-minimizing values of K and L have been computed, the corresponding value of λ can be determined either from equation 3a.1 or equation 3a.2.

For example, substituting $L^* = 20$ and $K^* = 80$ into equation 3a.1 yields

$$\lambda^* = \frac{\$10}{(2.5)(20)^{.5}(80)^{-.5}} = \frac{\$10}{1.25} = \$8.$$

Hence, if the firm produces 200,000 units of output by combining 20 production workers, each paid salary and benefits worth \$40,000 per year, with 80 units of capital (80,000 machine-hours at \$10 per machine-hour), the marginal cost of production is \$8.

Constrained Output Maximization

There is an alternative and equivalent way of expressing the firm's constrained optimization problem. When the firm strives to minimize the total cost of producing a given quantity of output, it simultaneously must strive to maximize the quantity of output it produces for a given total expenditure on inputs. Hence, we can restate the firm's optimization problem as one of determining the quantities of K and L that maximize output when the total cost of production is fixed at $1,600,000.

In this case, the firm's objective is to select an input mix that maximizes

$$Q = 5K^{.5}L^{.5} \quad \text{OBJECTIVE FUNCTION}$$

subject to the constraint that its input expenditures total to $1,600,000. In other words, the constraint on the firm's input choices is given by the total cost function

$$\$1,600 = \$10K + \$40L, \quad \text{CONSTRAINT}$$

where total cost, the price of labor, and units of capital are again denominated in thousands.

The Lagrangian for this output-maximization problem is

$$\mathcal{L} = 5K^{.5} L^{.5} + \lambda(1600 - 10K - 40L). \quad \text{LAGRANGIAN}$$

The values of K, L, and λ that maximize this function are again determined by setting the following three partial derivatives equal to zero.

$$\frac{\partial \mathcal{L}}{\partial K} = (2.5)L^{.5}K^{-.5} - \lambda 10 = 0 \qquad (3a.7)$$

$$\frac{\partial \mathcal{L}}{\partial L} = (2.5)K^{.5}L^{-.5} - \lambda 40 = 0 \qquad (3a.8)$$

$$\frac{\partial \mathcal{L}}{\partial \lambda} = 1600 - 10K - 40L = 0 \qquad (3a.9)$$

The solution technique for finding the optimal values of K and L proceeds exactly as before and yields the same answer. In particular, producing the maximum possible quantity of output for a total expenditure of $1,600,000 requires that the firm hire 20 units of labor and 80 units of capital.

When output is maximized subject to a total cost constraint, the Lagrange multiplier is interpreted as

$$\lambda = \frac{\Delta \text{ objective}}{\Delta \text{ constraint}} = \frac{\Delta Q}{\Delta TC} = \frac{1}{MC}.$$

Once the values of K and L are known, λ can be calculated from either equation 3a.7 or equation 3a.8. Using equation 3a.7,

$$\lambda = \frac{(2.5)(20)^{.5}(80)^{-.5}}{10} = \frac{1.25}{10} = .125$$

The inverse of λ ($= 1/.125$) is 8, which is the value of marginal cost at the production rate of 200,000 units per year.

APPENDIX 2:
Interpreting Regression Results

This chapter presents two "Studies in Managerial Economics" and reports regression results in both case studies. While we assume that the student has been exposed to the fundamentals of regression analysis in an introductory statistics class, this appendix offers a brief review of the basic concepts.[32]

To illustrate simple regression analysis, consider a firm that operates retail stores in seven cities. The firm's owner is interested in estimating the overall relationship between growth in retail sales and growth in consumers' incomes. The marketing department has collected the following observations on sales growth and income growth in the seven states where the firm's stores are located:

LOCATION (STATE)	AL	CO	IN	PA	OK	TN	TX
SALES GROWTH	4.0%	8.0%	5.0%	6.5%	5.0%	6.5%	7.0%
INCOME GROWTH	1.0%	7.0%	2.0%	6.0%	3.0%	5.0%	4.0%

Income growth is thought to be the principal determinant of sales growth and, as a first approximation, a linear relationship between the two variables is hypothesized. This relationship is represented by the equation

$$SALES = a + b*INCOME.$$

SALES and *INCOME* represent sales growth and income growth, respectively. The task of regression analysis is to estimate values of the coefficients a and b. If $\hat{a}$ and $\hat{b}$ represent the estimated values of these coefficients, then the predicted relationship between *SALES* and *INCOME* is

$$\widehat{SALES} = \hat{a} + \hat{b}*INCOME + \epsilon.$$

$\widehat{SALES}$ is the predicted value of sales growth for a given rate of income growth and ϵ is the regression error term. The error term picks up the cross-state variation in sales growth *not* explained by cross-state variations in income growth. It is assumed to have a zero mean and constant variance.

---

32 For a more detailed but still user friendly review of elementary statistics and regression analysis, see Harvey J. Brightman, *Statistics in Plain English* (Cincinnati, OH: South-Western Publishing Co., 1986).

Linear regression calculates the values of a and b that minimize the sum of the squared differences between $\widehat{SALES}$ and $SALES$. The sum of these squared differences is

$$\sum_{i=1}^{n} (SALES_i - \widehat{SALES_i})^2 = \sum_{i=1}^{n} (SALES_i - \hat{a} - \hat{b}*INCOME_i)^2,$$

where $n = 7$ represents the number of observations. In effect, the values $\hat{a}$ and $\hat{b}$ are the vertical intercept and slope of the straight line that "best fits" a scatter diagram of the observations of income growth and sales growth.

The formulas for calculating $\hat{a}$ and $\hat{b}$ are

$$\hat{b} = \frac{s_{(INCOME)(SALES)}}{s^2_{INCOME}}$$

and

$$\hat{a} = \overline{SALES} - \hat{b}*\overline{INCOME}.$$

In these formulas, $s_{(INCOME)(SALES)}$ is the estimated covariance of income growth and sales growth, s^2_{INCOME} is the sample variance of income growth, $\overline{SALES}$ is the mean value of sales growth, and $\overline{INCOME}$ is the mean value of income growth. The estimated covariance of income and sales growth and the sample variance of income growth are in turn calculated as follows:

$$s_{(INCOME)(SALES)} = \left(\frac{1}{n}\right) \sum_{i=1}^{n} (INCOME_i - \overline{INCOME})(SALES_i - \overline{SALES})$$

and

$$s^2_{INCOME} = \left(\frac{1}{n}\right) \sum_{i=1}^{n} (INCOME_i - \overline{INCOME})^2$$

With the observations on sales growth and income growth given above, these formulas yield the following estimated relationship between $SALES$ and $INCOME$:

$$\widehat{SALES} = \hat{a} + \hat{b}*INCOME = 3.64 + .59INCOME.$$

The estimated regression equation predicts that sales will increase by 3.64 percent if income growth is equal to zero and that a unit increase in the variable $INCOME$ will cause a .59 unit increase in the variable $SALES$. Because $INCOME$ and $SALES$ are measured in percentage terms, $\hat{b} = .59$ means that a one percent increase in income growth will increase sales growth by .59 percent.

The next step in regression analysis is to assess the statistical reliability of the estimated coefficients. In this example, we are interested in the statistical confidence to be placed in $\hat{b}$. The standard error of the regression coefficient, $\hat{\sigma}_b$, is a measure of the reliability of $\hat{b}$ and is calculated by the formula

$$\hat{\sigma}_b = \frac{1}{\sqrt{n}} \frac{s_{SALES}}{s_{INCOME}},$$

where s_{SALES} is the square root of the estimated regression variance (s^2_{SALES}), n is again the number of observations, and s^2_{INCOME} is again the sample variance of income growth. The formula for the estimated regression variance, s^2_{SALES}, is

$$s^2_{SALES} = \frac{1}{(n-2)} \sum_{i=1}^{n} (SALES_i - \widehat{SALES})^2.$$

Using these formulas, the standard error of $\hat{b}$ is equal to .113. The standard error of $\hat{b}$ can then be used to construct a confidence interval for $\hat{b}$. In particular, a 95 percent confidence interval for the true value of $\hat{b}$ is

$$\Pr[\,(\hat{b} - t\hat{\sigma}_b) < b < (\hat{b} + t\hat{\sigma}_b)\,] = .95,$$

where the value of t is taken from the tabulated values of Student's t distribution. Because $\hat{b} = .59$, $\hat{\sigma}_b = .113$ and the appropriate t-value is 2.571, the 95 percent confidence interval for b is

$$\Pr\{\,[.59 - (2.571)(.113)] < b < [.59 + (2.571)(.113)]\,\} = .95,$$

or

$$\Pr(.3 < b < .88) = .95.$$

The critical characteristic of this particular confidence interval is that it does not contain zero. When the 95 percent confidence interval does not contain zero, the estimated coefficient is said to be significantly different from zero at the 5 percent level. An equivalent and convenient test of significance is to calculate a t-statistic by dividing the estimated coefficient by its standard error. The calculated t-statistic is then compared with the tabulated value of t used in constructing the confidence interval.

When the absolute value of the calculated t-statistic is greater than the critical value of t for the 95 percent confidence interval, the coefficient is statistically different from zero at a 5 percent level of significance on a two-tailed test. In this example, the calculated t-ratio is 5.22 (.59 divided by .113). Because this t-ratio is greater than the t value of 2.571 that is used in computing the 95 percent confidence interval, $\hat{b}$ is significant at the 5 percent level.

For large samples, a 95 percent confidence interval is constructed using a t-value of 1.96. Because the empirical studies discussed in this text are typically large-sample studies, the appropriate t-value is 1.96. The reader can therefore determine whether a coefficient is significant at the 5 percent level by simply comparing the reported or estimated t-ratio with the critical value of 1.96. If the absolute value of the reported t-ratio is greater than 1.96, then the coefficient in question is significant at the 5 percent level on a two-tailed test.

CHAPTER

4

Production and Cost in the Short Run

OVERVIEW

The distinction between the long run and the short run is conceptually quite simple. In the long run, the firm can vary its usage of all inputs; in the short run, at least one input is fixed. Plant size is normally considered to be a fixed input because it is relatively costly to expand or contract the firm's production capacity in the short run. Raw materials and labor, on the other hand, are normally considered to be variable inputs because the employment of these productive resources can be more readily increased or decreased. (However, these inputs could be fixed if negotiated contracts with suppliers of raw material or labor constrain the firm's short-run behavior.)

An input can be classified as either fixed or variable on the basis of whether its usage varies directly with the quantity of output produced. For most firms, plant scale and the number of managers and support personnel do not vary immediately as output varies. On the other hand, if the firm varies its level of production in response to changing market conditions, the use of some inputs, like energy and raw materials, tends to change automatically while the use of other inputs, like administrative staff, changes only by managerial fiat.

Costs, like inputs, are divided into fixed and variable components. The costs associated with fixed and variable inputs are called fixed costs and variable costs, respectively. A fixed cost is defined as a cost that does not vary with changes in output and a variable cost is defined as a cost that does vary with changes in output. Because fixed costs do not decline when the firm reduces production (even if the firm shuts down), the short run can also be

119

defined as a period of time in which some costs are unavoidable. In the long run, all costs are variable and all costs are thereby avoidable in principle.

Chapter 3's analysis of production and cost in the long run demonstrates that production characteristics determine cost characteristics. If production is subject to constant returns to scale and there are no economies or diseconomies of scale, for example, then long-run marginal and average costs are constant over the relevant range of output. This fundamental duality between production and cost also applies in the short run as well.

The long-run analysis in Chapter 3 also shows that the least-cost combination of inputs defines economically efficient production. The selection of the least-cost input combination determines the plant size within which short-run production decisions will be made. This chapter extends the analysis in Chapter 3 by showing how productivity and cost vary in the short run as the firm varies input usage and output in a plant of given size.

APPLICATION

The demand characteristics of the Johnson Company's new all-weather coat are presented in Chapter 2. On the basis of this information, tentative annual sales of 200,000 units are forecast. For this level of production, the analysis in Chapter 3 shows that the least-cost combination of labor and capital consists of 20 production workers and 80 units of capital. The 80 units of capital (or 80,000 machine-hours because a unit of capital is defined as 1,000 machine-hours) establishes the optimal scale of the company's plant. Once the plant is built, management's short-run decisions to increase or decrease production are made under the constraint that production capacity is fixed.

Somewhat paradoxically, short-run analysis of production and cost is relevant even when the Johnson Company is still in the planning stage. After all, the actual production of the new product will eventually occur in a plant of a fixed size. The profit-maximizing price and profit-maximizing quantity of output, which are relevant from both long-run and short-run perspectives, must therefore be consistent with one another.

After answering the set of questions posed in Chapter 3, the company's owner starts thinking about the production and cost issues the firm will face once the plant is built and production begins. The following list of questions reflects the issues that Ms. Johnson believes are important.

1. The long-run production function is $Q = 5K^{.5}L^{.5}$. What is the short-run production function and how is it related to the long-run production function?
2. An isoquant map can illustrate many of the properties of the long-run production function. What are the properties of the short-run

production function and is there a convenient way of illustrating
these properties?

3. Productivity is an important issue in the employment of inputs.
What should the firm's productivity goal be in the short run? Is the
obvious answer that the firm should attempt to maximize the productivity of the variable input?

4. Cost minimization is a central theme of long-run production and
cost analysis. In the short run, what role does cost minimization
play? Avoidable costs are variable costs in the short run. Should the
firm attempt to minimize variable costs or should it strive to minimize total costs?

5. Long-run marginal and average costs for all-weather coats are constant for all output levels. Do similar properties characterize costs
in the short run? What characterizes the behavior of marginal and
average costs when the firm varies output in the short run? Will
the per unit cost of production remain the same or will it vary as
output varies?

THE SHORT–RUN PRODUCTION FUNCTION

Short-run and long-run production functions are intimately related to one
another. Indeed, they are two different ways of analyzing the same technological relationship between input usage and output. The short-run production function is based on a single plant size while the long-run production
function considers all possible plant sizes.

The two-input model of production can be represented by the
following function:

$$Q = f(K, L). \tag{4.1}$$

Q is the quantity of output produced, K is capital usage, and L is labor. By definition, both inputs are variable in the long run. If capital (plant size) is held
fixed in the short run, the **short-run production function** can be written as:

$$Q = f(K_0, L). \tag{4.2}$$

K_0 represents the fixed quantity of capital or plant size. The short-run production function is therefore derived directly from the long-run production
function by holding plant capacity fixed at some predetermined level.

As shown in Chapter 3, the long-run production function can be illustrated
graphically by a production map on which isoquants are drawn showing the
various technically efficient combinations of capital and labor that can produce a given quantity of output. The short-run production function can be
derived from this production map by simply holding capital fixed at some
level and allowing labor usage to vary. Figure 4.1 illustrates this derivation.

Part 1   Decision-Making Tools

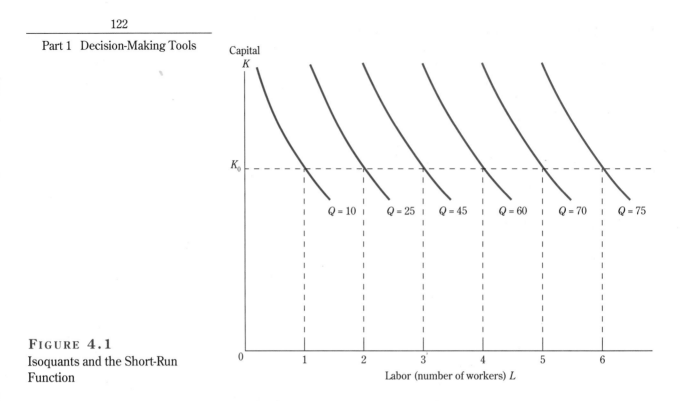

FIGURE 4.1

Isoquants and the Short-Run Function

In Figure 4.1, capital is held fixed at K_0 units and the employment of the variable input, labor, successively increases by one unit. The short-run production function is represented on this map by the impact of changes in labor usage on the level of output produced, holding plant capacity constant. As one unit of labor is successively added to the fixed input, output first increases at an increasing rate (until three units of labor are employed). Output then increases at a decreasing rate. For example, the addition of the first three units of labor causes output to increase in successively larger increments of 10, 15, and 20 units. The addition of the next three units of labor causes output to increase in successively smaller increments of 15, 10, and 5 units.

Because capital is held fixed at K_0, the relationship between labor usage and output can also be illustrated on a two-dimensional graph. In Figure 4.2a, the curve that represents the relation between employment and output for a fixed quantity of capital is conventionally called a **total product curve**. The shape of the total product curve in Figure 4.2a reflects the relationship between labor usage and output (total product) depicted in Figure 4.1. The total product curve is convex (from below) between the origin and point D because output first increases at an increasing rate as additional units of labor are successively combined with K_0 units of capital. The concave portion of the total product curve between points D and F indicates that output increases at a decreasing rate as more labor is employed over this range. Increases in labor usage beyond point F are associated with reductions in total product.

Total, Marginal, and Average Product

The discussion of Figures 4.1 and 4.2*a* emphasizes the relationship between changes in the employment of the variable input (labor) and changes in total product. This relationship is the **marginal product of labor**, MP_L. As defined in Chapter 3, the marginal product of labor is the change total in output associated with a change in labor usage, holding all other inputs constant. It can be expressed as the partial derivative of the production function with respect to L:

$$MP_L = \frac{\partial Q}{\partial L}. \tag{4.3}$$

In other words, the marginal product of labor is the slope of the short-run total product curve in Figure 4.2*a*.

The short-run production function in Figure 4.2*a* is divided into three regions. The upward sloping, convex region between the origin and point D

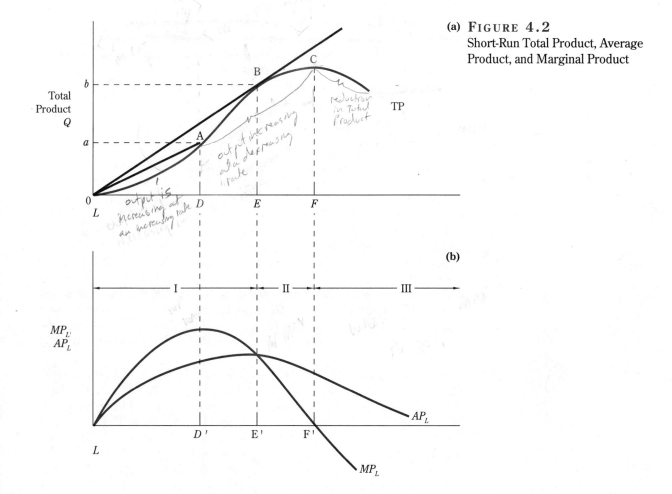

(a) **FIGURE 4.2**
Short-Run Total Product, Average Product, and Marginal Product

corresponds to the range of production over which output increases at an increasing rate as labor usage is increased. As shown in Figure 4.2*b*, labor's marginal product is rising in this region.

The marginal product of labor at any point on the total product curve is determined graphically by calculating the slope of a straight line drawn tangent to the total product curve at that point. Over the range of the total product curve between the origin and point *D*, the slopes of these tangents become successively steeper as additional units of labor are combined with a fixed quantity of capital. Labor's marginal product is consequently rising—each additional worker employed adds more to total product than the previous worker.

Between points *D* and *F* in Figure 4.2*a*, output increases at a decreasing rate. Labor's marginal product is declining over this range (the slopes of lines drawn tangent to the total product curve become successively flatter). At point *F*, the marginal product of labor is zero (a line drawn tangent to the total product curve at point *C* has a zero slope). Increases in labor beyond point *F* are associated with declining total product and a negative marginal product of labor.

The productivity of labor is measurable in two different ways. The marginal product of labor measures the productivity of the *last* unit of labor employed. Alternatively, the average product of labor measures the productivity of *all* the units of labor employed. The **average product of labor** is calculated by dividing total output by total labor input:

$$AP_L = \frac{Q}{L}. \tag{4.4}$$

As discussed above, the behavior of marginal product can be inferred from the curvature of the total product curve because marginal product is the slope of the total product curve. The convex portion of the curve implies that marginal product is increasing and the concave portion implies that marginal product is decreasing as labor usage increases. The behavior of average product also follows a definite pattern along the total product curve.

The behavior of labor's average product can be seen by referring to the straight line, or ray, drawn from the origin to point *B* on the total product curve in Figure 4.2*a*. The slope of this ray is *Ob/OE*. Because *Ob* is the quantity of output produced by *OE* units of labor, *Ob/OE* = *Q/L* is the average product of labor at point B. Hence, the slope of a ray drawn from the origin to a point on the total product curve is the average product of labor at that point.

Because the slope of the ray *OA* (i.e., *Oa/OD*) is smaller than the slope of the ray *OB*, the average product of labor at point A is less than the average product of labor at point B. In fact, if point *A* is arbitrarily placed anywhere between the origin and point *B*, the same conclusion follows. The implication is that the average product of labor is rising over the region from the origin to point *B* on the total product curve in Figure 4.2*a*.

We can make the same sort of comparison for points on the total product curve that lie to the right of point *B*. For example, a ray drawn from the origin to point C will have a smaller slope than the ray OB. Because the slope of the ray OB is greater than the slope of any other ray drawn to points that are either to the left or right of it, the average product of labor is at a maximum at point B. Hence, the average product of labor first rises, reaches a maximum at point B, and then falls. The average product curve is illustrated in Figure 4.2b.

If the marginal product curve rises, reaches a maximum, and then falls as shown in Figure 4.2b, then the average product curve must follow the same pattern. Moreover, the point at which marginal product is at a maximum must occur before (at a lower level of employment than) the point at which average product is at a maximum. The following table of hypothetical test scores demonstrates the intuition behind these relationships.

TEST NUMBER:	1	2	3	4	5	6	7	8	9	10
MARGINAL VALUES:	60	70	80	90	100*	90	80	70	60	50
TOTAL POINTS:	60	130	210	300	400	490	570	640	700	750
TEST AVERAGE:	60	65	70	75	80	82*	81	80	78	75

The table shows the numerical scores earned by a student on a series of ten weekly exams. The individual test scores are in the row labeled "marginal values." The first five test scores successively increase by ten points; the scores then successively decline by ten points. The highest test grade is earned on the fifth exam. The row labeled "total points" shows the student's cumulative exam points at the end of each week. The final row in the table shows the student's overall weekly test score average.

The "marginal value" of each successive test score determines whether the test average rises or falls. For example, because the score on the second exam (70) is higher than the student's average before the exam (60), the average rises (from 60 to 65). The grades on the next three exams successively increase, and this trend causes the exam average to continue to rise. This pattern follows from a general relationship between marginal values and average values: If the marginal value is greater than the previous average, the average must increase.

This is true even after the marginal value begins to fall. When the student's test performance starts to decline with the sixth exam, the average still rises (from 80 to 82) because the grade on the sixth exam exceeds the previous average (90 is greater than 80). But if marginal values continue to fall, the average must eventually decline. The average begins to fall with the seventh exam because the student's grade on the seventh exam is less than the previous average (80 is less than 82). As the table clearly shows, the row of marginal values reaches a maximum (exam 5) before the row of average values (exam 6).

Figure 4.2 shows the general relationship between marginal and average values. The marginal product of labor reaches a maximum at point A in the top panel where the slope of a line drawn tangent to the total product curve is as steep as possible. The average product of labor reaches a maximum at a higher level of employment (point B) where the slope of a ray drawn from the origin to the total product curve is as steep as possible. Note also that at the point where the average product of labor is at a maximum, marginal product is equal to average product. The marginal product of labor is equal to the average product of labor at point B because the slope of the ray and the slope of the line drawn tangent to the total product curve at that point are the same.[1]

The Short-Run Production Function with Cobb-Douglas Technology

As described above, the short-run production function is derived directly from the long-run production function by holding plant capacity (capital) fixed. Indeed, there is a "family" of short-run production functions associated with any given long-run production function. Each one of these short-run production functions shows how total output varies as the firm varies its usage of labor and other variable inputs, holding capital constant at a particular level.

Consider the Johnson Company's long-run production function for all-weather coats, $Q = 5K^{.5}L^{.5}$. Recall that Q is measured in thousands of all-weather coats, K is measured in units of 1,000 machine-hours, and L is measured by the number of production workers employed. If the firm builds a plant with a production capacity of 80,000 machine-hours of capital, the short-run production function is

$$Q = 5(80)^{.5}L^{.5} = 5(8.944)L^{.5} = 44.72L^{.5}. \qquad (4.5)$$

The isoquant map used in Chapter 3 to illustrate some of the properties of the long-run production function can also show the properties of this short-run production function. Figure 4.3 illustrates four isoquants for all-weather

FIGURE 4.3
Isoquants for the Production of All-Weather Coats

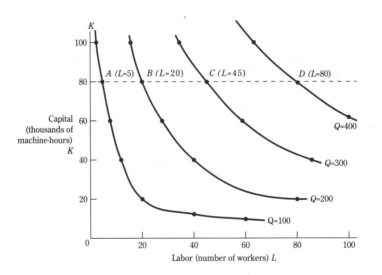

---

1 The marginal value of the student's test score is not exactly equal to the average test score when the average is at a maximum (exam 6) because of the discrete nature of the data used in the example.

FIGURE 4.4

Short-Run Total,
Average, and
Marginal Product
for All-Weather
Coats ($K_0 = 80$)

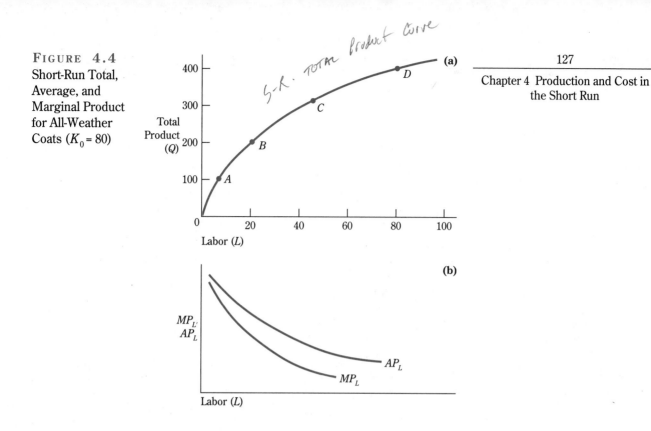

coat production. With capital usage held constant at 80 units, 100 units of
output can be produced by five production workers (point A); 200 units of
output can be produced by 20 production workers (point B); 300 units of output can be produced by 45 production workers (point C); and 400 units of
output can be produced by 80 production workers (point D).

These points are transferred to Figure 4.4a to construct a short-run
total product curve. Unlike the total product schedule illustrated previously in Figure 4.2a, the short-run total product curve for all-weather
coats in Figure 4.4a does not contain a region in which output increases
at an increasing rate. Rather, output increases continuously at a
decreasing rate as additional units of labor are combined with a fixed
quantity of capital.

We can verify this characteristic of the short-run production function for
all-weather coats by considering the algebraic expression for the marginal
product of labor:

$$MP_L = \frac{\partial Q}{\partial L} = (.5)(44.72)L^{-.5} = \frac{22.36}{L^{.5}}. \tag{4.6}$$

Equation 4.6 shows that the marginal product of labor declines continuously
as labor usage increases. In other words, this production function does not
contain a region where the marginal productivity of labor is rising. The rate

Including Management in the Production Function

The production function for all-weather coats used as an example in Chapters 3 and 4 explicitly includes only two inputs, capital and labor. All other inputs, such as materials and energy, are for simplicity assumed to enter the production function in fixed proportions. Another assumption is that only one type of labor enters the production function when, in fact, two broad types of human resources—production labor and managerial labor—are employed by nearly every firm.

Most empirical studies include production labor, but not managerial labor, as an explanatory variable in the production function. However, Robert Mefford recently included the quality of management in estimating a production function from plant-level data for a multinational manufacturer of consumer goods.[a] Mefford measured the quality of managerial inputs on the basis of performance evaluated in terms of plant managers' success in achieving targeted goals for output, cost, and quality.

The three most commonly used forms of the production function in empirical studies are the Cobb-Douglas production function, the constant elasticity of substitution (CES) production function, and the transcendental logarithmic (translog) production function. The basic empirical forms of these three models are represented by the following equations:

Cobb-Douglas:

$$\ln(Q) = \ln(a_0) + a_1 \ln(K) + a_2 \ln(L) + a_i Z_i$$

Constant Elasticity of Substitution:

$$\ln(Q) = \ln(b_0) + b_1 \ln(K) + b_2 \ln(L) + b_3 [\ln(K) - \ln(L)]^2 + b_i Z_i$$

Translog:

$$\ln(Q) = \ln(c_0) + c_1 \ln(K) + c_2 \ln(L) + c_3 [\ln(K)]^2 + c_4 \ln(K)\ln(L) + c_5 [\ln(L)]^2 + c_i Z_i$$

The notation, ln, represents the natural logarithm of the variable, Q represents output, K represents capital, L represents production labor, and Z_i represents any other variables that are included in the production function.

Estimates of Cobb-Douglas, CES, and Translog Specifications of the Production Function

	Cobb-Douglas COEFFICIENT (t-RATIO)	CES COEFFICIENT (t-RATIO)	Translog COEFFICIENT (t-RATIO)
$\ln(K)$	−0.096 (−3.53)	−0.127 (−4.419)	−0.847 (−1.58)
$\ln(L)$	1.158 (25.34)	1.169 (26.21)	1.928 (2.02)
$\ln(MGMT)$	0.175 (4.53)	0.149 (3.83)	0.139 (3.54)
TIME	0.014 (1.69)	0.020 (2.37)	0.018 (2.10)
SMALL	−0.100 (−2.45)	−0.105 (−2.66)	−0.098 (−2.46)
BIG	−0.065 (−1.95)	−0.068 (−2.11)	−0.063 (−1.59)
TECH*ln(K)	0.016 (2.69)	0.014 (2.49)	0.012 (1.96)
SKILL*ln(L)	0.009 (4.61)	0.008 (4.46)	0.009 (4.54)
$\ln(K)*\ln(L)$	——	——	0.115 (3.02)
$[\ln(L)]^2$	——	——	−0.088 (−1.98)
$[\ln(K)]^2$	——	——	−0.028 (−1.488)
$[\ln(K) - \ln(L)]^2$	——	− 0.042 (−2.74)	——

a Robert N. Mefford, "Introducing Management into the Production Function," *Review of Economics and Statistics* 66 (February 1986), pp. 96-104.

Mefford estimated each of the three production function specifications listed above. In addition to capital and production labor, the production functions include the variables ln(*MGMT*), logged value of managerial quality; *TIME*, a time trend variable to control for possible technological progress; *SMALL* and *BIG*, dummy variables that denote small and large plants, respectively; *TECH**ln(K), quality adjusted capital; and *SKILL**ln(L), quality adjusted labor. The regression estimates are presented in the above table.

The three functional forms yield comparable results. The variable of principal interest, *MGMT*, is positive and statistically significant in all three regressions, providing evidence that superior management is a valuable input in the production process.

---

at which total output increases falls continuously as additional units of labor are hired.[2]

Figure 4.4*b* graphs the marginal product of labor and the average product of labor for the Cobb-Douglas production function assumed. Because the marginal product of labor declines continuously in this special case, the average product of labor both declines continuously and is always greater than marginal product. Moreover, unlike the marginal product curve shown in Figure 4.2*b*, the marginal product curve in Figure 4.4*b* never becomes negative. This property of the production function for all-weather coats can be verified by referring to equation 4.6. No matter how large *L* is, the value of MP_L will always be a positive number.

THE LAW OF DIMINISHING MARGINAL RETURNS

The economic theory of production and cost exploits the observation that the production and cost functions for very different production processes share a number of common characteristics. For long-run production functions, the common property is returns to scale. Long-run cost functions are characterized by the presence or absence of economies (or diseconomies) of scale.

In the short run, all production functions (and, hence, all cost functions) share a common property called the **law of diminishing marginal returns.** Defined formally, the law of diminishing returns states that when additional units of a variable input are combined with some given quantity of a fixed input, a point is eventually reached at which the marginal product of the variable input begins to decline. Recall that marginal product is the change in total product attributable to a small change in the employment of the variable input. Diminishing marginal returns consequently occur in the range of the production function where each successive unit of the variable input employed contributes less to the firm's total output than the previous unit. In other words, diminishing marginal returns are associated with declining marginal productivity of the variable input.

---

2 The absence of a region of rising marginal productivity is not a general characteristic of short-run production functions, but is instead a special case due to the functional form (Cobb-Douglas) assumed in the application.

The law of diminishing marginal returns applies to *all* short-run production and cost functions. It is a technological fact of life, not an economic one. Because of the generality of the law of diminishing marginal returns, the economic theory of production and cost is not industry-specific or firm-specific. The theory applies to firms in the manufacturing sector, the service sector, or the agricultural sector.[3] While the law of diminishing marginal returns is quite general, its implications are usually illustrated with a farming example. Perhaps because farming is more standardized (and presumably more familiar) than other production processes, we can grasp the principle more readily before bringing it to bear in other settings like manufacturing or the provision of a service.

Suppose a farmer owns a 100-acre corn farm. Working alone, the farmer grows a total of 1,000 bushels of corn or 10 bushels of corn per acre. The fixed input in this example is the 100-acre corn farm. The variable input is labor because the farmer can hire additional workers to help plow, plant, fertilize, and harvest the crop. The law of diminishing marginal returns answers the following question: Is there a predictable relationship between the changes in output (corn production) that occur as more of the variable input (labor) is added to the fixed input (land)?

Before answering this question, note that only the number of workers changes. In particular, the *quality* of workers is assumed to remain constant throughout the following exercise. If some workers are more skilled than others, then as the farmer hires additional workers, two things would be happening at the same time. If both the quantity and quality of the input change, it is more difficult to predict the impact of increased labor usage on output. To avoid this problem, the theory of production assumes that the variable input is homogeneous. When the first worker is hired, it is assumed that this worker is identical in all respects to the farmer. The second worker hired (the farm's third laborer) is likewise assumed to be identical to the farmer and to the first worker hired.

The farmer working alone produces 10 bushels of corn per acre. What will happen to corn production per acre after the first worker is hired? There are three possibilities. When the first worker joins the production process, he or she can produce the same amount as the farmer, an amount greater than that produced by the farmer, or an amount less than that produced by the farmer. The following table depicts the three cases, where the marginal product of labor is measured in bushels per acre.

Although all three cases are possible, perhaps the most likely scenario is given by the middle column that shows increasing marginal returns when units of the variable input *are initially* added to the fixed input. Even though the farmer and the first worker (denoted as the first and second units of labor) are identical in all respects, the first worker hired adds more to total output than the farmer.

---

3 Because it applies to the short run, the law of diminishing marginal returns also operates independently of the returns to scale properties of the firm's long-run production function.

Labor	CONSTANT MARGINAL PRODUCT MP_L	INCREASING MARGINAL PRODUCT MP_L	DIMINISHING MARGINAL PRODUCT MP_L
1	10	10	10
2	10	20	9
3	10	30	8
4	10	40	7
.	.	.	.
.	.	.	.
.	.	.	.

Increasing marginal productivity can be attributed to specialization and the division of labor. When the farmer tends the crop alone, he or she is responsible for all aspects of the production process. Time and energy devoted to tilling, for example, diverts the farmer's attention from other jobs such as maintaining farm machinery, ordering supplies, and so on. As a result, some productive activities are neglected entirely and a less-than-optimal amount of effort is devoted to others. But when an additional worker is hired, the two can divide up some of the tasks—and work together on other jobs to complete them more quickly—thereby increasing the total corn yield to more than twice what it was with just one worker.

As units of the variable input are combined initially with the fixed input, the case in which marginal product first increases may be the most likely of the three possibilities. The law of diminishing marginal returns states, however, that the marginal product of the variable input will always *eventually* begin declining. If increasing marginal productivity occurs during the initial stages of production, at some point the gains from specialization and the division of labor will be exhausted as the farmer hires more workers. Hence, while the marginal productivity of labor may well increase initially, the farm will eventually reach a point at which an additional worker contributes less to total output than the previous worker.

Diminishing marginal returns are inevitable because the quantity of land available to the farmer is fixed during the short run. As additional units of labor are combined with this fixed quantity of land, the *rate* at which the output of corn can increase must eventually decline. If this were not so, that is, if the marginal product of the variable input increases without bound, one farmer could grow all of the world's corn in a flowerpot.

The point of diminishing marginal returns for a short-run total product curve like the one graphed in Figure 4.2a (see p. 123) is the point shown in Figure 4.2b at which the marginal product of the variable input is at a maximum. As we add units of the variable input beyond the point of diminishing marginal returns, average product continues to rise as long as marginal product is greater than average product. A point is eventually reached, however, at which average product is at a maximum. This point defines the boundary between Stage I and Stage II of the production function. Stage III is the region of the production function where the marginal product of the variable input is negative. No firm will operate in Stage III because total output can be increased there by hiring *fewer* units of the variable input. Production in either Stage I or Stage II is possible, however, depending on the revenue conditions faced by the firm.[4]

The total product curve for the special case of Cobb-Douglas technology in Figure 4.4*a* (see p. 127) indicates that output increases continuously at a decreasing rate as additional production workers are combined with a fixed quantity of capital. Marginal product starts declining immediately and diminishing marginal returns appear at all levels of employment in the production of all-weather coats.

SHORT–RUN COST CURVES

Chapter 3 shows that the firm's long-run cost curves can be derived directly from the long-run production function once the prices of inputs are known. It should be no surprise that a similar correspondence exits between the firm's short-run cost curves and the short-run production function.

Total Variable Cost, Marginal Cost, and Average Variable Cost

Once again let $Q = f(K_0, L)$ represent a short-run production function in which capital is the fixed input and labor is the variable input. Figure 4.2*a* (see p. 123) illustrates a total product curve for this production function; this curve is now reproduced in Figure 4.5*a*. Units of labor are measured on the horizontal axis.

The short-run total product curve in Figure 4.5*a* can be converted into a total variable cost curve by noting that the total variable cost of producing a given quantity of output is simply equal to the number of workers that must be hired to produce that quantity of output times the unit price of labor. **Total variable cost** (*TVC*) is calculated by multiplying the number of workers employed, L, times the wage rate or the unit price of labor, P_L:

$$TVC = P_L \times L.$$

Total variable cost depends on the quantity of output produced. The total quantity of output produced, in turn, depends (as determined by the production function) on the number of units of the variable input the firm combines

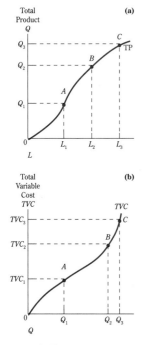

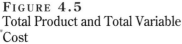

FIGURE 4.5
Total Product and Total Variable Cost

---

4 Production will take place only in Stage II if the firm faces a horizontal (perfectly elastic) demand curve. With a downward-sloping demand curve, however, production can take place in either Stage I or Stage II. See Chapter 8 for a more complete discussion of the impact of demand (revenue) conditions on the firm's production and pricing decisions.

with the fixed quantity of capital. The total variable cost curve associated with Figure 4.5a's production function is drawn in Figure 4.5b. In order to produce Q_1 units of output, for example, the firm must hire L_1 workers (point A in panel a). The total variable cost of producing Q_1 units of output is therefore equal to $TVC_1 = P_L \times L_1$ (point A in panel b). Points B and C on the total variable cost curve are derived similarly.[5]

Once the price of the variable input is known, the relationship between total output and employment of the variable input in Figure 4.5a can be converted into the relationship between total variable cost and total output in Figure 4.5b. Both the production function and the total variable cost function begin at the origin because no output can be produced if no units of the variable input are hired. If no units of the variable input are employed, total variable cost is zero. Moreover, the total variable cost schedule is concave (TVC increases at a decreasing rate) over the range of output where the total product schedule is convex (total product increases at an increasing rate), and vice-versa.

Figure 4.6 more closely examines the characteristics of a total variable cost curve having concave and convex regions. The curvature of the total variable cost curve is determined by the impact of successive increases in output on total variable cost. Total variable cost is increasing at a decreasing rate over the concave region of the total variable cost curve between the origin and point G in Figure 4.6a. Total variable cost is increasing at an increasing rate over the convex region between points G and I.

The rate of change in total variable cost is **marginal cost**. The marginal cost of production (MC) is the change in total variable cost divided by the corresponding change in output. Because variable cost is, by definition, the only cost that varies as output varies, marginal cost can alternatively be defined as the change in total cost (TC) divided by the change in output. Thus, the marginal cost of production can be expressed as:

$$MC = \frac{\Delta TVC}{\Delta Q} = \frac{\Delta TC}{\Delta Q}. \tag{4.7}$$

Marginal cost is the slope of the total variable cost (or total cost) schedule. The marginal cost curve in Figure 4.6b is consequently downward sloping when total variable cost increases at a decreasing rate. Marginal cost is upward sloping when total variable cost increases at a increasing rate. Setting aside the mechanics involved in the relationship between the curvature of the total cost curve and its slope, why is the marginal cost curve U-shaped?

To answer this question, retrace the steps followed in deriving the marginal cost schedule. Marginal cost declines when total variable cost increases at a decreasing rate. Total variable cost increases at a decreasing rate when total

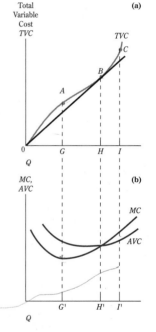

FIGURE 4.6
Short-Run Cost Curves (Variable Input Only)

---

5 This derivation assumes that the unit price of labor is unaffected by the firm's hiring decisions. In other words, it is assumed that the firm can hire as many workers as it wants at a price of P_L dollars per unit.

product increases at an increasing rate, that is, when the marginal product of the variable input is rising. In sum, marginal cost declines when the short-run production function exhibits increasing marginal returns to the variable factor. Marginal cost reaches a minimum at the point where the marginal product of the variable factor is at a maximum. And marginal cost eventually begins rising when, inevitably, diminishing marginal returns commence.[6]

The relationship between marginal cost and the marginal product of the variable input becomes clear when we consider the definitions of these two concepts. As defined above, marginal cost is the change in total variable cost (or total cost) associated with a change in output; that is,

$$MC = \frac{\Delta TVC}{\Delta Q}.$$

The change in total variable cost necessary to produce a change in output, in turn, is equal to the change in employment of the variable input times the unit price of the variable input; that is,

$$\Delta TVC = \Delta L \times P_L.$$

Combining these two expressions yields

$$MC = \frac{(\Delta L \times P_L)}{\Delta Q} = P_L \left(\frac{\Delta L}{\Delta Q} \right).$$

The term in parentheses, $\Delta L / \Delta Q$, is the *inverse* (or reciprocal) of labor's marginal product. In other words, $\Delta L / \Delta Q = 1/(\Delta Q / \Delta L) = 1/MP_L$. We can therefore write

$$MC = \frac{P_L}{MP_L}.$$

According to this expression, marginal cost is falling when the marginal product of the variable input is rising (increasing marginal returns). Marginal cost rises when the marginal product of the variable input is declining (diminishing marginal returns). Hence, there is a one-to-one relationship between marginal product and marginal cost.[7]

We can derive the average variable cost curve from the total variable cost curve by applying the same method used in deriving the average product of labor from the total product curve. **Average variable cost** (*AVC*) is defined as total variable cost divided by total output; that is,

---

6 It is important not to confuse increasing or diminishing marginal returns to the variable input with "returns to scale." The former refers to the relationship between an input and output when another input is held fixed (the short run), while the latter refers to the relationship between inputs and output when all inputs are variable (the long run).

7 Again assuming that the unit price of the variable input is held constant.

$$AVC = \frac{TVC}{Q}.$$

The average variable cost of production at point B in Figure 4.6a, for example, is equal to the slope of the ray OB. The slope of a straight line drawn from the origin to any other point on the total variable cost schedule will be greater than the slope of ray OB. Average variable cost is consequently at a minimum at point B. Hence, average variable cost first declines as output increases, reaching a minimum at point B, and then increasing thereafter.

The relationship between average variable cost and marginal cost is shown in Figure 4.6b. Average variable cost declines as long as marginal cost is declining and below average variable cost; average variable cost increases when marginal cost is both rising and above average variable cost. Marginal cost is equal to average variable cost when average variable cost is at a minimum: The slope of the ray OB is equal to the slope of a line drawn tangent to the total variable cost curve at point B.

Average variable cost is U-shaped for much the same reason that marginal cost is U-shaped. By definition, total variable cost is equal to the number of workers employed times the unit price of labor (i.e., $TVC = L \times P_L$). Hence, we can write

$$AVC = \frac{TVC}{Q} = \frac{(L \times P_L)}{Q} = P_L\left(\frac{L}{Q}\right).$$

The expression in parentheses is the reciprocal of labor's average product. In particular, $L/Q = 1/(Q/L) = 1/AP_L$. Combining these definitions yields

$$AVC = \frac{P_L}{AP_L}.$$

Average variable cost is consequently falling when the average product of the variable input is rising (Stage I of the production function). When the average product of the variable input is falling (Stages II and III of the production function), average variable cost is rising. The minimum point on average variable cost corresponds to the point at which average product is at a maximum.

Average Fixed Cost and Average Total Cost

The cost curves shown in Figure 4.6b provide convenient tools for analyzing production and cost in the short run. However, these curves only reflect the costs associated with the variable input. The effect of both variable and fixed inputs on the firm's costs of production is captured by the average total cost (ATC) curve.

The impact of fixed inputs on average cost is initially represented in Figure 4.7a as average fixed cost. **Average fixed cost** (AFC) is defined as total fixed cost (TFC) divided by output, Q:

$$AFC = \frac{TFC}{Q}.$$

Because fixed costs, by definition, do not change as the firm varies the quantity of output it produces, average fixed cost declines continuously as output increases. Figure 4.7a illustrates this property of average fixed cost.

The average variable cost and marginal cost curves from Figure 4.6 b are reproduced in Figure 4.7b. **Average total cost** (ATC) is computed by adding average variable cost to average fixed cost, that is,

$$ATC = AFC + AVC.$$

For example, the addition of average variable cost "ab" to average fixed cost "cd" results in an average total cost equal to "be." Put differently, the vertical distance between average total cost and average variable cost at any point is equal to average fixed cost ("ea" = "cd"). Moreover, because average fixed cost declines continuously as the firm expands production, the vertical distance between AVC and ATC becomes smaller and smaller as output increases. AVC is never equal to ATC, however, because AFC is never equal to zero. $AFC = TFC/Q$ is always a positive number no matter how large Q becomes.

Average total cost is a U-shaped curve that, like average variable cost, first declines, then reaches a minimum, and finally increases. Marginal cost is equal to average total cost when average total cost is at a minimum. The same reasoning we used previously to explain the relationship between average variable cost and marginal cost also explains the relationship between average total cost and marginal cost. As long as marginal cost is less than average total cost, average total cost declines. When marginal cost is greater than average total cost, average total cost increases. Finally, because ATC includes the costs associated with the fixed and variable inputs, AVC reaches a minimum before (at a lower level of output than) ATC.

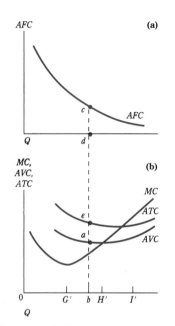

FIGURE 4.7
Short-Run Cost Curves (Fixed and Variable Inputs)

Short-Run Cost Curves with Cobb-Douglas Technology

The previous section derives the set of short-run cost curves generated by a short-run production function exhibiting both increasing and diminishing marginal returns to the variable input. We now return to the analysis of the short-run cost characteristics of the Johnson Company's proposed new product. The company produces all-weather coats using a Cobb-Douglas production technology that displays diminishing marginal returns throughout—the marginal product of labor declines continuously.

If capital is held fixed at 80 units (K_0 = 80, or 80,000 machine-hours), the short-run production function is $Q = 44.72L^{.5}$ (see equation 4.5 on p. 126). Total cost (TC) is the sum of the firm's expenditures on capital (total fixed cost, or TFC) and labor (total variable cost, or TVC) which, in general, can be written as:

$$TC = TFC + TVC = P_KK_0 + P_LL. \qquad (4.8)$$

Capital is denominated in units of 1,000 machine-hours and the price of capital is $10 per machine-hour per year. Labor is measured as the number of production workers employed. Individual workers can be hired by paying a compensation package worth $40,000 annually. Denominating this compensation in thousands of dollars, the unit price of labor is $40. Both the short-run production function and the cost equation are defined for a period of one year.

If total cost is also denominated in thousands of dollars, the short-run total cost function is:

$$TC = \$10K_0 + \$40L = \$10(80) + \$40L = \$800 + \$40L. \qquad (4.9)$$

The total cost of producing all-weather coats is the sum of total fixed cost (*TFC*) and total variable cost (*TVC*). Total fixed cost, in turn, is the cost of acquiring 80 units of capital (*TFC* = $800 or $800,000). Total variable cost depends on the number of production workers the firm employs (*TVC* = $40L).

The key concepts of average total cost, average variable cost, and marginal cost show how the firm's production costs vary as output varies, holding plant size (capital) fixed. Equation 4.9 must therefore be rearranged to express total cost as a function of output, Q, rather than labor, L. The short-run production function, $Q = 44.72L^{.5}$, can be rewritten so that labor is on the left-hand side as follows:

$$L = \frac{Q^2}{(44.72)^2} = \frac{Q^2}{2000}. \qquad (4.10)$$

Substituting equation 4.10 into equation 4.9 yields the following short-run total cost function:

$$TC = \$800 + \$40\left(\frac{Q^2}{2000}\right) = \$800 + \$.02Q^2. \qquad (4.11)$$

Writing the total cost function in this way underscores the idea that fixed costs are fixed. Total fixed cost (*TFC* = $800) is constant; it does not depend on the quantity of output produced. Total variable cost, on the other hand, is a function of output. In particular, dropping the $800 which represents the fixed cost of capital, total variable cost is:

$$TVC = \$.02Q^2. \qquad (4.12)$$

Average total cost and average variable cost are computed by dividing total cost (equation 4.11) and total variable cost (equation 4.12) by Q. These computations yield:

$$ATC = \frac{TC}{Q} = \frac{\$800}{Q} + \$.02Q \qquad (4.13)$$

and

$$AVC = \frac{TVC}{Q} = \$.02Q. \qquad (4.14)$$

Marginal cost is the derivative of either the total cost equation or the total variable cost equation. Marginal cost is consequently equal to:

$$MC = \frac{dTC}{dQ} = \frac{dTVC}{dQ} = \$.04Q. \qquad (4.15)$$

Equations 4.13, 4.14, and 4.15 can be used to calculate average total cost, average variable cost, and marginal cost at various levels of output. Keeping in mind that output is denominated in thousands of all-weather coats, the following table shows these costs for output levels of 100,000, 200,000, 300,000, and 400,000 units per year.

SHORT RUN COST DATA FOR ALL-WEATHER COATS

Q	100,000	200,000	300,000	400,000
ATC	$10	$8	$8.67	$10
AVC	$2	$4	$6	$8
MC	$4	$8	$12	$16

Figure 4.8 graphs average total cost, average variable cost, and marginal cost. The marginal cost curve for the Johnson Company's all-weather coat operation is linear and upward sloping throughout the relevant range of output. Marginal cost does not decline initially (as in Figure 4.7b, p. 136) because the Cobb-Douglas production function does not contain a region of increasing marginal returns to the variable input. If marginal cost rises continuously, average variable cost must also rise continuously.

On the other hand, average total cost does have the familiar U-shape. This is because average fixed cost falls continuously. The reduction in average fixed cost is large enough to initially offset the increase in average variable cost. Hence, average total cost declines initially. However, because average fixed cost is continuously falling and average variable cost is continuously rising, average total cost must eventually begin to rise.

Average total cost is at its minimum at an annual output rate of 200,000 all-weather coats. Marginal cost is equal to average total cost at this point.

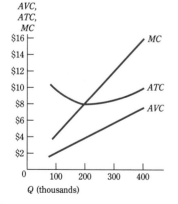

AVC,
ATC,
MC

FIGURE 4.8
Short-Run Cost Curve for
All-Weather Coats

The problem of selecting an efficient plant size provides a synthesis of short- and long-run cost analyses. The choice of an optimal plant size is, of course, a long-run issue. The process of selecting the plant size that is optimal for producing a particular level of output presupposes that the firm can consider varying its usage of all inputs, including capital and any other inputs treated as fixed in the short-run. However, the choice between plants of different sizes is based on differences in their respective short-run cost curves. The short-run cost characteristics of different plant sizes ultimately determine the long-run characteristics of production and cost.

Single-Plant Production

Consider a firm that plans to produce all of its output at a single production facility. Suppose that the firm can choose among three different plant sizes that, for simplicity, are called "small," "medium," and "large." The optimal plant size is the one that minimizes the total cost of producing the profit-maximizing level of output or, equivalently, the plant that minimizes the average total cost of producing the profit-maximizing output level.

Each of the three possible plant sizes generates a unique set of short-run average and marginal cost curves. Given information on the production function and input prices, the relationship between costs and output is derived for the fixed quantity of capital associated with each plant.

Consider the firm's choices when the short-run average cost (SAC) curves of the three plants have the relationship depicted in Figure 4.9a. Larger plant sizes enable the firm to achieve lower average production costs in this example. Such reductions in average cost will materialize with expansions in plant size if the **long-run production function** exhibits increasing returns to scale, if the firm is able to exploit economies of scale, or both.

If the firm plans to produce a relatively small quantity of output, say Q_1 units, the smallest plant size is the most efficient because the average total cost of producing Q_1 units of output (ATC_1) is lower than the average total cost of either the medium (ATC_2) or large plant (ATC_3) at this point. By similar reasoning, the smallest plant is more efficient than the others for producing any level of output up to Q_2 units.

The average cost of producing an output level between Q_2 and Q_3 units is lower for the medium-sized plant than for the small or large plants. Finally, if the firm plans to produce an output level of Q_3 units or more, the large plant is the most efficient.

Somewhat surprisingly, perhaps, the minimum average costs of producing Q_1, Q_2, or Q_3 units of output do *not* coincide with the minimum points of the short-run average cost curves that define the three possible plant sizes. As a general matter, the minimum point of a short-run average cost curve is conventionally referred to as **plant capacity**. The minimum point on the short-run average cost curve corresponds to the rate of output at which the *plant's* per unit costs of production are as low as possible. This definition of

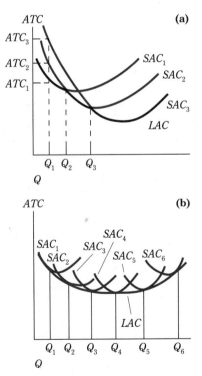

FIGURE 4.9
Long-Run Average Cost and
Alternative Plant Sizes

plant capacity is more useful than one that is based on the physical production limits of a plant because it recognizes that a plant can produce more or less than its "normal" output, but that the average cost of production will tend to rise when it does so.

Ignoring uncertainties in demand for the moment, the implication of Figure 4.9a is that the firm will tend to operate whatever plant it chooses at less than full capacity. That is, if the firm plans to produce either Q_1, Q_2, or Q_3 units of output, it will produce to the left of the minimum point on the short-run average cost curve that corresponds to the relevant efficient plant size. The underlying rationale for this conclusion is based on the linkage between short-run and long-run average production costs.

The darkened segments of the short-run average cost curves in Figure 4.9a represent the minimum average total costs of producing various possible levels of output when plant size is variable. The scalloped, darkened line in Figure 4.9a is the firm's long-run average total cost (LAC) curve. Long-run average cost declines initially, perhaps because the production function exhibits increasing returns to scale. Because the short-run average cost curves shift downward as plant size increases in this case, the firm is able to achieve lower average costs by shifting to a larger plant size and operating it below capacity than it would by operating a smaller plant at full capacity. The upward-sloping portion of the long-run average cost curve indicates that diseconomies of scale, due in part perhaps to decreasing returns to scale, will eventually arise as plant size increases.

The foregoing example can be generalized to include a continuum of alternative plant sizes. Figure 4.9b shows this generalization. The long-run average cost curve (LAC) is the "envelope" of points on the individual short-run average cost curves corresponding to plant sizes that are optimal for producing various possible levels of output. The smooth long-run average cost curve in Figure 4.9b implies that the firm can choose from a continuous number of alternative plant sizes as opposed to the discrete number of plants that characterize the scalloped long-run average cost curve in Figure 4.9a.

The short-run average cost curves of six representative plant sizes are drawn in Figure 4.9b. If the optimal level of production is Q_1 units, the optimal plant size is the one associated with SAC_1. Because the long-run average cost curve declines initially, an increase in the optimal level of output means that the optimal plant size also increases. As planned output expands from Q_1 to Q_2 to Q_3, the optimal plant size increases because expanding plant capacity lowers average production costs. Note once again that the points on the short-run average cost curves that define the long-run average cost curve do not correspond to the minimum points of the short-run average cost curves. When long-run average cost is declining, the points of tangency between long-run and short-run average cost occur to the left of (below) minimum short-run average cost.

The long-run average cost curve is horizontal between points Q_3 and Q_5. In this output range, scale economies are exhausted (and diseconomies of scale have not yet appeared). The long-run average cost curve now connects the minimum points of the short-run average cost curves. The point at which long-run average cost *first* reaches a minimum is called the **minimum efficient scale** (*MES*). Minimum efficient scale is represented by the plant size associated with Q_3 in Figure 4.9b.

Interpreting the minimum efficient scale of production warrants caution. From an engineering or technological point of view, every plant in Figure 4.9b is an efficient plant. The relatively small plant represented by SAC_1 is not necessarily inefficient relative to the larger plant represented by SAC_3. Plant efficiency is defined with respect to a planned rate of output. Plant SAC_1, for example, is the efficient plant size for producing Q_1 units of output; it is inefficient if the firm plans to produce a larger quantity of output. Minimum efficient scale simply indicates the smallest plant size which can attain minimum *long-run* average cost.

The long-run average cost curve in Figure 4.9b begins rising when planned output exceeds Q_5 units. Diseconomies of scale appear or the long-run production function exhibits decreasing returns to scale. If the firm plans to produce output level Q_6 with a single plant, the efficient plant size is represented by SAC_6. When long-run average cost is rising, the points of tangency between long-run and short-run average cost occur to the right of (above) minimum short-run average cost. Lower average costs can be achieved by operating a plant of given size above capacity than by building a larger plant and operating it at full capacity.

Multi-Plant Production

The choice of an optimal plant size is straightforward when production takes place in a single plant. The plant scale that minimizes the long-run average total cost of producing the profit-maximizing level of output is the optimal plant size in this case. However, many firms operate more than one production facility. If the production facilities operate at the same stage of the production process, the firm is said to be **horizontally integrated.** If the production facilities operate at successive stages of the production process, the firm is said to be **vertically integrated**. If the production processes of different plants are unrelated to one another, the firm is said to be a **conglomerate**. An analysis of the optimal strategies for choosing among these options is obviously a good deal more complicated than one that is limited to choosing the optimal plant size for a single production facility. Some brief remarks on the multi-plant operations of horizontally integrated firms are offered here.[8]

Multi-plant operations enable the firm to achieve a lower average total cost of production than single-plant operations when the cost penalties of a large plant are relatively high. An example is provided in Figure 4.10. Except for very low levels of output, the long-run average cost curve is horizontal over a wide range, after which the long-run average cost of single-plant

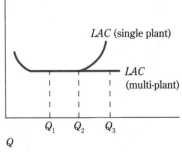

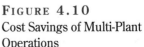

FIGURE 4.10
Cost Savings of Multi-Plant Operations

---

8 Chapters 12 and 13 provide detailed analyses of vertical integration. Conglomerate enterprises are discussed in Chapter 14.

production rises dramatically. The firm could produce output levels such as Q_1 or Q_2 within a single production facility or it could produce these output levels by operating two or more smaller plants of minimum efficient scale.

If the firm produces more than Q_2 units of output, however, multi-plant production will reduce average costs. For example, if Q_3 is twice Q_1, the firm can produce Q_3 units of output by operating two production facilities of plant size Q_1. The average cost of producing Q_3 units of output by operating two production facilities of plant size Q_1 is less than the average cost of production in a single facility of size Q_3. In essence, the firm is able to extend the horizontal section of the long-run average cost curve with multi-plant operations.[9]

INTERRELATIONS AMONG SHORT- AND LONG-RUN COST CURVES

The long-run average cost curve shows the *minimum* average cost of producing every feasible level of output when all inputs are variable. It is constructed as the "envelope" of individual short-run average cost curves, each of which represents the optimal plant size for producing a particular targeted level of output.

As defined in Chapter 3, the long-run marginal cost curve shows how long-run total cost changes when output changes. It indicates the *minimum* amount by which total cost increases when output is increased, all inputs being variable. Alternatively, long-run marginal cost shows the *maximum* amount that can be saved when output is reduced, all inputs again being variable. Short-run marginal cost, by contrast, shows how total cost changes when output changes, holding plant capacity fixed. How are long-run marginal cost and short-run marginal cost related to one another?

The answer to this question is that each point on the long-run marginal cost curve corresponds to a point on a short-run marginal cost curve. Figure 4.11 shows the relationship between short- and long-run marginal cost. Consider the plant size denoted by SAC_1 with the associated short-run marginal cost curve SMC_1. Following the discussion earlier in the chapter, SMC_1 intersects SAC_1 at SAC_1's minimum. At point A, corresponding to output Q_1, short-run average cost is equal to long-run average cost. Short-run and long-run *total* cost are consequently also equal to one another at point A.

Now consider a smaller quantity of output, such as Q_1', produced in plant size SAC_1. Short-run average cost exceeds long-run average cost and so short-run total cost is greater than long-run total cost at output Q_1'. If output is expanded from Q_1' to Q_1, both short-run and long-run total costs increase.

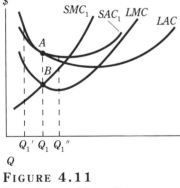

FIGURE 4.11
Short -Run and Long-Run
Cost Curves

---

9 As will be seen in Chapter 5, the profit-maximizing level of output depends on both demand and cost factors. A reduction in production cost will affect the firm's profit-maximizing quantity of output and the price of its product. The changes in price and output do not abrogate the above analysis, but only reinforce the profitability edge that a multi-plant firm can have over a single-plant firm.

Government Regulation and Short-Run Hospital Costs

Entry of new hospitals and expansions of existing hospital facilities are regulated in the United States by certificate-of-need (CON) regulations. An increase in the number of beds in an existing hospital or the construction of new hospital facilities must first be approved on a "need" basis by state health boards. Proponents argue that this requirement reduces costs by preventing "costly duplication" of hospital capacity. For many economists, however, CON regulations blatantly reduce competition and impair allocative efficiency by creating an artificial barrier to entry and expansion.

Despite (wishful?) thinking that CON requirements reduce hospital costs by preventing overexpansion, some 15 empirical studies have found that these regulations are associated with increased costs rather than lower costs.[a] In a recent study, however, John Mayo and Deborah McFarland report evidence that CON regulations have a negative effect on costs.[b] Mayo and McFarland estimate a two-equation model in which CON regulation is a determinant of the number of hospital beds and the number of hospital beds, in turn, is a determinant of total variable hospital cost. Mayo and McFarland conclude that CON regulations have a negative effect on hospital costs because (a) the number of hospital beds is negatively related to CON regulations and (b) the number of hospital beds is positively related to hospital variable costs.

The purpose of empirical research is to lend support to a theory or to provide evidence that fails to support the theory. Most scientific hypotheses are tested many times before any one empirical result is accepted. Mayo and McFarland's empirical study contradicts the evidence of many other studies. Which findings are accurate? Should one accept the studies reporting evidence that CON regulation increases hospital costs, or should one accept the study by Mayo and McFarland suggesting that CON regulation tends to reduce hospital costs? Rather than answering this question directly, it is more important in our opinion to recognize that differences in empirical models and statistical results are essential features of the scientific process. We must view all econometric results with skepticism. It is skepticism that spurs additional research on previously tested topics

In the spirit of skepticism, Keith Anderson has published a rebuttal to Mayo and McFarland's findings.[c] Anderson argues that CON regulation should be included directly as a determinant of hospital costs rather than following Mayo and McFarland's specification which includes regulation as an indirect determinant of cost. Anderson's reasoning is that the effects of CON regulation on hospital costs go beyond its simple impact on the number of hospital beds. For example, a hospital may propose to undertake a capital project to improve quality and attract additional patients and physicians. If the regulatory body rejects the project, the hospital can then substitute alternative improvements to meet these goals—alternatives that can affect hospital costs directly.

As a second criticism, Anderson argues that Mayo and McFarland's data set was too limited (their sample included 120 hospitals in the State of Tennessee). Anderson also argues that Mayo and McFarland's measure of the stringency of CON regulation—the share of applications for new beds approved by state and local regulatory authorities—is inappropriate.

a A bibliography of these studies is provided in Keith Anderson, "Regulation, Market Structure, and Hospital Costs: Comment," *Southern Economic Journal* 58 (October 1991), pp. 528-34.

b John W. Mayo and Deborah McFarland, "Regulation, Market Structure, and Hospital Costs," *Southern Economic Journal* 53 (January 1989), pp. 559-69.

c Anderson, "Regulation, Market Structure, and Hospital Costs: Comment."

Anderson examines the determinants of hospital variable costs using a sample of 2,069 hospitals. He measures the stringency of CON regulations by the number of years the regulations had been in place. In addition, the regulatory variable enters the cost function both linearly and as an interaction term with the number of hospital beds. Anderson finds that CON regulation has a positive, significant effect on hospital costs and, in fact, increases costs by approximately 10 percent. The following table reproduces Anderson's empirical results.[d]

DETERMINANTS OF HOSPITAL TOTAL VARIABLE COST

VARIABLE	DEFINITION	COEFFICIENT (t-RATIO)
PD	Patient days of care.	14.967 (0.53)
PD^2	PD squared.	−0.001 (−2.08)
WAGE	Average wage of nurses.	328.116 (1.74)
$WAGE^2$	Wage squared.	0.003 (0.76)
BEDS	Number of hospital beds.	111,721. (10.60)
$BEDS^2$	BEDS squared.	−259.176 (−5.38)
PD*BEDS	Interaction of PD and BEDS	1.128 (4.09)
PROFIT	Dummy equal to one if a for-profit hospital.	520,976. (0.69)
NONFED	Dummy equal to one if a state hospital.	2,398,270. (3.79)
CONAGE	Number of years that CON regulations have been in place.	27,200,072. (2.63)
BEDS* CONAGE	Interaction of BEDS and CONAGE	144.39 (0.48)

d The estimated coefficients associated with three dummy variables, *TEACHER*1, *TEACHER*2, and *TEACHER*3, are not reported in this table.

But if the firm moves from a point at which short-run total cost is greater than long-run total cost to a point at which they are equal, the *change* in short-run total cost (SMC_1) must be less than the *change* in long-run total cost (LMC). Hence, SMC_1 must be less than LMC at Q_1' (or at any other point to the left of A).

For example, suppose that the total cost of producing Q_1 units of output is $100. If the firm produces a smaller quantity of output, its total production costs will of course be lower. In accordance with Figure 4.11, suppose that the short-run total cost of producing Q_1' units is $90 and that the long-run total cost is $80 ($SAC_1$ is greater than LAC if short-run total cost is greater than long-run total cost). When the firm expands output from Q_1' to Q_1 units, short-run total cost increases by $10 ($SMC = $10) and long-run total cost increases by $20 ($LMC = $20). Short-run marginal cost is consequently less than long-run marginal cost at Q_1'.

A similar argument establishes the relationship between short- and long-run marginal costs to the right of point A. Short-run average cost again exceeds long-run average cost at output Q_1'', and so short-run total cost is greater than long-run total cost at that point. Hence, if output expands from Q_1 to Q_1'' units, the firm moves from a point at which SMC_1 is equal to LMC (point B) to a point at which SMC_1 is greater than LMC. The *change* in short-run total cost must therefore be greater than the *change* in long-run total cost. Hence, SMC_1 must be greater than LMC at Q_1'' (or at any other point to the right of A).

Short-run marginal cost is thus equal to long-run marginal cost when short-run average cost is equal to long-run average cost. Short-run marginal cost is less than long-run marginal cost to the left of the point of tangency between *SAC* and *LAC*, and short-run marginal cost is greater than long-run marginal cost to the right of the point of tangency between *SAC* and *LAC*. Following this argument for all possible plant sizes generates the long-run marginal cost curve shown in Figure 4.11.

STRATEGIES FOR STABILIZING PRODUCTION COSTS

In the real world, managers make production decisions in a dynamic environment where market conditions change unexpectedly. Demand is often uncertain, for example, and the firm must therefore be prepared to cope with the possibility that the quantity of output it sells in any period may not be equal to the quantity it produces.

If the long-run average cost schedule is U-shaped, there is only one plant size that is efficient for producing a given quantity of output. If the firm produces more or less than the quantity that is optimal for the given plant size, it will fail to minimize long-run total production costs. In other words, if the quantity of output produced is not the quantity at which short-run average cost is equal to long-run average cost, total production costs will be higher than they would be if the firm could adjust its plant size optimally.

By definition, plant size can be adjusted optimally only in the long run. Consider once again plant size SAC_1 in Figure 4.11 (p. 142), the optimal plant size for producing Q_1 units of output. Suppose that the firm experiences a reduction in demand to Q_1' units. If this demand reduction is permanent, the firm can achieve minimum long-run total costs by adjusting its plant size downward. On the other hand, if the demand change is only temporary so that the firm sells Q_1' units in some periods and, perhaps, Q_1'' units in other periods, plant size adjustments are obviously not practical.

Inventories and order backlogs enable the firm to stabilize its production costs in the face of uncertain demand. The basic function of inventories and order backlogs is to provide a buffer that smooths out differences in timing between the production of a product and its sale. In terms of Figure 4.11, if demand is on average equal to Q_1 units, the firm continues to produce this quantity in every period, thereby achieving minimum average (and total) production costs. Temporary changes in demand are accommodated by changing inventory or order backlog policies rather than changing production levels.

Inventories are accumulated stocks of finished goods. Like all economic decisions, the determination of the optimal inventory level requires a balancing of benefits and costs. The primary benefit of holding finished goods in inventory is the ability to handle temporary increases in demand by drawing down these stocks rather than stepping up the level of production or increasing the price of the product. When demand is higher than normal (Q_1''), the firm in Figure 4.11 can meet its production shortfall by drawing down its inventories.

When demand is lower than normal (Q_1'), on the other hand, the firm can add unsold goods to its inventories.

Holding inventories is costly, however. Storage costs must be borne, and the firm necessarily foregoes income it could have earned by reallocating the funds tied up in inventory holdings to alternative uses. Hence, finished goods should be stockpiled only up to the point where the additional benefit of adding one more unit to inventory is just equal to the additional cost.

Because inventories are not costless, inventory holdings alone may not completely balance the timing of production and sales. During periods of higher-than-normal demand, the firm can also use **order backlogs** rather than increase production or raise price. That is, customers are asked to wait for delivery of the product. The cost of this strategy, of course, is that the firm can put orders on backlog, but it cannot prevent customers from buying the product from a competitor who promises delivery sooner. To prevent customer loss from backorders, the firm can offer discounts for the inconvenience. This reasoning implies that it could also be in the firm's interest to offer discounts for advance orders. The more advance orders the firm has, the less uncertain demand is likely to be, and the smaller the problem of production instability.

SHORT-RUN PRODUCTION AND COST REVISITED

This chapter's opening application asks five questions about the production and cost characteristics of the Johnson Company's new product. This section applies the theory of production and cost in the short run to answer these questions.

The long-run production function is $Q = 5K^{.5}L^{.5}$. What is the short-run production function and how is it related to the long-run production function? The short-run production function is derived directly from the long-run production function by holding plant capacity fixed at a given level. If the quantity of capital is held constant at 80 units (80,000 machine-hours), the short-run production function is:

$$Q = 5(80)^{.5}L^{.5} = 5(8.944)L^{.5} = 44.72L^{.5}.$$

By this definition, there is a unique short-run production function corresponding to every feasible plant size.

An isoquant map can illustrate many of the properties of the long-run production function. What are the properties of the short-run production function, and is there a convenient way of illustrating these properties? The most important property of any short-run production function is the property of diminishing marginal returns to the variable input. The law of diminishing marginal returns states that a point is eventually reached on every short-run production function at which the marginal product of the variable input begins to decline. In general, the short-run production function is characterized initially by increasing marginal returns, followed by a region of diminishing marginal returns.

The short-run production function for all-weather coats exhibits diminishing marginal returns throughout. This property is due to the assumption of Cobb-Douglas production technology. The marginal product of labor in this special case is:

$$MP_L = \frac{\partial Q}{\partial L} = (.5)(44.72)L^{-.5} = \frac{22.36}{L^{.5}}.$$

As labor usage successively increases, MP_L successively declines.

Productivity is an important issue in the employment of inputs. What should the firm's productivity goal be in the short run? Is the obvious answer that the firm should attempt to maximize the productivity of the variable input? There are two ways to measure the productivity of a variable input: marginal productivity and average productivity. Both of these productivity measures decline continuously as labor usage increases in the production of all-weather coats. The goal of maximizing either marginal or average productivity in this case leads to the plainly silly answer that the firm should hire one production worker.

In general, the goals of maximizing marginal productivity or average productivity are not consistent with profit-maximization. Instead, depending on the revenue conditions it faces, the firm should always produce where the marginal product of the variable input is either increasing (Stage I) or diminishing (Stage II). The firm should never produce in Stage III, where marginal product is negative.

Cost minimization is a central theme of long-run production and cost analysis. In the short run, what role does cost minimization play? Avoidable costs are variable costs in the short run. Should the firm attempt to minimize variable costs or should it strive to minimize total cost? Cost minimization, like productivity maximization, is not an end to itself in the short run. Only in the special case of a flat long-run average cost schedule will production take place at minimum short-run average cost. If the long-run average cost schedule is U-shaped, production may occur above or below the plant capacity denoted by the minimum short-run average total cost.

Long-run marginal and average costs for all-weather coats are constant for all output levels. Do similar properties characterize cost in the short run? What characterizes the behavior of marginal and average costs when the firm varies output in the short run? Will the per unit cost of production remain the same or will it vary as output varies? Short-run average cost curves are always U-shaped because diminishing marginal returns are unavoidable. Short-run average cost curves are U-shaped independently of the shape of long-run average cost. With U-shaped long-run average costs, there is only one plant size that is optimal for producing a particular level of output. The efficient plant size is the one at which short-run average cost equals long-run average cost. The per unit cost of production therefore varies as output varies in the short run and, moreover, short-run average cost exceeds long-run average cost when plant size cannot be adjusted optimally.

Short-run marginal cost (*SMC*) is equal to short-run average cost (*SAC*) when *SAC* is at its minimum. Long-run marginal cost (*LMC*) is likewise equal to long-run average cost (*LAC*) when *LAC* is at its minimum. In addition, *SMC* is equal to *LMC* at the point where *SAC* is equal to *LAC*. *SMC* is less than *LMC* to the left of this point and *SMC* is greater than *LMC* to the right of this point.

SUMMARY

One of the most important elements of the theory of production and cost in the short run is the relationship among the total, marginal, and average values of these functions. In general, as additional units of the variable input are combined with some given quantity of the fixed input, the short-run production function first increases at an increasing rate. It then increases at a decreasing rate beyond the point at which diminishing marginal returns appear. The marginal product of the variable input first rises, reaches a maximum, and then declines. Average product also rises initially, reaches a maximum, and then declines. However, average product attains its maximum value after marginal product attains its maximum. Marginal product is equal to average product when average product is at its maximum.

The set of short-run total, marginal, and average product curves determines a set of total variable cost, marginal cost and average variable cost curves. The product curves are based on the output effects of changes in input usage. The cost curves are based on the cost effects of changes in output. Given that units of the variable input are obtainable at a constant price per unit, total variable cost increases at a decreasing rate when total product increases at an increasing rate. On the other hand, total variable cost increases at an increasing rate when total product increases at a decreasing rate.

Because marginal cost is the slope of the total variable cost (or total cost) schedule, the rate of increase in total variable cost (or total cost) determines the character of marginal cost. Marginal cost declines as output increases when total variable cost increases at a decreasing rate. Marginal cost increases as output increases when total variable cost increases at an increasing rate. If marginal cost decreases and then increases, average variable cost is U-shaped and, at its minimum, is equal to marginal cost. Average total cost is likewise U-shaped because it is the sum of U-shaped average variable cost and continuously declining average fixed cost. Marginal cost is also equal to average total cost when average total cost is at its minimum.

This chapter demonstrates the interrelationships between the short run and the long run. The long-run average cost curve is constructed as an envelope of points on individual short-run average cost curves. Each point on the long-run average cost schedule represents the minimum average (and total) cost of producing a particular level of output when all inputs are variable. The optimal size of a plant is defined as the plant size (the short-run average cost curve) on which the long-run average cost of producing a given level of output is at a minimum.

For large levels of production, multi-plant production can offset the effects of diseconomies of scale. Dynamic efficiency in the face of changing market conditions is as important as static efficiency. Firms may be able to stabilize their costs of production when demand uncertainties cause fluctuations in production by the use of inventories and order backlogs.

QUESTIONS

4.1 Derive the short-run production functions for all-weather coats when capital is fixed at 80 units and when capital is fixed at 100 units. Graph both of these short-run production functions on the same diagram.

4.2 Explain the differences between diminishing marginal productivity and decreasing returns to scale.

4.3 The average total cost curve is U-shaped both when the average variable cost curve is U-shaped and when the average variable cost curve is only upward sloping. Why?

4.4 Explain the relationship between the shape of the average variable cost curve and the total product curve.

4.5 Evaluate the following statement. If diminishing marginal returns did not characterize the production of corn, the world's entire supply of corn could be grown in a flower pot.

4.6 General Motors has recently closed down many of its assembly plants. Although the reason for shutting down any of its plants is because of its declining market share, the most inefficient plants are closed first. Why would General Motors tolerate inefficient plants in the first place? For example, shouldn't General Motors either replace or upgrade inefficient plants when demand is high? In this way, General Motors would have a set of equally efficient plants when demand falls and, perhaps, would not have to close down as many plants.

4.7 Classify the following costs as either fixed or variable.
   a. cost of raw materials
   b. managerial salaries
   c. insurance on plant and equipment
   d. transportation costs of the final product
   e. transportation costs for raw materials
   f. utility costs of the central office
   g. utility costs of the production facility
   h. insurance on production workers
   i. production worker wages
   j. property taxes
   k. accounting department wages and expenses

4.8 Suppose that the long-run average cost curve for a firm first declines and then remains flat over a wide range of output. This cost curve does not incorporate transportation costs. Suppose that transportation costs increase linearly as output increases. How does including transportation costs affect the minimum efficient scale of production and how does it affect the shape of the long-run average total cost curve?

4.9 Suppose that the long-run average cost curve for a firm is U-shaped like the one in Figure 4.11 (see p. 142). Draw a graph that shows the relationship between short-run marginal cost (*SMC*) and long-run marginal cost (*LMC*) for a plant that is optimal for producing the quantity of output corresponding to the minimum point on long-run average cost. Draw another graph that shows the relationship between *SMC* and *LMC* for a plant that is optimal for producing a level of output to the right of the minimum point of *LAC*.

PROBLEMS

4.1 Popeye's Pizza Parlors is a successful chain of pizza restaurants in the midwestern United States. Roger Daily, the owner and founder of the company, estimates that the daily fixed cost of operating one restaurant is $300 and that every pizza sold costs the firm $10 in labor, materials, and energy. He therefore estimates that the total cost function for an individual restaurant is:

$$TC = \$300 + \$10Q,$$

where Q represents the number of pizzas the restaurant produces and sells per day.
   a. What are the equations for total variable cost (*TVC*), total fixed cost (*TFC*), average total cost (*ATC*), average variable cost (*AVC*), average fixed cost (*AFC*), and marginal cost (*MC*)?
   b. Graph total cost and total fixed cost on a single diagram. Determine the shape of total variable cost from this graph.
   c. Graph average variable cost, marginal cost, and average total cost on a single diagram.
   d. What is the shape of the underlying short-run production function? How do diminishing marginal returns affect this production function? What characterizes the substitutability of capital and labor?
   Problems 4.2 through 4.4 continue the analysis in problem 4.1.
4.2 Roger Daily is a cautious manager. He asks three consulting firms to estimate the daily total cost function for one of his restaurants. These consulting companies are named MBA Consulting, ABD Consulting, and PHD Consulting. The MBA Consulting Company estimates the following daily total cost function for Popeye's Pizza:

$$TC = \$300 + \$10Q - \$.05Q^2,$$

where Q again represents the number of pizzas the restaurant produces and sells.
   a. What are the equations for total variable cost (*TVC*), total fixed cost (*TFC*), average total cost (*ATC*), average variable cost (*AVC*), average fixed cost (*AFC*), and marginal cost (*MC*)?
   b. Graph total cost and total fixed cost on a single diagram. Determine the shape of total variable cost from this graph.
   c. Graph average variable cost, marginal cost, and average total cost on a single diagram.
   d. What is the shape of the underlying short-run production function? How do diminishing marginal returns affect this production function? What characterizes the substitutability of capital and labor?

4.3 The ABD Consulting Company estimates the following daily total cost function
for Popeye's Pizza:

$$TC = \$300 + \$5Q + \$.05Q^2,$$

where Q again represents the number of pizzas the restaurant produces and sells.
a. What are the equations for total variable cost (TVC), total fixed cost (TFC),
average total cost (ATC), average variable cost (AVC), average fixed cost
(AFC), and marginal cost (MC)?
b. Graph total cost and total fixed cost on a single diagram. Determine the shape
of total variable cost from this graph.
c. Graph average variable cost, marginal cost, and average total cost on a single
diagram.
d. What is the shape of the underlying short-run production function? How do
diminishing marginal returns affect this production function? What characterizes
the substitutability of capital and labor?

4.4 The PHD Consulting company estimates the following daily total cost function
for Popeye's Pizza:

$$TC = \$300 + \$5Q - \$.05Q^2 + \$.0005Q^3,$$

where Q represents the number of pizzas the restaurant produces and sells.
a. What are the equations for total variable cost (TVC), total fixed cost (TFC),
average total cost (ATC), average variable cost (AVC), average fixed cost
(AFC), and marginal cost (MC)?
b. Graph total cost and total fixed cost on a single diagram. Determine the shape
of total variable cost from this graph.
c. Graph average variable cost, marginal cost, and average total cost on a single
diagram.
d. What is the shape of the underlying short-run production function? How do
diminishing marginal returns affect this production function? What characterizes
the substitutability of capital and labor?

CHAPTER

5

Product Pricing and Profit Analysis

OVERVIEW

This chapter presents the fundamental rule for determining the firm's profit-maximizing price. The profit-maximizing price occurs at the quantity of output where marginal revenue is equal to marginal cost. When marginal revenue is greater than marginal cost, the firm should reduce price to increase sales because under these circumstances each extra unit sold will add more to the firm's total revenue than it will add to total cost. On the other hand, when marginal revenue is less than marginal cost, the firm should increase price to reduce sales.[1]

From this perspective, there is a unique relationship between the profit-maximizing price, the optimal markup on direct (marginal) cost, and the elasticity of demand for the firm's product. When the demand for the firm's product is price sensitive at the profit-maximizing quantity (demand is relatively elastic because, for example, there are close substitutes available), the optimal markup tends to be lower and price will therefore be lower than when the demand for the product is price insensitive.

---

1 These decision rules apply when the demand curve is downward sloping and the firm is consequently a "price searcher." If the firm is instead a "price taker" that confronts a horizontal (perfectly elastic) demand curve, marginal revenue is constant and equal to price. Under these conditions, the firm is able to vary sales without varying price. Profit-maximization nevertheless still occurs at the point where marginal revenue (price) is equal to marginal cost. See Chapter 8 for a comparison of price-taker and price-searcher firms.

This chapter also presents an analysis of profits and clarifies the important distinction between accounting profits and economic profits. In addition, we present the concept of break-even analysis and show that, applied with care, this technique effectively compares the output-profit characteristics of alternative production processes or alternative investment opportunities. The last section explains the role of incremental analysis in managerial decisions. Incremental analysis is a generalization of marginal analysis and determines the profit implications of alternative courses of action the firm can take.

APPLICATION

Earlier chapters present the demand, production, and cost characteristics of the Johnson Company's new product. As estimated by an outside consulting team, the demand for the product, an all-weather coat, is represented by the following equation:

$$Q_x^d = 60 - 5P_x + 2.4P_y - 4P_z + 10I. \tag{5.1}$$

Q_x^d is the quantity of all-weather coats demanded during a one-year period and is measured in units of thousands of coats. P_x is the price the company charges for its all-weather coat, P_y is the price of a competing ski jacket, and P_z is the price of an all-weather hat that consumers may match with the all-weather coat. I is the average annual disposable income of prospective buyers and is measured in thousands of dollars.

The Johnson Company does not have direct control over four of the variables in equation 5.1. The price of the competing ski jacket is $50, the price of the all-weather hat is $20, and average annual consumer income is $40,000. Substitution of these values into equation 5.1 yields the demand equation:

$$Q_x^d = 500 - 5P_x. \tag{5.2}$$

Equation 5.2 shows the quantity of all-weather coats consumers are willing and able to buy at various possible prices, holding the other determinants of demand constant.

The firm can expect to sell 200,000 coats per year if it charges a price of $60. At this price, the absolute value of the point price elasticity of demand is:

$$\text{POINT } \eta_p = \left| -\frac{\partial Q}{\partial P} \frac{P}{Q} \right|$$

$$= \left| -5 \times \frac{60}{200} \right| = 1.5. \tag{5.3}$$

Demand is elastic at a price of $60 per unit. A one percent change in price leads to a 1.5 percent change in quantity demanded.

The inverse demand function for all-weather coats relates the price of the product to quantity demanded. It is given by the equation:

$$P_x = \$100 - \$.2Q_x^d. \tag{5.4}$$

The total revenue function, *TR*, is generated when the inverse demand function is multiplied by quantity:

$$TR = P_x Q_x^d = \$100Q_x^d - \$.2(Q_x^d)^2. \tag{5.5}$$

Marginal revenue is the slope of the total revenue function. Taking the required derivative yields:

$$MR = \frac{dTR}{dQ_x^d} = \$100 - \$.4Q_x^d. \tag{5.6}$$

As discussed in Chapter 3, the long-run production function for all-weather coats is specified as follows:

$$Q = 5K^{.5}L^{.5}. \tag{5.7}$$

Q represents output in thousands of coats per year, *K* represents capital in units of 1,000 machine-hours, and *L* represents labor in terms of the number of production workers employed. This particular Cobb-Douglas production function exhibits constant returns to scale throughout the relevant range of output. If capital and labor both increase in the same proportion, output also increases in this proportion.

The company has initially planned to produce 200,000 all-weather coats per year. The least-cost input combination for producing this quantity of output requires the employment of 80 units (80,000 machine-hours) of capital and 20 production workers. If each production worker gets salary and fringe benefits worth $40,000 annually and the price of capital is $10 per machine-hour per year, the total cost of production is $1,600,000 (= 20 x $40,000 + 80,000 x $10). The long-run average cost of production is consequently equal to $8 (= $1,600,000/200,000). Because long-run average cost is constant and equal to long-run marginal cost when production is characterized by constant returns to scale, the long-run marginal cost of production is also equal to $8.

The production function in equation 5.7 includes only those inputs that are substitutable in the production process. All-weather coat manufacture also requires fabric, buttons, and other inputs that enter the production function in fixed proportions. These inputs must be incorporated explicitly into the firm's costs of production. Assume that these inputs add $12 to the cost of producing each coat. Long-run total cost is therefore:

$$LTC = \$20Q. \qquad (5.8)$$

This equation implies that long-run average total cost and long-run marginal cost are:

$$LAC = LMC = \$20. \qquad (5.9)$$

Chapter 4 develops the characteristics of short-run production and cost. A specific short-run production and cost function are associated with a specific plant size or level of capital expenditure. The optimal (long-run total cost minimizing) plant size for producing 200,000 units of output requires a capital expenditure of $800,000. The short-run total cost function is consequently $STC = \$800 + \$.02Q^2$ (see equation 4.11 on p. 137). However, once again we must consider the inputs used in fixed proportions. If every coat produced requires $12 worth of materials and other inputs, the short-run total cost equation is:

$$STC = \$800 + \$12Q + \$.02Q^2. \qquad (5.10)$$

Short-run marginal cost is the slope of the short-run total cost function. Taking the required derivative yields:

$$SMC = \$12 + \$.04Q. \qquad (5.11)$$

The pieces are now in place to answer one of the most fundamental questions the Johnson Company's owner must ask: What is the profit-maximizing price for all-weather coats?

PROFIT-MAXIMIZING PRICING DECISIONS

The rule for determining the profit-maximizing price is simple and straightforward. The firm should set a price by determining the maximum amount consumers are willing and able to pay for the quantity of output at which marginal revenue is equal to marginal cost. The logic of this rule becomes apparent with the aid of Figure 5.1. Panel a of this graph shows the firm's total revenue, total cost, and profit schedules. In accordance with the discussion in Chapter 2, total revenue (TR) first rises, reaches a maximum, and then declines. The total cost (TC) function is drawn as a straight line to reflect the assumption of constant average cost.

Profit, π, is simply the difference between total revenue and total cost (i.e., $\pi = TR - TC$). The goal of profit maximization is achieved by determining the quantity at which this difference is as large as possible. In panel a of

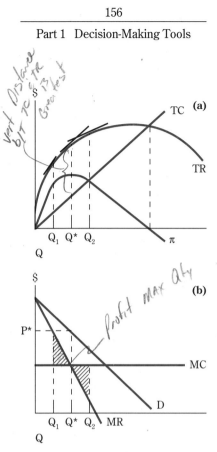

FIGURE 5.1
The Profit-Maximizing Output and
Price

Figure 5.1, the profit-maximizing quantity is Q^* units, the quantity of output at which the vertical distance between *TR* and *TC* is at a maximum. Q^* occurs at the point where the slope of the total revenue function, defined as **marginal revenue**, is equal to the slope of the total cost function, defined as **marginal cost**.

The conclusion that Q^* is in fact the profit-maximizing quantity is visually apparent in panel *a*. The underlying intuition becomes clear when we consider quantities either smaller or larger than Q^*. For example, suppose the firm produces $Q_1 < Q^*$ units. At Q_1, the slope of the total revenue function is greater than the slope of the total cost function—marginal revenue is greater than marginal cost. Hence, if the firm expands output in the direction of Q^*, total revenue will rise by more than total cost and the firm's profits will consequently increase.

The opposite relationships hold if the firm produces $Q_2 > Q^*$ units. The slope of the total cost function is greater than the slope of the total revenue function at this point—marginal cost is greater than marginal revenue. Hence, if the firm *reduces* output in the direction of Q^*, total cost will fall by more than total revenue falls and the firm's profits will again increase. Profits are consequently at a maximum at Q^* where marginal revenue is equal to marginal cost.

A similar conclusion is reached in panel *b* of Figure 5.1 which shows a linear demand schedule, its associated marginal revenue schedule, and a horizontal (constant) marginal cost schedule. The profit-maximizing quantity is again Q^* units, determined by equating marginal revenue with marginal cost. Imagine once more that the firm produces a quantity of output other than Q^*. If the firm produces $Q_1 < Q^*$ units, marginal revenue is greater than marginal cost. By producing one more unit of output, the firm will add more to total revenue than it will add to total cost, and profits will increase. (By increasing production from Q_1 to Q^*, the firm will increase its profits by an amount illustrated by the area of the shaded triangle between Q_1 and Q^*.) Now suppose that the firm produces $Q_2 > Q^*$ units. In this case, marginal cost is greater than marginal revenue. As the firm reduces output, profits will again increase because total cost declines more than total revenue declines. Profits are maximized at Q^* where marginal revenue is equal to marginal cost.[2]

The price corresponding to the profit-maximizing quantity of output in panel *b* of Figure 5.1 is P^* dollars per unit. That is, if the firm charges price P^*, consumers will, according to the demand schedule, be willing and able to buy Q^* units and the firm's profits will consequently be at a maximum. Hence, the profit-maximizing price is determined by the point on the demand schedule corresponding to the profit-maximizing quantity.

The Johnson Company's Profit-Maximizing Quantity and Price: Long-Run Analysis

In the long run, by definition, all costs are variable. The profit-maximizing firm should therefore produce the quantity at which long-run marginal cost

---

2 A mathematical treatment of profit maximization is provided in the appendix to this chapter.

is equal to marginal revenue. From the application in this chapter, the marginal revenue and long-run marginal cost equations for all-weather coats are

$$MR = \$100 - \$.4Q$$

and

$$LMC = \$20.$$

Setting marginal revenue equal to long-run marginal cost,

$$\$100 - \$.4Q = \$20,$$

and solving for Q yields

$$Q^* = \frac{\$80}{\$.4} = 200,$$

or 200,000 units.[3]

We can determine the profit-maximizing price by substituting the profit-maximizing quantity into the inverse demand function (see equation 5.4, p. 154). Performing this substitution results in a profit-maximizing price of $60 per unit. In particular,

$$P_x^* = \$100 - \$.2Q^* = \$100 - \$.2(200) = \$60.$$

At this price and quantity, the firm earns $12,000,000 (= $60 x 200,000) in total revenue. The total cost of producing 200,000 units of output is $4,000,000 (= $20 x 200,000). Total profit is consequently equal to $8,000,000 (= $12,000,000 – $4,000,000).

Figure 5.2 depicts the price-quantity combination that maximizes the Johnson Company's long-run profits from producing and selling all-weather coats. Marginal revenue is equal to long-run marginal cost at an output rate of 200,000 units per year. A unit price of $60 corresponds to this profit-maximizing quantity. The firm's profits are represented by the shaded rectangle, whose area is $40 x 200,000 = $8,000,000.[4]

The Johnson Company's Profit-Maximizing Quantity and Price: Short-Run Analysis

The discussion of production and cost in Chapters 3 and 4 shows that short-run and long-run concepts are closely related. The short-run production

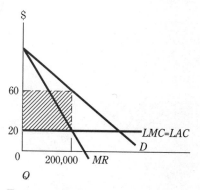

FIGURE 5.2

The Johnson Company's Long-Run Profit-Maximizing Output and Price

3 As determined in Chapter 3, the least-cost input combination for producing this quantity of output is one that consists of $800,000 worth of capital (80,000 machine-hours at price of $10 per machine-hour) and 20 production workers.

4 Total revenue is represented by the area of the rectangle defined by price times quantity, or $60 x 200,000 = $12,000,000. Long-run total cost is equal to the area of the rectangle defined by long-run average cost times quantity, or $20 x 200,000 = $4,000,000.

function, for example, is derived directly from the long-run production function by holding plant size (capital) fixed at a particular level. Given information on input prices, a set of short-run cost curves is then determined. Each set of short-run cost curves shows how average and marginal production costs vary as output is varied within a plant of given size. The long-run average total cost curve is the envelope of the short-run average total cost curves that define each possible plant size. It traces out the plant sizes that are optimal for (minimize the long-run average total cost of) producing every feasible level of output.

The close relationship between long-run cost and short-run cost means that once the profit-maximizing price and quantity have been determined by equating long-run marginal cost with marginal revenue, an optimal plant size has also been determined. The optimal plant size is the particular plant at which the long-run average cost of producing the profit-maximizing quantity is at a minimum. Furthermore, because short-run marginal cost is equal to long-run marginal cost when short-run average cost is equal to long-run average cost, the short-run profit-maximizing price and quantity, determined by equating the appropriate short-run marginal cost function with marginal revenue, is the same as the price-quantity combination that maximizes long-run profits.

From equation 5.11 (see p. 155), the short-run marginal cost function associated with a plant size of 80,000 machine-hours of capital is

$$SMC = \$12 + \$.04Q.$$

Setting marginal revenue, $MR = \$100 - \$.4Q$, equal to short-run marginal cost and solving for Q again yields a profit-maximizing quantity of 200,000 units. The profit-maximizing price is therefore $60 per unit.

Figure 5.3 diagrams the short-run cost functions corresponding to this optimal price-quantity combination. (For comparison purposes, this figure also shows the long-run average and marginal cost schedules. Recall that in the special case where long-run marginal cost is constant and equal to long-run average cost, long-run average cost is equal to short-run average cost when short-run average cost is at a minimum.) The total cost of producing 200,000 units of output is again $4,000,000 and total revenue is $12,000,000. The firm consequently earns a profit of $8,000,000.

The short-run cost curves come into play once the production facility is built and there is a change in either demand or input prices. If it is costly to vary plant size immediately in the face of such changes, then the firm will limit its responses to those it can implement by varying its usage of inputs other than capital. In other words, constrained to operate within a plant of given size, output variations are governed by the short-run production and cost functions, not long-run production and cost functions.

As an example, suppose that the average annual income of consumers (as measured by real disposable household income in the United States) increases from $40,000 to $42,200. This increase in income generates an increase in demand, causing the firm's demand and marginal revenue curves

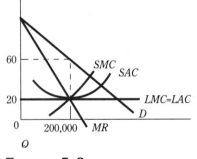

FIGURE 5.3

The Johnson Company's Short-Run Profit-Maximizing Output and Price to shift to the right. Holding all other variables constant, the new demand for all-weather coats will then be:

$$Q_x^d = 60 - 5P_x + 2.4P_y - 4P_z + 10I$$
$$Q_x^d = 60 - 5P_x + 2.4(50) - 4(20) + 10(42.2)$$
$$Q_x^d = 522 - 5P_x. \tag{5.12}$$

The inverse demand function, total revenue function, and marginal revenue function associated with the new demand schedule are

$$P_x = \$104.4 - \$.2Q_x^d, \tag{5.13}$$
$$TR = \$104.4Q_x^d - \$.2(Q_x^d)^2, \tag{5.14}$$

and

$$MR = \frac{dTR}{dQ_x^d} = \$104.4 - \$.4Q_x^d. \tag{5.15}$$

Short-run marginal cost is still represented by the equation $SMC = \$12 + \$.04Q$. Setting marginal revenue equal to short-run marginal cost and solving for Q yields a new profit-maximizing quantity of 210,000 units. Using equation 5.13, the new profit-maximizing price is thus $62.40. In order to continue to maximize profits, the firm should respond to the increase in demand by increasing both price and output.

In the short run, of course, plant capacity is fixed and so the firm can only increase output by hiring more production workers. In combination with 80 units of capital, the number of production workers required to produce 210,000 units of output is determined by the short-run production function (see p. 137),

$$L = \frac{Q^2}{2000}.$$

Substituting $Q = 210$ into this equation yields $L = 22.05$.[5] In other words, the firm must hire an additional 2.05 production workers to increase output from 200,000 units to 210,000 units in the short run.[6]

Because plant size cannot be adjusted immediately, the firm incurs a cost penalty to increase output in the short run. This cost penalty is illustrated by the movement along the short run average cost curve in Figure 5.4 which

[5] As shown in Chapter 4, the relationship between labor usage and output in the short run is determined by substituting $K_0 = 80$ into $Q = 5K_0^{.5}L^{.5}$ and solving for L.

[6] Obviously, the firm cannot literally hire .05 of a production worker. Labor usage can, however, be adjusted by hiring part-time employees or by varying the number of hours worked by existing employees.

shows the new and old profit-maximizing price-quantity combinations. According to equation 5.10 (p. 155), the short-run total cost of producing 210,000 units of output is $4,202,000. The average cost of production has therefore increased to $20.01 (= $4,202,000/210,000).

The total revenue earned by selling 210,000 all-weather coats at a price of $62.40 per unit is $13,104,000. Profit at the new price and quantity combination is therefore $8,902,000 (= $13,104,000 − $4,202,000). Although the firm's profits have increased in the short run as output and price increase in response to a higher demand, the firm can do even better in the long run by expanding the capacity of its plant. When the firm shifts to the optimal plant size for producing 210,000 units of output (the plant size at which short-run average cost is equal to long-run average cost), average production costs decrease to $20 and profits thereby increase.

ELASTICITY AND THE OPTIMAL MARKUP ON MARGINAL COST

There is a one-to-one relationship between the profit-maximizing price, P^*, marginal cost, MC, and the (absolute value of the) elasticity of demand at the profit-maximizing price, η_p^*. This relationship is as follows:

$$P^* = \frac{MC}{1 - \left(\dfrac{1}{\eta_p^*}\right)}. \tag{5.16}$$

Equation 5.16 is simply an application of the marginal-revenue-equals-marginal-cost rule for profit maximization because, as shown in the appendix,

FIGURE 5.4
Short-Run Price and
Production Responses to
an Increase in Demand

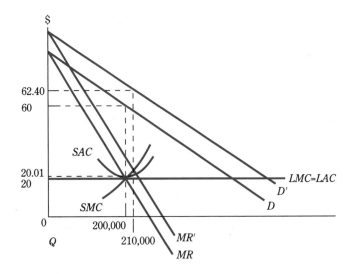

$MR = P[1 - (1/\eta_p)]$.[7] Equating marginal cost with marginal revenue expressed in this way (that is, writing $MC = P[1 - (1/\eta_p)]$, and solving for P) yields the expression in equation 5.16.

As an example, consider the demand and cost conditions for all-weather coats specified in equations 5.1 through 5.9 (see pp. 153-55). The long-run marginal cost of production is constant and equal to $20 per coat. The absolute value of the elasticity of demand at the profit-maximizing price-quantity combination, determined by setting marginal revenue equal to marginal cost, is 1.5. Substituting these values into the right-hand side of equation 5.16 yields

$$P^* = \frac{\$20}{1-\left(\dfrac{1}{1.5}\right)} = \frac{\$20}{1-.6667} = \frac{\$20}{.3333} = \$60,$$

the previously determined profit-maximizing price.

The one-to-one correspondence between P^*, η_p^*, and MC implies that the firm's profit-maximizing markup on marginal cost is also uniquely related to the elasticity of demand at the profit-maximizing price. In general, the markup on marginal cost is defined as

$$\text{MARKUP} = \frac{P - MC}{MC}.$$

In other words, the markup is the percentage by which price exceeds the firm's marginal cost of production. When the markup is calculated on the basis of long-run marginal cost and long-run marginal cost is constant and equal to long-run average cost, the markup represents the firm's percentage profit margin on sales. Moreover, because all costs are variable in the long run, the markup percentage calculated on the basis of long-run marginal cost is sometimes referred to as the markup on **direct cost**.

The appendix to this chapter shows that the profit-maximizing markup, MARKUP^*, is related to η_p^* in the following way:

$$\text{MARKUP}^* = \frac{-1}{1-\eta_p^*}. \tag{5.17}$$

As an application of this relationship, recall that the absolute value of the elasticity of demand for all-weather coats *at the profit-maximizing price* is 1.5. The profit-maximizing markup on marginal cost is consequently:

$$\text{MARKUP}^* = \frac{-1}{1-1.5} = \frac{-1}{-.5} = 2,$$

---

[7] The relationship among marginal revenue, price, and the elasticity of demand is discussed more fully in Chapter 2.

or 200 percent.[8] The firm's marginal production cost is equal to $20. The profit-maximizing price of $60 accordingly represents a 200 percent markup over marginal cost.

It might be tempting to think that markup pricing is a practical alternative to following the "theoretical" rule for determining price by setting marginal revenue equal to marginal cost. In fact, surveys of actual business pricing policies suggest that **markup pricing** is a common practice.[9] However, the markup on price that is consistent with profit maximization can be determined *only* from an analysis based on marginal revenue and marginal cost.

To see this conclusion, note that the elasticity of demand at the profit-maximizing price, η_p^*, appears in equation 5.17. How is the value of η_p^* determined? It is the particular value of the elasticity of demand at the point on the demand schedule corresponding to the quantity where marginal revenue is equal to marginal cost! Hence, the optimal markup on marginal cost provides no more information to the manager than is provided by an analysis based on marginal revenue and marginal cost. Nor does markup pricing provide a shorter, more practical way to calculate the profit-maximizing price. More to the point, *markup pricing cannot be used to determine the price and quantity that maximize the firm's profit*. The firm can determine the optimal markup percentage only *after* it has determined the profit-maximizing price.

The Defects in Markup Pricing Policies

The use (and misuse!) of markup pricing can be illustrated with an example based on the demand and cost characteristics of all-weather coats. The long-run marginal cost of producing all-weather coats is constant and equal to $20 per unit. The absolute value of the elasticity of demand at the profit-maximizing price is 1.5 and the profit-maximizing markup on marginal cost is 200 percent.

Now suppose that because of an increase in the price of fabric and other materials, long-run marginal cost increases to $25 per coat. If the firm mechanically applies the same percentage markup to the new level of marginal cost, it would raise the price of all-weather coats to $75. Is this the price that maximizes the firm's profits under the new circumstances? The answer is an unambiguous no.

To see the flaw in using the optimal markup percentage calculated at the initial profit-maximizing price-quantity combination to determine the price the firm should charge when marginal cost increases, calculate the firm's profits at a price of $75 per coat. Total revenue of course depends on price and quantity. The demand for all-weather coats is $Q_x^d = 500 - 5P_x$, and the firm can therefore expect to sell 125,000 coats at a price of $75 per unit. Total

---

8 Note that if demand is unit elastic (i.e., $|\eta_p| = 1$), the markup is undefined. If demand is inelastic (i.e., $|\eta_p| < 1$), on the other hand, the markup percentage is *negative*. These observations reinforce the conclusion that a profit-maximizing firm will only operate in the region of the demand schedule where demand is elastic (i.e., $|\eta_p| > 1$).

9 Survey evidence suggesting that many business decision makers use markup percentages to determine their prices is reported in a classic paper by Robert L. Hall and Charles J. Hitch, "Price Theory and Business Behavior," *Oxford Economic Papers* 2 (May 1939), pp. 12-45.

revenue is thus $9,375,000 (= $75 x 125,000). Although long-run marginal cost has increased to $25, it is still constant over the relevant range of output at the new, higher level. The long-run average cost of production also increases to $25. Total cost is $3,125,000 (= $25 × 125,000) and profit is therefore equal to $6,250,000 (= $9,375,000 – $3,125,000).

Now calculate the new price and profit following the marginal-revenue-equals-marginal-cost rule. The marginal revenue equation is $MR = \$100 - \$.4Q$. Setting marginal revenue equal to the new, higher marginal cost,

$$\$100 - \$.4Q = \$25,$$

and solving for Q yields a profit-maximizing quantity of 187,500 coats. In order to sell this quantity of coats, the firm must charge a price determined by substituting $Q^* = 187.5$ into the inverse demand function, $P = \$100 - \$.2Q$. This substitution yields a profit-maximizing price of $62.50.

Total revenue is consequently equal to $11,718,750 (= $62.50 × 187,500) and total cost is $4,687,500 (= $25 × 187,500). The firm therefore earns a profit of $7,031,250 (= $11,718,750 – $4,687,500). Profit is consequently $781,250 higher if the firm follows the marginal-revenue-equals-marginal-cost rule than if it mechanically applies the same markup when marginal cost is $25 that it used when marginal cost was $20.

The foregoing example shows clearly that the inappropriate use of markup pricing can lead the firm to fail to maximize its profits. What went wrong? That is, why did applying the old markup percentage to the new marginal cost figure cause the firm to forego over $781,000 in profits? The answer is that the elasticity of demand has changed and so the optimal (profit-maximizing) markup also changes. In particular, the absolute value of the point price elasticity of demand at the new profit-maximizing price-quantity combination is

$$\text{POINT} \quad \eta_p = \left| -\frac{\partial Q}{\partial P} \frac{P}{Q} \right| = \left| -5 \times \frac{62.50}{187.5} \right| = 1.67.$$

Demand has become more elastic and the optimal markup percentage is therefore reduced. Specifically, the optimal markup percentage is now

$$\text{MARKUP*} = \frac{-1}{1-1.67} = \frac{-1}{-.67} = 1.49,$$

or 149 percent, not 200 percent.

There is one *special* set of circumstances in which the firm can continue to use the same markup when the marginal cost of production changes. Consider the multiplicative demand function introduced in Chapter 2:

$$Q_x^d = (18.414429)P_x^{-1.5}P_y^{.6}P_z^{-.4}I^2. \tag{5.18}$$

This particular demand function exhibits a *constant price elasticity of demand*. Because the elasticity of demand is constant, the optimal markup on marginal cost will also remain constant as the firm varies sales in response to changes in production costs. A pricing policy of maintaining a constant markup when cost changes is consistent with profit maximization if the demand curve is nonlinear and exhibits constant elasticity. Absent more detailed information about the demand function, it may be rational for the firm to tentatively adopt the assumption of constant elasticity in order to economize on the costs of acquiring more precise information. However, once the firm has learned enough about demand to determine its elasticity characteristics, it should abandon the constant-markup assumption unless it finds that the demand function does in fact reflect constant elasticity.

In general, however, markup pricing rules can lead the manager astray. This is because *the markup pricing concept is based on the implicit (and erroneous!) assumption that cost is the sole determinant of price.* Hence, when faced with a \$5 increase in marginal cost, the Johnson Company attempts to pass all of the cost increase (plus a 200 percent markup) on to consumers in the form of a higher price. Faced with this higher price, consumers rationally reduce their purchases of all-weather coats. And, given the elasticity of demand at the new, higher price, the gain in revenue associated with charging a higher price is more than offset by the revenue lost when fewer units are sold.[10] The basic lesson is that the firm must take *both* demand and cost into account in determining the price that maximizes its profits. This is precisely the purpose of setting marginal revenue equal to marginal cost.

Demand Characteristics and Optimal Markups

When interpreted properly, the optimal markup percentage can be useful in evaluating the firm's pricing policies. In most cases, the manager does not have the luxury of being able to specify the mathematical equations of the demand curves for each of the firm's products. Therefore, he or she cannot know the precise relationships between all possible prices and quantities for every good sold. All successful managers nevertheless have a basic understanding of the sensitivity of sales to price changes, and many firms in fact use standard markup percentages to determine price. The formal relationship between the optimal markup and the elasticity of demand can guide the manager in judging whether the firm's prices are roughly consistent with the objective of profit maximization.

Most firms are multiproduct firms. As a rule, the demand curves for the firm's various products will have different price elasticities at the profit-maximizing level of sales. If that is the case, the firm should use a different markup percentage to determine the price it charges for each product. Other things being the same, the less sensitive any one product's sales are to a given change in price, the larger the markup should

---

10 When price rises to \$75 per coat, sales fall to 125,000 units. Marginal revenue at this level of sales is $MR = \$100 - \$.4(125) = \$50$. Because marginal revenue is greater than marginal cost (\$25) at this point, profits cannot be at a maximum. Profits will rise if the firm reduces price to increase sales because every additional unit sold will add more to total revenue than it will add to total cost.

be. Or, in the language of economics, the less elastic is demand at the profit-maximizing quantity, the greater is the optimal markup on marginal cost. Table 5.1 illustrates the relationships between various markups and their associated demand elasticities when the markups are determined in the manner consistent with profit maximization.

Every elasticity in Table 5.1 is greater than one if the negative sign is ignored. Hence, every elasticity in the table is an example of "elastic" demand. We need only consider elasticities greater than one because a firm will never set price so low that demand becomes inelastic (i.e., the absolute value of the elasticity coefficient is less than one). For example, when the elasticity of demand is –1.5, the optimal markup on marginal cost is 200% as computed in Table 5.1. As demand becomes more elastic (as sales become more sensitive to price changes), the optimal markup percentage falls. When the elasticity of demand is –21, for instance, the optimal markup percentage on marginal cost is only 5%. The conclusion is that price sensitive products should generally have much lower markups than products that are price insensitive.

What types of products have relatively sensitive demands (with an elasticity like –21) and what types of products have relatively insensitive demands (with an elasticity like –1.5)? Keep in mind that Table 5.1 refers to the elasticities of demand for the various products sold by a particular *firm*. Table 5.1 does not refer to the elasticity of the market or industry demand schedule. The aggregate demand for bread in the United States, for example, is undoubtedly quite inelastic. If the average price of bread increases by 10 percent nationwide, the total quantity of bread demanded will, in all probability, not decline by very much. But the demand for bread facing a particular grocery store in Wichita, Kansas, will be much more elastic because consumers in Wichita can easily shift their bread purchases to other stores if price increases at one of them. The degree to which consumers can switch to competing sellers or to competing products in response to a change in price— that is, the availability of substitutes—is one of the primary determinants of the elasticity of demand.[11]

TABLE 5.1   THE OPTIMAL MARKUP PERCENTAGE
AND THE ELASTICITY OF DEMAND

OPTIMAL MARKUP ON MARGINAL COST	PRICE ELASTICITY OF DEMAND
200%	–1.5
100%	–2.0
50%	–3.0
25%	–5.0
10%	–11.0
5%	–21.0

11 See Chapter 2 for a discussion of the determinants of the elasticity of demand.

Consider the product in question to be the services offered by a traditional supermarket versus those of a convenience store. In general, the sales of the convenience store will be less sensitive to price changes than the sales of the supermarket. The convenience store supplies a different product in the sense that it offers consumers the opportunity to buy one or two items in less time than would typically be spent in purchasing the same products in a full-line grocery store with a larger inventory to search through and longer lines at the check-out counter. The markup for products in a convenience store will therefore tend to be higher than the markup on equivalent items in a grocery store. Customers purchase "convenience" by paying the higher prices that correspond to the higher markups.

Now consider the product to be the services offered by two competing grocery stores. These stores can differ on a number of important dimensions, including location, cleanliness, friendliness of employees, variety of products, number of specialty items, freshness of produce, and so on. If, in the minds of consumers, one of the stores has a distinct advantage over the other along one or more of these dimensions, its sales will tend to be less sensitive to price changes than those of its competitor. Markups will tend to be higher in the store offering more of the characteristics consumers value because the elasticity of demand will tend to be lower. Of course, these amenities cannot be supplied costlessly. Managers must determine the profit-maximizing amount of cleanliness, friendliness, variety, and so on.

Now consider the product to be two different goods offered by a single grocery store. Consumers do not "comparison shop" to the same extent on all items. Frequency of purchase has an important impact on the elasticity of demand for different products. In general, consumers are more sensitive to price changes on items they purchase frequently than they are for items they buy infrequently. The markup on milk is typically very small because consumers buy milk quite often and they can therefore readily monitor and respond to price differences among stores. At the other extreme are items like spices. As a rule, spices do not appear on the average shopping list very often. Consumers buy spices much less frequently than most other grocery items and are consequently apt to have less information about price differences across competing grocery stores. Spices will therefore tend to have a relatively low elasticity of demand and a relatively high markup.[12]

As a last example of how demand elasticities and markups differ across products, consider competing brands of the same products offered by a grocery store. In the cereal section, for instance, there will usually be several national brands of cornflakes, a house brand, and, perhaps, an unlabeled "generic" brand. By contrast, there are fewer substitutes available for other types of ready-to-eat cereals that are more distinctive in terms of ingredients, shape, or nutritional value—some highly sugared children's cereals and

---

12 The elasticity of demand varies substantially even within the relatively narrow spice category, however. Markups tend to be much lower on salt, black pepper, and oregano, for example, than they are on more exotic—and less frequently purchased—spices like bay leaves or white pepper.

high-fiber adult cereals fall into this category. Because there are fewer substitutes for these cereals, the elasticity of demand for them will tend to be lower—and the markup higher—than for items like cornflakes for which competition among brands is more intense.

The foregoing examples show that pricing is a complex problem that goes far beyond the application of simple markup pricing rules. However, and perhaps paradoxically, this complexity means that managers who understand the marginal-revenue-equals-marginal-cost rule for determining the profit-maximizing price will be better equipped to tackle pricing decisions than those who fail to take its lessons to heart. Managerial intuition and experience are certainly valuable resources for making pricing decisions that approach the optimal price determined by following the principles of economics. But intuition can only carry the manager so far. A basic understanding of the economic theory of profit-maximizing price setting is essential to firm's long-run survival.

APPLICATION

This application continues the story of the Johnson Company's all-weather coat factory. The anticipated costs of the proposed investment project are now presented in greater detail.

In the planning phase of the project, the company's president spent $150,000 for research and development, $5,000 in legal fees to obtain a patent on the new product, and retained the services of a consulting firm that specializes in advising clients on the production and sale of new product lines. Ms. Johnson paid the consulting firm $20,000 for a report which contains the following projections.

Pre-production Costs:
1. A plant having the capacity to produce 200,000 coats per year requires an initial investment of $3,030,688 for the building and equipment. The plant has an estimated useful life of 12 years.
2. Production workers require a week of pre-production training at a total cost of $12,500.

Production Costs:
1. The cost of the materials required to produce each coat is $10.
2. The plant will also maintain a stock of material in inventory to meet unexpected orders from customers or to compensate for unexpected delivery delays from materials suppliers. For every 10 coats produced, the production manager thinks it advisable to hold enough material in inventory to produce one additional coat.
3. Each coat requires 30 minutes of labor to complete. Production workers earn $8 per hour.
4. The production manager earns a salary of $50,000 per year.

5. Utility costs are expected to increase by $1 for every additional coat produced.

Indirect Costs:

1. The Johnson Company consists of various production facilities and a central office. The central office is responsible for supervisory, accounting, and marketing activities. The accounting department estimates that the annual overhead expenses of the central office currently amount to $3 million. It estimates further that the variable cost of the firm's production facilities is $60 million. Because overhead is, on average, 5 percent of variable cost, the Johnson Company uses this percentage to allocate overhead among its different product lines.

The company plans to produce 200,000 coats per year and sell them for $60. Once the production facility is built, which of the costs listed above are fixed costs and which are variable costs? The firm expects annual revenue of $12,000,000 from the sale of all-weather coats. Given the consulting firm's cost projections, what *economic* profits can the company expect to earn each year?

FIXED COSTS AND VARIABLE COSTS REVISITED

The analysis of the behavior of firms in *Modern Managerial Economics* has stressed the critical role played by marginal cost in profit-maximizing pricing and production decisions. The distinction between fixed costs and variable costs lays the groundwork for determining marginal cost because only variable costs affect marginal cost. Costs that change as output changes are called variable costs. Costs that do not change as output changes are called fixed costs. Marginal cost is the change in variable cost that occurs in response to a change in output.

The cost projections for the Johnson Company's proposed all-weather coat factory are divided into fixed and variable costs in Table 5.2. While most of the process of separating expenses into the fixed and variable cost categories is fairly straightforward, important questions arise about the decision to assign "allocated overhead of 5 percent of total variable cost" to the fixed cost category. Unlike the other components of fixed cost, this cost is not constant but instead depends on and varies with total variable cost. Because total variable cost changes as output changes, the allocated cost figure will also vary with output.

For example, given that average variable cost is $16 in this example (the sum of $10, $1, $4, and $1), total variable cost is $3,200,000 when 200,000 coats are produced. Allocated overhead is 5 percent of total variable cost and is therefore equal to $160,000 at the targeted quantity of output. If the firm

TABLE 5.2 FIXED AND VARIABLE COSTS FOR ALL-WEATHER COATS

FIXED COSTS	VARIABLE COSTS
1. R&D cost of $150,000	1. Materials cost of $10 per coat
2. Patent expenses of $5,000	2. Inventory costs of material at $1 per coat
3. Consulting fee of $20,000	3. Production labor cost of $4 per coat
4. Investment in plant and equipment of $3,030,688	4. Utility expenses of $1 per coat
5. Training cost of $12,500 for production workers	
6. Production manager's salary of $50,000 per year	
7. Allocated overhead of 5 percent of total variable cost	

instead produces 210,000 coats, total variable cost rises to $3,360,000 and allocated overhead will increase to $168,000. Allocated overhead therefore varies as output varies because of the rule used to estimate it. Why is allocated overhead classified as a fixed cost rather than a variable cost?

The answer is that allocated overhead is a fixed cost because it represents the cost of the inputs supplied by the firm's central office. Recall that the central office in this example is responsible for supervisory, accounting, and marketing services. Top-level management determines the marketing policies that will affect the success or failure of the venture. It will set the price, choose the distribution system (discount store, specialty store, or catalog orders), and coordinate the firm's production, inventory, distribution, and sales activities. Because the usage of these managerial inputs will not vary significantly as output varies, they are essentially fixed inputs and the cost of using them is in effect a fixed cost.

The accounting department makes a record of the firm's transactions. Because the effort required to record sales of 210,000 units differs little from the effort required to record sales of 200,000 units, the firm's usage of accounting services will not vary as output varies. Consequently, the cost of accounting services is also appropriately regarded as a fixed cost. Similarly, the costs of advertising and other promotional activities are likely to be constant over a fairly large range of sales. In sum, because the central office's inputs do not tend to change with the volume of sales, central office costs are properly defined as fixed costs. The fact that overhead costs are allocated by a method that causes them to fluctuate with sales reflects the basic difficulty of attributing the costs of the central office's activities to different production facilities and to different product lines.

The basic difficulty is this: If the company's central office supplies services to several operating divisions or to several product lines, then the costs of these services may properly be regarded as **joint costs**. There is *no* theoretically correct way of allocating joint costs.[13] In the example at hand, the firm allocates overhead expenses on the basis of total variable costs. Alternative methods of allocation which use dollar value of sales or physical quantity of output are equally valid. There is no theoretical reason for preferring one method of allocation to another.

This observation points to the difficulty (discussed more fully below) of translating accounting costs into economic costs. As will be seen later, however, it turns out that while overhead expenses and other fixed costs affect the *level* of the firm's profits, they are irrelevant to determining the price-output combination at which those profits are at a maximum. Hence, when the firm allocates overhead expenses across product lines on the basis of total variable costs (or on any other basis, for that matter), the resulting cost figure provides only a "snapshot" of the product line's contribution to company overhead at that particular point in time. The fact that some bases used for calculating a product's contribution to overhead vary with output does not mean literally that overhead is itself a variable cost. It is not.

A second point about the allocation of central office expenses requires emphasis. The method of estimation assumes that central office expenses will increase if the firm decides to build the coat factory. Central office costs will be assumed not to vary as output varies once the coat factory is in place. But they are not assumed to be the same whether the coat factory is built or not. Once the new facility is in operation, management will have another set of decisions to make in addition to those it was making for its existing product lines. The accounting department will work with another set of cost, revenue, and tax figures. The marketing department will be required to develop another advertising campaign. Thus, the central office expense figure in Table 5.2 (see p. 169) is meant to reflect the additional costs associated with the introduction of a new product line. It does not represent a reallocation of pre-existing overhead costs.

ACCOUNTING PROFIT AND ECONOMIC PROFIT

The basic idea of profit is simple enough. Profit is total revenue minus total cost. But the notion of profitability raises a number of difficult conceptual issues. One factor that complicates the analysis of profits is that there is more than one definition of profitability. While accountants generate one measure of profitability from a given set of cost and revenue figures, the economist's assessment of the same set of numbers differs considerably. This section explains the distinction between accounting profit and economic profit.

---

13 For a classic debate on this topic, see the series of articles by Frank W. Taussig and Arthur C. Pigou, "Railway Rates and Joint Costs," *Quarterly Journal of Economics* 27 (February, May, and August 1913), pp. 378-84, 535-38, and 687-94.

The basic definition of profit—total revenue less total cost—must be modified to account for differences in the timing of revenue (cash inflows) and costs (cash outflows). The Johnson Company's all-weather coat factory, for example, is expected to have a useful life of 12 years, but the outlays necessary to build and equip the plant are incurred at the beginning of this period. The "cost" of producing coats in the first year should not include the full cost of the production facility but only a portion of that cost. The portion of cost allocated to the first year (or any other year) should represent the value of plant and equipment "used up" by the production of coats in that year. This is the concept of **depreciation**.

It should be obvious that the actual rate at which a tangible asset like a factory depreciates physically is quite difficult to determine. This example assumes the simplest possible depreciation scheme, namely that the factory is "used up" in equal amounts over its 12-year life so that the simple, straight-line method of depreciation can be applied. That is, the annual cost of producing coats associated with using the plant and equipment is assumed to be $252,557 (= $3,030,688/12). There are, however, a number of other equally valid depreciation rules available. Companies often adopt the rule that offers the most favorable tax treatment.

Because of differences in timing between acquisition and use of physical capital, the appropriate definition of profit in a given year is:

profit in a given year	=	**total revenue** from output produced in that year	minus	only those **costs** generated by production in that year

Accountants and economists agree that this is the proper definition of profits. There is little disagreement about the calculation of total revenue, which is simply the market value of the firm's sales (price times quantity sold). However, accountants and economists calculate costs quite differently.

Accounting Profit

If the Johnson Company produces 200,000 all-weather coats and sells them for $60 each, the accounting cost and profit for the first year of the factory's operation are determined by the calculations shown in Table 5.3.

Accounting conventions require firms to "expense" outlays other than those connected with the purchase of tangible assets in the period they are incurred. Therefore, the R&D, patent, consulting, and training costs will not show up on the firm's balance sheet in the factory's second year of operation. Accounting profit will consequently be higher by the sum of these costs in the second year and beyond. These costs sum to $187,500, so that accounting profits in the second and subsequent years will amount to $8,337,443.

Economic Profit

The economist would make two fundamental adjustments to the accountant's profit calculation. First, investments in physical *and* nonphysical assets

TABLE 5.3 Accounting Costs and Profit for All-Weather Coats

Accounting Total Cost			
			SOURCE
variable cost	=	$3,200,000	$16 times 200,000
			deprec. of physical assets (1/12 of $3,030,688)	$252,557
			+	
			R&D cost	$150,000
			+	
			patent costs	$5,000
			+	
fixed costs	=	$650,057	consulting	$20,000
			+	
			training	$12,500
			+	
			prod. manager's salary	$50,000
			+	
			overhead (5% of variable cost)	$160,000
total cost	=	$3,850,057		

Accounting Profit			
			SOURCE
total revenue	=	$12,000,000	$60 times 200,000
total cost	=	$3,850,057	calculated above
profit		$8,149,943	

would be depreciated. Second, the opportunity cost of the firm's resources would be treated as an implicit cost of production.

Depreciation of Tangible and Intangible Assets. The Johnson Company will spend $3,218,188 before producing one all-weather coat. This figure represents the sum of expenditures on physical capital (the $3,030,688 for plant and equipment) and nonphysical capital (the $187,500 sum of R&D, patent, consulting, and training costs). The company expects all of these expenses to generate a stream of future benefits that will accrue beyond the first year of production. Pre-production training, for example, will provide the factory's workers with skills and knowhow that will increase their productivity in future periods. Similarly, the expense of acquiring a patent will grant the firm an exclusive right to produce its coat for the legal life of the patent (17 years). The company should therefore capitalize and depreciate these costs at a rate that indicates their association with production over time.

Estimating the appropriate usage rate or depreciation rate for physical assets is quite difficult. The task is even more challenging for nonphysical assets. This is because the appropriate depreciation rate depends on the precise time shape of the stream of expected future benefits from each investment. Not only are these benefits uncertain (some of the workers trained initially may quit, for example), but the flow of benefits is likely to differ across different investments. Once again, however, we assume for simplicity that all assets depreciate equally over the 12-year life of the plant. The relevant depreciation cost in year one (and in subsequent years) is therefore one-twelfth of $3,218,188 or $268,182.[14]

Opportunity Cost of Investment. The $3,218,188 pre-production investment can be financed either by setting aside a portion of the profits earned by the firm in previous years (retained earnings), by issuing new stock, or by borrowing the funds. If the firm borrows the capital from outside lenders, the interest payments to these creditors will be an explicit cost that shows up in the accounting cost calculation. Because this cost does not appear in the calculation, we can assume that the firm uses retained earnings to finance the project. Suppose that the company could earn 10 percent on money deposited in a savings account. When $3,218,188 in retained earnings is used to finance the investment in the all-weather coat factory, the company forgoes the opportunity to earn interest on these funds. So this lost opportunity is therefore properly treated as an additional cost of production. At an interest rate of 10 percent, the opportunity cost of the investment is $321,818 per year.

Although we simplify matters here by assuming that the Johnson Company's next best alternative investment opportunity is to deposit funds in a savings account, economic profit calculations will normally include the rates of return generated by other possible available projects. For example, rather than producing and selling all-weather coats, the Johnson Company may be able to use its resources to enter new markets with its existing product line or to produce a number of other products. Both internal and external investment opportunities must be taken into account. The opportunity cost of the all-weather coat project is the value of the foregone opportunity that offers the next highest rate of return.[15]

We can now determine the economic cost of the resources used by the Johnson Company for the production of all-weather coats and judge the project's economic profitability. If the firm sells 200,000 coats at $60 each, its economic cost and profit in the first year of operation will be as shown in Table 5.4.

In order to interpret the $8,000,000 economic profit figure correctly, we must remember that the income that could have been earned in the firm's next best investment opportunity is included in total cost. In this example, it is assumed that the firm could deposit the initial investment of $3,218,188 in a savings account and thereby accrue interest of $321,818. Because this interest is treated as an additional cost of bringing the all-weather coat factory on line, the $8,000,000 economic profit calculation means that the firm will earn

---

14 For simplicity, the effects of the corporate and personal income taxes are ignored. See Chapter 15 for a more thorough discussion of capital budgeting.

15 The calculation of the firm's cost of capital is explained in detail in Chapter 15.

TABLE 5.4 ECONOMIC COST AND PROFIT FOR ALL-WEATHER COATS

Economic Total Cost			
			SOURCE
variable cost	=	$3,200,000	$16 times 200,000
			deprec. of investment (1/12 of $3,218,188) — $268,182
			+
			opportunity cost of investment (10% of $3,218,188) — $321,818
fixed costs	=	$800,000	+
			prod. manager's salary — $50,000
			+
			overhead (5% of variable cost) — $160,000
total cost	=	$4,000,000	

Economic Profit			
			SOURCE
total revenue	=	$12,000,000	$60 times 200,000
total cost	=	$4,000,000	calculated above
profit		$8,000,000	

$8,000,000 more by producing all-weather coats than it would earn by depositing the initial investment in the bank.

In the factory's first year of operation, accounting total cost is $3,850,057 while the economic cost of the resources required to produce the initial batch of 200,000 coats is $4,000,000. The firm's income statement will therefore show an accounting profit of $8,149,943, while its economic profit is $8,000,000. These figures do not necessarily indicate general relationships in the sense that accounting costs may be either higher or lower than the firm's corresponding economic costs. In this example, the accounting cost calculation incorporates factors that bias it both upward and downward from the firm's actual economic cost of production. On the one hand, accounting cost is higher than economic cost because it includes the full cost of intangible assets rather than the depreciated value of these assets. On the other hand, accounting cost is lower than economic cost because it excludes the opportunity cost of the resources used by the firm in financing the investment project.

Book Value versus Market Value. Although not illustrated by the current example, there is a third issue that distinguishes the accounting and economic definitions of cost and profit. The firm carries tangible capital on its accounts at its "book value" or original purchase price. For example, if a firm purchases a $1,000 machine having an expected useful life of ten years, the accounting cost of the machine is $100 in each of those years when the straight-line method of depreciation is used. At the end of the ten years, the machine is fully depreciated and, apart from maintenance or repair expenses,

Advertising, New Product Profit Expectations, and Investments in R&D

One of the fundamental principles of economic theory is that the profit-maximizing behavior of firms in a freely functioning competitive marketplace enhances the welfare of consumers. Disagreements about the applicability of this principle to actual markets often hinge on the interpretation of what constitutes a "competitive" environment. Advertising has often been singled out as a possible anti-competitive byproduct of the pursuit of profits in a market economy. In this regard, advertising is thought by some economists to be wasteful at best, insofar as it promotes "artificial" product differentiation. At worst, these economists argue, advertising is manipulative, thwarting the wants of consumers and fostering market power by creating brand loyalties that make it more difficult for new products and new firms to succeed in attracting customers.

However, other economists view advertising as an essential element of the competitive market process insofar as it serves as a means of communicating information to consumers about available alternatives. Seen in this light, advertising may promote the entry of firms offering new products or encourage the introduction of new products by existing firms. The latter relationship—the link between innovation and advertising—has recently been examined empirically by David Hula.[a]

Hula argues that one potential benefit of advertising is that it can serve as a catalyst for innovation. If advertising increases the likelihood of success of new products, then other things being the same, the firm's investments in the research and development (R&D) activities necessary to bring these new products to fruition will be more profitable. If this is the case, firms should be more willing to invest in R&D. Hence, R&D expenditures will be positively related to the firm's current total advertising spending and to the amount of future advertising it expects to devote to new products. According to Hula, the rationale for this relationship is that

> estimation of the demand for a new product is very imprecise, based largely upon a subjective impression that the new product fulfills a consumer need, perhaps also supported by some preliminary test marketing results. If the firm believes its past advertising is an

intangible capital asset creating consumer loyalty transferable to new products the firm may develop, or that it will have sufficient funding and creativity to advertise the new product effectively once it is developed, the demand for the new product as perceived by the firm will be greater, making the development and introduction of the new product more likely.[b]

In other words, R&D spending should be positively related to a firm's total advertising if either one of two conditions holds. One condition is that past advertising creates brand name capital for the firm that spills over to new products. The other condition is that advertising enhances the expected profitability of new products. Hula tests this hypothesis with the following three-equation regression model:

$$SALES = a_0 + a_1 ADV + a_2 R\&D + a_3 ASSETS + a_4 DUM,$$

$$R\&D = b_0 + b_1 ADV + b_2 DIV + b_3 TECH + b_4 PROFIT + b_5 SALES^2 + b_6 DUM, \text{ and}$$

$$DIV = c_0 + c_1 ADV + c_2 PROFIT + c_3 R\&D.$$

In this model, *SALES* represents the total sales (revenue) of a firm; *ADV* is the firm's expenditures on advertising; and *R&D* is its spending on research and development. *ASSETS* represents the total value of the firm's assets; *DUM* is a producer-consumer goods dummy variable that is set equal to one if the firm sells primarily to producers; *DIV* is an index of firm diversification; *TECH* is an index of technological opportunity; and *PROFIT* is the firm's net after-tax profit. The model was estimated with 1972 data for 191 firms from a wide variety of industries. The results of this estimation are as follows (*t*-ratios in parentheses):

---

a David G. Hula, "Advertising, New Product Profit Expectations, and the Firm's R&D Investment Decisions," *Applied Economics* 20 (1988), pp. 125-42.

b *Ibid*, p. 126.

$$SALES = 284.64 - 2.20ADV + 19.29R\&D$$
$$\quad\quad\quad\quad (-.60) \quad\quad (16.45)$$

$$+ .77ASSETS - 368.54DUM$$
$$(26.02) \quad\quad (-3.09)$$

$$R\&D = 8.56 + .93ADV - 3.30DIV + 11.62TECH$$
$$\quad\quad (2.89) \quad (-1.10) \quad\quad (3.85)$$

$$- .03PROFIT$$
$$(-0.80)$$

$$+ 0.91\text{x}10^{-6}SALES^2 + 17.29DUM$$
$$(9.09) \quad\quad\quad\quad (1.16)$$

$$DIV = 8.58 + .03ADV + .0006PROFIT - .0004R\&D$$
$$\quad\quad (1.07) \quad\quad (1.45) \quad\quad\quad (-0.03)$$

The key result is the coefficient associated with *ADV* in the *R&D* equation. Advertising is a positive and significant determinant of *R&D* spending. This result supports the thesis that advertising plays a positive social role by promoting innovation in the marketplace.

the costs associated with the machine disappear from the firm's accounts even if it continues to be used.

Moreover, events subsequent to the machine's acquisition can affect its value. For example, new technologies and new production methods can render the machine obsolete. Or an increase in the demand for the firm's product can make the machine more valuable. Such capital gains and losses do not appear on the firm's balance sheet, however. The accounting cost of a physical asset is always based on its depreciated original purchase price (which may be zero). Economic cost, by contrast, is based on the asset's *current* market price. In other words, economists "mark to market," writing the cost of physical assets up or down to reflect changes in their market values. The economic cost of production consequently falls when the market value of an asset declines. And the economic cost of production rises when the market value of an asset increases.

The accounting cost of physical capital changes only when the asset is actually sold and the new purchase price becomes the asset's new book value. Economic cost changes whenever market value changes, reflecting the fact that *if* the asset is sold it will now fetch either a higher or lower price, and the opportunity cost of production must change accordingly.

ECONOMIC PROFITS AND BREAK-EVEN ANALYSIS

A firm can judge the profitability of a proposed investment project only by comparing it to the profitability of other investment opportunities. Unlike accounting profitability measures, profit comparisons are built into the calculation of economic profits. An accounting profit of $100,000, for example, does not by itself provide any information about the relative worth of a proposed capital project. However, an economic profit of $100,000 indicates that the project under consideration will generate $100,000 more in profits than the next most profitable investment. As long as economic profit is greater than zero, the proposed investment is more profitable than the next best alternative investment and should therefore be undertaken.

An economic profit equal to zero provides a convenient benchmark for analyzing the profitability of an investment project. When economic profit is greater than zero, the project is more profitable than the next best alternative. When economic profit is less than zero, the project is less profitable than the next best alternative. When economic profit is equal to zero, the project earns the same return as the next best alternative. The implication, of course, is that firms should undertake projects that are expected to generate positive economic profits and reject projects that are expected to generate negative economic profits.[16]

Because economic profit calculations measure a project's relative profitability, it is sometimes useful to determine the quantity of output required for a proposed investment to achieve zero economic profits. In the application developed in this chapter, the Johnson Company will earn an annual economic profit of $8,000,000 if it sells 200,000 coats per year at a price of $60 each. This profit projection is contingent on an accurate forecast of sales at the $60 price. What if 200,000 coats are not sold? After all, even if the sales projection is reasonably accurate given the information available to the consulting firm, an unanticipated change in the economy could invalidate the forecast. Given this uncertainty, management may want to know how sensitive profits will be to alternative levels of sales.

The Assumptions of Linear Break-Even Analysis

The sensitivity of profits to sales can be gauged with a technique known as **break-even analysis**. One type of break-even analysis, called **linear** break-even analysis, assumes that price and average variable cost remain constant across various possible output levels. The economic theories of demand and cost suggest that this assumption is generally inappropriate. If this is the case, then the technique of linear break-even analysis is compromised. However, there are circumstances in which it may be reasonable to assume that price and average variable cost remain constant in the face of short-run variations in output.

Firms do not adjust prices instantly when demand and cost conditions change. Acquiring information is costly and it takes time to incorporate changes in demand or costs into the firm's pricing policy. There is also a direct cost of changing prices. These costs are called **menu costs** because the restaurant business provides a textbook example of the costs associated with changing prices. Restaurants do not raise their prices immediately when all tables are occupied and some customers are forced to wait in line, nor do they cut their prices immediately to fill empty tables when no one is

---

16 Strictly speaking, the set of acceptable capital projects contains all proposed investment opportunities whose expected future cash flows have a positive net present value when discounted at the firm's weighted average cost of capital. The estimation of net cash flows does incorporate the concept of economic profitability, however. See Chapter 15.

waiting. The logic of not changing prices is that the restaurant would incur costs to reprint its menu that would in all likelihood exceed the expected benefits. Moreover, the restaurant's owner recognizes that customers in general prefer to face an uncertain waiting time rather than face an uncertain price.

For reasons such as these, prices are not perfectly flexible in the short run. Because of the costs associated with monitoring market conditions, firms will often rely on short-run adjustments in output rather that simultaneously adjusting both price and output. At least during the short run, it may therefore be reasonable to assume that price will remain the same over some range of output even though holding price constant means that the firm may be operating at a point "off" its demand schedule. The assumption of constant price is only literally true in the case of a price-taker firm that confronts a horizontal demand schedule (see Chapter 8).

The firm may likewise assume that average variable cost is constant across different levels of output if it is not able (i.e., if it is too costly) to acquire the information required to more precisely estimate the average variable cost function. Many firms have access only to crude data that yield highly unreliable estimates of short-run average variable cost. In this case, the assumption of constant average variable cost may be the firm's best guess even though it is known in advance to be wrong.

The preceding comments about the assumptions of constant price and constant average variable cost do not necessarily invalidate the use of linear break-even analysis. They indicate, however, that linear break-even analysis, like most managerial tools, must be approached with a good deal of care. Because its assumptions are in general inappropriate, its results may be misleading, causing managers who rely exclusively on them to make poor business decisions.

Calculating the Break-Even Quantity

Given these limitations, linear break-even analysis begins by asking the question, "For a given price, at what level of output will zero economic profits be achieved?" The distinction between fixed cost and variable cost is critically important in answering this question because only variable costs increase as output increases. But fixed costs also affect a project's break-even quantity. The following paragraphs describe the relationship between fixed cost, variable cost, and the break-even quantity of output.

At the break-even quantity, total revenue equals total economic cost. Because total cost is the sum of fixed cost and variable cost, the break-even quantity occurs at the point where total revenue equals total fixed cost plus total variable cost; that is, where the project's economic profit is zero.

Both total revenue and total variable cost change as output changes. Total revenue is simply price times quantity and total variable cost is average variable cost times quantity.[17] Let P represent price, Q represent quantity, TFC

---

17 To reiterate, linear break-even analysis assumes that price and average variable cost remain constant as the firm varies the quantity of output it produces and sells. Total revenue ($P \times Q$)

represent total fixed cost, and AVC represent average variable cost. The break-even quantity of output occurs at the point where

$$P \times Q = TFC + (AVC \times Q).$$

Let Q_{BE} represent the level of sales at which this equality holds. Moving the quantity terms to the left-hand side,

$$(P \times Q_{BE}) - (AVC \times Q_{BE}) = TFC,$$

and solving for Q_{BE} yields

$$Q_{BE} = \frac{TFC}{P - AVC}.$$

In the all-weather coat example, total fixed cost is $800,000, price is $60, and average variable cost is $16. The break-even level of output for the proposed coat factory is therefore:

$$Q_{BE} = \frac{\$800,000}{\$60 - \$16} = \frac{\$800,000}{\$44},$$

$$= 18,182.$$

Hence, in order for the investment in the coat factory to earn at least as much as the next best alternative investment, which in this case was assumed to be the 10 percent interest rate paid on funds deposited in a savings account, the firm must sell 18,182 coats per year. Only if the firm's annual sales total more than 18,182 coats will the investment generate positive economic profits. Annual sales of fewer than 18,182 coats will incur economic losses.

The Contribution Margin

The difference between price and average variable cost is known as the **contribution margin** (*C-MARGIN*). To see the reasoning underlying this concept, suppose the firm produces one coat and sells it for $60. The direct cost (average variable cost) of producing this coat is $16. When the coat is sold, $16 of the revenue earned is used to cover the direct cost of the coat, leaving $44 toward covering the firm's fixed costs of production. If a second coat, which also has a direct cost of $16, is produced and sold for $60, it too will furnish $44 toward fixed cost. The same relationships hold for each successive coat until

---

and total variable cost (*AVC* x *Q*) consequently vary only because quantity varies and not because either price or average variable cost changes. These assumptions obviously do not hold in general. When the firm faces a downward-sloping demand schedule, it must reduce price to sell more units. Moreover, because production in the short run is always characterized by diminishing marginal returns, all short-run average variable cost curves are either U-shaped or, as in the special case at hand, linear and continuously rising (see Chapter 4).

the firm sells the 18,182nd coat, at which point all fixed costs are covered. Up to this point, each coat contributes $44 toward the payment of fixed costs.

After sales have covered all of the project's fixed costs (the break-even point has been reached), sales begin contributing to profits. When the 18,183rd coat is sold for $60 ($16 of which still goes to cover the direct cost of producing it), the remaining $44 is profit. Each additional coat sold beyond this point will likewise contribute $44 to profits. Hence, the difference between price and average variable cost ($44) is the contribution made by each unit of sales to either covering fixed cost or, once enough coats have been sold to cover fixed costs, to increasing profits.

A break-even chart is a useful way of illustrating the relationships among revenue, cost, and output when price and average variable cost are held constant. Figure 5.5 presents the linear break-even chart for all-weather coats. The total revenue schedule begins at the origin and increases by $60 for every additional coat sold. Total cost is $800,000 initially because fixed costs exist even when there is zero production. The total cost schedule increases by $16 for every additional coat produced because this figure represents the direct cost of producing each coat.

The vertical distance between total revenue and total cost represents economic profit or loss at various levels of output. If the firm produces no output, its loss is equal to total fixed cost ($800,000). When the firm produces its first coat, the loss falls by $44 to $799,956; when the second coat is produced and sold, the loss again falls by the amount of the contribution margin ($44). The firm incurs successively smaller and smaller losses until it sells 18,182 coats. At that point, total revenue is equal to total cost and economic profits are zero. Once sales are sufficient to cover fixed costs, profits begin rising by the amount of the contribution margin ($44) every time another coat is sold. Thus, the 18,183rd coat contributes $44 to economic profits, the 18,184th coat contributes another $44 to economic profits, and so on.

Once the profit-maximizing price and output levels are determined by equating marginal revenue with marginal cost, break-even analysis shows the level of sales at which the firm's economic profits are zero, *assuming that price and average variable cost are constant*. Note that the linear break-even chart in Figure 5.5 does not by itself provide any information about the predicted profit-maximizing quantity of sales. To see this limitation of break-even analysis, consider the following question: What quantity of coats should be produced according to Figure 5.5? The answer is an infinite amount! The difference between total revenue and total cost increases without bound with every unit increase in sales beyond the break-even point.

The linear break-even chart in Figure 5.5 is correctly interpreted as follows: it shows the relationship between economic profits and sales at a predetermined selling price of $60 and a predetermined direct cost of $16. It does not indicate whether $60 is the profit-maximizing price or, for that matter, what quantity of sales can be expected at the $60 price.

Despite its limitations, break-even analysis can, *when properly interpreted*, provide a convenient way of summarizing some of an investment project's properties. The following application demonstrates its usefulness. It shows

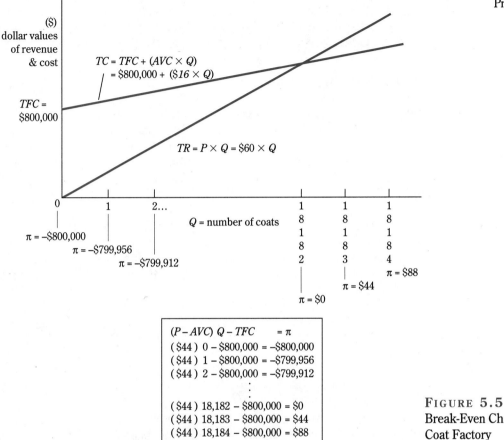

FIGURE 5.5
Break-Even Chart, All-Weather
Coat Factory

how break-even analysis can be a helpful tool for comparing the profit-output characteristics of two different investment projects.

APPLICATION

The theory of production and cost teaches that there is usually more than one way to produce most products. Suppose that the consulting firm retained by the Johnson Company's president provides her with two sets of cost estimates based on two different production technologies for manufacturing all-weather coats. The technology used to generate the cost estimates in the chapter's opening application is a "conventional technology." The consulting firm's second set of cost estimates is based on an alternative, more capital-intensive production technology.

Table 5.5 presents the costs of the two technologies. Assume that the profit-maximizing price is $58 if the robotic technology is used and that the profit-maximizing quantity is 206,896 coats. Apply break-even analysis to compare the output-profit characteristics of the two technologies. Which production technology should the firm adopt?

Profit Analysis for Alternative Technologies

Table 5.4 (see p. 174) summarizes the profitability of producing all-weather coats with the "conventional technology." The firm expects to earn an economic profit of $8,000,000 with this technology. Table 5.5 shows the changes in the firm's costs associated with adoption of the robotic technology. Investment in plant and equipment increases from $3,030,688 to $7,612,500; materials costs fall from $10 to $8 per coat; and production labor costs decline from $4 to $2 per coat.

The essence of the comparisons in Table 5.5 is that fixed costs are higher and variable costs are lower with the robotic technology. Table 5.6 presents the effect of these changes on profitability. Note that total cost, by chance, remains the same. The reduction in variable cost exactly

TABLE 5.5   PROJECTED COSTS OF PRODUCING COATS WITH ALTERNATIVE TECHNOLOGIES

CONVENTIONAL TECHNOLOGY	ROBOTIC TECHNOLOGY
Fixed Costs	Fixed Costs
1. Research and development cost of $150,000	1. no change
2. Patent expenses of $5,000	2. no change
3. Consulting fee of $20,000	3. no change
4. Investment in plant and equipment of $3,030,688	4. Investment in plant and equipment of $7,612,500
5. Training cost of $12,500 for production workers	5. no change
6. Production manager's salary of $50,000 per year	6. no change
7. Allocated overhead of 5 percent of total variable cost	7. no change
Variable Costs	Variable Costs
1. Material cost of $10 per coat	1. Material cost of $8 per coat
2. Inventory of material at a cost of $1 per coat	2. no change
3. Production labor cost of $4 per coat	3. Production labor cost of $2 per coat
4. Utility expense of $1 per coat	4. no change

offsets the increase in fixed cost if robotic technology replaces the conventional technology. Because the profit-maximizing price is lower with robotic technology, the profit-maximizing quantity rises. As a result, the robotic technology's total revenue can be higher, lower, or the same as the total revenue associated with the conventional production technology. In this example, total revenue is $12,000,000 for both production technologies.

Table 5.6 shows that the expected economic profits of the robotic production technology are exactly the same as those of the conventional technology. Based on profit considerations alone, the two investment choices are identical if demand and production costs have been estimated correctly. However, the two technologies are not identical if actual sales either fall short of projected sales or exceed them. Break-even charts can succinctly illustrate the trade-off between variable cost and fixed cost when sales forecasts are uncertain.

Figure 5.6 presents the break-even charts for the two alternative production technologies. By adopting the conventional technology, the firm will break even if it sells 18,182 coats at a price of $60. With robotic technology, the firm needs sales of 34,783 units to break even at the lower profit-maximizing price of $58. If there is uncertainty about the demand for the product, this higher break-even point means that producing all-weather coats with robotic technology exposes the firm to greater risk.

As shown in Figure 5.6, the contribution margin is $44 for the conventional technology and $46 for the robotic technology. Hence, beyond the break-even

TABLE 5.6   ECONOMIC COST AND PROFIT FOR THE PROPOSED ROBOTIC PRODUCTION TECHNOLOGY

ECONOMIC TOTAL COST

SOURCE

variable cost = $2,400,000	$12 times 200,000		
	deprec. of investment (1/12 of $7,800,000)	$650,000	
	+		
	opportunity cost of investment (10% of $7,800,000)	$780,000	
fixed cost = $1,600,000	+		
	prod. manager's salary	$50,000	
	+		
	overhead (5% of variable cost)	$120,000	
total cost = $4,000,000			

ECONOMIC PROFIT

SOURCE

total revenue = $12,000,000	$58 times 206,896	
total cost = $4,000,000	calculated above	
profit	$8,000,000	

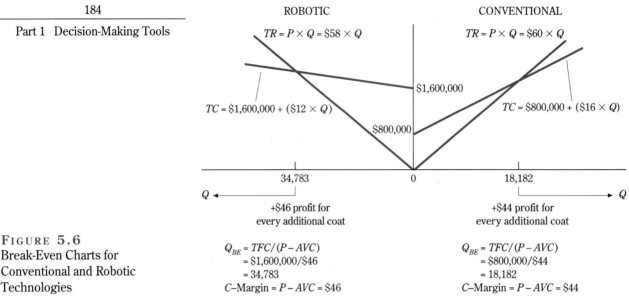

FIGURE 5.6
Break-Even Charts for
Conventional and Robotic
Technologies

points of the two technologies, every additional coat sold increases profits by an extra $2 if the robotic technology is adopted. Although the firm's chances of reaching the break-even level of sales are lower with robotic technology (because the break-even quantity is higher), the profit potential of this technology is higher because its contribution margin is larger. Managers who are relatively unwilling to take chances might therefore choose the conventional technology and those who are more inclined to accept risk might choose the robotic technology.

The relative mix of fixed and variable inputs in the production process is referred to as **operating leverage**. According to Webster's New World Dictionary, the word "leverage" is defined as an "increased means of accomplishing some purpose." A healthy athlete, for example, has more leverage in salary negotiations than does an injured athlete. The term operating leverage has a similar meaning. An increase in operating leverage refers to an increased potential for creating profits. As the previous example illustrates, if a firm chooses a production technology that relies more on fixed inputs and less on variable inputs, it has the potential for earning greater profits after it reaches the break-even level of output. However, the cost of this increased operating leverage is the potential for greater losses if the firm does not reach the break-even level of sales.

Beyond the break-even quantity, an increase in operating leverage means that profits become more sensitive to changes in sales, holding price and average variable cost constant. Consequently, one way to measure operating leverage is to calculate the percentage change in profits relative to the percentage change in sales. Like any other ratio of percentage changes, the percentage change in profits relative to the percentage change in sales is an elasticity which characterizes the responsiveness of the firm's profits to changes in sales. This particular elasticity is called the **degree of operating leverage** (*DOL*) and is defined as

$$DOL = \left(\frac{\Delta\pi}{\pi}\right) \div \left(\frac{\Delta Q}{Q}\right) = \left(\frac{\Delta\pi}{\Delta Q}\right)\left(\frac{Q}{\pi}\right).$$

The degree of operating leverage depends on the relative mix of fixed and variable inputs in the production process. A computational formula for *DOL* can therefore be written in terms of variable cost, fixed cost, and price (variable cost is represented by average variable cost and fixed cost is represented by total fixed cost). This computational formula is

$$DOL = \frac{(P-AVC)Q}{(P-AVC)Q - TFC},$$

where *P* is price, *AVC* is average variable cost, *Q* is sales, and *TFC* is total fixed cost.

If the firm adopts the conventional technology for producing all-weather coats, price is $60, average variable cost is $16, and total fixed cost is $800,000. With robotic technology, on the other hand, price is $58, average variable cost is $12, and total fixed cost is $1,600,000. The value of *DOL* will obviously vary with the level of sales chosen. Therefore we arbitrarily measure the degree of operating leverage for the conventional technology (*DOL$_C$*) and the robotic technology (*DOL$_R$*) at sales of 100,000 and then at sales of 200,000. At sales of 100,000, the operating leverage figures are:

$$DOL_C = \frac{(\$60-\$16)\,100,000}{(\$60-\$16)\,100,000 - \$800,000}$$

$$= \frac{\$4,400,000}{\$4,400,000 - \$800,000}$$

$$= \frac{\$4,400,000}{\$3,600,000} = 1.22,$$

and

$$DOL_R = \frac{(\$58-\$12)\,100,000}{(\$58-\$12)\,100,000 - \$1,600,000}$$

$$= \frac{\$4,600,000}{\$4,600,000 - \$1,600,000}$$

$$= \frac{\$4,600,000}{\$3,000,000} = 1.53.$$

Because it relies more on fixed inputs, robotic production has greater operating leverage for a given level of output than does conventional production. (If we calculate operating leverage at sales of 200,000 units, $DOL_C = 1.1$ and $DOL_R = 1.21$.) Note that the elasticity of profits with respect to changes in sales falls as sales increase for both types of technologies. This is a general characteristic of this measure of operating leverage.

INCREMENTAL PROFIT ANALYSIS

The economist's most basic tool is marginal analysis. Marginal always means "rate of change." It is defined for "small" changes in output. In particular, marginal revenue and marginal cost refer to the changes in total revenue and total cost associated with the last unit of output sold.

On the other hand, for considering a "large change" in a firm's operations, so-called **incremental analysis** applies. Incremental analysis represents a generalization of marginal analysis. Whereas marginal analysis is based on the changes in revenue and cost associated with a one-unit change in output, incremental analysis is based on the changes in revenue and cost associated with alternative courses of action or "lumpy" decisions. The firm uses incremental analysis, for instance, for evaluating the profit implications of introducing a new product, adopting a new production technology, expanding into a new territory, or increasing or decreasing output substantially.

Marginal analysis and incremental analysis share a common methodological principle. In both cases, the only relevant revenues and costs are those that will change because of the managerial choice under consideration. In marginal analysis, the only relevant revenues and costs are those that vary as output varies. In incremental analysis, the only relevant revenues and costs are those that change as the firm evaluates alternative courses of action. Hence, the manager's task is to separate revenues and costs into categories based on whether they are relevant or irrelevant to the decision at hand.

Like marginal analysis, incremental analysis is carried out in terms of the additional earned revenue and the additional incurred costs resulting from a decision to accept or reject a proposed project. Incremental analysis must *not* include the revenues that will be earned or the costs that will be borne regardless of the decision.

In marginal analysis, fixed costs are irrelevant because these costs do not change as output changes. In incremental analysis, irrelevant costs are divided into two categories: committed costs and sunk costs. **Committed costs** are those future obligations that must be met regardless of the firm's alternative courses of action. **Sunk costs** are those costs the firm has already incurred and hence, by definition, are immune to the manager's chosen course of action. Vested employee pension rights provide an example of a committed cost—the firm is obligated to pay retirement benefits independent of the course of action chosen. Previously purchased physical assets such as land, buildings, and equipment, as well as prior investments in brand-name capital, are common examples of sunk costs.

"Dumping," Irrelevant Costs, and the U.S. Semiconductor Industry

One of the paradoxes of government intervention in the marketplace is the belief that consumers sometimes require protection from prices that are "too low." For example, a policy of selling products at prices below "cost" is seen as a strategy that large firms may use to force smaller rivals out of business. Once below-cost prices have accomplished their purpose, the surviving firm forces consumers to accept a higher price than otherwise. This type of pricing is, for obvious reasons, called **predatory pricing**. More formally, predatory pricing occurs when a firm sells at a price below marginal cost with the intent of driving its competitors out of business.[a]

Predatory pricing evokes images of the era of the robber barons in American economic history–of the Rockefellers and Vanderbilts creating huge empires on the collective corpses of slain competitors. However, it is possible to make a strong case that predatory pricing can never be a rational business strategy. In a classic article, John McGee argues that predatory pricing is irrational because the predator's losses will always be greater than any of its victims' losses.[b]

McGee's reasoning is as follows: If all firms are equally efficient, then the predator must set price below its own cost in order to take sales away from its rivals. At the same time, the predator must expand its own output, for otherwise its rivals can continue to sell at the higher, nonpredatory price. Because the predator sells more output at the below-cost price while its rivals sell less output at this price, the predator's losses are greater than the losses of any one of its rivals. Conclusion? Predatory pricing will force the predator out of business before any rival is forced to exit the industry.[c]

Now suppose that the firms are not equally efficient; that is, the predator has lower costs than its rivals. In this case, the firm with lower costs should charge lower prices than its rivals if it behaves competitively. It will consequently be extremely difficult to distinguish (desirable) aggressive competitive behavior from (illegal) predatory behavior. James Miller and Paul Pautler summarize the current thinking about predatory pricing as follows: "If the historical literature is to be believed, cases of successful predation are exceedingly rare. And if the theoretical literature is to be believed, this is no accident."[d]

So-called dumping is the international trade equivalent of predatory pricing. There are currently antidumping laws that prohibit foreign firms from selling products in the United States at prices below their unit costs of production. In 1986, the U.S. Deparment of Commerce and International Trade Commission ruled that Japanese firms were illegally dumping semiconductors in the U.S. market. The charge eventually led to an agreement that regulates the price and quantity of Japanese semiconductors that the United States imports.

If domestic predatory pricing is irrational, should international predatory pricing be any different? In a recent article, Andrew Dick argues that the Japanese semiconductor firms did not engage in predatory behavior even though they in fact sold semiconductors at a price below their current unit costs of production.[e]

---

a Given the difficulty of estimating marginal cost, predatory pricing is often diagnosed in practice from prices below average variable cost. For a more complete discussion of the logic (or illogic!) of predatory pricing, see William F. Shughart II, *The Organization of Industry* (Homewood, IL: Richard D. Irwin, 1990), pp. 295-301.

b John S. McGee, "Predatory Price Cutting: The Standard Oil (N.J.) Case," *Journal of Law and Economics* 1 (October 1958), pp. 137-69.

c A counterargument to this reasoning is that the predator is typically more powerful financially than its prey and can therefore sustain losses more readily by borrowing in the capital market. However, this "deep pockets" theory has been successfully criticized in a number of articles. See, for example, George J. Stigler, "Imperfections in the Capital Market," *Journal of Political Economy* 75 (June 1967), pp. 287-92 and Frank H. Easterbrook, "Predatory Strategies and Counterstrategies," *University of Chicago Law Review* 48 (Spring 1981), pp. 263-337.

d James C. Miller III and Paul A. Pautler, "Predation: The Changing View in Economics and the Law," *Journal of Law and Economics* 28 (May 1985), pp. 495-502.

e Andrew R. Dick, "Learning by Doing and Dumping in the Semiconductor Industry," *Journal of Law and Economics* 34 (April 1991), pp. 133-59.

What the Department of Commerce failed to appreciate is that all *current* costs are not necessarily relevant in determining the firm's profit-maximizing price. This observation is especially valid when production includes "learning-by-doing" effects.[f] Learning-by-doing causes the firm's average and marginal costs of production to decline as the *cumulative* volume of output increases. When this is the case, the relevant marginal cost of production for pricing decisions is not the current cost but is instead the lower future cost implied by learning-by-doing.

There are two reasons for this. First, the firm has an incentive to reduce price below current cost in order to increase current sales and thereby accumulate the cost-reducing production experience sooner. Second, if the buyers of the firm's product know that learning-by-doing is likely to lead to lower costs (and price) in the future, they will rationally defer at least some of their purchases until these cost-savings (and lower prices) materialize. Hence, learning-by-doing is another case in which accounting costs do not accurately reflect the opportunity cost of the resources used in the production process. Accounting costs are biased upward when learning-by-doing is important.

There is evidence that learning-by-doing is a significant factor in the production of semiconductors. If this evidence is accurate, then the Japanese firms, although formally guilty of dumping, were not engaged in predatory pricing. Instead, they simply used the relevant cost of production that incorporated the cost-reducing aspects of learning-by-doing and set price accordingly.[g]

f The importance of learning-by-doing as a source of cost savings is discussed in Chapter 3.
g Dumping in international trade may also represent a form of third-degree price discrimination. Charging a lower price in a foreign market than in the domestic market is profitable if the demand for the firm's product is more elastic in the former than in the latter. See Chapter 6.

To illustrate the use of incremental analysis, suppose that the manager of a fast food restaurant evaluates the profit potential of opening at 6:00 a.m. in order to serve breakfast. The restaurant currently opens at 11:00 a.m. daily and only prepares lunch and dinner.

Only incremental revenues and costs are relevant to this decision. Specifically, the manager must compare the additional revenue expected from selling breakfast with the additional cost of preparing and serving this meal. The incremental cost of serving breakfast, in turn, includes the prices at which suppliers sell breakfast food items, the additional labor expense associated with paying the employees who will cook and serve this meal, additional lighting and other energy costs, and any expenses associated with kitchen remodeling or purchasing additional cooking and storage equipment.

Incremental analysis does not include costs which are independent of the manager's decision. In particular, the indirect costs associated with the restaurant's existing building and equipment are irrelevant. Because these costs will be borne whether or not the manager chooses to open earlier and serve breakfast, they have no impact on the profit potential of this decision. The costs of acquiring the existing building and equipment are sunk. They are therefore of no consequence to the manager's choice. The only relevant costs are the additional expenses of operating and maintaining this capital that are incurred by opening earlier.

The foregoing example illustrates the importance of excluding irrelevant costs in incremental analysis. At the same time, care must be taken to include all relevant opportunity costs in the calculation of incremental costs. For example, suppose that as part of the decision to serve breakfast, the restaurant's manager is considering whether to purchase an additional refrigerator to store orange juice and other perishable breakfast food items. The direct cost of purchasing this refrigerator is a relevant cost if the manager decides to buy it.

On the other hand, if the refrigerator is not acquired, incremental analysis must take into account the expected impact of the decision on the restaurant's lunch and dinner sales. Using existing refrigerator capacity to store orange juice reduces the space available for hamburger patties and other non-breakfast foods, thereby increasing the chances of losing sales later in the day if these items are out of stock. The foregone lunch and dinner sales revenue is, in this case, a relevant cost of the decision to serve breakfast.

Once expected revenues and costs have been categorized as relevant or irrelevant to the decision at hand, the principles of marginal analysis apply. If incremental revenue exceeds incremental cost, the firm's profits will increase if the project is undertaken. The manager should therefore accept the proposal. On the other hand, the manager should reject any proposed course of action for which incremental cost exceeds incremental revenue.

Summary

This chapter covers the basics of short-run and long-run profit analysis. The most fundamental concept in this discussion is the marginal-revenue-equals-marginal-cost rule for determining the firm's profit-maximizing quantity of output. The profit-maximizing price is the maximum price consumers are willing and able to pay for that quantity. This chapter also explains the proper allocation of cost into its fixed and variable components and clarifies the important distinction between accounting profit and economic profit.

This chapter also pointed out the limitations of linear break-even analysis. Break-even analysis, as explained in this chapter, can provide a rough-and-ready method for comparing the benefits and costs of alternative production processes or alternative investment projects that have different fixed cost-variable cost components. We must remember, however, that the assumptions of linear break-even analysis (constant price and constant average variable cost) are in general erroneous. A production process that relies more on fixed inputs than on variable inputs tends to have a greater profit potential at a given price because its contribution margin is higher. However, the chances of failing to achieve this greater profit potential are also greater if sales fall short of projections, because heavy reliance on fixed inputs drives the break-even point higher.

Incremental analysis, the last concept presented in this chapter, is a generalization of marginal analysis. Where marginal analysis is based on unit changes in output, incremental analysis is based on alternative courses of action. Marginal analysis and incremental analysis share a common methodological theme: they include only those revenues and costs that are

KEY TERMS
marginal revenue
marginal cost
direct cost
markup pricing
joint costs
depreciation
break-even analysis
linear break-even analysis
menu costs
contribution margin
operating leverage
degree of operating leverage
incremental analysis
committed costs
sunk costs
predatory pricing

affected by the change in question. These revenues and costs are referred to as marginal revenue and marginal cost and as incremental revenue and incremental cost in the two frameworks.

QUESTIONS

5.1 Should firms apply an "optimal" markup to average total cost to determine the prices they will charge? Why or why not?

5.2 Draw the graph of a profit-maximizing firm facing a downward-sloping demand curve and a long-run average cost curve which is declining continuously. Can you explain why such a firm is known as a "natural monopoly?"

5.3 What is the difference between marginal cost and incremental cost?

5.4 The historical cost of an input, rather than its current cost, is required for computing a firm's taxes and for stockholder reporting. What effect does the use of historical costs have on reported accounting profits in comparison to economic profits?

5.5 Comment on the following statement. Most firms do not calculate marginal revenue or marginal cost. The marginal-revenue-equals-marginal-cost rule is therefore irrelevant to actual business decisions.

5.6 As a general rule, will most of the firm's decisions be made "in the short run" or will most of them be made "in the long run"? How long does it take to get to the long run?

5.7 What are the assumptions used in linear break-even analysis? Comment on how these assumptions affect the usefulness of this technique.

5.8 During the "off-season," hotels located at popular vacation spots typically lower their room rates below the rates they charge during the peak tourist season. But the costs of building the hotel are sunk and, given that a few of the hotel's rooms are already occupied, the cost of serving one more guest is essentially zero. Why don't hotels allow guests to stay without charge during the off-season?

5.9 In the wake of Hurricane Andrew's destructive impact on South Florida, Home Depot, a leading hardware retailer, maintained the price of plywood at its pre-storm level despite a substantial increase in demand. Rather than raising price, Home Depot ordered the managers of its retail outlets to ration plywood by limiting the number of sheets any one customer could buy. Was this policy consistent with profit maximization? Why or why not?

PROBLEMS

5.1 The Cobalt Tool Company manufactures and sells a six-piece screwdriver set. The demand and cost equations for this product are as follows:

$$P = \$60 - \$2Q \text{ and } TC = \$50 + \$5Q + \$.5Q^2,$$

where P is price, TC is total cost, and Q is the quantity of screwdriver sets produced and sold (in thousands).

a. Determine the profit-maximizing price and quantity of screwdriver sets.

b. Determine the elasticity of demand at the profit-maximizing quantity and determine the level of the firm's profits.

c. Calculate the optimal markup on marginal cost.

5.2 Health-Co Incorporated produces a nutrient-rich drink that is often used as a diet supplement for the elderly. The demand and cost equations for this product are as follows:

$$Q = 600,000 - 10,000P \text{ and } TC = \$1,000 + \$2Q + \$.00005Q^2,$$

where P is price, TC is total cost, and Q is the number of 8-ounce cans of the product produced and sold.
   a. Determine the profit-maximizing price and quantity of the product.
   b. Determine the elasticity of demand at the profit-maximizing quantity and determine the level of the firm's profits.
   c. Calculate the optimal markup on marginal cost.

5.3 The Batesville Comfort Company sells window air conditioning units. The demand and cost equations for this product are as follows:

$$P = \$880 - \$.02Q \text{ and } TC = \$1,150,000 + \$80Q + \$.01Q^2,$$

where P is price, TC is total cost, and Q is the quantity of air conditioning units bought and sold.
   a. Determine the profit-maximizing price and quantity of window air conditioners.
   b. Determine the elasticity of demand at the profit-maximizing quantity and determine the level of the firm's profits.
   c. Calculate the optimal markup on marginal cost.

5.4 Dan Connor, Artie Zimmer, and Bob Bruss each earn $22,500 annually as automobile mechanics at a car dealership. They are considering opening a shop that specializes in fast-service oil changes. The projected annual cost of the building and equipment is $60,000. On average, an oil change requires $6 of materials (oil and oil filter). The average price of oil changes is $20 in the shops that currently provide this service. Dan, Artie, and Bob think that they can charge $25 for their oil changes because of the faster service they intend to provide.
   a. What are the accounting and economic cost functions for this oil-changing business?
   b. Based on the shop's economic costs, how many oil changes will each of the workers have to perform each day in order to break even?

5.5 Miracle Products Incorporated has successfully marketed a number of diverse "miracle products." The company's miracle car wax product can supposedly withstand burning; its miracle paint remover, they claim, can take off layers of paint with a single stroke of a rag; and its miracle edged knife set can cut through nails or tin cans. The company is considering production of a miracle juicer that it will sell for $300. The production of each juicer will require $75 in materials and 4 hours of labor. Workers earn $12 per hour in the company's production facility. Additional costs for utilities, management, and insurance are expected to be $23 for every juicer produced. The production equipment necessary for producing juicers costs $1,250,000.
   a. Calculate the break-even level of sales for the miracle juicer.
   b. The company expects to sell 10,000 units. What is the degree of operating leverage at this quantity?

Profit Maximization With The Calculus

In this appendix we use elementary calculus to derive the basic mathematical relationships that underlie the firm's profit-maximizing pricing decisions. The appendix to Chapter 2 provides a brief summary of the rules of differentiation.

All results are in general functional notation. The firm's demand curve (in inverse form) is assumed to be $p = p(Q)$, where p is selling price per unit and Q is the number of units of output produced during some given time period. The demand curve is downward sloping so that $dp/dQ < 0$. The total revenue earned during any period is simply price times quantity, or $p(Q)Q$. Total cost, c, depends positively on the rate of output chosen, that is, $c = c(Q)$, with $dc/dQ > 0$.

Given these assumptions, the firm's decision problem is to select the quantity of sales, Q, that maximizes

$$\pi = p(Q)Q - c(Q),$$

where π is profit (total revenue minus total cost). A necessary condition for a profit maximum is that a "small" change in output have equal effects on revenue and cost. The firm's output choice must therefore satisfy

$$\frac{d\pi}{dQ} = p + Q\left(\frac{dp}{dQ}\right) - \left(\frac{dc}{dQ}\right) = 0,$$

which implies that at the profit maximum

$$p + Q\left(\frac{dp}{dQ}\right) = \left(\frac{dc}{dQ}\right).$$

The left-hand side of this equality is the firm's marginal revenue (MR) schedule—it shows how total revenue changes when sales change. Note that because price and quantity vary inversely along the demand schedule ($dp/dQ < 0$), marginal revenue is less than price. Thus, when the firm reduces price in order to increase its sales, the extra revenue earned by selling more output is more than offset by the lower price now charged on all units sold.[18] The right-hand side of the equality is marginal cost (MC). The firm consequently maximizes profit by selecting the rate of output at which $MR = MC$. This is the basic pricing rule described in the text.

The second-order sufficient condition for profit maximization is that $d^2\pi/dQ^2 < 0$. Taking this derivative yields

$$\frac{d^2\pi}{dQ^2} = 2\left(\frac{dp}{dQ}\right) + Q\left(\frac{d^2p}{dQ^2}\right) - \left(\frac{d^2c}{dQ^2}\right) < 0.$$

The inequality can be rewritten as

$$\left[2\frac{dp}{dQ} + Q\frac{d^2p}{dQ^2}\right] < \frac{d^2c}{dQ^2}.$$

Hence, the marginal cost function must be more steeply sloped than the marginal revenue function at the point where they intersect if profits are to be maximized.

As stated in this chapter, the $MR = MC$ rule can be written in a slightly different form by considering the relationship between marginal revenue and the elasticity of the demand schedule. As has just been seen, $MR = p + Q(dp/dQ)$. Multiplying the second term on the right-hand side by (p/p) and then rearranging this expression for marginal revenue yields

$$MR = p\left[1 + \left(\frac{Q}{p}\right)\left(\frac{dp}{dQ}\right)\right].$$

Recalling that $\eta_p = |-(dQ/dp)(p/Q)|$ is the absolute value of the elasticity of demand, $MR = p[1 - (1/\eta_p)]$. This allows the $MR = MC$ rule to be written as

$$p\left[1 - \left(\frac{1}{\eta_p}\right)\right] = MC,$$

or as

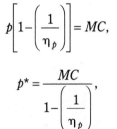

$$p^* = \frac{MC}{1 - \left(\dfrac{1}{\eta_p}\right)},$$

where p^* is the particular price that maximizes the firm's profit.

This expression indicates several characteristics of the profit-maximizing price. First, the firm will never voluntarily operate in the inelastic region of

---

18 If the firm finds it profitable to price discriminate—charge different customers different prices—marginal revenue will not necessarily be less than price. See Chapter 6 for a discussion of price discrimination.

the demand schedule. This conclusion follows from observing that if $\eta_p < 1$, $MR < 0$. In such a circumstance, the firm could increase profit by moving up the demand schedule (reducing sales and raising price) until it reaches the region where demand is elastic ($\eta_p > 1$) and $MR > 0$. Second, $p > MC$ if demand is elastic. Third, the greater is the elasticity of demand, the smaller is the amount by which price exceeds marginal cost.

The last result appears when we consider the optimal markup on marginal cost. In percentage terms, this markup will be $(p - MC)/MC$. To determine this markup, use the expression for the profit-maximizing price above, that is, $p = MC/[1 - (1/\eta_p)]$, subtract MC from both sides, and then divide through by MC and rearrange the right-hand side to obtain

$$\frac{p - MC}{MC} = \frac{-1}{1 - \eta_p},$$

which is the expression for the optimal markup stated in the text. Hence, the greater is the elasticity of demand (the larger is η_p in absolute value), the smaller is the optimal markup on marginal cost.

CHAPTER

6

Price Discrimination: Exploiting Information About Demand

OVERVIEW

The economist's most basic tool is marginal analysis. This simple yet powerful analytical concept focuses on the changes in revenue and cost associated with a given business decision or choice. For example, when the firm establishes a profit-maximizing quantity and thereby determines the price at which its product will be sold to consumers, the only relevant costs are those that change as output changes.

As explained in earlier chapters, in the long run all costs are variable and the long-run profit-maximizing quantity is the one that equates marginal revenue with long-run marginal cost. At this quantity, marginal revenue is also equal to short-run marginal cost for the optimal plant size. Once the production facility is built, only short-run marginal costs are relevant to output and pricing decisions. Fixed costs are irrelevant. Changes in demand or input prices require the firm to reevaluate the profit-maximizing quantity and price by equating marginal revenue with short-run marginal cost. Hence, only *marginal* cost and *marginal* revenue enter into the determination of the profit-maximizing price-quantity combination.

The examples presented thus far focus on a single product having a single profit-maximizing price and level of sales. Although these examples help expose the logic of marginal analysis, they do not do full justice to the tool's broad applicability. Marginal analysis can explain such diverse real-world business practices as offering discount prices to students and senior citizens, selling two items for the price of one, and charging the same price to different customers even though the costs of serving these customers differ. In these and other examples in this chapter, the profit-maximizing firm is able to exploit differences in demand among different groups of customers. This chapter explains how firms can develop profit-enhancing pricing strategies by acquiring more detailed knowledge about the demands for their products.

The first section of the chapter explains the circumstances in which profit considerations dictate discounts to students, senior citizens, children, and other groups of consumers. One of the necessary conditions for this sort of "third-degree price discrimination" to be profitable is that the elasticity of demand for the firm's product differ across different groups of customers. The second section develops the economics of "first-degree price discrimination." Relevant examples are "price skimming," a practice by which the firm introduces a new product at a high price and then gradually reduces the product's selling price over time, and "take-it-or-leave-it" offers. The third section discusses "second-degree price discrimination." The overall theme of the chapter is to show that many real world pricing practices have demand-based explanations that are logical extensions of marginal analysis.

APPLICATION

The Hartford Shoe Company manufactures and sells a full line of men's and women's shoes. One of its best-selling products is a tennis shoe endorsed by a popular U.S. Open champion. The demand schedule for the product is given by the equation,

$$Q = 25,000 - 250P,$$

where Q is the number of pairs of tennis shoes sold per year and P is the price of the tennis shoes. The total cost (fixed plus variable cost) of producing these shoes is

$$TC = \$243,120 + \$20Q.$$

In order to maximize profit, the firm must determine the quantity at which marginal revenue is equal to marginal cost. The marginal revenue function is derived from the total revenue function. Because marginal revenue is the change in total revenue with respect to a change in quantity, the total revenue function must first be expressed in terms of quantity only. Total revenue is then the product of price and quantity. In particular, the inverse demand schedule for the Hartford Company's tennis shoes is

$$P = \$100 - \$.004Q.$$

Total revenue (TR) can now be written in terms of Q as

$$TR = P \times Q = (\$100 - \$.004Q)Q = \$100Q - \$.004Q^2.$$

Marginal revenue (*MR*) is the derivative of total revenue with respect to Q that is;

$$MR = \frac{dTR}{dQ} = \$100 - \$.008Q.$$

The marginal cost function is likewise derived by taking the derivative of total cost with respect to Q. Performing this operation yields

$$MC = \frac{dTC}{dQ} = \$20.$$

At the profit-maximizing level of sales, marginal revenue is equal to marginal cost. Setting these two functions equal to one another (*MR* = *MC*),

$$\$100 - \$.008Q = \$20,$$

and solving for Q yields $Q^* = 10,000$. The profit-maximizing price is then determined by substituting the profit-maximizing quantity, Q^*, into the demand equation. The optimal price is consequently

$$P^* = \$100 - \$.004(10,000) = \$60.$$

At the profit-maximizing price-quantity combination, total revenue is $600,000 (= $60 x 10,000). The total cost of producing 10,000 pairs of tennis shoes is $443,120 (= $243,120 + $20 x 10,000). The Hartford Company's annual economic profit is therefore $156,880 (= $600,000 – $443,120).

After studying the firm's current pricing policy for tennis shoes, the head of the company's marketing department, David Cory, concludes that it must change. He drafts a plan for changing the price of tennis shoes and requests a meeting with Leslie Richardson, the company's president, to explain his plan. Ms. Richardson's initial reaction to the value of this proposal is negative. After all, $60 is "the" profit-maximizing price, isn't it? Why would the firm want to consider changing it? Despite her reservations, the president agrees to meet with Mr. Cory and listen to his idea.

When they meet, Mr. Cory explains that each retail store has a computer for recording transactions. When a clerk makes a sale, the customer supplies his or her name, address, phone number, and occupation. The clerk records the customer information in the computer along with information about the products purchased. The data base is developed so that the advertising department can target these individuals when mailing sales brochures. These records show that students have purchased 3,750 of the 10,000 pairs of tennis shoes sold during the past year. Mr. Cory proposes that the company attempt to increase the number of tennis shoes it sells to students by offering them a discount off the $60 price.

At this point, Ms. Richardson interrupts Mr. Cory's presentation and says, "Look, you obviously don't understand the basic concept of using marginal revenue and marginal cost to set a quantity and price that maximizes profits. Of course we can sell more tennis shoes to students and non-students alike by simply lowering price. The extra sales made at the lower price will increase the firm's revenue, but reducing price on the units that were being sold at the higher price will cause revenue to decline. The net effect on total revenue resulting from the change in sales that accompanies a change in price is called marginal revenue. As long as marginal revenue is greater than the marginal cost of producing tennis shoes, successive price reductions will increase our profits. But once we reach the point at which a price cut causes an increase in revenue that is less than the increase in the cost of producing the product, our profits start going down. We set the current price of $60 precisely because any further price reduction, and consequently any further increase in sales, will cause a decrease in profits."

After waiting a few moments to make sure his boss is finished lecturing him on the basics of product pricing, Mr. Cory continues with his argument. He assures Ms. Richardson that he understands the principles of marginal analysis. However, he reemphasizes the significance of the sales information showing that the company's tennis shoes are purchased by two different groups of customers. Mr. Cory states that this information is important because a number of other items carried by the company's retail outlets are sold almost exclusively to either students or to non-students. For example, the customer data base indicates that casual leather boating shoes are sold almost exclusively to students while dressy wing tips are sold almost exclusively to non-students.

The Hartford Shoe Company contracts with another company to do the actual production of the boating and wing tip shoes. The firm buys the wing tips for $30 and sells them at a price of $97.50, a markup of 225 percent. The firm also buys the boating shoes for $30 but sells them for $82.50, a markup of 175 percent. The two products do not differ significantly in terms of other factors that might affect the profit-maximizing pricing strategy (such as the availability of substitutes in competing stores). Therefore, Mr. Cory concludes that the different markups are related to the characteristics of the customers who purchase these products. If the firm uses different markups in the pricing of two separate items purchased by two separate groups of customers, Mr. Cory believes that this practice should also be followed, when feasible, in the pricing of a single item that is purchased by the same two types of buyers.

Mr. Cory's proposal is to sell the company's tennis shoes to non-students for $65 and to students for $55. These prices are based on the markup percentages applied to the items that are purchased almost exclusively by one of the two groups of customers. Because the marginal cost of producing the tennis shoes is $20, a 225 percent markup for non-students results in a price of $65; a 175 percent markup for students results in a price of $55. This price differential means that students will receive a discount of approximately 15 percent off the list price of $65. A 15 percent student discount is offered by other sellers and seems to be generally accepted by non-student customers. Furthermore, retailers can easily identify student customers by asking them to show their ID cards to qualify for the discount.

Should the Hartford Company institute a 15 percent student discount on tennis shoes? In other words, should the firm price discriminate, selling tennis shoes to different customers at different prices?

THE PROFIT CONSEQUENCES OF PRICE DISCRIMINATION

The Hartford Shoe Company currently sells tennis shoes at a price of $60 per pair to students and non-students alike. At this price, the company sells 10,000 pairs per year and these sales consequently generate $600,000 in total revenue. By assumption, the marginal cost of producing tennis shoes is constant and equal to $20 per unit, so that average variable cost is also constant and equal to $20. Total variable cost is therefore $200,000 (= $20 × 10,000). With fixed costs amounting to $243,120, the total cost of producing 10,000 pairs of tennis shoes is $443,120. The firm therefore earns an economic profit of $156,880 (= $600,000 − $443,120) when it charges all of its customers the same price.

The marketing department reports that students buy 3,750 pairs of tennis shoes; non-students buy the remaining 6,250 pairs. If the firm raises the price for non-students, these customers will buy fewer tennis shoes. If it offers a discount to student customers, it will sell more tennis shoes to them. The overall impact of these price changes on the company's profits depends on the change in sales to each of these two groups.

Sales to Non-Student Customers

The first step in analyzing the profitability of the proposed pricing policy is to estimate the quantity of tennis shoes non-student customers will buy if their price increases from $60 to $65. The problem is illustrated by the following:

$$P_1 = \$60 \qquad Q_1 = 6{,}250$$
$$P_2 = \$65 \qquad Q_2 = \,?.$$

In order to determine Q_2, the firm needs an estimate of the sensitivity of non-student purchases to a $5 price increase. As Chapter 2 explains, the elasticity of demand measures the degree to which sales respond to price changes, holding all other determinants of demand constant. If it is assumed that the profit-maximizing markup applied to wing tip shoes (which are sold almost exclusively to non-students) is a reasonable estimate of the profit-maximizing markup for tennis shoes sold to this same group of customers, the markup percentage can provide an estimate of the elasticity of demand for this group of customers.

Recall that the profit-maximizing markup and the absolute value of the elasticity of demand, η_p, are related to one another in the following way:

$$\text{MARKUP*} = \frac{-1}{1 - \eta_p{}^*}.$$

This equation can be rewritten by moving η_p to the left-hand side:

$$\eta_p{}^* = 1 + \frac{1}{\text{MARKUP*}}.$$

The price of the company's wing tip shoe style is based on a 225 percent markup on marginal cost. The absolute value of the elasticity of demand implied by this markup is consequently

$$\eta_p = 1 + \left(\frac{1}{2.25}\right) = 1 + .4444 = 1.4444.$$

We can now estimate the quantity sales at the proposed $65 price from the elasticity figure of 1.4444. This estimate assumes that the non-student public's demand schedule for tennis shoes is linear. Chapter 2 shows how to calculate the elasticity of demand with the following formula:

$$\eta_p = \left| -\left(\frac{\Delta Q}{\Delta P}\right) \times \left(\frac{P_2}{Q_2}\right) \right|$$
$$= \left| -\frac{(Q_2 - Q_1)}{(P_2 - P_1)} \times \left(\frac{P_2}{Q_2}\right) \right|.$$

For this problem, all values are known except Q_2. Substituting the known values into the equation results in

$$1.4444 = \left| -\frac{(Q_2 - 6{,}250)}{(\$65 - \$60)} \times \left(\frac{\$65}{Q_2} \right) \right|,$$

which when solved for Q_2 yields

$$Q_2 = 5{,}625.$$

What will happen if the profit-maximizing markup on the wing tip shoes sold to non-student customers is used as a guide in determining the sensitivity of those customers to a change in the price of tennis shoes? The company can expect to sell 625 fewer pairs to them if price is increased from \$60 to \$65 per pair. We can now analyze the impact of this reduction in sales on the firm's profits.

When all of the firm's customers are charged the same price of \$60, 6,250 pairs of tennis shoes are sold to the non-student public. If the price for this group of customers increases to \$65, 5,625 pairs will be sold to them. Will this change in the firm's pricing policy be profitable? One way of answering this question is to calculate the total profit contributions at the two prices. We can calculate the total profit contributions by subtracting the total variable cost of producing tennis shoes from the total revenue generated from selling them at the two prices under consideration. The total profit contributions at \$60 and at \$65 are as follows:

Total Profit Contributions: Non-Student Customers

price	$60	$65
total revenue	$60 × 6,250 = $375,000	$65 × 5,625 = $365,625
total variable cost	$20 × 6,250 = $125,000	$20 × 5,625 = $112,500
total profit contribution	$250,000	$253,125

The *total* profit contribution concept here is based on the (per unit) profit contribution *margin* introduced in Chapter 5. That is, when 6,250 pairs of tennis shoes are sold at a price of \$60 per pair, the firm earns \$250,000 over and above its total variable production costs. This \$250,000 first contributes to covering fixed production costs and then, after the break-even point is reached, begins contributing to profits. On the other hand, when 5,625 pairs of tennis shoes are sold at a price of \$65 each, the firm earns \$253,125 net of total variable cost that can allocated in the same way. Although the total profit contributions are not literally "profits," they are representative measures of the "relative profitability" of each price. The total profit contribution increases by \$3,125 when the firm raises the price for a pair of tennis shoes sold to the non-student public from \$60 to \$65.

Notice that the total profit contribution rises in this case even though the firm's total revenue on tennis shoe sales to the non-student public declines. (As Chapter 2 discusses, when demand is elastic a price increase necessarily causes total revenue to fall.) The total profit contribution rises because the reduction in total variable cost associated with producing fewer pairs of tennis shoes is greater than the reduction in total sales revenue at the proposed higher price.

The relationship between the profit contribution margin and the total profit contribution is easy to demonstrate. The profit contribution margin is price minus average variable cost. Because average variable cost is $20, the profit contribution margin is $40 when the firm charges a price of $60. The total profit contribution is simply $40 times 6,250 or $250,000. The profit contribution margin is $45 when the firm charges a price of $65 and the associated total profit contribution is $45 times 5,625 or $253,125.

Sales to Student Customers

The quantity of tennis shoes student customers can be expected to buy if their price decreases to $55 can also be estimated. We can then compare the profitability of sales to this group to the profits earned at the higher, non-discriminatory price of $60.

As before, calculating the expected volume of sales to students at the proposed $55 price is the first step in the analysis. The problem is illustrated by the following:

$$P_1 = \$60 \quad Q_1 = 3,750$$
$$P_2 = \$55 \quad Q_2 = ?.$$

Determining Q_2 again requires an estimate of the sensitivity of the student-customers' purchases to a $5 reduction in price. If the profit-maximizing markup for casual boating shoes (which are sold almost exclusively to students) is a reasonable guide to the profit-maximizing markup for tennis shoes purchased by students, this percentage markup can help estimate the elasticity of demand for this group of customers. The profit-maximizing price of boating shoes is based on a 175 percent markup on marginal cost. As discussed above, the absolute value of the elasticity of demand implied by the optimal markup is

$$\eta_p^* = 1 + \frac{1}{\text{MARKUP} *} = 1 + \frac{1}{1.75}$$
$$= 1 + .5714 = 1.5714.$$

Again assuming that the demand function for tennis shoes is linear, an estimate of the quantity of tennis shoes that students will buy at a price of $55 can be calculated by substituting the known price and quantity values into the formula for the elasticity of demand. Performing this substitution,

$$\eta_p^* = \left| -\frac{(Q_2 - Q_1)}{(P_2 - P_1)} \times \left(\frac{P_2}{Q_2} \right) \right|,$$

$$1.5714 = \left| -\frac{(Q_2 - 3{,}750)}{(\$55 - \$60)} \times \left(\frac{\$55}{Q_2} \right) \right|,$$

and solving for Q_2 yields

$$Q_2 = 4{,}375.$$

As the law of demand dictates, students can be expected to buy more pairs of tennis shoes at the proposed lower price of $55. Offering a discount to them generates 625 additional tennis shoe sales over and above the number sold at the higher, non-discriminatory price.

When tennis shoes are sold at a uniform price of $60, students buy 3,750 pairs. If price falls to $55 for this group of customers, they will buy 4,375 pairs. We can evaluate the profit consequences of this price change by calculating the total profit contributions associated with the two prices. These total profit contributions are shown in the following table:

Total Profit Contributions: Student Customers

price	$60	$55
total revenue	$60 × 3,750 = $225,000	$55 × 4,375 = $240,625
total variable cost	$20 × 3,750 = $75,000	$20 × 4,375 = $87,500
total profit contribution	$150,000	$153,125

Alternatively, we can calculate the total profit contributions directly from the respective profit contribution margins:

profit contribution margin	$40	$35
sales	× 3,750	× 4,375
total profit contribution	$150,000	$153,125

These calculations show that the total profit contribution rises by $3,125 if the firm charges students a price of $55 rather than $60. The total profit contribution on tennis shoes increases in this case for two reasons. First, because demand is elastic over the range of prices considered, offering student-customers a lower price causes total revenue to rise. Second, although the total variable cost of producing tennis shoes also increases, the increase in total variable cost is less than the corresponding increase in sales revenue.

Total Profit With and Without Price Discrimination

The above calculations indicate that if the price of tennis shoes increases to $65 for non-student customers, the total profit contribution will increase by $3,125. At the same time, if the price charged to student customers is reduced to $55, the total profit contribution on sales to this group will, coincidentally, also increase by $3,125. The total profit contribution therefore rises by $6,250 after the discount policy is introduced. Table 6.1 verifies this result, showing the calculation of the firm's profits with and without price discrimination.

The total profit contribution attributable to tennis shoe sales changes when the firm practices price discrimination, because of the impact of this pricing policy on profit contribution margins. The profit contribution margin for sales to both groups of customers is $40 at the initial non-discriminatory price of $60. With price discrimination, the profit contribution margin on sales to the non-student public rises to $45 and the profit contribution margin on sales to students falls to $35. Both of these changes work in the direction of increasing the firm's total profit contribution. On the one hand, while fewer pairs of tennis shoes are sold to non-student customers, this effect is more than offset by the fact that these sales carry a higher profit contribution margin. On the other hand, the lower profit contribution margin on sales to student customers is more than offset by the increase in the quantity sold to this group.

Winners and Losers from Price Discrimination

The Hartford Shoe Company sells 10,000 pairs of tennis shoes when it charges a uniform price of $60 to all customers. Non-student customers buy 6,250 pairs and student customers buy 3,750 pairs. The firm continues to sell

TABLE 6.1 TOTAL PROFITS WITH AND WITHOUT PRICE DISCRIMINATION

	Without Price Discrimination		With Price Discrimination	
	Non-Students	Students	Non-Students	Students
price	$60	$60	$65	$55
sales	6,250	3,750	5,625	4,375
revenue	$375,000	$225,000	$365,625	$240,625
total revenue	$600,000		$606,250	
total variable cost	$200,000		$200,000	
total fixed cost	$243,120		$243,120	
total economic profit	$156,880		$163,130	

10,000 pairs of tennis shoes when it price discriminates.[1] But fewer pairs are sold to non-students, whose price is increased, and more pairs are sold to students, who receive a discount. When the non-student price is raised to $65, their purchases drop to 5,625 pairs; when the student price is reduced to $55, their purchases rise to 4,375 pairs.

The non-student public is obviously made worse off when the firm price discriminates. Before price discrimination, 6,250 non-student customers purchased tennis shoes, paying a price of $60 per pair. When the price charged to them increases to $65, 5,625 non-students pay the extra $5 and the remaining 625 no longer buy this brand of tennis shoes at all. On the other hand, student customers are made better off when the firm price discriminates. Before price discrimination, 3,750 student customers paid $60 per pair of tennis shoes. When the price they are charged decreases to $55, all 3,750 of them enjoy a price that is $5 lower than before. Moreover, 625 student customers who were unwilling or unable to buy tennis shoes for $60 per pair are prompted to make purchases at the new lower price.

Price discrimination thus creates winners and losers among the firm's customer base. Economic theory provides no basis for assessing the overall welfare effects of this pricing policy, at least in the case of linear demands where total sales remain the same with and without a discrimination in price. Because it is not possible to say whether the winners gain more than the losers lose, the net impact of price discrimination on consumer welfare is ambiguous.

THE THEORY OF PRICE DISCRIMINATION

Price discrimination is "the act of selling the same article . . . at different prices to different buyers."[2] Defined in this way, price discrimination is practiced widely by business firms. Movie houses, amusement parks, and many retailers offer special discount prices to children, senior citizens, and military personnel; bars hold "ladies' nights," selling drinks at lower prices to women than to men; academic journals charge much higher subscription rates to libraries than to individual subscribers; long-distance telephone companies charge lower rates on evenings and weekends than during normal business hours; and physicians typically charge higher fees to high-income, insured patients than to low-income, uninsured patients. Many more examples could be added to this list.

---

1 This result is not general and holds only for linear demand schedules. With nonlinear demands, total sales can increase or decrease when price discrimination is introduced. The net impact depends on whether the increase in purchases by customers who pay a lower price is greater or smaller than the reduction in sales to customers who pay a higher price. The technical conditions under which price discrimination leads to an increase or decrease in total sales are described in Joan Robinson, *The Economics of Imperfect Competition*, 2E. (London: Macmillan, 1969). For a summary of the analytical results, see William F. Shughart II, *The Organization of Industry* (Homewood, IL: Richard D. Irwin, 1990), pp. 282-92.

2 Robinson, *Economics of Imperfect Competition*, p. 179.

We must raise a cautionary note at this point, however. Price discrimination is said to exist when the *same* product is sold at different prices to different customers. In other words, price discrimination is practiced when price differences do not reflect differences in cost but are instead purely a function of *demand*. This definition requires not only that the goods sold to consumers at discriminatory prices be physically identical, but also that all other aspects of the transaction be the same across buyers. For example, two identical new automobiles might be sold to different buyers at different prices. Price discrimination occurs under these circumstances only if the optional equipment, credit terms, warranty coverages, waiting times prior to delivery, and all other aspects of the sales transactions are the same for the two buyers. Otherwise, the price difference merely reflects the fact that different goods have been purchased.

It is therefore important to keep in mind throughout the following discussion that the goods sold at different prices are measured in units of constant quality—they are identical in every respect except the price at which they are sold. In other words, letting (P_1, P_2) and (MC_1, MC_2) represent the prices and marginal costs associated with selling a product to two distinct customer groups, price discrimination is practiced when

$$\frac{P_1}{MC_1} \neq \frac{P_2}{MC_2}.$$

That is, when price differences do not reflect cost differences.[3] The theory of price discrimination is composed of three parts: (a) the responses of consumers to price discrimination, (b) the conditions necessary for price discrimination to be profitable, and (c) the rule for determining the profit-maximizing price for each group of customers. Each of these parts of the theory of price discrimination is discussed below.

The Role of Consumer Responses to Price Discrimination

When a firm practices price discrimination, one group of customers pays a higher price for the same product than other customers. Children pay less than adults for watching the same movie at the same time. Restaurants often charge senior citizens less for the same meal than their younger patrons.[4] Grocery stores sell food items at lower prices to coupon clippers than to other customers. Businesses located in towns with relatively large student or military populations commonly offer merchandise at discount prices to these

---

3 Hence, price discrimination also exists when the *same* price is charged to two different groups of customers if the costs of supplying them differ.

4 The fact that restaurants often offer low-priced menus for children is probably not an example of price discrimination, however. The food selection on these menus is often quite limited and the portions are smaller. Hence, the lower meal prices for children in all likelihood reflect lower costs.

groups. Leaded and unleaded gasoline are sold at different prices.[5] Price discrimination is one of the most common pricing practices used by businesses.

Firms price discriminate because it increases their profits. However, as with every other business practice, firms must consider consumers' reactions to the pricing policy prior to implementing it. After all, if customers think that a firm's discount policy is in some sense "unfair," they will simply shift their purchases to other firms that do not price discriminate or they will not purchase the product at all. For example, almost all theaters charge different admission prices to children and adults. If most adults considered this practice unfair, the theater industry would not have as many customers or be as profitable. Hence, the perception of fairness by consumers is an important element in determining the profitability of price discrimination. If price discrimination creates ill-will among potential customers, its potential for increasing the firm's profits will decline.

Price discrimination can draw ill-will from another quarter. The practice of charging different prices to different customers is illegal where the effect of doing so is, in the language of Section 2 of the Clayton Act, to "substantially lessen competition or tend to create a monopoly." Of course, no one would argue that offering discounts to children and senior citizens makes the movie theater or restaurant market less competitive. However, manufacturers and wholesalers who grant lower prices to retail grocery chains who buy in bulk than to small, independent, retail grocers have been found guilty of violating the antitrust laws.[6] Defending oneself against a charge of unlawful price discrimination is "impossible"—the burden is on the seller to prove that any differences in prices charged are justified by differences in the costs of serving various customer groups.[7] The manager is forewarned.

Conditions Necessary for Price Discrimination to be Profitable

In the price discrimination example outlined in the chapter's opening application, non-students are charged $65 for the Hartford Company's tennis shoes because this price reflects a 225 percent markup on the $20 marginal cost of production. Furthermore, students are charged $55 for a pair of tennis shoes, a price generated by applying a 175 percent markup to marginal cost. If the 225 percent markup for non-student customers is the profit-maximizing markup for that group, the non-students' demand for tennis shoes has an

---

5 The production costs of leaded and unleaded gasoline are nearly equal, and the price differential between them at the wholesale level is only about 1 cent per gallon. Yet, the retail price of regular unleaded gasoline is about 10 cents per gallon higher than that of regular leaded gasoline, suggesting that price discrimination is being practiced. See Barry Nalebuff, "Puzzles: Noisy Prisoners, Manhattan Locations, and More," *Journal of Economic Perspectives* 1 (Summer 1987), pp. 190-91.

6 See, for example, *FTC* v. *Morton Salt Co.*, 334 U.S. 37 (1948). The law on price discrimination is discussed in Chapter 18.

7 Robert H. Bork, *The Antitrust Paradox: A Policy at War with Itself* (New York: Basic Books, 1978), p. 399.

Two groups must have diff. η ρ

elasticity of 1.4444 at the $65 price. If the 175 percent markup for student customers is the profit-maximizing markup for that group, the students' demand for tennis shoes has an elasticity of 1.5714 at the $55 price.

As this example illustrates, in order for price discrimination to increase the firm's profits, two (or more) customer groups must have different elasticities of demand. The group of customers with the more elastic demand is, by definition, more sensitive to price changes than the other group. The group that is more sensitive to price changes, namely the student customers, is in turn charged a lower price than the group with the less elastic demand. Students, children, coupon clippers, senior citizens, and military personnel are offered discount prices because firms believe that their purchases are more price sensitive than those of other customers.[8]

In order to practice price discrimination, the firm must be able to identify and separate consumers into groups on the basis of their elasticities of demand at low cost. This is the second condition necessary for practicing profitable price discrimination. Children can, by and large, be identified through simple observation while senior citizens, students, and military personnel usually carry identification cards which verify their status. Discriminating in price in this way is practical because firms typically post prices for the higher-priced, lower-elasticity group and then offer discounts to those customers whose demand is more elastic. It is the customer's responsibility to prove that he or she qualifies for the lower price. This voluntary self-selection system lowers the seller's cost of implementing and policing a price discrimination policy.

Self-selection also operates in the use of cents-off coupons as a method of price discrimination. Retailers print coupons and distribute them through the mail or local newspapers. Although the coupons are available to virtually all potential customers, only those who are the most price sensitive will bother to clip them and take them to the store to be redeemed. In this way, the customers identify themselves as having relatively elastic demands.

The absence of a significant resale market is the third condition necessary before price discrimination can be practiced profitably. If students purchase the Hartford Shoe Company's tennis shoes for $55 and resell them to non-students for $60, the additional profits earned by charging different prices to different customers evaporate. The resale market would probably not be significant in this example because transactions between students and non-students involve a cost. Students would have to search for non-students who just happen to want to buy a pair of tennis shoes of a particular size at a particular time, or the non-student customer would have to find a student willing to earn $5 by making the purchase in his or her behalf.

The cost of preventing the development of a resale market in goods sold at discriminatory prices explains why movie theaters offer children discounts on admissions but not on popcorn. It is easy for the theater's manager to prevent adults from entering on children's tickets. But it would not be so

---

8 The economic determinants of the elasticity of demand are discussed in Chapter 2.

easy to prevent children from buying popcorn at discount prices at the concessions stand and then taking it back for their parents to eat.

In sum, the following three conditions are necessary for price discrimination to be an effective, practical tool for increasing a firm's profits:

1. Consumers can be divided into two or more subgroups that have different elasticities of demand.
2. The firm can readily identify each type of customer.
3. There is not a significant resale market for the good.

The Price Discrimination Rule

The previous chapter shows that the profit-maximizing quantity of a product (and, hence, the firm's profit-maximizing price) occurs at the point where marginal revenue is equal to marginal cost. This same rule applies when firms practice price discrimination. In the tennis shoe example, following the rule means that the marginal revenue from sales to non-student customers should be equal to marginal cost and that the marginal revenue from sales to student customers should also be equal to marginal cost. Moreover, because the firm assumes the marginal cost of producing a pair of tennis shoes to be constant and equal to $20, the marginal revenue from sales to both groups should also be equal to $20 when profits are at a maximum.

Marginal revenue is defined as the change in total revenue that results from a "small" change in sales (and therefore from a small change in price). What is the marginal revenue of selling tennis shoes to non-student customers and to student customers? To answer this question, recall that we have determined the relationships between price and quantity for these two groups as follows:

NON-STUDENTS		STUDENTS	
$P_1 = \$60$	$Q_1 = 6{,}250$	$p_1 = \$60$	$q_1 = 3{,}750$
$P_2 = \$65$	$Q_2 = 5{,}625$	$p_2 = \$55$	$q_2 = 4{,}375$

When the non-student price increases by $5, this group buys 625 fewer pairs of tennis shoes. If the effect of a $1 price change is assumed to be constant over this range (i.e., the demand schedule is assumed to be a straight line), then sales fall by 125 pairs (625 divided by 5) each time price increases by $1. Similarly, when the student price is reduced by $5, sales to this group increase by 625 pairs. If the effect of a $1 price change is again assumed to be constant, then sales increase by 125 pairs each time price decreases by $1. (It is only coincidental that a $1 change in price causes the quantity demanded by both non-students and students to change by the same amount.)

A $1 change in price causes the quantity demanded by both students and non-students to change by 125 pairs of shoes. We can use this observation to generate the price and sales figures necessary to calculate marginal revenue from non-student sales when price is $65 and marginal revenue from student sales when price is $55. Table 6.2 shows these calculations.

We have already determined that non-students will purchase 5,625 pairs of tennis shoes when the price is $65. Because a $1 price change causes sales to change by 125 units, sales at prices of $66 and $64 will be 5,500 and 5,750, respectively. We can then calculate total revenue from sales to non-student customers at the three prices by simply multiplying price times quantity.

Marginal revenue is the change in total revenue divided by the change in sales. When price is reduced from $66 to $65, for example, total revenue increases by $2,625 and sales increase by 125. The marginal revenue associated with reducing price from $66 to $65 is therefore $21 (= $2,625/125). Because marginal revenue ($21) is greater than marginal cost ($20), lowering price from $66 to $65 increases the firm's profits. However, as shown in Table 6.2, if price decreases from $65 to $64, then the marginal revenue from each of the 125 extra shoe sales is only $19. Because marginal revenue from this increase in sales is less than marginal cost, profits would fall if price were lowered below $65.

The marginal revenue figures for student demand are calculated in the same way as the marginal revenue figures for non-student demand. Table 6.2 shows that the marginal revenue associated with reducing price from $56 to $55 is $21, and that the marginal revenue associated with reducing price from $55 to $54 is $19. The $55 student price is therefore profit-maximizing. The $65 price for non-students is profit-maximizing because it too is associated with marginal revenue of $21. This marginal revenue figure is approximately equal to the marginal cost figure of $20; any further discrete reduction in price would reduce the firm's profits because marginal revenue would then be less than marginal cost.

TABLE 6.2 MARGINAL REVENUE FROM NON-STUDENT AND STUDENT SALES AT THEIR PROFIT-MAXIMIZING PRICES

Non-Student Demand and Marginal Revenue			
PRICE (P)	QUANTITY (Q)	TOTAL REVENUE (TR)	MARGINAL REVENUE (MR)
$66	5,500	$363,000	
+ $1 <	> − 125		
$65	5,625	$365,625	$2,625/125 = $21
− $1 <	> + 125		
$64	5,750	$368,000	$2,375/125 = $19
Student Demand and Marginal Revenue			
PRICE (P)	QUANTITY (Q)	TOTAL REVENUE (TR)	MARGINAL REVENUE (MR)
$56	4,250	$238,000	
+ $1 <	> − 125		
$55	4,375	$240,625	$2,625/125 = $21
− $1 <	> + 125		
$54	4,500	$243,000	$2,375/125 = $19

Photocopying, Academic Journal Articles, and the Profitability of Price Discrimination

How many times have you gone to your college or university library and found that all of the copying machines were being used and you had to wait your turn to copy a friend's class notes, an article assigned for class, or a reference for a research paper? Causal empiricism of this sort illustrates the immense impact that the introduction of photocopying machines has had on the users of published materials.

From the users' standpoint, photocopying has been an enormous time-saver. However, publishers of copyrighted material may be injured if widespread photocopying causes a reduction in the sales of their products. As an example, *Consumer Reports* is in the business of selling information about product quality and price across a wide variety of consumer goods. A potential subscriber to *Consumer Reports* may be less inclined to purchase the magazine because of the opportunity of photocopying articles from this publication at the library. In theory at least, copyright laws limit this type of free-riding behavior because they grant to the copyright holder the exclusive right to reproduce their copyrighted materials. But given the widespread availability of photocopying machines, it is costly to limit illegal photocopying. Moreover, "fair use" copying done in support of research, teaching, and news reporting is conditionally exempted from possible infringement of the copyright laws.

Although the substitution of copying for purchasing can reduce the demand for copyrighted material, S. J. Liebowitz has argued recently that photocopying can also increase the value of published material and, by extension, increase its demand and potential profitability.[a] Because the articles published in academic journals are probably more photocopy-intensive than books or general interest magazines, Liebowitz uses the market for professional journals to illustrate the potential impact of photocopying on the profitability of publishing copyrighted material.

Consider two periods for the market for academic journal articles. In the first period, the technology for widespread photocopying does not exist and journals are sold to both institutional buyers (primarily libraries) and to individuals at the same price. Further assume that the demand elasticities of the two groups of customers are similar and that this explains why only one price is charged. If photocopying is introduced in the second period, what happens to the demand for journal subscriptions? The demand on the part of individual subscribers may well fall because individuals can now substitute copying for purchasing. However, the demand by libraries should increase because journal articles become more valuable to the library's customers.

The decrease in demand by individual subscribers and the increase in demand by institutional subscribers mean that the profit-maximizing price will fall for the first group and rise for the second group. If the publisher is able to successfully price discriminate between these two groups, then photocopying can increase the publisher's profits if the demand-raising effect is sufficiently large relative to the demand-lowering effect of photocopying.

Liebowitz's theory is consistent with experience in the market for journal articles. Prior to the introduction of photocopiers in 1959, discriminatory pricing was generally not practiced by the publishers of professional journals, but it had become the dominant form of pricing by the 1980s. The theory also implies a testable relationship between the observed price differential and the intensity of photocopying. Liebowitz uses citations as a proxy for photocopying intensity in testing this relationship. He reasons that journals containing articles cited more often by academic researchers would tend to be photocopied more intensely than journals containing less frequently cited articles. If photocopying intensity is in turn inversely correlated with the researcher's elasticity of demand,

a S. J. Liebowitz, "Copying and Indirect Appropriability: Photocopying of Journals," *Journal of Political Economy* 93 (October 1985), pp. 945-57.

then the publishers of more frequently cited journals should charge relatively higher prices to their institutional subscribers.

Based on data for 80 economics journals, Liebowitz estimates a simple regression model of the library-individual subscription price differential. The results are as follows (t-ratios in parentheses):

$$\frac{P_{lib}}{P_{ind}} = 1.38 + .0071CITES + .578PUB - .160AGE$$
$$(2.14) \qquad (3.36) \qquad (1.01)$$

The dependent variable, P_{lib}/P_{ind}, is the ratio of the subscription prices charged to libraries and to individuals by the journal's publisher. The independent variables are defined as follows: *CITES* is the number of citations per page received by a journal, *PUB* is a dummy variable that is equal to one if the journal had its price determined by a commercial publishing firm rather than by a not-for-profit professional organization, and *AGE* is a dummy variable equal to one if the journal was in existence prior to the introduction of photocopying machines in 1959. The positive relationship between the subscription price differential and citations per page supports Liebowitz's theory that photocopying promotes profit-maximizing price discrimination in the market for academic journals.

To summarize, when a firm charges different prices to two (or more) groups of customers, the profit-maximizing price for each group is the price at which marginal revenue is equal to marginal cost. In an example with discrete changes in prices and sales, the firm's objective is to select the quantity at which marginal revenue is as close to marginal cost as possible, provided that marginal revenue is greater than marginal cost.

PRICE DISCRIMINATION OF THE THIRD DEGREE

The Hartford Company's student discount policy is an example of **third-degree price discrimination**. As the previous discussion indicates, price discrimination of the third degree involves separating customers into two or more subgroups based on differences in their elasticities of demand, charging a higher price to the group whose demand is less elastic.

This section investigates third-degree price discrimination in more detail. Subsequent sections address first- and second-degree price discrimination.

Third-Degree Price Discrimination: A Mathematical Treatment

The profit-maximizing prices for tennis shoes sold to non-students and to students were determined initially by applying the optimal percentage markups for two other products that the firm sells exclusively to each of these customer groups. Enough information is now available to construct the equations for both groups' demands for tennis shoes. The quantity demanded by the non-student public is represented by Q_d^N and the quantity demanded by students is represented by Q_d^S.

Non-Student Customers. Letting P^N denote the price at which tennis shoes are sold to non-students, the demand function for this customer group is:

$$Q_d^N = 13{,}750 - 125P^N.$$

The slope of the demand schedule is –125 because the quantity of tennis shoes non-students are willing and able to buy changes by 125 pairs each time price changes by $1. The first term in the demand equation—its intercept—is 13,750. This is the quantity of tennis shoes the firm would "sell" to non-students if it charged a zero price.[9]

Once the demand function is known, we can derive the marginal revenue function from it. The profit-maximizing quantity of tennis shoes is then determined by equating marginal revenue and marginal cost. In particular, the inverse demand function is

$$P^N = \$110 - \$.008Q_d^N.$$

Total revenue (*TR*) is simply price times quantity, or

$$
\begin{aligned}
TR = P^N \times Q_d^N &= (\$110 - \$.008Q_d^N) \times Q_d^N \\
&= \$110Q_d^N - \$.008(Q_d^N)^2.
\end{aligned}
$$

Marginal revenue (*MR*) is the derivative of total revenue with respect to quantity. Taking this derivative yields

$$MR = \frac{dTR}{dQ_d^N} = \$110 - \$.016Q_d^N.$$

Marginal cost is assumed to be constant and equal to $20 per unit. We find the profit-maximizing quantity by determining the quantity at which marginal revenue is equal to marginal cost. Setting *MR* = *MC* (ignoring the subscript),

$$\$110 - \$.016Q^N = \$20,$$

and solving for Q^N yields

$$Q^{N*} = \frac{\$90}{\$.016} = 5{,}625.$$

Finally, we find the profit-maximizing price by substituting the profit-maximizing quantity, Q^{N*}, into the non-students' demand equation. The optimal price for non-students is consequently

---

9 The intercept can be determined by noting that non-students purchase 6,250 pairs of tennis shoes at a price of $60 per pair. Substituting this information into the general equation for a linear demand schedule, $Q_d^N = a - bP^N$, yields 6,250 = a – 125(60). The intercept, a, is consequently equal to a = 6,250 + 7,500 = 13,750.

$$P^{N*} = \$110 - \$.008(5,625) = \$110 - \$45 = \$65.$$

Student Customers. The equation for student demand is

$$Q_d^S = 11,250 - 125P^S.$$

Following the steps outlined above, if the firm produces 4,375 pairs of tennis shoes and sells them at a unit price of $55, it will maximize its profits on sales to this group of customers.

Third-Degree Price Discrimination: A Graphical Treatment

The theory of price discrimination can be usefully summarized graphically. There are two important elements to the theory. First, after identifying and separating consumers into two or more groups that have different elasticities of demand for the product in question, profit-maximizing price discrimination consists of selecting the quantities of output to be sold to each customer group in such a way that marginal revenue equals marginal cost across all submarkets. With two distinct customer groups, for example, the profit-maximizing rule involves setting

$$MR_1 = MR_2 = MC.$$

MR_1 and MR_2 are the marginal revenues associated with sales to each of the two groups and MC is the common marginal cost of selling in the two submarkets.

The intuition here is quite simple. Suppose that this equality does not hold; that is, suppose that $MR_1 < MC$ while $MR_2 > MC$. The firm's total profits can then be increased by shifting sales away from the first market (where the last unit sold has added more to total costs than it has to total revenue) so that more output can be sold in the second market where additional sales will add more to total revenue than to total cost.

We can show a second element of the theory of price discrimination by writing the profit-maximizing rule in elasticity form. Recalling that $MR = P[1 - (1/\eta_p)]$,[10] the rule for setting marginal revenue equal to marginal cost across two distinct customer groups can be rewritten as

$$P_1\left[1-\left(\frac{1}{\eta_1}\right)\right] = P_2\left[1-\left(\frac{1}{\eta_2}\right)\right] = MC,$$

where P_1 and P_2 are the selling prices in each submarket and η_1 and η_2 are the absolute values of the respective demand elasticities of the two groups of customers.

Two important implications follow from this expression for profit-maximizing price discrimination. First, if the demand elasticities in the two submarkets

---

10 This relationship is derived in Chapter 2.

are the same (i.e, if $\eta_1 = \eta_2$), then the same price will be charged in both submarkets. Hence, price discrimination is possible only if distinct customer groups have different sensitivities to price. Second, given that marginal revenue is positive only in the region of the demand schedule where demand is elastic (η is greater than 1 in absolute value), profits will be at a maximum when a higher price is charged in the submarket where demand is relatively inelastic. That is, $P_1 > P_2$ if $\eta_1 < \eta_2$, and vice-versa.

Figure 6.1 summarizes these ideas. The graphs are based on the following equations, which describe the revenue and cost conditions in each of the two distinct submarkets for tennis shoes:

	Non-Students	Students
inverse demand function	$P^N = \$110 - \$.008Q_d^N$	$P^S = \$90 - \$.008Q_d^S$
marginal revenue function	$MR = \$110 - \$.016Q_d^N$	$MR = \$90 - \$.016Q_d^S$
marginal cost function	$MC = \$20$	$MC = \$20$

Panel c of the figure shows the market demand for tennis shoes which is derived by summing horizontally the demands of non-students (panel a) and students (panel b). The market demand schedule has a "kink" in it at $90 because at prices above that level, only non-students are willing and able to purchase tennis shoes. The quantity of tennis shoes that will be sold at any price below $90 is simply the number demanded by non-students plus the number demanded by students.

The profit-maximizing quantity of tennis shoes is determined in panel c by equating marginal revenue with marginal cost. This exercise yields optimal sales of 10,000 pairs of shoes and an optimal price of $60 per pair. If the firm charges the same price to all of its customers, its total profit contribution is $400,000—a $40 profit contribution per pair times 10,000.

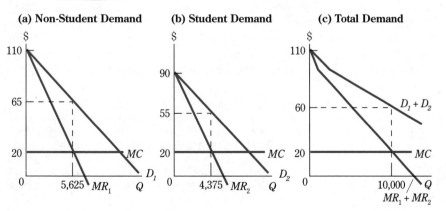

(a) Non-Student Demand   (b) Student Demand   (c) Total Demand

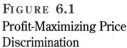

FIGURE 6.1
Profit-Maximizing Price Discrimination

Opening New Markets by Price Discriminating

In 1973, E. I. du Pont de Nemours was granted a patent for a superstrength synthetic fiber called Kevlar®.[a] Kevlar®'s strength characteristic—it has a strength-to-weight ratio five times greater than steel—makes it an obvious choice for products such as tire belts and bullet-resistant vests. After Kevlar® was patented, du Pont invested heavily in developing new applications for the product. After several years of research the company found that pulped Kevlar® could be used in friction/sealer products. The synthetic fiber now appears in such diverse applications as undersea cables, aircraft components, and missile casings, in addition to the aforementioned products.

Du Pont's pricing policy played a major role in opening new markets for Kevlar®. Prior to Kevlar®'s development, asbestos was the principal material used in friction products and gaskets. In order to successfully compete with asbestos, du Pont sold Kevlar® to the friction/sealer market at a price lower than the price it charged to other buyers. A similar policy was adopted when du Pont, again after years of research and development expenditure, successfully applied Kevlar® as a tire-belting material. In this case, Kevlar® competed with low-cost substitutes such as steel and fiberglass and du Pont again adjusted its price downward for this particular market.

One of du Pont's rivals filed a suit in which it charged that du Pont's policy of price discrimination was an abuse of the protection afforded by its patent on Kevlar® and was, in addition, a violation of the antitrust laws prohibiting price discrimination. Patents are conventionally viewed as a method of encouraging the research and development expenditures necessary for successful innovation. For society, the granting of patent rights involves a tradeoff between the welfare loss associated with monopoly power and the welfare gains associated with lower costs and/or higher quality products.[b] In weighing this tradeoff, the U.S. courts have limited the manner in which patent holders may exploit their position. Price discrimination has repeatedly been challenged on the grounds that it is an abuse of the monopoly privileges granted to a patentee.

Jerry Hausman and Jeffrey MacKie-Mason have defended price discrimination associated with successful innovations that are protected from competition by a patent. In particular, price discrimination can allow a firm access to markets that it could not otherwise penetrate if forced to use a uniform pricing policy. By opening up new markets, price discrimination can result in an expansion of output, thereby helping to offset a patent's social cost that comes from granting monopoly power. Du Pont's Kevlar® is a case in point. Its successful penetration of the markets for friction/sealer material and tire-belting material depended on setting prices that reflected the substitutability of competing products in these markets. Recall that du Pont invested in the technology necessary for entry into these markets *after* the original patent was granted. There would have been fewer incentives for investments of this sort if price discrimination could not have been practiced.

Hausman and MacKie-Mason also argue that penetrating new markets by price discriminating allows firms to achieve the cost savings associated with scale economies and learning-by-doing. In the case at hand, Hausman and MacKie-Mason report that learning-by-doing caused unit costs to fall by 60 percent with each doubling of cumulative output during the first ten years of Kevlar®'s production. They also reported that du Pont successively built larger, lower-cost plants for producing Kevlar® as the new markets were developed. At least in the case of this product, price discrimination appears to have benefited society by allowing du Pont to increase production and to achieve lower costs from learning-by-doing and scale economies.

a The material for this case study is taken from Jerry A. Hausman and Jeffrey K. Mackie-Mason, "Price Discrimination and Patent Policy," *Rand Journal of Economics* 19 (Summer 1988), pp. 253-65.

b From society's viewpoint, the optimal patent life ends at the point where the marginal benefit of a patent is equal to its marginal cost. This model is developed in W. D. Nordhaus, *Invention, Growth, and Welfare: A Theoretical Treatment of Technological Change* (Cambridge, MA: MIT Press, 1972).

Now turn to panels *a* and *b*, which show the profit-maximizing prices and quantities in the two distinct submarkets for tennis shoes. Setting marginal cost equal to marginal revenue in the non-student market yields an optimal quantity of 5,625 shoes and an optimal price of $65 per pair. Raising price in the market where demand is relatively inelastic generates a profit contribution of $253,125 (a $45 profit contribution per pair times 5,635 pairs).[11] Similarly, the marginal-cost-equals-marginal-revenue rule dictates that the firm sell 4,375 pairs of tennis shoes to students at a price of $55 per pair. Doing so yields a profit contribution of $153,125 on sales to that group of customers. In total, then, the firm earns a profit contribution of $406,250—an increase of $6,250 over and above the profit contribution earned with a single-price policy—by exploiting differences in consumers' sensitivities to price.

PRICE DISCRIMINATION OF THE FIRST DEGREE

Many business practices seem inconsistent with the marginal-revenue-equals-marginal-cost pricing rule at first blush. Previous sections of this chapter show that the widely used strategy of charging two (or more) different prices for the same product to two (or more) different groups of customers is a logical extension of marginal-cost pricing, rather than an exception to the rule. The profit-maximizing price for one group of customers is lower than the profit-maximizing price for the other customer group simply because the first group's demand is more elastic. Price discrimination of the third degree exploits this difference.

Price discrimination of the first degree extends the marginal-revenue-equals-marginal-cost rule to its logical extreme. The term **first-degree price discrimination** means that the firm has enough information about the demand for its product so that it can sell each unit of output at a different price. The price charged for each unit is the maximum amount the consumer is willing and able to pay for that unit.

The informational requirements of first-degree price discrimination would seem to limit its usefulness. But there are real-world examples that approximate this scheme, such as the pricing policies of colleges and universities. Students who apply for financial aid must supply their schools with detailed information about family income, assets, and liabilities. The poorest applicants receive the largest need-based scholarship awards and therefore pay the lowest net prices (tuition and fees less financial aid) for their educations. Applicants from wealthier families receive little or no financial aid and consequently pay substantially higher net prices for their college educations.

---

11 Comparing any two linear demand schedules, the elasticity of demand is smaller in absolute value (demand is less elastic) at every price on the demand curve that intersects the vertical (price) axis farther away from the origin. By inspection, then, demand is less elastic in the non-student market than in the student market.

Financial aid awards are typically so finely scaled that nearly every student pays a different price for the same good. Importantly, the existence of price discrimination in the pricing of college admissions has nothing to do with the social consciousness or sense of fairness of college administrators. The practice of charging different prices to different customers based on differences in their willingness and ability to pay is simply a matter of rational, profit-maximizing behavior in a setting where customers are economically separable and a resale market is unlikely to emerge.

Two other examples of first-degree price discrimination are discussed in more detail below. One of these examples is "price skimming," a strategy for charging consumers different prices for the same good based on differences in the timing of their purchases. The other example is an "all-or-none" offer which requires the consumer to purchase multiple units of a good or nothing at all.

"Price Skimming"

The practice of **price skimming** is one example of price discrimination of the first degree. It is a pricing strategy often used when a new product is introduced to the market. Price skimming takes advantage of the fact that some consumers are willing and able to pay higher prices than others. The firm introduces the product at a relatively high price and then successively reduces the price over time, thereby "skimming the cream" off the demand schedule.[12]

Estimating the demand schedule for the new product is the first and most critical step in implementing a price skimming strategy. The firm must forecast sales at various possible prices for a product that has not yet been sold. It must take account of the impact of the new product's introduction on sales of its own existing products as well as those products sold by other firms with which the new product is likely to compete.

The firm then divides prospective customers into groups along the new product's estimated demand schedule. These customer groups are defined by the maximum prices they are willing to pay for the new product. The firm first sells to the group of customers willing to pay the highest price for the new product. It then reduces price and sells to the group of customers willing to pay the next highest price; and so on.

Although the price-skimming strategy has obvious similarities to the earlier example of discriminating in price between student customers and non-student customers, there is also a noticeable difference. With a price-skimming strategy, there is potentially an infinite number of prices that, charged sequentially, will maximize the firm's profits over time. The seller must consequently make judgments concerning the initial price when the product is introduced and the schedule of price reductions that will follow. Because of

---

12 Alternative pricing strategies for new products are discussed more fully in Chapter 9.

the complex nature of these judgments, gaining insights into the practice of price skimming requires a theoretical treatment of the pricing policy.

Panels *a* and *b* of Figure 6.2 illustrate the potential profitability of first-degree price discrimination. These graphs are based on the equations that represent the revenue and costs for the Hartford Shoe Company's tennis shoes. Panel *a* shows the single price and output that result from equating marginal revenue with marginal cost. As discussed previously, we can estimate the "profitability" of each unit of sales by its "profit contribution." At a unit price of $60 and an average variable cost of $20, the total profit contribution of the 10,000 pairs of tennis shoes sold is $400,000. This total profit contribution is represented by the area of the rectangle *ABCD* in panel *a*.

Panel *b* illustrates first-degree price discrimination. This graph includes no separate marginal revenue curve because *price equals marginal revenue* when each unit of output is sold at the maximum price consumers are willing and able to pay for it. Because the demand curve represents the relationship between quantity demanded and price, it also represents marginal revenue in panel *b*.

In other words, the firm begins at the demand schedule's vertical intercept. It introduces its product at a price slightly below $100 per pair. Suppose that the Hartford Company charges an introductory price of $95 per pair. At that price, it can expect to sell $Q = 25{,}000 - 250P = 25{,}000 - 250(95) = 1{,}250$ pairs of tennis shoes. Total revenue increases by $118,750 (= $95 × 1,250) and so marginal revenue is $95 (= $118,750/1,250). The firm then reduces the price of tennis shoes to, say, $90 per pair and sells an additional 1,250 pairs. Total revenue increases by $112,500 (= $90 × 1,250); marginal revenue declines to $90 (= $112,500/1,250) on sales to this group of customers. And so on.

As usual, the firm maximizes profits by producing at the point where marginal revenue is equal to marginal cost. This equality holds at point *F* in panel *b*. The practice of first-degree price discrimination in panel *b* is consequently more profitable than the single price solution in panel *a*. When the firm sells each unit of output at its maximum demand price, the total profit contribution is equal to the area of the triangle underneath the demand curve above marginal cost, or area *EFG* (= $800,000) in panel *b*.

The graphs in Figure 6.2 show that quantity increases from 10,000 units in the single-price case to 20,000 units in the case of first-degree (or "perfect") price discrimination. It would be a mistake, however, to make a direct comparison between the $60 price in panel *a* and the $20 "price" in panel *b*. Because each unit of output sells at a successively lower price along the demand curve in panel *b*, a price of $20 is charged only on the 20,000th unit. In other words, $20 simply marks the point at which additional sales are no longer profitable.

This chapter earlier shows how to derive the single profit-maximizing price and quantity in panel *a* from the demand and cost equations. We can also derive the profit-maximizing quantity for perfect price discrimination from these equations. Table 6.3 displays the relevant calculations. In comparing the two pricing policies, notice that solving for the profit-maximizing quantity in the case of first-degree price discrimination simply involves using the inverse demand function as the marginal revenue function.

(a) A Single Profit-Maximizing Price

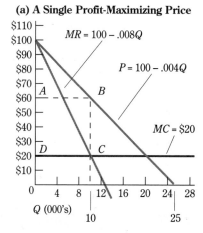

(b) First-Degree Price Discrimination

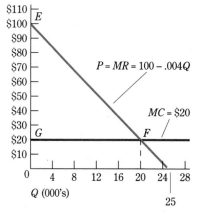

FIGURE 6.2

The Cases of a Single-Price Policy and First-Degree Price Discrimination

TABLE 6.3   A COMPARISON BETWEEN A SINGLE-PRICE POLICY AND FIRST-DEGREE PRICE DISCRIMINATION

	SINGLE-PRICE POLICY	FIRST-DEGREE PRICE DISCRIMINATION
demand	$Q = \$25,000 - \$250P$	$Q = \$25,000 - \$250P$
inverse demand	$P = \$100 - \$.004Q$	$P = \$100 - \$.004Q$
marginal revenue	$MR = \$100 - \$.008Q$	$MR = \$100 - \$.004Q$
marginal cost	$MC = \$20$	$MC = \$20$
MR = MC yields	$Q^* = 10,000$	$Q^* = 20,000$
optimal price	$P^* = \$60$	$P^* = \$20$ on the last unit sold

The practice of first-degree price discrimination presupposes that the seller possesses a great deal of information about the demand for its product and can therefore institute a policy of charging a different price for each unit of output produced. It is unlikely that any firm will find it economical to acquire such detailed information about demand that it will be able to capture the entire profit contribution area of *EFG* in the graph shown in panel *b* of Figure 6.2. Rather, it is more plausible to think that a firm could identify a discrete set of profitable prices such as those used to analyze the Hartford Company's price-skimming strategy. In such cases, the firm separates customers into groups on the basis of their maximum demand prices and all customers within each group pay the same price. This variant of the price-discrimination model—price discrimination of the second degree—will be discussed more fully later.

The seller is not the only beneficiary of first-degree price discrimination. As Figure 6.2 clearly shows, perfect price discrimination results in the production of a greater quantity of output than would be produced with a policy of charging the same price to all customers. Hence, while some consumers pay higher prices than they would under a single-price policy, first-degree price discrimination results in the production and sale of additional units of output that the firm would not produce and sell otherwise.

A caveat is necessary at this point, however. The optimal price-skimming rule assumes that the firm's prospective customers do not "learn" its pricing strategy and, moreover, that they do no react negatively to it. If, on the one hand, buyers who pay higher prices become disappointed when they observe the same product later being sold to others at lower prices, the ill-will created may diminish the firm's profits on future sales or on other product lines as customers shift their purchases to competitors who do not engage in price skimming. On the other hand, if prospective customers expect selling prices to decrease over time, they may defer their purchases to future periods. Either one of these customer reactions can cause the pricing strategy to unravel, with the result that the profits associated with price skimming are less than the profits earned by charging a single profit-maximizing price on all units sold.

"All-or-None" Offers

An alternative and perhaps more widely used pricing strategy by which a seller can approximate price discrimination of the first degree is to require consumers to purchase multiple units of a product at a stated price per unit or buy nothing at all. This pricing strategy is known as an **all-or-none offer** and is illustrated in Figure 6.3. This figure reproduces the demand schedule in panel *b* of Figure 6.2, except that to make the example more realistic, all prices are divided by 100 and all quantities are divided by 1,000.

As conventionally drawn, the demand schedule assumes that buyers are free to purchase either the indicated quantity or any smaller quantity at the posted selling price.[13] In Figure 6.3, for example, if the market price is $.20 per unit, consumers have the option of purchasing any number of units they wish at that price up to and including 20 units. A different demand schedule must be drawn if buyers have only the choice of either purchasing 20 units of the product or nothing at all. This all-or-none demand curve lies to the right of the ordinary demand curve. It is constructed as follows.

The seller first determines the profit-maximizing quantity of sales using the reasoning of first-degree price discrimination. If each unit of output can be sold at the maximum price consumers are willing and able to pay for it, profits will be maximized at point *F* where the price charged on the last unit sold is equal to marginal cost. The total amount consumers spend when first-degree price discrimination is practiced is then calculated. These expenditures are represented in the diagram by the entire area underneath the demand curve up to the profit-maximizing quantity. In this example, consumers' total expenditures are equal to the total profit contribution triangle (area *EFG*) plus the rectangle representing the total cost of producing 20 units of output. Specifically, the total profit contribution is equal to $8,[14] and total cost is equal to $4 ($.20 times 20 units).

When the firm practices first-degree price discrimination, consumers consequently spend $12 to purchase the indicated quantity. Next, the all-or-none demand curve is drawn so that consumers' total expenditures (price times quantity) on this offer will be equal to their total expenditures on the ordinary offer. Dividing these total expenditures ($12) by the profit-maximizing

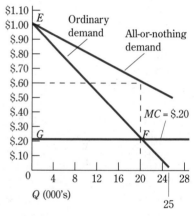

FIGURE 6.3
Ordinary and All-or-Nothing
Demand Curves

---

13 See Milton Friedman, *Price Theory* (Chicago: Aldine, 1976, p. 15).
14 The formula for the area of a triangle is $(1/2)bh$, where b is the length of the base and h is the triangle's height. In this example, $(1/2)bh = (1/2)(20)($.80) = 8.

Block Booking in the Motion Picture Industry

"Block booking" was a marketing technique once widely used in the motion picture industry to distribute feature films to theater chains and to television stations for exhibition to their audiences.[a] Motion picture distributors commonly assembled a number of films into a block and required exhibitors to lease the entire block of pictures on a take-it-or-leave-it basis. These blocks normally contained films of varying quality so that if an exhibitor wanted to obtain the right to show one or more of the "hit" movies in a particular package, he or she also had to accept several box-office "bombs."

George Stigler has put forth an ingenious argument that block booking represents a form of price discrimination.[b] The film distributor's ability to discriminate in price arises from the fact that different exhibitors place different values on individual motion pictures. These differences in value, in turn, are driven by differences in audience preferences across local exhibition markets. Light comedies are more popular among some audiences; serious dramas are more popular among others. Moreover, local theater owners and local TV station managers are likely to have more information about the preferences of local audiences than do the distributors. If this were not so, the distributors could simply charge rental rates for individual films that reflected these preferences and so approximate first-degree price discrimination.

Consider the stylized facts in the following table which shows the hypothetical values placed on two films by two exhibitors. Assuming that the rental rate for a particular movie will be the same for both exhibitors, the distributor would rent *Ernest Saves Christmas* for $2,500 and rent *The Hunt for Red October* for $7,000 if the films are priced separately. (Setting a higher price for either film would cause one of the exhibitors not to rent it and thereby reduce the distributor's gross receipts.) The distributor's total revenue under this pricing policy would be $19,000. Of course, if the distributor has perfect information about the relative values of the films to the two exhibitors, perfect price discrimination would yield $20,500 in revenue, but this degree of precision of demand measurement is ruled out by assumption.

Film Values to Two Exhibitors

EXHIBITOR	THE HUNT FOR RED OCTOBER	ERNEST SAVES CHRISTMAS
A	$8,000	$2,500
B	7,000	3,000

With block booking, however, the distributor can charge a rental rate of $10,000 for the pair of films and will earn $20,000 in total. By setting the price of the block equal to the *minimum* value placed on it by exhibitors (exhibitor A values it at $10,500 whereas exhibitor B values it at $10,000), the distributor receives an additional $1,000 in revenue over and above the amount that would have been earned had the films been priced separately. Hence, block booking is equivalent to confronting exhibitors with an all-or-none offer and in this regard is a form of first-degree price discrimination.[c]

a Block booking is no longer used widely, having been declared illegal by the Supreme Court. See *U.S.* v. *Paramount Pictures, Inc.,* 334 U.S. 131 (1948) and *U.S.* v. *Loew's Inc.,* 371 U.S. 38 (1962).

b George J. Stigler, "A Note on Block Booking," in George J. Stigler, *The Organization of Industry* (Homewood, IL: Irwin, 1968), pp. 165-70.

c Some questions have been raised recently about Stigler's analysis of the purposes and effects of block booking. On closer examination of the contracts between the distributors and exhibitors of feature films, it turns out that the actual rental rates charged on film packages varied substantially across local exhibition markets, a fact that is inconsistent with the price discrimination hypothesis. An alternative hypothesis for block booking is that it represented an inventory-management tool for the contracting parties which conserved resources by reducing the incentives of exhibitors to haggle over the values of individual films and promoted efficient risk-sharing between distributors and exhibitors. See Roy W. Kenney and Benjamin Klein, "The Economics of Block Booking," *Journal of Law and Economics* 26 (October 1983), pp. 497-540.

quantity of sales (20 units) yields an average price of $.60 per unit. Hence, if the seller requires that consumers either purchase 20 units of the product at a price of $.60 per unit or buy nothing at all, consumers will spend $12. When the cost of producing these units is deducted, $12 yields the same profit ($8) that would have been earned with the more complicated pricing strategy of selling each unit of output at a different price.

Confronting consumers with an all-or-none choice is thus equivalent to price discrimination of the first degree. Moreover, like perfect price discrimination, all-or-none pricing policies result in the production and sale of additional units of output that the firm would not produce and sell otherwise. Although it requires similarly precise information about demand, an all-or-none pricing policy has advantages in implementation insofar as all units of output are sold at the same price per unit. These advantages in implementation help explain why this selling technique is used in a number of industries, including the marketing of gem-quality diamonds and the leasing of motion pictures (see the accompanying case study).[15]

PRICE DISCRIMINATION OF THE SECOND DEGREE

Second-degree price discrimination requires less information about demand than is assumed in the case of first-degree price discrimination. Rather than selling each unit of a product at a different price (equal to the maximum amount a consumer is willing and able to pay for it), the firm separates customers into two or more groups and charges the same price to all buyers in a given group. Higher prices are then charged to groups of buyers having higher demand prices for the good in question.

Price discrimination of the second degree is illustrated in Figure 6.4 which reproduces Figure 6.3 and shows the hypothetical demand facing the seller of some good or service. This representation assumes constant marginal production costs and determines the profit-maximizing quantity of sales by equating marginal revenue with marginal cost. In this example, the optimal level of sales is 20 units. The first 4 units are sold at a price of $.84, the second 4 at $.68, the third 4 at $.52, the fourth 4 at $.36, and the last 4 units sell at a price equal to the firm's marginal cost of $.20.[16]

Because all groups of customers pay the same price for all of the units, marginal revenue is constant within each block of 4 units and equal to price. That is, each unit sold to the group having the highest demand price adds

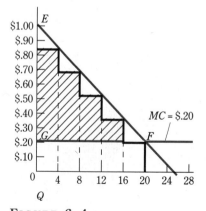

FIGURE 6.4
Second-Degree Price Discrimination

---

15 For an interesting discussion of the selling method used by De Beers to market its uncut, gem-quality diamonds to wholesalers and jewelry manufacturers, see Roy W. Kenney and Benjamin Klein, "The Economics of Block Booking," *Journal of Law and Economics* 26 (October 1983), pp. 497-540.

16 Because the equation of the inverse demand curve is $P = \$1 - \$.04Q$, price must be reduced by $.16 to sell an additional 4 units.

$.84 to the firm's total revenue; each unit sold to the group having the next highest demand price adds $.68 to total revenue; and so on. The marginal revenue "curve" is thus represented by the solid "step function" underneath the demand schedule. The total profit contribution associated with these sales is accordingly represented by the shaded areas within triangle *EFG*.

There are numerous examples of this type of price discrimination. One of the most common is the practice of charging a lower unit price for a product to customers who buy larger quantities. Catsup is typically sold in various sized bottles, for example. A ten-ounce bottle might be sold for $1, a 20-ounce bottle for $1.80, and a 30-ounce bottle for $2.40. With this pricing strategy, the average price of ten ounces of catsup declines from $1 to $.90 to $.80 as the customer buys successively larger bottles. These price differences may partially reflect differences in costs. Unit packaging costs or transportation costs could well be lower for larger sized bottles of catsup than they are for smaller bottles. However, even if all costs are constant across bottle sizes, it will still be profitable for the firm to price them differently if the customers who buy the various bottle sizes have different demand characteristics. Just as importantly, if the characteristics of demand do not vary across customer groups, then the firm will not profit from offering quantity discounts (in this case, the demand curve in Figure 6.4 would be very flat).

Charging different prices to different groups of customers is profitable when the firm can exploit differences in demand. Second-degree price discrimination exploits differences in the maximum prices consumers are willing and able to pay for a particular good or service, but does so more crudely than perfect price discrimination. The typical buyer of a ten-ounce bottle of catsup, for instance, may be from a single-person household that buys catsup infrequently and exhibits a strong sense of brand loyalty. On the other hand, the typical buyer of a 30-ounce bottle of catsup may shop for a five-person household that buys catsup regularly and frequently makes price comparisons. The first group of customers will in all likelihood be willing and able to pay a higher price for catsup than the customers in the second group, and the firm's markup on marginal cost should therefore be greater on the smaller bottle of catsup.

Second-degree price discrimination is a method of charging different prices to different groups of customers that relies on a process of self-selection. Customers with higher demand prices will tend to buy smaller quantities at higher average unit prices, and customers with lower demand prices will tend to buy larger quantities at lower average unit prices. It is also true, however, that such a pricing policy will tend to encourage increased consumption of the good or service sold in this way because average price declines as quantities rise. In other words, pricing a 20-ounce bottle of catsup at $1.80 is equivalent to offering the customer the opportunity of buying an additional ten ounces of catsup for $.80, provided that he or she buys the first ten ounces at the "regular" price of $1. All customers who buy 20 ounces of catsup therefore pay an average price of $.90 for each ten-ounce unit of catsup. Because individuals will buy more of an item at lower prices than at higher prices, second-degree price discrimination tends to increase the quantity sold to any one customer.

Public utilities widely practice second-degree price discrimination. Long-distance telephone services, for example, are typically priced on a declining schedule in which the highest rates are charged on the first three minutes of conversation. Anyone who talks longer than this can buy the next block of time at a lower rate, and so on.

Quantity discounts of this sort are a subset of a more general pricing practice known as **product bundling**.[17] Product bundling involves selling two or more products together at a price that is less than the sum of the prices that would be charged if the products were purchased separately. For example, restaurants often offer their patrons the opportunity to purchase a meal that includes a trip to the salad bar, a main course, and a beverage at a price that is less than the customer would pay if the items were ordered a la carte. Personal computers are generally bundled with a video terminal, a keyboard, and disk operating system software. Automobile companies regularly run special deals and offer air conditioning or some other optional feature at "no cost." Universities and colleges typically charge a lower tuition rate per credit hour for a full course load than for a partial course load.

In these examples, firms assemble different products into a bundle and offer them on a take-it-or-leave-it basis ("no substitutions allowed"). Such bundling prevents buyers from rejecting individual elements of a package of products, some of which may be "over-valued" (have relatively high markups over marginal cost) and some of which may be "under-valued" (have relatively low markups over marginal cost) at the bundle's selling price.

Preventing consumers from rejecting elements of the bundle economizes on transaction costs. On the one hand, bundling may simply reflect the seller's ability to assemble products into cost-effective packages due to superior information about the quality and performance characteristics of the bundle's complementary components. The efficiency advantages associated with the seller's superior information would be lost if buyers were permitted to unbundle the package unilaterally. On the other hand, bundling may be appropriate in situations where the seller cannot easily discover or cheaply control the underlying variance in the quality of individual products. Precise estimates of the values of the elements of the package would require both buyers and sellers to engage in costly, duplicative search.

Consider, for example, a personal computer system that contains a keyboard, a video terminal, and a printer. Bundling these items into a package prevents wasteful haggling over the prices of the individual system components. Negotiating individual prices would require both the buyer and the seller to acquire more precise information about the quality and performance characteristics of the particular brands and models in the system under consideration. Neither party would necessarily have an advantage in

---

17 See Walter J. Adams and Janet L. Yellen, "Commodity Bundling and the Burden of Monopoly," *Quarterly Journal of Economics* 90 (August 1976), pp. 475-98.

this regard. The buyer is unlikely to be a computer hardware expert. And while the seller may know the average performance characteristics and specifications of the system's components, information about the particular components at issue could only be acquired by conducting additional tests. In such cases, it may be economical for buyers to rely on the brand name capital of sellers in making their purchase decisions. Sellers, in turn, have incentives to strive to maintain their reputational capital by offering product bundles of the promised average quality.[18]

In the case of quantity discounts, the firm packages and sells several units of the same good as a bundle. In the catsup example, the unit is ten ounces of catsup. Similarly, when the pizzeria offers a medium pizza for $8 or two for $12, it too is engaging in product bundling. Bundling of this sort is explained more by considerations of price discrimination than by the transaction-cost argument laid out in the previous paragraph.

The prevalence of price discrimination in its many forms has important implications about the relevance of marginal-cost pricing. The last several sections of this chapter present examples showing that many pricing strategies which at first blush seem inconsistent with the marginal-revenue-equals-marginal-cost rule are in fact dictated by marginal analysis. These examples differ from the pricing policies described in earlier chapters only in their presumption that the firm acquires and exploits more detailed information about the demand for its products.

What may seem abstract when written in equation form is often a part of ordinary business practice. Moreover, firms need not calculate demand, marginal revenue, and marginal cost precisely to behave in a manner consistent with marginal principles.[19] Success is defined by results, not motivation. Business practices that are successful—that is, increase profits—will become standard practices through imitation. Firms that do not adopt proven successful practices will eventually fail and leave the market. Firms that better understand the principles of marginal analysis will therefore fare better than those that do not.

Still, however, the analysis does not do justice to the dynamic forces of competition which determine the practices that are successful and guide firms to perform their ultimate social function, namely the production and sale of goods and services that are valued by consumers. In an ever-changing marketplace, business practices that are successful at one point in time may not be successful at another point.

Sears once dominated the retailing industry by frequently offering sales throughout the year. Sales promotions are yet another example of price discrimination. Some customers are less patient and less sensitive to price and will therefore make purchases even when the items they want to buy

---

18 Roy W. Kenney and Benjamin Klein, "The Economics of Block Booking." *Journal of Law and Economics* 26 (October 1983), pp. 497-540.

19 Armen A. Alchian, "Uncertainty, Evolution, and Economic Theory," *Journal of Political Economy* 58 (June 1950), pp. 211-21.

are not on sale. Conducting a sale is simply a strategy for targeting other customers who are more patient and more sensitive to price. However, as Sears ultimately discovered, price discrimination (like all business practices) is subject to the constraints imposed by the competitive marketplace.

Consumers are not passive and, over time, Sears' marketing strategy apparently lost its appeal. As prospective customers became more accustomed to the regularity of sales, fewer and fewer of them were willing to make purchases at non-sale prices. In addition, Sears' selling technique imposed a cost on customers who were price conscious—the cost of gathering the information necessary to take advantage of sale prices. This dissatisfaction led to the success of retailers like Wal-Mart, K-Mart, Toys "R" Us, and Circuit City who offer "everyday low prices." In 1989, Sears recognized that its sales strategy was no longer competitive and switched to a policy of cutting its "regular prices" across-the-board and drastically reducing the number of sales.

SUMMARY

This chapter has explained how firms can develop profit-enhancing pricing strategies by acquiring more detailed knowledge about the demand for their products. It has also shown a diverse set of pricing practices to be consistent with the marginal-revenue-equals-marginal-cost pricing rule. The widespread use of these pricing practices indicates that firms are much more knowledgeable about the demand characteristics of their products and their customers than most of us (including economists) give them credit for. Discount policies, price skimming, quantity discounts, and product bundling are common pricing practices whose profitable use requires fairly detailed information about demand.

One of the more subtle points of this chapter is that the market provides information that helps the firm both acquire information about the relevant characteristics of demand and make complex pricing decisions. The market rewards firms that adopt successful practices which exploit the demand characteristics of their customers. Over time, the firm's rivals will copy these successful pricing practices. Ideas are difficult to monopolize. Critics of managerial economics often argue that firms cannot possibly acquire all of the information necessary to estimate a demand and marginal revenue schedule and it is therefore silly to expect them to use the marginal-cost pricing rule. Although that criticism may be true literally, in some ways the firm possesses more information than is indicated by a simple demand equation. Firms operate in a dynamic, competitive environment. Accurate knowledge of this environment leads to successful business practices, and the rewards of these practices lead other firms to adopt them.

KEY TERMS
price discrimination
third-degree price discrimination
first-degree price discrimination
price skimming
all-or-none offer
second-degree price discrimination
product bundling

6.1 Comment on the following statement: The most common form of price discrimination is the failure to price discriminate.

6.2 What conditions are necessary before price discrimination is possible?

6.3 Movie theaters often charge different prices for matinees and evening performances. Is this an example of price discrimination?

6.4 Explain the difference between first-degree and second-degree price discrimination.

6.5 Third-degree price discrimination occurs when the firm charges two or more different prices to different customers according to differences in their demand characteristics. What is the relationship between elasticity and the price that a customer is charged?

6.6 In a conventional auction the auctioneer starts the bidding with a low price and price is then bid upward. In a so-called "Dutch auction" the auctioneer starts at a high price and then slowly lowers the price. Discuss the reasons why the seller may prefer the "Dutch auction" system. If the seller prefers the "Dutch auction," why would any seller use the conventional auction method?

6.7 Evaluate the following statements: Profit-maximization requires that the firm set a price such that marginal revenue is equal to marginal cost. The marginal costs of some products are close to zero (for example water, electricity, or computer time) and, according to the marginal-cost pricing rule, these products should be sold at a "zero price." These types of goods provide an obvious exception to using the rule of setting marginal revenue equal to marginal cost in order to maximize profits.

6.8 Explain an "all-or-nothing" marketing strategy.

6.9 True or False: If the demand for a firm's product increases, then the firm must raise price in order to maximize profits.

6.10 Two examples of industries that use "all-or-nothing" marketing strategies were given in this chapter—gem-quality diamonds and the leasing of motion pictures. What do these industries have in common that is required for an all-or-nothing marketing strategy?

6.11 The U.S. Postal Service charges $.29 to mail a first-class letter to any address in the 50 states or the District of Columbia. Is this pricing policy an example of price discrimination? Why or why not?

PROBLEMS

6.1 The East Asia Electronic Company sells small compact disc players in Japan and the United States. The elasticity of demand for CD players is 4 in Japan and 10 in the United States. The price of a CD player in Japan is $60. If the company can successfully separate these two markets and if transportation costs are ignored, how much should it charge for a CD player in the United States?

6.2 The Copeland Roofing Company has two types of clients: builders and homeowners. The cost of roofing an average home is $2,000 in materials and labor (the principal variable costs). The demand functions for the clients are:

$$Q_B = 120 - .02P \qquad \text{(builders)}$$
$$Q_H = 80 - .01P \qquad \text{(homeowners)}$$

a. What are the profit-maximizing prices and outputs for the two groups of customers?
b. What are the profit contributions of the sales to each group?
c. What are the elasticities of demand at the profit-maximizing prices for the two groups?
d. If the firm charges the same price to both types of customers, how much profit will it earn?

6.3 The Granger Hat Company sells two different types of hats. It sells a relatively unique hunter's hat that is produced in a special shade of "hunter's orange." The color is easily spotted by other hunters but is (supposedly) not easily seen by deer and other game. The company also makes ordinary baseball hats that are sold in convenience stores. The marginal cost of producing both hats is the same; it is constant and equal to $4.50 per hat. The demands for the two types of hats are given by the following equations:

$$P_H = 24.5 - .0005Q_H \qquad \text{(hunter's hat)}$$
$$P_B = 14.5 - .000125Q_B \qquad \text{(baseball hat)}$$

a. Determine the profit-maximizing price and quantity for both types of hats.
b. Determine the elasticity of demand at the profit-maximizing quantity for each product.
c. How much extra profit does the company earn by price discriminating?

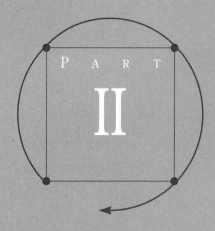

The Firm and the Market

The Boundaries of the Firm

OVERVIEW

This chapter presents and synthesizes modern theories that highlight the importance of **transaction costs** and property rights in shaping the economic activities undertaken by the firm. We address the fundamental question of why the firm emerges as an economic entity by comparing the market and the firm as alternate institutions for guiding the allocation of society's scarce productive resources. Also discussed are critical factors influencing the choice between the firm and the market, such as information costs, asset specificity, team production and shirking, and principal-agent relationships.

The chapter emphasizes the superiority of market procurement in terms of efficient resource allocation and cost containment, and suggests that managerial decision makers should be biased in favor of this approach. Whether the market option is chosen in any particular instance nevertheless depends on a host of considerations. Important factors include the number of independent suppliers ready to meet the buyer's requirements; the extent to which assets used in the production process are specialized to particular orders or customers; the degree of uncertainty about future costs, prices, and supply availabilities; and the frequency with which orders are placed.

These and other critical issues surrounding the choice between the market and the firm are discussed in detail. The aim is to provide a theoretical framework that we will apply throughout Parts II and III to analyze a rich set of decision-making problems that managers must confront.

Consider a decision faced by the head of the manufacturing unit of a company that produces small internal combustion engines. These engines are assembled and sold to other firms that manufacture lawn mowers, tillers, lightweight tractors, and similar gasoline-powered garden equipment. In consultation with the manager of the company's purchasing department, the unit must choose a strategy for obtaining the spark plugs installed by production workers just before testing and crating the engines for shipment.

There are three options to consider. One option is to purchase spark plugs as needed from independent suppliers that specialize in manufacturing engine parts meeting the company's specifications. The second option is to negotiate contracts with one or more of these suppliers that provide for scheduled deliveries of spark plugs to the engine assembly plant. Finally, the firm can acquire an ownership interest in an existing supplier or build a new manufacturing facility to produce the spark plugs for itself.

Which of these options should the firm select? This chapter emphasizes that there are costs associated with each of them. These transaction costs include the costs of acquiring information, the costs of monitoring and appraising performance, and the costs of coordinating related business activities. Put another way, transaction costs are "search and information costs, bargaining and decision costs, and policing and enforcement costs."[a]

More specifically, when the firm chooses the spot-market option, the purchasing department must periodically search for and evaluate information about the prices, specifications, and availabilities of the various brands and models of spark plugs produced by outsiders. More formal relationships with independent parts suppliers force the firm to bear the costs of negotiating, writing, and enforcing contractual terms. In addition, market contracting may leave the firm vulnerable to exploitation by a supplier who attempts to take advantage of gaps in the contract by seeking more favorable terms than had been agreed to initially.

Ownership integration entails its own set of costs. The costs of bringing the transaction inside the boundaries of the firm include the costs of acquiring specialized information about the prices, specifications, and availabilities of the equipment and materials used in the manufacture of spark plugs. In addition, the costs of monitoring and appraising the performance of the "captive" production facility must be weighed.

---

a Carl J. Dahlman, "The Problem of Externality," *Journal of Law and Economics* 22 (April 1979), p. 148.

NEOCLASSICAL AND MODERN THEORIES OF THE FIRM COMPARED

The neoclassical theory of the firm, as presented in nearly all microeconomics texts and as laid out in some of its details in Part I of this book, is chiefly a theory of production and cost. The theory stresses the technological, revenue, and cost constraints faced by firms in transforming scarce productive resources into goods and services valued by consumers. It focuses on equilibrium conditions and derives rules for determining optimal output quantities, optimal input combinations, and optimal prices. In doing so, the organizational structure of the firm is taken as given and rivalry between firms is often explicitly ruled out. The firm emerges for purely technological reasons (economies of scale in production) in the neoclassical model.[1]

Some very important questions about the nature of the firm are not specifically addressed by neoclassical theory. For one, the neoclassical production function that relates outputs to inputs does not focus on the issue of resource ownership. Which of the raw materials, capital, and other physical resources employed in the production of a good or service will the firm own and which will it purchase or lease from other firms? Which of the production workers will be full-time employees of the firm and which will be hired as temporary consultants or contractors? Which employees will be paid a salary, which will be paid an hourly wage, and which will be paid on commission? In short, by focusing on the technological relationships between inputs and outputs, neoclassical theory abstracts from the institutional details that describe how the firm acquires productive resources and how the owners of these resources are compensated.

A related set of questions concerns the determinants of the functions the firm will perform. Which of the business activities associated with the production and sale of a good will the firm undertake within its organization and which will be performed by outsiders? For example, does the firm market its own product directly to consumers or does it instead wholesale its product through a network of independent distributors? If the former strategy is chosen, are the firm's retail outlets wholly owned or are they operated as franchises? Is advertising copy prepared in-house or by an independent advertising agency? What about accounting, personnel, maintenance, and transportation? Which of these functions will be brought inside the ownership boundaries of the firm and which will be performed by other firms?

Managers who consciously guide the allocation of the firm's resources are likewise not a principal focus of neoclassical theory. What organizational structure does the firm adopt and what methods do managers employ to

---

1 To the neoclassical economist, the firm "is effectively defined as a cost curve and a demand curve, and the theory is simply the logic of optimal pricing and input combination." See Martin Slater, "Foreword," in Edith T. Penrose, *The Theory of the Growth of the Firm*, 2E. (White Plains, NY: M. E. Sharpe, 1980), p. ix, quoted in Ronald H. Coase *The Firm, the Market, and the Law* (Chicago: University of Chicago Press, 1988), p. 3.

coordinate the various business functions the firm chooses to undertake? How do managers appraise and control the performance of the people, equipment, and materials under their supervision? How do the firm's managers identify and exploit market opportunities?

Finally, neoclassical theory does not specifically address important questions concerning the ownership structure of firms in the economy. Indeed, the neoclassical firm is implicitly assumed to be a sole proprietorship owned and operated by a single individual. But the ownership and management functions are separate in the large, modern business enterprise. What institutional features of the corporate form of organization serve to reduce the costs imposed on shareholders due to their limited control of managerial decision making? What actions can owners and managers take to align their separate interests more closely?

More fundamentally, what forces help shape the ownership structure the firm will adopt? Why are some firms organized as sole proprietorships, some as partnerships, and some as corporations? Why are some corporations closely held while the ownership of others is dispersed widely? Why are some business enterprises operated for profit while others are operated not for profit?

The modern theory of the firm seeks answers to these critical questions. It does not deny the importance of purely technological factors in influencing the extent to which economic activities are integrated within the firm. But the modern theory emphasizes that the determinants of the boundaries of the firm are not exclusively (or even mainly) technological in nature. In the modern theory, the firm is a complex set of contractual interrelationships among resource owners.

Each one of these contractual relationships—the acquisition of an input, the employment of a worker, the transfer of a finished good to a customer, and so on—is a **transaction** that could be carried out either within the firm or on the market. By making the transaction the unit of analysis, the modern theory of the firm attempts to explore piece-by-piece the economic forces that determine the boundaries of business enterprise.

In a sense, neoclassical theory treats the firm as a technological "black box" that transforms inputs into outputs efficiently by setting marginal revenue equal to marginal cost in the product market and marginal cost equal to marginal revenue product in resource markets. The assumptions made by the neoclassical model help simplify the analysis and in so doing generate a rich set of insights into the behavior of the firm. The modern theory takes these insights as a starting point and applies them in analyzing novel questions about the nature of the firm.

THE COASIAN FIRM

Nearly all subsequent work on the determinants of the functions and structure of the business firm owes its origins to Ronald Coase.[2] Coase's important

---

2 Ronald H. Coase, "The Nature of the Firm," *Economica* 4 (November 1937), pp. 386-405.

contribution followed from asking the simple question, Why do firms exist? After all, the market efficiently collates vast amounts of information about resource values across space and over time. The market then condenses this information into a set of relative prices that coordinate the production and distribution of goods by guiding resources (through explicit profit signals) into their most highly valued uses.

Essentially the same resource allocation functions are carried out within the firm. The owners and managers of business enterprises assign tasks, establish rewards, monitor performance, and coordinate the production and distribution of goods. They do so without the benefit of explicit price and profit signals, however. Instead, resource allocation decisions within the firm are accomplished by administrative command. The firm reassigns workers, develops new products, and scraps old equipment not because relative prices have expressly changed but because managers have ordered it so.[3] The firm's management is therefore more like the bureaucracy of a centrally planned socialist economy than it is like the hypothetical decision maker of neoclassical theory who allocates resources instantaneously and efficiently in response to market signals.

Coase wondered why it is that two different institutions—the firm and the market—perform the same basic functions. His insight was that these two alternate methods of coordinating economic activities exist because there are costs associated with the use of the price system. The firm emerges in the attempt to economize on these costs.

The Costs of Using the Market

At the heart of Coase's theory is his identification of the costs of using the market. Any market exchange or transaction requires both parties to bear search and information costs. Buyers, for example, must canvas prospective suppliers to obtain information on their locations, the physical characteristics and prices of goods for sale, delivery schedules, credit terms, warranty provisions, and so on. Suppliers, in turn, must gather information about buyers' locations, preferences, and credit worthiness, the prices and terms offered by rival sellers, and so forth.

Both parties must update their information periodically as new buyers and sellers enter the market (and as existing ones leave), as new technologies emerge, as new products and new marketing techniques appear, and as the "particular circumstances of time and place" change.[4] In short, "the most obvious cost of 'organising' production through the price mechanism is discovering what the relevant prices are."[5]

---

3 Managers do use market prices as benchmarks for their internal resource allocation decisions. For some evidence on this score, see Andrew Whinston, "Price Guides in Decentralized Organizations," in W. W. Cooper, H. J. Leavitt, and M. W. Shelly, eds., *New Perspectives in Organization Research* (New York: Wiley, 1964), pp. 405-48.

4 Friedrich A. Hayek, "The Use of Knowledge in Society," *American Economic Review* 35 (September 1945), p. 521.

5 Coase, "The Nature of the Firm," p. 390.

The parties to a transaction may be able to economize on the resources they invest in acquiring market information by contracting to buy or sell over a specified interval. Coase recognized, however, that the institution of contracts is itself costly. Besides the obvious costs of negotiation and enforcement, all contracts are incomplete in the sense that they fail to cover every possible future contingency. Long-term contracting might therefore bind one or both of the parties to terms and conditions which unforeseen events later render unfavorable. Short-term contracts may help the two parties avoid being locked into unfavorable terms. But by requiring the parties to renegotiate their agreement more frequently, short-term contracts force them to bear more of the search and information costs they sought to economize on in the first place.

Coase suggested that the economic rationale for the firm is found in the entrepreneurial drive to conserve on the resources that would otherwise be consumed in using market prices as a guide to resource allocation decisions. Internalizing some business decisions under the direct control of an entrepreneur-manager economizes on transaction costs and these cost savings provide an efficiency basis for the emergence of the firm. That is, for some transactions, the firm may be more efficient than the market in the sense that search and information costs, bargaining and decision costs, and policing and enforcement costs are lower.

The Costs of Administrative Command

The alternative to market coordination of economic activities is of course not free. Coase identified two costs of directing resources by administrative command that limit the size and scope of the firm.

First, the total costs of internal organization rise as additional transactions are removed from the market and placed within administrative control. Planning and decision making become more complex and more costly as the firm coordinates more activities and functions.

Second, there is greater risk of failing to make the best use of productive resources as more transactions are organized within the firm. Errors in assigning tasks, establishing rewards, and monitoring performance become more likely as less reliance is placed on the market. (These rising costs of planning and coordination are analogous to the diseconomies of scale that limit the size of firms in the neoclassical model.)

Determining the Optimal Firm Size

According to Coase, "a firm will tend to expand until the costs of organising an extra transaction within the firm become equal to the costs of carrying out the same transaction by means of an exchange on the open market or the costs of organising another firm."[6] Figure 7.1 illustrates Coase's theory graphically.

---

6 *Ibid.*, p. 395.

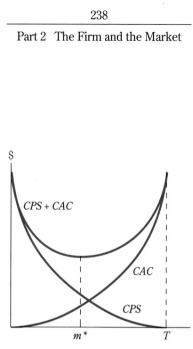

FIGURE 7.1
The Costs of Resource Allocation
in the Coasian Firm

The vertical axis measures total cost. The number of technically separable transactions, m, that are carried out under the direction of the firm's managers is measured along the horizontal axis. Thus, as one moves along the horizontal axis, the number of resource-allocation decisions that are made by administrative command increases relative to the number of decisions that are guided by the price system. Point T, at the far right of the diagram, represents the total number of technically separable transactions involved in the production of some good or service.

The two relevant cost categories identified by Coase are plotted in the figure. The curve labeled CPS represents the total cost of using the price system. This cost is at its maximum when the owners of resources make all resource-allocation decisions in response to market price signals. One might think of a general contractor who, using nothing more than a rented desk and a telephone in a leased office, arranges the construction of a ten-story apartment building. There is no construction firm per se. All labor and materials are obtained on the open market from independent suppliers and subcontractors who submit bids on various parts of the job.

As more transactions come under administrative command—implying that an equal number of technically separable resource-allocation decisions are removed from the market—the total cost of using the price system declines. At point T, all transactions are coordinated by entrepreneurial direction. The cost of using the price system is zero at that point because the firm has completely superseded the market in the production of the given output. At point T, the general contracting firm has expanded to encompass all of the functions and activities associated with the construction of the building. Not only are all construction workers, electricians, plumbers, and architects full-time employees of the firm, but the company has integrated backward into the production of all of the materials and equipment necessary to complete the job. The firm now produces its own dynamite, steel, concrete, glass, heating and air conditioning equipment, construction machinery, hardware, paint, carpeting, and so on.

The cost savings from removing transactions from the market do involve some sacrifice, however. Increasing the size and scope of the firm means that internal resource allocation decisions become more complex. The total costs of administrative command and control are represented by the curve labeled CAC in Figure 7.1. These costs are zero at the far left of the diagram when the firm makes all resource-allocation decisions in response to market price signals; they are at a maximum when all relevant transactions take place under entrepreneurial direction (point T).

Those decisions that are on net least costly to administer by conscious command will be the first to be removed from the market. As a larger share of the entire production process is taken off the market and internalized within the firm, the total cost of administratively directing additional transactions increases. The CAC curve is consequently convex to the horizontal axis—the marginal cost of administrative command rises as management successively removes resource-allocation decisions from the market. The *CPS* curve is likewise convex because those transactions that are least expensive to carry out on the market will be internalized within the firm last. That is, the marginal transaction-costs savings become successively smaller as the firm makes additional resource allocation decisions internally.

Marginal analysis determines the optimal size of the firm. According to Coase, the firm expands until the marginal costs of internal decision making are just equal to the marginal costs of using the market. This point is labeled m^* in Figure 7.1, where the slope of *CAC* is equal to (the negative of) the slope of *CPS*. The point m^* also corresponds to the firm size at which the vertical sum of *CAC* and *CPS* is at its minimum.

Any change from m^* in the number of transactions internalized within the firm relative to the number carried out on the market causes the total cost of resource allocation to increase. In moving from m^* to m^* + 1, for example, the costs of directing resources by administrative command rise by more than the costs of using the price system fall. Similarly, a decrease (below m^*) in the number of internalized transactions causes the cost of using the market to increase by more than is saved by reducing the complexity of internal resource allocation decision making. Thus, m^* is the optimal number of transactions to be carried out within the firm.

Changes in the underlying parameters that determine the relative positions of the *CAC* and *CPS* curves will change the value of m^*. Advances in auditing techniques or organizational innovations, for instance, may improve the entrepreneur's ability to monitor and coordinate the production process. This reduction in the costs of administrative command would cause the *CAC* curve to shift downward. And, other things being equal, such a change would lead to an increase in the optimal number of transactions carried out within the firm. By contrast, any parameter shift that causes the cost of using the price system to fall relative to the cost of administrative command will lead to a reduction in the number of internally directed resource allocation decisions.

Coase's theory of the firm has been accused of lacking empirical content—of being tautological—even by his admirers, but its influence is beyond question.[7] This is because the particular factors Coase identified as shaping the size and scope of business enterprises shifted the focus of research away from treating the firm as a technological "black box" and toward an analysis of the rich and varied transactions that constitute the activities of firms in the economy.

---

7 For example, see Armen A. Alchian and Harold Demsetz, "Production, Information Costs, and Economic Organization," *American Economic Review* 62 (December 1972), pp. 777-95; and Oliver E. Williamson, *The Economic Institutions of Capitalism: Firms, Markets, Relational Contracting* (New York: Free Press, 1985).

Why do Hospitals have Exclusive Contracts with Physicians?

Hospitals typically engage the services of two types of physicians. Admitting physicians have the privilege of admitting patients to the hospital and managing their care. Hospital-based physicians supply ancillary services to patients, such as anesthesiology, radiology, and pathology, at the request of the admitting physicians.[a]

Although hospital-based physicians do not themselves admit patients or directly supervise their care, they are an important input into the production of hospital services. They perform and interpret critical diagnostic tests and they consult with admitting physicians, offering medical advice that is indispensable in managing the patient's hospital stay. Admitting physicians presumably choose hospitals to patronize partly on the basis of their perceptions of the quality of the services provided by the hospital-based specialists.

As it does with the other ancillary services it supplies (nursing, food, and janitorial services, for example), the hospital has three options for seeing that the services of hospital-based physicians are made available. The hospital can hire the specialists as full-time employees, it can contract with an outside professional corporation to be the sole supplier of these services, or it can adopt an "open-staff" policy under which admitting physicians personally select specialists from among the independent hospital-based physicians who themselves have staff privileges.

Many hospitals have chosen the second alternative, namely arranging for hospital-based physicians' services (particularly the anesthesiology and radiology specialties) to be supplied through exclusive contracts with independent professional corporations. That is, the hospital administrator signs a contract with a local group of anesthesiologists or radiologists. This contract gives the specialists' professional corporation the exclusive right to supply these ancillary medical services to the hospital's admitting physicians.

These exclusive contracts have been the subject of a substantial amount of litigation. The issue reached the Supreme Court in 1983 on a case challenging an exclusive contract for anesthesia services at a New Orleans hospital.[b] Edwin Hyde, an independent anesthesiologist, sued Jefferson Parrish Hospital, claiming that its exclusive contract with a local group of anesthesiologists injured competition by preventing him and other independent anesthesiology specialists from practicing at the hospital.

Why did Jefferson Parrish Hospital enter such an exclusive contract? Note that the selection of anesthesiologists is up to the hospital under all three of its options for offering the services of these specialists to admitting physicians. That is, whether anesthesiology services are supplied by full-time hospital employees, through exclusive contract with an outside professional corporation, or by independent specialists who have staff privileges, it is the hospital that selects the anesthesiologists who will assist admitting physicians in managing the care of their patients. The hospital will therefore bear essentially the same search and information costs in arranging for anesthesiology services no matter what policy it adopts. These are the costs of identifying and retaining the services of qualified specialists who will work well with the hospital's admitting physicians.

There are other transaction costs that do vary according to the type of arrangement the hospital makes for securing the services of anesthesiologists, however. Consider decision-making costs. If anesthesiologists are full-time hospital employees, the hospital administrator or the administrative head of the surgery department will be responsible for determining work schedules, making operating room assignments, monitoring medical record keeping, and, in general, planning and coordinating the activities of the providers of anesthesiology services with those of the hospital's admitting physicians to maintain a smoothly functioning patient care environment.

a This case study is drawn from William J. Lynk and Michael A. Morrisey, "The Economic Basis of *Hyde*: Are Market Power and Hospital Exclusive Contracts Related? "*Journal of Law and Economics* 30 (October 1987), pp. 399-421.

b *Jefferson Parrish Hospital Dist. No. 2* v. *Edwin G. Hyde,* 104 Sup. Ct. 1551 (1984).

At the other extreme, with an open-staff policy, the admitting physician will bear these decision-making costs, engaging the services of anesthesiologists on a case-by-case basis. Admitting physicians will personally select providers from among those specialists having staff privileges who are available at the time surgery is scheduled. Operating room assignments for anesthesiologists may tend to be haphazard or ad hoc under these conditions (from the hospital administrator's point of view), and conflicts between admitting physicians may thereby arise. The costs of search and decision making may be particularly high when the patients of admitting physicians require emergency surgery.

Exclusive contracts help economize on these decision-making costs. In particular, when the hospital engages an outside professional corporation to supply anesthesiology services under exclusive contract, the anesthesiology firm assumes primary responsibility for arranging employee work schedules, making operating room assignments, transcribing anesthesiologists' notes, adding the notes to patients' medical records in a timely manner and, in general, planning and coordinating their employees' activities with those of the hospital's admitting physicians. The hospital administrator must still be responsible for evaluating the level and quality of anesthesiology services the contractor supplies, but he or she can do so by monitoring output (performance) rather than inputs.[c] The routine, day-to-day decisions concerning staffing, work scheduling, and record keeping shift to the outside professional corporation.

Exclusive contracts also help solve a "free-rider" problem that may exist under alternate employment policies for hospital-based physicians. These problems can arise when cooperation between the hospital and the providers of ancillary medical services "could produce long-lived gains for all parties, but where, once the investment is made, one party has the ability to appropriate all of the gains."[d]

For example, the hospital and the anesthesiologists would both benefit from a program designed to upgrade the surgery department—purchasing better equipment, improving surgical scheduling procedures, providing additional training to the nurse anesthetists who assist in the operating room, and so forth. The benefits of such a program will be shared by all of the anesthesiologists who work at the hospital. Therefore, the incentive for any one of them to bear a share of the program's costs (spending more time helping train operating room assistants, participating in advisory committee work, writing reports, and so on) depends critically on the nature of the employment relationship.

If the anesthesiologists are either full-time hospital employees or independent specialists with staff privileges, the hospital will capture the bulk of the benefits of upgrading the surgery department. The hospital may then choose to share the gains by hiring new anesthesiologists or by granting staff privileges to additional specialists. The resulting dilution of the original anesthesiologists' benefits would make the entire sequence unprofitable for them, making it less likely that the improvement would be made in the first place. Put another way, "if anesthesiologists are compensated only for time spent in surgery, a free-rider problem develops: since all anesthesiologists benefit, each has the incentive to avoid personally undertaking the costs of the beneficial activity, and therefore no one does it."[e]

When anesthesiology services are supplied exclusively by an independent professional corporation, however, the benefits of participating in upgrading the hospital's surgery department will be reflected in the value of an ownership position in the outside firm. That is, the professional corporation's profits will rise to the extent that the improvements lower the costs of supplying anesthesiology services. This occurs when, for example, operating room assistants are better trained or scheduling procedures are more efficient.

This increase in profitability will raise the anesthesiologist-owners' wealth, thereby enabling each of them to capture a portion of the returns to their joint investment. In short, "within a firm of anesthesiologists,

c See, generally, Armen A. Alchian and Harold Demsetz, "Production, Information Costs, and Economic Organization," *American Economic Review* 62 (December 1972), pp. 777-95.
d Lynk and Morrisey, "Economic Basis of *Hyde*," p. 404.
e *Ibid.*

these [mutual] gains can be explicitly recognized, and tasks of general benefit can be assigned and compensated."[f] Because the hospital can be expected to capture a share of the benefits of upgrading the surgery department as well, cooperation between the hospital and the anesthesiologists becomes more likely and the improvements are therefore more apt to be undertaken.

The above discussion suggests a Coasian efficiency rationale for the emergence of the firm. Negotiating exclusive contracts with outside professional corporations to engage the services of anesthesiologists and other hospital-based specialists lowers the hospital's (and admitting physicians') decision-making costs and helps overcome free-rider problems. Transaction costs are lower than they would be if anesthesiologists were salaried employees of the hospital or if an open-staff policy were in effect.

Not all hospitals sign exclusive contracts, however. This observation suggests that the relative superiority of one method of engaging the services of hospital-based physicians over another varies with the size and scope of the hospital's activities, its internal organizational structure, and the market environment in which it operates.[g] To reiterate Ronald Coase's conclusion, "a firm will tend to expand until the costs of organising an extra transaction within the firm become equal to carrying out the same transaction by means of an exchange on the open market or the costs of organising another firm."

---

f *Ibid.* pp. 404-5.
g Empirical evidence suggests, though, that there is no statistically significant relationship between hospitals' market shares and their propensity to adopt exclusive contracts for hospital-based physicians. This evidence casts doubt on the notion that exclusive hospital contracts are injurious to competition. In fact, the Court determined that the exclusive anesthesiology contract challenged by Dr. Hyde did not constitute an antitrust law violation. See Lynk and Morrisey, "Economic Basis of *Hyde.*"

THE TRANSACTION-COST APPROACH

Information about resource values is not free—resources must be invested to discover "what the relevant prices are."[8] Rather than assuming this difficulty away, however, the modern theory of the firm makes it the center of attention. The modern approach treats contracts and firms as alternate means of conserving on the costs of acquiring information. The institutions of contracts and firms may also assist the parties to an exchange in economizing on other costs of transacting, including bargaining and decision costs and policing and enforcement costs. Hence, the growing literature in this line of research has been collectively referred to as "transaction-cost economics" or as the "new institutional economics" to highlight its emphasis on the rules that govern exchange.[9]

In a very real sense, contracts are a pervasive feature of economic life: "If each individual is a private input owner—of his own labor, if nothing else— then almost all individuals in society are bound by contracts when they compete and interact."[10] Because the transaction-cost approach underscores the importance of the institutions of exchange, the critical task is to characterize

---

8 Coase, "The Nature of the Firm," p. 390.
9 Oliver E. Williamson, "Transaction-Cost Economics: The Governance of Contractual Relations," *Journal of Law and Economics* 22 (October 1979), pp. 233-61.
10 Steven M. S. Cheung, "The Contractual Nature of the Firm," *Journal of Law and Economics* 26 (April 1983), p. 18.

transactions in terms of the factors that help determine which institution—markets, contracts, or firms—is optimal in any particular case.

Characterizing Transactions

Oliver Williamson has argued that the crucial features of transactions are uncertainty, the frequency with which they recur, and the extent to which the parties are required to make investments in transaction-specific assets.[11] The third of these characteristics is perhaps the most important.

Specialized assets create incentives for **opportunistic behavior**, which Williamson defines as "self-interest seeking with guile."[12] The crux of the matter is this: certain exchanges require that one of the parties invest in an asset that is highly specialized to the transaction. (The construction of a pipeline from an oil refinery to an isolated distribution terminal where gasoline is sold to wholesalers is a relevant example.) Because the value of the asset is much higher in its current use than in its next best alternative use, once the investment is made the parties are "locked into" their relationship to a significant degree. The buyer cannot readily turn to alternate suppliers, nor can the seller turn to alternate customers without suffering a substantial loss.

By the same token, however, each can take advantage of the other by opportunistically attempting to obtain more favorable terms than had been agreed to prior to the investment being undertaken. The buyer can refuse to make any further purchases unless price decreases, and the seller can refuse to make any further deliveries unless price increases. In short, the value of the specialized asset over and above its value in the next best alternative use can be *appropriated* by post-contractual opportunistic behavior.[13]

Williamson refers to transactions of this kind as "idiosyncratic"—in the presence of specialized assets the benefits of the transaction are contingent on avoiding opportunistic self-interest-seeking in its execution.[14] Specialized institutional arrangements are obviously needed for governing such transactions.

The frequency with which transactions recur also influences the institutional arrangements made for governing the interactions between the parties to an exchange. When transactions take place infrequently, explicit contracts or other formal mechanisms will usually be unnecessary except in the presence of the aforementioned specialized assets. Only if the buyer and seller expect to maintain a continuing relationship does the need for a formal governance structure arise. The assurance of such a long-term relationship is in fact necessary to induce the parties to make investments in any physical or human capital that is specialized to the transaction.

---

11 Williamson, "Transaction-Cost Economics," p. 246.

12 Williamson, *Economic Institutions of Capitalism*, p. 47.

13 See Benjamin Klein, Robert G. Crawford, and Armen A. Alchian, "Vertical Integration, Appropriable Rents, and the Competitive Contracting Process," *Journal of Law and Economics* 21 (October 1978), pp. 297-326.

14 Williamson, "Transaction-Cost Economics," p. 240-241.

Uncertainty, or the absence of perfect information about resource values over time, also affects the choice of relying on market price signals, contracts, or the firm for governing transactions. Generally speaking, uncertainty hinders the use of long-term contracting as a routine mechanism for governing transactions. By definition, the inability of the parties to foresee the future in perfect detail makes it impossible (prohibitively costly) for them to anticipate and make provisions for every possible contingency. It therefore becomes imperative that they devise a mechanism (a "governance structure") for working things out when unexpected events reveal gaps in the contract.

Governance Structures

As discussed previously, variations in three critical features of transactions—uncertainty, frequency, and degree of asset specialization—lead to the emergence of alternate institutions for governing exchange. Abstracting for the moment from the uncertainty dimension, the various possibilities are laid out in Table 7.1, adapted from a classification scheme proposed by Williamson, which provides a useful way of organizing the discussion, but not in a way that everyone accepts.[15]

The Market. In the absence of specialized assets, market governance is preferable to other institutions regardless of the frequency with which transactions recur. This is because the market creates powerful incentives for all

TABLE 7.1   TRANSACTION CHARACTERISTICS AND GOVERNANCE STRUCTURES

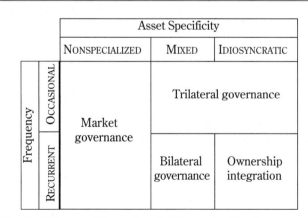

		Asset Specificity		
		NONSPECIALIZED	MIXED	IDIOSYNCRATIC
Frequency	OCCASIONAL	Market governance	Trilateral governance	Trilateral governance
	RECURRENT		Bilateral governance	Ownership integration

Source: Oliver E. Williamson, "Transaction-Cost Economics: The Governance of Contractual Relations," *Journal of Law and Economics* 22 (October 1979), p. 253. © The University of Chicago Press. Reprinted by permission.

---

15 *Ibid.*, p. 253. Coase himself, for example, does not think that asset specificity is an important key to understanding the choice between long-term contracting and ownership integration. See Ronald H. Coase, "The Nature of the Firm: Influence," *Journal of Law, Economics, and Organization* 4 (Spring 1988), pp. 33-47.

parties to use resources efficiently (hold costs down) and to honor their commitments. Spot market transactions between buyer and seller are enforced mainly by the threat of loss of future business. When resources are unspecialized, both parties can turn to alternatives without difficulty. Consequently, one party's threat to terminate the business relationship credibly prevents opportunistic behavior by the other. Market governance thus relies on the fact that, inasmuch as the reputations of both buyer and seller are contingent on satisfactory performance, each has incentives to behave responsibly.

This repeat-purchase mechanism disciplines recurrent market transactions. When exchanges between buyer and seller take place frequently, both parties can readily consult their own experiences. The buyer can continually monitor its supplier's compliance with the implicit promise made to deliver goods of certain quality at appointed times at specified prices. The customer's ability to shift to alternate supply sources at low cost provides the seller with a strong incentive to fulfill these expectations. For its part, the seller can readily verify its customer's compliance with the implicit promise made to accept delivery and to pay promptly. The supplier's capacity to shift to alternate buyers provides the customer with a strong incentive to fulfill these expectations.

In the absence of specialized assets, market governance will usually be cost-effective even when transactions take place infrequently. This is because information of the sort just discussed will be available from other market participants who have dealt with the buyer or seller in the interim. The parties to the exchange can therefore consult the experiences of others when they have not themselves engaged in the transaction recently.

Because of the superiority of market governance in terms of efficient resource allocation and cost control, there should be a presumption in its favor. Indeed, market governance may be more powerful than Williamson's classification scheme suggests. The reputations of buyers and sellers are specialized resources in the sense that their capital values are contingent on satisfactory performance. Because they have low salvage value, investments in reputational capital are analogous to the posting of a bond that assures noncheating behavior.

Investments in other types of nonsalvageable, transaction-specific assets—brand names, trademarks, elaborate storefronts, expensive advertising campaigns and celebrity endorsement contracts, and so on—may have similar purposes and effects.[16] The value of such investments will be lost if market commitments, expressed or implied, are not honored. The point is that instead of creating incentives for opportunistic behavior, certain idiosyncratic capital may in fact serve as a guarantee against it.

Contracts. Market governance generally will not suffice when the exchange requires one or both of the parties to invest in highly specialized

---

16 Benjamin Klein and Keith B. Leffler, "The Role of Market Forces in Assuring Contractual Performance," *Journal of Political Economy* 89 (August 1981), pp. 615-41.

or idiosyncratic assets. Even though buyer and seller both have an interest in seeing the transaction through to completion on the initial terms, circumstances may arise that make it wealth-maximizing for one of them to engage in opportunistic behavior. More explicit or formal governance structures are necessary to help avoid such possibilities.

First, consider the case of transactions that recur infrequently. Even when the assets involved are highly specialized, it will not usually pay to supersede the market entirely by internalizing the transaction within the firm. For example, an electric utility may place an order for a heavy turbine generator to replace or expand its existing power generating capacity only once every ten or fifteen years. Such equipment is highly transaction-specific in the sense that each turbine must meet the customer's unique technical and performance specifications. Therefore, both parties are vulnerable to being "held up" once the order has been placed. Nonetheless, because of the infrequency of orders, it will obviously not be economical for the utility company to build its own heavy turbine generators.

How then are the parties to limit the incentives of each to engage in post-contractual opportunistic behavior? How is the buyer able to avoid having to pay a higher price than agreed to if the seller pleads unexpected cost overruns? How is the seller able to avoid having to accept a lower price than agreed to if the buyer pleads unexpected financial emergencies? Nonperformance can be redressed in the courts, but litigation is itself costly and may in the end prevent the transaction from being completed on any terms.

Third-party assistance (or what Williamson refers to as **trilateral governance**) offers an alternative mechanism for reducing transaction costs under these circumstances. The buyer and seller can agree when they sign the contract to bind themselves to arbitration in the event that disputes arise. Binding arbitration has at least three advantages over other governance structures. First, the contract need not (as indeed it cannot) specify each party's responsibilities under all possible contingencies. Second, because the parties can reasonably expect unbiased decisions from an independent arbitrator, the chances increase that the parties will resolve their dispute in a manner that permits the transaction to go through to completion. Finally, private, third-party arbitration is usually subject to fewer delays and is therefore less costly than seeking redress through the courts.[17]

When transactions recur frequently and the assets involved are only moderately specialized (see the "mixed" case in Table 7.1 on p. 244), time-consuming arbitration may not be cost-effective. **Bilateral governance**, where the parties specify in their contract permissible adaptations to various contingencies, is appropriate in such circumstances. "Escalator" clauses are a relevant example. Buyer and seller agree that the buyer will pay some fraction of any cost

---

17 See Bruce L. Benson, *The Enterprise of Law: Justice without the State* (San Francisco: Pacific Research Institute, 1990) for a description of the evolution and growing importance of private dispute resolution mechanisms.

increases resulting from a rise in the general level of prices. More sophisticated formulas can account for increases in the prices of raw materials or other inputs that represent a significant share of the cost of the final product.

Bilateral governance is transaction-cost reducing in the sense that specifying permissible adjustments ahead of time allows the parties to extend the term of the contract beyond the duration it would have otherwise. The parties thereby avoid renegotiation costs of shorter-term contracts. It should be stressed, however, that such a governance structure will be economical only if the events that trigger an adjustment are verifiable to both parties at low cost. Because disputes about whether or not an adjustment is in fact warranted may themselves cause a bilateral agreement to unravel, verification costs may lead to the emergence of alternative governance mechanisms.[18]

Ownership Integration. Recurrent transactions involving highly specialized assets will generally occur within the governance structure of the firm. The incentive for buyer and seller to engage in opportunistic behavior decreases when the two parties merge their separate profit streams into a single economic entity. Because there is less for one party to gain by attempting to take advantage of the other, adaptations to unforeseen events can be made immediately and in whatever form is jointly wealth maximizing.

Consider the case of a resort hotel and a golf course built next to each other at a popular vacation spot.[19] Weather, scenery, and other attributes of the site generate a stream of **rents** for the owners of each enterprise—the values of both the hotel and the golf course are higher in their present location than they would be at the next best attractive resort area. Moreover, the value of each asset is partly dependent on the existence of the other: the hotel owner benefits from the patronage of guests who want to play golf, and the owner of the golf course benefits from golfers having a convenient place to stay.

If the hotel and golf course are separately owned, each is vulnerable to being "held up." Once the investments necessary to build the resort have been made, the owner of the golf course can attempt to capture all of the location-specific rents by opportunistically raising the course's greens fee. Similarly, the owners of the hotel can attempt to capture all of the location-specific rents by opportunistically raising the hotel's room rates. Because each owner is interested only in personal wealth maximization, neither has an incentive to consider the impact of his or her pricing policy on the other.

18 For an application of these ideas to political markets, see W. Mark Crain, William F. Shughart II, and Robert D. Tollison, "Legislative Majorities as Nonsalvageable Assets," *Southern Economic Journal* 55 (October 1988), pp. 303-14.

19 See Klein, Crawford, and Alchian, "Vertical Integration, Appropriable Rents, and the Competitive Contracting Process," for this and other examples of the incentives for ownership integration created by the existence of appropriable rents.

And, knowing that the risk of appropriation exists (or that it will cost something to prevent opportunistic behavior), the resort may not be built in the first place. In such a situation, the transaction-cost minimizing solution is for the hotel and the golf course to be jointly owned.[20]

In sum, the transaction-cost approach views the firm as an institutional structure that emerges to govern a specialized set of transactions characterized by their frequency and their asset specificity. Under this approach, however, defining the firm is not an all-or-nothing proposition. The boundaries must be derived transaction by transaction.

The transaction-cost approach also emphasizes that the boundaries of the firm are not rigid. As technologies change, the characteristics of transactions change, and this may in turn lead to changes in governance structures. As assets become more transaction specific, for instance, and the gains from opportunistic behavior thereby increase, the costs of contracting across ownership boundaries will generally increase by more than the costs associated with internal-to-the-firm decision making. Other things being the same, we would expect market contracting to give way to ownership integration in such circumstances. Similarly, if the degree of resource specialization is held constant, ownership integration will tend to replace explicit contracting as the uncertainty surrounding transactions increases.[21]

In sum, a market economy will contain a continuum of governance structures, running from discrete exchanges on the spot market completely unencumbered by explicit contractual terms to the formal internalization of transactions within the firm, each structure being optimal (transaction-cost minimizing) for the given circumstances. The firm emerges as an economic entity in the transaction-cost approach because of its superiority in conserving resources that would otherwise be lost through opportunistic behavior or through an inability to adapt to changing market conditions when transactions take place across ownership boundaries.

TEAM PRODUCTION

Further insights into the nature of the firm are provided in an important paper by Armen Alchian and Harold Demsetz.[22] Alchian and Demsetz underscored the firm's role in capturing the benefits associated with **team production**. They define this as production in which (1) several different types of resources are employed, (2) the final product is greater than the sum of the separate contributions of each of the cooperating resources, and (3) not all of the resources used in the production process are owned by the same individual.

20 The choice between ownership integration and contracting is discussed more fully in Chapters 12 and 13.
21 Harold B. Malmgren, "Information, Expectations, and the Theory of the Firm," *Quarterly Journal of Economics* 75 (August 1961), pp. 399-421.
22 Alchian and Demsetz, "Production, Information Costs, and Economic Organization."

The Merger of General Motors and Fisher Body

A realistic illustration of the hold-up problem that plagues transactions involving idiosyncratic capital—and the incentives for ownership integration that such opportunistic behavior creates—is apparent in the events preceding the merger of General Motors with Fisher Body Company in 1926.[a] By 1919, the manufacture of automobiles had shifted away from the use of wooden bodies to the use of closed metal bodies. In that year, General Motors entered a ten-year contract to have Fisher Body Company supply its requirements of stamped automobile body parts. Fisher agreed to manufacture the dies for stamping body parts to General Motors' designs and specifications, and to ship the parts to GM for assembly. In return, General Motors agreed to pay Fisher a price for stamped body parts equal to Fisher's cost (exclusive of interest on invested capital) plus 17.6 percent.

The contract contained an exclusive dealing clause whereby General Motors committed to buy substantially all of its automobile body parts from Fisher. The agreement also included provisions for binding arbitration in the event of disputes regarding price. General Motors attempted to protect itself further by specifying that the price it would pay to Fisher would not exceed the price paid by other automobile manufacturers to Fisher for similar body parts or be greater than the average market price of body parts produced by suppliers other than Fisher.

The contractual agreement did not work out in practice, however. General Motors' automobile sales increased dramatically in the ensuing years, and its demand for metal body parts rose substantially beyond the level it had anticipated at the time of the agreement with Fisher. GM became increasingly unhappy with the terms of the contract and with the price it was being charged for body parts. GM argued that the contract price for parts should be reduced because Fisher's output per unit of capital had increased significantly and so its average production costs had declined.

Fisher refused to renegotiate price and at the same time also rejected GM's proposal to relocate its body parts manufacturing plant closer to the auto maker's assembly facility, a move that General Motors claimed was necessary for increased production efficiency.[b] Finding the circumstances intolerable, General Motors began negotiations in 1924 for the purchase of Fisher's remaining stock. (GM had earlier acquired a minority ownership interest in the body parts supplier.) In 1926, these negotiations culminated in a merger agreement.

The relationship between General Motors and Fisher Body prior to their merger is a classic example of post-contractual opportunistic behavior in the presence of idiosyncratic capital. The manufacture of dies for stamping metal body parts in accordance with General Motors' designs and specifications gave these dies a value highly specialized to the transaction

a Benjamin Klein, Robert G. Crawford, and Armen A. Alchian, "Vertical Integration, Appropriable Rents, and the Competitive Contracting Process," *Journal of Law and Economics* 21 (October 1978), pp. 297-326. The GM-Fisher Body case is discussed more fully in Benjamin Klein, "Vertical Integration as Organizational Ownership: The Fisher Body-General Motors Relationship Revisited," *Journal of Law, Economics, and Organization* 4 (Spring 1988), pp. 199-213. Also see Richard N. Langlois and P. L. Robertson, "Explaining Vertical Integration: Lessons from the American Automobile Industry," *Journal of Economic History* 49 (1989), pp. 1-15.

b Fisher's refusal to relocate its own production facilities to a site closer to GM's plant was in large part due to the fact that transportation costs were fully reimbursable under the agreed-upon price formula. All of the benefits of Fisher's relocation would have therefore gone to GM. Fisher's inability to pass through any of its capital costs in calculating the prices of body parts created another difficulty for GM—Fisher shifted to a more labor-intensive production process that resulted in higher costs and higher parts prices than would have been charged otherwise. See Benjamin Klein, "Contract Costs and Administered Prices: An Economic Theory of Rigid Wages," *American Economic Review Papers and Proceedings* 74 (May 1984), p. 335.

between GM and Fisher. In a given model year, GM could not easily turn to an alternate supplier without suffering a costly production delay. Once the dies had been manufactured, Fisher's options likewise decreased because there were no demanders of its output comparable to General Motors. Fisher could not very well market the parts stamped from GM's designs to another automobile manufacturer.

An appropriable rent therefore existed in the dies,[c] and both parties had an incentive to behave opportunistically. Combining ownership of the designs and the dies through merger removed this incentive because it was now in each party's interest to behave in ways that enhanced their joint profits. Adaptations to unforeseen events such as unanticipated changes in demand could thereafter be made immediately and in whatever form promoted their mutual interests.[d]

c An economic *rent* is defined as a payment received by the owner of a resource over and above the resource's value in its next best alternative use.

d There are, of course, contractual alternatives to complete ownership integration for solving the transaction-cost problems associated with idiosyncratic capital. One of these alternatives is what David Teece calls "quasi-vertical integration." Under this arrangement, the downstream firm acquires an ownership interest in the specialized asset that generates appropriable rents, but not the whole supplier. In the automobile industry, for example, the downstream firm that performs final assembly operations might own the specialized dies used to manufacture stamped body parts, but not go so far as to acquire a full ownership interest in its parts supplier, relying instead on a contractual agreement to govern the supplier's production of parts. However, such an arrangement may leave the upstream firm vulnerable to exploitation by an opportunistic customer who threatens to switch suppliers. See Kirk Monteverde and David J. Teece, "Appropriable Rents and Quasi-Vertical Integration," *Journal of Law and Economics* 25 (October 1982), pp. 321-28.

The last two of these characteristics are the key elements of the team production idea. The final product the team produces is not determined by simply adding up the individual team members' contributions. Assembling the various resources together yields an increment of output above and beyond that which would be obtained if they were employed separately. This synergistic effect, which could be due to economies of scale or scope, the benefits derived from specialization and the division of labor, or some other technological factor, is the driving force behind cooperative production activities.

The Gains from Specialization

The productivity benefits of team production have been recognized at least since Adam Smith told his famous story of a pin factory more than 200 years ago.[23] Axel Leijonhufvud has cleverly used Smith's example to drive home the importance of the benefits stemming from specialization and the division of labor.[24] Suppose that pin manufacturing involves five separate operations, each of which requires a different pin-making tool. With "crafts production," each of five workers, proceeding at his or her own pace, performs all of the steps necessary to make a pin. In this case, the daily output of pins is simply the sum of the number of pins each worker is able to produce in a day.

23 Adam Smith, *An Inquiry into the Nature and Causes of the Wealth of Nations* (New York: Modern Library, 1937), pp. 4-5. (First published in 1776).

24 Axel Leijonhufvud, "Capitalism and the Factory System," in Richard N. Langlois, ed., *Economics as a Process* (Cambridge: Cambridge University Press, 1986), pp. 203-23.

Now suppose that the production process is rearranged into a "factory system," so that each worker specializes in one of the five pin-making operations and the five workers perform their tasks in sequence. Worker A specializes in the first operation, say straightening the wire, which he or she then turns over to worker B, who cuts it to proper length, and so on. Team production replaces production by individuals.

Switching from crafts production to factory production generates a number of important benefits. First, factory production saves physical capital. With crafts production, each worker must be equipped with a complete set of pin-making tools and four of the five tools are always idle as each of the separate manufacturing operations is being performed. Factory production, by contrast, requires only one set of tools, not five, and no tool is ever idle.

Second, and more important to the team production idea, factory production conserves on human capital insofar as no one worker need possess all of the skills and abilities necessary for making a complete pin. Each worker must learn only those particular skills that are appropriate to one narrowly defined task. Because "proficiency is gained by concentration of effort,"[25] such specialization generates increased productivity—the output of the team is much larger than the sum of the outputs produced by the five workers making pins independently.

The Incentives to Shirk

The productivity benefits of team production come at a cost, however. Switching from crafts production to factory production requires standardization of the product and increased monitoring and coordination of the individual worker's activities. No individual can any longer be free to work at his or her own pace. Each must instead work at the pace of the team—if one workstation is unstaffed, no pins can be made. Put another way, the third characteristic of team production poses a problem in organization. Because not all of the resources used in the production process are owned by the same individual (if nothing else, each worker is the owner of his or her own labor), the firm must find a way of organizing and capturing the benefits of team production.

Alchian and Demsetz highlighted a particular cost of organization associated with team production, namely the increased incentives of team members to **shirk**. "Shirking" is evading responsibilities, neglecting details, reducing work effort in order to consume more leisure on the job, and so forth. This becomes a problem in a team production setting because the increased output derives from the cooperative interaction of the team members. It is therefore difficult (costly) to identify and to compensate them for their individual contributions.

Given that there is a less direct link between any one individual's effort and the compensation received in payment for that effort, a team member

---

25 Charles E. Ferguson, *Microeconomic Theory*, 3E. (Homewood, IL: Richard D. Irwin, 1972), p. 235.

will bear only a portion of the total cost associated with the reduction in output due to his or her shirking. As a first approximation, if there are n team members, each bears only $1/n$ of any money income loss that results from the increased consumption of leisure on the job.

Because the individual's opportunity cost of leisure is less than the opportunity cost facing the team as a whole, he or she will rationally choose to consume more of it (up to the limit of detection), thereby reducing the total output of the team. But all team members face the same incentives. If they all choose to consume additional leisure on the job, total output will fall even further. Thus, while the team as a whole would be better off (their money incomes would be higher) if shirking were not possible, each has an incentive to engage in behavior that makes them jointly worse off.

At the extreme, shirking may dissipate all of the productivity gains associated with team production. One possible solution to the problem of controlling shirking is to add a member to the team who specializes in observing and metering the effort of each team member.[26] But the hiring of a **monitor** does not completely solve the shirking problem, because monitors may themselves shirk. The question then becomes, Who will monitor the monitor?

Property Rights and Residual Claims

The **classical capitalist firm** provides a solution to the shirking problems of team production activities. Instead of having the team hire the monitor, the monitor hires the team. He or she contracts with each team member to perform specific tasks with a stipulated level of effort. In exchange, the monitor agrees to pay each team member an income share equal to that member's expected contribution to output. The monitor thus becomes a **residual claimant**—he or she has the right to keep all of the income generated by the team's productive activities not owed by contract to the individual team members. The greater the income (output) generated (the less the shirking), the larger the monitor's residual will be. This type of ownership arrangement thus provides the monitor with a profit motive to keep shirking to a minimum.

The existence of a monitor with a claim to the residual income generated by team production is one component of the bundle of **property rights** associated with ownership of the classical capitalist firm. Alchian and Demsetz point out that in order to play the role of residual claimant effectively, the owner-monitor must also (1) be the central party to all contracts with team inputs, (2) have the right to observe input behavior, which includes the tasks of assigning duties, establishing rewards, and metering performance, (3) be able to alter the membership of the team unilaterally, and (4) have the right to sell the residual claim.

---

26 Cheung, "The Contractual Nature of the Firm," p. 8, relates that a group of workers in pre-revolutionary China, whose job it was to pull a large wooden boat with ropes while marching along a riverbank, jointly agreed to hire a taskmaster to whip them!

The last of these rights is especially important. **Alienability** of the residual claim enables the owner-monitor to capture in the sales price of the firm the discounted value of any organizational innovations he or she discovers that reduce costs or increase revenue. The owner's ability to profit personally from such discoveries provides an economic incentive for putting them into operation.

Alchian and Demsetz' insights about the shirking-information problem of team production help shed additional light on the purposes and effects of the various organizational and financial structures adopted by firms in the economy. Part III explores these implications more fully. The common denominator is that different ownership arrangements entail different combinations of shirking and information costs.

As just one illustration of the power of the team-production insight, consider the relationship between the size of the team and the magnitude of the shirking-information cost problem. In general, the larger the team, the more costly it will be for the owner to acquire information about and to monitor the performance of individual team members. This observation suggests that multi-owner arrangements such as those found in **partnerships** and other types of **profit-sharing firms** will be appropriate only in specialized circumstances.

Dividing the residual claim among several owners predictably increases the incentive of any one of them to shirk because he or she will bear only a portion of the total cost of doing so. Owner shirking includes neglecting details, failing to monitor the performance of employees effectively, and allocating resources in ways that enhance the owner's personal welfare (purchasing a plusher office carpet, incurring unnecessary travel and entertainment expenses, and so on). This behavior reduces the market value of the firm.

But because the bulk of this reduction in the firm's market value will fall on the other owners, each has an incentive to engage in more shirking than if he or she bore the full cost of such behavior. However, the number of owners may be "small" or the firm may be engaged in work that a single, nonexpert owner would have difficulty monitoring, such as providing medical or legal services. In these cases, the higher shirking incentives the owners face individually may be more than offset by their ability to evaluate one another's performance more effectively.

Widespread sharing of the residual claim by larger teams, such as that observed in **employee-owned firms** in the United States and **socialist** ("labor-managed") **firms** elsewhere, will have an adverse impact on business performance. This is because while having a share in the residual claim increases the cost of shirking to an individual employee, he or she will still not bear the full consequences of such behavior. With equal profit sharing, the larger the team, the smaller each ownership share is, and the more the cost of shirking to the individual owner diverges from the cost to the firm as a whole. Moreover, as the number of owners increases, the ability of each owner to acquire information about and to monitor the performance of the others declines. Thus, employee ownership of large enterprises is likely to result in losses from owner shirking that exceed any gains associated with giving the employees a financial stake in the performance of the firm.

It should be noted, however, that owner shirking is not completely unconstrained. One can make a profit by taking over a firm where such behavior has risen to unacceptable levels. That is, if owner shirking lowers the value of the firm, taking steps to limit shirking will cause the firm's market value to rise. An outsider (or one of the existing owners) who perceives such an opportunity can therefore buy out a majority of the employee-owners by offering them a premium over and above the current market price of their shares. This owner can then implement improvements to reduce shirking, raise the firm's market value, and thereby realize a profit. Thus, as long as the ownership rights to employee-owned firms are alienable, the market for corporate control places limits on owner shirking.[27] (This disciplinary margin is of course not available for socialistic or government-owned enterprises, which helps explain their poor performance relative to that of privately owned capitalist firms.)[28]

The Role of the Firm in a Team-Production Setting

The shirking-information costs of team production recognized by Alchian and Demsetz are a complement to, rather than a substitute for, the insights about the nature of the firm identified by Coase and Williamson. In the team-production framework, the firm emerges as a specialized institution for collecting, collating, and utilizing information about cooperative production activities. Because the owner-monitor gains more knowledge about the productivities of team inputs, opportunities for the profitable employment of cooperating resources are available at lower cost within the firm than on the market. The metering problem associated with team production thus provides an additional efficiency rationale for the emergence of the firm as an economic entity.

The basic insight is this: Team production yields an increment of output over and above that which would be produced if the team members worked separately and independently. At the same time, however, because team inputs are not owned by the same individual, the firm must find a way to organize the team so that the productivity gains thereby generated are not dissipated by team members' shirking.

The classical capitalist firm offers a solution to this problem by providing the firm's owner with a profit motive to hold shirking to a cost-effective minimum. The owner's ability to do so is enhanced by organizing the team within

---

27 Henry G. Manne, "Mergers and the Market for Corporate Control," *Journal of Political Economy* 73 (April 1965), pp. 110-20.

28 For some recent evidence supporting this conclusion, see Anthony E. Boardman and Aidan R. Vining, "Ownership and Performance in Competitive Environments: A Comparison of the Performance of Private, Mixed, and State-Owned Enterprises," *Journal of Law and Economics* 32 (April 1989), pp. 1-33. Also see Chapter 16 of this book.

a single firm. Compared to the case where some or all of the team inputs are employed by other firms, this arrangement provides the owner-monitor with a greater opportunity to gather information about, to evaluate, and to reward the performances of individual team members.

While it may be true that familiarity breeds contempt, it also nourishes the acquisition of information. The owner-monitor obtains more and better knowledge about the productivities of the human and physical resources under his or her daily supervision than could possibly be obtained if those same inputs were employed under the proximate control of the owners of other firms. By using this information properly, the owner can limit shirking and thereby capture more of the productivity benefits of team production than would be possible otherwise.

The relationships between the owner-monitor and the resources used in team production are only a subset of the activities of business firms in which the interests of contracting parties may diverge, however. Principal-agent theory provides a framework for a broader treatment of this topic.

PRINCIPAL-AGENT RELATIONSHIPS

A principal-agent relationship exists whenever one individual (the **principal**) delegates authority to another (the **agent**) whose decisions have an impact on the principal's welfare. Principal-agent relationships are quite common. Examples are the relationships between voters and their elected representatives in the legislature, Congress and the bureaucracy, labor union members and the officers they designate to negotiate with management, homeowners and real estate agents, clients and lawyers, and investors and stockbrokers. The agency relationships of particular interest here are those that exist within and among firms—between employers and employees, between suppliers and customers, and between owners (stockholders) and managers, for example.

As in all other aspects of economic life, the principal's delegation of decision-making authority to an agent involves a tradeoff. On the one hand, by delegating decision-making authority to another, the principal economizes on the resources that he or she would otherwise invest in gathering information about an activity requiring specialized or expert knowledge. On the other hand, and assuming that each party seeks to maximize its own welfare, the interests of principal and agent will never dovetail perfectly. This divergence of interests means that the decisions of the agent will potentially impose a welfare loss on the principal. Put another way, because the agent's choice may not be the same as the choice the principal would make personally given the same information, the agent may fail to maximize the principal's wealth.

Consider the incentives facing a real estate agent who is retained to sell a client's house. Real estate agents are typically paid a fixed commission by the seller, which is expressed as a percentage (normally six percent) of the price at which the house is ultimately sold. While it is obviously true that a

Why is Corporate Ownership Prohibited in the National Football League?

The National Football League (NFL) includes in its constitution and bylaws provisions stating that no franchise can be owned by a corporation.[a] Therefore, only individuals can own NFL teams. [b] Moreover, NFL franchises tend to be more tightly held—there are fewer owners per team—than is typical of firms in most industries. Indeed, ownership concentration seems to be the norm across the major professional sports (football, baseball, basketball, hockey, and soccer).[c]

One explanation for the concentrated ownership structure observed in professional sports is that franchises are closely held because of the amenity potential offered by the output of these firms. Victory in the Super Bowl, the National Basketball Association Championship, or the World Series provides the winning team's owners with a substantial amount of personal satisfaction that would be greatly diluted if widely shared.

Such an indulgence of tastes by the owners of professional sports franchises implies that ownership must be concentrated in order to facilitate owner control of managerial decision making. Concentrated ownership also increases the personal enjoyment derived from being "the" owner of, say the New Orleans Saints, rather than being one of a thousand owners, even if profits are sacrificed in the process. Sports ownership therefore connotes a world of utility maximization, not profit maximization, and to this end ownership structure has tended toward fewer effective owners (limited partnerships and closely held family enterprises).

There is an alternative, profit-maximizing explanation of ownership structure in professional sports, however. This explanation derives from treating the league rather than the individual sports franchise as the proper unit of analysis. While it is true that professional sports teams have separate balance sheets and income statements, in no meaningful sense are these entities independent of one another. Sports franchises are interdependent in a quite fundamental way.

No one club has anything of value to offer the marketplace (except perhaps an old-fashioned barnstorming tour) outside a league format with a regular season schedule, playoffs, and a championship. The Chicago Bulls may have a separate identity for tax purposes, but they cannot produce anything of value unless they are a member of the National Basketball Association (NBA) and thus have access to a schedule of NBA opponents. In sports, the relevant unit of analysis is the league, which competes for customers (fans) with other live and televised sporting and entertainment events.

The interdependence fostered by a league format presents an economic problem for individual team owners. Teams may compete against each other on the field, but off the field they share common interests. Because of this fact, sports leagues have evolved elaborate systems of controls over such matters as player selection and compensation, revenue sharing, franchise location and expansion, and investments in franchises.

These control systems serve to overcome a shirking-information problem among team owners. The welfare of the league is at a maximum when "competitive

---

a This case study is based on Arthur A. Fleisher III, William F. Shughart II, and Robert D. Tollison, "Ownership Structure in Professional Sports," in Richard O. Zerbe, Jr., ed., *Research in Law and Economics*, vol. 12 (Greenwich, CT: JAI Press, 1989), pp. 71-75.

b This restriction excludes the Green Bay Packers, whose preexisting (nonprofit) corporation was "grandfathered" into the NFL's constitution.

c Harold Demsetz and Kenneth Lehn, "The Structure of Corporate Ownership: Causes and Consequences," *Journal of Political Economy* 93 (December 1985), pp. 1155-77.

balance" prevails. Balance of this kind enhances attendance and television ratings across the league, making all teams financially better off than they would be under a situation of one- or two-team dominance and generally uninteresting competition among teams. Put another way, a professional sports league is a joint venture of individual team owners.

As in other cases of jointness and shared responsibilities, controlling shirking is the basic economic problem. Incumbent owners must guard against the possibility that one of them will purposely reduce the on-field competitiveness of his or her team by hiring cheap, low-caliber players and losing lots of games while at the same time continuing to share in joint league revenues from such sources as national television contracts. Concentrated ownership helps facilitate owner monitoring and control of shirking.

With fewer owners per team, each bears a greater share of the cost of any one owner's shirking, which is manifested in lower team revenues throughout the league. This greater per-owner cost of shirking both reduces each owner's incentive to degrade team quality and increases the incentives of all to monitor and to control shirking by other owners. In short, concentrated ownership serves to increase the profitability of the league as a whole by lowering the costs to individual team owners of acquiring information about and reducing shirking.

The profit-maximization objective would seem to explain the prevalence of provisions in professional sports league constitutions and franchise contracts requiring careful review of prospective league franchise investors, how many franchises there are, where the franchises are located, and so on. The profit-maximization hypothesis about ownership concentration in professional sports is testable. It predicts that owner-ship will be more concentrated the greater the extent of revenue sharing among team owners. More revenue sharing implies a greater potential for owner shirking because each franchise's income is thereby less closely tied to the quality of the team it fields.

The profit-maximization hypothesis therefore predicts that ownership will be more concentrated in the NFL, which has been called the most "socialistic" of all major professional sports leagues insofar as it has the greatest amount of revenue sharing among team owners.[d] This is precisely what we noted at the outset: The NFL bans corporate ownership of its franchises. By disallowing incorporation and thereby restricting ownership to small groups of individuals, the NFL has responded to profit-maximizing incentives to control the potential for shirking among its owners. The other major professional sports leagues operate with less revenue sharing and do not specifically restrict ownership to individuals. In fact, as of 1980, the NBA had three corporate owners (not including the Boston Celtics, who subsequently "went public"), and ten Major League Baseball teams had corporate owners. This evidence is broadly consistent with a profit-maximizing theory of ownership structure in professional sports.

d Robert C. Berry and Glenn M. Wong, *Law and Business in the Sports Industry, Vol. I: Professional Sports Leagues* (Dover, MA: Auburn House Publishing Co., 1986), p. 8. All three major sports leagues jointly share on a pro rata basis revenues from national (but not local) television contracts. Each league has a different arrangement for sharing live gate receipts, however. There is no sharing of live gate receipts in the NBA (100 percent goes to the home team); there is an 80-20 split in favor of the home team in professional baseball, and a 60-40 split in favor of the home team in the NFL.

---

higher sales price leads to a higher commission for the agent, the marginal benefit to the agent of higher selling prices is rather small—the agent only realizes an additional $60 in commission income for every $1,000 increase in price. Consequently, the agent may not work as hard in seeking out buyers willing to pay top dollar as the homeowner would like. The agent may rationally try to convince the principal to accept a lower price than could be obtained by waiting longer to sell. This is because the bulk of the benefits of searching for additional buyers who would be willing to pay more than the current top offer will go to the homeowner.

A similar divergence of interests exists between investors and stockbrokers who are also usually paid on fixed commission. Stockbrokers earn commission income based on the market value of the shares they buy or sell on their clients' accounts. They may therefore have an incentive to buy and sell more often than would be consistent with the principal's objective of maximizing the value of his or her own stock portfolio.

Agency Costs

Principal-agent theory focuses on the actions that the two parties can take to economize on the costs of their relationship. These costs can be divided into three categories.[29]

First, the principal can invest time and resources in monitoring the agent's activities, and he or she can attempt to create incentives for the agent to behave in ways that are more likely to lead to desired outcomes. Among the efforts the principal may undertake to monitor and control the behavior of the agent are laying down operating rules, making the agent's compensation contingent on observable results, and auditing the agent's records. The resources that the principal invests in such efforts fall into the category of **monitoring costs**.

Second, the agent will in some cases invest real resources for the purpose of guaranteeing his or her performance to the principal. These are **bonding costs**. Finally, any reduction in welfare suffered by the principal due to the agent's failure to maximize the principal's wealth is the **residual loss** associated with the principal-agent relationship.

Total **agency costs** are the sum of the monitoring costs, the bonding costs, and the principal's residual loss. The special object of principal-agent theory is to analyze the role that monitoring and bonding activities play in reducing the residual loss of the principal and to examine the agency costs associated with various organizational structures that might be adopted for governing the principal-agent relationship.

Responses to Agency Problems in the Modern Corporation

Consider the "separation of ownership from control" that characterizes the modern corporation. The stockholders (the principals) delegate decision-making authority respecting the day-to-day operations of the firm to managers (the agents) whose specialized knowledge enables them to make more profitable use of the firm's resources than could the nonexpert, absentee owners. At the same time, however, the managers' discretionary decision-making authority (along with their superior information about the firm's resources) allows them room for taking actions that further their own self-interests rather than those of the stockholders.

---

29 Michael C. Jensen and William H. Meckling, "Theory of the Firm: Managerial Behavior, Agency Costs, and Ownership Structure," *Journal of Financial Economics* 3 (1976), p. 308.

Managers may consequently fail to maximize stockholders' wealth (impose a residual loss on the firm's owners) by, for example, neglecting details, overconsuming the perquisites of office, and avoiding risk. Is such a divergence of interests consistent with economic efficiency? Put another way, what features of the corporate form of business organization help economize on the agency costs of the separation of ownership from control?

As discussed above, one source of agency costs in the firm—owner shirking—is disciplined by the market for corporate control. This mechanism also constrains the divergence of interests between owners and managers. One can make a profit by taking over a poorly managed enterprise and replacing incumbent managers with other individuals who are willing and able to take steps that increase stockholder wealth. The managerial labor market imposes similar constraints[30]. Managers who consistently direct the resources of the firm in ways that diminish its market value will in the long run command lower salaries as they compete for jobs against individuals more adept at managing business enterprises. But these margins of control are available to nearly all types of business organizations. What are some of the unique control mechanisms of the corporate organizational structure?

Share Transferability. A critical feature of the corporate form of business organization is the alienability of ownership rights. **Share transferability** limits the residual losses managers may impose on owners because stockholders are free to sell their equity claims if they find the divergence between management's resource-allocation decisions and those that would maximize their own wealth becoming too large. Moreover, stockholders can sell their shares without consulting the other owners of the firm.

Share transferability thus promotes economically efficient specialization by owners and managers. Managers, whose comparative advantage lies in appraising and coordinating the productive resources under their supervision, can specialize in overseeing the day-to-day operations of the firm. Owners, on the other hand, can specialize in risk taking. They need only monitor the market price of their shares to determine whether or not their agents are acting in their best interest. Share transferability—along with the existence of an active market in equity claims—provides a crucial monitoring function that helps reduce the residual loss associated with the principal-agent relationship between the owners and managers of the corporation.

This institutional feature of the corporation is less readily available to the owners of other types of business organizations. In partnerships, for example, the ownership and management functions are combined and shared jointly by the active partners. An individual partner cannot sell his or her ownership interest without the approval of all of the other partners. Indeed, a partnership must be dissolved if any co-owner wants to withdraw from the

---

30 Eugene F. Fama, "Agency Problems and the Theory of the Firm," *Journal of Political Economy* 88 (April 1980), pp. 288-307.

firm. This means that partners who fail to make managerial decisions that maximize the welfare of the partnership as a whole can only be replaced by terminating the entire enterprise and then reconstituting the firm under a new partnership agreement. The absence of share transferability makes it more costly for the owners of partnerships to sell out if they become dissatisfied with "management." Other things being the same, the residual losses of the owners of partnerships will therefore tend to be larger than those of the owners of corporations.

Contingent Pay. Principal-agent theory also sheds light on the structure of managerial compensation. As mentioned previously, one method of controlling the residual loss associated with the principal-agent relationship is for the principal to provide the agent with incentives to behave in ways that are compatible with the principal's desired outcomes. Generally speaking, the owners of the corporation will want their managerial agents to pursue the goal of maximizing expected long-run profits. This objective maximizes the present value of the net cash flows accruing to the firm's assets, thereby maximizing the market value of the owners' equity claims. The managers of the corporation, however, may have a more compressed time horizon (because, after all, their personal association with the firm will not last forever). Therefore, they may be more interested than the stockholders in short-run gains.

Among other things, this divergence between the basic objectives of owners and managers may lead the managers to undertake investment projects with more immediate and, perhaps, more risky payoffs than the owners would wish. Such a situation is especially likely if the managers' compensation is tied to current performance outcomes. Suppose, for example, that top management's pay consists of a flat salary plus a bonus tied to the firm's performance over the past quarter or the past year. This performance might be measured by sales or profit growth or earnings per share. In this case, the manager-agent has a clear incentive to forsake some investment projects with a positive net present value—projects whose benefits are realized far into the future but whose costs are more immediate. Likewise, he or she might undertake other investment projects with a negative net present value—projects whose benefits begin accruing in the short term but whose costs show up only at a much later date.

One solution to this time-horizon problem is to make management's compensation partly contingent on the firm's expected long-run profitability. An obvious way of doing this is to include in management's compensation package an option to buy company stock at some predetermined price per share at some future date. If the option price is set no lower than the current stock price, the manager has a greater incentive to undertake investment projects having a positive net present value (and to avoid those having a negative net present value). This conclusion follows because regardless of the short-run profit consequences, undertaking projects that increase the firm's discounted net cash flows (and hence increase the market value of equity claims on the firm) will increase management's wealth along with that of the other owners.

Stock options will of course not cause management's interests to dovetail perfectly with those of the firm's owners. Given that management will have an option to buy only a limited number of shares, they will still not bear the full costs of any investment decision that reduces the market value of the firm. But making stock options and bonuses a part of management's compensation package will clearly reduce agency costs by providing managers with a greater incentive than they would have otherwise to behave in ways that serve owners' interests rather than their own.

Deferred compensation schemes have similar purposes and effects. Stock options and bonuses that can be exercised by the manager only upon retirement, generous pension plans, and the like create incentives for managers to place greater weight on the long-run profit consequences of their resource-allocation decisions. Should they do otherwise and be demoted or fired, their deferred compensation will decrease or disappear. A manager's consent to an employment contract that includes compensation provisions that are either contingent on satisfactory performance or are payable only when the employment relationship ends in a voluntary and mutually agreeable fashion is equivalent to the posting of a bond that guarantees behavior acceptable to the firm's owners. In short, managerial compensation is one of several control devices employed by the corporate form of business organization to help reduce agency costs and thereby increase the present value of the firm (stockholder wealth).

As the above examples illustrate, principal-agent theory provides a generalization of the shirking-information cost problem that characterizes team production. And, as we have seen, the theory generates important insights about the ownership structure of the firm and managerial compensation. Principal-agent theory has also helped answer questions concerning the internal organizational structure of the firm and its financial structure.[31] This set of problems is not only interesting in its own right but also promises to shed light on broader questions concerning the nature of the firm and the manager's role in it.

SUMMARY

This chapter has stressed the idea that the firm and the market represent alternative institutions for guiding the allocation of society's scarce productive resources. Beginning with Ronald Coase's fundamental insight that it is costly to use either the market price system or internal-to-the-firm decision making to coordinate the allocation of resources, the chapter has laid out the principal factors affecting the choice between these alternative methods of governing exchanges between buyer and seller. This discussion has addressed the fundamental question of why the firm emerges as an economic entity.

KEY TERMS
transaction costs
transaction
opportunistic behavior
trilateral governance
bilateral governance
rent
team production

---

31 These issues are explored fully in Part III.

Transaction costs, which include search and information costs, bargaining and decision costs, and policing and enforcement costs, make up one set of factors. In any exchange, both buyer and seller must invest real resources in acquiring information about prices, in striking a bargain, and in monitoring compliance with the agreed-upon terms. As such, the choice between the firm and the market is determined partly by the goal of economizing on the costs of transacting.

Another set of factors includes the degree of uncertainty surrounding the transaction, the frequency with which the transaction recurs, and the extent to which the parties must invest in transaction-specific assets. The more these factors increase, the more vulnerable a market transaction becomes to disputes concerning permissible adaptations to unanticipated events. These factors may encourage one self-interest-seeking party to take advantage of the other by opportunistically appropriating the rents created by investments in transaction-specific capital.

Team production supplies a third rationale for the emergence of the firm as an institution for governing transactions between buyer and seller. The advantages of the firm over the market in this regard consist of management's opportunity to acquire superior information about the productivities of the resources under its direct control. And, at least in the case of the classical capitalist firm, there are further incentives for utilizing this information in ways that reduce shirking and therefore enhance productivity and profits.

A final set of factors includes the costs that surround the principal-agent relationships between customer and supplier, between employer and employee, and between owner and manager. Alternative ownership arrangements (property rights assignments) have important consequences in terms of the twin objectives of promoting efficient specialization and limiting the divergence of interests between principal and agent.

This chapter has emphasized the superiority of market procurement because of the incentives it provides to contain costs and allocate resources efficiently. Only in specialized circumstances will it be optimal for market exchange to give way to other, more formal mechanisms for governing a transaction. Spot-market transactions, market contracting, and ownership integration all have advantages and disadvantages. The task of identifying the institutional structure that will be optimal for governing a transaction in any particular case is one of management's most important challenges.

QUESTIONS

7.1 The collapse of the Soviet Union, which the *Wall Street Journal* has referred to as "ACNE" (the Association of Countries with No Economies), demonstrated that resources are allocated much more efficiently when decisions are guided by market-based price signals than when made by administrative command. On the other hand, Ronald Coase insists that the firm emerged as an economic entity precisely because it helps economize on the costs of using the price system to allocate resources. Reconcile these two apparently conflicting observations. In other words, why does central planning "work" in one case but not the other?

7.2 The production and sale of a college textbook involves a large number of distinct functions and activities. Discuss the factors that help explain the following observations about the organization of the typical textbook publishing company.

a. Editors and sales representatives are full-time employees of the firm, but the authors of textbooks are not.

b. Copy-editors who read and correct the final manuscript in preparation for typesetting freelance their work on a contract basis.

c. The design and layout of the text are performed by the publisher, but the manufacture of the finished product is carried out by an independent printing company. *Hint:* The design and layout process determines the book's page length, and printing costs are an increasing function of page length.

7.3 Under Major League Baseball's old "reserve clause," a drafted player was assigned to one team and could not play for another unless traded or released from his contract by the team's owner. Under the current system of "free agency," players can, with certain restrictions, negotiate with other teams and market their baseball skills to the highest bidder. Under which regime are players more prone to injury? That is, would you expect the typical player to spend more time on baseball's disabled list under the reserve clause or under free agency? Why?

7.4 The sight of a dead animal along the side of the road is distasteful to most drivers. Explain why no one ever stops to remove it.

7.5 Many franchisors like McDonald's, Burger King, and Wendy's own and operate a substantial fraction of their franchise outlets. Explain why the company-owned outlets tend to be larger (measured in terms of gross sales) and to be located closer to national or regional headquarters than independent franchisees. Also explain why there seems to be a tendency for the proportion of company-owned outlets to decline as the franchisor continues to expand.

7.6 For each of the following situations, compare the advantages and disadvantages of having the activities carried out by two separate firms versus having them performed by a single firm.

a. A pipeline transports crude oil from an oil field to a petroleum refinery that produces gasoline.

b. A public university wants to offer food services to faculty and students.

c. A greeting card manufacturer wants a readily available supply of envelopes and card stock.

d. Disneyland wants to make hotel rooms available to its customers.

7.7 Why is the residual loss imposed by elected representatives on voters likely to be larger than the residual loss imposed by corporate management on stockholders?

7.8 In a labor-managed firm, the company's assets are owned jointly by the employees. In a capitalistic firm, the company's assets are owned by the stockholders. The number of owners of the firm is usually smaller in the first case than in the second, yet labor-managed firms typically have higher operating costs and lower profit margins than their capitalistic counterparts. Why, given that they have fewer owners, do labor-managed firms fare so poorly?

7.9 The reasoning commonly used by textbook authors to explain why blast furnaces and rolling mills are jointly owned is that having these two activities take place within the same firm improves production efficiency by avoiding the cost of reheating steel ingots prior to further processing. Is this explanation complete? Can you think of another reason for the joint ownership of blast furnaces and rolling mills?

7.10 In 1984 and 1985, T. Boone Pickens twice attempted to acquire a controlling ownership interest in the Phillips Petroleum Company of Bartlesville, Oklahoma. The management of the Phillips Company was ultimately able to block Pickens' takeover bid by buying back the common stock he had accumulated. Phillips' management paid a substantial price premium to do so—Pickens made $89 million on the transaction. Does the economy benefit from such corporate "greenmail" or was Pickens the only winner? Explain. As part of your answer, consider what actions Phillips' management had to take in order to raise the cash necessary to buy back Pickens' stock.

7.11 Provide a theoretical explanation for why most of the major independent accounting firms are organized as partnerships rather than as publicly traded corporations.

7.12 The corporate form of business organization is distinguished by limited liability— in the event of bankruptcy, the financial liability of any one of the owners (stockholders) is limited to the value of his or her original investment in the firm. What role, if any, does limited liability play in reducing the agency costs between the owners and managers of the corporation?

CHAPTER

8

The Firm and Its Rivals

OVERVIEW

Part I focused on the revenue and cost constraints facing the manager of an individual firm. The object of that analysis was to derive rules for guiding the manager's selection of a level of production and a selling price consistent with the goals of maximizing both short-run and long-run profit. In so doing, Part I did not consider explicitly the firm's interactions with its rivals. But all firms operate in a broad market environment where rivalry is more or less a fact of life. In some markets, large numbers of small sellers vie for the patronage of consumers; in other markets, a small number of large firms compete head-to-head; and in still other markets, there may be only one seller of a product having no close substitutes.

This chapter applies the economic theory of the firm to analyze the impact of rivalry on managerial decisions. Two stylized market models are discussed. One of these models is the **price-taker** model which assumes that the quantity of output produced by an individual firm is so small relative to the industry total that the firm's own production decisions have no impact on market price. The second model is the **price-searcher** model of Part I which assumes that the demand curve for the firm's product is downward-sloping. We will summarize this model and then extend it to describe an industry in which several large firms recognize their mutual interdependence so that each explicitly takes its rivals' reactions into account.

The overall theme of the chapter is to show how the nature of the rivalry between firms constrains the manager's choices. Marketplace competition determines what variables the manager can control, what level of profit the firm can expect to earn, and how external factors such as government policy or the entry of new rivals will affect the firm's pricing and production decisions. Plainly, managers must understand these market constraints if they are to pursue strategies that are consistent with their organization's long-run prosperity.

APPLICATION

Your employer, Excessive Holding Company, recently acquired two firms, Pizzarama and Free Spirits. Both companies are wholly owned subsidiaries of Excessive Holding Company and will operate independently of each other. The markets in which they compete are very different as is the level of competition each firm faces.

Pizzarama is a chain of pizza parlors located in the Midwest. There are many rival firms. Entry barriers to potential new firms in the industry are minimal. Start-up costs are low. For all intents and purposes, consumers are unable to distinguish pizza prepared by Pizzarama from its competitors' pizza. Labor and food costs make up the majority of the expenses associated with a Pizzarama operation. Because competition is so intense, Pizzarama has little, if any, influence on the price it charges its customers. Pizza consumers are very sensitive to price changes and are always looking for cheap pizza.

Free Spirits is a franchised liquor distributor operating in one Southern state. Entry of new competitors to the market is costly and requires governmental approval. Currently, there are just a few competing distributors offering distinctive national brands and providing a range of customer recognition and loyalty. Free Spirits has some discretion over the price it sets for its goods. Lower prices will attract new consumers and increase the volume of purchases by current consumers. Rival firms carefully monitor shifts in competitors' strategies to enhance their own market shares.

The CEO of Excessive Holding Company assigns you as the Chief Operating Officer of these two companies. Your goal is to maximize each company's profits. How would you determine the price you will charge for the products sold by Pizzarama and Free Spirits? What level of output will you select to achieve the optimal level of profit for Pizzarama and for Free Spirits?

PRICE TAKERS AND PRICE SEARCHERS

Business firms are created primarily to increase the wealth of their owners by producing and selling goods and services valued by consumers. For this purpose, the owners of capital, labor, land, raw materials, and other productive resources enter into contractual relationships with one another in order to coordinate the utilization of inputs in the production process and to share in the revenues generated by the firm. Because specialization of resource ownership promotes efficiency and effectiveness, teamwork among resource owners is critical to the success of the enterprise.

Some of the problems associated with organizing resources within the firm are addressed in Chapter 7. Other internal-to-the-firm issues will be discussed in upcoming chapters.

This chapter positions the firm in the context of an economic market, analyzing how it responds to competitive market forces and interacts with its rivals both in the short run and in the long run. It is not the intent of this chapter to elaborate on the industrial organization of markets, but rather to provide some basic insights into how a firm relates with other firms in an economic market setting.

For simplicity, firms are categorized as either price takers or price searchers.[1] Those firms lacking the ability to influence the market price for the good or service they sell are referred to as price takers. In particular, the quantity of output produced by a price-taker firm is such a small portion of the industry total that significant expansions or contractions in its volume of production have no impact on the market price of the firm's product. The good or service produced by the price-taker firm, in the view of the consumer, is homogeneous—it is indistinguishable from the goods or services produced by other firms competing in the market.

As it seeks to maximize profit, the price-taker firm behaves as if the market-determined price of its product is an uncontrollable operational constraint. A Kansas wheat farmer, for example, is unable to differentiate his or her wheat from the wheat produced by other growers. If one farmer attempts to charge a price slightly higher than the price charged by other farmers, consumers will stop buying that farmer's wheat and switch their purchases to another grower who sells at the lower market price. Consumers cannot distinguish among the wheat supplied by different farmers. One farmer's wheat is as good as another's. Because any wheat farmer can produce and sell all of his or her crop at the market-determined price, there is no incentive for the farmer to reduce price below the market price in order to sell more wheat. Consequently, all wheat farmers accept the current price in the wheat market and, hence, behave as price takers.

This does not mean that the price taker has no business decisions to make. It simply means that the firm has no discretion over what price to charge. A wheat farmer still must decide what crop to produce, how much acreage to plant, what combination of inputs to use in the production process, how much of the crop to hold in inventory and how much to ship to market,

---

1 Armen A. Alchian and William R. Allen, *Exchange and Production: Competition, Coordination, and Control*, 3E. (Belmont, CA: Wadsworth Publishing Co., 1983), pp. 205-62.

when to sell the crop (spot market or futures market), and whether to continue to operate the farm or to shut down and pursue another career.

A price searcher, by contrast, is a firm that has some influence over the price it charges, subject to the cost and demand constraints of the marketplace. Customers in a price-searcher market view the goods or services offered by rival sellers to be heterogeneous or distinguishable from one another, but substitutable. The automobiles produced and sold by Toyota, Ford, Honda, and Chrysler, for example, are all distinct and offer the car buyer a wide variety from which to choose, but car manufacturers compete for customers in the same market.

Some goods differ in quality or ease of access, or are preferred by consumers to competing goods. The reputation of the supplier, the perceived quality associated with a brand name, and the dependability of the retailer all influence the customer's preferences as well as the price differentials among competing goods or services. When the products offered by rival sellers in a market are differentiated from one another in the minds of consumers, the demand curve facing any one firm is downward-sloping. Hence, unlike the price-taker firm, the price-searcher firm has the ability to raise price without losing all of its sales.

Under these circumstances, the firm must search for the profit-maximizing price. Moreover, in addition to the questions to be answered by a price taker, the price searcher must also determine what level of product quality to supply, how to distinguish its good from competing goods in the minds of the consumer, how to respond to its rivals' initiatives, what level and mix of advertising and promotional activities to undertake, how much to invest in the research and development of new products or the improvement of existing products, and what pricing strategies to employ.

This chapter presents these two distinctive market models. In discussing the two general categories of price-taker and price-searcher firms, we intend to emphasize the importance of market constraints to managerial decisions. The traditional organizational structures of perfectly competitive firms, monopolistically competitive firms, oligopolistic firms, and monopolistic firms are not discussed explicitly because many critical managerial decision-making problems can be analyzed without the additional complexity required to make finer distinctions between industrial organization types. In most instances, it is possible to develop useful and accurate business strategies using the economic predictions derived from the two general market models of the price taker and the price searcher.

PRICE-TAKER MARKETS

The distinguishing feature of a price-taker market is that no individual buyer or seller has the ability to affect the market-determined price. This characteristic is assured by the five following assumptions.

"Large" Number of Buyers and Sellers. The number of buyers and sellers is so large that no one of them can, acting alone, influence market

Dynamic Competition in the U.S. Economy

The market structure models in this chapter provide a theoretical framework for analyzing firm behavior and industry performance. Firm and industry profitability play key roles in characterizing performance in these models. As we shall see, entry and exit drive economic profits to zero in price-taker markets and in "open" price-searcher markets. On the other hand, firms in either "closed" price-searcher markets or oligopolistic markets enjoy market power that enables them to earn positive economic profits in the long run. Market power and the above-normal profits associated with it tend to misallocate scarce productive resources and therefore reduce society's welfare.

The most commonly used index of market structure is the four-firm concentration ratio, defined as the market share of the industry's four largest firms. Many cross-sectional studies have shown that industry profitability and market concentration are positively related. One interpretation of these studies is that the firms in concentrated industries possess market power and are therefore responsible for the resource misallocation characteristic of the static price-searcher model.

However, the association between high concentration and market power has been attacked both theoretically and empirically. The recently developed theory of contestable markets stresses the role that *potential* entry plays in determining firm conduct and industry performance in highly concentrated markets comprising only a few firms or even a single firm. A contestable market is defined as one in which barriers to entry and exit are low. Contestable markets force firms to set price at levels consistent with earning a normal profit (zero economic profit) because to do otherwise would invite the entry of new firms that would drive price and profits down. Hence, as long as there are no significant barriers to entry or exit, firms in either oligopolistic industries or single-firm industries are expected to earn zero economic profits in the long run.

An empirical implication of the theory of contestable markets is that economic profits are only temporary unless significant barriers to entry exist. Malcolm Coate examined the rate of decay of profits across 233 manufacturing industries over the period 1958 to 1984.[a] To do so, he estimated the following linear regression model:

$$PCM = a + bLPCM + cGROW + dCR4.$$

PCM is defined as the industry price-cost margin (an index of profitability), *LPCM* is the value of the price-cost margin lagged one year, *GROW* is the real growth rate in industry output, and *CR*4 is the four-firm concentration ratio.

Coate reported the following coefficient estimates (the constant term was not reported; *t*-ratios are in parentheses):

$$PCM = a + .678LPCM + .0142GROW + .0403CR4$$
$$(65.3) \qquad (4.29) \qquad (5.58)$$

The coefficient associated with *LPCM* indicates that current profits are 67.8 percent of the previous year's profits, on average. Above-normal profits consequently tend to decay at a rate of about 30 percent per year. Importantly, Coate did not find any systematic relationship between the rate at which profits decay and industry concentration. For example, he found that profits were stable over time for 26 industries which had an average four-firm concentration ratio of 34.4 percent as opposed to the overall sample average of 39.6 percent.

Barry Keating provided additional insights into the dynamic competitiveness of the U.S. economy by ranking industries according to their profitability (return on net worth) and following changes in the rankings over time.[b] The accompanying table shows the ten most profitable industries in 1969 and their subsequent rankings in 1973 and 1981.

a Malcolm B. Coate, "The Effect of Dynamic Competition on Price-Cost Margins," *Applied Economics* 23 (1991), pp. 1065-76.
b Barry Keating, "An Update On Industries Ranked By Average Rates Of Return," *Applied Economics* 23 (1991), pp. 897-902.

RANKING BY RETURN ON NET WORTH			
INDUSTRY	1969	1973	1981
NEWSPAPERS	1	7	11
MOVIE THEATERS	2	252	13
PERSONAL SERVICE	3	25	139
OFFICE AUTOMATION	4	85	105
CABLE TV OPERATORS	5	6	56
CONSULTING & PR	6	155	74
INSURANCE SERVICES	7	12	14
BLDG. MAINTENANCE	8	43	151
FINANCIAL SERVICES	9	69	68
REAL ESTATE	10	188	192

Only two industries that were ranked in the top ten in 1969 remained in the top ten in 1973; not one of the top ten industries in 1969 was also ranked in the top ten in 1981. The table is consistent with the general conclusion that profits are highly unstable in the dynamically competitive U.S. economy.

price. The purchases made by any one customer and the quantity sold by any one firm are so small (relative to the total) that decisions about how much to buy or sell are made under the assumption that the prevailing market price will not change.

Homogeneous Product. The product produced and sold by each firm in a price-taker market is assumed to be indistinguishable from that offered by every other firm. This homogeneity applies not only to the physical characteristics of the good but to all other aspects of its production and sale. Compared to rivals, no firm has any advantages on any dimension of competition that consumers value, including product quality, credit terms, warranty periods, location, pre- and post-sale services, and so on. Buyers select among firms solely on the basis of price. They are otherwise indifferent about the identity of the seller from whom they make their purchases.

"Free" Entry and Exit. Firms are able to enter and exit the market freely. Artificial barriers to the movement of productive resources into or out of the industry, such as those created by government regulation or by the ownership of essential raw materials, do not exist.

Perfect Factor Mobility. There are no specialized resources in a price-taker market. Factors of production can move freely among various uses. A worker, for example, is equally productive in each possible job assignment. Land, labor, and capital can be reallocated readily among various uses both within and across firms.

Perfect Knowledge. All relevant information in a price-taker market is freely accessible to all buyers and sellers. Buyers know the locations of every seller and the prices they charge. Sellers have complete knowledge of the prices, availabilities, and productivities of all inputs. They know the locations of all buyers and the prices they are willing to pay. Any changes in these data become fully and instantaneously available to all market participants.

The Demand Schedule of the Price-Taker Firm

Consider a firm operating in the price-taker market defined by the demand (D) and supply (S) schedules depicted in Figure 8.1. The forces of demand and supply dictate that the market equilibrium price is P' per unit and that the equilibrium quantity bought and sold is Q' units. Because the firm can sell each unit it produces in the market for P' dollars, the demand curve (d) confronting the price-taker firm is horizontal or perfectly elastic. If the firm charges a price higher than P', consumers will shift their purchases to competitors who continue to charge P' and quantity demanded for this firm will be zero. Likewise, the price taker has no incentive to lower price below P' because it can sell all it produces at that price.

If the firm produces q units of output, total revenue (TR) is price times quantity, or $TR = P' \times q$. Marginal revenue (MR) is the change in total revenue associated with the sale of each additional unit produced. Because the price-taker firm can sell all it wants at P', marginal revenue from the sale of each succeeding unit is equal to the market price; that is, $MR = P'$.[2] As depicted in Figure 8.1, the price-taker firm's demand schedule (d) is precisely the same as its marginal revenue schedule (MR). Each price-taker firm views the demand and marginal revenue for its product as being identical and horizontal at the market-established price.

Short-Run Profit Maximization for a Price-Taker Firm

Like all firms, the price-taker maximizes profit by selecting the quantity of output at which marginal revenue (MR) is equal to marginal cost (MC). Because, as just discussed, the price-taker's marginal revenue schedule is constant and equal to the market-determined price (P), the rule for profit maximization in this case is for the firm to produce where $P = MC$.

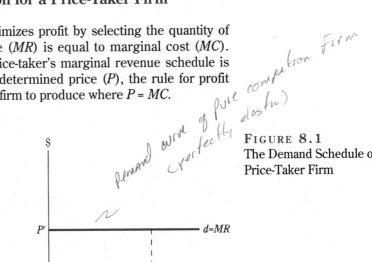

FIGURE 8.1
The Demand Schedule of the Price-Taker Firm

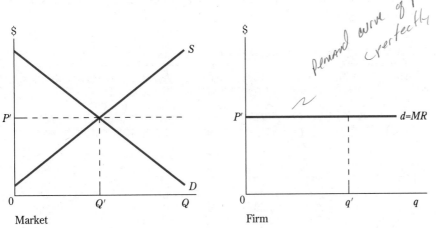

Market   Firm

---

2 Because $TR = P' \times q$, $MR = dTR/dq = P'$ for all q.

For example, suppose that a price-taker firm faces the hypothetical short-run production costs displayed in Table 8.1. Suppose further that the market-determined price is $105 per unit. What output level should the firm produce to maximize profit?

Because each unit sold adds $105 to the firm's total revenue, the total revenue schedule for a price of $105 is computed in Table 8.2 by multiplying price times quantity. The profit earned at each level of production is calculated by subtracting the total cost of producing those units from the total revenue generated from the sale of those units; that is, $\pi = TR - TC$. For example, according to Table 8.1, the firm incurs a total fixed cost (TFC) of $10 regardless of the quantity of output it produces. When the firm produces four units of output, the total variable cost (TVC) of production is $270, so that the total cost of production is equal to $280. The firm can sell these four units in the marketplace for $105 per unit; total revenue is thus $420. The firm's profit is consequently $140.

As shown in Table 8.2, the maximum profit ($245) occurs at output level $q = 7$. Other output levels generate profit, but not as much as when the firm produces and sells seven units. Had the firm decided to produce an eighth unit, it would have earned an additional $105 in revenue, but would have incurred an additional cost (marginal cost) of $110, reducing profits from $245 to $240. The eighth unit should not be produced. Whenever the marginal cost of producing one more unit of output exceeds the marginal revenue associated with selling that unit (MC > MR), profits will decline if output increases.

On the other hand, had the firm not produced the seventh unit of output (stopping at six units), it would have saved the $100 in variable cost required to produce the seventh unit. But by not selling the seventh unit, the firm would have lost the opportunity to earn $105 in revenue. The firm's profits cannot be at a maximum if it fails to produce a unit of output for which marginal revenue is greater than marginal cost (MR > MC). Hence, if the market-determined price is $105, profits are at a maximum when the price-taker firm produces $q = 7$.

TABLE 8.1 HYPOTHETICAL SHORT-RUN COSTS

TOTAL OUTPUT (q)	TOTAL FIXED COST (TFC)	TOTAL VARIABLE COST (TVC)	TOTAL COST (TC)	AVERAGE FIXED COST (AFC)	AVERAGE VARIABLE COST (AVC)	AVERAGE TOTAL COST (ATC)	MARGINAL COST (MC)
0	$10	$0	$10	—	—	—	—
1	10	90	100	$10	$90	$100	$90
2	10	170	180	5	85	90	80
3	10	230	240	3.33	76.67	80	60
4	10	270	280	2.50	67.50	70	40
5	10	320	330	2	64	66	50
6	10	380	390	1.67	63.33	65	60
7	10	480	490	1.43	68.57	70	100
8	10	590	600	1.25	73.75	75	110
9	10	710	720	1.11	78.89	80	120

TABLE 8.2 Profit or (Loss) at Three Market-Determined Prices

| | $P = \$105$ | | | | $P = \$64$ | | |
Total Output	Total Revenue	Marginal Revenue	Profit		Total Revenue	Marginal Revenue	Profit
0	$0	—	($10)		$0	—	($10)
1	105	$105	5		64	$64	(36)
2	210	105	30		128	64	(52)
3	315	105	75		192	64	(48)
4	420	105	140		256	64	(24)
5	525	105	195		320	64	(10)
6	630	105	240		384	64	(6)
7	735	105	245		448	64	(42)
8	840	105	240		512	64	(88)
9	945	105	225		576	64	(144)

| | $P = \$59$ | | |
Total Output	Total Revenue	Marginal Revenue	Profit
0	$0	$59	($10)
1	59	59	(41)
2	118	59	(62)
3	177	59	(63)
4	236	59	(44)
5	295	59	(35)
6	354	59	(36)
7	413	59	(77)
8	472	59	(128)
9	531	59	(189)

The profit-maximization rule for the price-taker firm is shown graphically in Figure 8.2 using continuous cost and revenue functions. The firm maximizes profit at the level of output (q_1) which equates marginal revenue with marginal cost, $MR = MC$.[3] In this example, the market-established price, P_1, determines the price-taker's marginal revenue (demand) schedule which is then equated with marginal cost (point A). At a price of P_1, the firm thus sets $P_1 = MR = MC$, produces q_1 units of output and earns a maximum profit denoted by the area of the shaded rectangle P_1ABC.[4]

---

3 The firm selects the level of output that maximizes $\pi = TR - TC$. Taking the required derivative, $\partial\pi/\partial q = \partial(TR)/\partial q - \partial(TC)/\partial q$ and setting the right-hand side equal to zero, yields the marginal-revenue-equals-marginal-cost rule, $\partial(TR)/\partial q = \partial(TC)/\partial q$. Total revenue is of course price times quantity, $P \times q$. For the price-taker firm, however, price is constant (the firm can sell all it produces at the market-determined price), and so P is treated as a constant in taking the derivative of total revenue. Hence, $\partial(TR)/\partial q = P$, and the profit-maximization rule simplifies to $P = MC$.

4 The shaded area is equal to the difference between price and average total cost ($P_1 - C$) times q_1 units produced.

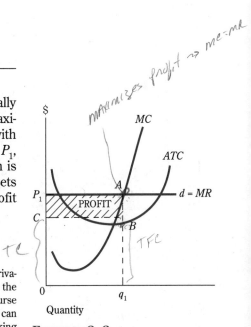

FIGURE 8.2
Short-Run Profit Maximization for a Price-Taker Firm

The Shut-Down Decision. Suppose that for reasons outside the firm's control, the market equilibrium price declines from $105 to $64 per unit. How should the profit-maximizing firm respond?

Referring to the profit calculations in Table 8.2, it is apparent that the firm incurs an economic loss at each output level if the market price of its product falls to $64. Should the firm go out of business? By definition, total fixed cost is incurred regardless of the quantity of output the firm produces. Hence, if the firm decides to shut down, its total losses will amount to $10 in this example.

Is there a level of production that would enable the firm to lose less by continuing to operate rather than shutting down? The figures displayed in Table 8.2 suggest that if the firm remains in business and produces $q = 6$ units of output, it will lose $6 rather than the $10 it would lose by shutting down. Loss minimization is the counterpart to profit maximization when the firm faces losses. Because it is obviously better to lose $6 than to lose $10, the firm should continue to operate and produce six units of output if market price declines to $64.

Viewed differently, at $q = 6$, $TVC = \$380$ and $TR = \$384$. This means that by producing and selling six units of output, the firm earns sufficient revenue both to cover its total variable costs of production and make a $4 contribution towards covering its total fixed cost. The $4 contribution to total fixed cost reduces the firm's short-run economic losses from $10 to $6.

Figure 8.3 graphically depicts a comparable situation. At every possible level of output, the market price of P_2 is less than the firm's average total cost. Hence, regardless of what output level the firm decides to produce, its total costs will exceed total revenue and economic losses will result. However, as long as the firm can operate at a level of production at which price (marginal revenue) exceeds average variable cost, total revenue will be greater than total variable cost ($TR > TVC$) and its losses will be less than total fixed cost.

In particular, given a market price of P_2, the firm will produce q_2 units of output (determined by setting $P_2 = MR = MC$). Total revenue at this level of output, $P_2 \times q_2$, is represented by the area $0P_2Gq_2$. The total cost of producing q_2 units is represented by the area $0EFq_2$. This follows from observing that average total cost at q_2 is E and that $TC = E \times q_2$. Total cost can be divided into its total variable cost (area $0VRq_2$) and total fixed cost (area $VEFR$) components.[5]

If the price-taker shuts down, it will lose TFC or the area $VEFR$. On the other hand, by producing and selling q_2 units, total revenue ($0P_2Gq_2$) covers both total variable cost ($0VRq_2$) and part of total fixed cost (VP_2GR). The economic loss sustained by producing q_2 units (P_2EFG) is therefore less than the loss that would be incurred if the firm were to shut down ($VEFR$).

What will happen to the price taker if the market price declines further to $59? As Tables 8.1 and 8.2 reveal (see pp. 272–273), each possible output

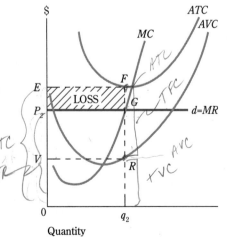

FIGURE 8.3

Short-Run Loss Minimization for a
Price-Taker Firm

_____

5 At q_2, average variable cost is V and average fixed cost is $E - V$. Hence, $TVC = V \times q_2$ and $TFC = (E - V) \times q_2$.

level now generates losses in excess of total fixed cost. Using the marginal rule for profit maximization (loss minimization), the best the price-taker can do if it continues to operate is to produce five units of output and lose $35. When compared to the loss of $10 that would be incurred by shutting down, it should be obvious that the firm will minimize losses by suspending operations. In this example, the firm incurs a total variable cost of $320 at $q = 5$, but generates only $295 in total revenue. Hence, by continuing to operate, the firm would lose the total fixed cost of $10 and an additional $25 by failing to cover all of its variable production costs. Consequently, at a price of $59, the price taker's optimal (loss-minimizing) strategy is to shut down.

Figure 8.4 graphically illustrates this situation. At a market price of P_3, the marginal-revenue-equals-marginal-cost rule dictates that the firm produce q_3 units of output. The total revenue generated from the sale of q_3 units is represented by the area OP_3Kq_3. Total cost at this point is the area $OHIq_3$, and so economic losses of P_3HIK result. By producing, the firm is not able to cover its total variable costs (area $OLJq_3$). The firm's economic losses (area P_3HIK) exceed total fixed cost (area $LHIJ$) by the amount that total revenue is less than total variable cost (area P_3LJK).

In order to minimize losses, the price taker rationally shuts down if market price is P_3. Shutting down makes sense for any price below the minimum of the average variable cost curve because when $P < AVC$, $TR < TVC$. Whenever total revenue is less than total variable cost, the losses the firm incurs by continuing to produce are greater than the losses sustained by shutting down (TFC).

In sum, if a firm cannot earn sufficient revenue to cover its variable costs of production, then suspending operation minimizes losses. By producing when $TR < TVC$, the firm's economic losses are greater than its total fixed costs. This shut-down rule implies that *regardless of the magnitude of total fixed costs* a firm should not undertake any investment project for which the additional cost (marginal cost) of purchasing the variable inputs is expected to exceed the additional revenue (marginal revenue) generated by the sale of the output.

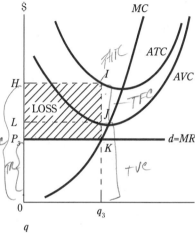

FIGURE 8.4
The Price-Taker's Shut-Down Decision

The Irrelevance of Fixed Costs. In the short run, every business is faced with commitments to compensate the owners of resources whose usage cannot be readily altered in response to changing market conditions. Total fixed cost is the sum of the payments to the owners of fixed resources and should not be included in the firm's decision-making calculus. These fixed resources may be the physical plant and equipment that define the firm's production capacity and constrain its ability to adjust output in the short run. After a fixed input has been acquired or after an irrevocable commitment has been made to compensate its owner, the firm must ignore its cost in making profit-maximizing decisions in the short run.

Including total fixed costs in the decision-making process merely clouds the issue without providing managers with any additional useful information. Recovering these costs is certainly desirable and the ability to do so will determine the long-run survival of the firm. But once a fixed input has been purchased, it is not necessary to cover total fixed cost in order for it to be economical to utilize the fixed input in the short run. By definition, the firm incurs total fixed cost whether or not any revenue is earned. Hence, total fixed cost is not relevant to economic or management decisions.

The same is true if there is a change in total fixed cost. For example, suppose the hypothetical firm described in Tables 8.1 and 8.2 (see pp. 272–273) experiences a $5 increase in total fixed cost because of a legal judgment against it. Given a market price of $64, will the firm alter the quantity of output it produces? The answer is no. The firm will still minimize its losses by producing 6 units of output. The total economic loss has increased from $6 to $11, but the decision to produce or to shut down is unaffected.

The irrelevance of fixed cost often confuses households as well as businesses. For example, once a consumer purchases a share of stock, the original purchase price becomes immaterial to future investment decisions. Whether the stock price subsequently goes up or goes down, the initial purchase price is a fixed cost and should not enter into subsequent decisions. If a share of stock is purchased for $100 and its market price later falls to $87, then the stockholder has a piece of paper worth $87. Ignoring any favorable tax treatment of capital losses, the stockholder's decision to hold this asset or to trade it should be made on the basis of how best to invest $87. Nothing is gained by fretting over the $13 capital loss.

The same is true if the stock appreciates from $100 to $113. Ignoring any favorable tax treatment for capital gains, the stockholder owns an asset worth $113 no matter what the original purchase price. The relevant decision is how best to invest $113. The original price is a fixed cost. Becoming mesmerized by a $13 capital gain only muddles the stockholder's wealth-maximizing decisions.

Similarly, suppose that a consumer purchases a new car for $15,000. At the end of the first year of ownership, the value of the car may have depreciated to $10,000. The initial purchase price is a fixed cost and must be ignored. The car is worth $10,000 and that is the value of the asset relevant for deciding whether to trade it in or to keep the year-old car for a second year.

Amateur gamblers are often victimized by their own inability to ignore fixed costs. Should an inexperienced gambler enter into a poker game and lose the first hand, he or she must treat the loss as a fixed cost.[6] Too often an amateur will "double down" in the hope of getting even, when, in reality, the last hand is history and should not be considered in subsequent betting decisions. Nor is the amateur "playing with someone else's money" if he or she wins the first hand. Playing poker is like tossing an unbiased coin—the previous toss has no impact on subsequent tosses.

Total fixed cost is irrelevant to decisions about whether or not to produce and to decisions about how much to produce. The profit-maximizing firm will produce if total revenue is greater than total variable cost ($TR > TVC$). This is equivalent to requiring that market price be greater than minimum

---

6 Ignoring the wealth effect of the lost hand.

average variable cost $(P > \text{min. } AVC)$. Total revenue measures the value placed by consumers on the quantity of the good or service produced by the firm. And total variable cost measures the total value of the additional resources used to produce the output. Therefore, the profit-maximizing firm will produce in the short run whenever it can add value to the resources used in the production process. Likewise, the firm will avoid utilizing resources whose value exceeds the value of the goods and services produced. If a price-taker firm decides to produce, then it will maximize profits by

1. expanding production whenever $P = MR > MC$,
2. contracting production whenever $P = MR < MC$, and
3. producing where $P = MR = MC$.

The Supply Curve of the Price-Taker Firm and Industry

The price-taker firm's supply curve shows the quantity of output the firm is willing and able to supply at each possible market price. Figure 8.5 shows a graphical derivation of the supply schedule.

In the short run, provided that price exceeds minimum average variable cost, the price-taker maximizes profits or minimizes losses by producing the quantity of output at which the market-determined price is equal to marginal cost. As market price varies, the firm moves along its marginal cost curve to find the new level of production which is most profitable to produce.[7] The price-taker firm's marginal cost curve above the minimum of average variable cost is consequently identical to the firm's short-run supply curve because it shows the quantity supplied by the profit-maximizing price-taker at each possible market price. For prices below minimum average variable cost, of course, the firm produces no output because at these prices total revenue is less than total variable cost. The firm will shut down operations at any price below minimum average variable cost.

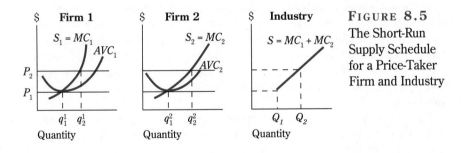

FIGURE 8.5
The Short-Run Supply Schedule for a Price-Taker Firm and Industry

---

7 This assumes that the prices of the inputs used by the firm do not vary with changes in quantity of goods produced. In other words, the suppliers of inputs are themselves price-takers. The firm can employ as many units of the variable inputs as it wants without affecting their market-determined prices.

At the far left of Figure 8.5, the price-taker's supply curve is S_1; it is identical to MC_1 above minimum average variable cost. The supply curve of the second firm is likewise denoted by $S_2 = MC_2$ (above minimum AVC).

In the short run, the **industry** (or **market**) **supply curve** is the horizontal summation of all the price-taker firms' supply curves and is denoted by "S". At a market-determined price of P_2, for example, firm 1 supplies q_2^{1} units of output and firm 2 supplies q_2^{2} units. In total, these two industry members produce $Q_2 = q_2^{1} + q_2^{2}$ units if the market price is P_2. Similarly, if market price is P_1, industry output is $Q_1 = q_1^{1} + q_1^{2}$. No output will be produced at prices below P_1 because at those prices neither firm would earn enough revenue to cover its variable production costs. This derivation holds for any arbitrary number of firms. The industry supply curve in the short run is simply the horizontal sum of the relevant portions of the individual firm's marginal cost schedules (above minimum average variable cost).

It should be noted that not all firms will necessarily have the same minimum average variable cost. Different firms may exit from the market at different prices. Furthermore, the configurations of all firms' short-run cost curves will not necessarily be the same. At any market price, some firms may earn a profit while other firms incur losses or shut down. Regardless of the profit-loss situation of individual price-takers, however, the short-run industry supply curve is derived by summing the quantities supplied by each firm at each price.

Long-Run Profit Maximization for the Price-Taker Firm

As defined in Chapter 3, the long run can be usefully thought of as a planning period. In the short run, the firm is constrained by past plant capacity decisions and operates with at least one fixed input. In the long run, the planning horizon is sufficiently distant to allow managers the freedom to consider varying the usage of all inputs. They can make decisions about which markets to enter and which to exit. And they can make judgments about the optimal scale of operations for the markets in which the firm wishes to compete.

In the long run, of course, profit-maximizing firms follow the same decision rule they do for shorter time horizons. As such, a price-taker firm maximizes profits by producing the quantity of output that equates marginal revenue or price to long-run marginal cost. If, at that output level, market price is greater than long-run average cost, the firm will earn positive economic profits. If market price is less than long-run average cost, economic losses will result.

Figure 8.6 depicts the relationship between long-run marginal cost (LMC) and long-run average cost (LAC).[8] Assume that the market is initially in equilibrium at price P' and quantity Q'. The price-taker firm accepts the price of P' and maximizes profits by producing q' units of output. At that

---

8 See Chapter 3 for a derivation of these long-run cost schedules.

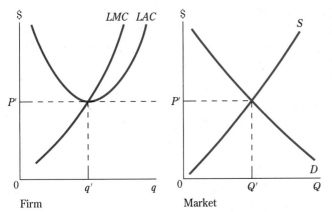

FIGURE 8.6
Long-Run
Equilibrium for
the Price-Taker
Firm and Industry

279

Chapter 8   The Firm and Its Rivals

quantity of output, market price equals long-run marginal cost and is also equal to the minimum of long-run average cost. Total revenue equals total cost and the firm consequently breaks even (economic profits are zero).

Because the revenue earned by the firm just covers the opportunity costs of productive resources employed, the price-taker has no incentive to leave the market. The firm's owner earns a "normal" rate of return on his or her investment. Zero economic profit means that the owner's rate of return in this market is equal to the rate of return available on the next best alternative investment opportunity. Because the firm can do no better in any other market, there is no incentive to withdraw from this market.

When economic profit is zero for existing firms, no outside firm has an incentive to enter the market (and no established firm has an incentive to expand). Hence, the market situation in Figure 8.6 is referred to as a **long-run equilibrium**. This equilibrium is stable, and market price and quantity will remain the same until a change in some external economic force changes the profit-loss picture for the representative firm.[9]

Analyzing the long-run impact of changing market conditions on the price-taker market requires an understanding of how production decisions in the market for final goods and services affect input prices. Two market types are studied. First, a constant cost market is analyzed. In such a market we assume that changes in final product output do not affect input prices. Stated differently, a constant cost market is one in which the industry employs such a small portion of the total quantity of productive resources available that changes in the usage of these resources by the firms in the industry will not affect the market prices of the resources.

---

9 Every firm in the price-taker market will earn zero economic profits in long-run equilibrium. Should one firm employ a unique resource that enables it to achieve lower costs than its rivals, other firms will compete for that resource, thereby raising the resource's market price. The higher input price would drive the firm's average and marginal costs of production upward, and this process would continue until the costs of the firm were comparable to those of other firms.

Second, an increasing cost market is analyzed. Here we assume that resource prices move in the same direction as the utilization of productive resources by the firms in the market for the final good or service. (Resource prices are not affected by the production decisions of individual price-taker firms, however.) For instance, as the demand for the final good or service increases, the industry consumes more resources. This increased utilization of productive resources raises the market prices of resources and these higher input prices, in turn, increase the costs of production of firms in the final product market.

Constant Cost Industry. Assume that the price-taker market depicted in Figure 8.7 is in long-run equilibrium at point A with market demand D' and market supply S'. The market price of the final good is P' and the industry produces and sells Q' units of output. Each price-taker firm produces q' units at this price and earns an economic profit of zero.

Now let the market demand for the final good or service increase to D''. Initially, market price increases to P^*. At this higher price, the price-taker expands production to q^* units and earns a positive economic profit denoted by the area of the shaded rectangle in Figure 8.7. The additional quantities supplied by the existing firms restore short-run industry equilibrium at point B.

The positive economic profits of existing firms in this market serve as a signal that attracts new entry. Profits in excess of normal indicate that the rate of return available on investments in this industry exceed the opportunity cost of the resources employed by it. This signal encourages entrepreneurs to enter and to share in these profits. With the entry of new firms, market supply begins to increase or shift to the right. Based on the definition of a constant cost market, however, input prices remain unchanged as entrepreneurs acquire the resources necessary to enter and to bring new production capacity on line. Therefore, the entry of additional producers does not affect the average and marginal cost curves of existing firms.

As market supply increases in response to the entry of additional firms, the market price of the final product is driven downward. As price declines from P^*, existing firms cut back production from the q^* level. But as long as the market price remains above P', positive economic profits persist. The

FIGURE 8.7
The Long-Run
Supply Schedule
for a Constant
Cost Price-Taker
Industry

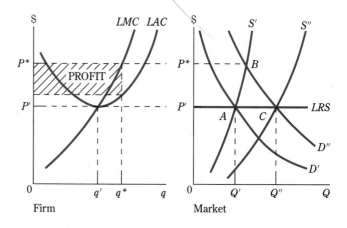

profit signal therefore continues to attract entry until, eventually, market supply increases to S''. At S'', market price is driven back to the original price of P' and profit levels return to zero. The entry of new firms ceases at this point. A new, stable long-run equilibrium is restored at point C. Note that while total industry output has increased to Q'' units, each firm still produces q'. In other words, the entry of new firms accounts for the entire increase in industry supply, and each new firm enters with a plant of the same scale as the original firms.[10]

Points A and C are two points on the industry's **long-run supply** (*LRS*) **schedule**. For a constant cost industry, the *LRS* schedule is horizontal (or perfectly elastic), indicating that the industry is willing and able to supply a wide range of possible output levels at the same price per unit.[11]

In long-run equilibrium, the constant cost price-taker firm charges the market-determined price, produces the level of output at which market price equals long-run marginal and average cost, and earns a zero economic profit. Because the long-run supply schedule of the constant cost price-taker industry is horizontal, the long-run supply price of the industry's product is also constant.

Short-run fluctuations in market price are eliminated in the long run by the entry and exit of firms. Temporary increases or decreases in price send profit signals to which entrepreneurs respond. Shifts in market demand cause the number of firms in the industry to increase or decrease. The greater is demand, the greater is the number of firms that will in the long run supply the good or service to the marketplace. The lower is demand, the fewer are the firms that will supply the product. Because resource prices remain unchanged as firms enter and exit the constant cost industry, long-run equilibrium is restored when market price returns to the original level and zero economic profits are reinstated.

Increasing Cost Industry. If we assume increasing costs, the foregoing analysis changes in one important way: The market prices of resources consumed by an industry vary as industry output expands or contracts. This is due chiefly to the fact that the input requirements of a price-taker industry are large relative to available supplies. Therefore, a change in the number of firms desiring to purchase resources will affect the market prices of these resources.

Refer to Figure 8.8. Assume that the increasing cost industry is initially in equilibrium at point A, determined by the intersection of demand, D', and supply, S'. The typical price-taker firm is consequently in long-run, zero-profit equilibrium at price P' and quantity q'.

---

10 The adjustment process in response to a reduction in demand proceeds symmetrically. Existing firms would experience economic losses initially and would cut back production in response to the fall in market price. Over time, some firms would be forced to exit the market. Market supply would decline and market price would increase. This adjustment process would continue until the economic losses were eliminated and a new long-run equilibrium was restored at P'. Fewer units of output would be produced and sold when equilibrium was restored because fewer producers would remain viable. These surviving firms would again earn an economic profit of zero.

11 Resource supply schedules are themselves horizontal (or perfectly elastic) in this case, implying that input owners are price-takers.

FIGURE 8.8
The Long-Run
Supply Schedule
for an Increasing
Cost Price-Taker
Industry

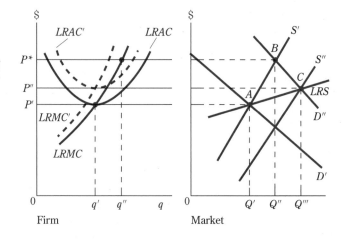

Now suppose that the demand for the industry's good or service increases to D''. Initially, the market adjusts to a new, short-run equilibrium at point B, charging price P^*. At P^*, the representative firm expands production to q'' and earns a positive economic profit. But a profit in excess of normal levels again attracts new firms to the market. As these new firms enter, two factors affect the profits of existing suppliers adversely. First, as new production capacity is brought on line and market supply thereby increases, competition drives the market price of the industry's product downward. This reduction in market price, in turn, forces existing firms to contract production below q'' and accept lower profits.

Second, in an increasing cost industry, the growing number of producers increases the demand for resources, pushing resource prices higher. Input prices are bid upward because the industry must attract resources away from increasingly valuable alternative uses.[12] As resource prices increase, the representative firm's marginal and average production costs increase (shift upwards). These two forces create a two-way profit squeeze by raising production costs and, simultaneously, lowering revenue.

This process continues as long as firms earn positive economic profits. New firms will continue to enter until the rate of return on investments in the industry has returned to normal. Once profit is eliminated, a new long-run equilibrium emerges. In Figure 8.8, the new long-run equilibrium occurs at point C. Market supply has increased to S'' and market price is P''. The price-taker firm's long-run average and marginal costs have increased to $LRAC'$ and $LRMC'$, respectively. Profit for the price-taker has returned to zero.

Points A and C represent two points on the industry's long-run supply schedule. The long-run supply schedule for an increasing cost industry is positively sloped as indicated by the curve labeled LRS in Figure 8.8. The industry responds to an increase in demand by adjusting both the number of

---

12 Resource supply schedules are upward sloping in this case, indicating that higher prices are necessary to call forth larger input quantities to particular uses.

suppliers and their cost structures. Market price does not return to the original level because the cost of doing business increases when the industry expands. In other words, because input prices are bid upward as more inputs are consumed, the industry is willing and able to supply a larger quantity of output only if it can sell that output at a higher price.[13]

An increasing cost price-taker industry will in the long run charge the market-determined price, produce where price equals long-run marginal and average cost, and earn an economic profit of zero. The industry's long-run supply curve is positively sloped. To expand production, the increasing cost industry must attract resources away from increasingly valuable alternative uses. The market price of the industry's output must rise to compensate for higher input prices and production costs.

Normative Implications of the Price-Taker Model

The price-taker model describes the workings of markets consisting of large numbers of independently acting buyers and sellers. Due to the assumptions made in constructing the model, the interaction of price-taker firms leads to an optimal allocation of society's scarce productive resources. This model therefore serves as a benchmark for evaluating market performance.

Because market price is equal to marginal cost in long-run equilibrium, the price-taker industry achieves **allocative efficiency**. Marginal cost, it will be remembered, is always measured in terms of opportunities foregone. From society's point of view, marginal cost represents the value of the next best alternative sacrificed when resources are used to produce the last unit of a particular good or service rather than devoting those resources to some other use. Hence, when industry output expands to the point at which market price is equal to long-run marginal cost, the marginal value consumers place on the last unit purchased (the amount they are willing to pay for that unit) is just equal to the marginal value (opportunity cost) of the resources used to produce the last unit of output.

Moreover, because market price is equal to minimum average cost in long-run equilibrium, the price-taker industry also achieves **production efficiency**. The industry's good or service is produced at the lowest possible cost per unit or, to put it another way, output is produced by the optimal number of firms, each of which employs its production capacity at the efficient (cost-minimizing) rate.

---

13 The price-taker industry responds to a reduction in demand symmetrically. Market price falls, initially forcing existing firms to incur economic losses. Some firms will exit the industry as a result and the accompanying reduction in supply puts upward pressure on the price of the industry's product. At the same time, because the surviving firms consume fewer inputs, the market prices of these productive resources decline. As resource prices decline, the costs of production are reduced for the remaining firms (their marginal and average cost curves shift downward). These market forces tend to eliminate the industry's economic losses. A new, stable equilibrium is eventually reached at a lower output price and a lower level of production due to fewer firms in the market.

The combination of allocative efficiency and production efficiency that characterizes long-run equilibrium in the price-taker model helps explain why the model often serves as a benchmark for judging the performance of real-world markets. Remember, however, that the price-taker model is not meant to be a literal description of reality. The assumptions of model-builders should not be interpreted as establishing necessary conditions for the existence of "competition." Put in the reverse, actual markets may fail to satisfy one or more of the assumptions of the price-taker model (large numbers of buyers and sellers, homogeneous product, free entry and exit, perfect factor mobility, and perfect knowledge). But this does not mean that those markets are noncompetitive. The price-taker model is nothing more or less than a very powerful abstraction that focuses attention on how market forces help keep prices in line with costs.

PRICE-SEARCHER MARKETS

In many markets, rival products are viewed by consumers as good, but not perfect substitutes for one another. The industry's products are heterogeneous in the sense that, in the minds of consumers, the goods of various firms differ along one or more dimensions. Heterogeneity exists because suppliers differ in their locations, the qualities of their products, their promptness of delivery, their willingness to insure customer satisfaction, their ease of access, their reputations, and so on.

Buyers also differ in their tastes and preferences, the lengths of their time horizons, their perceptions of quality, their knowledge of products, and the opportunities available to them to search for and purchase competing goods. For these reasons and more, suppliers possess varying amounts of what is known as "market power," or the ability to raise price without losing all of their customers. For example, gas stations, automobile manufacturers, soft drink companies, shoe retailers, grocery stores, druggists, and universities are all able to differentiate their products from their close competitors and, to some extent, create customer loyalty. These firms can raise their prices without fear of losing the business of every customer.

Consumers differ in terms of the information available to them when making a purchasing decision. Whether a consumer is buying a new car with a turbo-charged engine and a fuel injection system or a new pair of basketball shoes, choices are constrained by the limited amount of prepurchase knowledge he or she has acquired. The more time and effort the consumer devotes to gathering information about the prices and attributes of alternative goods, the better informed are his or her purchase decisions. Unfortunately, gathering facts and figures about a particular item is costly. The consumer eventually reaches a point in the search for information at which the expected gains from continued search do not warrant the additional cost of continuing the search. Never will consumers have full and complete information on which to base any purchase decision.

Because rival products are heterogeneous or differentiated in the minds of consumers, the demand schedule confronting an individual seller is downward sloping. The law of demand consequently applies to the firm as well as to the industry. As the firm increases the price of its product, holding all other variables constant, consumers respond by reducing their purchases. Unlike the price-taker, a firm confronted by a downward-sloping demand curve can increase the price of its product without losing all of its sales. Moreover, it must reduce the price of its product in order to increase its sales. Such a firm is known as a price-searcher because it must search for the price and quantity combination that maximizes its profits.

In addition to making all other business decisions, the price-searcher must decide which price to charge and what level of output to produce. This does not mean that the price-searcher's options are unlimited. The price-searcher firm is constrained both by the cost of production and by the demand for its product. A price-searcher firm cannot force consumers to purchase its product or service; it must operate within the revenue constraints imposed by its customers.

Short-Run Profit Maximization for the Price-Searcher Firm

Part I derives the price-searcher's rule for profit maximization. That rule dictates that the firm select the quantity of output at which marginal revenue equals marginal cost. The firm's profit-maximizing price is then determined by the point on the demand schedule that corresponds to this quantity. Figure 8.9 illustrates the marginal-revenue-equals-marginal-cost rule. Profits are at a maximum for this price-searcher firm if it produces q_1 units of output and sells at a price of P_1 dollars per unit.

Having the ability to search for the profit-maximizing price does not guarantee that the firm will in fact earn positive economic profits. After all, Ford created the Edsel and the Coca-Cola Company introduced New Coke. McDonald's has repeatedly tried to market the McRib sandwich without much success and it has also failed with (Mc?) pizza.

Consider Figure 8.10. At every level of output, price is less than the average total cost of production. Under these circumstances, the firm earns insufficient revenue to cover the total cost of production and sustains economic losses. Should the firm shut down?

To answer this question, the firm must first determine the optimal production level if it decides to produce. The point of profit maximization or loss minimization occurs at q_2 units. By charging a price of P_2 dollars per unit, the firm earns $0P_2Aq_2$ dollars in total revenue. The total cost of producing q_2 units is $0CBq_2$ and so an economic loss of P_2CBA is incurred. If the firm chooses not to produce, then its total losses would be equal to total fixed cost (area $FCBE$). Because $P_2CBA < FCBE$, the firm minimizes its losses by continuing to operate and produce q_2 units of output. This conclusion is consistent with the price-taker's shut-down decision: As long as total revenue is greater than total variable cost ($TR > TVC$), the firm should continue to produce in the short run.

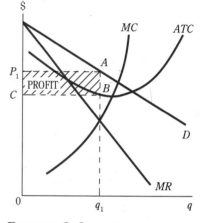

FIGURE 8.9
Short-Run Profit Maximization for a Price-Searcher Firm

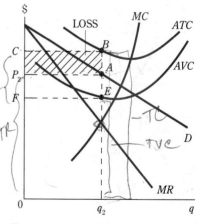

FIGURE 8.10
Short-Run Loss Minimization for a Price-Searcher Firm

Hence, like the price-taker, the price-searcher maximizes profit by producing where marginal revenue is equal to marginal cost. In the short run, the price-searcher likewise earns a profit, operates at a loss, or shuts down, depending upon the demand and cost conditions it faces in the marketplace. The advantage that a price-searcher has over a price-taker, however, is that it may be able to earn positive economic profits in the long run. Whether it can do so or not depends on the conditions of entry into the price-searcher's industry.

Long-Run Profit Maximization for the Price-Searcher Firm

As we have emphasized, the long run is a planning horizon and, as such, it allows the price-searcher firm the opportunity to position itself strategically with respect to its rivals. Strategic positioning for the price-searcher is critical, as is the case in any market. This is because the existence of economic profits will attract new entrants and economic loses will send some existing firms scurrying to locate another market that offers the prospect of earning at least a normal return on their investments.

When resources can enter and exit an industry freely, that is, when barriers to entry and exit are low, the market is called an **open market**. If, on the other hand, rivals find it difficult to enter or to exit in response to price and profit signals, the market is called a **closed market**. Long-run adjustments by the price-searcher firm differ considerably between these two market types. Each is analyzed below.

"Open" Market. Consider a price-searcher firm operating in an open market as presented in Figure 8.11.[14] The local restaurant market supplies a relevant example. In any city or town, consumers have a variety of dining out options. Barriers to entry and exit are relatively low, as evidenced by the large number, wide assortment, and high turnover rates of fast-food restaurants, upscale and downscale eating places, ethnic restaurants, pizza establishments, steak houses, diners, and so on. Each offers a distinct menu and a distinct ambience but all compete in essentially the same market.

Suppose that the demand schedule facing one of the price-searcher firms in an open market is D_1, initially producing positive economic profits[15]. Such profits would be short-lived because other firms would be attracted to the market by the prospect of earning an above-normal rate of return. Two important demand effects materialize as new competitors introduce distinct but substitutable products to the marketplace.[16] First, the demand for the

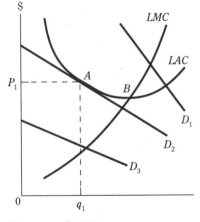

14 Such a market is known as **monopolistically competitive** because it combines the downward-sloping demand curve of the price-searcher ("monopoly") model with the free entry and exit of the price-taker ("competitive") model.

15 To avoid cluttering the diagram, we omit the marginal revenue schedules associated with the various demand schedules drawn in Figure 8.11. The profit-maximizing quantity in all cases is determined by equating marginal revenue with long-run marginal cost.

16 For simplicity, we assume a constant cost industry. If the industry is instead an increasing cost industry, then the *LAC* and *LMC* schedules would also shift upward due to higher input prices, thereby creating a two-way squeeze on profits or losses.

FIGURE 8.11
Long-Run Equilibrium for a
Price-Searcher Firm

price-searcher's product declines (shifts downward) as some of its customers shift their purchases to the new entrants' products. Second, the demand for the price-searcher's product becomes more elastic as the number of substitutes increases. Consumers become more sensitive to price changes as the range of available options widens.

For both of these reasons, D_1 eventually shifts to D_2. The incentive to enter the market ceases as the profits of the existing firms drop to zero at the point of tangency between D_2 and LAC. At point A, the firm's price (P_1) is equal to long-run average cost. Total revenue is equal to total cost (area $OP_1 Aq_1$).

Similarly, if D_3 had been the original demand schedule, the price-searcher would sustain economic losses initially. Some firms in the market would be forced to look elsewhere for profit opportunities. Two demand effects would again materialize as exit proceeds. First, the demand for the surviving firms' products would increase (shift outward) as the customers of the exiting firms look for remaining alternatives to buy. Second, the demand for the price-searcher's product becomes less elastic as the number of substitutes declines. With fewer available options, consumers become less sensitive to price changes.

D_3 consequently shifts toward D_2. As long as firms incur losses, they will continue to exit the market. Eventually, losses are eliminated as demand increases and becomes tangent to long-run average cost (point A). A zero-profit, long-run equilibrium is thereby restored.

In sum, long-run equilibrium for a price searcher firm in an open market occurs at the point where marginal revenue is equal to long-run marginal cost and price is equal to long-run average cost. Because there are no barriers to entry or exit in an open market, competitive market forces assure that economic profits are zero. The rate of return on investments in the industry is equal to the rate of return on the next best available investment opportunity. The price-searcher firm's revenue is just sufficient to cover the opportunity costs of all resources employed in the production process. There is consequently no incentive to leave or to enter the market when long-run equilibrium is reached.

"Contestable" Market. The foregoing discussion emphasizes the role of actual entry and exit in assuring a zero-profit, long-run equilibrium for the price-searcher firm and industry in an open market. The physical movement of resources into and out of the industry may not be necessary to guarantee this result, however, if the market is "contestable."[17]

A **contestable market** is one in which both entry and exit are costless. Costless entry means that potential newcomers do not bear any costs not borne by firms already in the industry. Outsiders have access to the same production technology as insiders; they face no cost disadvantages relative

---

17 William J. Baumol, John C. Panzar, and Robert D. Willig, *Contestable Markets and the Theory of Industry Structure* (San Diego, CA: Harcourt Brace Jovanovich, 1982).

Identifying Profit Opportunities in an Open Price-Searcher Market

The retail gasoline market has undergone significant change over the past several decades. Once self-service gasoline stations appeared in the early 1970s, their market share rose dramatically. By 1979, more than 50 percent of the gasoline sold in the United States was customer-pumped at self-service stations.[a]

In addition to the shift to self-service gasoline sales in the 1970s, there was also a basic change in the composition of ownership of retail gas stations. Locally owned, independent dealers were increasingly replaced by self-service outlets owned by the major gasoline refiners. While almost all gasoline was sold by locally owned, independent dealers before 1970, refiner-owned stations accounted for some 12 percent of the market in 1978.

The independent retailers of gasoline charged that these two events—the emergence of self-service gasoline stations and the forward integration of refiners into gasoline retailing—were related. In particular, they argued that the major gasoline refiners sought to gain control of retail gas prices by replacing independent retailers with refiner-owned, self-service stations.[b] By "monopolizing" the retail market for gasoline, refiners could increase their downstream profits, thereby offsetting the impact of crude oil embargos and other events in the 1970s that had reduced the profitability of their refining operations.

Owen Phillips and David Schutte offered an alternative explanation for the evolution of self-service gas stations. They explored the competitive market forces that determine the relative profitability of self-service and full-service operations. Phillips and Schutte first constructed a model of the profit incentive of a full-service retailer to switch to a self-service sales policy. From this model, Phillips and Schutte constructed the following index (H) of the relative profitability of self-service operations:

$$H = \frac{\eta_{sf} r_s}{r_f} - \frac{\eta_{fs} r_f}{r_s} + \eta_{ff} - \eta_{ss}.$$

In this index, η_{ff} and η_{ss} are the own-price elasticities of demand for full- and self-service products, η_{sf} and η_{fs} are the cross-price elasticities of demand for self- and full-service products, and r_s and r_f are the revenues the seller expects from self-service and full-service sales.

If the two cross-price elasticities are equal to one another (i.e., $\eta_{sf} = \eta_{fs} = \delta$), then we can write the profit incentive index in a more interpretable form as

$$H' = \delta \left(\frac{r_s^2 - r_f^2}{r_f r_s} \right) + \eta_{ff} - \eta_{ss}.$$

There are two circumstances in which H' will be positive and it will consequently be profitable to switch from full-service to self-service operations. In the first case, the self-service product generates more revenue than the full-service product ($r_s > r_f$) and the numerator of the term in the parentheses is positive. The index H' is then positively related to the value of δ and inversely related to the absolute value of η_{ff}. Put differently, if the revenue from self-service sales is expected to be greater than the revenue from full-service sales, the incentive to switch to self-service is higher the more substitutable the two products are for one another in the minds of consumers.

The second case occurs if the self-service product generates less revenue than the full-service product ($r_s < r_f$) and the numerator of the term in parentheses is negative. The index H' is then negatively related to δ and the incentive to switch to self-service is higher the less substitutable the two products are for one another.

The central thesis of Phillips and Schutte's paper is that the prevalence of self-service operations in a market should be positively related to the value of H or H'

a Material for this case study is taken from Owen R. Phillips and David P. Schutte, "Identifying Profitable Self-Service Markets: A Test in Gasoline Retailing," *Applied Economics* 20 (1988), pp. 263-72.

b U. S. Department of Energy, *The State of Competition in Gasoline Marketing*, Final Report DOE/PE-0026, Washington, D. C.

in that market. To test this thesis, Phillips and Schutte first noted that there is a wide geographic variation in the market shares of self- and full-service retail gasoline dealerships. For example, in 1976 only 6 percent of Philadelphia's gasoline pumps were self-service while the figure was 50 percent in Houston. In general, a higher proportion of gasoline is sold by self-service stations in the South and West than in the East.

Based on a sample of 31 cities, Phillips and Schutte estimated the demand for full- and self-service gasoline and then calculated estimates of H for these cities. The sample means for prices, quantities, and elasticities were $q_f = 321$, $q_s = 164$, $p_f = \$.9757$, $p_s = \$.9515$, $\eta_{ff} = -39.91$, $\eta_{fs} = 13.75$, $\eta_{ss} = -36.39$, and $\eta_{sf} = 86.35$. The estimates suggest that sales at full-service pumps are slightly more responsive to changes in own-price than are self-service sales ($\eta_{ff} > \eta_{ss}$ in absolute value). More importantly, the cross-price response is quite large. At the sample means, a 1 percent increase in the price of gasoline at the full-service pump leads to an 86 percent increase in self-service sales. Although full-service sales are considerably less responsive to a change in the self-service price, the evidence suggests strongly both that consumers consider the two to be readily substitutable and that sellers in this industry lack market power. Gasoline retailers apparently compete in an open price-searcher market.

Finally, Phillips and Schutte found the simple correlation coefficient between H and the proportion of self-service pumps across the 31 cities in the sample to be .81. This finding led the authors to conclude that market forces associated with demand characteristics in self- and full-service markets play a central role in the proportion of the gasoline market that is accounted for by self-service stations.

---

to the established firms. Costless exit means that any firm leaving the industry can recover all expenses incurred during entry. All productive resources are salvageable in the sense that they are either consumed (fully depreciated) during the time the firm is in operation or can be sold in active secondhand markets for a price equal to their acquisition cost less normal depreciation.

Under these circumstances, established firms cannot sell their output at any price greater than long-run average production cost. Any attempt to do so would invite "hit-and-run" entry by outsiders who would collect a share of the incumbent firms' profits by undercutting their prices, and then depart the industry when returns fall back to normal. Realizing their vulnerability to entry, the incumbents have no choice except to price their product at average cost. The industry equilibrium is a zero-profit equilibrium because every "wedge" between price and average cost represents a profit opportunity that outsiders will exploit. In a contestable market, potential entry is as good as actual entry.

"Closed" Market. A closed market is one for which important barriers to entry or exit exist. Resources are no longer free to move into or out of the industry at will. Closed markets can be created by the activities of the incumbent firms, by the characteristics of the industry's production technology, or by public policies toward business.

Incumbent firms may be able to erect barriers that prevent new competitors from entering the industry. First, to the extent that existing firms control essential resources used in the production process, entry is blocked because potential newcomers have no access to the inputs

The Role of Michael Jordan in Assuring Contractual Performance

In a contestable price-searcher market, established sellers are vulnerable to "hit-and-run" entry by outsiders who undercut the prevailing market price. One strategy a new entrant may use to attract customers away from established firms is to manufacture a product of inferior quality but misrepresent it. If consumers find it difficult to judge quality, the entrant may in the short run be able to make inroads into the established firms' profits by selling a low-quality product (which is presumably cheaper to produce) at a high-quality price.

How can the established firms protect themselves against such tactics? Just as importantly, what prevents the existing firms themselves from fooling consumers by selling low-quality goods at high-quality prices? Unless consumers are convinced that the incumbents will not cheat them in this way, they will not be willing to pay the price premium necessary to motivate sellers to offer high-quality products.[a] The fundamental problem is that the established firms cannot charge prices in excess of average cost without inviting entry. At the same time, they must adopt a strategy that convinces consumers that high price represents a signal of high quality and that serves as a guarantee of noncheating behavior.

One solution to this problem is for the established sellers to make investments in firm-specific, nonsalvageable capital.[b] Michael Jordan's endorsement contract with Nike is an example of such an investment.[c] The multimillion dollar payment made to Michael Jordan to appear in Nike's advertising campaigns is worthless if Nike fails to continue to produce shoes of the implicitly promised quality. Cheating the consumer by selling low-quality shoes at high-quality prices will result in the forfeiture of this investment—Nike will lose future business and lose the value of the brand name capital built up through Michael Jordan's association with the firm.

Michael Jordan's endorsement contract serves an additional economic function. The payments made to him raise Nike's average costs of production and these higher average production costs dissipate the positive economic profits that would otherwise invite entry to the industry. A zero-profit, long-run equilibrium is reached by price competition among established sellers, which lowers the premium consumers must pay to motivate the supply of high-quality products, and by nonprice competition (investments in firm-specific capital) which raises unit production costs. Both factors serve as a guarantee that high-quality products will in fact be supplied. Michael Jordan is more than just a great basketball player—he is also an important input in the production of Nike shoes and other consumer products.

a This is the famous "lemons" problem discussed by George Akerlof, "The Market for 'Lemons': Quality Uncertainty and the Market Mechanism," *Quarterly Journal of Economics* 84 (1970), pp. 488-500. See Chapter 11 for a more complete discussion of price-quality tradeoffs.
b Benjamin Klein and Keith Leffler, "The Role of Market Forces in Assuring Contractual Performance," *Journal of Political Economy* 89 (August 1981), pp. 615-41. We apologize to Ben and Keith for stealing their title for this case study.
c Other firm-specific investments such as elaborate storefronts, costly television advertising campaigns, financial support for the U. S. Olympic Team, and so on have similar purposes and effects.

required to produce a product that would compete with existing products. The mineral spring owned by the Perrier Company may fit into this category. Such entry barriers also exist in industrial diamonds and bauxite (an ore essential to the production of aluminum).

Second, the established firms may enter into a collusive agreement to limit competition among themselves. Collusion may make the entry of new firms more difficult because the potential entrant must compete against cartel members acting in concert rather than against individual firms acting independently of one another. Of course, the higher-than-normal returns earned by the colluders also invite the entry of outside firms desiring to share in the cartel's profits.[18]

Third, established firms often possess significant brand name capital. Consumer awareness of existing products discourages new competitors who would have to undertake expensive advertising campaigns to overcome entrenched consumer loyalties. Potential competitors may have higher costs than incumbent firms because they must advertise more per unit sold in order to create their own brand name recognition. Investments in firm-specific brand name capital, as just seen in the Michael Jordan case study, also serve to close markets by erecting barriers to exit. Locational advantages may likewise provide established firms with a competitive edge that is difficult (costly) for new entrants to overcome.

The economies of scale associated with many capital-intensive production processes may erect technological barriers to entry. Because long-run average production costs decline sharply in the presence of scale economies, there is a tendency for established firms to expand, thereby raising the minimum efficient scale at which potential entrants can expect to survive. High start-up costs impede the entry of new rivals that would otherwise enter and compete with established firms.

Legal barriers to entry close markets in yet another way. Patents provide one example of government-enforced property rights that prevent the entry of new rivals. Laws establishing licensing requirements, providing copyright or trademark protection, setting safety standards, bestowing exclusive franchises, and imposing import quotas are but a few of the ways that government intervention into the economy can create closed markets.[19]

However they are created, though, barriers to entry and exit short-circuit the natural workings of the market that would otherwise keep prices in line with costs and rates of return in line with opportunity costs. Refer again to Figure 8.11 (see p. 286). If the demand schedule confronting the price-searcher is D_1, the firm will earn a positive economic profit. Potential rivals desiring to share in these profits cannot do so because entry is blocked. Hence, the incumbent firms earn positive economic profits not only in the short run, but in the long run as well. Barriers to entry, in essence, protect the profits of existing

---

18 Collusion is discussed more fully below.
19 Public policies toward business are discussed in detail in Part IV.

firms. Because of this, consumers are denied the opportunity to select from the larger and more diverse set of options that would be available otherwise.

Normative Implications of the Price-Searcher Model

In contrast to the price-taker model, long-run equilibrium for the price-searcher industry in both open and closed markets is characterized by price greater than long-run marginal cost. Allocative efficiency is consequently not achieved. Productive resources are allocated *in*efficiently because the value consumers place on the last unit of output produced by the price-searcher exceeds the opportunity costs of the resources employed to produce the last unit.

Likewise, the price-searcher does not achieve production efficiency. This conclusion follows from observing that in a closed market, price is greater than long-run average cost. Moreover, while the price is equal to long-run average cost in an open price-searcher market, price is not equal to *minimum* long-run average cost in either an open or closed market. Hence, the price-searcher does not produce its product at the lowest possible unit cost. From the consumer's point of view, too few resources and too few firms are employed in the production of the industry's output.

A comparison of the characteristics of long-run equilibrium suggests that the price-searcher supplies a smaller quantity of output (and consequently charges a higher price) than would be the case if the good or service were instead supplied by a price-taker industry facing the same demand and cost conditions. This is somewhat of a false comparison, however. The price-taker model applies only when the good or service produced is homogeneous or undifferentiated. If, on the other hand, consumers value product differentiation, the assumptions of the price-searcher model come into play. Heterogeneous goods cannot be produced by a price-taker industry because, by definition, price-searching behavior begins when demand curves are downward sloping. Put differently, the benchmark performance characteristics of the price-taker industry can only exist if product differentiation is eliminated.

It is nevertheless true that output is lower and price is higher with price-searching than with price-taking behavior. One way of thinking of these differences is that the allocative and production inefficiency of the price-searcher firm and industry represent market failures that must be redressed by appropriate government intervention.[20] Another way of thinking about these differences is that allocative and production inefficiency are the "prices" consumers must pay for the product variety they value.[21]

---

20 See Part IV.

21 Edward H. Chamberlin, *The Theory of Monopolistic Competition*, 8E. (Cambridge, MA: Harvard University Press, 1962), pp. 93-94.

Up to this point, firms have made market decisions without explicitly considering the possible reactions of their rivals. By assumption, of course, individual price-taker firms have no power to influence the market and can therefore safely ignore their competitors. Price-searchers, by contrast, have some discretion over the prices they charge and, moreover, they can take actions to further differentiate their own products from those sold by rival firms.

In some price-searcher markets—those in which there are relatively few competitors—one firm's actions have a direct impact on its rivals. For example, other things being the same, if one firm lowers its price, its sales will increase at competitors' expense. These competitors will, in all probability, retaliate in an attempt to win back their lost customers. A firm that does not take its rivals' likely responses into consideration when initiating a price reduction will sell far fewer additional units than it might have expected to sell otherwise. Similarly, if a firm raises its price and rivals do not follow, a substantial market share and profit reduction can be predicted.

Paul Sweezy referred to an industry composed of a few firms who recognize their mutual interdependence as an **oligopoly**.[22] In such an industry, firms will find it in their best interest to anticipate the probable reactions of other sellers to any policy change they plan to initiate. A number of theories have been proposed to model the behavior of mutually interdependent firms. Three models that provide a framework for solving managerial problems of this type are outlined below.

The "Kinked" Demand Curve Model

The simplest oligopoly model is the "kinked" demand curve model. Paul Sweezy proposed the model in an attempt to rationalize the observation that the prices charged by industries composed of a few large firms tend to be more stable over time than would be expected in a highly competitive market environment subject to changing demand and cost conditions. The fundamental assumption of the Sweezy model is that each firm believes that its rivals are reluctant to follow price increases, but respond immediately to match price cuts.

Figure 8.12 illustrates the reactions anticipated by an oligopolist charging price P and producing output Q. Beginning at point A, a firm can either raise or lower its price. Demand curve D is relevant for proposed price increases. Assuming that rivals will hesitate to match any price higher than P, the firm can expect its sales to fall substantially as consumers switch to lower-priced alternatives. On the other hand, if rivals quickly match any attempt to charge a price lower than P, the firm cannot expect its sales to increase significantly. Hence, demand curve D' is relevant for proposed price reductions.

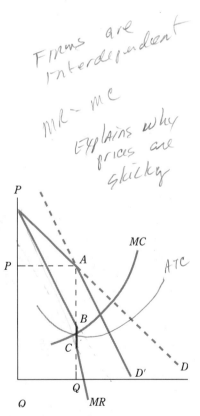

Firms are interdependent

MR = MC explains why prices are sticky

FIGURE 8.12
The "Kinky" Oligopoly Demand Schedule

Because the Sweezy model presumes an asymmetry in rivals' reactions to price changes, the effective demand curve faced by the firm is derived by splicing the relevant segments of D and D'. Starting at point A, demand curve D applies for any price increase and demand curve D' applies for any price reduction. The asymmetry in rivals' reactions generates a "kink" at point A, the prevailing price-quantity combination.

Figure 8.12 also shows that the kink in demand caused by these asymmetric reactions introduces a "jump" or discontinuity into the firm's perceived marginal revenue schedule.[23] This discontinuity occurs at output level Q. Each segment of the marginal revenue schedule corresponds to the relevant region of one of the two demand schedules that determine the location of the kink at point A. The length of the vertical segment of the marginal revenue schedule, BC, is a function of the differences in the elasticities of demand for price changes above and below P. These demand elasticities, in turn, depend on the extent to which rival firms react to price changes.

Given the marginal cost schedule MC, the firm maximizes its profits by producing Q units of output and selling them at a price of P dollars per unit. Indeed, the firm will continue to produce Q units of output and charge a price of P dollars as long as marginal cost cuts marginal revenue anywhere in marginal revenue's vertical range. The kinked demand curve model thus provides a justification for price rigidity in oligopolistic industries. Marginal production costs can rise as high as B or fall as low as C without causing the firm to change its price-output decision.

The Sweezy model's prediction that prices in oligopolistic markets tend to be inflexible seems to be consistent with the idea that firms are hesitant to reduce price because they fear that price reductions will trigger a "price war" that could well threaten their survival. The periodic fare wars among the major commercial airlines and price wars among local gasoline stations lend support to these fears. The threat of retaliation to a price reduction forces the oligopolist to continue to charge the same price even when production costs have fallen.

Concern with long-run survival may also help explain why firms hesitate to raise price even when production costs have increased. Realizing that its customer base could be damaged significantly if competitors do not follow, the firm's best strategy may be to hold price at the initial level and absorb higher production costs in the form of lower profits.

This is especially true if price increases create a **ratchet effect**. When a price increase is not matched by rival firms, some customers shift their allegiances and become customers of competitors. The firm may then lose some of its ability to attract old customers back by simply lowering price. If this is the case, then point A in Figure 8.12 no longer applies. After raising price, the firm

---

23 See George J. Stigler, "The Kinky Oligopoly Demand Curve and Rigid Prices," *Journal of Political Economy* 55 (October 1947), pp. 434-49; and D. Smith and W. Neale, "The Geometry of Kinky Oligopoly: Marginal Cost, the Gap, and Price Behavior," *Southern Economic Journal* 37 (January 1971), pp. 276-82.

may decide to charge P again, but rivals counter and charge lower prices. In essence, demand curve D' shifts to the left, and the kink moves up along demand schedule D to a lower volume of sales and a lower level of profits.

The ratchet effect may cause the firm to lose market share permanently. Once price has been increased, price reductions, even if they are not matched, are no longer as effective in attracting customers. For example, we know of a restaurant in South Carolina that was doing a booming business. People waited in line to be served old-fashioned, southern-style meals. Because of its popularity, the restaurant's manager decided to double the prices on the menu. Large numbers of customers soon shifted to competing restaurants. When the manager realized his mistake, he switched back to the old menu. But the restaurant's competitors responded by lowering their prices and the restaurant never regained its original share of the market.

The kinked demand curve model describes why oligopolistic firms may be reluctant to change price in response to changes in cost. However, the model provides no explanation for how the prevailing price is determined in the first place.[24] We need more sophisticated theories to more fully understand the interactions of rivals in a dynamic market setting.

A Simple Game Theory Model

Game theory provides a framework for modelling the options managers face in oligopolistic markets. In any game, one player wins by out-maneuvering or out-performing another player. In a tennis match, winning depends on the ability to react to the opponent's play and adjust one's game strategy in ways that neutralize the other player's strengths. In chess, a player wins not only by reacting to the opponent's individual moves but by developing a series of moves and replies that overwhelm the other player's anticipated strategy. The same is true in an industry composed of relatively few interdependent firms. The manager pursues production and sales strategies based on the most likely responses of rivals.

Game theory was introduced into economics in the early 1950s by John von Neumann and Oskar Morgenstern.[25] The basic elements of a game are the *players*, a set of interdependent *strategies*, and a set of *payoffs* associated with each possible course of action. Games may be *cooperative* or *noncooperative* depending on whether or not the players have opportunities to coordinate their strategy choices. Interdependence is the key characteristic of any

---

24 Moreover, Sweezy's fundamental assumptions are questionable despite their superficial appeal. Systematic (as opposed to anecdotal) empirical evidence seems to suggest that oligopolistic firms are no more reluctant to follow price increases than they are to match price cuts. See Stigler, "Kinky Oligopoly Demand Curve;" Julian A. Simon, "A Further Test of the Kinky Oligopoly Demand Curve," *American Economic Review* 55 (December 1969), pp. 971-75; and Walter J. Primeaux and Mark R. Bomball, "A Reexamination of the Kinky Oligopoly Demand Curve," *Journal of Political Economy* 82 (July/August 1974), pp. 851-62.

25 John von Neumann and Oskar Morgenstern, *Theory of Games and Economic Behavior* (Princeton, NJ: Princeton University Press, 1953).

game—the payoff associated with any player's move or choice depends on the move or choice made by the other players.

The most basic type of game consists of two players each of whom can pursue two possible strategies. Consider the **payoff matrix** shown in Table 8.3. The cells show the economic profits of two oligopolistic firms under two possible courses of action. (A two-firm oligopoly is known as a **duopoly**.) Each firm has the option of either maintaining its price at the current level or reducing price by five percent. For example, if both firms independently decide to keep prices unchanged, firm A earns a profit of $60 and firm B earns a profit of $40. Should firm A decide to reduce price by 5%, its profit increases to $65, provided that firm B does not match the price cut. Firm B can likewise increase its profit by $5 by instituting a 5% price cut, provided that firm A continues to charge the initial price. If both firms simultaneously reduce their prices by 5%, their profits both decline by $10.

What is the optimal pricing strategy for each firm to follow? If the firms are averse to risk, they might follow a **maximin strategy**. A maximin strategy maximizes the game's minimum expected payoff. Firm A observes that by maintaining a constant price, the lowest profit it will earn is $55. On the other hand, the lowest profit firm A can expect from reducing price by 5% is $50. The optimal strategy for firm A under the maximin rule is to maintain price at the current level. This strategy guarantees that the worst firm A will do is earn a profit of $55 no matter what firm B does.

If Firm B likewise adopts the maximin strategy, it too will choose to maintain price at the initial level. This conclusion follows from observing that if Firm B holds its price constant, the lowest profit it can expect to earn is $35. By reducing price by 5%, on the other hand, firm B's lowest expected profit is $30. The maximin strategy guarantees that firm B will do no worse than earn a profit of $35 if it maintains price at the current level. Firm B consequently avoids cutting its price.

Both firms will maintain a constant price if *both* follow the rule of maximizing their minimum expected profit. It should be obvious, however, that one firm can profit at the other's expense if the rival continues to play the maximin strategy in every market period. If firm B follows the rule of maximizing its minimum expected payoff, for example, firm A can increase its profit to $65 by reducing price. Firm B faces a similar incentive if it thinks that firm A will

TABLE 8.3   A PRISONERS' DILEMMA DUOPOLY GAME

		Firm B	
		MAINTAIN PRICE	REDUCE PRICE
Firm A	MAINTAIN PRICE	A = $60 B = $40	A = $55 B = $45
	REDUCE PRICE	A = $65 B = $35	A = $50 B = $30

adhere to the maximin strategy. The strategy of maintaining a constant price may therefore unravel over time as each firm strives to take advantage of the other.

The payoff matrix in Table 8.3 illustrates a classic **prisoners' dilemma**.[26] Because one firm's expected profit is a function of the strategy followed by its rival, the two players' choices are interdependent in a fundamental way. Both firms will be better off (their profits will be higher) if they both maintain price at its current level. But because each firm can increase its own profits by cutting price while the other continues to charge the initial price, there are strong incentives to follow a strategy that makes both firms worse off.

The prisoners' dilemma game is very simple, but it does illustrate how mutual interdependence affects the payoffs to cooperation and competition in an oligopolistic market. Strategies for keeping cooperation alive are among the principal topics of research in modern game theory. The important point here is that disaster awaits managers who fail to incorporate the expected responses of rivals into their decision-making calculus.

Cartels

The classic prisoners' dilemma game illustrates that there are often mutual gains from cooperation among the firms in an oligopolistic market. A **cartel** forms when competitors explicitly agree to act in concert. The incentives for firms to cooperate or collude have been recognized for more than 200 years. In 1776, Adam Smith observed that "people of the same trade seldom meet together..., but the conversation ends in a conspiracy against the public...."[27] In the United States, cartels are illegal under the Sherman Act of 1890 for purposes of domestic trade, but U. S. firms are permitted to participate in cartels formed for purposes of international trade.

The most recognizable cartel is the Organization of Petroleum Exporting Countries (OPEC). However, there are many other examples of both legal and illegal collusive behavior in the United States. The National Collegiate Athletic Association (NCAA), for example, has cartelized intercollegiate athletics.[28] Similarly, eight Ivy League schools and the Massachusetts Institute of Technology were recently charged with conspiring to fix the offers of financial aid to entering students.[29]

---

26 Two suspects are interrogated in separate rooms. The police have no physical evidence so that if neither suspect confesses, they both go free. However, each is told that if the other suspect does not admit to any wrongdoing, his sentence will be reduced if he shows good faith efforts to cooperate with the authorities. Both suspects of course confess and both go to jail.

27 Adam Smith, *An Inquiry into the Nature and Causes of the Wealth of Nations*, (New York: Modern Library, 1937), p. 128. (First published in 1776.)

28 See, for example, Robert E. McCormick, "Colleges Get Their Athletes for a Song," *Wall Street Journal*, 20, August 1985, p. 24.

29 "U.S. Charges 8 Ivy League Universities, MIT with Illegally Fixing Financial Aid," *Wall Street Journal*, 23 May , 1991.

As George Stigler demonstrated, the joint profits of firms competing in an industry can be increased if the firms mutually agree to limit the quantity of output they produce.[30] We can demonstrate this result by treating two or more conspirators as a single multi-plant firm. Refer to Figure 8.13. Suppose the industry contains two firms, A and B. The market demand schedule is D and the corresponding marginal revenue schedule is MR. The cartel's marginal cost of production, MC_c, is the horizontal summation of the marginal cost curves of the two individual firms; that is, $MC_c = MC_a + MC_b$. The cartel maximizes profit at the level of output at which marginal revenue is equal to marginal cost, or $MR = MC_c$.

The cartel must, in turn, allocate production to the individual firms in a way that equates their individual marginal costs with the cartel's overall marginal cost (i.e., $MC_a = MC_b = MC_c = MR$). Put differently, each unit of output should be allocated to the low marginal cost producer to maximize overall cartel profits. For example, if at some given level of production $MC_a > MC_b$, then the cartel can increase joint profit by expanding production in firm B and contracting production in firm A until the marginal costs of the two firms are equal to one another.

In Figure 8.13, the cartel maximizes profits by producing Q_c units of output and selling them at a price of P_c dollars per unit. Following the profit-maximizing rule of equating marginal costs with marginal revenue across the two firms, draw a horizontal line from the point at which $MR = MC_c$. The intersection of this line with the marginal cost schedules of firm A and firm B determines the quantity of output each should produce. Firm A produces q_a units and firm B produces q_b units. Both firms charge P_c and the cartel sells $Q_c = q_a + q_b$ units. The total cartel profit is the sum of the two shaded areas in the figure.

By mutually agreeing on the quantity of output each firm will produce and on the selling price, the cartel enables its two members to jointly earn higher

FIGURE 8.13
Cartel Production Quotas

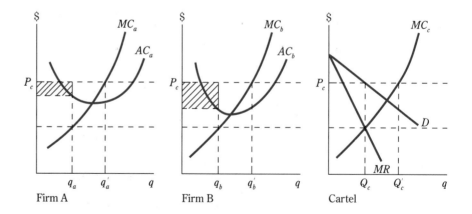

Firm A   Firm B   Cartel

30 George J. Stigler, "A Theory of Oligopoly," *Journal of Political Economy* 72 (February 1964), pp. 44-61.

profits than they would be able to earn otherwise. But the collusive agreement must be strictly enforced, because the conspiracy contains the seeds of self-destruction. After agreeing to charge price P_c, each firm can increase its own profits by expanding production beyond the quantity established by the cartel.

This conclusion follows because at price P_c, both firms are producing a quantity of output at which marginal cost is less than price. Independent expansions of production to either q_a' or q_b' would enhance the cheater's profit, *provided* that the other cartel member adheres to the original agreement. Unfortunately for the cartel (but fortunately for consumers), the collective response would be to expand production to $Q_c' = q_a' + q_b'$ units, resulting in a surplus of $Q_c' - Q_c$ at the cartel price. The surplus would force price to decline, effectively destroying the cartel. Instead of earning above-normal profits, cheating causes the cartel agreement to unravel, thereby returning the market to the zero-profit, price-taker solution.

These incentives to cheat on the cartel agreement are even stronger if some members are more efficient (have lower production costs) than their co-conspirators. In Figure 8.13, for example, the relatively low-cost firm (firm B) can expand its market share and profit substantially by cutting price below P_c. Hence, the members of a cartel must be prepared to devote some of the conspiracy's profits to the job of monitoring compliance with their agreement to restrict production. To be successful, this enforcement mechanism must serve to detect and punish cheating behavior without triggering a destructive price war.

As Stigler pointed out, fixing market shares is the most obvious method of enforcing a cartel agreement. The cartel establishes production quotas for each member (such as q_a and q_b in Figure 8.13); evidence of cheating is then obvious when any firm produces more than its assigned quota. The cartel must then penalize the cheater in a way that deters future violations of the cartel's rules. Enforcement can be quite costly. In 1990, for example, the members of OPEC disagreed on the proper allocation of revised crude oil production quotas. One member in particular (Kuwait) began exceeding its assigned limit. A possible explanation of Iraq's invasion of Kuwait, which triggered the Persian Gulf War, is that Saddam Hussein was playing the role of cartel policeman.

Collusion is driven by the goal of raising the conspirators' joint profits. The ability to reach this goal depends not only on deterring cheating by existing members but dealing with the prospect of new entry by outsiders seeking a share of the cartel's profits. Cartels are consequently more likely to be successful in markets in which there are significant barriers to the entry of new firms. With minimal barriers to entry, the colluders must convince new entrants to join in the conspiracy. Doing so requires increasing and reassigning production quotas. Moreover, the accommodation of new members will make cheating more difficult to detect, thereby increasing the incentives of all members to engage in it and shortening the agreement's expected life.

The theory of oligopoly suggests that private cartels are inherently unstable. The same profit motive that provides incentives for firms to act cooperatively provides equally powerful incentives for cooperation to break down.

SUMMARY

This chapter has placed the firm in a market context and presented two basic theoretical models. In a price-taker market, it is assumed that the quantity of a homogeneous good produced by an individual firm represents such a small share of the industry total that the firm's own production decisions have no impact on market price. The firm consequently takes the market-determined price as given and maximizes profits by selecting the quantity of output at which marginal cost is equal to price.

Depending on demand and cost conditions, the price-taker firm may earn an economic profit or sustain an economic loss in the short run. In the long run, however, the movement of resources into and out of the industry eliminates profits and losses. New firms enter until economic profits are competed away and existing firms exit until any economic losses disappear. Long-run equilibrium for the price-taker industry reflects allocative efficiency (price equal to marginal cost), production efficiency (price equal to minimum average cost), and zero economic profits.

The product supplied by a price-searcher industry, by contrast, is heterogeneous. The representative firm consequently faces a downward-sloping demand schedule. Because marginal revenue is less than price in this case, profit maximizing behavior entails searching for the quantity at which marginal cost is equal to marginal revenue. Long-run profitability depends on conditions of entry into the price-searcher industry. In an "open" market, short-run profits are dissipated by the actual entry of new resources and they are dissipated by the threat of potential entry if the market is "contestable." Only if the market is "closed" is the price-searcher able to earn positive economic profits in the long run.

This chapter has also extended the price-searcher model to describe oligopolistic markets in which competitors recognize their mutual interdependence. While powerful incentives exist for the firms to behave cooperatively in this case, there are equally powerful forces leading to the breakdown of cooperation.

The market models in this chapter provide valuable insights into the competitive market process. The price-searcher model, in particular, will be applied throughout the remainder of *Modern Managerial Economics* to address a rich set of issues of critical importance to managerial decision-making.

QUESTIONS

8.1 The law of demand clearly states that, other things being the same, consumers will buy more of a good as its price falls. If the law of demand is valid, then why is the demand curve confronting a price-taker firm horizontal or perfectly elastic?

8.2 If you were asked to determine whether tennis shoes are sold in either a price-taker market or a price-searcher market, what kinds of information would you seek?

8.3 No Crash Airlines is scheduled to fly from Memphis to Wichita. If the flight is made, the airline incurs operating costs of $5,000. If the flight is not made, No

Crash Airlines still incurs a fixed cost of $1,000. If 50 passengers wish to take this flight, then what is the minimum ticket price No Crash Airlines can charge each passenger and still make it economically sensible to take off?

8.4 Assume that wine grapes are produced in a price-taker, constant cost industry. Suppose there is a change in tastes by older people away from beer to wine. If you work for a wine manufacturer, what can you expect to happen to the market price of wine in the short run? How will your firm respond in the short run? What will happen to the market price of wine in the long run? What change in sales, if any, can your firm expect in the long run?

8.5 In what sense are allocative inefficiency and production inefficiency the "cost" of product variety?

8.6 Your friend manages a price-taker firm and faces the following situation: Price = $10, average total cost = $12, average fixed cost = $5, and marginal cost = $10. Your friend hires you as a consultant. What recommendations would you make?

8.7 A price-searcher firm is earning a positive economic profit. Suppose that the government levies a lump-sum tax on this firm equal to its profits. What impact would this tax have on the firm's output and pricing decisions in the short run? What adverse consequences might this tax have in the long run?

8.8 A price-searcher firm operating in a closed market is earning a positive economic profit. Will the firm still earn an economic profit if it is sold to a new owner? Why or why not? Use a diagram to illustrate the cost and revenue schedules of the new and old owners.

PROBLEMS

8.1 Figure 8.14 depicts the average and marginal cost functions of Sweet Sweat, a price-taker clothing firm that produces t-shirts for people to wear during aerobic workouts. Use the information in the figure to answer the following questions:
   a. If the market price of a t-shirt is $8.00, how many t-shirts will Sweet Sweat manufacture? What is the profit or loss of Sweet Sweat at this price?
   b. If the price of t-shirts is $7.00, how many t-shirts will Sweet Sweat manufacture? What is the profit or loss of Sweet Sweat at this price?
   c. If the price of t-shirts falls to $6.00, will the firm shut down? If not, what quantity of output will it produce?
   d. At what price will Sweet Sweat stop producing t-shirts?

8.2 Pizza Supreme and Pizza King are the only two pizza firms in Keystone, Pennsylvania. Their market shares are recorded in Table 8.4 for the strategies of either increasing their prices by 10% or maintaining prices at their current levels. Assuming that the two firms do not collude and that both managers follow a maximin strategy, what pricing strategies will Pizza Supreme and Pizza King pursue?

TABLE 8.4

		Pizza Supreme	
		MAINTAIN PRICE	INCREASE PRICE
Pizza King	MAINTAIN PRICE	PS = 40% PK = 60%	PS = 30% PK = 70%
	INCREASE PRICE	PS = 60% PK = 40%	PS = 50% PK = 50%

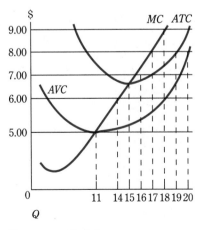

FIGURE 8.14

Topics in the Pricing of Products And Resources

OVERVIEW

This chapter considers four advanced pricing issues. The first topic, **transfer pricing**, involves the optimal pricing of goods and services that the firm exchanges internally among its divisions or units. Transfer pricing decisions are critical to the firm's overall profitability. Indeed, selecting the prices at which resources are transferred within the firm is every bit as important to profit as selecting the prices at which final products are sold to consumers.

The pricing decisions that face the multi-product firm are the second major topic of Chapter 9. Under this heading, we discuss the pricing of joint products, or products that are interdependent in the production process. Oil refining supplies a relevant example of such a production process in which the manufacture of one product (gasoline, for instance) necessarily implies that one or more other products (kerosene, fuel oil, and so on) will also be produced. What is the optimal price of each joint product given that a change in the quantity produced of one of them will affect the quantities produced of the others?

The chapter also considers the pricing of products that are interrelated in demand. How does General Motors, for example, solve the problem of determining the profit-maximizing prices of Buicks and Oldsmobiles given that the price it charges for one model has an impact on the sales of the other?

The third major topic in this chapter is **multi-part pricing**. Examples of this pricing strategy include discounts for volume purchases, the practice of charging admissions or membership fees for the privilege of purchasing the firm's product, and variable rates on utilities with either higher or lower rates beyond certain levels of consumption. Long-distance telephone charges are usually highest for the first three minutes of a conversation; many amusement parks charge an admission fee and then require customers to purchase a ticket for each ride; and many private country clubs require members to buy an annual membership plus pay a "greens fee" for each round of golf played. What is the profit-maximizing multi-part price given that the initial charge limits the number of customers who will be willing and able to pay the subsequent charges?

How a firm assigns production quotas to its various plants producing the same product is the chapter's fourth topic. **Multi-plant firms** operate at various locations within a country and around the world as divisions of multi-national enterprises. Differences in technology, taxes, and the prices of raw materials and labor create differences in production costs among the plants. What is the optimal allocation of output among the plants that will maximize the firm's overall profit? How can the multi-plant firm adjust to the varying cost structures of its individual production facilities?

The issues raised by transfer pricing, by multi-product pricing, by multi-part pricing, and by multi-plant firms are unquestionably complex. It is nevertheless true that the basic principles of marginal analysis can help untangle the analysis and thereby provide straightforward rules that serve as useful guides to profit-maximizing pricing decisions in these more complicated cases.

APPLICATION

There are three basic steps in the manufacture of carbonated soft drinks. In the first stage, the firm produces flavoring syrups according to closely guarded recipes. These syrups are then sold under exclusive license to independent bottling companies who combine them with carbonated water to produce the final product. After filling various containers, the bottlers then distribute the packaged soft drinks to retail outlets which sell the product to consumers.

Although each stage of the soft drink production process involves a variety of inputs, consider the aluminum cans that will be filled by the independent bottling companies. Suppose that one of these bottlers has decided to obtain its requirements of this input by acquiring a can manufacturing facility. Assume that marginal production costs for the plant are constant and equal to five cents per can. Independent manufacturers, who supply other soft drink bottlers and many other firms that use aluminum cans to package their products, charge their customers prices as high as ten cents per can.

The internal pricing problem confronting the vertically integrated bottler is this: At what price should the firm's can manufacturing facility transfer aluminum cans to the downstream bottling division? Is the optimal (profit-maximizing) transfer price equal to the can division's marginal production cost of five cents per can, or should the can division instead charge the bottling unit the market-determined price of ten cents per can?

The answer to this question could not be more important. The transfer pricing option chosen by the firm will partly determine the bottling division's costs and, hence, help establish the quantity of soft drinks that will be produced and distributed to retailers. The quantity of soft drinks the bottling division produces will, in turn, determine the number of aluminum cans it will order from the firm's manufacturing facility. The bottling division's requirements will likewise feed back to influence the number of cans the upstream division will sell in the external market to other customers. In short, the price at which cans are transferred internally affects the quantities produced at both stages of production, the allocation of profits between the two divisions, and the firm's overall profitability.

The following section derives rules for determining the optimal transfer price. The discussion begins with a simple transfer pricing problem in which there are no outside customers for the good or service. We then proceed to more complicated cases like the one confronting the bottler who faces both internal and external markets for an intermediate input.

TRANSFER PRICING

Along with the tremendous expansion in the scale and scope of the modern business corporation has come a trend toward decentralized managerial decision making.[1] As firms diversified into new products and new markets, it became increasingly difficult for a small group of top managers to both cope with the myriad details of the organization's daily operations and devote their attention to the planning, appraisal, and coordination functions essential to the enterprise's long-term survival.

The structural innovation that helped reduce the information overload on top managers and paved the way for the development of the modern business organization is known as the **multidivisional** or *M-form* **firm**. Each of the semi-autonomous operating divisions of the multidivisional firm, which may be set up along product, brand, or geographic lines, is regarded as a "profit center." Each of these divisions is responsible for all of the business functions related to its own product or territory—input purchasing, manufacturing, accounting, marketing, and so on. And each division is judged on the basis of the profitability of its own operations.

---

1 See Chapter 1 for a summary of the historical evolution of the modern business firm.

Although the multidivisional firm offers distinct advantages over other types of business organizations in terms of decentralized decision-making authority and performance evaluation, these benefits by no means emerge automatically. If the firm evaluates its operating units on the basis of their profitability, divisional managers will rationally strive to maximize their own divisions' profits. The pursuit of such an objective is consistent with the goal of maximizing the overall profitability of the firm when the firm's various units have no dealings with one another. But conflicts that impair the company's global profitability may arise in more typical cases where one division supplies goods or services to another.

The crux of the matter is this: The price at which the firm transfers a good or service between divisions affects the revenues of the selling division and the costs of the buying division. The price-output decisions and profitability of each division consequently depend on the transfer prices at which goods and services are "sold" within the firm. What is more important, however, is that the transfer price that is optimal (profit-maximizing) from the point of view of one division's manager may not be optimal from the standpoint of the company's overall profitability.

This basic conflict between the objectives of the firm as a whole and the objectives of its semi-autonomous divisions emerges because a transfer price serves two functions in the multidivisional firm. One function of a transfer price is to act as a measure of the *marginal value* of the resources used in a given division. In this role, the transfer price guides divisional resource-allocation decisions according to the familiar marginal-cost-equals-marginal-revenue rule. And, thereby, management can determine both the optimal level of output and the optimal input combination for producing that output.

The other function of a transfer price is to serve as a measure of the *total value* of the resources used in the division. That is, because the transfer price affects divisional revenues or costs, it plays a role in evaluating the overall performance (profitability) of the division. As the following discussion shows, these two functions may clash. The transfer price that is appropriate for making optimal internal resource-allocation decisions may not be appropriate for evaluating a division's contribution to the firm's global profitability.

In what follows, we derive basic rules for determining optimal transfer prices by adopting a number of simplifying assumptions.[2] First, we assume that a multidivisional firm produces a single product and that the production process takes place in two stages. The firm manufactures its product in the first, or upstream, stage. This product is then transferred from the manufacturing division to the marketing, or downstream, division which sells it to final consumers.

Second, we assume that the divisions of the firm are independent in two important respects. In the case where an outside market for the manufacturing

---

2 The discussion relies on the analysis of transfer pricing presented in Jack Hirshleifer, "On the Economics of Transfer Pricing," *Journal of Business* 39 (July 1956), pp. 172-84.

division's product exists, the external demand function facing the manufacturing division is assumed to be independent of the demand function facing the firm's marketing division. In other words, this assumption of **demand independence** means that the manufacturing division's sales to outside customers have no impact on the demand for the final product sold by the marketing division. The marketing division's sales to its customers likewise do not affect the external demand for the manufacturing division's product. (Interrelated demands are considered in the section on multi-product pricing later in the chapter.)

Technological independence is also assumed. This means that the operating costs of one division are not affected by the level of operations carried out in the other. For example, suppose that the manufacturing division expands production by hiring more workers. In this case, the divisions are technologically independent if the marketing division's unit price of labor is not affected by the manufacturing division's hiring decisions.

The third simplifying assumption is that the multidivisional firm employs a **fixed-proportions technology**.[3] This assumption means that one—and only one—combination of inputs can produce a specified output. In particular, it is assumed that in order for the company's marketing division to sell one unit of the final product, exactly one unit of output from the manufacturing division is required.

With these simplifying assumptions in mind, we analyze three cases. The optimal transfer price is determined when (1) no external market for the manufacturing division's product exists, (2) there is a price-taker external market (the price charged to outside customers is equal to marginal cost), and (3) there is a price-searcher external market (the price charged to outside customers includes a markup over marginal cost).

No External Market

The analysis of transfer pricing begins with the case in which the firm's manufacturing division sells all of its output to the downstream marketing division. No external market for the intermediate product exists. This assumption means that if the manufacturing division's production rate exceeds the marketing division's requirements, the excess output must be discarded.[4] Similarly, if the marketing division's requirements exceed the production capacity of the manufacturing division, additional units of the intermediate product cannot be obtained from outside suppliers. In short, with no external market, if the firm is to maximize profit, then the quantity of the intermediate product produced by the manufacturing division must be exactly equal to the quantity demanded by the marketing division.

---

3 See Chapter 3 for a more complete discussion of this assumption.

4 The analysis thus assumes that inventories cannot be carried from period to period. All units produced by the manufacturing division during a given period must be sold by the marketing division during that period.

Figure 9.1 shows the revenue and cost functions necessary for determining the optimal transfer price in this case. D_F is the demand curve for the final product sold by the firm's marketing division and MR_F is the marginal revenue associated with this final product demand. The firm's overall marginal production cost, MC, is equal to the manufacturing division's cost of producing an additional unit of the intermediate product, MC_M, plus the marketing division's cost of selling an extra unit of the final product, MC_F. Hence, the quantity of the final product that maximizes total profit is Q_F, determined by equating MR_F with $MC = MC_M + MC_F$. P_F is the optimal final product price that corresponds to this profit-maximizing quantity.

The manufacturing division likewise determines its optimal quantity of output by equating marginal revenue with marginal cost. In order to assure that the manufacturing division produces exactly Q_M $(= Q_F)$ units, a transfer price equal to the manufacturing division's marginal cost at the profit-maximizing output level is required. Setting the transfer price equal to MC_M at Q_F yields an optimal transfer price of P_T dollars per unit. Once a transfer price of P_T is established, the manufacturing division in essence faces a horizontal demand curve for its output. Each additional unit of the intermediate product produced and transferred to the marketing division increases the manufacturing division's revenue by P_T dollars. Equating the marginal revenue of the manufacturing division, $MR_M = P_T$, with its own marginal cost, MC_M, yields the desired result: the quantity of output produced by the manufacturing division is exactly equal to the quantity that maximizes the firm's profits on final product sales.

We can verify the conclusion that a transfer price of P_T dollars per unit is consistent with the objective of maximizing the firm's global profits as follows. Once the internal transfer price is established, the marginal cost of the marketing division is equal to MC_F'. MC_F' is determined by adding the price paid to the manufacturing division for a unit of the intermediate product, P_T, to the cost of selling an extra unit of output to final consumers, MC_F. Equating $MC_F' = MC_F + P_T$ with the marginal revenue associated with final

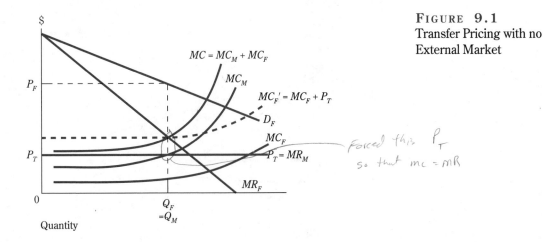

FIGURE 9.1
Transfer Pricing with no External Market

product demand, MR_F, yields a profit-maximizing output rate of Q_F units and a corresponding profit-maximizing price of P_F dollars per unit.

To summarize, when there is no external market for an intermediate product, the optimal transfer price is equal to the marginal cost of producing the intermediate product at the quantity of output that maximizes the profits associated with final product sales.

Price-Taker External Market

When an external market for the intermediate product exists, it is no longer necessary for the manufacturing division's output rate to be identically equal to the number of units required by the company's marketing division. If, on the one hand, the manufacturing department has the capacity to produce more units of the intermediate product than the marketing division requires, the firm can sell the surplus output externally to outside customers. On the other hand, if the manufacturing department produces fewer units of the intermediate product than the marketing division requires, the firm can purchase additional units of the product externally from independent suppliers.

This section considers the case where the external market for the intermediate product is a price-taker market. As established in Chapter 8, this assumption means that the market-determined price of the manufacturing division's product is equal to marginal production cost.

Figure 9.2a illustrates the transfer-pricing problem when the manufacturing division has excess production capacity and consequently sells part of its output to the marketing division with the remainder being sold in the external market. As before, D_F represents the demand for the final product distributed by the company's marketing division and MR_F is the marginal revenue associated with these final product sales. With a price-taker external market for the intermediate product, the manufacturing division faces a horizontal (perfectly elastic) demand curve for its output. It can sell as many units of the intermediate product to outside customers as it wants to at the market-determined price.

FIGURE 9.2a
Transfer Pricing with a
Price-Taker External Market:
Outside Sales

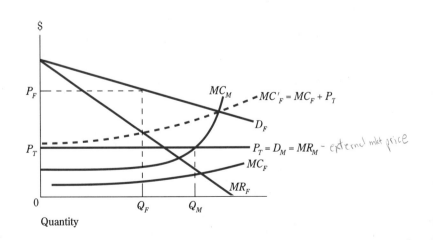

Suppose that the market-determined price of the intermediate product is P_T dollars per unit. The manufacturing division's external demand curve, D_M, is therefore illustrated by the horizontal line drawn at P_T. Because each unit of the intermediate product sold externally increases the manufacturing division's total revenue by P_T dollars, the external demand curve also represents divisional marginal revenue, MR_M.

Equating divisional marginal revenue, MR_M, with divisional marginal cost, MC_M, yields an optimal output of Q_M units of the intermediate product. The profit-maximizing price-output decisions of the manufacturing division determine the optimal transfer price. Because the manufacturing division can sell as many units of the intermediate product as it wishes externally for P_T dollars per unit, it would have no incentive to sell its output internally at any price less than P_T. Moreover, because the marketing division can obtain its own intermediate product requirements from outside suppliers at this same price, it would have no incentive to pay the manufacturing division any price higher than P_T dollars per unit.

With a price-taker external market for the intermediate product, the optimal transfer price for intracompany sales is therefore equal to the market-determined price of P_T dollars per unit. Once the firm has established this internal transfer price, the marketing division goes about selecting its own optimal price-output combination by setting divisional marginal revenue equal to divisional marginal cost. As before, we determine the marketing division's marginal cost, MC_F', by adding the price paid to the manufacturing division for a unit of the intermediate product, P_T, to the cost incurred in selling an extra unit of output to final consumers, MC_F. Equating $MC_F' = MC_F + P_T$ with the marginal revenue associated with final product sales, MR_F, yields a profit-maximizing output rate of Q_F units and a corresponding profit-maximizing price of P_F dollars per unit. In Figure 9.2a, Q_F is less than the profit-maximizing output rate of the manufacturing division, Q_M. The excess units of the intermediate product produced by the manufacturing division, $Q_M - Q_F$, are sold to outside customers at a price of P_T dollars per unit.

The same analysis would apply if the production capacity of the manufacturing division fell short of the marketing division's requirements. This case is depicted in Figure 9.2b. The manufacturing division again determines its optimal output rate, Q_M, by equating the market-determined price of the intermediate product with divisional marginal cost. The marketing division's marginal cost, MC_F', is set equal to the marginal revenue from final sales, MR_F, yielding the profit-maximizing output rate of Q_F units and price of P_F. Because $Q_F > Q_M$, the entire manufacturing division's output is transferred to the marketing division at an internal price equal to the market-determined price, P_T. The marketing division then purchases the remainder of its requirements of the intermediate product, $Q_F - Q_M$, from outside suppliers.

Hence, with a price-taker external market for the intermediate product, the optimal transfer price is equal to the market price of the intermediate

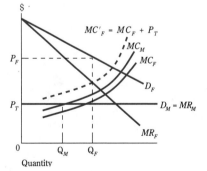

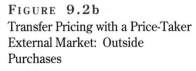

FIGURE 9.2b
Transfer Pricing with a Price-Taker External Market: Outside Purchases

product.[5] It is worth noting, however, that with a price-taker external market the market price of the intermediate product is equal to the marginal cost of producing it. Therefore, the conclusion of the previous section that marginal-cost pricing should guide intracompany transfers still holds.

Price-Searcher External Market

In the case of a price-taker external market for the intermediate product just analyzed, internal exchange confers no advantages on either division of the firm. The selling division's prices for intracompany transfers and outside customers are the same, and the buying division makes intracompany purchases at the same price it pays to outside suppliers. The two divisions are effectively independent firms that happen to operate under common ownership.

The transfer pricing problem becomes substantially more complicated with a price-searcher external market for the intermediate product. In this case, the manufacturing division faces a downward-sloping external demand curve for its output. The intermediate product is therefore sold to outside customers at a price that includes a markup over marginal production cost. Is this same market-determined price of the intermediate product the optimal (profit-maximizing) transfer price for intracompany sales?

Although the analysis is somewhat complicated, the answer is flatly no. We reach this conclusion with the aid of Figure 9.3, which presents the

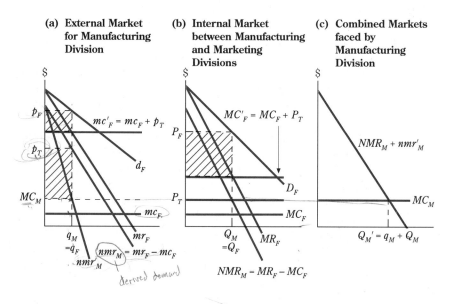

FIGURE 9.3
Transfer Pricing with a Price-Searcher External Market

5 For evidence that firms rely on market prices as guides to their internal resource allocation decisions, see Andrew Whinston, "Price Guides in Decentralized Organizations," in W. W. Cooper, H. J. Leavitt, and M. W. Shelly, eds., *New Perspectives in Organization Research* (New York: Wiley, 1964), pp. 405-48.

transfer-pricing problem as an example of third-degree price discrimination.[6] The model of third-degree price discrimination is useful in this context because the company's manufacturing division effectively sells its output in two separate markets. The external market for the intermediate product is illustrated in panel *a* and the internal market consisting of the firm's own marketing division is illustrated in panel *b*.

We must make some additional assumptions to simplify the analysis and to facilitate comparisons between the price-output decisions in the two markets for the intermediate product. In particular, we assume that both internal and external purchasers of the manufacturing division's output face identical final product demands and that both incur identical marginal costs of marketing the intermediate product to final consumers. Moreover, marginal marketing costs and the manufacturing division's marginal production costs are assumed to be constant throughout the relevant ranges of output.

With these assumptions in mind, the first step is to derive the demand curves for the intermediate product in the respective submarkets. In panel *a*, d_F is the demand curve for the final product distributed by the independent producers and mr_F is the marginal revenue associated with this final product demand. The demand curve for the intermediate product is *derived* from the marginal revenue associated with final product demand. We begin this derivation by noting that the maximum price a producer in the external market would be willing to pay for an extra unit of the intermediate product is equal to the additional revenue earned by selling that unit to final consumers, mr_F, net of the additional cost of marketing that unit, mc_F.

In other words, the demand for the intermediate input (or what Hirshleifer calls the "net marginal revenue" or nmr_M schedule)[7] in the external market is derived by subtracting the marginal cost of marketing the final product from the final product's marginal revenue. Hence, $nmr_M = mr_F - mc_F$ is the effective demand curve confronted by the manufacturing division in the external market for the intermediate product. The schedule labeled nmr'_M is the marginal revenue associated with this effective input demand schedule.

The net marginal revenue associated with intracompany sales of the intermediate product is derived in a similar fashion in panel *b* of Figure 9.3. D_F is the demand for the marketing division's final product and MR_F is the marginal revenue associated with this final product demand. The marginal cost of selling the intermediate product to final consumers is again subtracted from the marginal revenue associated with final product sales to obtain the net marginal revenue for the marketing division. Hence, $NMR_M = MR_F - MC_F$ is the marketing division's effective demand curve for the intermediate product produced by the manufacturing division.

The NMR_M schedule shows the maximum price the marketing division is willing to pay for various quantities of the intermediate product. We derive this by netting out the marginal cost of marketing a unit of the final product,

---

6   Price discrimination is introduced and discussed in Chapter 6.
7   Hirshleifer, "On the Economics of Transfer Pricing."

MC_F, from the additional revenue earned on the last unit sold, MR_F. NMR_M is the relevant marginal revenue schedule for intracompany sales of the intermediate product. The objective of maximizing the firm's overall profitability dictates that the external and internal demands for the intermediate product be treated differently.

Given the submarket demands for the intermediate product derived in panels a and b, the manufacturing division's profit-maximizing level of output is determined in panel c. Equating the manufacturing division's marginal production cost, MC_M, with the horizontal sum of the marginal revenues earned by selling in the internal and external markets, $NMR_M + nmr_M'$, yields an optimal output of Q_M' units of the intermediate product. The quantities of the intermediate product sold internally and externally are then determined according to the **equi-marginal principle**. Following this rule requires setting marginal cost at the manufacturing division's overall profit-maximizing level of production equal to marginal revenue in each separate submarket.

In panel a, equating marginal manufacturing cost with marginal revenue yields optimal external sales of q_M units of the intermediate product. (Recall that marginal revenue in the external market, nmr_M', is determined from the derived external demand curve for the intermediate product, nmr_M.) The profit-maximizing price in this submarket is p_T dollars per unit, which is the point on the external demand curve corresponding to q_M. This price-output combination maximizes the manufacturing division's profits on external sales of the intermediate product. These profits, $(p_T - MC_M) \times q_M$, are indicated by the lower shaded rectangle in panel a.

The external producers, in turn, purchase q_M units of the intermediate product at a price of p_T dollars per unit. Their marginal cost of selling the final product to ultimate consumers is accordingly equal to the sum of the price paid per unit of the intermediate product, p_T, plus the marginal marketing cost, mc_F. Equating $mc_F' = mc_F + p_T$ with the marginal revenue associated with final product sales, mr_F, yields an optimal final product output of q_F ($= q_M$) units and an optimal final product price of p_F dollars per unit. The external producers consequently earn an economic profit on final product sales represented by the upper shaded area in panel a.

Panel b shows the price-output decisions in the internal market. Equating marginal manufacturing cost with net marginal revenue on intracompany sales of the intermediate product, NMR_M, yields an optimal quantity of Q_M units. The optimal transfer price is P_T dollars per unit which is equal to the manufacturing division's marginal cost of producing the intermediate product. Once the firm has established this internal transfer price, the marketing division goes about selecting its own optimal price-output combination by setting divisional marginal revenue equal to divisional marginal cost.

As before, we determine the marketing division's marginal cost, MC_F', by adding the price paid to the manufacturing division for a unit of the intermediate product, P_T, to the cost of selling an extra unit of output to final consumers, MC_F. Equating $MC_F' = MC_F + P_T$ with the marginal revenue associated with final product sales, MR_F, yields a profit-maximizing output rate of Q_F ($= Q_M$) units and a corresponding profit-maximizing price of P_F dollars per unit.

Because the manufacturing division transfers its output internally at a price equal to marginal production cost, it earns no economic profit on intracompany sales of the intermediate product. (Recall that with constant marginal cost, average cost is equal to marginal cost.) All of the firm's profits are consequently earned by the marketing division on sales to final consumers. These profits are indicated by the shaded area in panel b.

In total, then, the manufacturing division produces $Q_M{}' = q_M + Q_M$ units of the intermediate product. It sells q_M of these units to outside customers at a markup ($p_T > MC_M$) and it transfers Q_M of these units to the company's marketing division at a price equal to marginal cost ($P_T = MC_M$). The firm's overall profits from following this strategy are equal to the profits earned by the manufacturing division on external sales of the intermediate product— the lower shaded area in panel a—plus the profits earned by the marketing division on final product sales—the shaded area in panel b.

Setting the transfer price on intracompany sales of the intermediate product equal to the manufacturing division's marginal cost yields larger profits for the firm as a whole than would be earned if the internal and external markets were instead treated the same.[8] Such a policy would reduce overall profitability even though the manufacturing division can increase its own profits by treating intracompany sales on a par with external sales.

If the firm restricts the quantity of the intermediate product it transfers to the marketing division to q_M ($< Q_M$) units and thereby raises price to p_T ($> P_T$) dollars per unit, the apparent profitability of the manufacturing division will double under the linear demand and constant marginal cost conditions assumed in Figure 9.3 (see p. 310). As a result of this strategy, however, the marketing division's profits would be reduced from the total indicated by the shaded area in panel b to an area equal in size to the upper shaded area in panel a. The reduction in the marketing division's profits would more than offset the increase in the manufacturing division's profits. Therefore, the firm's global profits would fall.

The logic of this section can help solve the transfer-pricing problem in the chapter's opening application. Recall that a soft-drink bottler's aluminum can manufacturing subsidiary incurred constant marginal production costs of five cents per can while independent can manufacturers charged their customers a price of ten cents per can. The transfer-pricing rule derived above suggests that as a first approximation, the profit-maximizing strategy is for the bottler's can manufacturing division to set a price of five cents per can on intracompany sales and sell any cans produced over and above the bottling division's requirements at a price of ten cents per can in the external market.

The Opportunity Cost of Internal Transfers. One question that may come to mind at this point is whether the marginal-cost transfer-pricing

---

8 This result is proved algebraically in Chapter 12. It is shown there that avoiding the markup over marginal cost included in the market-determined price of an intermediate input is one of the basic economic motives for combining successive stages of production under common ownership.

rule adequately accounts for the opportunity cost of intracompany sales of the intermediate product. After all, when the can manufacturing division transfers one unit of output to the bottling division at a price of five cents, doesn't it forego the opportunity to sell that unit to an outside customer for ten cents? In other words, isn't five cents "lost" on each internal transaction?

The answer is no. The reason is that the revenue sacrificed when a sale is made internally rather than externally is *not* represented by the price difference between internal and external sales. The revenue sacrificed is instead the amount the external sale would have contributed to the can manufacturing division's total revenue. The opportunity cost of the internal sale is consequently measured by marginal revenue in the external market—not price. Because marginal revenue is equal to marginal cost at the profit-maximizing level of production, the marginal-cost transfer-pricing rule properly accounts for the revenue foregone in the external market.

Price "Squeezes" and Efficient Resource Allocation. The fact that the firm sells the intermediate product in the external market at a markup but makes intracompany transfers at a lower price has sometimes been interpreted as evidence of anticompetitive behavior on the part of the multidivisional firm. Indeed, the price differential between internal and external sales of an intermediate product is often characterized as a "price squeeze" designed to place external customers at a competitive disadvantage relative to the company's own buying division. While a thorough examination of this so-called price squeeze is beyond the scope of the present discussion, two points are worth making.

First, the price differential between internal and external sales is the result of rational, profit-maximizing behavior on the part of a seller facing two distinct, price-searcher submarkets for its output. Second, the lower price charged on intracompany sales serves to increase the total output of the final product beyond the quantity the firm would produce if all transactions in the intermediate product took place at its market-determined price. Because the output of the final product is greater with marginal-cost transfer pricing, its price is lower than otherwise. The benefits to consumers of this lower final product price must be balanced against any potential "injury" to outside purchasers of the intermediate product before any general conclusions are drawn.

Using Transfer Prices to Evaluate Divisional Performance. A clear-cut transfer price equal to the selling division's marginal cost emerges from the foregoing analysis. However, caution is warranted when using transfer prices to evaluate divisional contributions to overall company profitability. Suppose, for example, that the chief executive officer of the firm depicted in Figure 9.3 (see p. 310) must decide whether or not to abandon the manufacturing subsidiary.

It would be a mistake for the CEO to conclude that the manufacturing division makes no contribution to company profits over and above those profits earned on external sales of the intermediate product. This is because the profit contribution of the manufacturing division also includes the incremental profits of the marketing division attributable to its ability to purchase the intermediate product from the manufacturing division at a price equal to marginal cost rather than at the market-determined price it would otherwise pay outside suppliers.

The marketing division likewise contributes to the profits of the manufacturing division by selling additional units of output to final consumers that would not be sold if the two divisions operated independently of one another and transactions between them took place at the market-determined price of the intermediate product. Hence, a correct decision about whether or not to abandon a subsidiary requires a careful examination of the cost and revenue functions of the firm as a whole.

When we assume demand independence and technological independence, the optimal transfer pricing rule is a straightforward application of the marginal-revenue-equals-marginal-cost principle.[9] In particular, for the cases examined in this section, the general rule that maximizes the firm's overall profitability is to set the transfer price equal to the marginal cost of the selling division. The optimality of marginal-cost transfer pricing holds directly both when there is no external market for the intermediate product and when the external market is a price-searcher market. A price-taker external market for the intermediate product is just a special case of the general rule. As has been shown, the transfer price should equal the market price of the intermediate product in this case, but this market price also equals the marginal cost of the selling division when the external market is a price-taker market.[10]

The analysis in this section has important practical implications for the multidivisional firm. Chapter 14 will describe in detail the advantages of organizing the firm into semi-autonomous "profit centers." Among the most important of these advantages are the increased incentives provided to divisional managers to use the resources under their command efficiently and the streamlined information flows which facilitate divisional performance evaluation by the company's top managers. However, the potential gains associated with organizing the firm in this way may be lost because of an improper transfer-pricing policy.

In particular, following the customary rule of pricing intracompany sales at "market" will, except in one very special case, have serious adverse consequences for the firm's overall profitability. Of equal practical importance, the divisional "profit" calculated on the basis of the established transfer price—even if that price is properly set equal to the marginal cost of the selling division—should not be used to make non-marginal, incremental decisions like those involved in determining whether to expand or abandon a subsidiary.

---

9 The complications introduced by demand dependence and by technological dependence are discussed in Hirshleifer, "On the Economics of Transfer Pricing."

10 It is worth noting that the optimality of marginal-cost transfer pricing does not depend on the structure of the final product market. That is, transferring resources within the firm at a price equal to the selling division's marginal cost maximizes overall company profits whether the final product market is a price-taker market or a price-searcher market. See *Ibid.*

Transfer Pricing in College Athletic Budgets

Stories alleging that many big-time intercollegiate athletic programs operate in the red have surfaced recently and become part of the conventional wisdom.[a] Two *USA Today* writers, for example, published a report claiming that over half of the nation's top college athletic departments lose money. Among the biggest alleged losers are Auburn University and the University of Michigan. These two traditional sports powerhouses purportedly run huge deficits despite the fact that each reports athletic revenues in excess of $18 million annually. Similar assertions have appeared in *College Sports, Inc.*, a book written by an Indiana University English professor, and in newspaper sports columns across the country.

At the same time, however, economists have vocally criticized the National Collegiate Athletic Administration (NCAA) and its member schools for their monopolistic practices that limit payments to college athletes and thereby enhance the profitability of college athletic programs.[b] Indeed, Harvard economist Robert Barro has characterized the NCAA as the country's most efficient cartel.

That college sports is big business is beyond dispute. Notre Dame's college football television package alone is worth $36 million. The NCAA will receive $1 billion over seven years for broadcast rights to the men's national championship basketball tournament. Over 40 college athletic programs report cash inflows in excess of $10 million per year. The obvious question is, How do such money machines find a way to operate in the red?

The answer is found in the transfer-pricing policies adopted by college athletic departments. Most intercollegiate athletic departments operate as semi-autonomous "profit centers" and maintain their own sets of accounts separate from their schools' academic programs. The typical athletic department reports cash inflows from such diverse revenue sources as ticket sales, TV and radio broadcasts, and alumni contributions. Expenses consist principally of coaches' salaries,

travel, maintenance of athletic facilities, and scholarships that cover the tuition, fees, books, and room and board of student-athletes.

It is the last item that is chiefly responsible for the budget deficits that are so apparently widespread throughout college sports. Scholarship expenses are typically reported on the athletic department's books at the average cost per student-athlete (about $8,000 per year) rather than at the **marginal cost** to the college or university of providing educations to these student-athletes. Given that few schools operate anywhere near full capacity, the extra instructional expense incurred by academic departments in educating the average scholarship athlete is far less than the $8,000 "cost" carried on the athletic department's accounts. The school will hire few, if any, additional faculty to teach the 200 to 300 athletes typically on scholarship, and will build no new classroom space or laboratory facilities to accommodate them.

When the marginal-cost transfer-pricing rule is applied to scholarship outlays, athletic department deficits shrink dramatically. Once reported expenses are adjusted downward to reflect the fact that the additional cost of awarding one more scholarship is essentially nil, about a $5 million improvement in the bottom line materializes in the budget of the representative top college sports program. This adjustment is often large enough to turn an apparent deficit into a multi-million dollar surplus.

a The following discussion is based on Brian L. Goff and William F. Shughart II, "Close Look Shows College Sports No Drain on Schools' Resources," *Washington Times*, 9 August 1992, p. c3. Also see Melvin V. Borland, Brian L. Goff, and Robert W. Pulsinelli, "College Athletics: Financial Boon or Burden?," in Gerald W. Scully, ed., *Advances in the Economics of Sport*, vol. 1 (Greenwich, CT: JAI Press, 1992), pp. 215-35.

b William F. Shughart II, "Protect College Athletes, Not Athletics," *Wall Street Journal*, 26 December 1990, p. 6.

What motivates college athletic departments to carry scholarship expenses at average cost rather than at marginal cost and thereby put their budgets in the red? One answer is that athletic deficits yield substantial fund raising benefits. Imagine the task of pumping boosters for more money while simultaneously reporting a sizable budget surplus. The danger in this strategy, however, is that the adoption of an improper transfer pricing policy may lead uninformed outside observers to conclude erroneously that college athletic programs are money losers and should therefore be abandoned when, in fact, just the opposite is true.

In sum, selecting the prices at which the firm transfers raw materials and other inputs internally is every bit as important to the firm's profitability as selecting the prices at which final products will be sold to their ultimate consumers. The conclusion in this section is that the marginal cost of the selling division is the benchmark to use for pricing intracompany transfers.

MULTIPLE PRODUCT PRICING

Up to this point, production processes that yield a single product have been the focus of attention. The profit-maximizing rule for such a single-product firm is to select the quantity of output at which marginal revenue is equal to marginal cost. How is this rule affected when a firm produces more than one final product? Some production processes produce two or more goods simultaneously. These goods are called **joint products** or **joint complements**. When one good is produced, a complementary good is produced as a byproduct. For example, heating oil and gasoline are joint products, lumber and sawdust are joint products, and beef and hides are joint products.

Similarly, two or more goods which consumers view as substitutes for one another can often be produced using similar processes and resources. These goods are called **joint substitutes**. This case differs from the previous one because the firm must forego the production of one substitute good to produce the others. When the firm's resources are utilized to produce one good they cannot at the same time be utilized to produce the substitute good. Examples of substitutes in production are blue jean pants and blue jean jackets, Ford and Mercury automobiles, regular beer and light beer, cola and cherry cola, and cheese and sausage pizzas.

Joint Complements

The analysis of joint complements proceeds in two steps. First we assume that two joint products are produced in fixed proportions. Milling one board foot of lumber produces a certain amount of sawdust. Slaughtering one steer produces one hide. Next, we consider joint products that can be produced in variable proportions. There are two important questions to answer in each of these cases. First, how many units of each joint product should the firm produce? Second, how many units of each good should the firm *sell*?

317

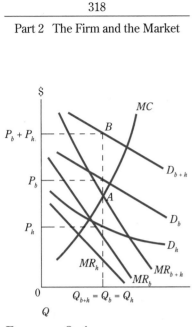

FIGURE 9.4
Joint Production of
Complements—Fixed Proportions
Technology (No Excess
Production of Hides)

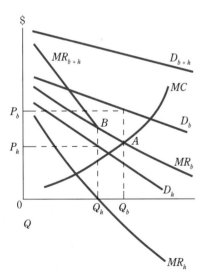

FIGURE 9.5
Joint Production of
Complements—Fixed Proportions
Technology (Excess Production of
Hides)

Joint Products with Fixed Proportions. Consider the situation depicted in Figure 9.4. Two complements, beef (b) and hides (h), are produced using a single production process. D_b and MR_b denote the demand and marginal revenue schedules associated with beef; D_h and MR_h denote the demand and marginal revenue schedules associated with hides. Each steer slaughtered yields a given quantity of beef and one hide. Of course, if the producer wants to market only one of these goods, then the option of discarding the other can be exercised as long as the cost of disposal is minimal. Fortunately for this firm, consumers value both beef and hides as revealed by their respective demand curves. How does the firm determine the overall demand for the steers that yield these joint products?

To the producer, the value of a steer is equal to the value of the beef plus the value of the hide. The value associated with any quantity of beef or hides is the vertical distance between the horizontal axis and the corresponding points on D_b or D_h. For example, at output level $Q_{b+h} = Q_b = Q_h$, the value of beef to consumers (the amount they are willing to pay) is P_b and the value of hides is P_h. The value of the joint product at Q_{b+h} is consequently equal to $P_b + P_h$, shown on the joint demand curve, D_{b+h}, as point B. The essential idea here is that the total value of a unit of the joint product is the *vertical sum* of the value of beef plus the value of hides. In other words, the composite price the producer could charge for each joint unit produced is the price of beef plus the price of hides. Hence, D_{b+h} is the demand for steers. It is derived by vertically summing the separate demand curves for beef and hides at each possible level of joint output.

We can determine the profit-maximizing quantity of steers by locating the level of output at which joint marginal revenue equals marginal cost. Joint marginal revenue, MR_{b+h}, in turn, is the schedule marginal to D_{b+h}; it is the vertical sum of MR_b and MR_h. Following this rule, the profit-maximizing quantity of steers occurs at point A in Figure 9.4. At point A, $MR_b + MR_h = MR_{b+h} = MC$. At this profit-maximizing output level, the firm raises and slaughters $Q_{b+h} = Q_b = Q_h$ steers and charges prices of P_b and P_h for beef and hides, respectively. Equal quantities of beef and hides are produced and sold in this hypothetical example. Is this always the case for joint complements in production?

The answer to this question is no. Although there are many reasons why joint complements may not be produced and sold in exactly the same proportions, Figure 9.5 illustrates one of the more important reasons. In Figure 9.5, the marginal revenue schedule for one of the goods becomes negative in the relevant range of production; that is, the demand for one of the goods becomes inelastic before the profit-maximizing quantity of the other is reached. This condition holds for hides at output levels greater than Q_h. At Q_h, $MR_h = 0$. In such a situation, if the firm expands sales beyond Q_h, then $MR_h < 0$ and the total revenue associated with hides actually declines with additional units sold. The profit-maximizing firm will rationally cease marketing hides when the last unit sold adds nothing to total revenue.

Given the revenue and cost conditions depicted in Figure 9.5, the profit-maximizing firm raises and slaughters Q_b steers. (The profit-maximizing quantity of steers occurs at point A where joint marginal revenue is equal to marginal cost, $MR_{b+h} = MC$.)[11] Q_b units of beef are sold at a price of P_b dollars per unit. Q_h ($< Q_b$) hides are sold at a price of P_h per unit. The excess production of hides, $Q_b - Q_h$, is discarded. Even if the marginal cost of production is zero, expanding the sale of hides beyond Q_h would reduce the firm's total profits. Jointness in production does not translate into jointness in sales beyond Q_h.

Joint Products with Variable Proportions. The analysis is slightly more complicated when joint complements can be produced in variable proportions rather than fixed proportions. With variable proportions technology, a firm produces two or more goods as byproducts of the same production process, but their relative quantities can be varied. A barrel of crude oil, for example, yields different quantities of gasoline and heating oil depending on processing temperature and other variables under the refinery's control.

Figure 9.6 shows a hypothetical variable proportions production function for gasoline and heating oil. TC_1 and TC_2 are **isocost curves**. They show all of the combinations of gasoline and heating oil that can be produced for a given total expenditure. The various combinations of gasoline and heating oil on TC_1 cost TC_1 dollars to produce. Combinations of the joint products lying on TC_2 cost TC_2 ($> TC_1$) dollars to produce.

The slope of an isocost curve at a particular point is the ratio of the joint products' marginal production costs at that point. For example, if it costs the firm \$.25 to produce an additional gallon of gasoline ($MC_G = \$.25$) and it costs \$1 to produce an additional gallon of heating oil ($MC_O = \$1$), then the slope of the isocost curve ($-MC_O/MC_G = -\$1/\$.25 = -4$) indicates the number of gallons of gasoline the firm must forego producing in order to expand production of heating oil by one gallon while holding total cost constant. Because of jointness in production, the firm can expand its output of one product only by reducing its production of the other. Given the marginal production costs assumed, the firm must reduce gasoline production by four gallons in order to produce one more gallon of heating oil so as to hold total production costs constant.

TR_1 and TR_2 are **isorevenue lines**. They show all of the joint product combinations that generate the same amount of total sales revenue. The gasoline and heating oil combinations lying on TR_1 generate TR_1 dollars in total revenue for the firm and the joint product combinations lying on TR_2 generate TR_2 ($> TR_1$) dollars in total revenue.

The slope of an isorevenue line is equal to the ratio of the joint products' marginal revenues.[12] The slope of the isorevenue line shows the rate at

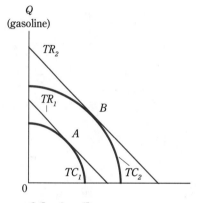

Q
(gasoline)

FIGURE 9.6
Joint Production of
Complements—Variable
Proportions Technology

---

11 In Figure 9.5, the joint marginal revenue schedule, MR_{b+h}, is identical to MR_b beyond Q_h (point B). Instead of adding the negative marginal revenue associated with hides beyond Q_h, the firm stops selling hides and disposes of the surplus. The joint marginal revenue schedule is equal to the vertical sum of the marginal revenues of the two goods only as long as the individual marginal revenues are positive.

12 For purposes of simplicity, the isorevenue schedules are drawn as straight lines. The marginal revenues associated with the two products are assumed to be constant, implying that

which the firm can vary its sales of gasoline and heating oil while holding total revenue constant. For example, if $.50 in additional revenue is earned by selling one more gallon of gasoline ($MR_G = \$.50$) and $1.50 in additional revenue is earned by selling one more gallon of heating oil ($MR_O = \$1.50$), then the slope of the isorevenue line ($-MR_O/MR_G = -\$1.50/\$.50 = -3$) indicates that the firm must sell one gallon of heating oil for every three gallons of gasoline not sold in order to hold total revenue constant.

The firm's decision problem is to select the combination of gasoline and heating oil that yields the highest profit. Optimal (profit-maximizing) joint product combinations occur at the point of tangency between isocost and isorevenue schedules. For example, if the firm budgets an expenditure of TC_1 dollars, point A represents the profit-maximizing combination of gasoline and heating oil. This combination yields $TR_1 - TC_1$ dollars in profit.

We reach the conclusion that point A corresponds to a profit maximum by noting that every other joint product combination that yields TR_1 dollars in total revenue costs more than TC_1 dollars to produce. Likewise, every other combination of gasoline and heating oil that can be produced for an expenditure of TC_1 generates less than TR_1 dollars in total revenue. The same is true at Point B. If the firm spends TC_2 dollars to produce gasoline and heating oil, then no other combination of the joint products is as profitable as the combination at point B.

For joint products that can be produced in variable proportions, profit-maximizing behavior requires the firm to produce the particular combination of the joint products at which the ratio of their marginal revenues is equal to the ratio of their marginal costs. For the example at hand, ignoring algebraic signs, the profit-maximizing rule is to select the combination of gasoline and heating oil at which $MR_O/MR_G = MC_O/MC_G$. Alternatively, profit maximization requires that the marginal revenue per dollar spent on the last unit produced must be equal across the joint products; that is, $MR_O/MC_O = MR_G/MC_G$. If an inequality between these ratios exists, then the firm has an opportunity to increase profit. To do so requires the firm to reduce production of the product yielding relatively low marginal revenue per dollar of marginal cost and to increase production of the good yielding relatively high marginal revenue per dollar of marginal cost. Reallocating production in this way generates an increase in the firm's total profit.

One note of caution is warranted at this point. While the equi-marginal principle can help determine the profit-maximizing combination of joint complements in production, determining the profitability of individual joint products is problematic. This is because there is no theoretically correct way of allocating common costs of production. We have no way of knowing, for example, what share of the rancher's feed costs should be allocated to beef as opposed to hides, or what share of the refinery's central office expenses

---

gasoline and heating oil are sold in price-taker markets. If the joint products are instead sold in price-searcher markets, the isorevenue schedules would be nonlinear. The rule for determining the profit-maximizing quantities of the two goods is not affected by the type of market assumed, however.

should be allocated to gasoline as opposed to heating oil. Because common costs cannot be allocated in a sensible manner, the average total production costs of individual joint products are completely arbitrary and, hence, so are their individual contributions to total profits.

Many firms of course attempt to quantify their "fully allocated costs," but, unfortunately, these figures are by and large meaningless. Fortunately, however, managers can, using marginal revenue and marginal cost, determine the profit-maximizing combination of two or more joint products even if they cannot determine exactly how much of this total profit each has contributed.

Joint Substitutes

The most common type of multi-product firm produces goods that consumers view as substitutes.[13] General Motors produces Oldsmobiles and Buicks. Nike produces Air Jordans® and The Force 180's® basketball shoes. Nintendo® and Super Nintendo® video games are made by the same company. The differences between jointly produced substitutes often appear to be more cosmetic than functional. Different models of dish washing machines, for example, supply essentially the same services to households, but the extras, such as additional cycles and water temperatures, can lead to significant differences in tastes and preferences among consumers and, hence, create differences in final prices.

The same is true for many other products. In recent years, some products are differentiated chiefly by the signature of a sports celebrity. Michael Jordan, Charles Barkley, and David Robinson all endorse different types of Nike basketball shoes. Different versions of the same good compete with one another for the consumer's dollar. Likewise, the different models compete for the limited resources of the firm. How should the firm allocate resources among each of two or more substitute goods in order to maximize profit?

Consider the problem of determining the optimal allocation of resources across a two-good production process. The firm can use its resources to manufacture either Nintendo (N) or Super Nintendo (S) video games. For simplicity, we assume that the marginal production costs of the goods are identical. In other words, the costs incurred in producing either one more Nintendo or one more Super Nintendo game are the same. Assume further that the cost of switching the production process from one good to the other is zero or negligible. A final simplifying assumption is that the demands for these substitute goods are independent of one another—the demand for Nintendo games is unaffected by the price of Super Nintendo games, and vice-versa.

Figure 9.7 illustrates the relevant revenue and cost schedules. D_N and D_S represent the demand for Nintendo and Super Nintendo, respectively. MR_N

---

13 For a detailed examination, see Eli Clemens, "Price Discrimination and the Multiple Product Firm," *Review of Economic Studies* 19 (1950-51), pp. 1-11.

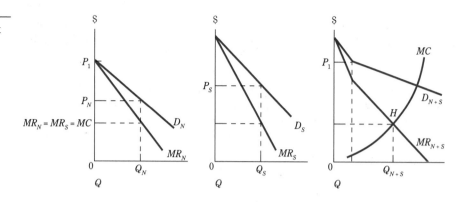

FIGURE 9.7
Joint Production of Substitutes

and MR_S are the corresponding marginal revenue schedules and MC is the joint marginal cost of producing video games.[14]

In contrast to the analysis of joint complements, the joint demand for substitutes is the *horizontal summation* of the demands for each of the individual goods. The joint demand for Nintendo and Super Nintendo is represented in the far right panel of Figure 9.7 by the schedule labeled D_{N+S}. The production of a Nintendo video game prevents a Super Nintendo game from being produced with the same resources. Consequently, for each Nintendo game manufactured and sold, the producer foregoes the opportunity to manufacture and sell a Super Nintendo game.

At any given price, the number of video games the firm can expect to sell is equal to the number of Nintendo games demanded at that price (determined along D_N) plus the number of Super Nintendo games consumers are willing and able to buy at that price (determined along D_S). Hence, at each price the quantity demanded of Nintendo is added to the quantity demanded of Super Nintendo to find the total demand, D_{N+S}. For prices above P_1, the quantity demanded of Nintendo is zero, so the total demand for video games is identical to the demand for Super Nintendo. The joint marginal revenue curve (MR_{N+S}) is derived from D_{N+S} and corresponds to the horizontal sum of MR_N and MR_S.

The opportunity cost of producing another unit of either type of video game is the revenue sacrificed by not producing and selling the other. The firm must therefore equate the marginal revenue of Nintendo and the marginal revenue of Super Nintendo in order to maximize its profits. If, for instance, $MR_N > MR_S$, then the firm can increase its total revenue by expanding the production of Nintendo by one unit and contracting the production of Super Nintendo by one unit. Because the firm manufactures no additional video games when it reallocates production in this way, the firm's total cost is unaffected and profit therefore increases by $MR_N - MR_S$. Producing more Nintendo

14 If the marginal costs of producing the two goods differ, then the joint marginal cost (MC) schedule would be derived by summing the marginal cost curves for N and S horizontally. The analysis would not change significantly.

games reduces MR_N because price must decrease to sell more of them. At the same time, producing fewer Super Nintendo games increases MR_S. The marginal revenue differential accordingly shrinks, and such a reallocation will continue to be profitable until MR_N is equal to MR_S.

The equi-marginal principle teaches that the firm's profits will be at a maximum when production is distributed between substitute goods in such a way that joint marginal revenue is equal to the joint marginal cost of production. And, furthermore, the marginal cost of producing the optimal total quantity is set equal to the marginal revenue of each good; that is, $MR_{N+S} = MR_N = MR_S = MC$. This profit maximum occurs at point H in Figure 9.7. Setting joint marginal revenue equal to marginal cost yields an optimal total quantity of Q_{N+S} video games. To determine the allocation of resources among Nintendo and Super Nintendo games, the marginal revenue in each market is set equal to the common value of joint marginal revenue and marginal cost at the profit maximum. Thus, the firm produces Q_N Nintendo games and Q_S Super Nintendo games. (Note that by definition $Q_N + Q_S = Q_{N+S}$.) To sell these profit-maximizing quantities, the firm will charge prices of P_N and P_S, respectively.

In sum, a profit-maximizing firm that produces substitute goods will allocate its production capacity such that joint marginal revenue is equal to the marginal revenues associated with the individual goods and to the overall marginal cost of production. The analysis here has obvious similarities to the analysis of transfer pricing with an external price-searcher market and the analysis of third-degree price discrimination. These similarities illustrate the power of the equi-marginal principle.

APPLICATION: MICKEY MOUSE MONOPOLIES

When the authors of *Modern Managerial Economics* were teenagers, Disney World had not yet been built, nor had the Disney organization opened the doors of its theme parks in Europe or Japan. But our childhoods were not completely bereft of culture, for the Magic Kingdom did exist at its original location in Southern California. In those early days 25 years ago, Disneyland's pricing policy consisted of an entry fee to the park plus per-ride charges. For a fee of roughly $12, customers acquired an admission pass plus a booklet containing a limited assortment of tickets for use on the park's numerous rides. Once inside the park, customers could purchase additional tickets on an individual basis if they wanted to ride any of the attractions more often than permitted by the number of tickets included in the admission booklet. The individual ticket prices ranged from about $.25 for the smaller rides up to around $1 for the larger, more popular rides.

If one visits Disneyland today, however, the ticket booklet has disappeared—the per-ride charges are zero. The admission price of about $30 entitles the customer to an unlimited number of rides, provided of course that he or she is willing to wait in the very long lines that accumulate during peak periods at the most popular attractions.

What explains this change in Disneyland's pricing policy? How should Disneyland's management decide what combination of entry fee and per-ride ticket prices to charge? The following section discusses the economics of these various pricing strategies.

MULTI-PART PRICING

The pricing strategy originally adopted by Disneyland—the combination of an entry fee plus per-ride charges—is known in the economics literature as a **two-part tariff**.[15] The customer must pay a lump-sum charge for the right to purchase a good or service. Membership dues for private clubs (e.g., country clubs and dinner clubs) and for social organizations (e.g., Rotary and Lions), installation fees for cable television and for telephone service, student activity fees at universities, and cover charges at night clubs and bars are examples of the lump-sum fee required before the consumer is allowed to buy the product or service sold by the supplier.

In addition, the customer pays for each unit of the product or service consumed. Country club members pay for meals, club functions, golf carts, tennis courts, and locker room services. Rotarians and Lions pay monthly activity fees. Users pay monthly charges for cable television and for telephone services. Tuition is assessed on the number of credit hours taken by a student. Once admitted into a bar, the consumer is charged for drinks. Why is multi-part pricing practiced? Is it discriminatory?

A Two-Part Tariff for a Single Customer

Consider a single consumer with the demand curve for amusement park rides depicted in Figure 9.8. Assume for simplicity that the amusement park has no fixed costs. With marginal cost constant at *MC*, the amusement park could charge a price of *B* dollars per ride, determined by setting marginal revenue equal to marginal cost. The consumer would purchase *q* rides and enjoy **consumer surplus** equal to the area of the triangle *BCE*.[16] The amusement park earns an economic profit of *ABEG* by adopting this profit-maximizing single-price policy.

Through the practice of two-part pricing, the amusement park can increase its profits considerably. This two-part pricing strategy involves charging a lump-sum entry fee equal to the area of the triangle *ACF* plus a

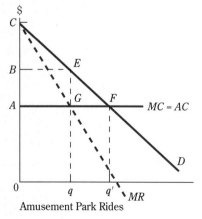

FIGURE 9.8
Two-Part Pricing—Single Consumer

15 See Walter Y. Oi, "A Disneyland Dilemma: Two-Part Tariffs for a Mickey Mouse Monopoly," *Quarterly Journal of Economics* 85 (February 1971), pp. 77-96.

16 As a reminder, the value of consumer surplus on each unit purchased is the difference between the maximum price the consumer would have been willing to pay and the actual price paid to purchase that unit.

price of A dollars for each ride. Assuming for simplicity that the income effect of such a lump-sum charge is zero, the consumer would purchase q' rides once inside the park and be left with no consumer surplus.[17] The amusement park's profit is equal to the area ACF. (Total revenue is the area ACF plus the area 0AFq', and the total cost of production is equal to 0AFq'.)

The amusement park has effectively transformed the consumer surplus and deadweight loss associated with the single-price policy into profit. This is the maximum profit the amusement park can extract from this customer. Raising the lump-sum charge above the value of the area ACF would force the consumer to stop purchasing amusement park rides and spend all of his or her income on other goods.

Two-Part Tariffs for Two Customers

The foregoing analysis suggests that when more than one customer is served, the first-best profit strategy for the amusement park is to assess a lump-sum tariff equal to the value of each customer's consumer surplus plus a ticket price equal to the marginal cost of operating rides. Such a pricing policy is similar to the second-degree price discrimination case discussed in Chapter 6. In effect, the amusement park price discriminates by assessing different lump-sum tariffs on customers who would otherwise enjoy varying amounts of consumer surplus. Because the legality of such a policy of price discrimination may be of concern to the business enterprise, what would happen if the amusement park charges a uniform tariff and price to every consumer?

Consider the situation illustrated in Figure 9.9, which shows two consumers with demand curves D and D', respectively. We again assume that the amusement park has no fixed costs and that the marginal cost of operating rides is constant and equal to MC. Assume further that no resale of goods takes place among consumers.[18] If the amusement park charges a single per-ride ticket price of A dollars (equal to marginal cost), then the first consumer would buy X tickets and enjoy consumer surplus of ABC, while the second consumer would buy Y tickets and enjoy consumer surplus of AKJ.

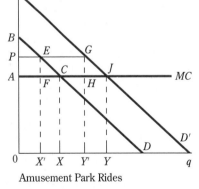

FIGURE 9.9
Two-Part Pricing—Two Consumers

---

17 The consumer purchases q' rides once inside the park because the admission fee becomes a sunk cost after it has been paid. The entry fee accordingly has no impact on the consumer's decision concerning how many tickets to buy. He or she purchases tickets until the marginal benefit of rides is equal to marginal cost (point F).

18 Transaction costs and shipping costs often preclude consumers from reselling goods. Should the tariff be excessive, however, a resale market may emerge. Consider, for example, the problem faced by Sam's Wholesale Club, a unit of the Wal-Mart Company. By paying a membership fee, consumers have the opportunity to purchase a variety of household items in bulk at a substantial discount. If the membership fee is set "too high," consumers have an incentive to resell items purchased at Sam's to nonmembers at a price higher than the Club price but lower than the price these nonmembers would pay for the same items elsewhere. Such a resale market reduces the number of memberships sold and the profitability of two-part pricing. The firm adopting a multi-part pricing strategy must therefore be aware of the potential for resale markets to develop and incorporate this possibility into its selling policies by, for example, limiting the number of items members are allowed to buy on any one visit.

Uniform Tariffs. If the amusement park's owner cannot identify consumers a priori on the basis of their demands for rides or if the owner wants to avoid an allegation of illegal price discrimination, then a uniform lump-sum tariff must be established for both consumers. The maximum lump-sum tariff the amusement park can assess while still keeping both consumers in the market is equal to the area ABC. Any lump-sum tariff larger than ABC will eliminate the first consumer from participating in the market. Given an admission fee of ABC and a per-ride ticket price of A, the amusement park earns a profit equal to *twice* the area ABC.

The amusement park's owner will also want to consider the profit implications of alternative two-part pricing strategies. One of these alternatives is to increase the lump-sum tariff beyond ABC. Such an increase in the admission fee would eliminate the first consumer because he or she is not willing to pay more than ABC to enter the park. In the limit, the amusement park could set the lump-sum tariff equal to the area AKJ and charge a ticket price equal to marginal cost. The park's profit under this strategy would be equal to the area AKJ with only one consumer being served.

An increase in the admission fee is profitable depending on whether the area AKJ is greater or less than twice the area ABC. If $AKJ > 2ABC$, then the amusement park can increase profit by imposing a lump-sum tariff of AKJ and eliminating the smaller demander. If $AKJ < 2ABC$, then the amusement park will charge the lower admission fee of ABC and serve both customers.

Differential Tariffs. Price-discriminating admission fees offer yet another alternative pricing policy. If the amusement park's owner can identify and separate customers into groups based on their demand for rides, then differential admission fees can be charged. For example, if D' represents the demand schedule of "thirtysomething" adults and D is the demand schedule of senior citizens, a policy of offering discounted admission to seniors can increase the park's profits over and above the profits earned by either of the previous pricing strategies. In this case, the park sets its "regular" admission fee equal to AKJ and offers a discounted fee equal to ABC to senior citizens. If marginal-cost ticket prices are then charged to all customers, the park's total profit is $ABC + AKJ$.

The Optimal Two-Part Tariff. Finally, the amusement park's owner may be able to increase profit by increasing the price of rides. Suppose the amusement park raises ticket prices to P dollars. Under this policy, the first consumer buys X' tickets and enjoys consumer surplus equal to the area PBE. The second consumer buys Y' tickets and enjoys consumer surplus equal to PKG. With a ticket price of P, the largest lump-sum tariff the amusement park can charge and still keep both customers in the market is equal to the area PBE.

Suppose the amusement park charges the area PBE as a uniform lump-sum tariff to both consumers. For the first consumer, the park's profit is the area $OPEX' + PBE - OAFX'$. This profit is lower (by the area FEC) than the profit earned when ticket price equals marginal cost and an admission fee of

ABC is charged. For the second consumer, the park's profit is the area *0PGY'* + *PBE* – *0AHY'*. This profit is higher (by the area *EGHC*) than the alternative marginal-cost pricing policy.

Increasing the ticket price necessarily reduces the lump-sum tariff charged to both consumers (*PBE* < *ABC*). But the additional profit earned by selling tickets at a price greater than marginal cost tends to offset the revenue foregone on admission fees. The relative magnitude of these effects determines whether the amusement park's owner should consider raising ticket prices. In other words, the net change in profit is equal to the increase in profit from the second consumer minus the lost profit from the first consumer. The decision to increase ticket prices and lower the lump-sum tariff depends on which of these effects is greater. The amusement park should raise ticket prices if *EGHC* > *FEC*; it should continue to charge a ticket price equal to marginal cost if *EGHC* < *FEC*.[19]

In a two-consumer model, selecting the optimal two-part pricing policy requires the amusement park to consider all possible combinations of ticket prices and admission fees in order to choose the one combination that maximizes profit or maximizes the difference between *EGHC* and *FEC*.[20] Generalizing to more than two consumers obviously makes the optimal pricing decision more complex. Regardless of how complicated it may be to select the profit-maximizing price and lump-sum tariff combination, however, the rationale for a two-part pricing policy is fairly straightforward. By assessing a lump-sum tariff for the right to purchase a good or service that approximates the value of consumer surplus, a firm can increase its profits over and above the profits that would be earned under a single-price policy.[21]

MULTI-PLANT PRODUCTION

With the advent of "just-in-time" production where suppliers locate production facilities close to major customers to reduce inventory costs and to improve their ability to fill orders in a timely manner, multi-plant firms are increasingly common in today's global economy. The potential market for many products is large relative to the capacity of any one production facility. Therefore, the firm may have to operate several plants manufacturing the same product to achieve its optimal level of output. The management challenge unique to multi-plant firms is to allocate production among the various plants to achieve minimum production costs and maximum profit.

---

19 Oi discusses a case in which the firm lowers its ticket price below marginal cost and increases the lump-sum tariff enough to increase profit overall. This result is based on several limiting assumptions. See Oi, "Disneyland Dilemma," for more on this possible pricing strategy.

20 See Oi for a detailed analysis of the problem of selecting the optimal, nondiscriminatory two-part pricing model.

21 Discount pricing represents an alternative multi-part pricing strategy. See Chapter 6 for a discussion of this alternative in the context of second-degree price discrimination.

Because the production facilities of a firm are often located in different geographic regions, the company's top managers face differences in the prices of raw materials and labor. Because the production facilities of a firm are often located in different political jurisdictions, the company's top managers face differences in governmental tax and regulatory policies.[22] Multinational firms face a whole host of additional differences, including differences in currency values (exposing them to exchange rate risk) and the potential risk of nationalization of their plants. All of these factors and more lead to differences in cost structures across the production facilities of the multi-plant firm.

Table 9.1 illustrates a hypothetical two-plant firm with different marginal production costs for each facility. Inspection of Table 9.1 indicates that if the firm decides to produce one unit of output, plant 1 should produce it because $MC_1 < MC_2$. It costs the firm an additional \$3.20 to produce the first unit of output in plant 1 and it costs an additional \$3.35 to produce that unit in plant 2. Thus, the minimum marginal cost of the firm (MC_f) for the first unit of output is \$3.20. The firm should use plant 2 to produce a second unit of output. The marginal cost of the second unit in plant 1 is \$3.50 compared with a marginal cost of \$3.35 for the first unit produced in plant 2. The firm's marginal cost (MC_f) for a second unit of output is \$3.35. Hence, if two units of output are produced, the firm will produce one unit in each of its plants. By similar reasoning, the third unit of output will be produced in plant 1.

In order to determine the firm's overall profit-maximizing quantity, refer to the demand and marginal revenue schedules in the last two columns of Table 9.1. The price-searcher firm maximizes profits by producing the quantity of output at which marginal revenue is equal to marginal cost. This profit

TABLE 9.1 HYPOTHETICAL COSTS OF A TWO-PLANT FIRM

OUTPUT	MC_1 PLANT 1	MC_2 PLANT 2	MC_f FIRM	PRICE	MR
1	\$3.20	\$3.35	\$3.20	\$10.00	—
2	\$3.50	\$3.55	\$3.35	\$9.50	\$9.00
3	\$3.80	\$3.75	\$3.50	\$9.00	\$8.00
4	\$4.10	\$3.95	\$3.55	\$8.50	\$7.00
5	\$4.40	\$4.15	\$3.75	\$8.00	\$6.00
6	\$4.70	\$4.35	\$3.80	\$7.50	\$5.00
7	\$5.00	\$4.55	\$3.95	\$7.00	\$4.00
8	\$5.30	\$4.75	\$4.10	\$6.50	\$3.00
9	\$5.60	\$4.95	\$4.15	\$6.00	\$2.00
10	\$5.90	\$5.15	\$4.35	\$5.50	\$1.00

22 Local and state governments often compete for jobs by offering incentive packages to firms that establish plants in their jurisdictions. So-called enterprise zones grant firms a state income tax credit for each employee hired, low interest rate industrial construction loans, cheap land for plant sites in industrial parks, and forgiveness of property taxes for a specified number of years. Such incentives obviously affect the cost structure of the firm significantly.

maximum occurs at seven units of output and a corresponding price of $7. (Marginal cost is less than marginal revenue at this point, but if the firm expands production to eight units, total cost rises by more than total revenue and total profit consequently declines.)

The least-cost allocation of the profit-maximizing quantity is for plant 1 to produce three units of output and plant 2 to produce four units. Assuming continuous revenue and cost functions, the firm must allocate production among its plants so that the marginal cost of the last unit produced in each plant is equal to the marginal cost of production for the firm as a whole. And, furthermore, marginal cost must be equal to the marginal revenue of the last unit sold. In other words, the equi-marginal principle dictates that

$$MC_1 = MC_2 = MC_f = MR.$$

If the foregoing equality does not hold, the firm can increase its profits by reallocating production from the high-cost plant to the low-cost plant. For example, had the firm decided to produce four units in plant 1 and three units in plant 2, the marginal cost of the seventh unit would have been $4.10. By reducing production in plant 1 by one unit, the firm realizes cost savings of $4.10. Producing one more unit in plant 2 adds $3.95 to total cost. There are consequently net cost savings of $.15 and a net increase in profit of $.15. The profit-maximizing firm would rationally decide to reassign production of the seventh unit away from plant 1 to plant 2.

Figure 9.10 illustrates the equi-marginal principle using continuous revenue and cost functions. MC_f is derived from MC_1 and MC_2 using the methodology of Table 9.1. The firm maximizes profits (minimizes losses) by producing $q_1 + q_2$ units of output, determined by setting $MR = MC_f$. The profit-maximizing quantity of output is allocated across plants so that the cost of the last unit produced in each facility is equal to the firm's overall marginal cost and to marginal revenue. Plant 1 accordingly produces q_1 units and plant 2 produces q_2 units.

In general, the equi-marginal principle dictates that the firm concentrate production activities in its relatively low-cost or efficient plants. As the example

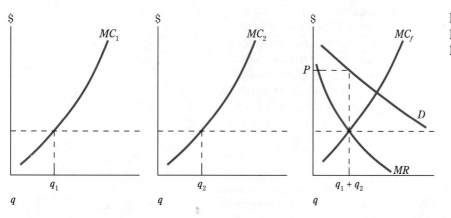

FIGURE 9.10
Production Allocation for the
Multi-Plant Firm

at hand indicates, however, it can still be profitable for the firm to employ older, less efficient facilities as long as these plants exhibit cost advantages over at least a portion of the relevant region of production.

But the manager must be prepared to close outmoded facilities if circumstances warrant. For example, suppose that plant 1's labor force unionizes and the facility's marginal cost of production increases by $1.50 at each level of output. The firm's overall marginal cost of production would therefore be recalculated as shown in Table 9.2. The firm now maximizes profits (minimizes losses) by producing six units of output—all of which are produced in plant 2. Essentially, the cost increase in plant 1 forces the firm to close plant 1, to expand production in plant 2 from four to six units, and to contract production overall from seven to six units. When one plant's costs increase, the firm's overall cost of production changes, thereby forcing the profit-maximizing firm to reassign more production away from higher cost plants to lower cost plants.

Plant relocation offers an alternative to closure. State and local governments have realized that reducing the operating costs of a plant might attract the company's owner to relocate a production facility to their geographic area. Through tax breaks and low interest loans, municipalities are cutting the cost of doing business for prospective companies wishing to relocate their plants. For example, suppose that the firm in Table 9.2 could relocate plant 1 and reduce its marginal cost of production by $2.00 per unit of output. What would happen? Table 9.3 illustrates this case.

By relocating, plant 1 reduces its cost of production. Recalculating the firm's overall marginal cost indicates that the profit-maximizing level of output returns to seven units. Thus, it becomes economical for the firm to produce four units of output in plant 1 and to reduce production in plant 2 to three units. Total profit has increased. The firm must compare the present value of these additional profits to the cost of relocating the plant before making a final relocation decision. But the value of the economic development incentives offered by the municipality should be transparent.

TABLE 9.2 TWO PLANT FIRM—INCREASED COST AT PLANT 1

OUTPUT	MC_1' PLANT 1	MC_2 PLANT 2	MC_f FIRM	PRICE	MR
1	$4.70	$3.35	$3.35	$10.00	—
2	$5.00	$3.55	$3.55	$9.50	$9.00
3	$5.30	$3.75	$3.75	$9.00	$8.00
4	$5.60	$3.95	$3.95	$8.50	$7.00
5	$5.90	$4.15	$4.15	$8.00	$6.00
6	$6.20	$4.35	$4.35	$7.50	$5.00
7	$6.50	$4.55	$4.55	$7.00	$4.00
8	$6.80	$4.75	$4.70	$6.50	$3.00
9	$7.10	$4.95	$4.75	$6.00	$2.00
10	$7.40	$5.15	$4.95	$5.50	$1.00

Multinational Production

Because the multinational corporation operates production facilities in at least two countries it is, by definition, a type of multi-plant firm. Thus, the theory of multi-plant production also provides a conceptual framework for explaining the existence of multinational enterprises (MNE).

Multinational firms exist for two reasons. First, international plant location is determined by cross-country cost differences. A plant locates at the lowest-cost production site for serving its particular market. Second, plants in different countries will operate under common administrative control if either costs are lower or revenue is higher than when the plants are managed separately. Richard Caves argues that the existence of intangible assets provides the most fruitful explanation for why multi-plant (and multinational) enterprises are more profitable than single-plant operations.[a]

An intangible asset can take a variety of forms. It can be technological in nature—the ability to produce a product at lower cost than rivals or produce a better product at the same cost. It can be promotional in nature—the skill to promote a product so that customers recognize its advantages over rival products. It can also be dynamic in nature—the ability to respond to changing market conditions more quickly than rivals, or the initiative to introduce innovations that rivals cannot readily copy.

Caves presents the following simple example that shows the connection between intangible assets and the existence of multi-plant and multinational firms. Suppose there are seven soap factories in seven different countries and each is under separate managerial control. The employees of one of these factories discover a way to improve the product. The product improvement adds little to cost and cannot be imitated by the other firms. How can management maximize the rents derived from this product improvement? One option is to expand production in its single plant and export the product to other countries. However, if the multi-plant production that currently characterizes the world economy is locationally efficient, then the export solution entails excessive transportation costs.

A second option is for the innovating firm to license its discovery to the six other firms. A drawback to this option is that the seller may not be able to capture the full value of the innovation. In order to capture the full value of the intangible asset, the innovator must convince potential licensees of its true worth. However, if the employees of the innovating firm reveal too many of the details of the innovation they risk losing it. On the other side of the bargaining process, yet-to-be-convinced firms may feel that the innovation's value is overstated. Thus, both the seller and the buyer may act in ways that cause the intangible asset to be underpriced.

In light of the cost of exporting products and the problems of selling or licensing an intangible asset, the most profitable option for the innovating plant may be to merge with the six other soap plants. The production facilities of the new MNE would then share the intangible asset and maximize the joint profit potential from exploiting the innovation.

At the same time, of course, the expected benefits of multinational operations must be balanced against the expected costs. When a firm acquires foreign subsidiaries, its managers must learn the peculiarities of the new markets. They must transfer home-office personnel abroad or hire foreign nationals to manage the overseas production facilities. Either choice involves a cost because home-office personnel must acquire specialized knowledge about the foreign market, and foreign nationals must acquire specialized knowledge about the home office's product and production process.

a Richard E. Caves, *Multinational Enterprise and Economic Analysis* (Cambridge: Cambridge University Press, 1982).

We can extend the transaction-cost approach to explain the dynamic development of a firm from a domestic enterprise into a multinational enterprise. Once again assume that a firm develops an intangible asset. Because of information costs, it is economical for the firm to expand in the domestic market first. However, the marginal returns to domestic production eventually decline, and expanding to serve overseas markets becomes more attractive.

Caves and Pugel find empirical support for this characterization of multinational development. A significant difference between firms that choose to expand multinationally and those that do not is the market share the former group had already attained in the domestic market.[b] This result supports the hypothesis that the successful firm first expands in the domestic market before incurring the transaction costs of expanding internationally.

b Richard E. Caves and Thomas A. Pugel, *Intraindustry Differences in Conduct and Performance*, Monograph Series in Finance and Economics, 1980-2 (New York: Graduate School of Business Administration, New York University, 1980).

TABLE 9.3 TWO PLANT FIRM—REDUCED COST AT PLANT 1

OUTPUT	MC_1'' PLANT 1	MC_2 PLANT 2	MC_f FIRM	PRICE	MR
1	$2.70	$3.35	$2.70	$10.00	—
2	$3.00	$3.55	$3.00	$9.50	$9.00
3	$3.30	$3.75	$3.30	$9.00	$8.00
4	$3.60	$3.95	$3.35	$8.50	$7.00
5	$3.90	$4.15	$3.55	$8.00	$6.00
6	$4.20	$4.35	$3.60	$7.50	$5.00
7	$4.50	$4.55	$3.75	$7.00	$4.00
8	$4.80	$4.75	$3.90	$6.50	$3.00
9	$5.10	$4.95	$3.95	$6.00	$2.00
10	$5.40	$5.15	$4.15	$5.50	$1.00

The foregoing discussion suggests that each plant manager has a vested interest in continually seeking cost savings that maintain his or her plant's position in the company's overall strategic plan. Firms are very sensitive to shifts in costs among their various production facilities. Slight cost shifts may significantly affect the future success or failure of an individual plant.

SUMMARY

KEY TERMS
transfer pricing
multi-part pricing
multi-plant firms
multidivisional firm

This chapter has covered four advanced pricing topics. At the outset, we evaluated the pricing of resources transferred or exchanged internally within the firm in three market situations. First, a good or service is transferred within the firm at a price equal to the marginal cost of producing it when no external market exists. Second, the firm internally transfers a good or service at the market-determined price established in a price-taker external market.

The market-determined price is equal to marginal cost in this case. Third, when a price-searcher external market exists, the firm internally transfers a good or service at a price equal to marginal cost, but sells it at a mark-up to outside customers.

The production and pricing of joint products was this chapter's second major topic. First, joint complements are two or more goods produced simultaneously by a single production process. Profit maximization in this case requires the firm to vertically sum the demands for the individual goods and produce the quantity of output at which joint marginal revenue is equal to marginal cost. Both of these goods are then sold only if the marginal revenue associated with each joint complement is positive at the profit-maximizing quantity. Second, joint substitutes are two or more goods that can be produced using the same production process; but in this case the production of one good precludes the production of the other. The demand for joint substitutes is equal to the horizontal sum of the demands for the individual goods. In order to maximize profit, joint marginal revenue is set equal to joint marginal cost. The common value of joint marginal revenue (= marginal cost) is in turn set equal to the separate marginal revenues of the substitute goods.

Multi-part pricing is a third advanced pricing policy that may enable the price-searcher firm to generate profits in excess of those earned by charging a single profit-maximizing price. For discriminating two-part pricing, the optimal strategy is to charge a price equal to marginal cost plus a lump-sum tariff equal to the consumer surplus of each customer for the right to buy the good or service. For non-discriminating two-part pricing, the firm can either set price equal to marginal cost and charge a tariff equal to the small demander's consumer surplus or set a price greater than marginal cost and reduce the tariff accordingly.

Finally, multi-plant firms maximize profits by equating the marginal cost of production in each plant to the firm's overall marginal cost of production at the point where the firm's marginal cost is equal to marginal revenue.

KEY TERMS

demand independence
technological independence
fixed-proportions technology
equi-marginal principle
marginal cost
joint products
joint complements
joint substitutes
isocost curves
isorevenue lines
two-part tariff
consumer surplus

QUESTIONS

9.1 Suppose that Textile West has obtained a patent on an innovative textile manufacturing process. Textile West uses the process to produce a certain type of fabric for itself. Textile West also licenses other firms to use the process for a fee of $F per year. Because these other companies have to pay this licensing fee, their costs of production are higher than those of Textile West. Hence, Textile West will be able to sell its product for a lower price than its rivals. True, false, or uncertain? Explain your answer.

9.2 You are the vice-president of the manufacturing division of a single-product company that produces and sells sunscreen lotion in a price-taker market. You are allowed to set the price you charge the retailing division. Suppose that the retailing division markets the lotion under conditions of increasing marginal cost. How do you determine the transfer price? Suppose the market price of sunscreen lotion increases. What will happen to the transfer price?

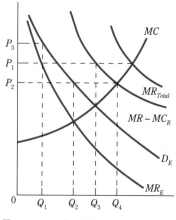

FIGURE 9.11

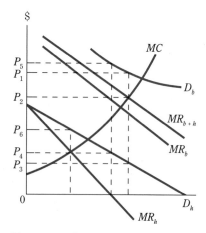

FIGURE 9.12

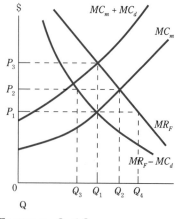

FIGURE 9.13

9.3 Your company, ABC, Inc., has two retail divisions—a U.S. retailer and an international retailer. Both divisions sell their product in price-taker markets. The U.S. price is P_u and the international price is P_i. The President and CEO of the firm has set the following company policies:
a. The manufacturing vice-president sets the transfer price.
b. The vice-president of each retail division determines the quantity of the intermediate good to purchase.
c. No division can buy from or sell to outside firms.
d. No collusion among retailing vice-presidents is allowed.
You are the vice-president of ABC's manufacturing division. What is the optimal transfer price and quantity of the intermediate good produced and sold in each retail market if (a) the transfer price is the same for both divisions, or (b) the transfer price is allowed to be different because $P_i > P_u$?

9.4 A two-part price enables the firm to increase its profits over and above those it would earn under a single-price policy. Given the profitability of two-part pricing, why do you think that Disneyland abandoned it? That is, why do you think that Disneyland now charges an admission fee but does not levy a separate charge for rides?

9.5 For a multi-plant price-searcher firm with plant A and plant B, if $MC_B > MC_A$ what should the firm do?

9.6 General Motors has several divisions producing substitute goods. Describe how the vice-presidents of the Buick and Oldsmobile divisions will determine price and quantity produced in their respective divisions to maximize General Motors' overall profits.

PROBLEMS

9.1 Duke Power generates electricity at the Oconee Nuclear Power Plant according to the wholesale marginal cost (MC) schedule depicted in Figure 9.11. The "total" marginal revenue is the horizontal sum of the marginal revenue of the external market (MR_E) and the retail marginal revenue (MR) of Duke Power minus the retail marginal cost (MC_R) of distributing its wholesale electricity.
a. Duke Power would sell _____ units of electricity to external retailers (such as Blue Ridge Electric Coop) at a price of _____.
b. Duke Power would transfer _____ units of electricity to its retail division at a price of _____.

9.2 Because beef and hides are perfect complements in production, a profit-maximizing firm would set the price of beef at _____ and the price of hides at _____ given the market conditions depicted in Figure 9.12. Note: MR_{b+n} is the vertical sum of MR_b and MR_h.

9.3 Use Figure 9.13 to answer parts (a) and (b) of this problem separately. Assume you are the vice-president of the manufacturing division of CCS, Inc. MC_m is your division's marginal cost of producing an intermediate good and MC_d is the distribution (retailing) division's marginal cost of processing the intermediate good into a final product. MR_F is the firm's marginal revenue from selling the final product. The goal is to maximize the firm's profit and not the profit of any one division. Assume that the demand for the final product is independent of the demand for the intermediate good.

a. Suppose there is no external market for the intermediate good. A centralized firm would produce _____ units of output. Defend your answer.

b. Suppose there is no external market for the intermediate good and a decentralized firm produces this product. If you want to maximize the manufacturing division's profits while not jeopardizing the firm's profits, then you would set a transfer price of _____ and produce _____ units of the intermediate good for sale to the distribution division. Defend your answer.

9.4 Use the information shown in Figure 9.14 to answer parts (a) and (b) of this problem. Your manufacturing division sells the intermediate good to either your company's distribution division or to a price-searcher external market. Assume the demand for your company's final product is independent of the demand for your intermediate good. MC_m and MC_d are the marginal costs of the manufacturing and distribution divisions, respectively. MR_F and MR_e are marginal revenues of your firm's final good and your division's good in the external market, respectively. Let $MR^* = MR_e + (MR_F - MC_d)$.

a. You would produce _____ units and sell _____ units to the distribution division at a transfer price of _____.

b. From part (a), you would also sell _____ units of the intermediate good in the external market for price _____.

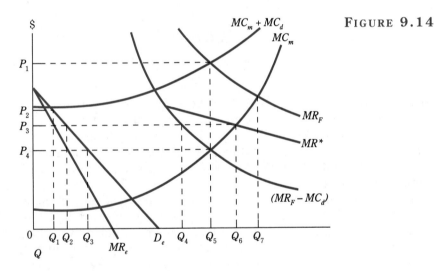

FIGURE 9.14

Strategic Management Decisions

OVERVIEW

Managerial decisions are not made in a static environment. Firms are forced to adopt long-run strategies because of the constant change that characterizes a dynamically competitive marketplace. Successful long-term planning is forward-looking. It provides a methodological framework for identifying strategies that enable the firm to respond to changes in its internal and external environments.

The formulation of strategic goals is the first step in long-term planning. Strategic goals are broad statements of the firm's objectives for the future. Although the appropriate time horizon for long-term planning varies from firm to firm and from industry to industry, the conventional rule-of-thumb is to base a strategic plan on objectives to be met over a three- to five-year time span. Peter Drucker's best-selling book, *The Practice of Management*, suggests eight strategic managerial goals. These are market standing, innovation, productivity, physical and financial resources, profitability, managerial performance and development, worker performance and attitude, and public responsibility.[1]

---

1 Peter F. Drucker, *The Practice of Management* (New York: Harper & Brothers, 1954), pp. 65-83.

The importance of drawing up a strategic plan is now a part of the conventional wisdom in the study of management. How does this standard management practice square with the goal of the firm in economic theory? As stressed in Chapter 1, there is only one objective that ensures the firm's long-term survival in a competitive environment—the goal of maximizing the value of the firm, which is equivalent to maximizing the present value of future profits. At first glance, there seems to be a contradiction between the ways in which economic theory and management theory view the objective(s) of the firm. While economic analysis singles out long-run profit maximization, Drucker's list relegates profitability to only one of eight strategic goals.

Economic theory's single-goal approach and management theory's multi-goal approach are more consistent with one another than one might think at first blush. Achieving the objective of long-run profit maximization requires the manager to confront a complex set of interrelated decisions. A strategic plan supplies a useful framework for organizing these decisions. Microeconomic analysis provides an invaluable set of tools that the manager can then apply to evaluate these strategies in a logically consistent fashion.

Chapter 10 presents four examples of economic analysis for strategic decisions. The common denominator is time. The first section explores the effects of entry on the firm's profit-maximizing price and quantity. Should the firm select the price and quantity that are optimal in a static market environment and wait for entry to occur, thereby taking advantage of its lead time over rivals? Alternatively, should the firm respond immediately to entry by reducing price in order to hold on to its market share in the face of new competition? The value of these pricing strategies depends on the characteristics of the good being produced, the existence of barriers to entry of new competitors, and consumers' future price expectations.

The second section considers the related issue of entry deterrence. If entry affects profits adversely, can the firm successfully adopt strategies that limit the entry of new firms into its market?

The third section discusses how managers can incorporate "learning-by-doing" effects into the firm's production and pricing decisions. How does knowing that accumulated production experience reduces the firm's costs affect the time path of product price? Should the manager select a price today that reflects expected future production costs, or should price instead be lowered gradually over time as cumulative output grows and the firm's cost curves shift downward?

The final section of the chapter introduces the economics of advertising. How do the advertising and promotional activities of the firm and its rivals affect future sales? How is the content of an advertising message affected by the characteristics of the product being sold? We will use the economics of information and search theory to analyze the manager's decision to advertise. Essentially, advertising lowers consumers' costs of gathering information and, thus, reduces the full price of the product or service (price plus the cost of search). Marginal analysis determines the optimal amount of advertising for a firm.

The applications in Chapters 2 through 5 are based on the Johnson Company's plan to market a new all-weather coat. Prior to the product's introduction, the company's top managers meet to outline a strategy for responding to future developments in the market. At the start of the meeting, the company's president reviews the demand and cost conditions shown in equations 10.1 and 10.2 that were used to calculate the project's expected profitability.

$$P = \$100 - \$.2Q, \tag{10.1}$$

$$STC = \$800 + \$12Q + \$.02Q^2. \tag{10.2}$$

P is the price of all-weather coats, Q is quantity (measured in thousands), and STC is short-run total production cost.

The profit-maximizing price and quantity are determined by equating marginal revenue with marginal cost. The marginal revenue and marginal cost equations are

$$MR = \$100 - \$.4Q \text{ and} \tag{10.3}$$

$$MC = \$12 + \$.04Q. \tag{10.4}$$

Setting $MR = MC$ yields a profit-maximizing quantity of 200,000 coats. From equation 10.1, the profit-maximizing price associated with this quantity is $60. Finally, total revenue is $12,000,000; total cost is $4,000,000; and profit is $8,000,000.

Following this review, the management team begins discussing a definitive set of strategic goals that will serve as a framework for future decision making. Based on this discussion, the president draws up the following list of five objectives in each of three major areas—the firm's financial performance, its marketing strategy, and its production capability.

FINANCIAL GOALS
_____

1. Profitability
2. Cash flow
3. Dividends
4. Return on invested earnings
5. Outside debt

MARKETING GOALS
_____

1. Market share
2. Growth in sales
3. Reputation for service and quality

4. Penetration into foreign markets
5. Effective advertising

PRODUCTION GOALS

1. Operating costs
2. Raw material cost
3. Inventory cost
4. Capacity utilization
5. Flexibility in response to changing market conditions

The next step for the management team is to specify a "realistic but challenging" target for each of the objectives. For example, the profitability goal could be defined as achieving a 20 percent return on sales, and the market share goal could be defined as achieving sales equal to 30 percent of the coat market. However, it is clear from the ensuing discussion that the managers must address a number of important issues before narrowly defining any strategic goals. In particular, the following issues appear to be the most important stumbling blocks in defining strategic goals that are both realistic and challenging.

Issue 1. The firm's marketing strategy will focus on the all-weather coat's superior versatility. The Johnson Company's coat is light enough to use as a rain jacket in warm weather and has sufficient insulating features to be worn comfortably in cool weather. Product innovation inevitably invites imitation by other firms. **How should the firm's pricing and output targets change as new competitors enter the market?**

Issue 2. Rather than responding passively to the entry of new competitors, why not anticipate their entry and adopt strategies that enable the firm to maintain its market share by reducing competitors' incentives to enter? **How can the firm price the all-weather coat so that a sufficient profit is maintained but there is minimal incentive for other firms to enter the market?**

Issue 3. The production department has advised the management team that short-run average cost is likely to decline as workers gain production experience and become more adept at their tasks. **If learning-by-doing characterizes the production process, how does this affect current and future pricing and production decisions?**

Issue 4. The success of the Johnson Company's new product is contingent on informing consumers of its advantages relative to products already on the market. **What are the basic principles that define a successful advertising strategy?**

This chapter shows how economic analysis can provide important insights into these important questions. Firms must address issues of this sort before specifying "realistic and challenging" strategic goals.

The price-taker and price-searcher models in Chapter 8 provide a starting point for discussing the effects of entry on the firm's profit-maximizing price and output decisions. **Pure monopoly** is defined as a closed price-searcher market in which a single firm sells a product having no close substitutes. **Oligopoly** is defined as a price-searcher market that is dominated by a few large firms.[2] Oligopolistic markets are usually characterized by high—but not necessarily insurmountable—barriers to entry. The model of **monopolistic competition** assumes that there are many firms selling differentiated products in an open price-searcher market. Finally, the **price-taker model** of "perfect competition" assumes that there are many firms selling a homogeneous product and that these firms have complete freedom to enter and exit the industry.

The model of pure monopoly can safely be ignored in studying the effects of entry because it, by definition, represents the case of a single firm.[3] The remaining three market structure models make one of two possible behavioral assumptions. The oligopoly model assumes that the sellers recognize their mutual interdependence, while the models of monopolistic competition and perfect competition assume that the sellers make decisions independently of one another. Simply stated, managerial decisions in the models of monopolistic competition and perfect competition exclude the possible reactions of rivals, while managerial decisions in the model of oligopoly are explicity based on those expected reactions.

Put in these terms, it may seem that oligopoly theory is more "realistic" and that actual managerial decision-making is more closely related to the theory of oligopoly than it is to either the model of monopolistic competition or the model of perfect competition. However, realism is a very imperfect criterion for choosing one theory over another. By definition, all theories are simplifications and are therefore "unrealistic." For example, a completely realistic road map would be much less useful than one that sacrifices some realism for simplicity. Someone who is driving from Dallas to New Orleans does not need to know the location of every dirt road along the way. The usefulness of a map lies in its ability to help travelers get from one point to another; the usefulness of a theory lies in its ability to predict.

This section analyzes the effects of entry when firms make their decisions independently. Thus, the discussion of entry's effects on the pricing and production decisions of the firm takes a long-run perspective. We first describe possible sources of barriers to entry. The impact of entry on price and output in an open price-searcher model is then analyzed.

---

2 The main issue here is the degree to which the market is "contestable." See Chapter 8.

3 Few private firms are monopolistic in the sense assumed by the model of pure monopoly. Even monopolies based on exclusive patent rights are vulnerable to entry by firms that "invent around' the patent and market substitutable goods. See the section on "The Effects of Advertising" for an example taken from the pharmaceutical industry.

The term **barriers to entry** is used to describe any disadvantage faced by potential entrants to an industry that is not also faced by the established firms. More precisely, an entry barrier can be defined "as a cost of producing (at some or every rate of output) which must be borne by a firm which seeks to enter an industry but is not borne by firms already in the industry."[4]

Other definitions of entry barriers have been proposed, but all of them tend to focus attention on the differing opportunities facing industry "insiders" versus "outsiders." The entry barrier concept raises two important issues. One of these issues relates to whether barriers to entry exist for reasons outside the control of the established firms (because of conditions of demand or cost, for example) or whether industry insiders can themselves erect barriers to entry.[5] Another more fundamental question is, What actually constitutes a barrier to entry?

Three possible sources of entry barriers are usually identified. The first of these is **economies of scale**. If production in an industry exhibits economies of scale, then the long-run average costs of production decline as the rate of output increases. In order to compete successfully with the established firms, new entrants must be prepared to enter with a plant of sufficient size (minimum efficient scale) to take advantage of these scale economies. Firms entering with smaller plant sizes would be forced to operate at a unit cost disadvantage relative to the existing firms.

Capital requirements are a related possible barrier to entry. The investment necessary to finance the construction of a plant of minimum efficient scale may be so large that new firms are either unable to raise the capital needed to enter or face differentially higher costs of doing so. Because most new business ventures fail, potential entrants may be forced to borrow at higher interest rates or to issue stock at lower prices than their established rivals. Moreover, suppliers may refuse to extend credit to the newcomer or, if they do, demand stricter terms; workers may demand higher wage rates to accept jobs with a firm having uncertain prospects; and so on.

Finally, entry may be deterred by the existence of **sunk costs**. Sunk costs are costs that an established firm cannot avoid even if it ceases production. If sunk costs cannot be recovered under any circumstances, they will not affect the pricing and output decisions of the firm that has incurred them. The newcomer, by contrast, must take such costs into account when deciding to enter because they have not yet been borne. Hence, the necessity of investing in specialized capital raises the incremental costs of production to the potential entrant above those of the established firm which, by definition, treats sunk costs as a bygone.[6]

---

4 George J. Stigler, "Barriers to Entry, Economies of Scale, and Firm Size," in George J. Stigler, *The Organization of Industry* (Homewood, IL: Richard D. Irwin, 1968), p. 67.

5 See the section on "Strategic Entry Deterrence" below.

6 William J. Baumol and Robert D. Willig, "Fixed Costs, Sunk Costs, Entry Barriers, and the Sustainability of Monopoly," *Quarterly Journal of Economics* 96 (August 1981), pp. 405-31.

The entry barrier concept highlights the idea that there are substantial advantages to being first. Industry pioneers benefit from taking the lead in exploiting scale economies, establishing reputations, and investing in highly specialized capital. These **"first-mover" advantages** may raise barriers to entry by forcing newcomers to bear costs that are not being borne by firms that entered the industry in the past. On the other hand, latecomers may benefit from the pioneering investments of first-movers who, by demonstrating the profitability of a new product or new market, reduce the costs of subsequent entry.[7]

In any case, entry—or the threat of it—is the mechanism by which a market system helps keep prices in line with costs. Entry is triggered by the existence of positive economic profits in an industry and, in the limit, it drives those profits to zero. How far this process goes depends on the importance of barriers to entry. The following section explores two of the possibilities.

The Effects of Entry

Figure 10.1 helps to explain the possible effects of entry on the established firm's profit-maximizing price and quantity. The initial revenue conditions are described by the linear demand schedule, D_0, and the marginal revenue schedule associated with it, MR_0. We determine the profit-maximizing price and quantity, P_0 and Q_0, as usual by equating marginal revenue with marginal cost. Total revenue is represented in the diagram by area OP_0AQ_0, total cost is $OEBQ_0$, and total profit is the difference between the two, or EP_0AB.

Entry shifts the demand curve for the firm's product to the left. The introduction of new products provides consumers with alternatives that were previously unavailable. The quantities they are willing and able to buy from any one seller therefore decline. In addition to the leftward shift, entry can also affect the demand schedule's slope. Whether it does or not depends on how product differentiation is affected.

Product differentiation explains why the firm's demand schedule slopes downward. If entry increases the availability of close substitutes, making it more difficult for the firm to differentiate its product from those offered by rivals, differentiation decreases (the industry's product becomes more homogeneous) and the demand schedule becomes flatter. On the other hand, if product differentiation is not affected, entry causes a parallel shift in the firm's demand schedule.

In any event, a downward shift in demand causes the firm's profits to decline. Economic profits can at most fall to zero in the long run; otherwise the firm would exit the industry. Economic profits are zero when the firm's demand schedule is tangent to its average total cost curve.

Figure 10.1 presents two cases. In the first case, entry causes the established firm's demand schedule to shift to the left, but its slope remains unchanged. Under this assumption, economic profits fall to zero when the

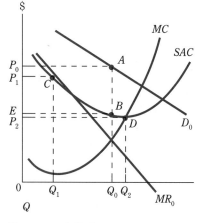

FIGURE 10.1
Range of Post-Entry Price-Output Combinations

7 Harold Demsetz, "Barriers to Entry," *American Economic Review* 72 (March 1982), pp. 47-57.

new demand schedule is tangent to its short-run average cost curve at a point like C. The new profit-maximizing price and quantity are P_1 and Q_1.[8] Entry forces the firm to reduce both price and sales.

In the second case, the demand curve shifts to the left and also becomes flatter as product differentiation declines. Entry is again assumed to continue until the firm's economic profits drop to zero. In the limit, the post-entry demand schedule becomes perfectly elastic. The firm's demand schedule is tangent to its short-run average cost curve at point D when entry ceases. At the new long-run, zero-profit equilibrium the firm has reduced its selling price to P_2 and increased its sales to Q_2 units.

The two cases in Figure 10.1 illustrate the general range of price and output responses to entry if economic profits fall to zero. Depending on entry's effects on product differentiation and the slope of the demand curve, the post-entry price will lie somewhere between P_1 and P_2, and post-entry sales will range from a low of Q_1 to a high of Q_2.

Figure 10.2 illustrates the effects of entry on the price and quantity of the Johnson Company's all-weather coats. One difference between this case and the previous one is that the initial level of production (Q_0) occurs at the point of the minimum average total cost curve. The graph shows that entry forces the price of all-weather coats to fall from $60 to somewhere between $26.53 (point A) and $20 (point B); the post-entry quantity of coats varies from 60,000 to 200,000 coats. (These prices and quantities are derived mathematically in the appendix to this chapter.)

To summarize, when a firm competes in an open price-searcher market, the existence of positive economic profits attracts new rivals to enter the industry. Entry continues until economic profits fall to zero—that is, until price is equal to average cost. Entry's effects on the established firm's sales and on the relationship between price and marginal cost depend on how the introduction of new alternatives affects product heterogeneity. In general, the more substitutable new products are for existing products, the flatter the firm's post-entry demand schedule will be, the less post-entry sales will fall (they may even increase), and the closer post-entry price will be to marginal cost.

In an open price-searcher market, the firm responds to entry by reducing price. Its sales may increase or decrease depending on the relative sizes of entry's two effects on the demand curve—it shifts inward and becomes flatter. How profitable the introduction of a new product will be therefore depends in part on the length of the seller's lead time over rivals. The longer it takes new rivals to enter, the longer the incumbent will earn positive economic profits and the more the value of the firm will increase by undertaking the investment necessary to bring the new product to market. Because lead time over rivals is such a critical factor in determining the profitability of a new

---

8 To avoid cluttering the diagram, the new demand and marginal revenue schedule corresponding to this profit-maximizing price-quantity combination are not shown. If they were, marginal revenue would intersect marginal cost at Q_1 units of output.

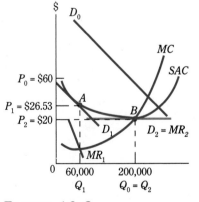

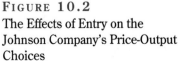

FIGURE 10.2

The Effects of Entry on the Johnson Company's Price-Output Choices

product, it is natural to ask whether there are strategies available to the firm that increase this advantage. That is, rather than responding passively to entry, can an established firm actively discourage new rivals from entering the industry and thereby increase the length of time over which it earns positive economic profits? The following section addresses this question.

STRATEGIC ENTRY DETERRENCE

The concept of strategic entry deterrence refers to actions that an established firm might take to block or delay the entry of new rivals. If an industry insider can convince outsiders that entry is unprofitable, then it may be able to prevent the competitive expansion of industry output that will otherwise cause its own profits to decline over time.

Two general points about entry-deterring strategies are worth making at the outset. First, as we shall see below, the established firm must sacrifice current profits to prevent or delay the entry of rivals. As such, the decision to engage in strategic entry deterrence is essentially a capital-budgeting problem. On the one hand, if the established firm accepts the fact that entry is inevitable, its economic profits will be relatively high in the short run. These profits will then decline steadily over time as entry forces market price downward until, eventually, profits fall to zero.

On the other hand, if the established firm chooses to undertake an entry-deterring strategy, its profits will be lower initially. But these profits will remain above normal over time if the firm successfully deters entry. Depending on the length of time required for new rivals to enter, the interest rate chosen for discounting expected future profits, and the cost of deterring entry, one of these two strategies will have a higher present value than the other. "Investing" in strategic entry deterrence is consequently worthwhile only if the expected rate of return to it is at least as great as the rate of return available on the firm's next best alternative investment opportunity.

Second, entry-deterring strategies make sense only if the established firm either dominates the industry (existing competitors are small "fringe" suppliers who passively follow its pricing decisions) or convinces its existing rivals that acting in concert to deter entry is in their mutual best interest. If the established firm faces uncooperative competitors within the industry, it will have little room for taking actions that deter or delay the entry of outsiders. Hence, the notion of strategic entry deterrence presupposes either that the established firm possesses significant market power or that the problems of reaching and enforcing a collusive agreement among industry insiders have been solved.[9]

---

9 See Chapter 8 for a discussion of the theory of collusion.

Limit-Entry Pricing

The limit-entry pricing model suggests that an established firm can prevent new rivals from entering the industry yet at the same time enjoy positive economic profits. It does so by charging a price low enough to convince potential entrants that entry is unprofitable, but high enough to earn continued economic profits. In short, the established firm sacrifices current profits (by producing a quantity of output greater than the quantity at which marginal revenue equals marginal cost) in order to prevent entry from reducing its profits to zero.

Figure 10.3 graphs the limit-entry pricing model. Market demand is labeled D and all firms, including potential entrants, are assumed to have access to the same production technology represented by long-run average cost schedule LAC. The problem faced by the established firm is to determine a price-output combination that makes entry unprofitable at minimum efficient scale. (The minimum efficient plant size is shown in the figure as short-run average cost curve SAC_M.)

To solve the limit-entry pricing problem, an assumption must be made about how the established firm will respond to entry. In the most familiar version of the model, potential entrants believe that the established firm will maintain its output at the pre-entry level if entry in fact occurs.[10] Under this assumption, the quantity the entrant can expect to sell at any price is equal to the total market demand at that price minus the quantity sold by the established firm.

The limit-entry price is calculated by determining the point at which the potential entrant's residual demand curve, d, is just tangent to LAC. An output rate of Q_L accomplishes this purpose. If the established firm sells Q_L units and charges a price trivially below p_L, the remaining market demand is not large enough to support entry at minimum efficient scale. The established firm has left the potential entrant no output for which the post-entry price will cover its average production costs. Assuming that the established firm holds its output steady at Q_L in the face of entry, any amount supplied by the entrant would force market price below p_L and below the entrant's average production costs.

The limit-pricing model therefore seems to offer the established seller a profitable entry-deterring strategy. It contains a fatal flaw, however. Potential entrants will simply not believe that the established firm will hold its output steady if entry in fact occurs. To see why this is so, suppose that despite the apparent lack of market opportunities, a new firm enters by building a plant of minimum efficient scale, Q_M. If the established firm continues to produce Q_L units, industry output ($Q_M + Q_L$) exceeds the quantity at which market demand intersects long-run average cost. Market price therefore falls below LAC and both the entrant *and* the established firm suffer economic losses.

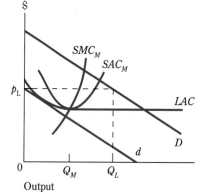

FIGURE 10.3
The Limit-Entry Pricing Model

10 Paolo Sylos-Labini, *Oligopoly and Technical Progress* (Cambridge, MA: Harvard University Press, 1962).

But the established firm's total losses are greater than those of the entrant because Q_L is greater than Q_M.

How can the established firm limit its losses in response to entry? The only way of doing so is to reduce production below Q_L. But as the established firm's output declines, the entrant's residual demand schedule, d, shifts to the right. This increase in demand opens up a range of output over which price is greater than average cost and entry is potentially profitable. The bottom line is that the assumption on which the limit-entry pricing model rests is not logically consistent. Knowing that the established firm must reduce output to accommodate entry, the potential entrant calculates whether it can cover its costs at the post-entry price and, if so, enters. The pre-entry price is irrelevant to the entry decision and, as such, cannot be used strategically to deter entry, at least in the way suggested by the limit-pricing model.

Although limit-entry pricing is illogical in the context of the model outlined above, the idea has been rehabilitated recently. The new argument is that charging a price below the profit-maximizing price can successfully delay or deter entry if potential entrants believe that the established firm is more efficient (has lower costs of production) than is in fact the case. Alternatively, responding to entry by charging prices below cost may pay dividends by helping the established firm develop a reputation as an aggressive competitor that is willing to sustain heavy losses to punish any newcomer that dares to enter.

The first of these theories assumes that an informational asymmetry exists between industry insiders and outsiders. The second requires that the threat of entry disappear at some point so that the established firm can raise price to recoup the losses it suffers from aggressive below-cost pricing. In both of these cases, however, the only way for the established firm to limit the market opportunities of potential entrants is to take sales away from them by increasing output. Increased industry supply and lower industry price are the expected responses to entry, and strategies to deter entry are consequently difficult to distinguish from the normal workings of the competitive market process.

Raising Rivals' Costs

Established firms may be able to deter entry by adopting a strategy that raises potential rivals' costs more than their own. Trade protectionism supplies the clearest example of this strategy. If foreign producers are required to pay a tariff or comply with a regulation that domestic producers can avoid, then entry by international competitors into the domestic market is more costly and less likely.

The idea of raising rivals' costs is more general, however. There is evidence, for example, that the ban on television advertising of cigarettes raised the market value of existing brands by making it more difficult for manufacturers to inform smokers about the availability of newer brands.[11] Similarly, the

---

11 Lynne Schneider, Benjamin Klein, and Kevin Murphy, "Government Regulation of Health Information," *Journal of Law and Economics* 24 (December 1981), pp. 575-612.

average price of eyeglasses is significantly higher in states where advertising by optometrists is prohibited and new entrants presumably find it more costly to attract the attention of consumers than they would otherwise.[12]

There are many other possibilities for achieving success in this way. For instance, suppose two different production technologies yield the same minimum average cost. One of these production technologies is relatively capital-intensive; the other is relatively labor-intensive. The capital-intensive firms join with a labor union to negotiate a collective bargaining agreement that raises wage rates industrywide. The higher wage rates raise the industry's average production costs, but the costs of the labor-intensive firms increase by more than the costs of the capital-intensive firms who, by assumption, employ fewer workers per unit of output. These differentially higher production costs force some of the labor-intensive firms out of the industry and deter entry of new labor-intensive rivals.

The examples above suggest that a successful strategy of raising rivals' costs must impose differentially higher costs on potential entrants and, moreover, that these costs must be unavoidable. Hence, implementing a strategy to raise rivals' costs generally requires the cooperation of a government regulatory agency to promulgate and enforce compliance with rules that increase some firms' costs of doing business more than others.[13] This is because any avoidable cost, like any abnormal profit, serves as an invitation to entry.

LEARNING-BY-DOING

Time plays a central role in strategic managerial decision-making. The long-term success of a new product depends on the firm's ability to respond to changes in demand and cost conditions that occur over time. At first blush, it may seem that time has already been incorporated explicitly into the theory of production and cost. After all, Chapter 3 has discussed production and cost in the long run, and Chapter 4 has presented short-run production and cost analysis. But the distinction between the short run and the long run has very little to do with the length of the manager's time horizon.

Rather than defining a time horizon, the short run and long run refer to constraints that bind the manager's choices. In the long run, the firm is not constrained by prior commitments and can choose any technically feasible production process. In the short run, the firm faces one or more constraints that limit its input choice set. Moreover, there are as many short runs as there are possible constraints on the firm's activities. The period of time during which at least one input is treated as fixed (the "short run") can be very short or very long depending on how costly it would be to vary the usage of the particular input in question.

---

12 See the section entitled "The Effects of Advertising" for additional examples.

13 See Part IV for a discussion of why government regulators may have incentives to impose regulations that benefit some firms at the expense of others.

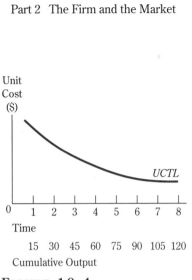

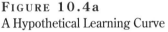

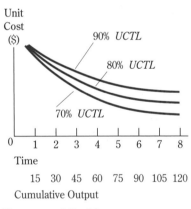

FIGURE 10.4a
A Hypothetical Learning Curve

FIGURE 10.4b
Classifying Learning Curves

Unlike short-run and long-run cost curves, which relate the firm's marginal and average costs to the quantity of output produced *per unit of time*, the effect of time on costs is explicitly incorporated into a concept known as the **learning curve** or the *experience curve*. The learning curve shows how the firm's unit costs of production vary over time.

Figure 10.4a illustrates a hypothetical learning curve. Note that the horizontal axis can be measured either in units of time or in terms of the accumulated quantity of output the firm has produced up to a particular point in time. The substitutability of time and cumulative output underscores an important dimension of learning curves: The rate of output in each period is held constant. We have labeled the curve in Figure 10.4a as a *unit cost time line* (UCTL) to underscore the role of time in its construction and to differentiate the learning curve from the more familiar long-run average cost curve.

The learning curve in Figure 10.4a is downward sloping, indicating that the firm's unit costs of production decline over time or, equivalently, as cumulative output increases. Its shape reflects the increased proficiency that workers gain with experience, or **learning-by-doing**. Learning-by-doing characterizes many everyday activities as well as many production processes. Children become more proficient at tasks like tying shoes or riding bicycles as they gain more experience; teenagers gradually become better drivers; and students who spend more time thinking about end-of-chapter questions perform better on in-class exams.

A convenient classification scheme for learning curves is based on the percentage reduction in unit costs associated with each doubling of cumulative output. A 90-percent learning curve, for example, indicates that unit costs decline to 90 percent of their previous level with each doubling of cumulative output; an 80-percent learning curve indicates that each doubling of cumulative output causes unit costs to decline to 80 percent of their previous level; and so on.

Figure 10.4b presents the graphs of three representative learning curves. Each curve is convex to the origin, indicating that unit costs decline at a decreasing rate as cumulative output increases. This property is illustrated in Table 10.1:

TABLE 10.1 A HYPOTHETICAL 80-PERCENT LEARNING CURVE

Time Period	Cumulative Production	Unit Cost Time Line	
1	15	$100.0	
			–$20.00
2	30	80.00	
⋮			–$16.00
4	60	64.00	
⋮			–$12.80
8	120	51.20	
⋮			–$10.24
16	240	40.96	
⋮			–$8.19
32	480	32.77	
⋮			–$6.56
64	960	26.21	

With each successive time period or with each doubling of cumulative output, learning-by-doing results in successively smaller reductions in unit costs.

Profit-Maximizing Decisions and Learning Curves

Learning-by-doing can be incorporated into the marginal analysis that serves as the basis for profit-maximizing production and pricing decisions. Because learning-by-doing increases labor productivity over time, it causes the short-run average cost curve to shift down as cumulative output increases. Figure 10.5 illustrates the impact of learning-by-doing on the firm's short-run average cost curve. (Although it is not shown in the figure, learning-by-doing results in lower marginal production costs as well.)

Anything that reduces costs also creates an opportunity for the firm to increase profits. Figure 10.6 illustrates the opportunity to increase profitability when learning-by-doing characterizes the production process. For simplicity, we assume that the firm is a price-taker; it faces a horizontal (perfectly elastic) demand curve. Price (P) and marginal revenue (MR) are identical when the price-taker model is assumed. In period 1, the firm maximizes profits by equating marginal revenue with marginal cost; $q_{t=1}$ units of output is the profit-maximizing quantity. At this rate of output, the firm earns economic profits equal to the area of rectangle $aPbc$. If learning-by-doing does not characterize the production process, then the firm simply produces the same quantity in the second period if everything else remains the same.

Now assume that workers gain proficiency with experience. In particular, suppose that if the firm produces one more unit of output ($q_{t=1} + 1$) in period 1, learning-by-doing causes a downward shift of the cost curves in the second period (to $MC_{t=2}$ and $ATC_{t=2}$). How does producing this extra unit of output affect the firm's profits? The profit-maximizing quantity in period 2 now becomes $q_{t=2}$, and the firm earns a profit equal to the area of rectangle $ePfg$ in this period. However, the firm will earn profits equal to the area of rectangle $aPbc$ if it maintains output $q_{t=1}$ in both periods. The additional profit associated with the one-unit increase in period 1's output is the difference between

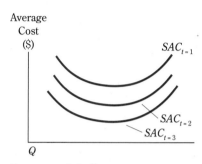

Average Cost ($)

FIGURE 10.5
Impact of Learning-by-Doing on Short-Run Average Costs

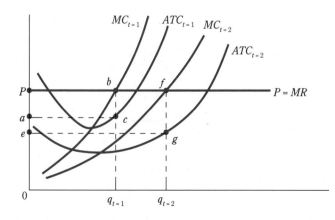

FIGURE 10.6
Learning-by-Doing in a Two-Period Model

these two figures, or $ePfg - aPbc$. Because this additional profit occurs one period in the future, its present value is equal to $(ePfg - aPbc)/(1 + r)$, where r is the discount rate or interest rate.

Although producing one more unit today increases future profits by $(ePfg - aPbc)$, it also causes current profits to fall. Profits decline because in order to take advantage of learning-by-doing in the first period, the firm produces beyond the point at which marginal revenue is equal to marginal cost. The loss associated with this increased output is simply the difference between marginal cost and marginal revenue at $q_{t=1} + 1$. Taking account of both factors, when the firm increases production in the first period by one unit beyond $q_{t=1}$, the net effect on profits (E) is

$$E = \left[\frac{ePfg - aPbc}{(1+r)}\right] - (MC - MR)q_{t=1+1}.$$

Hence, the firm should increase current production as long as E is positive (the discounted value of the increase in future profits more than offsets the loss of current profits caused by expanding output).

The two-period model can be easily extended to a multi-period setting. If the learning effect of producing $q_{t=1} + 1$ in the current period results in lower costs in each of n future periods, then if the firm expands production in the first period, the net effect on profits is

$$E = \sum_{t=1}^{n} \left[\frac{\Delta\pi_t}{\left(1+r\right)^t}\right] - (MC - MR)q_{t=1+1}.$$

The term $\Delta\pi_t$ represents the change in period t's profits resulting from the expected future cost reduction associated with producing one more unit of output today.

If E is positive, the firm's "true" marginal cost curve is lower than the unadjusted-for-learning marginal cost curve. As shown in Figure 10.7, learning-by-doing shifts the marginal cost curve downward from $MC_{t=1}$ to $(MC_{t=1} - E)$. The profit-maximizing output level in period 1 consequently increases from

FIGURE 10.7
Learning-by-Doing in an n-Period Model

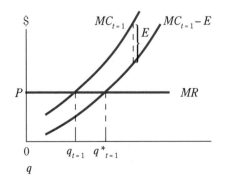

$q_{t=1}$ to $q^*_{t=1}$. If the firm is able to anticipate reductions in future costs associated with learning-by-doing, then it can increase total profits by increasing current production levels.

Strategic Implications of the Learning Curve

Firms can develop effective competitive strategies in a number of different areas, including pricing, product cost, product quality, and customer service. The learning curve provides an additional tool that forward-looking managers can use to their advantage. Although the example in the previous section assumed a perfectly elastic demand curve, this was done only to simplify the graphical presentation. The lessons in that section apply equally to firms with downward-sloping demand curves, and it is these firms that can use the concept of the learning curve to gain an advantage over their rivals.

Learning effects are relatively unique because they are dependent on cumulative output or, as we saw earlier in this section, on the actual passage of time. This is one aspect of production that conveys, by definition, an advantage to being the first firm to introduce a product. The firm can fully exploit this first-mover advantage by reducing price during the new product's introductory phase, increasing production and sales, and driving down its unit costs over time. This strategy can provide the incumbent firm with a head start over potential entrants that allows it to maintain a dominant position in the industry.

In this case, the firm is able to create a "barrier to entry" by reducing price and increasing its own sales. From the standpoint of the consumer, this type of entry barrier is fairly innocuous because entry from outside the industry is simply replaced by entry from within the industry. Price cuts that would be forced by the entry of new rivals are replaced by the established firm's own price reductions; increases in output that would occur over time as new firms enter are replaced by an expansion of sales by the incumbent firm.

ADVERTISING AND PROMOTION

The principles of economics are helpful in analyzing a wide range of business decisions. Advertising and promotional activities are among the most important strategies of firms which lend themselves to study using the economic tool of marginal analysis. Altering the level and mix of advertising and promotional effort may significantly affect the firm's profitability. Successful managers understand how such non-price competition affects consumers and, therefore, the demand for their goods or services.

In one view, advertising is a subject better addressed by psychologists and sociologists. Advertising is manipulative. Firms advertise to artificially differentiate their products. By convincing buyers that one firm's product is somehow better than the products of its rivals, advertising generates brand loyalty that reduces consumers' sensitivity to price changes and allows the seller to charge a higher price (and to earn higher profits) than otherwise.

If advertising is primarily persuasive rather than informative, it may make markets less competitive by deterring entry. Advertising may act as a barrier to the entry of new firms for two reasons. First, if advertising is subject to economies of scale, it may increase the capital requirements of newcomers by forcing them to enter with a larger plant size to attain minimum unit costs. Second, because the effects of advertising may be cumulative, a new firm may have to advertise more than an established firm to achieve the same level of sales. The new entrant may have to spend more on advertising per unit sold than established firms, causing its average production costs to be higher.

The economic theory of advertising, on the other hand, starts from the premise that advertising communicates essential information to consumers. Advertising brings the existence of products to the attention of prospective buyers, providing them with facts about price, quality, design and performance specifications, sellers' locations, and so on. By making consumers aware of available alternatives, advertising increases their sensitivity to price changes and enhances the competitiveness of markets.

The economic theory of advertising thus views advertising as an informative medium that reduces buyers' costs of searching for products that satisfy given tastes and preferences. The psychological view of advertising suggests that advertising creates or manipulates those tastes and preferences. In order to understand the economics of advertising, one must first understand the economics of information.

The Economics of Information

George Stigler introduced his pioneering work on the economics of information by stating that "information is a valuable resource: knowledge is power."[14] Prospective buyers have limited knowledge of the locations of alternative sellers, the prices they charge, and the attributes of the goods they sell. Because of buyer ignorance, prices vary widely at any moment of time even for a homogeneous good.

As long as consumers realize that prices are dispersed, it may be worth their while to acquire additional price information. The expected benefit of search is measured in terms of the probability of finding a lower price. This is true even if the good is heterogeneous or its quality is variable. In that case, engaging in search may help avoid a disappointing purchase decision. Other things being the same, the consumer's disappointment will tend to be greater the higher the price he or she pays.

The chief cost of search is the opportunity cost of the searcher's time. Time spent gathering price information is time that cannot be used to earn income or to enjoy leisure activities.

---

14 George Stigler, "The Economics of Information," *Journal of Political Economy* 64 (June 1961) p. 213.

As with all other economic decisions, the optimal amount of search is determined by equating marginal benefit with marginal cost. As long as the additional benefits of search exceed the additional costs, the consumer will rationally continue to gather information. But because the consumer's time is valuable, it will not pay to search indefinitely for lower prices. The marginal costs of search will eventually become equal to the marginal benefits and an optimal stopping point will be reached.

The economic theory of information suggests that the consumer will tend to search more when the dispersion of prices is great and when the good's price represents a large fraction of her budget. These conclusions follow because the potential savings (the expected marginal benefits) of search are greater. On the other hand, those consumers whose time has relatively high opportunity costs (e.g., people with high incomes and people who value leisure highly) will search less than consumers whose time is less valuable.

The economic theory of information also suggests that the pattern of search depends in part on the degree to which selling prices are correlated over time. Consumers will search more in any one period the more the information acquired in that period can be utilized in future periods. Because knowledge of prices is accumulated over time, experienced buyers will tend to pay lower prices than newcomers to the market.

In short, Stigler recognized that information about prices is valuable to buyers. It represents an important input into the consumer's purchase decisions because it reduces the full price he or she pays for a good or service. **Full price** is defined as the sum of the product's money price and the value (opportunity cost) of the time devoted to search.

Because price information is valuable to the consumer, suppliers have an incentive to supply it. They do so through various forms of advertising. By providing information to potential buyers about the available alternatives, advertising lowers the cost of search and thereby reduces the consumer's full price. Advertising does not eliminate price dispersion completely, because no combination of advertising media is capable of reaching all possible buyers within the relevant time period. The identities and locations of sellers change, experienced buyers exit the market (or they simply forget previously acquired information), and new customers enter. The supplier must produce a continuous stream of advertising messages to maintain a given stock of information in the minds of the relevant consumers.

If nothing else, advertising that conveys information about sellers' identities helps prospective buyers eliminate irrelevant alternatives. By increasing the stock of information consumers have in hand before beginning their search, advertising reduces the time they have to spend canvassing sellers in the search for lower prices. Advertising thus enables consumers to accumulate a given amount of price information at a lower cost. Contrary to conventional wisdom, advertising results in lower, not higher, prices. Advertising reduces the time cost component of a good's full price. Even advertising of the sort that many media critics condemn as pure puffery—advertising containing pleasant images and little or no hard data about price or performance

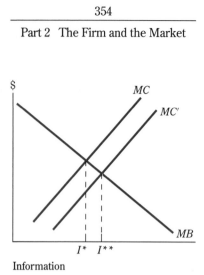

Information

FIGURE 10.8
Optimal Search

specifications—is valuable to consumers because it brings information about available alternatives to their attention.

Figure 10.8 summarizes these ideas. The schedule labeled *MB* represents the marginal benefits of search to an individual consumer. Its downward slope indicates that the benefits of search are subject to diminishing returns. For a given distribution of prices in a market, the probability that the consumer will contact a seller who charges a price that is lower than the prices charged by sellers approached earlier tends to fall with additional search. *MC* represents the consumer's marginal cost of search. This marginal cost schedule is upward sloping because additional time devoted to search requires the consumer to sacrifice increasingly valuable alternatives.

The optimal amount of price information for the consumer is determined by the marginal-benefit-equals-marginal-cost rule. The optimal information set is I^*. When marginal benefit is equal to marginal cost, the consumer should stop searching and purchase from the seller who quotes the lowest price among those sellers in information set I^*. Advertising expands the optimal amount of information by reducing the consumer's marginal cost of search. This reduction in marginal cost is represented by the downward shift of *MC* to *MC'*. With a lower marginal cost of search, the optimal information set expands to I^{**}. With more information in hand, the consumer can expect to pay a lower price than he or she would have paid with a more costly search.

The Content of Advertising Messages

Stigler's theory of information leads to an entirely different conclusion about the purposes and effects of advertising than has been drawn from the psychological or sociological models. Rather than viewing advertising as manipulating consumers' purchase decisions, Stigler's theory suggests that advertising reduces the full price of those purchases in a setting where information is incomplete and acquiring and communicating knowledge about selling prices is costly.

The seller's decision to advertise is subject to the same marginal calculus as the buyer's decision to acquire information. Advertising is economical up to the point where the marginal expected benefit, measured in terms of additional sales revenue, is equal to marginal cost. Because advertising is costly, it will never pay the seller to attempt to communicate information to all possible buyers just as it will never pay any one of those buyers to become fully informed.

Although price is obviously a critical input into consumers' purchase decisions, advertising messages convey a variety of information. Some advertising communicates explicit information about price; other messages contain the endorsements of celebrities or extol the product's image. The specific content of advertising messages depends in large part on the characteristics of the advertised product.

Search and Experience Goods

Phillip Nelson made an important contribution to the economic theory of advertising by pointing out the distinction between two broad categories of products.[15] He argued that advertising serves entirely different functions for each of these categories. In Nelson's model, consumers face the problem of searching over heterogeneous goods that differ in quality. He defines quality as the physical attributes of goods or the buyer's subjective evaluation of those attributes.

The product categories identified by Nelson are search goods and experience goods. **Search goods** are products whose quality consumers can judge at the time of purchase. For example, the style and fit of a dress can be evaluated in the store, its fabric content can be determined, its seams can be tested for strength, and so on. Because the buyer can determine the quality of a search good prior to purchase, sellers have little to gain from attempting to mislead potential customers. Thus, advertising messages for search goods will consist mainly of direct information describing specific product characteristics and prices. The quality claims made in advertisements for search goods will correspond to the quality consumers find when they inspect the products at the time of purchase. If not, the advertiser will lose sales when consumers' expectations are not fulfilled, and the investment in advertising will have been wasted.

In the case of **experience goods**, by contrast, consumers can determine quality only after use. The proof of the pudding is in the tasting. Caviar and coffee, for example, are experience goods because the buyer cannot judge product quality until after consuming them. Advertising claims about the quality of experience goods are of little value to the consumer because the claims cannot be verified prior to purchase. As a result, advertising messages for experience goods will contain indirect information that stresses the identity and reputation of the brand name. Any quality information will tend to be of a very general nature—"less filling!, tastes great!;" "new and improved;" and so on.

The inability of consumers to verify the advertising claims of the sellers of experience goods prior to purchase provides firms with an opportunity to misrepresent the quality of their products to first-time buyers. A profit can be made in the short run by selling a low-quality product at a high-quality price. But hit-and-run tactics of this sort will tend to be unprofitable in the long run as disappointed customers switch their purchases to competitors who do not make misleading advertising claims. Advertising claims for experience goods are also disciplined by the information supplied to the market by third parties who specialize in rating the performances of consumer goods. Furthermore, first-time buyers can avoid disappointing purchase decisions by consulting the experiences of friends and acquaintances.

---

15 Phillip Nelson, "Information and Consumer Behavior," *Journal of Political Economy* 78 (March/April 1970), pp. 311-29; and Phillip Nelson, "Advertising as Information," *Journal of Political Economy* 82 (July/August 1974), pp. 729-54.

As mentioned in Chapter 8, the fact that an experience good is advertised at all provides some assurance of quality to consumers. This is so not because consumers are misled by pleasant images or celebrity endorsements, but because an advertising campaign represents a nonsalvageable investment in the seller's brand name capital. A firm's expenditures on advertising and promotion are an implicit guarantee that it will not cheat consumers by failing to deliver the implied quality because cheating will result in the forfeiture of this investment. If it does cheat, the firm will sacrifice future business and lose the value of the brand name capital built up through advertising. In this sense, an advertising campaign is equivalent to posting a forfeitable performance bond that provides a signal of quality to potential buyers.[16]

Credence Goods

A firm's investments in brand name capital are even more critical in the case of credence goods, a subset of Nelson's experience goods category.[17] **Credence goods** are goods whose quality is difficult to evaluate both before and after purchase. Automobile repairs are a relevant example. Most consumers rationally lack the specialized knowledge necessary to determine whether the work suggested by a mechanic is in fact required. Was a complete tune-up needed or would replacing the fuel filter have been enough to stop the car from backfiring? Consumers are likewise often incapable of judging the quality characteristics of medical, legal, and investment advice. Low-quality professional services may not come to light for weeks or months after purchase.

Because the cost of determining the quality of a credence good before and after purchase is high, incentives exist for suppliers to use advertising to transmit false information to consumers. A profit can be made by selling a low-quality credence good at a high-quality price. Investments in brand name capital cannot completely solve the quality assurance problem if buyers cannot determine quality after the fact. It is nevertheless true that investments in brand name capital ("Mr. Goodwrench") help limit hit-and-run tactics by new entrants and by firms without established reputations who must charge lower prices for low-quality products.

The Economics of Advertising

The advertising-as-information model suggests that the main purpose of advertising is to increase the demand for the firm's product by reducing consumers' costs of search. The firm must provide a continuous stream of advertising messages to achieve that goal because consumers' knowledge is

---

16 Benjamin Klein and Keith Leffler, "The Role of Market Forces in Assuring Contractual Performance," *Journal of Political Economy* 89 (August 1981), pp. 615-41.
17 Michael R. Darby and Edi Karni, "Free Competition and the Optimal Amount of Fraud," *Journal of Law and Economics* 16 (April 1973), pp. 67-88.

Pricing New Products to Signal Quality

Consumers initially possess limited information about the quality of new products. The physical characteristics of the product and the seller's advertising and promotional activities provide some information about product quality. In addition, however, because it generally costs more to produce a high-quality product than a low-quality product, price differentials among competing products may provide consumers with information about differences in product quality. The idea that higher price implies higher quality does not imply that consumers know the precise relationship between price differentials and quality differentials or that the relationship is consistent across all products. The signaling model requires only that consumers can associate price and quality.[a]

Kyle Bagwell and Michael Riordan have modeled the firm's pricing decision for products of uncertain quality.[b] They begin with the premise that uninformed consumers rationally infer high quality from a high price. Why are high prices an efficient means of signaling product quality? What prevents low-cost, low-quality producers from setting high prices that mislead uninformed consumers into believing that their products are of high quality? The answer to these questions is based on the reactions of consumers to inappropriate price signals. Low-cost, low-quality producers that introduce products at high prices will suffer substantial sales losses over time as consumers become better informed. If consumers recognize this constraint on false price signals, then uninformed consumers will rationally infer higher quality from a higher price.

Bagwell and Riordan argue that the most efficient way of transmitting information about a new, high-quality product is to initially set a "high price" (one that is higher than the profit-maximizing price would be if perfect information is assumed), and then gradually reduce the product's selling price over time. That is, part of a new product's price acts as a quality signal for uninformed consumers. As consumers subsequently acquire more information about product quality, the value of the signaling component of price declines and the firm should therefore reduce its price over time.

Bagwell and Riordan's theory of price signaling predicts a declining time trend in the prices of high-quality products, price differentials among competing brands, and a positive correlation between price and quality. David Curry and Peter Riesz have tested these predictions with price and quality data from *Consumer Reports*.[c] Their data set consisted of a sample of 62 products and 4,000 individual brands. They tested the following three hypotheses with these data:

H_1: The average price of all brands of a specific product line declines over time. (Price is measured in constant dollars.)

H_2: The variability of prices across different brands decreases over time.

H_3: Price and product quality become more positively related to one another over time.

In testing the first of these hypotheses, Curry and Riesz regressed the mean price for each of the 62 products in their sample on a linear time trend and found that 85 percent of the estimated coefficients were negative. They also performed a sign test to determine whether positive and negative coefficients for the linear trend were equally likely; they rejected the null

a Firms selling high-quality products may also have an incentive to advertise their products more heavily than the suppliers of low-quality products. The reasons why more heavily advertised brands tend to be of higher quality and consumers can therefore rely on advertising as a quality signal are discussed in James M. Ferguson, "Comment," *Journal of Law and Economics* 19 (August 1976), p. 342.

b Kyle Bagwell and Michael H. Riordan, "High and Declining Prices Signal Product Quality," *American Economic Review* 81 (March 1991), pp. 224-39.

c David J. Curry and Peter C. Riesz, "Prices and Price/Quality Relationships: A Longitudinal Analysis," *Journal of Marketing* 52 (January 1988), pp. 36-51.

hypothesis. In testing H$_2$, Curry and Riesz found that the variability of prices within a product line fell over time in 79 percent of the sample. A sign test again rejected the null hypothesis that positive and negative coefficients were equally likely. Finally, Curry and Riesz found that price and product quality were positively related to one another over time in only 35 percent of the product lines included in their sample. They were not able to reject the null hypothesis associated with H$_3$. The evidence suggested that the numerical value of the rank correlation between price and quality generally declines over time.

In sum, Curry and Riesz's results support two of the predictions of the price signaling model developed by Bagwell and Riordan. New products include a price premium that serves as a signal of quality. As consumers subsequently learn more about the quality differentials of products available in the market, the price premium of the high-quality brands tends to fall. This sequence of events and the logic behind it are consistent with the null hypotheses H$_1$ and H$_2$; they are inconsistent with the null hypothesis H$_3$.

limited and the identities of buyers and sellers change. People who purchase a product today may not demand it next period. Tastes and preferences may change over time, rivals may introduce new products, and consumers may simply forget. Because of turnover in the market, firms must advertise in every period to inform prospective buyers about the relative merits of their goods or services.

Optimal Advertising

Viewed in this way, advertising responds to consumers' demands for information that reduces the full prices of the products they wish to purchase. By lowering the search cost component of full price, advertising increases the quantities consumers are willing and able to buy at given money prices. Figure 10.9 illustrates the impact of advertising on demand. Without advertising, the firm's demand schedule is D_1 and consumers purchase q_1 units at a money price of P dollars per unit. Advertising increases demand to D_2. Consumers are now willing and able to buy q_2 units at money price P.

The more the firm advertises, the more the demand for its product increases. Eventually, however, the marginal impact of advertising declines. The law of diminishing marginal returns causes increases in demand to become progressively smaller as additional advertising is undertaken. The diminishing marginal returns to advertising are illustrated in Figure 10.9 by the fact that an equal increase in advertising expenditures shifts the demand curve by successively smaller amounts. The increase in demand from D_2 to D_3 is less than the increase from D_1 to D_2.

In addition to increasing demand, advertising affects the elasticity of demand for the firm's good or service. By differentiating its product from competing products, the firm's own advertising fosters brand loyalty and therefore tends to make consumers less sensitive to subsequent price changes. On the other hand, advertising by the sellers of competing products increases consumers' awareness of available alternatives and therefore tends to make them more sensitive to subsequent price changes. The overall

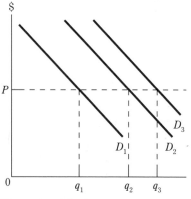

FIGURE 10.9

The Effects of Advertising on Demand

impact of advertising on the elasticity of any one seller's demand schedule depends on which of these effects dominates.

In a market setting where information is imperfect and search is costly, the optimal quantity of advertising is determined by the marginal-benefit-equals-marginal-cost rule. From the seller's point of view, marginal benefit is measured in terms of the additional sales revenue expected to be generated by a particular advertising message. This additional sales revenue, in turn, depends on the number of prospective buyers the advertising message reaches, the ad's effectiveness in conveying information to consumers, and so on.

As discussed above, the marginal impact of advertising on sales tends to decline as advertising expenditures increase. As an ad appears more often or in more places, it reaches progressively fewer new buyers. The declining marginal benefit of advertising is illustrated in Figure 10.10 by the down-ward-sloping schedule MB_A. Alternatively, the marginal benefit of advertising *at a given selling price* is equal to the difference between price and marginal production cost; that is, $MB_A = P - MC$.[18] Because the firm's marginal costs of production rise as the firm's advertising expenditures increase and it sells more units of output, it follows that the marginal benefits of advertising decline.

The marginal cost of advertising, MC_A, rises with additional advertising. This is because the firm must sacrifice increasingly valuable alternative investment opportunities as it spends more resources on advertising and promotion. Put differently, diminishing marginal returns to advertising imply increasing marginal costs.[19]

It is profitable for the firm to continue to expand its advertising and pro-motional activities as long as marginal benefit exceeds marginal cost. The optimal quantity of advertising occurs at the point where the last dollar spent on advertising yields one dollar in additional benefit. Figure 10.10 depicts this equilibrium condition. The profit-maximizing quantity of advertising is A^* where the marginal benefit of advertising $(P - MC)$ is equal to the marginal cost of advertising (MC_A).

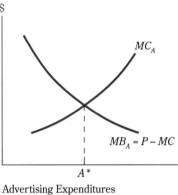

Advertising Expenditures

FIGURE 10.10
Optimal Advertising

18 Let the firm's profit function be $\pi = PQ(A) - C[Q(A)] - P_A A$, where P is the firm's selling price, $Q(A)$ is the quantity of output sold, C is total production cost, P_A is the price per unit of advertising, and A is the number of units of advertising the firm purchases. The notation $Q(A)$ indicates that the firm's sales depend on advertising intensity. The profit-maximizing quantity of advertising is found by partially differentiating the profit function with respect to A. Taking this derivative yields $\partial\pi/\partial A = P(\partial Q/\partial A) - (\partial C/\partial Q)(\partial Q/\partial A) - P_A$. The first term on the right-hand side of this expression, $P(\partial Q/\partial A)$, is the increase in total revenue associated with a one unit increase in advertising, holding selling price constant. The second term, $(\partial C/\partial Q)(\partial Q/\partial A)$, is the additional cost of producing the extra units of output sold when advertising is increased by one unit, and P_A is the price paid by the firm to purchase a unit of advertising. Setting this derivative equal to zero and rearranging yields the marginal-benefit-equals-marginal-cost rule: $P - \partial C/\partial Q = P_A/(\partial Q/\partial A)$.

19 As derived in the previous footnote, the marginal cost of advertising is $P_A/(\partial Q/\partial A)$. Because the marginal impact of advertising on sales declines as additional advertising is undertaken, the denominator of this expression becomes progressively smaller as A increases. Holding the unit price of advertising constant, it follows that $P_A/(\partial Q/\partial A)$ rises as more advertising is purchased.

The foregoing discussion suggests that advertising and promotional activities are treated like any other input in the firm's production function. Profit-maximizing firms advertise to increase their sales and, in doing so, follow the same marginal-benefit-equals-marginal-cost rule that determines the optimal quantities of all other productive resources.

One complication not addressed here is that advertising and promotional activities typically have cumulative effects that carry over to future periods. Advertising during this period not only increases sales in this period, but in subsequent periods as well. A great deal of controversy exists among economists about the proper method of depreciating the future streams of benefits associated with advertising because the patterns of these benefits are often uncertain at the time firms make their investments in advertising. The stream of future benefits may also vary from advertising campaign to advertising campaign. Hence, a complete analysis of the firm's optimal advertising decision requires solving a capital budgeting problem that balances the present value of expected marginal benefits and costs.[20]

The Optimal Mix of Advertising Media

In the above discussion, we assume each unit of advertising to be homogeneous. While this assumption is helpful in determining the optimal quantity of one type of advertising, managers often face the problem of allocating a given advertising and promotional budget across a number of different advertising media. Package inserts, in-store displays, radio and television commercials, billboard and newspaper ads, and so on represent alternative methods of conveying information to consumers. Firms use these various advertising media to attract the attention of prospective buyers because no one of them is capable of reaching all members of the intended audience at any one time.

Indeed, much of the modern discipline of marketing is devoted to studying techniques for identifying and targeting ads toward specialized segments of the consumer population. Location, time of day, reading and television viewing habits, age, income, and other demographic characteristics all enter into the selection of the types and mix of advertising media that are consistent with the objective of profit maximization.

The determination of the optimal advertising mix is a straightforward application of the equi-marginal principle.[21] Consider a firm that can advertise in a weekly news magazine or on television. Advertising in each medium exhibits diminishing marginal returns. That is, the more units of advertising the firm purchases in any one medium, the smaller the expected increase in sales. For purposes of simplicity, assume further that the effectiveness of advertising in one medium is independent of the other. In other words,

---

20 See, for example, Thomas R. Stauffer, "The Measurement of Corporate Rates of Return: A Generalized Formulation," *Bell Journal of Economics* 2 (August 1971), pp. 434-69.
21 See Chapter 9 for other applications of this principle.

magazine and television ads reach different segments of the targeted consumer population.

Let MB_M represent the marginal benefit per dollar spent on magazine ads. That is, $MB_M = (P - MC)/P_M$, where P is the price of the firm's product, MC is the cost of producing an additional unit of output, and P_M is the unit price of magazine advertisements. Similarly, if P_{TV} is the unit price of television ads, the marginal benefit per dollar spent on that medium is $MB_{TV} = (P - MC)/P_{TV}$. The equi-marginal principle states that the optimal advertising mix is determined by allocating the firm's advertising budget in such a way that the marginal benefit of the last dollar spent is the same across advertising media. If MB_M is not equal to MB_{TV}, the firm can increase its profits without increasing its total advertising expenditures by reallocating its advertising budget toward the medium in which expected marginal benefits are higher.

For example, if $MB_M < MB_{TV}$, the firm's profits will increase by $(MB_{TV} - MB_M)$ if \$1 of its advertising budget shifts from magazine to television advertising. As this reallocation process continues, MB_{TV} declines and MB_M increases. It stops when profits no longer increase, that is, when $MB_{TV} = MB_M$. At that point, the marginal benefit per dollar spent on magazine ads is equal to the marginal benefit per dollar spent on television commercials. This budget allocation corresponds to the optimal (profit-maximizing) advertising mix.

Ads placed in one medium may reinforce or complement the effectiveness of advertising in other media. Interrelationships among the effectiveness characteristics of various advertising media obviously complicate the analysis, but the rule for determining the optimal advertising mix remains the same. The allocation of advertising dollars is optimal when the marginal benefit per dollar spent is equal across advertising media.

Table 10.2 presents some information on the advertising mixes chosen by the firms in selected consumer goods industries. While all of these industries devote the largest share of their advertising budgets to television, the variation in the distribution of expenditures across media is quite large. For example, retailers as a group spend more than half of their advertising budgets on newspaper ads, while firms in the sporting goods and toy category devote little attention to that medium. Table 10.2 reveals the diversity in the types of advertising messages businesses use to attract the attention of consumers. In most cases, all available advertising media are exploited to some degree to promote the industry's products.

The Effects of Advertising

There are two contradictory views about the purposes and effects of advertising. One view suggests that by creating brand loyalty and by erecting barriers to entry, advertising makes markets less competitive and advertisers more profitable. The other view suggests that by responding to consumers' demands for information about available alternatives, advertising lowers barriers to entry and makes markets more competitive.

TABLE 10.2 TOTAL U.S. ADVERTISING SPENDING IN SELECTED CONSUMER GOODS INDUSTRIES IN 1990 ($1,000)

ADVERTISING MEDIUM	RETAIL	AUTOMOTIVE	FOOD	ENTERTAINMENT	SNACKS AND SOFT DRINKS	BEER AND WINE	SPORTING GOODS AND TOYS
Total Ad Spending	$6,494.2	$5,700.7	$3,874.0	$3,063.6	$1,231.0	$751.5	$635.3
Magazine	249.1	901.2	449.3	44.4	64.5	45.5	126.7
Sun. Magazine	119.7	25.5	34.7	3.0	3.5	3.5	1.2
Newspaper	3,823.1	809.2	45.4	611.3	22.4	10.3	6.8
Outdoor	68.9	53.0	11.0	47.2	10.1	20.0	.2
Network TV	356.0	1,790.0	1,663.5	875.1	452.1	302.1	140.4
Spot TV	1,499.1	1,664.8	1,025.2	1,170.8	382.8	210.4	233.4
Syndicated TV	20.6	115.7	351.7	147.2	168.4	45.2	82.8
Cable TV	38.7	114.1	124.7	62.3	52.8	37.0	40.2
Network Radio	101.5	106.7	75.1	14.8	29.4	5.0	.6
Spot Radio	217.6	120.5	93.4	87.5	45.1	72.4	2.9

Source: *Advertising Age*, 6 January 1992.

Economists have conducted a great deal of research to test these two hypotheses empirically.[22] These studies have examined the links between advertising and profits, between advertising and barriers to entry, and between advertising and prices.

Advertising and Profitability. One of the first major studies of the relationship between advertising intensity and profitability was published in 1967 by William Comanor and Thomas Wilson.[23] They sought to explain the variation in profit rates (after-tax returns on equity) across a sample of 41 consumer goods industries. The explanatory variables included demand growth, book value of assets, and the ratio of advertising expenditures to sales. Comanor and Wilson found that an average profit rate of 12 percent was earned by industries that advertised heavily, compared with an overall average profit rate of 8 percent across all industries. They concluded that this significant difference in profitability was due to entry barriers created and maintained by advertising.

Comanor and Wilson's study contains several flaws, however. Most important, they treated advertising as a current expense, making no attempt to account for the fact that advertising and promotional activities represent investments in brand name capital in much the same way that purchases of plant and equipment represent investments in physical capital. Both types of investment generate returns beyond the period in which expenses are incurred and both should therefore be capitalized and depreciated over their expected useful lives. Later researchers made such adjustments and considered

22 A survey of this literature is contained in Robert B. Ekelund, Jr. and David S. Saurman, *Advertising and the Market Process: A Modern Economic View* (San Francisco: Pacific Research Institute for Public Policy, 1988).
23 William S. Comanor and Thomas A. Wilson, "Advertising, Market Structure, and Performance," *Review of Economics and Statistics* 49 (November 1967), pp. 423-40.

the significant differences across industries in the way that current advertising affects sales in future periods. Their results suggest that the positive relationship between advertising intensity and profitability identified by Comanor and Wilson disappears when these adjustments are made.[24]

Advertising and Barriers to Entry. A more fundamental issue is whether advertising, either because it creates brand loyalty among buyers or because it is characterized by significant economies of scale, actually impedes the entry of new firms and thus raises the prices and profits of established sellers. In an important study, Jean Lambin found a statistically significant degree of inertia (brand loyalty) among the consumers of the products in his sample, which included soft drinks, electric shavers, hair spray, gasoline, laundry detergents, and cigarettes.[25] The critical question, of course, is whether advertising *causes* such loyalty. Lambin examined this issue by relating brand loyalty to three measures of advertising intensity.

He found that a firm's own advertising has a measurable influence on its sales and market share. On average, across all of the products and brands in his sample, a 10 percent increase in advertising led to a 1 percent increase in the advertiser's market share. By reinforcing the identities of brand names in the minds of existing customers and by attracting the attention of new buyers, advertising seems to increase the demand for a firm's product in the way predicted by economic theory. However, Lambin also found that the advertising expenditures of rivals had a larger, *negative* effect on any one firm's sales. On average, a 10 percent increase in the advertising expenditures of the sellers of rival products reduced a given brand's market share by more than 1.5 percent. Lambin also reported evidence suggesting that the more intensely all the firms in an industry advertise, the less stable are the market shares of the individual industry members.

Hence, Lambin's findings are consistent with the idea that when industry advertising increases, consumers receive information about a variety of available brands from a number of different sources. This increased advertising intensity causes some consumers to continue to purchase the same brand, perhaps because advertising reduces the cost to them of recalling the identities of desirable products or continues to provide them with assurance of quality. But increased industry advertising also causes other consumers to switch their purchases to rival sellers. Indeed, Lambin's results suggest that the switching effect tends to dominate the inertia effect, so that brand loyalty declines overall. The basic conclusion seems to be that firms may not be able to increase their market shares through advertising, given that rivals are free to advertise.

Even if advertising does not create strong brand loyalties among consumers, advertising may still erect barriers to entry if it exhibits significant economies of scale. If new entrants must advertise more intensely than existing

---

24 See, for example, Robert Ayanian, "Advertising and Rate of Return," *Journal of Law and Economics* 18 (October 1975), pp. 479-506.

25 Jean J. Lambin, *Advertising, Competition, and Market Conduct* (Amsterdam: North-Holland, 1976).

firms or if advertising expenditures per unit sold decline with increases in output, then newcomers may face a cost disadvantage relative to established sellers. However, Lambin's findings point to the conclusion that advertising expenditures are subject to diminishing, not increasing, returns to scale. Similar results have been reported by other researchers.[26] There also seems to be little empirical support for the notion that large-scale advertisers reach potential customers at a lower cost than their smaller rivals.[27]

On the other hand, a firm's investments in brand name capital differ in one important way from its investments in physical capital.[28] If entry is unsuccessful, physical capital like buildings and equipment can be resold to recover at least part of the costs of entry. By contrast, none of the information or goodwill generated by the unsuccessful entrant's advertising and promotional activities can be recouped in this way. Hence, because of the inherent riskiness of marketing a new product, potential entrants to an industry face a cost disadvantage relative to established firms, whose investments in brand name capital are sunk and consequently do not influence their pricing and output decisions. The unique, nonsalvageable characteristics of start-up advertising expenditures may therefore erect entry barriers in the sense that the cost of doing business is higher for newcomers than for incumbents, at least until (and if) the new brand becomes established.

Such a disadvantage has been documented in the market for prescription drugs.[29] In 1958, Merck & Company introduced Diuril®, a patented diuretic that represented a major breakthrough in the treatment of fluid retention. Within two years, ten other firms were marketing therapeutically equivalent products, having successfully "invented around" Merck's patent. But despite entry and the introduction of improved substitutes by its competitors, Merck still held a 33 percent market share in 1971. Merck maintained its leadership position even though it spent much less than its rivals on advertising and promotion and charged substantially higher prices. The implication of this story is that the company which is the pioneer in successfully marketing a new product may enjoy "first-mover" advantages that are difficult for later entrants to overcome.

Other researchers have argued that advertising lowers the risk of entry by making information about the existence of new products available to consumers. In fact, some evidence suggests that the rate of new entry tends to

26 James M. Ferguson, *Advertising and Competition: Theory, Measurement, Fact* (Cambridge, MA: Ballinger, 1975) and Julian L. Simon, "Are There Economies of Scale in Advertising?," *Journal of Advertising Research* 5 (April 1969), pp. 15-20.

27 David M. Blank, "Television Advertising: The Great Discount Illusion, or Tonypandy Revisited," *Journal of Business* 41 (January 1968), pp. 10-38; and John L. Peterman, "The Clorox Case and the Television Rate Structures," *Journal of Law and Economics* 11 (October 1978), pp. 321-422.

28 Ioannis N. Kessides, "Advertising, Sunk Costs, and Barriers to Entry," *Review of Economics and Statistics* 68 (February 1986), pp. 84-95.

29 Ronald S. Bond and David F. Lean, *Sales, Promotion, and Product Differentiation in Two Prescription Drug Markets* (Washington, D. C. : Federal Trade Commission, 1977).

be higher in industries in which advertising plays a major role than in industries where advertising is less intense.[30]

Advertising and Prices. Although the link between advertising and entry is controversial, there is at least one area in which the impact of advertising seems to be well-established: Consumers pay higher prices when advertising is restricted. In a famous paper on this topic, Lee Benham compared the prices of eyeglasses in states that regulated advertising by optometrists in 1963 to states where no such regulations were in place.[31] He found that the average price of a pair of eyeglasses was $37.48 in states that banned advertising by optometrists, but only $17.98 in states which did not restrict advertising. Benham also reported that the benefits of advertising did not seem to depend on the dissemination of *price* information to consumers. The average price of a pair of eyeglasses was only slightly higher in states that allowed optometrists to advertise but prohibited the inclusion of prices in their ads than the prices charged in states that imposed no advertising restrictions.

Other studies have reproduced this finding in a variety of markets. Increased amounts of advertising (or fewer restrictions on the content of advertising messages) have been shown to be associated with lower prices for toys, gasoline, contact lenses, prescription drugs, legal services, and beer. In addition, the weight of the empirical evidence points to the conclusion that the lower prices associated with fewer restrictions on advertising are not accompanied by lower product quality.

The evidence that restrictions on advertising result in higher prices for consumers casts doubt on the idea that advertising creates insurmountable brand loyalties and barriers to entry. Still, the theory and evidence on advertising remain unsettled and the conclusions remain controversial. Does advertising make it easier for firms to enter markets by enabling them to inform consumers about the availability of new products or does it instead create loyalties to existing products that place new entrants at a disadvantage? Perhaps both points of view are correct: considered in isolation, one firm's advertising and promotional activities tend to increase the demand for its product and make that demand less elastic. Given that all firms are free to advertise, however, advertising may reduce the demand for the product of any one seller and make that demand more elastic.

SUMMARY

This chapter has raised some important strategic managerial decision-making issues and has addressed four interrelated topics. The first of these considers

KEY TERMS
pure monopoly
oligopoly
monopolistic competition
price-taker model
barriers to entry

---

30 Kessides, "Advertising, Sunk Costs, and Barriers to Entry."
31 Lee Benham, "The Effect of Advertising on the Price of Eyeglasses," *Journal of Law and Economics* 15 (October 1972), pp. 337-52.

the impact of entry on the firm's pricing and output choices. While the entry of new competitors always forces the established firm to reduce price, whether entry leads to a reduction or to an expansion of the established firm's output depends on how product differentiation is affected.

The chapter then asked whether strategies are available to the established firm that enable it to actively deter or delay the entry of new competitors. The discussion under this heading included the limit-entry pricing model and strategies for raising rivals' costs.

Third, learning-by-doing characterizes the production process when accumulated experience leads to increased productivity and lower unit costs. When the learning curve is important, the firm may rationally decide to expand current output beyond the simple one-period, profit-maximizing quantity to more quickly take advantage of the cost savings associated with accumulated production experience. Current profits are sacrificed in return for higher future profits.

Fourth, advertising provides consumers with information about the price and quality attributes of the advertised product. This information is valuable to consumers to the extent that it lowers their costs of search and thereby reduces the full prices of the products they wish to buy. The content of advertising messages is a function of whether the product being advertised is a search good, an experience good, or a credence good. In any of these cases, however, one firm's advertising tends to increase the demand for its product and make that demand less elastic. Advertising by rival sellers tends to reduce the demand for any one firm's product and make that demand more elastic.

QUESTIONS

10.1 George Stigler defined a barrier to entry "as a cost of producing (at some or every rate of output) which must be borne by a firm which seeks to enter an industry but is not borne by firms already in the industry." Determine whether each of the following factors constitutes a barrier to entry based on this definition. Explain your reasoning in each case.
   a. Economies of scale.
   b. A minimum efficient plant size that accounts for a substantial fraction of total industry sales.
   c. A widely known brand name or trademark.
   d. Access to low-cost supplies of an essential input.
   e. A patent.
   f. Learning-by-doing.

10.2 First-mover advantages are the benefits enjoyed by the firm that first introduces a new product that turns out to be successful. List and explain at least three specific first-mover advantages. Can you think of any disadvantages of being first?

10.3 The labor economics literature makes a distinction between *specific* human capital, defined as the stock of skills and abilities which enhance worker productivity in a particular firm (and that firm only), and *general* human capital, defined as the stock of skills and abilities which enhance the productivities of workers no matter where they are employed. Reading ability is an example of general human capital; the offensive scheme and play calling signals of the New Orleans Saints is an example of the firm-specific human capital that must be acquired by the team's rookie quarterback. Investments in worker training which add to the stock of either firm-specific or general human capital translate in a learning-by-doing fashion into increased proficiency and lower unit production costs. Explain why the firm would be willing to fully pay for training that enhances specific human capital, but would require the worker to pay at least part of the cost (in the form of lower wages, perhaps) of training that enhances general human capital.

10.4 In 1972, the Federal Trade Commission issued an antitrust complaint against Kellogg, General Mills, and General Foods, the leading U.S. producers of ready-to-eat breakfast cereals. Among other things, the companies were accused of engaging in "brand proliferation" to deter the entry of new rivals. In other words, the FTC charged the established firms with continually introducing new cereal brands to preempt access to scarce grocery store shelf space, thereby strategically limiting the market opportunities of potential competitors. Evaluate the FTC's charge.

10.5 From time to time, firms have been accused of introducing "fighting brands"— generic versions of their products which they sell at prices below cost in order to protect the market shares of their principal brands against the forces of new entry. Evaluate the economic logic of this strategy for deterring entry.

10.6 In an open price-searcher market, an established firm can respond to entry either by reducing output or by increasing it. What determines which of these responses the firm will adopt?

10.7 Some products are said to "sell themselves." Other things being the same, would a profit-maximizing firm advertise more or less when its product sells itself than when it does not?

10.8 Why are the ads for search goods more likely to contain specific information about product price than the ads for experience goods?

PROBLEMS

10.1 Bob Dorsey, founder and president of NeuralNet, Inc., has developed a proto-type high-speed parallel processor that represents a major step forward in computing technology. Based on data gathered from users of existing supercomputers, the following demand and cost information has been estimated for the new neural network machine:

$$P = \$54 - \$1.5Q$$
$$TC = \$200 + \$6Q + \$.5Q^2.$$

P is price, TC is total production cost, and Q is the number of machines produced and sold per year. (Prices and costs are measured in millions of dollars.)

a. Calculate NeuralNet's output, price, and economic profits if no other firms are expected to enter the industry.

b. Calculate the range of possible price-output combinations if NeuralNet's profits are subsequently eliminated by entry. Assume that the cost function remains unchanged and that one potential long-run equilibrium results from a parallel shift in the demand schedule while in the other equilibrium the demand schedule becomes perfectly elastic.

10.2 Group Decision Support Systems, Inc. (GDSS), markets computer software that is capable of real-time Spanish-English translations. The software is used to help the managers of multinational firms overcome language barriers when they meet to coordinate their divisional production plans. GDSS has estimated the following demand and cost schedules for its product:

$$P = \$150 - \$.1Q$$
$$TC = \$3,000 + \$50Q + .15Q^2.$$

P is price, *Q* is quantity, and *TC* is the firm's total production cost.

a. Calculate GDSS's output, price, and economic profits if no other firms are expected to enter the industry.

b. Calculate the range of possible price-output combinations if GDSS's profits are subsequently eliminated by entry. Assume that the cost function remains unchanged and that one potential long-run equilibrium results from a parallel shift in the demand schedule while in the other equilibrium the demand schedule becomes perfectly elastic.

c. In light of the calculations in (b), is entry likely to occur? Why or why not?

The Mathematics of Entry's Impact on Price and Quantity

The following two equations characterize the pre-entry demand and cost conditions for the Johnson Company's all-weather coat:

$$P = \$100 - \$.2Q \text{ and}$$
$$STC = \$800 + \$12Q + \$.02Q^2.$$

P is the price of all-weather coats, Q is quantity (measured in thousands), and STC is short-run total production cost.

Before entry occurs, the firm earns a yearly economic profit of $8,000,000 by producing 200,000 coats and selling them at a price of $60 each.[32] Now assume that new firms enter the industry such that economic profits fall to zero while the slope of the demand curve remains the same. The latter assumption is made to hold constant the extent to which the Johnson Company's product is differentiated in the minds of consumers from the products supplied by the new entrants. If the demand curve's slope remains unchanged, product differentiation is unaffected by entry. The following four steps explain the influence of entry on price and output.

Step 1. Entry causes a leftward, parallel shift in the demand curve. The post-entry demand curve has the same slope as the pre-entry demand curve. Because the slope of the pre-entry demand curve, $P = \$100 - \$.2Q$, is $-.2$, the slope of the post-entry demand curve is also equal to $-.2$.

Step 2. The assumption that economic profits are driven to zero by entry implies that the post-entry demand curve is tangent to the short-run average cost curve at the new equilibrium. The slope of the demand curve and the slope of the short-run average cost curve are equal to each other at this point of tangency. The slope of the demand curve is $-.2$. The slope of the short-run average total cost curve is determined by, first, finding the equation for short-run average cost (SAC) from short-run total cost. In other words, if

$$STC = \$800 + \$12Q + \$.02Q^2,$$

32 To review the steps followed in determining the profit-maximizing quantity and price, refer to the application at the beginning of this chapter or to Chapter 5's appendix.

then

$$SAC = \frac{STC}{Q} = \$800Q^{-1} + \$12 + \$.02Q.$$

The slope of short-run average cost is the derivative of this equation with respect to quantity, or

$$\frac{d(SAC)}{dQ} = -\$800Q^{-2} + \$.02.$$

Step 3. The quantity at which the slopes of the post-entry demand curve and the short-run average cost curve are equal is determined by solving

$$-.2 = -800Q^{-2} + .02$$

for Q. This exercise yields $Q = 60$, or 60,000 all-weather coats.

Step 4. Although the slope of the post-entry demand curve is known, its intercept is not. Hence, the profit-maximizing price corresponding to a quantity of 60,000 coats cannot be calculated from the unknown equation for the demand curve. But price can be determined from the short-run average cost equation. The reason is that when economic profits are zero, average revenue (or price) is equal to average total cost. The price corresponding to sales of 60,000 coats is therefore:

$$P = SAC = \$800(60)^{-1} + \$12 + \$.02(60)$$
$$= \$13.33 + \$12 + \$1.20$$
$$= \$26.53.$$

A different price-quantity solution emerges when entry affects the slope of the firm's demand curve as well as shifting it to the left. At the extreme, the post-entry demand curve becomes perfectly elastic (horizontal). Price and quantity are calculated by the following two steps in this case.

Step 1. Because entry drives economic profits to zero, price is again equal to average total cost. If the post-entry demand curve is perfectly elastic, then price and average total cost are equal to one another at the minimum of average total cost. The equation for short-run average total cost is

$$SAC = \$800Q^{-1} + \$12 + \$.02Q.$$

Short-run average cost is at a minimum at the point where its slope is equal to zero. The quantity corresponding to this minimum point is found by taking the first derivative of SAC,

$$\frac{d(SAC)}{dQ} = -\$800Q^{-2} + \$.02 = 0,$$

and solving for Q. This calculation yields $Q = 200$, or 200,000 units.

Step 2. Price is again found by following step 4 above. Substituting $Q = 200$ into the equation for short-run average total cost,

$$P = SAC = \$800(200)^{-1} + \$12 + \$.02(200),$$

yields an optimal price of $20 per coat.

In conclusion, if entry causes economic profits to fall to zero, the Johnson Company can expect to sell between 60,000 and 200,000 all-weather coats per year and to charge a price somewhere in the range of $26.53 and $20 per unit.

CHAPTER

11

Managing Quality

OVERVIEW

It may come as a shock to learn that only 20 or 30 years ago, "Made in Japan" was synonymous with cheap, low-quality products. The ability of Japanese firms to compete successfully on an international scale depended critically on overcoming this image. They did so with a vengeance. A seemingly single-minded emphasis on reducing manufacturing defects and enhancing reliability enabled Japanese automobile and electronics companies to completely reverse consumers' perceptions and to ultimately set the world standard for product quality.

As a result of the competitive edge achieved by Toyota, Sony, Nippon Electric Company (NEC), and other Japanese industrial giants, quality has become a driving force in today's highly competitive global economy. In an effort to match their foreign rivals' success, many U.S. firms have made improving quality a top priority as they struggle to meet the demands of consumers and to regain their once dominant shares of the world market. "Total quality management" (TQM) is now widely viewed as *the* key to business survival in the 1990s and beyond.

This chapter provides detailed coverage of the economics of quality. Quality is one of the many nonprice attributes of a product that firms may exploit to secure a competitive advantage. Nonprice competition, which includes advertising and promotional activities, pre- and post-sale services, timeliness of delivery, warranty protection, geographic location, product quality, and a host of other factors, is a substitute for price competition. As such, the profit-maximizing firm must select an optimal combination of price and non-price characteristics that balances marginal benefits and marginal costs.

The determination of an optimal level of product quality thus follows the same rules applied in Chapter 10's analysis of strategic management decisions. The goal of quality improvement also raises issues related to property rights and economic incentives, the internal organization of the firm, make-or-buy decisions, inventory control, and reputational capital.

The chapter begins with a general discussion of price and nonprice competition. We then apply economic principles to help guide the manager through the philosophical teachings of the modern quality revolution.

APPLICATION

The president of the Johnson Clothing Company has become increasingly concerned with the quality of the products her firm sells to consumers. Although the term "quality" has a number of different meanings, she is convinced that the company's future success depends on improving product quality in two related directions. One area of concern is the production process. Reducing the number of items rejected on final inspection can conserve valuable materials and production time, avoid delivery delays, and slash inventory costs. Her second worry relates to the perceptions of consumers. The company's ability to attract first-time buyers depends on marketing a product line with few obvious defects. And, perhaps more importantly, repeat business hinges on consistently meeting customers' expectations about comfort, fit, durability, and reliability.

Ms. Johnson's apprehensions about quality prompt her to attend a seminar on "Total Quality Management" (TQM). Upon returning to the office, she calls a meeting of the firm's production and marketing managers to discuss a list of 14 objectives discussed at the seminar. (Table 11.1 presents a copy of the list.) She asks the two managers to evaluate these objectives for improving quality and to recommend whether the company should implement a TQM program.

This chapter supplies economic tools that are helpful in appraising the merits of the TQM philosophy. Although many of the items listed in Table 11.1 seem to rely more on psychology than on economics, the principles of marginal analysis are helpful in studying the tradeoffs involved in managing quality. To the extent that consumers value quality (are willing to pay for it), taking steps to improve product quality can increase the firm's sales and profits. But quality improvements are not a free lunch: They require the firm to invest more of its scarce resources in quality control and to provide appropriate incentives for employees and suppliers to meet more stringent quality standards. Thus, like all economic choices, implementing a program of quality management requires the firm to determine the optimal level of quality.

TABLE 11.1 THE ELEMENTS OF TOTAL QUALITY MANAGEMENT

1. Create constancy of purpose for improvement of product and service.
2. Adopt the new philosophy.
3. Cease dependence on mass inspection.
4. Stop awarding business on the price tag alone.
5. Continuously improve quality.
6. Institute training.
7. Institute leadership.
8. Eliminate fear.
9. Break down barriers between staff areas.
10. Eliminate motivational slogans.
11. Eliminate numerical goals.
12. Improve pride of workmanship.
13. Institute a vigorous program of education and retraining.
14. Take action to accomplish the transformation.

Source: Adapted from Mary Walton, *Deming Management at Work* (New York: Perigee Books, 1991), pp. 17–19.

PRICE AND NONPRICE COMPETITION

In order to simplify the analysis of the profit-maximizing firm, economists place price competition at center stage. The firm's objective in economic theory is to determine the particular price-output combination which maximizes profits. Competition is chiefly a matter of varying price and production in response to changing market conditions.

But firms compete for customers in a variety of other ways. They advertise, they supply pre- and post-sale services, they offer warranties and guarantees, they introduce new and improved products, they redesign their packaging, and so on. Such nonprice competition is valuable to consumers. It reduces their costs of search and it provides them with additional product characteristics from which to choose. Indeed, product heterogeneity is defined by the extent to which nonprice variables differ across sellers.

Economic models of the firm and industry assume that nonprice variables are held constant during the period of analysis. This assumption is explicit in the case of price-taker markets (see Chapter 8), where the product is homogeneous. In the price-taker model, the goods or services of any one firm are identical in all respects to those offered by its rivals. By assumption, nonprice competition has no role to play in the price-taker model and consumers make their purchase decisions solely on the basis of price. They are otherwise indifferent as to the identity of the seller from whom they buy.

The price-searcher model introduces product heterogeneity. Downward-sloping demand curves follow directly from the assumption that the products of rival sellers differ in terms of their nonprice characteristics. But demand curves are constructed in the price-searcher model by asking consumers how many units of a particular firm's product they are willing and able to buy at various possible prices, *holding all other things constant*. These "other things" include money income, tastes and preferences, the prices of related goods—and all nonprice attributes of the seller's product that consumers value. In other words, as price varies along the demand schedule, consumers vary their purchases of a good with given nonprice characteristics. The seller's advertising expenditures, warranty and credit policies, point-of-sale services, and so on are the same at every point on its demand schedule. It follows that if the firm changes any of the nonprice attributes of its product, the entire demand schedule will shift in or out and become steeper or flatter depending on how consumers respond to the change.

As stated at the outset, holding nonprice variables constant in studying the behavior of the profit-maximizing firm and industry helps simplify the analysis. This assumption also rests in part on an "empirical judgment" that "price competition is much more effective in increasing output and reducing profits than non-price competition."[1] Put differently, the tendency of economic models of the firm to emphasize price competition over nonprice competition is based on the following conjecture: It is cheaper for a firm to sell an extra unit of output by cutting price than by increasing its expenditures on some controllable nonprice variable. This conjecture, in turn, presupposes that marginal production costs do not rise as rapidly as the marginal costs of advertising, quality improvements, or other nonprice variables.

Whether this empirical judgment is valid or not, it is nevertheless true that price is only one dimension of competition. If consumers value the nonprice characteristics of products, then it is no longer obvious that one form of competition is "better" than another. Indeed, a wide range of selling techniques exist across firms and industries. This observation suggests that the perceived costs and benefits of price and nonprice competition differ under varying market circumstances. The relevant managerial question then becomes: What is the optimal mix of price and nonprice variables?

In answering this question, it is important to keep in mind that, like all economic decisions, the choice between price and nonprice competition involves a tradeoff. In a sense, price and nonprice characteristics are substitutes for one another. Consider product quality (defined more fully below). Improving the quality of a product without raising its price is equivalent to offering consumers a price cut. But high-quality goods are more costly to produce than low-quality goods. At the same time, consumers are generally willing to pay more for high-quality products. The firm thus faces a choice of varying the price of a product of given quality, varying quality at a given price, or varying both price and quality. Which of these actions is most

---

1 George J. Stigler, "Price and Nonprice Competition," *Journal of Political Economy* 72 (February 1968), pp. 149-54. Reprinted in George J. Stigler, *The Organization of Industry* (Homewood, IL: Richard D. Irwin, 1968), pp. 23-28.

profitable depends on the marginal cost of increasing product quality and the marginal value consumers place on quality improvements.

QUALITY DEFINED

"Quality" has a number of different interpretations. Two aspects of product quality are of particular importance to economists. One of these definitions of quality relates to the production process; the other refers to a set of characteristics that affect consumers' perceptions of product quality.

Quality of a Production Process

The quality of a production process is usually judged by the frequency with which defective items show up at points of intermediate or final inspection. Defects are costly to the firm because, depending on their severity, rejected items must either be reworked or repaired, cannibalized for salvageable parts, or scrapped. In any case, the firm loses valuable materials and production time, and unit production costs are higher than they would be otherwise.

Until the industrial revolution, production took place on a small scale. Individual artisans worked independently at their own pace and bore full responsibility for the quality of their products. Quality was essentially determined at the point of sale and the artisan was not paid for any item failing to meet the buyer's requirements. The individual worker shouldered the full cost of the time and materials wasted due to the production of defective or substandard items.

As markets expanded and the demand for manufactured products increased, traditional crafts production was supplemented by the **putting-out system**. Under this arrangement, a merchant or artisan contracted with other individuals to supply parts or components of the final product. The merchant or artisan delivered necessary materials to the worker's location, paid an agreed-upon piece rate for each finished item meeting specifications, and then assembled and sold the final product. The artisan and the piece-rate workers shared the cost of substandard production under the putting-out system. The worker was not paid for defective items and so received no compensation for lost production time, but the merchant or artisan bore the expense of wasted materials.

With the advent of assembly lines and mass production processes,[2] quality control became a statistical problem. Assembly line methods are characterized by the specialization and division of labor, the production of a large volume of output, and the standardization and interchangeability of parts and components of the final product. Mass production methods require increased supervision to prevent bottlenecks from developing either because of a failure to coordinate output rates at various points

---

2 The shift from crafts production to factory production is discussed more fully in Chapter 15.

along the production line, or because the parts or components produced at one stage fail to meet the design specifications and tolerances required at later stages. In short, the adoption of mass production methods placed a premium on reducing quality variations—parts and components had to meet more precise engineering standards.

Inspection of the final product initially became the standard procedure for maintaining quality. An inspector graded and either accepted or rejected each item as it came off the assembly line. But as assembly lines became more efficient and productive, the notion of inspecting every finished product gave way to statistical quality control. In the 1930s, W. A. Stewhart, a statistician at Bell Laboratories, applied the tools of probability and statistics to develop techniques for sampling and testing goods for desired characteristics.[3] Inspectors sampled and tested materials and parts obtained from outside suppliers before they entered the production process. Partially assembled items were likewise sampled and tested at various points along the assembly line.

Statistical quality control is basically a problem of determining the optimal sample size from which measurements will be taken. The first step in solving this problem is to specify the size of the allowable error. In other words, how much can a particular measurement deviate from its design specification before the item is rejected? Let L be the allowable error in the sample mean ($\pm .01$ inch in the diameter of a 1 inch part, for example).

The next step is to express the allowable error in terms of a confidence interval. This step involves specifying how large of a Type I error is acceptable, that is, how large of a chance can be taken that an item will pass inspection when the error in fact exceeds L. Assuming that the sample mean is normally distributed and that a five percent chance that the actual error exceeds L is acceptable, then it can be shown that

$$L = \frac{2\sigma}{\sqrt{n}},$$

where σ is the population standard deviation around the mean and n is the size of the sample taken.

Replacing the unknown σ with its sample estimate, s, and solving for n yields the required sample size

$$n^* = \frac{4s^2}{L^2}.$$

The formula for n^* suggests that other things being the same, the optimal sample size will be larger the greater is the variance of measurements around the mean, the smaller is the allowable error, and the narrower is the

3 Daniel T. Seymour, *On Q: Causing Quality in Higher Education* (New York: Macmillan, 1992), p. 8.

confidence interval.[4] Hence, in order to improve the quality of the production process (i.e., to reduce acceptable errors), the firm must devote more of its resources to quality control. This requires larger sample sizes, additional inspectors, and more precise testing and measurement.

The fact that quality control is costly suggests that it will never pay the firm to adopt a zero-defect policy. Reducing the frequency with which defects occur allows the firm to conserve materials and production time, eliminate bottlenecks, reduce inventory holdings, and avoid delivery delays. But the additional benefits of quality improvements must be balanced against the additional costs of achieving them. Because it is not worth spending more than $1 to avoid a dollar's worth of waste, the profit-maximizing firm should invest resources in improving the quality of its production process only up to the point where marginal benefit is equal to marginal cost.

This lesson is just as relevant to the notion of total quality management, which stresses that product quality is not solely the responsibility of the firm's manufacturing division. A total organizational commitment to quality requires devoting additional resources to training and education, to motivational programs that instill pride of workmanship, and so on. The firm must sacrifice increasingly valuable alternative resource uses to enhance its overall commitment to quality. Because the marginal cost of quality improvement tends to rise and its marginal benefits tend to decline, the firm will eventually reach a point at which further increases in quality are no longer profitable.

Quality in the Model of Consumer Behavior

The benefits of improving the quality of the production process are not limited to reducing production costs. Obviously defective items cannot be sold, and hidden defects that impair the product's performance, durability, or reliability threaten to devalue the firm's reputational capital. When a consumer makes a purchase that fails to meet his or her expectations, the seller must bear the costs associated with repairing or replacing the defective item, accepting the item's return, or, if no adjustment is made, the risk of loss of future business.

While some aspects of product quality can be measured objectively, the consumer's subjective evaluation of a product's quality characteristics is also critical in determining how much he or she is willing to pay for it. Durability (the length of the product's useful life) and reliability (the frequency with which breakdowns occur) are nonjudgmental attributes which can be verified with experience. Other quality characteristics, such as "taste," "feel," or

---

4 The formula for the optimal sample size must be adjusted if the sample mean cannot be assumed to be normally distributed, but the relationships between n, L, and s^2 continue to hold. In addition, if the computed value of n represents 10 percent or more of the population, a correction factor should be applied. The revised sample size, n', that takes proper account of the finite population correction is $n' = n/(1 + \phi)$, where $\phi = n/P$ (P is the size of the population from which the sample is taken). See George W. Snedecor and William G. Cochran, *Statistical Methods*, 6E. (Ames: Iowa State University Press, 1967), pp. 516-18, or any other elementary statistics text.

"look," are highly subjective and are therefore likely to be rated differently by different consumers.

Generally speaking, consumers are willing to pay more for high-quality products than for low-quality products. How much more they are willing to pay depends on the marginal value they place on additional quality. These marginal valuations are likely to differ substantially across consumers. A quality improvement that extends the tread life of an automobile tire by 50,000 miles, for example, is worth more to some car owners than to others, depending on driving habits, age of vehicle, and so on.

Moreover, whether or not any one consumer is satisfied with the quality of a product depends on how well it meets his or her expectations. Some consumers want to buy low-priced, low-quality goods. These consumers will only be dissatisfied if they buy a low-quality good at a high-quality price.

THE ECONOMICS OF QUALITY

Economic theory explains how and why events occur in a complex world where it can be difficult to separate causation from correlation. *All* theories simplify the real world. For example, the annual rate of inflation, by definition, realistically depends on the price changes that occur in every single market for goods and services in the economy. However, macroeconomic theory proposes that inflation can be explained and predicted tolerably well without having to investigate the underlying reason for every market price change. Macroeconomic theory instead suggests that the growth rate in the money supply relative to the growth of output of goods and services is an important determinant of the average rate of change in all prices in an economy.

Although economic theories simplify the real world, they are no less relevant for decision makers. Because economic theory helps explain why events occur, the basic philosophy of this text is that economic theory helps managers solve business decision-making problems in ways that more fully achieve the goals of the firm. An example of this linkage (discussed later in the chapter) is the common practice of using highly paid celebrities to advertise a product. Why is this practice so common? Economic theory provides an answer to this question and managers who understand the answers provided by theory can make better decisions than those who never ask the most basic of all questions: Why?

The topic of this section is the economics of quality. Its overall theme is that imperfect information plays a key role in understanding the sale and purchase of products with different quality characteristics. The first subsection develops the case in which there is perfect information in a market. The second subsection discusses markets in which sellers are able to differentiate the quality of their products, but buyers cannot—the case of "lemons" markets. The third subsection analyzes the market for information and demonstrates that differences in search costs across consumers can explain their purchases of high- and low-quality products. The fourth subsection considers the more general relation between relative prices and quality choices. The fifth subsection then turns to the responses of producers to imperfect information and explains the practice of signaling the quality of products to consumers. The last subsection considers the case of a company that successfully developed a quality-based competitive strategy, but with an additional twist—the government penalized them for their success.

Fully Informed Customers and Optimal Quality

In order to simplify the analysis, consider a product that has only a single quality characteristic.[5] The product is gasoline and quality is measured in terms of the mileage derived from each gallon of fuel. Although the market explicitly deals with the quantity of gasoline bought and sold, the demand and supply of gasoline is more fundamentally related to its quality attribute, miles per gallon.

There is a direct relationship between the quantity of the good produced by a firm and the firm's production of the quality attribute desired by consumers. Let q_i represent the *quantity* of the good produced by some arbitrary firm i, let g_i represent the **quality grade** of its product, and let a_i be the associated **quality attribute** of the product. The ith firm's production of the quality attribute, a_i, is then given by

$$q_i g_i = a_i. \tag{11.1}$$

In other words, if firm A sells 1,000 gallons of gasoline per day with a quality grade of 20 miles per gallon, it is actually selling 20,000 units of "mileage" per day to its customers. If firm B sells 1,500 gallons of gasoline per day with a quality grade of 15 miles per gallon, it is actually selling 22,500 units of "mileage" per day to its customers.

The price of gasoline sold by the ith firm (p^{gas}) is then determined by the quality grade of its gasoline (g_i) and the price that consumers are willing to pay for the attribute (p^a):

$$p^{gas} = g_i p^a. \tag{11.2}$$

Thus, if firm A sells gasoline with a quality grade of 20 miles to the gallon (20 *mpg* = g_i) and the price of a "*mpg*" is five cents (p^a = \$.05), then the price of firm A's gasoline is \$1.00 per gallon. If firm B sells gasoline with a quality grade of 25 miles to the gallon, then the price of its gasoline is \$1.25 per gallon. More generally, if one firm's gasoline gets, for example, 25 percent greater mileage than another, its price will be 25 percent higher.

Figure 11.1 illustrates the ith firm's profit-maximizing decision about the level of quality (g_i). The quality attribute, a_i, is measured on the horizontal axis and the price of this attribute, p^a, is measured on the vertical axis. The firm

---

5 The presentation in this section is drawn from Jack Hirshleifer, *Price Theory and Applications*, 2E. (Englewood Cliffs, NJ: Prentice-Hall, 1980), Chapter 12.

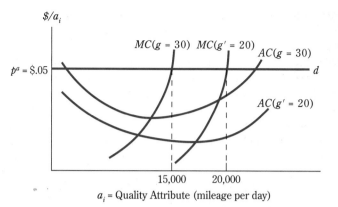

FIGURE 11.1
A Unique
Optimal Quality
Level

381

Chapter 11   Managing Quality

a_i = Quality Attribute (mileage per day)

is assumed to be a competitive price-taker *in the market for the attribute.* The firm consequently faces a perfectly elastic demand curve, d, for this attribute.

In Figure 11.1, the firm can choose either quality grade $g = 30$ *mpg* or quality grade $g' = 20$ *mpg*. If it chooses quality grade g, it produces 15,000 units of mileage per day and if it chooses quality grade g', it produces 20,000 units of mileage per day. In this case, quality level $g' = 20$ mpg maximizes the firm's profits because it minimizes the average cost of producing the desired attribute. It is important to note that there is no specific relationship between the position of the average cost curves and the quality grade. The lower average cost curve could just as easily represent the higher quality grade, in which case the firm would maximize its profits by producing the 30 miles-per-gallon gasoline. Also note that Figure 11.1 represents the case in which the average cost curve for one level of quality is everywhere below the other.

If firms are heterogeneous, then the optimal quality level can vary across them. In the example used above, firm A can sell gas that gets 20 miles to the gallon for $1.00 per gallon and firm B can sell gas that gets 25 miles to the gallon for $1.25 per gallon. Figure 11.2 illustrates the case of varying optimal quality levels across firms. This figure includes three average cost curves. As opposed to the cost curves in Figure 11.1, the curves in Figure

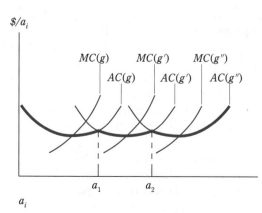

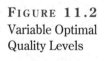

FIGURE 11.2
Variable Optimal
Quality Levels

11.2 overlap one another. The lowest cost of producing quality attributes less than a_1 is illustrated by the darkened portion of average cost curve $AC(g)$; the lowest cost of producing quality attributes between a_1 and a_2 is illustrated by the darkened portion of average cost curve $AC(g')$; and the lowest cost of producing quality attributes greater than a_2 is illustrated by the darkened portion of average cost curve $AC(g'')$. Because a_i varies with the quantity of output sold by the firm, the optimal quality chosen by the firm can also vary with output.

Suppose that gasoline is sold by a single firm rather than by a set of competitive firms. In the case in which there is a unique optimal quality level (as depicted in Figure 11.1), the monopolist will choose that quality level because the quality level with the lowest average cost maximizes profits. Although the monopolist produces less output than competitive firms, it does not have any incentive to reduce the quality of the product when there is a unique optimal quality level. The situation is more complicated in the case of variable optimal quality levels as shown in Figure 11.2. In this case the quality grade that represents the lowest average cost of producing the quality attribute, a_i, varies as output varies. If we view the producers in a market alternatively as, first, a single seller and then as a set of competitive firms, it is reasonable to assume that the single seller will be larger than the representative competitive firm. However, there is no general reason to believe that the quality grade for a large firm is necessarily higher or lower than that of smaller firms.

The implication of the above analysis is straightforward. When consumers are fully informed they will only pay for the attribute quality of the good. If quality varies across firms, then the price of the products will vary in proportion to their attribute quality and *consumers will be indifferent between buying low-quality and high-quality products*. In a world of perfectly informed consumers, product differentiation is a largely superfluous market characteristic. It occurs but is unimportant because low-quality and high-quality products differ in price by an amount that exactly compensates for their differences in quality.

Uninformed Customers and "Lemons" Markets

Because all theories rely on assumptions, the simplifying assumption of "perfect information" in the previous section does not automatically limit the usefulness of the model. However, we can ask the question: Does the perfect information model adequately reflect and predict the way that actual markets work? Although the answer to this question is a resounding yes (in our opinion), the development of economic models with imperfect information has increased our understanding of certain types of decisions in labor markets, capital markets, and product markets.

The development of models of imperfect information has not abrogated the usefulness of traditional microeconomic models that assume perfect information. The price-taker model with its assumption of perfect information still plays a fundamental role in the economist's effort to understand how markets work. Economists do *not* try to determine whether consumers possess perfect information or whether markets work perfectly. Rather, the more subtle question is whether there are alternative institutional arrangements that provide a *better* way of allocating resources than is provided by an unfettered market system. For example, if imperfect information is an important factor in the allocation of resources, then two types of questions arise. How does imperfect information affect the performance of a market system? Is there a way to improve performance by government rule-making or direct intervention? The latter question is more difficult and provides the foundation for (often acrimonious) debate.

One of the first explanations of potential problems posed by markets with imperfect information was provided by George Akerlof.[6] Sellers typically have more information than buyers in the used car market. That is, there is **asymmetric information** in this market. The potential impact of asymmetric information on market outcomes can be illustrated with a simple example. Suppose there are 100 potential buyers and sellers of used cars. Some of the used cars are of inferior quality—they are "lemons" that frequently break down and require their owners to spend an inordinate amount of time with the local (trustworthy?) mechanic. Assume that 50 of the cars are lemons or low-quality used cars and 50 of the cars are high-quality used cars.

Each buyer and seller has a **reservation price** that he or she is willing to pay and accept, respectively, for a used car. Suppose the reservation prices of the two groups are those shown in Table 11.2. If buyers and sellers can both distinguish low-quality from high-quality cars, then the market price of low-quality cars will be between $5,000 and $6,000 and the market price of high-quality cars will be between $10,000 and $11,000. Buyers and sellers do not know each other's reservation price and of course it is in the interest of each to keep that information from the other. Whether final prices favor the seller (closer to the buyer's reservation price) or the buyer (closer to the seller's reservation price) depends on the bargaining skills of each.

Now assume that only the seller of a used car can differentiate low-quality cars from high-quality cars. Buyers cannot distinguish lemons from high-quality used cars prior to purchase. If buyers know that they have a 50-50 chance of driving home a lemon when they buy a used car, then the

TABLE 11.2 HYPOTHETICAL RESERVATION PRICES FOR USED CARS

	SELLERS' RESERVATION PRICE[a]	BUYERS' RESERVATION PRICE[b]
low-quality used cars	$5,000	$6,000
high-quality used cars	$10,000	$11,000

a The *minimum* price sellers are willing to accept.
b The *maximum* price buyers are willing to pay.

6 George Akerlof, "The Market for Lemons: Quality Uncertainty and the Market Mechanism," *Quarterly Journal of Economics* 84 (1970), pp. 488-500.

reservation price for a used car of completely unknown quality is $8,500 (the average of $6,000 and $11,000).

How does this new reservation price affect the market for used cars? If buyers are only willing to offer $8,500 for any used car regardless of quality, then according to the schedule of seller reservation prices, only lemons will be offered in the market. Sellers are not willing to part with a high-quality used car for less than $10,000. But, of course, once buyers realize that only lemons are available in the market, then their reservation price drops to $6,000. The final result is that *only low-quality lemons are bought and sold in the market for a price between $5,000 and $6,000.*

The implication of imperfect information is that low-quality products can crowd out high-quality products, a phenomenon known as **adverse selection**. Because the sale and purchase of high-quality products makes both sellers and buyers better off, the loss of the mutual gains from trading high-quality products, by definition, means that the amount of quality provided by the market is less than optimal. There is "market failure" because sellers of low-quality lemons impose a negative externality on the sellers of high-quality cars. When low-quality cars are offered for sale, they adversely affect the perceived value of high-quality cars if buyers cannot differentiate low- and high-quality. Low-quality cars prevent the market for high-quality cars from functioning properly.

The Market for Information

As a consequence of imperfect information, low-quality goods can drive out high quality goods and create a **"lemons" market**. However, the existence of imperfect information gives buyers and sellers incentives to invest resources in gathering information. That is, there is a market for information, and the amount of "imperfect information" is not rigidly set by predetermined forces but rather is endogenously determined by the actions of both buyers and sellers.

Figure 11.3 illustrates the market for information. Time spent searching for information is measured on the horizontal axis and the marginal benefits and costs of search are presented on the vertical axis. The more time economic agents spend searching for information, the less imperfect information exists in the market. The marginal cost of search is upward-sloping, indicating that increasingly valuable alternatives must be sacrificed as additional time is devoted to gathering information. The second hour of search is more costly than the first hour, the third hour of search is more costly than the second hour, and so on. The reason that the marginal costs of search are increasing is intuitively obvious. The first half-hour of search for a used car would be at the expense of the least-valued activity of the day, which might have been watching a re-run of *Gilligan's Island*. The second half-hour of search would be at the expense of the next-least-valued activity of the day (for example, the loss of 30 minutes from a normally scheduled hour-long lunch break). And so on.

The marginal benefit curves in Figure 11.3 are downward-sloping. The downward slope reflects the proposition that each successive hour of search

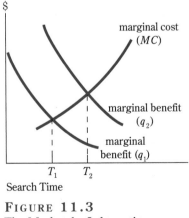

FIGURE 11.3
The Market for Information

Are Cherries Lemons?

A **"lemons" market** is one in which low-quality products drive out high-quality products because buyers cannot gauge product quality prior to purchase. All products, regardless of quality, consequently sell for the same price. Only low-quality products are bought and sold in a lemons market. Note that "lemons" are not defective products that no one wants to buy. Lemons are instead products that can be sold only at a lower price that reflects their differentially lower quality. A lemon can be a good buy just as easily as a high-quality product—if the price is low enough.

The conditions leading to a lemons market seem to characterize the market for cherries. Growers sort and sell cherries on the basis of size. There are ten different size categories of cherries. Size 10 is the largest-size, highest-quality category and size 1 is the smallest-size, lowest-quality category.

There are two standard methods of marketing cherries. Growers can choose to sort all of their cherries into each of the ten quality categories before they sell them or they can choose to sort cherries into one of three mixed-size categories (which we label as categories *A*, *B*, and *C*). Mixed-size category *A* includes cherries of sizes 10, 9, 8, and 7; mixed-size category *B* includes cherries of sizes 6, 5, and 4; and mixed-size category *C* includes cherries of sizes 3 and 2.[a] The smallest cherries are not included in any of the mixed-size categories.

At the time of sale, buyers of mixed-size cherries do not know the actual size distribution (quality distribution) of the cherries they purchase. For example, a buyer of cherries in mixed-category *B* knows only that the lot contains cherries of sizes 6, 5, and 4. The actual number of cherries of each size is unknown. Because sellers possess this information but buyers do not, cherries may be lemons. In other words, mixed-size lots would tend to contain proportionately more of the smallest size fruit. Buyers, in turn, would recognize this practice and respond by lowering the price they are willing to pay.

Economists Robert Rosenman and Wesley Wilson have investigated the way in which buyers and sellers cope with asymmetric information in the market for mixed-size cherries.[b] First, consider their analysis of why some firms find it more profitable to sort cherries into each of the ten size categories while other firms find it more profitable to sort cherries into the three mixed-size categories. Firms that sort cherries into all ten categories can be called "sorting firms" and firms that only sort into the three mixed-size categories can be called "non-sorting firms."

Three factors influence the decision to be a sorting firm or a non-sorting firm. A firm will find that it is more profitable to be a non-sorting firm as (a) the cost of sorting cherries increases; (b) the proportion of smaller cherries increases; and (c) the price differential between large and small cherries decreases.

Suppose that firm *A* represents the average sorting firm and that firm *B* represents the average non-sorting firm. For simplicity, assume that each firm produces 100 cherries in each of the ten size categories; that is, both firms sell fruit of the same quality. However, assume that firm *A*'s sorting costs are less than firm *B*'s cost of sorting so that firm *A* *normally* chooses to sort its cherries into ten size categories while firm *B* *normally* chooses to sort its cherries into three mixed-size categories.

Now suppose that the quality of firm *A*'s cherries turns out to be unusually low during a particular growing season. In other words, it has proportionately more cherries in the smallest size categories to sell. An

a In practice, Category *B* is defined as sizes 4 and larger and category *C* is size 2 and larger.
b Robert E. Rosenman and Wesley W. Wilson, "Quality Differentials and Prices: Are Cherries Lemons?," *Journal of Industrial Economics* 39 (December 1991), pp. 649-58.

increase in the proportion of small cherries increases the likelihood that the firm will sell in the three mixed-size categories. If average quality drops enough, firm A will switch from being a sorting firm to being a non-sorting firm. If it does, both firm A and firm B will market fruit in the three mixed-size categories, but the quality of firm A's cherries will be *less than* the quality of firm B's cherries.

Observing the switches of firms from being sorters to being non-sorters thus provides buyers with a way of differentiating relatively low- and high-quality cherry sellers in the market for mixed-size fruit. The prices of unsorted cherries sold by firms that normally sort their cherries should be less than the prices of unsorted cherries sold by firms that normally do not sort. A similar conclusion follows if we instead assume that both firms initially have the same costs of sorting but their cherries differ in quality.

Rosenman and Wilson's empirical results are consistent with the above analysis and indicate that seller characteristics indeed act as an effective signal of product quality. They report evidence that sorting firms that sell in the mixed-category market charge lower prices than non-sorting firms that sell in this market. This finding indicates that even when buyers are hampered by imperfect information, market signals allow them to differentiate low- and high-quality products.

---

yields a smaller expected benefit than the previous hour of search. The dispersion of quality in the market affects the position of the marginal benefit curve. For example, suppose there are two different quality selections in the market. Quality selection one, q_1, occurs when consumers can only choose between a low-quality product and a high-quality product. Quality selection two, q_2, occurs when consumers can choose between low-, moderate-, and high-quality products (or, alternatively, there is a larger difference between low- and high-quality products). Holding the amount of search time constant, the marginal benefit of search is expected to be greater the greater is the dispersion of quality in the market. Thus, the demand for search is higher when the market is characterized by quality dispersion q_2 than it is with quality dispersion q_1.

As shown in Figure 11.3, the optimal amount of search time varies positively with the dispersion of quality in the market. Search time T_2 is optimal given quality selection two and search time T_1 is optimal given quality selection one. The opportunity now exists for consumers to search out "best buys" in the economy. This differs from the case presented in the first subsection above in which perfect information was assumed and price differentials exactly offset quality differentials. Note, however, that the two cases are similar if we define the **full price** of the product as the product's money price plus the cost of search. That is, unless the consumer is just lucky, the search for "best buys" involves a cost which makes the full prices of these products comparable to the full prices of "less-than-best buys." If this were not the case then only one or the other would actually be bought and sold.

The presence of search costs can explain why high-quality and low-quality goods appeal to different classes of consumers. Again using the full information case as a reference point, high- and low-quality goods are exactly the same in that model because product price differentials compensate for quality differentials. However, the full prices of high- and low-quality goods can differ among consumers according to differences in their opportunity costs of search. For example, because their time is less valuable, low-income consumers generally have lower opportunity costs of searching than high-income consumers. In this context, the full prices of "best buys" that are associated with buying low-quality goods will be less for low-income consumers than for high-income consumers. Similarly, the full prices of "best buys" that are associated with buying high-quality goods will be less for high-income consumers than for low-income consumers.

Relative Prices and Quality Choices

As shown in the previous section, one of the reasons firms market both low- and high-quality goods is that the cost of search varies across consumers. When search costs are included in the prices of products, low-quality products have a relatively lower price than high-quality products for some consumers while just the opposite is true for others. (Remember that this discussion assumes that consumers demand the attributes of a product rather than the product itself.) The relationship between changes in relative prices and quality can explain other examples of consumer choice among different levels of quality.

The following example demonstrates the effect that relative prices have on quality choices. Calvin and Susan were married for three years before they had any children. As a childless couple, they habitually ate out twice a month. Sometimes they ate a $40 meal at a high-quality restaurant and sometimes they ate a $10 meal at a low-quality restaurant. Since having twins, they have to pay a babysitter $10 to take care of the children while they are out. How does having to pay a babysitter affect Calvin and Susan's decision to eat at high- and low-quality restaurants?

The relative price of eating at the two restaurants depends on whether the couple has to pay for a sitter or not. A high-quality meal is four times more expensive than a low-quality meal ($40 versus $10) before the couple have children; the same high-quality meal is only two and a half times more expensive than a low-quality meal ($50 versus $20) when the $10 babysitting fee is added to the costs of both meals. Because the relative price of a high-quality meal is lower after the couple have children, we would expect the couple to eat out at the higher quality restaurant more often after they had children than before.

Armen Alchian and William Allen provided the initial insight into explaining the relationship between relative prices and quality choices. Their original analysis is presented next.

Shipping the Good Apples Out

The **Alchian and Allen hypothesis** shows how fixed costs can affect the relative prices of low- and high-quality products.[7] Suppose that most of the

---

7 Armen A. Alchian and William R. Allen, *University Economics*, 2E. (Belmont, CA: Wadsworth Publishing Co., 1967), pp. 63-64. Also see Armen A. Alchian and William R. Allen, *Exchange & Production: Competition, Coordination, & Control*, 3E. (Belmont, CA: Wadsworth Publishing

apples sold in California are grown in the state of Washington. Assume that there are just two quality grades of apples, high-quality apples and low-quality apples. Assume further that it is *not* costly to separate low-quality apples from high-quality apples. The appearance of the apple not only indicates its physical appeal; it is also indicative of its taste and texture.

Now suppose that apples are grown uniformly across the state of Washington so that the transportation cost of supplying apples to consumers in Washington is negligible. In the state of Washington, a basket of high-quality apples sells for $20 while a basket of low-quality apples sells for $10. Now suppose that it costs $10 to ship a basket of apples from Washington to California and that this cost applies equally to both low-quality and high-quality apples. If the price of apples in California increases by the full amount of the cost of transportation, then the prices of baskets of high- and low-quality apples there will be $30 and $20, respectively.

Whereas high-quality apples are twice as expensive as low-quality apples in Washington ($20 is twice as much as $10), they are only one and a half times as expensive in California ($30 is one and a half times larger than $20). In sum, it is cheaper to buy high-quality apples in California than it is in Washington. If the effects of population differences are held constant and if preferences for high- and low-quality apples are comparable in the two states, then relatively more high-quality apples will be bought and sold in California than in Washington. Apple producers will tend to ship the high-quality apples out of the state in which they are grown.

Signaling by Producers

For a number of reasons, economics has long been known as "the dismal science." One reason for this reputation is the economist's insistence that self-interest is the single most important motivating force of human action. The economist claims that even seemingly selfless acts, like donating money or clothing to the victims of a natural disaster, are motivated by self-interest. It is certainly true that many people derive a sense of personal satisfaction from aiding the less fortunate. But more of such aid is forthcoming the more favorable is the tax treatment of charitable donations. This suggests that self-interest plays a large role in explaining noble behavior.

The optimal amount of any activity or behavior depends on its benefits and costs. In a previous subsection, the optimal amount of time spent searching for information is determined by equating the marginal benefit of search with the marginal cost of search. By the same token, "optimal" amounts of illegal, immoral, and unethical behaviors are determined by the respective marginal benefits and marginal costs of those activities. With respect to the behavior of firms, there are undoubtedly firms that purposely mislead or cheat their customers, illegally dispose of hazardous

Co., 1983), pp. 36-37, and Eugene Silverberg, *The Structure of Economics: A Mathematical Analysis*, 2E. (New York: McGraw-Hill, 1990), pp. 384-89.

wastes, and so on. But not all firms, and hopefully not most firms, engage in these activities because the market imposes considerable costs on these types of activities.

A *balanced* view of firm behavior considers both the incentives and disincentives of engaging in "unfair" practices toward customers. Yet all too commonly, writers categorically state that firms have free rein to manipulate, mislead, and cheat consumers. This perspective is perhaps nowhere more pronounced than in the related areas of imperfect market information, quality differentiation of competing products, brand names, and advertising. Consider the following statements from a popular consumer economics textbook:

> The consumer has become dependent upon brand names, and the manufacturers have accentuated and stimulated this dependency by spending billions of dollars on advertising that keeps brand names constantly before the consumer. In some respects, what has developed is a *Pavlovian response: consumers buy Brand X because the ads tell them to buy Brand X.*[8]

> Consumers simply cannot rely solely on brand names as guides to quality. The quality of a product is determined by the producer, and *the producer can improve or deteriorate the quality as he or she sees fit and still continue to use the same brand name.*[9]

> For many years the American Dental Association (ADA) has assured consumers that a simple solution of salt and soda is as effective a dentifrice as most products available in retail stores, with the exception of the toothpastes that contain fluoride. But the ADA is no match for the dentifrice-makers who spend millions of dollars telling consumers that if they use a particular product they will have gleaming, white teeth, no mouth odors, and fewer cavities.[10]

These assertions paint a pretty shabby picture of consumers. In our opinion, consumers are more sophisticated than dogs salivating in response to a dinner bell. Producers do not have carte blanche to manipulate consumers. And, somewhat peevishly, we wonder if the authors of the last quote have ever tried brushing their teeth with baking soda and salt.

Given that imperfect information exists in most markets, just what is the role of advertising in either educating or misleading consumers about product quality? Even though economists unsentimentally view behavior as a function of self-interest and do not think that firms practice honesty or morality for their own sakes, there are still strong theoretic reasons for believing that firms use advertising to signal product quality. This theoretical reasoning is explained next.

---

8 Leland J. Gordon and Stewart M. Lee, *Economics for Consumers*, 7E. (London: D. Van Nostrand Company, 1977), p. 314 (emphasis added).

9 *Ibid.*, p. 316 (emphasis added).

10 *Ibid.*, p. 319.

Advertising as a Quality Signal

Recall the "lemons" market in which car buyers have less information about product quality than sellers. The possibility exists that only lemons will be sold in this type of market—a prospect that injures both buyers and sellers of high-quality cars. Buyers have an incentive to search for information that helps them differentiate the two quality levels, and sellers have an incentive to provide information that achieves the same purpose.

Suppose that a manufacturer of a high-quality product, say a brand of refrigerator that breaks down less often than the brands sold by its competitors, wants to convey this information to consumers. At first glance advertising seems to be, at best, an imperfect means of communicating information about quality. The consumer does not initially have any more reason to believe the promotional campaign of this manufacturer than it does the campaigns of the manufacturers of low-quality refrigerators.

To consider the firm's options, suppose for simplicity that high-quality refrigerators last one year. On the first day of the year, the firm hopes to sell 200 refrigerators for a price of $2,000. If each refrigerator costs the company $1,000 to produce, then it will earn $200,000 in profits (total revenue is $400,000 and total cost is $200,000). On the last day of the year, all the refrigerators wear out and, if the firm in this example has properly represented the quality of its product, it hopes to sell another 200 refrigerators and earn another $200,000 in profits. However, this favorable sequence of events will materialize only if the high-quality refrigerator company can successfully differentiate its products from other, lower quality brands. Unfortunately, all refrigerators look alike to consumers.

The manufacturer might first consider a money back guarantee if its product fails to perform as promised. Warranties and guarantees are important, but imperfect, strategies for insuring product quality. Suppose the worst case happens and all the refrigerators fail the day after consumers take delivery (either because of outright fraud or imperfect information on the seller's part). Consumers still have no guarantee that the manufacturer (a) will not skip town if fraud is involved or (b) has the funds necessary to cover all warranties if the firm is honest, but inept. This flaw can be overcome if the manufacturer guarantees its guarantee by, for example, depositing $400,000 into a bank account to fully reimburse customers whose refrigerators do not last one year. But there is still one last hurdle to overcome. The manufacturer cannot have the ability to withdraw any of the funds during the period in question. Otherwise, a fraudulent manufacturer could deposit the funds at the beginning of the first day and withdraw them immediately after all refrigerators had been sold.

If the product's one-year life is extended to n years, the firm not only has to keep $400,000 in an untouchable bank account for n years—it can *never* withdraw those funds if it wants to continue to sell refrigerators in the future. Irretrievable investments of this sort are called **sunk costs**. Now suppose that it is impractical for the firm to create a sunk-cost bank account; that is, the firm cannot credibly commit itself to leave the funds untouched. The firm can approximate the effect of the $400,000 bank account by spending this amount on advertising, *provided* that consumers realize that only the producers of high-quality products will find it rational to pursue such a strategy.

Why would only high-quality firms be willing to make nonsalvageable investments in advertising? First, consider the case of the fraudulent or incompetent firm that sells refrigerators that fail the day after they are sold. If the firm spends $400,000 on advertising and its refrigerators all fail on day two, a loss of $200,000 will be incurred (total profit of $200,000 on sales less the $400,000 advertising costs). Contrast this with the case of the legitimate high-quality firm that spends $400,000 on advertising to promote its product. It continues to stay in business and to earn $200,000 in profits every year. In a sense, the firm earns interest on its sunk cost expenditures, but *only if* its quality claims are truthful and lead to continued future sales.

One final piece of the story remains to be told. If consumers learn from experience, then it may not be necessary for firms to provide explicit information about product quality. Consumers will be able to infer quality from the firm's willingness to invest in advertising. After all, there are only so many ways of saying, "Buy our refrigerators because they last one year." So-called promotional advertising that contains no hard facts or blunt promises can also send a clear **signal** about the firm's belief in the quality of its product. Recall the question of why firms often employ athletes or other high-profile celebrities to appear in their advertising campaigns. The answer is that these individuals are obviously highly paid and can therefore signal the firm's willingness to make expenditures that will be worthless if it fails to deliver products of the promised quality. Consumers, in turn, can use this willingness to invest in nonsalvageable capital as a signal of the quality of the seller's product.

Successful Product Differentiation: The ReaLemon Case

Consumers rely on brand names to differentiate competing products of varying quality. High and low-quality brands in a market are generally referred to as premium and non-premium brands, respectively. Brand status and market share are not related systematically to one another; premium products dominate some markets while non-premium brands dominate others. The relative market shares of premium and non-premium brands depend on a number of factors, including consumers' perceptions of relative quality; the price differential between premium and non-premium brands; the importance of the product in the consumer's budget; the cost of gathering information about quality differences; and the cost of making a disappointing purchase. This section looks at a case in which a premium brand also held a dominant market-share position—a combination that suggests a successful, quality-based competitive strategy.[11] The causes and consequences of this strategy are discussed below.

---

11 However, remember that long-run profit maximization is the ultimate objective of the firm. Market share is only important to the extent that it is an indicator of the firm's success in maximizing long-run profits.

ReaLemon, the Borden Company's premium brand of processed lemon juice, held a dominant share of its market in the 1970s.[12] In order to successfully compete with the ReaLemon brand, other manufacturers of processed lemon juice sold their products for prices about 25 percent lower than the price of ReaLemon. As an example, a bottle of ReaLemon sold for about 60 cents while a rival brand, Golden Crown, sold for about 45 cents per bottle. Although there were other lemon juice manufacturers, this discussion focuses only on the ReaLemon and Golden Crown brands.

Firms that sell non-premium brands can be just as successful and as profitable as firms that sell premium brands. Per unit profit for these products is the difference between price and average total cost. If we assume that price is indicative of consumers' perceptions of quality, then non-premium brands are defined as products that sell for lower prices than premium brands. The non-premium brand can be more profitable (per unit of sales) if its costs are sufficiently lower than those of the higher-priced premium brand. This was not the case in the processed lemon juice market, however. Golden Crown lemon juice sold for about 25 percent less than ReaLemon, but it didn't have a significant cost advantage over ReaLemon. ReaLemon was profitable; Golden Crown was not.

What factors explain the importance of brand status in determining market shares in the processed lemon juice market? If processed lemon juice is a fairly standardized product, then a brand's status should not play an important role in marketing the product. An additional factor that could lessen the importance of brand differences in this market is the way that processed lemon juice is typically consumed—it is used as an ingredient in recipes rather than being consumed directly.

However, there are reasons to believe that brand status is important in the processed lemon juice market. The quality of processed lemon juice, in general, is determined by its ability to approximate the taste of fresh lemon juice. Processed lemon juice is a convenient, but inferior, substitute for fresh lemon juice. Consumers judge the relative quality of different brands of processed lemon juice on the basis of how well they perform compared to fresh lemon juice. Two brands of processed lemon juice might look about the same, smell about the same, and even taste about the same, but it is still possible that fairly slight differences between brands can seem substantial when the brands are compared with the quality of fresh lemon juice. One brand can be just a little more bitter or just a little sharper than another. Small differences can cause one of the brands to be a poor substitute, relative to the other brand, for fresh lemon juice.

One aspect of lemon juice production that can accentuate taste differences among brands is the necessity of using preservatives in the production process. The taste of processed lemon juice is apparently sensitive to even small variations in the addition of preservatives to the product.[13] Thus,

---

12 Material in this section is drawn from Clement C. Krouse, "Brand Name as a Barrier to Entry: The ReaLemon Case," *Southern Economic Journal* 51 (October 1984), pp. 495-502.
13 *Ibid.*, p. 499.

quality control of the production process is an important part of maintaining a brand's quality status in this industry.

In the 1970s, the price difference between a one-ounce serving of ReaLemon and Golden Crown was less than one penny. On the surface, the money cost of trying alternative brands was insignificant. However, because of the way that processed lemon juice is used, the actual cost of brand switching could be perceived as being much higher than indicated by the price difference between brands. Processed lemon juice is most commonly used in recipes. The cost of the lemon juice is usually small relative to the cost of other ingredients. The principal cost of a lemon cake is in flour, sugar, milk, and eggs; the principal cost of lemon chicken is the cost of the chicken. Choosing an inferior brand of processed lemon juice can ruin a favorite recipe and cause the loss of the money spent on all of the recipe's other ingredients.

The Borden Company successfully dominated the market for reprocessed lemon juice with a quality-based strategy. However, ReaLemon was not an unqualified success. Golden Crown filed an antitrust suit against ReaLemon, and won. Basically, the courts concluded that Golden Crown was unable to compete because Borden charged too *low* a price for ReaLemon. If Borden had charged a higher price, then Golden Crown could have raised its price to a profitable level.

The finding that Borden unlawfully monopolized the processed lemon juice market was based on two key arguments. First, the premium status of the ReaLemon brand name represented a barrier to entry. Second, Borden used this advantage to engage in **predatory pricing**—charging a price that did not fully reflect its quality edge with the intent of driving its rivals from the market. According to the court,

> Borden engaged in a number of acts and practices, heretofore described.... These acts and practices include geographically discriminatory prices, promotional allowances tailored to combat competition in particular areas where competition had arisen, granting to selected key retail stores special allowances designed to eliminate, hinder or restrict sales of competitive processed lemon juices, and taking steps selectively to reduce the retail price of its premium priced product to a level so low as to make it virtually impossible for other producers of processed lemon juice to sell their products at prices above their own cost.[14]

The court felt that advertising had an undue influence on consumers' purchases of premium-brand products. This influence led to consumer attachment to the premium brand that could only be negated by a "disproportionately" large price difference. In the court's mind, Golden Crown's failure was no fault of its own but was instead caused by irrational consumers who preferred the ReaLemon brand to the Golden Crown brand regardless of actual differences in quality.

---

14 *Ibid.*, p. 496.

The marketing of **durable goods** requires the firm to address an important set of issues not raised in the case of nondurables. Durable consumer goods are much like capital goods in the theory of the firm. They provide the consumer with a flow of services over time. Indeed, durable consumer goods are not demanded for their own sake, but rather for the future flow of services the consumer anticipates receiving over the product's expected useful life.

The demand for a consumer durable (the amount the buyer is willing to pay) is equal to the net present value of these future services to the consumer.[15] The net present value of the future flow of services in turn depends on the purchaser's subjective assessment of the utility derived from consuming them, the expected length of the product's useful life, anticipated maintenance or repair expenses, and the amount, if any, for which the product can be resold.

By definition, a durable good generates a flow of services into the future. On the surface, this observation seems to imply that the demand for durable goods will be greater than the demand for nondurables which, once consumed, disappear. Moreover, other things being the same, consumers would seem to be willing to pay more for a good that is more durable (has a longer expected useful life) because the more durable good generates a flow of services farther into the future. Considered in isolation from the other factors that influence the demand for consumer durables, this is indeed the case.

There is an important complication that weakens these conclusions, however. Once a new durable good has been sold, ownership rights pass to the purchaser, who may subsequently choose to resell it. Used consumer durables create competition for the good's original producer by reducing the demand for new durables. The durability of the new good, in turn, affects the price at which the original purchaser can expect to resell it. And, other things being the same, the higher this expected resale price, the more the original purchaser is willing to pay.

In sum, the built-in durability of a product (its expected longevity) has two opposing effects on the price at which the firm will be able to sell it. On the one hand, by increasing its resale value, improved durability raises the price consumers are willing to pay for a new durable good. On the other hand, by making used goods better substitutes for new goods, improved durability reduces the demand for new durables, thereby reducing the price consumers will pay for them.

Table 11.3 illustrates the first of these effects. Suppose that a college junior is considering purchasing a new compact disc player that she intends to sell after graduation. The student places a subjective value of $300 on the pleasure of listening to her CD collection over the coming year. Given this subjective consumption value, she will be willing to pay $300 at most for a compact disc player if she cannot resell it at the end of the year. On the other hand, if the student expects to be able to resell the CD player for $50

---

15 The net present value concept is discussed more fully in Chapter 15.

TABLE 11.3 THE DEMAND FOR DURABLE GOODS AS A FUNCTION OF RESALE VALUE

CONSUMPTION VALUE	EXPECTED RESALE PRICE[a]	PRESENT VALUE OF RESALE PRICE[b]	DEMAND PRICE
$300	$0	$0	$300.00
300	50	45.45	345.45
300	100	90.91	390.91
300	150	136.36	436.36
300	200	181.82	481.82
300	250	227.27	527.27

a At the end of one year.

b Assuming an interest rate of 10 percent. The discount factor is $1/(1+r)$, where r is the rate of interest.

following graduation, the present value of this amount enters into the calculation of the price she is willing to pay for it. In this case, she consumes $300 worth of services and then receives $50 when she later sells the CD player. At an interest rate of 10 percent, the present value of $50 received one year from today is $50/1.1 = $45.45. This resale opportunity raises the amount the student is willing to pay for a new CD player from $300 to $345.45.

Table 11.3 shows that the amount consumers will pay for a new CD player rises as its resale value rises. But higher resale values imply that used CD players are better substitutes for new CD players. Better substitutability between new and used durable goods tends to reduce the price consumers will pay for new durables. At the extreme, suppose that new and used CD players are perfect substitutes for one another. If the college student is indifferent between purchasing a new or a used CD player, she will not be willing to pay more than $300 for a new one.

Hence, product durability is a double-edged sword. If the seller increases the durability of new products, it raises the price consumers are willing to pay for them. But as durability continues to increase, used goods become better substitutes for new goods and the price consumers will pay for new durables declines. In the limit, if the firm produces a CD player that is perfectly durable (lasts forever), new and used goods must sell at the same price. As far as the seller is concerned, producing a perfectly durable good is the same as producing a nondurable good having no resale value.

This important result is known in the economics literature as the **Coase conjecture**.[16] Consider a firm that produces and sells a perfectly durable widget in a closed price-searcher market. Suppose that the marginal costs of widget manufacture are constant and equal to $50 per unit. In addition, assume that marginal revenue is equal to marginal cost at an output rate of 100 widgets per year and that the corresponding profit-maximizing price is

16 Ronald H. Coase, "Durability and Monopoly," *Journal of Law and Economics* 15 (April 1972), pp. 143-50.

$75 per unit. Can the firm sell widgets for $75? The answer is no. Knowing that widgets last forever and that once production begins a used widget market will develop, the firm cannot credibly commit itself to never reducing the price of widgets in the future.

The firm cannot make a commitment not to reduce price because as additional new widgets are sold, more and more of them will find their way into the resale market. Because second-hand widgets are by definition perfect substitutes for new widgets, the market prices of both new and old widgets will tend to fall as their supply increases. Hence, to continue to sell the same number of new widgets in the future, the firm must reduce its price below $75. And, knowing that the price will eventually fall, consumers will not now be willing to pay $75. At what price will consumers be willing to purchase new widgets today? No more than $50—the marginal-cost price at which both new and old widgets will ultimately sell.

The foregoing discussion suggests that from the firm's point of view, a consumer durable has an optimal expected useful life. "Planned obsolescence" is a rational, profit-maximizing response to the tradeoff posed by product durability. The determination of optimal durability requires the firm to balance the effects of increased longevity in the markets for both new and used products. Generally speaking, as new and used durables become better substitutes for one another, the likelihood increases that greater durability will affect the seller's profits adversely.[17]

Although optimal durability must be determined on a case-by-case basis, we can gain some insights into the problem by observing the extent to which the sellers of consumer durables help promote the development of resale markets. Many new car dealers, for example, go to great lengths to help customers sell their used vehicles. The fact that new car dealers are willing to undertake such activities suggests that increasing the resale values of used cars will raise the prices and profitability of new car sales. On the other hand, textbook publishers go to great lengths to discourage their customers from reselling books in the second-hand market. They change editions frequently so that new books become obsolete sooner. This observation suggests that publishers think that the existence of an active resale market reduces the prices and profitability of new book sales.

OPTIMAL CONSUMER PRODUCT SAFETY

Consumer product safety is an aspect of quality that raises issues of critical importance to the firm. If the users of a product face a risk of injury or death, the seller's exposure to financial losses in the form of negligence lawsuits and impaired brand-name capital may well swamp any other factor that enters into the determination of optimal quality.

---

17 See, for example, Daniel K. Benjamin and Roger C. Kormendi, "The Interrelationship Between Markets for New and Used Durable Goods," *Journal of Law and Economics* 17 (October 1974), pp. 381-402.

Recycling and Market Power

The introduction of new technologies over the past decade or so have made it increasingly economical for firms to reuse previously processed materials. Used glass, paper, and aluminum products, for example, are now recycled into new products on a fairly large scale. The ability to reprocess inputs of these kinds has an obvious impact on the pricing and production decisions of the suppliers of virgin materials. On the one hand, the greater the output (the lower the prices) of virgin materials, the more of these materials will eventually find their way into the hands of reprocessors. On the other hand, the lower the output (the higher the prices) of virgin materials, the more economical the recycling alternative becomes.

To what extent does the existence of a secondary market in reprocessed materials affect the ability of suppliers of virgin materials to charge prices in excess of their marginal production costs? This was a critical issue in the famous antitrust decision against the Aluminum Company of America (Alcoa) in 1945.[a] Alcoa was found guilty of possessing an unlawful monopoly of the domestic market for raw aluminum ingots. In writing his opinion of the case, Judge Learned Hand elected to define the relevant market as consisting of all primary domestic aluminum ingot production plus aluminum ingot imports. On this basis, Alcoa was effectively a monopolist, accounting for 90 percent of total domestic sales.

Judge Hand's market definition excluded other primary metals, such as steel and copper, that a substantial number of users apparently viewed as feasible substitutes for aluminum.[b] More importantly, Judge Hand also excluded secondary (reprocessed scrap) aluminum from the relevant product market. Secondary aluminum accounted for approximately 40 percent of all domestic aluminum supplies and had it been included in the market definition, Alcoa's share of domestic sales would have dropped from 90 percent to 33 percent, a figure that is still high but almost certainly not high enough to constitute an illegal monopoly.

Judge Hand's decision to exclude secondary aluminum—a decision that almost certainly led him to find Alcoa guilty of unlawful monopolization—remains a subject of controversy among economists who have studied the case. The demand for aluminum products was growing rapidly during the time covered by the antitrust complaint, and Alcoa's production of raw aluminum ingots was consequently also expanding. Taking account of these facts, a number of economists have argued that a competitive market for secondary aluminum placed a major constraint on the prices Alcoa charged for primary aluminum.[c] It has also been argued, on the other hand, that Alcoa purposely reduced the rate of increase in its production of virgin aluminum ingots in anticipation of future recycling. By limiting the supply of aluminum available for reprocessing, Alcoa may have been able to charge higher prices for primary aluminum than it could have charged otherwise.[d]

a U. S. v. Aluminum Co. of America, 148 F.2d 416 (2d Cir. 1945).

b Merton J. Peck, Market Control in the Aluminum Industry (Cambridge, MA: Harvard University Press, 1961), pp. 31-34, estimates that aluminum's cross-price elasticity of demand with respect to the price of steel was on the order of 2.0, and perhaps even higher with respect to the price of copper. See Chapter 2 for the definition and interpretation of the cross-price elasticity of demand.

c See, for example, Darius W. Gaskins, "Alcoa Revisited: The Welfare Implications of a Secondhand Market," Journal of Economic Theory 7 (March 1974), pp. 254-71, and Franklin M. Fisher, "Comment," Journal of Economic Theory 9 (November 1974), pp. 57-59.

d Peter L. Swan, "Alcoa: The Influence of Recycling on Monopoly Power," Journal of Political Economy 88 (February 1980), pp. 76-99.

As mentioned earlier, however, a strategy of restricting the production of primary aluminum ingots is a double-edged sword. By raising the price of primary aluminum, Alcoa would have in effect encouraged a secondary market in reprocessed aluminum to develop more rapidly. The higher the price of primary aluminum, the more profitable reprocessing becomes, and the more competition Alcoa would then face from the secondary market. Hence, while reducing the output and raising the price of virgin aluminum may have allowed Alcoa to earn higher profits in the short run than it would have earned otherwise, these profits would have been competed away more quickly by reprocessors. Indeed, the fact that Alcoa and other major producers of primary aluminum have themselves become heavily involved in the recycling business in recent years suggests that reprocessed aluminum places a significant constraint on the price and profitability of primary aluminum.

Consumer product safety became a major concern in 1965 following the publication of Ralph Nader's book, *Unsafe at Any Speed*. In this book, Nader charged that the placement of the fuel tank in General Motor's Chevrolet Corvair made the vehicle vulnerable to exploding on impact if involved in a rear-end collision. Nader charged further that GM was not only aware of the Corvair's safety defect, but had knowingly suppressed the information. The negative publicity generated by *Unsafe at Any Speed* led to the enactment of a series of consumer product safety laws, culminating in 1972 with the establishment of the federal Consumer Product Safety Commission. *Unsafe at Any Speed* also triggered a flurry of consumer lawsuits that raised producers' legal liability for safety defects considerably.

Difficult though it may be to accept emotionally, the optimal number of safety defects is not zero. Because firms can reduce safety defects only by investing additional resources in design, testing, and inspection, it will never pay any firm to completely eliminate the possibility of harm to individuals who purchase its product. Just as importantly, the risk of injury or death to a firm's customers depends partly on the care they themselves exercise. Used improperly, virtually every product is potentially dangerous and even the most safety conscious company cannot protect consumers from their own carelessness.

Nor do consumers demand absolute product safety. Because safe products are more costly to produce than unsafe ones, consumers rationally weigh the marginal value of reductions in the risk of injury or death against the marginal expense of purchasing additional safety. Tradeoffs of this kind occur every day. Anyone who has chosen to drive rather than to fly to their vacation destination has implicitly accepted a higher accident risk in return for lower out-of-pocket travel expenses.

Hence, as with all economic choices, the profit-maximizing firm improves its product's safety features up to the point where marginal benefit is equal to marginal cost. Marginal benefit is here measured in terms of the amount consumers are willing and able to pay for safety improvements. Marginal cost consists of the value of the resources the firm has to invest directly in reducing consumers' accident risk plus its expected financial exposure to tort claims. The firm's legal liability, in turn, depends on the frequency with which product use will result in physical harm times the average size of the monetary damages it expects to pay to injured parties.

The cost-benefit analysis necessary to determine optimal safety is complicated by an unsettled question in product liability law. One side of the debate holds that the main purpose of the law is to provide *compensation* to consumers for the harm they suffer on account of safety defects. In other words, product liability law serves as an insurance policy that enables consumers to recover the monetary value of whatever injuries they sustain due to the use of an unsafe product. Under this view, if found liable, the firm would expect to pay a monetary award equal to the consumer's medical expenses plus the present value of any income he or she loses because of the injury.

The second purpose attributed to product liability law is *deterrence*, that is, preventing consumers from being harmed in the first place. Generally speaking, the damages calculated under the deterrence principle exceed those required under the compensation principle. And, indeed, assessing damages at the level required to achieve deterrence provides incentives for the firm to "overinsure," that is, to supply products that are excessively safe.[18] This conclusion follows because the firm chooses a price-safety combination in response to consumers' demands that in effect insures them ahead of time for perceived risk. (To reiterate, a compensating reduction in product price is required for consumers to accept an increased chance of product-related injury or death.)

Legal theories of compensation and deterrence aside, the reality of today's liability laws for products is that the firm's financial exposure to tort claims is both large and uncertain. Because public policy makers and the courts increasingly seek deterrence rather than compensation (as illustrated by the award of punitive damages), firms should use deterrence values in assessing their potential liability. Failure to do so can have disastrous consequences.

Consider the Ford Pinto, a safety defect case remarkably similar to the one exposed in *Unsafe at Any Speed*.[19] The Ford Motor Company made a conscious decision in the early 1970s not to make an inexpensive change in the Pinto's design that would have reduced its fuel tank's vulnerability in rear-end collisions. Ford calculated that it would cost $11 per vehicle (or a total of $137.5 million for the 12.5 million cars and light trucks having a faulty fuel tank design) to eliminate 180 burn deaths, 180 burn injuries, and 2,100 burned vehicles. Based on typical products liability awards at the time, the company expected to pay $200,000 in compensation for fatalities, $67,000 for burn victims, and $700 for damaged vehicles. Ford therefore estimated the total expected benefit of correcting the Pinto's design defect to be $49.6 million, a figure far lower than the $137.5 million total cost.

---

18 See W. Kip Viscusi, *Reforming Products Liability* (Cambridge, MA: Harvard University Press, 1991), pp. 89-94.

19 *Ibid.*, pp. 111-13.

The flaw in Ford's reasoning was not that it attempted to explicitly assign dollar values to the benefits and costs of correcting the Pinto's design defect, but that it seriously underestimated its financial exposure to tort claims. Using deterrence values rather than insurance values to assess Ford's legal liability, figures of $5 million per fatality and $2.5 million per burn victim were more appropriate. Proper calculation of the total expected benefits of making the design improvement ($1.352 billion) using these deterrence values of life show them to be ten times greater than the cost.

Financial exposure to tort claims is not the only cost of selling defective products that injure or kill their purchasers. Market forces penalize the owners of firms whose products fail to deliver the expected level of safety. This penalty is in the form of a reduced market value (stock price) which reflects the loss of brand name capital incurred by the firm when information about safety defects becomes publicly available.

The negative impact of information about safety defects on the value of the firm is considerably larger than the direct cost of recalling products either to destroy them or to correct the deficiency. In a study of the automobile and pharmaceutical industries, for example, Gregg Jarrell and Sam Peltzman found that the announcement of a product recall destroys between 1.5 percent and 6 percent of the firm's market value.[20] (They also reported evidence of negative spillover effects on the competitors of the firm whose product is recalled.) Similarly, in a study of the commercial airline industry, Mark Mitchell and Michael Maloney found that a fatal crash reduces the market value of an air carrier by about 2.5 percent, *provided* that the airline is at fault.[21] According to their results, no adverse consequences followed from accidents caused by factors outside the airline's control, suggesting that the market assigns blame correctly and fairly.

Negative publicity can damage the value of a brand name unless the firm takes dramatic steps in response. Several years ago, cyanide was discovered in several Tylenol® capsules. Johnson & Johnson, the maker of Tylenol®, removed its pain-killer from the market worldwide. The company redesigned the product, developed tamper-resistant packages, and took steps to reduce the chances of pill contamination during the manufacturing process. Despite the high cost of removing Tylenol® from the marketplace, such quick and decisive action enabled Johnson & Johnson to recover from the cyanide-poisoning episode in a relatively short period of time. Market forces evidently provide powerful incentives for firms to sell products that deliver the level of safety demanded by consumers.

---

20 Gregg Jarrell and Sam Peltzman, "The Impact of Product Recalls on the Wealth of Sellers," *Journal of Political Economy* 93 (June 1985), pp. 512-36.

21 Mark L. Mitchell and Michael T. Maloney, "Crisis in the Cockpit? The Role of Market Forces in Promoting Air Travel Safety," *Journal of Law and Economics* 32 (October 1989), pp. 329-55.

Perhaps the most basic characteristic of the 14 elements of Total Quality Management (TQM) listed in Table 11.1 (see p. 374) is their assumption that firms operate in a dynamically competitive environment. TQM stresses the importance of quality competition among firms; economic theories of competition have traditionally emphasized price competition among firms. In truth, both are important dimensions of a competitive market because consumers purchase products on the basis of their perceptions of value per dollar spent. This section discusses the elements of the TQM philosophy in the context of the economic theory of the firm.

Elements 1, 2, 5, and 14 in Table 11.1 are related to each other. The four elements are: create constancy of purpose for improvement of product and service; adopt the new philosophy; continuously improve quality; and take action to accomplish the transformation. From the perspective of economic theory, it is acceptable to emphasize the importance of quality competition but not in a way that confuses quality with the firm's ultimate objective of long-run profit maximization.

For a quality-based strategy to be successful, the firm must successfully market quality. If consumers are ignorant of the quality attributes of a firm's product, it does the firm no good to "continuously improve quality." Economic theory can provide important insights into consumer behavior in markets characterized by imperfect information. Consumers' efforts to learn about quality differentials among competing products are a function of the cost of search for that particular class of products. Search goods, experience goods, and credence goods differ according to the costs involved in gathering information about quality differences.[22] An understanding of this aspect of consumer behavior can aid a quality-based competitive strategy.

Element 4 advises that firms should stop awarding business because of the price tag alone. This element explicitly recognizes the important interrelationship among quality, price, and value. That is, element 4 suggests that when the firm purchases inputs it should not limit itself to the low-priced supplier but should also consider the value of the supplier's product (quality relative to price). This reasoning is not only true; it points out a possible weakness in elements 1, 2, 5, and 14 because these elements of TQM seem to equate product quality with product value. Just as firms must consider both price and quality in determining value when they purchase supplies, consumers base purchases on value and not just quality. Neither lower price nor higher quality alone translates into better value.

Elements 6 (institute training) and 13 (institute a vigorous program of education and retraining) underscore the benefits of training and educating workers. The weakness in these statements is that they fail to recognize the cost of these activities. How does the firm decide whether to emphasize general-skills education or job-specific skills? Economic theory recognizes

---

22 The categories of search, experience, and credence goods are defined in Chapter 10.

that all choices of the firm involve an opportunity cost and it can provide guidance in making those choices.

Element 3 (cease dependence on mass inspection) refers to the firm's technological choices. That is, this element of TQM maintains that technology which uses inspection to keep manufacturing defects from reaching customers is, in the long run, more costly than designing a product and production process that minimize defects in the first place. This is essentially an empirical question rather than a theoretical question. However, the theory of imperfect information shows that the cost of search is an important consideration in purchasing products and, therefore, also emphasizes the importance of variations in product quality.

Elements 7 (institute leadership) and 9 (break down barriers between staff areas) are concerned with management's role in the production process. These points maintain that a cooperative relationship between managers and workers is more productive than an adversarial relationship and, similarly, that competition among staffs and departments should be replaced by mutual cooperation. Relatedly, elements 8 (eliminate fear) and 12 (improve pride of workmanship) deal with labor's role in the production process. Again, adversarial relations between workers and managers are less productive than cooperative relations. These four elements are concerned with the psychology of labor relations, a subject that is not within the purview of economic theory.[23]

Elements 10 and 11 suggest that firms should eliminate motivational slogans and numerical goals. Both of these recommendations are corollaries of TQM's emphasis on the carrot rather than the stick in promoting labor productivity. Motivational slogans imposed from above are not consistent with the philosophy that labor and management should work as a cooperative team in the production process. Nor are numerical goals consistent with TQM. This philosophy argues that workers should gain motivation from the incentive to do a quality job rather than from goals dictated by management.

SUMMARY

Chapter 11 has focused on product quality to analyze the tradeoff between price competition and nonprice competition. Like all economic choices, the determination of optimal product quality requires the firm to balance the marginal benefits of quality improvements against the marginal costs of achieving them. Examined through the lens of marginal analysis, investments in product quality are no different from investments in advertising and promotional activities, pre- and post-sale services, or any other nonprice variable the profit-maximizing firm may exploit to distinguish its product in the minds of consumers from the products offered by rival sellers.

Key Terms

putting-out system
quality grade
quality attribute
asymmetric information
reservation price
adverse selection
lemons market
full price
Alchian and Allen hypothesis

---

23 But see Chapters 7, 14, and 16, which discuss the importance of property rights and the internal organization of the firm in providing workers and managers with incentives to cooperate.

The chapter highlights two important aspects of product quality. One relates to the frequency with which defective or substandard items are produced. Production defects are costly, wasting valuable production time and materials, delaying deliveries, and forcing the firm to hold larger inventories. Improving the quality of the production process is also costly, however. The frequency with which defects occur can only be reduced by investing additional resources in quality control. Hence, it is never economical for the profit-maximizing firm to adopt a policy of zero production defects. Resources should be invested in improving the quality of the production process up to the point at which marginal benefit is equal to marginal cost.

This chapter has also defined the concept of quality in terms of the value consumers place on various nonprice product characteristics. Consumers' perceptions of quality are affected by the product's durability, reliability, safety features, and a host of other factors. Whether or not it will be profitable for the firm to improve product quality along any of these margins again requires a balancing of benefits and costs.

We have examined the benefits and costs of quality improvements in the context of "lemons" markets, the pricing of durable goods, and consumer product safety. We have addressed the complex tradeoffs posed in each of these cases and derived rules for determining optimal quality, optimal durability, and optimal product safety. As with many of the issues discussed in other chapters, economic theory does not provide rote answers to the questions raised by product quality. But the powerful tool of marginal analysis does help the manager identify the important factors that must be taken into account when decisions about product quality are being made.

Key Terms
sunk costs
signal
predatory pricing
durable good
Coase conjecture

QUESTIONS

11.1 Evaluate, using economic reasoning, the following elements of the Total Quality Management philosophy:
a. Cease dependence on mass inspection.
b. Continuously improve quality.

11.2 Many shoppers rely on a well known brand name or trademark as a signal of quality and are willing to pay a premium for it. Does this behavior make economic sense? Why or why not?

11.3 Product guarantees and warranties often stipulate that adjustments or repairs be made by factory authorized dealers. Provide an economic explanation for this requirement.

11.4 Toyota has chosen to compete in the luxury car market by introducing the Lexus.® Lexus® models are not sold through Toyota dealerships and the Toyota name is not mentioned in Lexus® advertisements. Explain why Toyota adopted this marketing strategy for its luxury car.

11.5 Explain, using economic analysis, the following observations:
a. College football fans who travel longer distances to attend games purchase relatively higher priced seats than fans who live closer to the stadium.
b. Crack cocaine, a highly potent version of the illegal narcotic, became more readily available after the federal government instituted its "War on Drugs."

c. Tourists tend to eat at more expensive restaurants while traveling than they do at home.

11.6 One of the authors of *Modern Managerial Economics*, who lives in Oxford, Mississippi, recently took two business trips, one to Colorado Springs and the other to Memphis, Tennessee. On which trip did he buy more expensive presents for his two children? Why?

11.7 Suppose that the federal excise tax on gasoline increases by five cents per gallon. Do you expect this tax hike to differentially affect the sales of premium and regular grades of unleaded fuel? Why or why not?

11.8 Suppose you intend to lease either a new Mercedes-Benz or a new Chevrolet Camaro for one year. In which case would you expect the rental rate to be a greater fraction of the car's selling price? Explain.

11.9 Appliance manufacturers sell their products only in two or three basic colors. Given the multitude of possible colors, what is the economic rationale for limiting the color selection to just white, black, and beige?

11.10 Explain why you might expect a greater proportion of the used cars sold through newspaper ads to be "lemons" than those sold by franchised new car dealers.

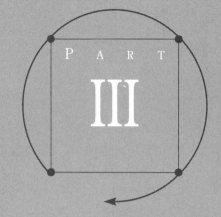

The Organizational Structure of the Firm

Make-or-Buy Decisions: The Economic Theory of Vertical Integration

OVERVIEW

Managers must make important and difficult choices about whether to obtain inputs employed in the production process from outside suppliers or to instead produce them internally. Chapters 12 and 13 build on the theory introduced in Chapter 7 by discussing in detail the costs and benefits of these two alternative means of procuring labor services, raw materials, capital equipment, and other essential resources. We will compare the costs of negotiating and enforcing contracts with outside suppliers to the organizational and incentive problems posed by ownership integration.

This chapter lays the groundwork for evaluating make-or-buy decisions. The economic theory of vertical integration identifies the purposes and effects of merging two or more successive stages of production under common ownership. The economic motives for integrating backward into the production of an important input and for integrating forward into the distribution of a final product are described under various assumptions. These assumptions concern the nature of the firm's production technology and the competitive characteristics of the markets in which the firm buys and sells.

The next chapter focuses on organizational choices for governing transactions in downstream retail markets. We will compare and contrast ownership integration with contractual alternatives such as resale price maintenance, franchising arrangements, requirements contracts, and tie-in sales. The goal of these two chapters is to provide the theoretical tools necessary to evaluate a wide range of make-or-buy decisions.

The International Business Machines Corporation (IBM) and Digital Equipment Corporation (DEC) have three things in common.[a] They both make computers, they are among the most vertically integrated of high-tech manufacturers, and they are currently the industry's worst performers.

The manufacture of one computer requires hundreds of individual parts and components. These parts run from simple items like switches and fans to complex silicon chips and disk drives that are critical to the product's performance. There are three ways to procure these parts and components. One option is to buy them on an as-needed basis in the "spot" market from independent suppliers who specialize in the manufacture of particular computer parts. A second option is to contract with one or more of the independent suppliers who agree to produce parts to the computer manufacturer's designs and specifications. The third option is for the computer manufacturer to fill its own parts requirements by buying an established supplier or by building its own parts manufacturing facility.

Both IBM and DEC embraced this last option with a vengeance, making virtually every part of their own computer products. Their reasons for doing so were fear of supply interruptions of critical parts due to reliance on outside suppliers and fear of losing technological expertise to foreign manufacturers. But these benefits came at a cost. IBM, in particular, grew stodgy and inflexible. The firm became wedded to in-house technologies that were leap-frogged by smaller, highly specialized "niche" companies. Lacking the pricing discipline of market competition, IBM found that its comparative advantages in memory-chip design and manufacture were offset by an inability to control parts costs. And the overhead burden of the administrative organization required to supervise and coordinate the production and assembly of hundreds of parts increasingly dulled the firm's competitive edge.

As a result, competition in the early 1990s forced IBM to undertake a series of painful downsizing measures. The firm shed high-cost manufacturing facilities and either laid off or offered early retirement to tens of thousands of employees. But the lesson of this chapter is that IBM's survival does not depend on becoming a completely "hollow" assembler of parts produced by others. Indeed, most successful companies are neither completely hollow nor completely vertically integrated. Striking a balance between making and buying is tricky, however. Fortunately, there are general economic principles that serve as useful guides in solving make-or-buy problems. This chapter lays out those principles.

---

a The following discussion is based in part on G. Pascal Zachary, "Getting Help: High-Tech Firms Find It's Good to Line Up Outside Contractors," *Wall Street Journal*, 29 July 1992, p. A1.

The transformation of a product from raw materials to its final sale involves many distinct (technologically separable) production and distribution functions. These functions could be carried out by separately owned, specialized firms or they could all be accomplished under common ownership within a single, **vertically integrated** organization.

In the first case, all transactions will take place across the ownership boundaries of firms. Some raw materials and intermediate goods will be bought and sold on the open market. Contracts of varying duration and complexity will govern other transactions of this kind. Indeed, any given market transaction may involve a mix of formal and informal relationships between buyer and seller. For example, a firm may purchase raw materials in the spot market but contract with a trucking company to transport the raw materials to its production facility. In the second case, the vertically integrated firm will simply transfer raw materials and intermediate goods from its upstream divisions to its downstream divisions at appropriate internal prices.[1]

Which option is chosen in any particular case depends on which minimizes the sum of production costs and transaction costs. As we have seen, a number of factors determine the boundaries of the firm. The important considerations include critical features of the transaction itself—the frequency of occurrence, the need to invest in specialized assets, and the degree of uncertainty involved.[2] Because these factors vary from transaction to transaction, all firms are integrated to some degree and no firm is completely vertically integrated. Moreover, the extent of vertical integration in the economy is not rigid. As firms adapt to changing market circumstances, the pattern of integration and disintegration will change across industries and over time.

This section investigates the economic theory of vertical integration. The analysis begins by focusing on technological and price-cost incentives to integrate successive stages of production. Subsequent sections discuss additional rationales for vertical integration, including those that stress the importance of transaction costs and government policy. A key lesson in this section is that vertical integration is typically motivated by the additional profit that results from transferring an input internally at a price equal to its marginal production cost rather than purchasing that same input from an outside supplier at a price that includes a markup over marginal cost. Merging successive stages of production under these circumstances leads to an expansion in sales of the final product and a corresponding reduction in its price.

1 Jack Hirshleifer, "On the Economics of Transfer Pricing," *Journal of Business* 30 (July 1956), pp. 172-84. Transfer pricing is discussed in Chapter 9.

2 Oliver E. Williamson, "Transaction-Cost Economics: The Governance of Contractual Relations," *Journal of Law and Economics* 22 (October 1979), pp. 233-61. These issues are discussed more fully in Chapter 7.

The analysis of the motives for vertical integration in this section is based on some simplifying assumptions. There are only two successive stages of production. The first (upstream) stage manufactures an intermediate input, I. This input is then transformed into a final product, F, in the second (downstream) stage of production. We assume that the production of one unit of F requires exactly one unit of I. Furthermore, we assume that marginal production costs at both stages are constant throughout the relevant range of output choices.

The theoretical presentation is divided into two cases. The first is the single-markup case. There we assume that, prior to any ownership integration, the firm sells the intermediate input to downstream buyers at a price that includes a markup over marginal cost. The final product is assumed to be sold at a price equal to marginal cost in a price-taker market. In the second (double-markup) case, selling prices before integration include markups over marginal cost at both stages of production. For each of these two cases, we discuss the incentives for vertical integration and derive ownership integration's impact on price, sales, and profit at the upstream and downstream stages of production. Throughout these examples, fixed costs are assumed to be zero so that marginal, average variable, and average total costs are equal to one another.

The Single-Markup Case. Vertical integration confers no advantages on the firms at either stage of production when economic profits are earned at only one production stage in the absence of ownership integration. The dairy industry provides a relevant example. As a result of agricultural marketing order programs sanctioned by the federal government during the 1930s, dairy farmers may sell all the milk they produce at a guaranteed price. Thus, although the market demand schedule for milk is downward sloping, with constant costs and no barriers to the entry of new producers, dairy farmers will expand output until the marginal cost of the last gallon of milk sold is just equal to the price at which the government will purchase that gallon. Dairy farmers earn only a "normal" rate of return (zero economic profit) under these circumstances. At the same time, the containers in which the farmers ship the milk to processors might be purchased from independent upstream suppliers whose prices include markups over marginal cost.

Figure 12.1 presents the revenue and cost schedules necessary for analyzing the single-markup case.[3] D_F represents the demand for the final product manufactured and sold by the downstream industry and MR_F is the associated marginal revenue schedule.[4] D_I is the downstream industry's

---

3 The following discussion relies heavily on Roger D. Blair and David L. Kaserman, *Antitrust Economics* (Homewood, IL: Richard D. Irwin, 1985), pp. 297-301.

4 Because the downstream industry will, by assumption, sell its product to customers at a price equal to marginal cost, the marginal revenue schedule associated with D_F is not relevant in determining optimal production at the second stage when transactions in the intermediate input take place across ownership boundaries. However, MR_F does come into play in discussing the motives for vertical integration in the single-markup case. See the mathematical example below.

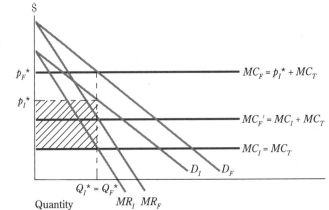

FIGURE 12.1
Fixed-Proportions
Technology with a
Single Markup

derived demand for the intermediate input produced upstream. Keeping in mind that $F = I$ (one unit of I is required to produce one unit of F), we construct this derived demand schedule by subtracting from the final product's price the cost incurred by the downstream industry in transforming a unit of the input into a unit of output. This cost is denoted by the schedule labeled MC_T.[5]

In other words, the maximum amount the downstream industry would be willing to pay for a unit of I is equal to the price for which it can sell a unit of F minus the cost of transforming I into F. Graphically, we derive D_I by subtracting MC_T from D_F and so the vertical distance between D_F and D_I is equal to MC_T. Once D_I is derived in this way, we determine the marginal revenue associated with sales of the intermediate input to the downstream industry, MR_I.[6]

Both upstream and downstream industries will maximize profit by producing where marginal revenue equals marginal cost. When transactions between the successive stages of production take place across ownership boundaries, the upstream suppliers select the rate of output at which the marginal cost of producing the intermediate input, MC_I, equals the marginal revenue associated with sales to downstream customers, MR_I. Setting $MR_I = MC_I$ yields optimal production of Q_I^* units and an optimal unit price of p_I^*. (The profit-maximizing price of I is determined by the point on the downstream industry's derived demand for the input, D_I, corresponding to Q_I^*.) The upstream industry's total profit is therefore equal to the area of the shaded rectangle defined by $(p_I^* - MC_I)Q_I^*$.

Given this price and quantity of the intermediate input, the downstream industry's marginal cost is $MC_F = p_I^* + MC_T$, the price of the input plus the

---

5 For simplicity—mainly to avoid cluttering the diagram—MC_T and MC_I are assumed to be equal.

6 The derivation of the marginal revenue schedule from the demand schedule is explained in Chapter 2. As shown there, when the demand schedule is linear, the marginal revenue schedule is also linear with a slope equal to twice that of the demand schedule. With linear revenue and cost schedules, the vertical distance between MR_F and MR_I is equal to MC_T for the same reason that D_F and D_I differ by that amount.

marginal cost of transforming the input into a unit of output. Equating MC_F with the price of the final product (determined along D_F), yields a profit-maximizing output of Q_F^* ($= Q_I^*$ because of the one-to-one correspondence between I and F) and a final product price of $p_F^* = MC_F$. The downstream industry consequently earns zero economic profit.

An algebraic example. We can see these same relationships with the aid of a simple mathematical example. Let the inverse market demand curve for the final product be

$$p_F = \$50 - \$.5Q_F.$$

Further assume that the marginal cost of producing the intermediate input that is used in a one-to-one ratio in the manufacture of the final product is constant and equal to $10 (i.e., $MC_I = \$10$), and that the marginal cost of transforming a unit of I into a unit of F, MC_T, is likewise equal to $10.

As discussed above, the derived inverse demand for the intermediate input is

$$p_I = p_F - MC_T.$$

This expression follows from noting that the maximum amount the downstream producers will be willing to pay for a unit of I is equal to the amount for which they can sell a unit of F less the cost of transforming I into F. Substituting $p_F = \$50 - \$.5Q_F$ and $MC_T = \$10$ into the right-hand side of this relationship yields

$$p_I = \$40 - \$.5Q_F = \$40 - \$.5Q_I$$

because $Q_F = Q_I$ by assumption. The marginal revenue associated with the derived input demand function is then

$$MR_I = \$40 - \$1Q_I.$$

Applying the marginal-revenue-equals-marginal-cost rule, the upstream industry maximizes profit by producing where

$$\$40 - \$1Q_I = \$10.$$

Optimal production at the first stage is determined by solving this expression for Q_I, which yields $Q_I^* = 30$. The intermediate input is sold to downstream buyers at a unit price of $p_I^* = \$40 - \$.5(Q_I^*) = \$40 - \$.5(30) = \$25$, and at this optimal price and quantity, the upstream producers earn total profits amounting to $\pi_I^* = (p_I^* - MC_I)Q_I^* = (\$25 - \$10)30 = \$450$.

Marginal cost at the second stage of production is $35 because the industry pays $25 for each unit of I on which it then spends $10 transforming the input into a unit of F. Setting $p_F = MC_F$, the final product industry maximizes profit by producing 30 units of output. Specifically, solving

$$\$50 - \$.5Q_F = \$35$$

yields $Q_F{}^* = 30$, which are each sold to consumers of the final product at a price of $p_F{}^* = MC_F = \$35$.

The absence of a motive for vertical integration. Although the downstream industry pays a price for the intermediate input that includes a markup over marginal cost,[7] no incentive for vertical integration exists under the stated assumptions. To see this result, suppose that the upstream and downstream producers combine under common ownership. The integrated firm would then maximize its profits by selecting the quantity of output at which the marginal revenue of the final product, MR_F, is equal to marginal cost. The relevant marginal cost in this case is $MC_F{}'$, which is found by summing the marginal cost of producing the input, MC_I, and the marginal cost of transforming the input into output, MC_T.

Rather than selling I at the market-determined price, $p_I{}^*$, as it did prior to merger, the upstream division of the integrated enterprise simply transfers the intermediate input to the downstream division at an internal price equal to marginal cost. (The upstream division consequently earns zero economic profit.) The downstream division, in turn, produces $Q_F{}^*$ units of the final product (the output level at which $MR_F = MC_F{}'$) and sells them at price $p_F{}^*$. The integrated firm's total profits, $(p_F{}^* - MC_F{}')Q_F{}^*$, are exactly equal to the profits earned by the upstream producers prior to ownership integration.[8]

Hence, no economic incentive for vertical integration exists in the single-markup case. The only consequence of integration is that profits are collected in the final product market rather than in the market for the intermediate input. Total sales at both stages of production are the same and the price paid by consumers of the final product is unaffected.

An algebraic proof that profits are unaffected by vertical integration. We can verify this important result mathematically. With full ownership integration, the firm maximizes profits at the downstream stage of production by equating MR_F with $MC_F{}' = MC_I + MC_T$. Using the same assumptions as before, $MC_F{}' = \$20$, and so optimal final product sales are found by solving

$$\$50 - \$1Q_F = \$20.$$

Hence, $Q_F{}^* = 30$ is the profit-maximizing quantity. Substituting this value into the final product demand schedule yields

---

7 The markup is 150 percent in the previous numerical example.

8 Demonstrating the equality of profits with and without integration requires showing that $(p_I{}^* - MC_I)Q_I{}^* = (p_F{}^* - MC_F{}')Q_F{}^*$. With fixed-proportions technology assumed, $Q_F{}^* = Q_I{}^*$. The profit equality thus holds if $(p_I{}^* - MC_I) = (p_F{}^* - MC_F{}')$. Substituting $p_F{}^* = p_I{}^* + MC_T$ and $MC_F{}' = MC_I + MC_T$ on the right-hand side of this relationship yields $p_I{}^* - MC_I = p_I{}^* + MC_T - (MC_I + MC_T) = p_I{}^* - MC_I$, which completes the proof.

$$p_F{}^* = \$50 - \$.5(30) = \$35,$$

which is the same price paid by the consumers of the final product in the absence of ownership integration.[9] Total profits are accordingly $\pi_F{}^* = (p_F{}^* - MC_F{}')(Q_F{}^*) = (\$35 - \$20)\,30 = \$450$. This figure is the same as the profit earned upstream before the merger.

The Double-Markup Case. This section analyzes the motives for merger when, in the absence of ownership integration, prices that include markups over marginal cost are charged at each of two successive stages of production. In contrast to the single-markup case described above, replacing market exchange with internal transfer pricing of an intermediate input not only increases the integrated firm's profit but, in addition, causes final product output to expand and final product price to fall. Hence, a strong incentive for vertical integration exists. And, moreover, such integration improves the allocation of society's scarce productive resources.

All of the assumptions in the previous section continue to hold. The main complication introduced here concerns the derivation of the downstream industry's derived demand for the intermediate input. Figure 12.2 shows the relevant revenue and cost schedules for analyzing the double-markup case.

First consider the resource-allocation decisions made at each stage of production when no vertical integration exists, that is, when transactions between upstream and downstream producers take place across the ownership boundaries of their firms. The upstream supplier's marginal cost is again denoted as MC_I and, as before, we determine the downstream industry's marginal cost, MC_F, by adding the price it must pay for a unit of the intermediate input to its own cost of transforming I into F (i.e., $MC_F = p_I + MC_T$, where p_I is the unit price of I charged by the final product industry's suppliers).

---

9 Note that although the final product price remains the same with and without integration of successive production stages, the markup over marginal cost paid by the final product's buyers following integration is smaller than the markup charged on sales of the intermediate input prior to integration. Following the merger of upstream and downstream producers, final product price includes a 75 percent markup over marginal cost. (Recall that the price of the intermediate input included a 150 percent markup when transactions took place across ownership boundaries.) This difference in the optimal markup is a consequence of the fact that the derived demand for the input is *less elastic* than the demand for the final product at any given quantity. The proof of this statement follows from noting that for a linear demand schedule, the elasticity of demand can be calculated at any point on the horizontal axis by taking the ratio of the distance between the given quantity and the demand schedule's horizontal intercept to the distance between the origin and the given quantity. Because this ratio is obviously smaller at any point on D_I than it is at the corresponding point on D_F (because D_I's horizontal intercept lies to the left of the horizontal intercept of D_F), it follows that D_I is less elastic at $Q_I{}^*$ $(= Q_F{}^*)$ than is D_F. Consequently, the optimal markup will be higher on sales of the intermediate input than on sales of the final product. For the geometric computation of demand elasticity, see Roger L. Miller and Roger E. Meiners, *Intermediate Microeconomics*, 3E. (New York: McGraw-Hill, 1986), pp. 145-47. Chapter 5 discusses the relationship between the elasticity of demand and the optimal markup over marginal cost.

FIGURE 12.2

Fixed-Proportions
Technology with
a Double Markup

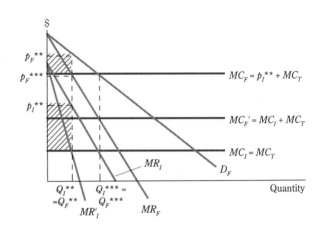

For any input price, then, the quantity of I purchased downstream will be determined by the intersection of MR_F with the sum of the input price and MC_T. As a result, $MR_F - MC_T = p_I$ is the downstream industry's *effective* derived demand for the intermediate input. This effective input demand function is labeled MR_I because, as shown below, it is identical to the schedule that is marginal to the demand schedule for I, D_I, derived in the single-markup case.[10] The schedule labeled MR_I' is the curve marginal to MR_I, the effective derived input demand in the double-markup case.

The upstream industry maximizes its profit by equating marginal revenue, MR_I', with marginal cost, MC_I. Q_I^{**} units of I are accordingly produced and this quantity of output is sold to the downstream industry at a price of p_I^{**} per unit. (The optimal price of the intermediate input is determined by the point on the downstream industry's effective demand for I, MR_I, corresponding to Q_I^{**}.) The supplier industry's total profit is therefore equal to the area of the rectangle defined by $(p_I^{**} - MC_I) Q_I^{**}$—the lower shaded rectangle in Figure 12.2.

Given this price and quantity of the intermediate input, the downstream industry's marginal cost is $MC_F = p_I^{**} + MC_T$. Equating MC_F with the marginal revenue of the final product, MR_F, yields a profit-maximizing output of Q_F^{**} ($= Q_I^{**}$ because of the one-to-one correspondence between I and F) and a final product price of p_F^{**}. The downstream industry earns profits equal to $(p_F^{**} - MC_F) Q_F^{**}$, which are represented by the area of the upper shaded rectangle in the figure.

An algebraic example. We can derive these same optimal prices, quantities, and profits with the aid of the simple mathematical example in the previous section. Recall that we assumed the inverse demand for the final product to be $p_F = \$50 - \$.5Q_F$, with associated marginal revenue of $MR_F = \$50 - \$1Q_F$. The

10 MR_I is the "net marginal revenue" schedule used in the analysis of optimal transfer pricing. See Chapter 9 for a discussion.

marginal costs of producing the intermediate input and of transforming a unit of I into a unit of F are both constant and equal to $10; that is, $MC_I = MC_T = \$10$.

As shown above, the effective demand for the intermediate input in this case is

$$p_I = MR_F - MC_T.$$

This relationship follows from noting that the downstream industry maximizes its profit by equating the marginal revenue associated with final product sales, MR_F, with its own marginal cost, which is the sum of the price paid for each unit of I and the cost of transforming I into F. Setting $MR_F = p_I + MC_T$ and solving for p_I gives the above expression for the derived demand for the intermediate input.

Substituting $MR_F = \$50 - \$1Q_F$ and $MC_T = \$10$ into the right-hand side of the inverse demand for I yields

$$p_I = \$40 - \$1Q_F = \$40 - \$1Q_I,$$

because $Q_F = Q_I$ by assumption of one-to-one fixed-proportions technology.[11] The marginal revenue associated with this effective input demand function is

$$MR_I' = \$40 - \$2Q_I.$$

Applying the marginal-cost-equals-marginal-revenue rule for profit maximization, the upstream industry produces where

$$\$40 - \$2Q_I = \$10,$$

which when solved for the optimal output rate yields $Q_I^{**} = 15$. The corresponding optimal input price is $p_I^{**} = \$40 - \$1Q_I^{**} = \$40 - \$1(15) = \$25$, which represents a 150 percent markup on marginal cost. This is the same unit price (and the same percentage markup on marginal cost) charged to downstream producers in the single-markup case, but only half as much I is sold as before (15 units versus 30 units). At this price and quantity, the input suppliers' total profit is consequently $\pi_I^{**} = (p_I^{**} - MC_I) Q_I^{**} = (\$25 - \$10)15 = \$225$.

Marginal production cost downstream is now equal to $35—each unit of the final product is manufactured by purchasing a unit of I for $25 and then transforming it into F by spending an additional $10. Equating this marginal cost with the marginal revenue associated with final product sales,

$$\$50 - \$1Q_F = \$35,$$

---

11 The demand for I derived in the single-markup case was $p_I = \$40 - \$.5Q_I$. The marginal revenue associated with this demand function was $MR_I = \$40 - \$1Q_I$. Hence, $p_I = MR_I$ in the double-markup case.

yields the profit-maximizing output rate at the second stage of production: $Q_F^{**} = 15$. The corresponding optimal price of the final product is then determined to be $p_F^{**} = \$50 - \$.5Q_F^{**} = \$50 - \$.5(15) = \$42.50$. This selling price, which includes a 142 percent markup over marginal cost, generates a profit downstream equal to $\pi_F^{**} = (p_F^{**} - MC_F)Q_F^{**} = (\$42.50 - \$35)15 = \$112.50$.

The incentives for vertical integration in the double-markup case.
Final product consumers are worse off with a double markup than with a markup at only one stage of production. A double markup reduces final product output by half and raises final product price. Moreover, when summed, total profits at the upstream and downstream stages of production are lower with a double markup—total profit amounts to $337.50 versus the $450 in profit earned by the input suppliers in the single-markup case. Hence, the producers of the intermediate input and the final product can increase their joint profits by vertically integrating. At the same time, such ownership integration will lead to an expansion in final product sales and a reduction in final product price, thereby benefiting the integrated firm's customers.

Figure 12.2 can help demonstrate this conclusion (see p. 414). If the input suppliers integrate forward into the final product market (or if the downstream producers integrate backward into the intermediate product market), the intermediate input, I, will be transferred from the integrated company's upstream division to its downstream division at the upstream division's marginal production cost rather than at the market-determined price charged when such transfers were made across ownership boundaries. Hence, the downstream division will maximize its profits by producing where the marginal cost of the final product, $MC_F' = MC_I + MC_T$, is equal to marginal revenue, MR_F. Equating the marginal revenue of the final product with the lower marginal production costs made possible by vertical integration yields an optimal output rate of Q_F^{***} ($> Q_F^{**}$) units and an optimal final product price of p_F^{***} ($< p_F^{**}$). This price and quantity of sales generate total profits of $\pi_F^{***} = (p_F^{***} - MC_F')Q_F^{***}$.

That such integration would in fact occur can be demonstrated by showing that the total profits of the integrated enterprise are greater than the sum of the profits earned at the separate stages of production prior to the merger of ownership interests. When market exchange governs transactions in the intermediate input, the upstream suppliers earn profits of $(p_I^{**} - MC_I)Q_I^{**}$ and the profits of the final product's producers are $(p_F^{**} - MC_F)Q_F^{**}$. Noting that $MC_I = MC_F' - MC_T$, $MC_F = p_I^{**} + MC_T$, and $Q_F^{**} = Q_I^{**}$, the two separate profit expressions can be combined to yield $(p_F^{**} - MC_F')Q_F^{**}$. By comparison, the integrated enterprise's profits have just been shown to be equal to $(p_F^{***} - MC_F')Q_F^{***}$. Because the output of the final product doubles following integration (i.e., $Q_F^{***} = 2Q_F^{**}$), it can be shown with a little algebra that total profits will rise following integration as long as $(p_F^{**} - MC_F')$

$< 2(p_F{}^{***} - MC_F{}')$.[12] Inspection of Figure 12.2 demonstrates compliance with this condition.

An algebraic example of the profitability of vertical integration. More specifically, consider the resource-allocation decisions of the integrated enterprise in the context of the mathematical example used throughout the previous discussion. In the wake of ownership integration between successive stages of production, the downstream division will produce where MR_F is equal to $MC_F{}'$. Following the profit-maximization rule requires solving

$$\$50 - \$1Q_F = \$20$$

to get $Q_F{}^{***} = 30$. In order to sell 30 units of the final product, price must be reduced to $p_F{}^{***} = \$50 - \$.5(Q_F{}^{***}) = \$50 - \$.5(30) = \$35$. At this price and quantity, the integrated enterprise's profit amounts to $(p_F{}^{***} - MC_F{}')Q_F{}^{***} = (\$35 - \$20)30 = \$450$. This figure exceeds by \$112.50 the combined profits of the upstream and downstream producers prior to integration.

An Assessment of Vertical Integration in the Fixed-Proportions Case. It is no coincidence that final product sales, final product price, and total profits are the same following vertical integration in the double-markup case as they were with or without ownership integration in the single-markup case. Nor should it be surprising that in the double-markup case just considered, the increase in total profits following a merger between successive stages of production is exactly equal to the profits earned by the producers of the final product prior to the merger. Both of these outcomes are due to a single fact: When the market-determined prices at each of two technologically separable stages of production include markups over marginal cost, ownership integration eliminates one (and only one) of these pricing distortions. Integration eliminates the markup over marginal production cost formerly applied on sales of the intermediate input to the final product's manufacturers.

This reduction in input price lowers marginal production costs downstream. However, vertical integration by itself has no impact on final product demand, and so the marginal revenue side of the optimal production rule in the final product market remains unchanged. Hence, in the single markup case where the final product price must equal marginal cost, an integrated firm is bound by the same constraint. An input supplier consequently gains no advantage from acquiring an ownership interest in one or more of its downstream customers. Final product price (and final product sales) remain

---

12 Substitute $Q_F{}^{***} = 2Q_F{}^{**}$ in the integrated firm's profit expression and then subtract from it the combined profits of upstream and downstream producers prior to merger. This subtraction yields $(2p_F{}^{***} - p_F{}^{**} - MC_F{}')Q_F{}^{**}$, which will be positive—total profit will increase following ownership integration—if the expression in parentheses is positive. Writing the required inequality as $2p_F{}^{***} > p_F{}^{**} + MC_F{}'$, subtracting $MC_F{}'$ from both sides, and then rearranging yields the stated condition.

the same with or without integration in this case. Therefore, the reduction in marginal production cost in the final product market made possible by vertical integration simply transfers existing profits from the first stage to the second stage of production.

Demand conditions downstream similarly constrain the integrated firm in the double-markup case. By eliminating the markup over marginal cost included in the market-determined price of the intermediate input, the firm can fill this demand more efficiently. Vertical integration reduces marginal cost at the second stage of production; it does not raise marginal revenue there. This change in the marginal-revenue-equals-marginal-cost calculus dictates that the integrated firm expand final product sales and reduce final product price. Put differently, vertical integration in the double-markup case enables the firm to search for *lower* final product prices that may enhance its profitability; merger does not free the firm to search for higher final product prices.

Indeed, from the point of view of the producers of the final product, vertical integration is profitable precisely because by raising their own production costs, the markup added to the manufacturing cost of the intermediate input by their upstream suppliers prevents them from producing enough units of the final product to fully exploit market demand.[13] By eliminating the market-determined "wedge" between input price and marginal cost, common ownership of both stages of production relaxes this constraint.

To summarize, if production in the downstream industry is subject to fixed-proportions technology, there is no profit motive for vertical integration unless prices already include a markup over marginal cost at both stages of production. If this is the case, ownership integration results in an unambiguous improvement in consumer welfare, because more units of the final product are made available at a lower price. A markup at only one stage provides no profit advantage through vertical integration. This observation has two important implications.

First, vertical integration does not allow a firm that charges a markup at one stage of production to transfer or extend that same markup to another stage of production. Second, in the absence of a double markup, the *only* reason for firms to vertically integrate is if combining two or more stages of production reduces cost. The previous diagrams show that if integration lowers the marginal cost of producing the intermediate input or the final product, or both, combining operations will induce the integrated enterprise to expand final product output beyond (and lower its selling price below) the indicated levels. Hence, with fixed-proportions technology, vertical integration may not make consumers of the final product better off, but it will surely not make them worse off.

---

13 Similarly, vertical integration is profitable from the upstream suppliers' point of view because the markup added to the production cost of the final product by their downstream customers prevents them from selling enough units of the intermediate input to fully exploit market demand.

Variable-Proportions Technology

Variable-proportions technology describes a production process in which different combinations of inputs can produce the same quantity of output. Thus, the firm can substitute one input for another while maintaining a constant output rate. The previous section hints at a motive for vertical integration that exists under these circumstances. When transactions in an intermediate input take place across ownership boundaries and the market-determined price includes a markup over marginal cost, downstream buyers tend to substitute away from the input. They tend to employ relatively more of other productive resources as they go about selecting the cost-minimizing input combination. Consequently, the input substitution opportunities made possible by variable-proportions technology in the downstream market may prevent the input supplier from fully maximizing its profit.[14]

Optimal Input Combinations With and Without Integration. Part I's discussion of production and cost theory is the basis for analyzing the motives for vertical integration in the variable-proportions case. To minimize the cost of producing any particular level of output, a profit-maximizing firm selects the combination of inputs at which the ratio of the marginal products of the inputs (the marginal rate of technical substitution) is equal to the ratio of the input prices. Put differently, cost-minimizing production requires that the marginal product per dollar spent be the same across the last units of all inputs employed.

This rule can be stated more concisely in the simple case where the firm uses only two variable inputs to produce some good or service. Let the quantities of these inputs be denoted by A and B, their marginal productivities as MP_A and MP_B,[15] and their unit prices as p_A and p_B. Suppose that neither input is sold at a markup initially. Given these assumptions and definitions, the optimal (cost-minimizing) input combination for the firm is the one where

$$\frac{MP_A}{MP_B} = \frac{p_A}{p_B} \quad \text{or} \quad \frac{MP_A}{p_A} = \frac{MP_B}{p_B}.$$

Now let the supplier of one of these inputs, say A, add a markup to its marginal production cost to set the price at which A will be sold to downstream

---

14 The motives for vertical integration in the variable-proportions case are discussed in Meyer L. Burstein, "A Theory of Full-Line Forcing," *Northwestern University Law Review* 55 (March-April 1960), pp. 62-95; John M. Vernon and Daniel A. Graham, "Profitability of Monopolization by Vertical Integration," *Journal of Political Economy* 79 (September-October 1971), pp. 924-25; and Frederic R. Warren-Boulton, "Vertical Control with Variable Proportions," *Journal of Political Economy* 82 (July-August 1974), pp. 783-802.
15 Recall that an input's marginal product is defined as the increase in total output associated with employing one more unit of the resource, all other inputs held constant.

customers. That is, the unit price of A increases from p_A to $p_A + m$, where m is the dollar amount by which A's market price exceeds the supplier's marginal production cost. The *ceteris paribus* impact of this price increase is that the downstream consuming industry will no longer be employing the combination of inputs that is optimal for producing the final product. That is, the markup on A causes

$$\frac{MP_A}{\left(p_A + m\right)} < \frac{MP_B}{p_B} .$$

If the producers of the final product continue to purchase the same quantities of A and B as they did before the price of A increased, total production cost will not be at a minimum.

To restore equality between the marginal productivities per dollar of input usage, the downstream producers will reduce their purchases of A, thereby raising A's marginal product, and increase their purchases of B, thereby lowering B's marginal product. The substitution of the now relatively cheaper input (B) for the now relatively more expensive input (A) will continue until

$$\frac{MP_A}{\left(p_A + m\right)} = \frac{MP_B}{p_B} .$$

At the new, more B-intensive input combination, the cost of producing the final product will again be at a minimum for the given input productivities and prices.

Note that while the downstream industry's substitution of B for A minimizes the cost of producing the final product at the new input-price ratio, the industry is unlikely to maintain the same rate of output as before. If it did so, its total production costs would be higher than when it employed the old, more A-intensive input combination. In other words, the markup added to the marginal cost of producing A by the upstream supplying industry forces the downstream consuming industry to use an inefficient input combination—inefficient compared with the combination used without the markup—to manufacture the final product.

This distortion in input proportions supplies a motive for vertical integration. In particular, by integrating forward into the final product market a manufacturer of input A can adopt the more A-intensive production process that was optimal in the absence of the markup. As a result of the lower total production costs made possible by transferring A internally at a price equal to marginal cost, the integrated firm's profit increases, final product output expands, and final product price declines.

A similar motive for vertical integration exists for the downstream consuming industry. By integrating backward into the manufacture of A, a final product producer can reinstate the previous more A-intensive production process. Total cost is lower (and profit is higher) when the producer transfers A internally at a price equal to marginal cost rather than purchasing A from outside suppliers at a markup over marginal cost. Final product output increases and final product price decreases in the process.

A Diagrammatic Explanation. The motives for vertical integration in the variable-proportions case are made more clear with the aid of a diagram. Figure 12.3 depicts the necessary production relations and cost schedules.

In the figure, the curves labeled Q_0 and Q_1 are familiar isoquants. As defined in Chapter 3, each isoquant shows the various combinations of inputs A and B the firm can use to produce some particular quantity of output. For example, the firm can produce Q_0 units of output using a relatively B-intensive production process (such as point Z_0). Or it can, by substituting A for B along the isoquant, continue to produce the same quantity of the final product using a more A-intensive process lying to the right of Z_0 on Q_0. This is the essence of variable-proportions technology. Which particular input combination the firm will in fact employ to produce Q_0 depends on the relative prices of the inputs.

The rate at which existing technology allows the firm to substitute one input for another while holding the level of output constant is the marginal rate of technical substitution (*MRTS*). It is the (negative of the) slope of an isoquant at a particular point. Chapter 3 shows that the *MRTS* is equal to the ratio of the marginal productivities of the two inputs. That is, the *MRTS* of input B for input A is equal to MP_A/MP_B.

The rate at which the *market* allows the firm to substitute one input for another while holding total expenditures constant is represented by the slope of the firm's budget or isocost line. Each isocost line, denoted by the labels C_iC_i' in Figure 12.3, shows the various combinations of inputs A and B that can be purchased on the market *at given factor prices* for a given budget. The slope of any isocost schedule is equal to the negative of the input-price ratio (i.e.,$-p_A/p_B$).[16]

To summarize, the slope of an isoquant shows the rate at which input substitution is technologically feasible; the slope of an isocost line shows the rate at which inputs can be substituted on the market. The output-maximizing (or cost-minimizing) input combination for the firm is therefore the one at which these two rates are equal, that is, where the marginal rate of technical substitution equals the factor-price ratio. This is the rule stated in the previous section, namely that optimal production takes place where $MP_A/MP_B = p_A/p_B$.

Suppose now that downstream manufacturers purchase inputs A and B to produce Q_0 units of some final product. Further assume that while input B is sold in a price-taker market at a price equal to its suppliers' marginal

---

16 As a reminder, with the unit price of input A equal to p_A and the unit price of input B equal to p_B, the total cost of producing given a level of output is $C = p_A A + p_B B$. Holding total cost constant at some stipulated level, say C_0, and solving for B, the equation of the isocost schedule is $B = C_0/p_B - (p_A/p_B)A$. The slope of this straight line is thus $-p_A/p_B$.

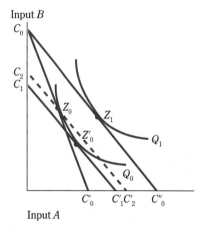

Input B

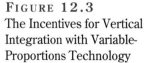

Input A

FIGURE 12.3
The Incentives for Vertical Integration with Variable-Proportions Technology

production cost, the price of A includes a markup over its marginal production cost. These factor prices generate an isocost schedule for the final product industry that is drawn as C_0C_0', with a slope equal to $-(p_A + m)/p_B$, where, as before, m is the dollar amount by which A's market price exceeds the marginal cost of producing it. Faced with these market-determined input prices, the downstream industry minimizes the cost of producing Q_0 units of the final product by selecting the relatively B-intensive input combination at point Z_0, where C_0C_0' is just tangent to the Q_0 isoquant. (The slopes of the isoquant and isocost lines are equal at Z_0, or $MP_A/MP_B = (p_A + m)/p_B$.)

By contrast, had the price of A included no markup, isocost line C_0C_0'', with a slope equal to $-p_A/p_B$, would have been relevant for the downstream industry. For the *same* total cost incurred in using the input combination Z_0 to produce Q_0 units of the final product, the downstream industry could have expanded its output to Q_1 units by operating at point Z_1 and using a relatively more A-intensive production process.[17]

Put differently, Q_0 units of output could have been produced at a *lower* total cost if neither input had been sold at a markup. This result is made apparent by referring to isocost line C_1C_1', which is drawn parallel to C_0C_0'' (has a slope equal to $-p_A/p_B$) but tangent to Q_0. Using the input combination Z_0' (in which A and B are employed in the same ratio as at point Z_1), the total production cost of Q_0 units declines by the vertical distance between C_0 and C_1.

Indeed, Q_0 units can be produced more cheaply even if the inefficient combination Z_0 is used when A and B are both available at prices equal to their suppliers' marginal production costs. We can measure these savings by referring to isocost curve C_2C_2', which passes through Z_0 with a slope equal to $-p_A/p_B$. Hence, the vertical distance, $C_0 - C_2$, represents the cost inefficiency imposed on the downstream industry by the markup pricing of input A. (This same vertical distance measures the profits earned by the unintegrated suppliers of A from selling A to the manufacturers of the final product at a markup.)

An input supplier can earn even higher profits by integrating forward into the downstream industry, however. Additional profits are possible because vertical integration will correct the distortion in the final product manufacturer's input usage caused by the markup included in the market price of input A. Under common ownership of the two stages of production, the integrated enterprise's upstream division will transfer input A to the downstream division at a price equal to marginal cost. Facing relative input prices of p_A/p_B, the downstream division will in turn select the efficient, A-intensive input combination Z_0', rather than the inefficient, B-intensive combination Z_0 chosen by its formerly independent customer. Due to this cost reduction, the

---

17 The downstream industry's total cost of production is represented by the vertical intercept of the isocost line, that is, by C_0/p_B. Because C_0C_0' and C_0C_0'' have the same vertical intercept, total expenditures on inputs are the same on both of these isocost lines.

integrated company's profits will increase by the vertical distance between C_2 and C_1.[18]

This profit opportunity provides the input supplier with an incentive to vertically integrate when variable-proportions technology is used to produce the final product. Overcoming the downstream industry's tendency to substitute away from an input sold at a markup over marginal cost enables the integrated firm to produce the final product more efficiently. This increased production efficiency leads to an expansion in final product output and a reduction in final product price, thereby benefiting the industry's ultimate consumers.[19]

OTHER ECONOMIC MOTIVES FOR VERTICAL INTEGRATION

The preceding discussion identifies a production efficiency motive for vertical integration. In particular, when production in the final product market is subject to variable-proportions technology and when the market-determined price of an input includes a markup over marginal production cost, forward integration by the input's supplier can improve the efficiency of downstream production. This is because transferring an input internally at price equal to marginal cost leads the integrated firm to select an input combination that is more efficient than the one chosen by its customers before integration.

There are a host of other reasons why a firm at one stage of a production process might find it profitable to integrate with a firm at some other stage of production. The objective of reducing transaction costs drives most of these other motives for vertical integration. As Ronald Coase has pointed out, it costs something to transfer a good or service across the ownership boundaries of firms.[20] Market transactions involve discovering what the relevant prices are, communicating information about the kinds and qualities of

---

18 The vertical distance between C_2 and C_1 is the *minimum* profit increase attributable to forward integration. This is because it has been assumed that the integrated firm will continue to produce Q_0 units of the final product. If the integrated firm finds it optimal to increase the amount of final output produced, the increase in profit will be greater than that depicted in Figure 12.3.

19 Whether or not vertical integration in the variable-proportions case leads to an increase or decrease in the price of the final product depends on a number of factors, including the elasticity of demand for the final product and the elasticity of the derived demand for the input sold at a markup prior to integration. However, even when the extreme assumption is made that the sole supplier of an input sold at a markup across ownership boundaries acquires *all* of the producers of the final product, final product price declines under most plausible elasticity values. See Fred M. Westfield, "Vertical Integration: Does Product Price Rise or Fall?," *American Economic Review* 71 (June 1981), pp. 334-46. Earlier models reaching the opposite conclusion are Richard L. Schmalensee, "A Note on the Theory of Vertical Integration," *Journal of Political Economy* 81 (March-April 1973), pp. 442-49; and Warren-Boulton, "Vertical Control with Variable Proportions."

20 Ronald H. Coase, "The Nature of the Firm," *Economica* 4 (November 1937), pp. 386-405.

Vertical Integration and Disintegration in the U.S. Auto Industry

The prospect of overcoming an input-price distortion is one important consideration in the make-or-buy decision. The seller of an intermediate input sold at a markup over marginal production cost has an incentive to integrate forward into the downstream consuming industry. And the buyer of that input has an incentive to integrate backward into the upstream producing industry. For buyer and seller, integration replaces market exchange at price greater than marginal cost with internal transfer of the input at price equals marginal cost.

Elementary economic theory suggests that there will tend to be low markups and little or no incentive for vertical integration in price-taker markets where large numbers of suppliers produce relatively homogeneous goods or services. In such cases, buyers (and sellers) can easily turn to alternatives. The threat of losing future business consequently provides strong incentives for both parties to behave responsibly and to honor their commitments.

Economic theory also suggests that market exchange will give way to ownership integration as the transaction between buyer and seller becomes more specialized. If one or both of the parties is required to invest in transaction-specific capital, then incentives exist to engage in opportunistic behavior or "self-interest seeking with guile."[a]

Kirk Monteverde and David Teece applied this concept in explaining the extent of vertical integration in the U. S. automobile industry by considering what they called the "applications engineering effort associated with the development of any given automobile component."[b] This activity refers to the time and the resources the firm must invest in designing, testing, and developing a particular part or component system into a final product that is ready to go into full-scale production. The more such effort is required for any input, the more vulnerable is the buyer to being "held up" by an independent supplier.

Monteverde and Teece hypothesized that internal procurement would be more likely for parts requiring greater applications engineering effort, and this is what the data in Table 12.1 show. Some parts and component assemblies, like those of the automobile's mechanical and electrical systems, are technically complex, have low tolerance for error, and require substantial engineering and design effort to "package"— the auto industry's term for meeting the constraint that all of the components must fit physically within the dimensions of the vehicle body. The manufacturers tend to make these parts and assemblies rather than buy them. By contrast, standardized parts like exterior ornamentation, paint and primer, locks, and carpeting are typically obtained by both auto makers from outside suppliers.

Table 12.1 also shows, however, that Ford and GM did not always choose the same option for obtaining their supplies of a given part. One interesting difference between the two companies relates to procurement of spark plugs. Very early in its organizational history, GM integrated backward into the production of spark plugs and began obtaining all of its requirements from its wholly owned subsidiary, AC. Prior to the early 1960s, on the other hand, Ford purchased its spark plugs from Champion, then the largest independent supplier of this part. Chrysler, too, had purchased spark plugs from an independent supplier, Autolite, and both Champion and Autolite had sold spark plugs to the third-largest domestic automaker, American Motors.

a Oliver E. Williamson, *The Economic Institutions of Capitalism: Firms, Markets, Relational Contracting* (New York: Free Press, 1985), p. 47.

b Kirk Monteverde and David J. Teece, "Supplier Switching Costs and Vertical Integration in the Automobile Industry," *Bell Journal of Economics* 13 (Spring 1982), p. 207.

TABLE 12.1 MAKE-OR-BUY DECISIONS FOR TWO U.S. AUTO MAKERS

PART CATEGORY	FORD	GM	PART CATEGORY	FORD	GM
Body			Spindle assembly	*	*
Body sheet metal	*	*	Driveshaft assembly	*	*
Exterior ornamentation			Wheels	*	*
Paint (topcoat)			Wires		
Primer			Rear axle	*	*
Bumpers	*	*	Drums		
Body lamps	*	*	Master brake cylinder		
Sealed beam bulbs		*	Power brake booster		*
Weatherstrip			Parking brake		
Mirrors—outside			Muffler		
Mirrors—inside		*	Tailpipe/ inlet pipe		
Interior trim	*	*	Brakes		
Interior ornamentation		*	Disc caliper & rotor		*
Carpeting & mats			Front suspension	*	*
Headlining	*	*	Rear suspension	*	*
Safety belts					
Inertia locks			**Transmission**		
Lock—cylinders			Automatic transmission assembly	*	*
Door handles		*	Automatic transmission cases	*	*
Hinges—door, hood decklid	*	*	Manual transmission assembly		*
Window regulator— power		*			
Window regulator— manual	*	*	**Fuel**		
Glass	*		Fuel tank	*	*
Windshield wiper motor	*	*	Gas cap		
Windshield washer system	*	*			
Crash pad		*	**Engine**		
Seat frame & springs			Engine stampings	*	*
Seat pad		*	Cylinder head	*	*
Seat tracks—manual and electrical		*	Block	*	*
Lamp bulbs		*	Manifold—intake & exhaust	*	*
Head restraints	*	*	Crankshaft	*	*
Headlamp assembly	*	*	Camshaft	*	*
Sealers & insulation			Piston	*	N/A
Armrests		*	Piston ring		
Grill			Valves—intake & exhaust	*	N/A
Frame			Radiator	*	*
Jack & wrench			Fan		
Engine mounts			Air cleaner	*	*
			Air cleaner element		*
Emission Components			Carburetor		*
Catalytic converter		*	Fuel pump		*
Air pump		*	Starter	*	*
Carbon canister	*	*	Distributor	*	*
Substrate & coating			Spark plugs		*
PCV & other valves			Ignition coil	*	*
			Oil filter	*	*
Chassis					
Wheel covers & hub caps—optional			**Electrical**		
Wheel covers & hub caps—standard		*	Instrument cluster & panel	*	*
Coil springs	*	*	Speedometer cable assembly		*
Leaf springs		*	Fuel sender	*	*
Shock absorbers	*	*	Alternator	*	*
Upper & lower arms	*	*	Regulator	*	*
			Battery		*

PART CATEGORY	FORD	GM
Horn	*	*
Battery cables		*
Wiring harness		*
Radio	*	*
Tape player		*
Speakers		*
Antenna		*
Speed control system	*	*
Clock		
Switches		
Steering		
Manual steering gear	*	*
Power steering gear	*	*
Steering linkage		*
Steering column	*	*
Steering wheel		*
Power steering pump		*
Steering assembly	*	*
Ventilation		
Air conditioning assembly	*	*
Evaporator	*	*
Expansion valve		*
Vacuum motors		*
Blower wheels		
Blower motors	*	*
Heater assembly	*	*
Heater core	*	*
Compressor		*
Clutch		*
ATC components		*
Condensor	*	*
Dehydrator/ receiver		N/A
Hose assemblies		N/A
Other		
Tubing—brake & fuel lines		
Antifreeze		
Oils & greases		
Steel		
Standard parts & fasteners		
Vinyl	*	
Water pump assembly	*	*
Oil pump	*	

Note: "*" indicates that 80 percent of component requirements were produced internally as of 1976; "N/A" indicates that information on the method of procurement was not available.

Source: Kirk Monteverde and David J. Teece, "Supplier Switching Costs and Vertical Integration in the Automobile Industry," *Bell Journal of Economics* 13 (Spring 1982), pp. 208-9.

In 1961, Ford acquired Autolite. It did so after rejecting the option of building its own spark plug manufacturing facility. An internal company study had concluded that the construction of such a facility would take from 5 to 8 years to complete. Moreover, even when the production facility came on-line, Ford would be at a disadvantage in marketing its own spark plugs to independent mechanics for use as replacement parts because it lacked an established distribution network and a recognized brand name for spark plugs.

However, the government successfully challenged the Ford-Autolite merger and 11 years later ordered Ford to divest the spark plug manufacturing assets it had acquired (see *Ford Motor Co.* v. *U.S.*, 405 U.S. 562 [1972]). In bringing the suit, the Department of Justice alleged that Ford's acquisition of Autolite had eliminated the possibility that Ford would enter the spark plug industry *de novo* and that the prospect of Ford's potential entry had helped keep market prices in line with costs. Moreover, the court held that the acquisition injured competition in the market for spark plugs because it prevented independent suppliers from competing for Ford's spark plug business.[c]

More recent events promise to change the organizational structure of the U.S. automobile industry considerably. Under pressure from global competitors, Ford has sold off its glassmaking facilities and GM is undergoing draconian downsizing in an effort to cut costs. Both companies are embarked on courses leading to much heavier reliance on outside parts suppliers. These events suggest that both Ford and GM allowed "make" decisions to live far beyond their usefulness. An appreciation of the economic forces that help shape the structure of the firm is evidently indispensable to management.

c For a critique of the Supreme Court decision finding in the government's favor and thereby compelling Ford to buy rather than make, see William F. Shughart II, *The Organization of Industry* (Homewood, IL: Richard D. Irwin, 1990), pp. 439-40.

resources to be exchanged, specifying desired quantities and delivery schedules, negotiating and enforcing contractual agreements, and so on. Of course, a firm must spend resources to coordinate and monitor exchanges between buyer and seller within its own organization. But if the cost of using internal organization to govern a transaction is lower than the corresponding cost of market governance, a clear incentive for ownership integration exists. We explore a number of the possibilities below.

Avoiding the "Hold-Up" Problem

Certain exchanges between buyer and seller require that one (or both) of the parties invest in an asset that is highly specialized to the transaction. A specialized asset is a productive resource whose value is much higher in its current use than in its next best alternative use.[21] When such assets are required, the parties are "locked into" their relationship to a significant degree. The buyer cannot turn to alternative suppliers and the seller cannot turn to alternative customers without incurring considerable switching costs. Thus, while both parties will benefit by completing the transaction on the agreed-upon terms, each has an incentive to take advantage of the other once the transaction-specific investment has been made. The buyer can refuse to make the promised purchases unless price is reduced, and the seller can refuse to make the promised deliveries unless price is increased. In short, the value of the specialized asset in its current use above its value in its next best alternative use can be appropriated opportunistically by one of the parties to the transaction.

Consider the case of a printing press owned and operated by party A.[22] Suppose that publisher B obtains printing services from A by leasing the press at a contracted rental rate of $5,500 per month. The next best alternative use of the printing press is rental to publisher C who is willing to pay at most $3,500 per month for printing services. Assume that the press owner's monthly operating costs are $1,500 and that the press has a scrap value of $1,000 (expressed as a monthly rental equivalent). The **quasi-rent** on the machine is $3,000 (= $5,500 − $1,500 − $1,000), the monthly revenue minus operating costs minus salvage value.

Under the stated conditions, publisher B can appropriate most of this quasi-rent even if the press owner later earns only a normal profit at the contracted rental rate. This opportunity exists because the press is worth only $3,500 per month in its next best use (rental to publisher C). If publisher B unilaterally cuts its monthly payment to $3,500, party A will still supply printing services to B, assuming that moving the press to C's location costs something.

---

21 See Chapter 7 for a complementary discussion of the role of transaction-specific capital in promoting ownership integration.

22 The following example is taken from Benjamin Klein, Robert G. Crawford, and Armen A. Alchian, "Vertical Integration, Appropriable Rents, and the Competitive Contracting Process," *Journal of Law and Economics* 21 (October 1978), pp. 297-326.

Hence, *the appropriable portion of the quasi-rent* is the $2,000 difference between the monthly rental rate of $5,500 and the $3,500 monthly value of the press to publisher *C*.

In fact, if no such alternative were available to the press owner, publisher *B* could credibly threaten to appropriate the entire quasi-rent ($3,000) by offering to pay only $2,500 per month for printing services. At the same time, if publisher *B* has no other supplier of printing services, the press owner can "hold up" its customer by demanding a monthly rental rate of more than $5,500. In short, both parties have an interest in maintaining their contractual relationship. But once the press has been installed, each has an incentive to take advantage of the other.

Of course, the expected gains of opportunistic behavior must be weighed against its expected costs. Firms that opportunistically attempt to appropriate the quasi-rents created by investments in transaction-specific capital can expect to lose future business or be required to deal on less favorable terms. To compensate for the increased risk that future commitments will not be honored, suppliers will demand higher prices from—or more frequent payments by—customers who have behaved opportunistically in the past. Similarly, buyers will offer lower prices to—or demand more frequent deliveries from—sellers who have a reputation for behaving opportunistically. It is nevertheless true that not all contingencies affecting a contractual relationship involving specialized capital can be foreseen, events that trigger permissible adaptations cannot be readily verified by both buyer and seller, and enforcing contracts is costly. Therefore, circumstances may arise in which it is wealth-maximizing for one of the parties to appropriate quasi-rents from the other.

As the assets involved in a transaction become more specialized to that transaction, more appropriable quasi-rents are created. The potential gains from opportunistic behavior increase. Ownership integration is a specialized organizational response to this hold-up problem. Removing the transaction from the market and merging the separate profit streams of buyer and seller into a single economic entity reduces the incentives for behaving opportunistically. Potential hold-up problems are less likely when the transaction takes place within the firm, because everyone involved can more readily recognize and share the benefits of cooperation.

Ownership integration is a profitable response to the hold-up problem if the additional administrative costs of bringing the transaction within the firm are outweighed by the savings from avoiding the opportunistic behavior associated with contracting across ownership boundaries. When ownership integration passes this test, it clearly leads to an improvement in social welfare by reducing transaction costs.

Promoting the Exchange of Information

Removing a transaction from the market and placing it within the firm reduces incentives for behaving opportunistically. Vertical integration also increases the likelihood that buyer and seller will use the specialized information each possesses in mutually beneficial ways.

Knowledge is dispersed and often contradictory.[23] Sellers have superior information about their own products, including knowledge of production costs, performance characteristics, quality variation, and prospects that supply interruptions will occur. Buyers, on the other hand, have superior information about their own input requirements, demand conditions in final product markets, and so on.

When transactions take place across ownership boundaries, each party has incentives to use its informational advantages for its own benefit. These divergent incentives can raise the costs to the buyer and seller of negotiating contracts as each hoards its specialized knowledge or engages in strategic posturing to shift the gains from trade more in its own favor. Informational asymmetries may also raise contract enforcement costs by requiring both parties to invest resources in monitoring compliance with the agreed-upon terms and in verifying claims that trigger permissible adjustments to those terms. Have the supplier's production costs in fact increased unexpectedly, so that price must increase? Has downstream demand in fact fallen unexpectedly, warranting a reduction in customer purchases?

Ownership integration offers an alternative to market contracting in the presence of asymmetric information that reduces transaction costs by bringing the specialized knowledge of buyer and seller within the firm. Each party is less able to appropriate the returns to any informational advantages he or she possesses. Therefore, there are fewer incentives for hoarding or strategically misrepresenting relevant facts. Because buyer and seller jointly profit from sharing their specialized knowledge, ownership integration provides rewards for disclosing and exploiting information that would not exist otherwise.

Responding to Fiscal, Regulatory, and Monetary Policies

An important principle established by the economic theory of vertical integration is that an incentive for the merger of successive stages of production under common ownership exists whenever the market-determined price of a resource includes a markup over the supplier industry's marginal production cost. Forward integration by an upstream seller and backward integration by a downstream buyer are profitable under these circumstances because removing the transaction from the market allows the firm to transfer the resource internally at a price equal to marginal cost. The integrated firm consequently employs the socially optimal input combination for producing the final product.

Similar incentives for vertical integration exist in the presence of any distortions in market-determined prices, including those associated with government fiscal, monetary, and regulatory policies. Price controls, taxes, and other public policies often drive an artificial "wedge" between price and marginal cost at one stage of the production process. These distortions

---

23 Friedrich A. Hayek, "The Use of Knowledge in Society," *American Economic Review* 35 (September 1945), pp. 519-30.

encourage ownership integration by penalizing external (market) transactions more than internal transactions.

Consider government tax policy. Obviously, if the sale of an intermediate input is subject to a tax, backward integration enables the purchaser to avoid the tax. More generally, vertical integration may allow a firm to reduce its overall tax burden by reallocating taxable activities to the stage of production at which marginal tax rates are lowest.

An interesting example of the incentives for ownership integration created by tax policy is provided by the "depletion allowance" that was granted to the U.S. oil industry until 1974.[24] In brief, the depletion allowance permitted domestic petroleum companies to take a corporate income tax deduction equal to a percentage of the value of the crude oil and natural gas they recovered during the tax year. As established in the Revenue Act of 1924, the allowance could not exceed 50 percent of the gross income of oil and gas wells, which the government defined as taxable income less expenses directly related to the extraction of these natural resources.

Downstream petroleum refineries had a clear incentive to integrate backward into oil and gas production to take advantage of this tax break. Vertical integration allowed the oil companies to shift income to the upstream extraction stage by artificially reducing the prices of refined petroleum products and artificially inflating the internal transfer price of crude oil. In this way, the "gross income" of oil and gas wells increased relative to income from the sale of refined petroleum products. Therefore, a greater proportion of total corporate income qualified for the favorable tax treatment provided by the depletion allowance. Tax policy was an important factor in promoting the vertical integration of oil extraction and refining operations. Evidence for this is furnished by the fact that after 1974, when the depletion allowance ended for large oil and gas producers, many of these companies sold off significant parts of their refining and marketing operations.[25]

We can also see the effects of government policies on the organization of production by considering the incentives for backward integration created by so-called **rate-of-return regulation**. This public policy approach, common in public utility regulation, involves setting an output price that allows the owners of the regulated firm to earn only a "fair" return on their investment. Specifically, the regulatory agency establishes a price for the firm's output such that no more than some predetermined percentage of the value of invested capital (the "rate base") is earned in any given year. Because the allowed rate of return is typically greater than the unit cost of capital, the regulated firm has an incentive to purchase more capital than it would in the absence of regulation.[26]

---

24 Ben Bolch and William W. Damon, "The Depletion Allowance and Vertical Integration in the Petroleum Industry," *Southern Economic Journal* 45 (July 1978), pp. 241-49.

25 *Ibid.*, p. 248.

26 Harvey Averch and Leland J. Johnson, "Behavior of the Firm under Regulatory Constraint," *American Economic Review* 52 (December 1962), pp. 1052-69.

This incentive to overinvest in capital follows from observing that even though rate-of-return regulation fixes the firm's profit *rate*, the *level* of the utility's profits is an increasing function of the value of the rate base. For example, if the allowed rate of return is fixed at 10 percent, the firm will earn a profit of $100,000 if its capital stock is valued at $1,000,000. Raising the value of the rate base to $1,500,000 increases profits to $150,000, and so on. By effectively lowering the cost of capital, rate-of-return regulation thus distorts the firm's input choices, leading it to select a production technique that is more capital-intensive than the efficient (cost-minimizing) input combination.

Backward integration into an unregulated input supply industry provides the regulated firm with an alternative strategy for artificially padding its rate base and increasing its allowable profits. Specifically, by charging the downstream division a sufficiently high internal transfer price for the unregulated input, the integrated company can inflate its average production costs at the regulated stage. Thus, the regulatory agency can be induced to set a higher price for the final product than it would set otherwise to preserve the targeted rate of return. At the same time, by artificially inflating the internal transfer price of the input, backward integration allows the regulated firm to shift its profits from the regulated division to the unregulated division and thereby circumvent the rate-of-return constraint.

Finally, monetary policy may also affect the extent to which firms vertically integrate.[27] During periods of unanticipated inflation, not only is the general price level rising continuously, but prices of individual products tend to be more variable as well.[28] The additional instability in the structure of market prices has two possible effects on the organization of production activities. First, the cost of using the price system to guide resource allocation decisions increases. The less reliably market prices signal resource values and profit opportunities, the more costly it is to transact across the ownership boundaries of firms. Contracts are more difficult to negotiate and enforce if buyer and seller are uncertain as to whether a given price change reflects an underlying change in the real value of a resource (a relative price change) or is part of the general inflationary trend (a nominal price change). Second, to the extent that managers use market prices as benchmarks, the increased price variability associated with inflation tends to raise the cost of internal resource allocation decisions.

Some recent empirical evidence suggests that, holding other things constant, increases in the inflation rate tend to increase the extent of vertical integration in the economy.[29] The unstable market price signals associated with unanticipated inflation apparently raise the cost of transacting across the ownership boundaries of firms by more than they increase the cost of

27 Donald J. Boudreaux and William F. Shughart II, "The Effects of Monetary Instability on the Extent of Vertical Integration," *Atlantic Economic Review* 17 (June 1989), pp. 1-10.

28 Richard W. Parks, "Inflation and Relative Price Variability," *Journal of Political Economy* 86 (February 1978), pp. 79-95.

29 Boudreaux and Shughart, "Effects of Monetary Instability."

transacting within the firm. In this sense, the vertically integrated firm may have evolved, at least partially, as an organizational response to the discoordinating effects of inflationary monetary policy.

Government tax, regulatory, and monetary policies almost always distort resource allocation decisions. By vertically integrating to insulate a transaction from such policies, the firm at least partly overcomes the distortion. To the extent that ownership integration allows firms to transfer resources internally at marginal cost, the allocative efficiency of competitive market exchange is restored. However, if vertical integration is profitable only because of these outside forces, combining successive stages of production under common ownership can at best neutralize the distortion. Vertical integration can never increase allocative efficiency beyond the point that would exist in the absence of such policies. And in some cases (as, for example, when firms manipulate internal transfer prices to exploit differential tax rates or regulatory policies) it may further magnify the adverse consequences of public policies toward business.

Two Reasons for Not Integrating

Opportunities for reducing cost provide a basic incentive for vertical integration. These cost-saving opportunities can be, and often are, purely technological in nature. But ownership integration is *not* always required to take advantage of production cost savings.[30]

Reducing Production Costs. Economists often use the steel industry to illustrate how the integration of successive stages of production can produce significant savings from improved scheduling to minimize equipment downtime and start-up costs. Combining the smelting operation with subsequent processing stages at the same production site avoids substantial reheating costs by enabling the metal to remain at high temperature from the blast furnace stage through the carbon burn-off and rolling and drawing stages.

This observation does not by itself explain why the blast furnace and the processing equipment are typically owned by the same firm, however. In principle, transactions between these two stages of production could take place across ownership boundaries under a contract in which the owner of the blast furnace agrees to operate at the processor's location and to supply all of the processor's requirements for molten steel of a given carbon content at a given price. Despite the production cost savings that would result, no blast furnace owner would voluntarily submit to such an arrangement. Once the blast furnace is installed, the processor could opportunistically appropriate the difference between the equipment's value in its current location and its value in the next best use (quasi-rent) by refusing to pay the price for molten steel

---

30 The following examples are taken from Paul H. Rubin, *Managing Business Transactions: Controlling the Cost of Coordinating, Communicating, and Decision Making* (New York: Free Press, 1990), pp. 12-16.

Price Discriminatory Vertical Integration

As defined in Chapter 6, price discrimination is the practice of selling the same good or service to different customers at different prices. In its most common form, the firm separates customers into two or more groups and charges a higher price to the customers whose demand is less elastic. A necessary condition for this pricing strategy to be successful is that the firm must be able to prevent **arbitrage**, that is, prevent the customers to whom a lower price is charged from reselling the units they buy to customers that would otherwise pay a higher price. If this condition cannot be satisfied, the firm will make no sales at the higher price and would earn larger profits by simply charging the same price to all buyers.

Forward integration by the supplier of an intermediate input can, by reducing arbitrage possibilities, facilitate price discrimination under certain circumstances.[a] The Aluminum Company of America (Alcoa) provides a useful illustration. Alcoa produces raw aluminum ingots that it sells to downstream customers who fabricate a variety of final products—rolled aluminum sheets, aluminum foil, wire and cable, cans, and so on. The elasticity of the derived demand for raw aluminum would be expected to differ across these various end uses, depending on the elasticity of final product demand and the substitution possibilities on the supply side of the final product market. For example, because wire can be made from aluminum or copper, the elasticity of wire manufacturers' derived demand for aluminum ingots will be determined in part by the willingness of consumers to substitute copper wire for aluminum wire and on the ability of producers to substitute copper for aluminum in the wire fabrication process.

For simplicity, assume that raw aluminum has only two end uses—wire and soft drink cans. Assume further that while wire can be manufactured from either aluminum or copper, there is no good substitute for aluminum in the production of cans. Other things being the same, the derived demand for aluminum ingots on the part of wire fabricators will be more elastic than that of can manufacturers, and Alcoa will want to

charge a higher price on the aluminum it sells to the latter. By exploiting this difference in demand elasticities, Alcoa's profits will be higher than if it charges the same price to all of its customers. However, because raw aluminum ingots are homogeneous, price discrimination could easily be defeated by arbitrage. Wire fabricators would have an incentive to resell some of the ingots they purchase to can manufacturers,[b] from whom Alcoa could not then continue to extract the higher price.

Alcoa could successfully price discriminate between the two downstream consuming industries by integrating forward into the manufacture of the downstream product with the *more* elastic derived demand for raw aluminum ingots.[c] If Alcoa integrates into the fabrication of aluminum wire, it can expand the use of aluminum ingots for that purpose by reducing the ingots' internal transfer price. At the same time, Alcoa could raise the price of ingots (above the price it would charge without price discrimination) on its sales to the unintegrated can industry, which has a less elastic derived demand for aluminum. Thus, complete forward integration into the industry with the more elastic derived input demand facilitates price discrimination. It allows the upstream supplier to charge an implicitly lower price to one group of customers without generating the resale competition that would otherwise erode its higher price to the second consuming industry.

a Martin K. Perry, "Price Discrimination and Forward Integration," *Bell Journal of Economics* 9 (Spring 1978), pp. 209-17.
b The resale price would be greater than the price paid for ingots by wire fabricators but less than the price Alcoa charges to can manufacturers. The wire fabricators would accordingly earn a profit on resales, and the can manufacturers would benefit by obtaining aluminum at a lower price than they would otherwise pay to Alcoa.
c Perry, "Price Discrimination and Forward Integration."

It is worth stressing that the opposite tactic of integrating forward into the downstream industry with the less elastic derived input demand would not accomplish the same purpose. If Alcoa integrates only into the production of cans, for example, theory dictates that it raise the internal transfer price of aluminum ingots above the price it would charge without price discrimination. This higher price would tend to reduce the quantity of aluminum consumed by its downstream division, causing the output of the final product to decline and its market price to increase. At the same time, Alcoa would lower the price on the ingots it sells to the unintegrated wire fabricators.

Doing so would cause the profitability of the price discrimination strategy to break down, however. New firms would purchase aluminum ingots at their now lower market price and enter into the production of cans in direct competition with Alcoa's integrated downstream division. This new entry would expand the supply of cans and reduce their market price, making it impossible for Alcoa to maintain the higher transfer price that makes price discrimination profitable.

Put another way, the price discrimination strategy would be defeated because the new rivals in the can industry would enjoy a cost advantage due to their access to relatively cheap aluminum. This cost advantage would force Alcoa to lower its internal transfer price to the price at which ingots are sold to its unintegrated customers. Of course, Alcoa could avoid this possibility by integrating into both consuming industries. But it could not thereby earn higher profits than are available through integration with the wire fabricators alone. Hence, the profit-maximizing set of industries for the price-discriminating input supplier "contains all but the one with the least elastic derived demand."[d]

d *Ibid.*, p. 211.

that had been agreed to previously. Nor would the processor want to commit to purchase all of its molten steel under a contract that leaves it vulnerable to opportunistic price increases by the owner of the blast furnace.

In short, "the firm will never integrate for production cost reasons alone."[31] **Economies of scale**—reductions in average production costs attributable to increases in the firm's planned rate of output—are the principle reason for this conclusion.[32] Unless each order is unique, an outside supplier that fills the orders of several customers will be able to manufacture the input at lower unit cost than any one buyer who integrates backward to produce the smaller quantity necessary to satisfy its own input requirements. Ownership integration generally entails a production-cost penalty in the presence of economies of scale. Thus, the goal of economizing on **transaction costs**,[33] not production costs, is the driving force behind the integration of successive stages of production under common ownership.

Securing a Reliable Source of Supply. The claim is often made that vertical integration into upstream intermediate product markets is necessary

---

31 Oliver E. Williamson, *The Economic Institutions of Capitalism: Firms, Markets, Relational Contracting* (New York: Free Press, 1985), p. 94.

32 Economies of scale are defined and discussed more fully in Chapter 3.

33 Carl J. Dahlman, "The Problem of Externality," *Journal of Law and Economics* 22 (April 1979), p. 148, defines transaction costs as "search and information costs, bargaining and decision costs, and policing and enforcement costs."

to gain a "secure source of supply" of an essential input. For example, Alcoa was at one time the only U.S. producer of raw aluminum ingots. Aluminum production involves removing the impurities (iron, silicon, and oxygen, primarily) from bauxite ore. Alcoa realized large production cost savings by locating its smelting operations near bauxite mines, thereby reducing transportation costs and maintaining a reliable flow of raw material for the ore processing stage.

A reliable source of bauxite supply was important to Alcoa both because the ore is an essential input in the production of aluminum and because a steady flow of raw material permitted fuller employment of the production capacities of smelters and other capital. Supply interruptions are indeed costly to the firm. A protracted interruption in supply forces the firm to idle equipment and lay off workers. Even after delivery resumption, the firm loses additional production while it recalls employees and restarts equipment. While it may be possible to avoid some of the costs associated with supply interruptions by maintaining larger inventories of raw materials than otherwise, holding inventories is itself costly.

Thus, a firm that wants to ensure a reliable supply of an essential input would do well to acquire an ownership interest in one or more of its upstream suppliers. But ownership integration is not necessary for this purpose alone. Paper and ink were essential inputs into the manufacture of this book, for example, but the publisher did not merge with a paper company and an ink supplier to avoid the costs of potential supply interruptions. Similarly, Alcoa could have negotiated long-term contracts with independent mine owners that guaranteed the delivery of specified quantities of bauxite ore at specified prices.[34]

But the potential hold-up problems associated with such contracts are obvious. Once Alcoa had installed smelters near a particular mine, the mine's owner could opportunistically appropriate the quasi-rents created by Alcoa's investment (quasi-rents equal to the cost of moving the smelting operations to a new location) by demanding a higher price for ore than had been agreed to initially. With no equivalent customers for the bauxite, the mine's owner would likewise be vulnerable to opportunistic behavior by Alcoa. Thus, it is the presence of transaction-specific capital—and not the pressure to establish a dependable source of supply—that explains common ownership of bauxite mines and ore smelters in the aluminum industry.

---

34 Alcoa did in fact enter into long-term contracts with ore suppliers in the early 1900s. However, these contracts were invalidated by the courts in 1912 when the government objected to provisions specifying that the mine owners could not sell bauxite to any firm other than Alcoa. These provisions, it was alleged, prevented new firms from entering the aluminum industry to compete with Alcoa by denying them access to an essential input. Hence, part of the explanation for Alcoa's ownership of bauxite mines can be traced to its inability to legally enforce a contract provision that kept mine owners from opportunistically diverting bauxite supplies to other customers and thereby extracting a higher price from Alcoa. For detailed histories of the U. S. aluminum industry and Alcoa's role in developing it, see Merton J. Peck, *Market Control in the Aluminum Industry* (Cambridge, MA: Harvard University Press, 1961) and *U. S. v. Aluminum Company of America*, 148 F.2d 416 (2d Cir. 1945).

KEY TERMS
vertical integration
fixed-proportions technology
derived demand
variable-proportions technology
"hold-up" problem
quasi-rent
rate-of-return regulation
arbitrage
economies of scale
transaction costs

This chapter has summarized the economic principles that influence a firm's decision to make or buy one of the inputs used in the production of a final product. One set of these principles focuses on the use of vertical integration to narrow the "wedge" between price and marginal cost associated with transactions across the ownership boundaries of firms. In particular, under the assumption that production is subject to fixed-proportions technology, a profit motive for vertical integration exists when the market-determined prices of the intermediate input and the final product both include markups over marginal production costs. Ownership integration of successive production stages is profitable in this case because it allows the integrated firm to transfer the input internally at a price equal to marginal cost and thereby exploit the demand for the final product more fully by increasing output and reducing price. No such motive exists in the case where price exceeds marginal cost at only one stage of the production process.

This chapter has derived a similar incentive for ownership integration under the more general assumption of variable-proportions technology. There, a market-induced distortion in input prices causes the downstream buying industry to adopt a suboptimal input combination for producing the final product by curtailing its purchases of the input sold at a markup over marginal cost. By again enabling final product producers to transfer units of the intermediate input internally at a price equal to marginal cost, vertical integration results in improved production efficiency and higher profits.

This chapter has also highlighted economic motives for vertical integration based on the goal of reducing the costs of transacting across ownership boundaries. Ownership integration provides benefits by lessening the incentives of buyer and seller to engage in opportunistic behavior and by promoting the sharing of specialized information between parties to a transaction.

The choices of firms to make or buy likewise depend in part on public policies toward business. In this regard, ownership integration enables the firm to reduce its overall tax liability, to evade regulatory constraints on its allowed rate of return, and to dodge some of the discoordinating effects of inflationary monetary policy. The goal of price discriminating among downstream consuming industries provides an additional economic motive for vertical integration.

Just as importantly, the chapter has stressed two reasons that firms should *not* integrate. The goals of reducing production costs and securing a reliable supply of an essential input are not by themselves able to explain why firms might decide to make rather than buy. Because these objectives can in principle be attained through market contracting, ownership integration is better explained by transaction-cost rather than production-cost reasoning.

12.1 Consider the manufacturing and retailing stages of production. Other things being the same, if a sales tax is levied at the retail level, will there be more of an incentive to vertically integrate these two stages of production than there had been in the absence of the tax? What if the tax is expanded to apply to purchases by retailers? Explain your reasoning.

12.2 In 1984, AT&T and the Department of Justice settled an antitrust case against AT&T. In the settlement, AT&T agreed to break itself into several smaller firms. It would continue to provide long-distance telephone service, but it would spin off its affiliated local telephone service companies who would thereafter provide local telephone service independently of "Ma Bell." Prior to the settlement, AT&T had acquired ownership control of Western Electric Company, a manufacturer of telephones and other communications equipment. Explain why the government was concerned that AT&T had used its ownership interest in Western Electric to limit the effectiveness of federal regulation of long-distance and local telephone rates and why the breakup of AT&T helped to address these concerns.

12.3 One of the candidates in the 1992 presidential election campaign raised the issue of tax policy toward multinational firms. The candidate's allegation was that the domestic divisions of multinational corporations commonly overstate the prices of goods and services transferred to the U.S. from their overseas divisions, and understate the prices of goods and services transferred from U.S. to foreign divisions. Assuming the allegation is true, provide an explanation for the transfer pricing policies of multinational firms. Should the market prices of internally transferred goods and services be used as guides for calculating the U.S. tax liabilities of multinational firms? Why or why not?

12.4 An input supplier that vertically integrates forward can increase its profits by selling to its downstream subsidiary at a price below the marginal cost of producing the input being transferred. Whatever profits the upstream division sacrifices in pursuing this strategy will be more than made up for by the additional profits earned by the downstream division. True, false, or uncertain? Explain.

12.5 You are the sole producer of an input, I, sold to a price-taker final product industry that uses I in fixed proportions to manufacture F. I has no other uses. Your firm earns profits of P dollars annually. While the Federal Trade Commission is not watching, you manage to buy all of the producers of F and become a price-searcher in that market. Are your profits greater than P? Why or why not?

12.6 Why did the Aluminum Company of America (Alcoa) have a strong interest in owning the mines from which it obtained supplies of bauxite ore? Why were long-term contracts with mine owners viewed as an inadequate substitute for ownership?

12.7 Critically evaluate the government's reasoning in opposing the Ford-Autolite merger. Did the Supreme Court's divestiture order prevent a reduction of competition in the market for spark plugs? Why or why not?

12.8 Explain why automobile manufacturers typically buy paint and primer from outside suppliers but produce their own transmission assemblies.

12.9 Suppose you were asked to draw up a list of the functions and activities of a public university (food services, security, parking control, housing, data processing, and instruction, to name a few) that could be provided by private firms rather than by state government. What criteria would you apply in composing this list?

12.1 Frank's Pastry Shop sells only one product—chocolate donuts. For each dozen chocolate donuts purchased by a customer, Frank requires exactly one donut box, which he buys from one of a large number of paper products suppliers at a price of $.25. The inverse demand for chocolate donuts on a daily basis is

$$p = \$5 - \$.025Q,$$

where Q is measured in units of dozens of donuts. Assuming that the supplier's marginal production costs are constant and equal to $.25 per box and that the marginal cost of producing donuts is likewise constant and equal to $.50 per dozen, determine the pastry shop's profit-maximizing daily sales, price, and profits from selling chocolate donuts. Would Frank find it profitable to integrate backward into the production of donut boxes under these circumstances? Why or why not?

12.2 Frank's Pastry Shop sells only one product—chocolate donuts. For each dozen chocolate donuts purchased by a customer, Frank requires exactly one donut box, which he buys from one of a small number of paper products suppliers. The inverse demand for chocolate donuts on a daily basis is

$$p = \$5 - \$.025Q,$$

where Q is measured in units of dozens of donuts. Assuming that the supplier's marginal production costs are constant and equal to $.25 per box and that the marginal cost of producing donuts is likewise constant and equal to $.50 per dozen, determine the donut box supplier's profit-maximizing price, sales, and profits. Determine the pastry shop's profit-maximizing daily sales, price, and profits from selling chocolate donuts under these circumstances. Would Frank now find it profitable to integrate backward into the production of donut boxes? Why or why not?

Make-or-Buy Decisions: Contractual Alternatives to Ownership Integration

OVERVIEW

The preceding chapter has offered a number of reasons why a profit-maximizing firm might want to vertically integrate into an earlier or later stage of the production process. Efficiency considerations play an important role in that discussion. Cost savings from ownership integration result from such sources as eliminating a "wedge" between market price and marginal cost, avoiding opportunistic behavior, and overcoming informational asymmetries between buyer and seller.

But the efficiency benefits of vertical integration can often be realized by other means. Removing a transaction from the market reduces the cost of using the price system to guide resource allocation decisions, but it also increases the cost of administering transactions within the governance structure of the firm. Planning becomes more complex and errors in assigning tasks, establishing rewards, and monitoring performance become more likely as the size of the firm increases and as its scope expands. Ownership integration is therefore profitable only if the savings realized by placing less reliance on market exchange exceed the added cost of internal decision making.

For this reason, market contracting offers an economical alternative to vertical integration in a wide range of circumstances. Indeed, in the real world we see a continuum of institutional structures for governing transactions between buyer and seller. Some are unwritten, implicit spot-market contracts enforced only by the threat of withdrawal of future business. Others are explicitly stated contractual guarantees of varying duration and complexity enforced by the courts or some other third party. And others develop all the way to formal ownership integration.

This chapter considers some important contractual substitutes for vertical integration. The discussion highlights additional features of the special relationship between buyer and seller by focusing on downstream retail markets rather than on upstream intermediate product markets.

APPLICATION

Automobiles and light trucks are marketed to consumers through a network of independently owned and operated dealerships. Individual dealers make wholesale purchases from one or more of the major domestic and foreign automakers and then resell the vehicles to buyers at a markup. General economic conditions aside, the volume of cars sold in any model year is determined in large part by dealer sales and service effort.

Automobile and truck sales are complex transactions. Prospective buyers face a wide range of options, and the cost of a new vehicle represents a significant fraction of the average person's budget. Therefore, consumers have strong incentives to search across dealers to gather information about price, performance, style, reliability, and credit terms prior to purchase—information which dealers must accordingly be prepared to furnish. Moreover, consumers want the vehicles they buy to deliver dependable service over a number of years. So purchase decisions also hinge not only on the quality reputations of the automakers themselves, but on those of the local dealers who will be called upon to make the adjustments and repairs necessary to honor any expressed or implied warranties.

For these reasons, car and truck dealerships are subject to an elaborate system of controls imposed on them by the automobile manufacturers. Some of these controls were aptly described by a representative of the old Packard Motor Company during hearings before the Federal Trade Commission nearly a century ago. According to this auto industry executive, the

Packard Company . . . require[s] of the dealer that he have a location in a convenient and conspicuous place in the city; they require him to have a repair shop of certain dimensions; they require him to have a force of a certain size, and a certain number of these men must be factory-trained, expert men. The size of this repair [shop] must bear a relation to the number of cars in use in the territory. There must be given to the purchaser what is known as free service, which means that for the first thirty days all adjustments that the car may need shall be given free. . . .[a]

a Federal Trade Commission, *Conference on Resale Price Maintenance*, 7 vols. (Washington, D. C.: Federal Trade Commission, 1917), pp. 670-71. Quoted in Andrew N. Kleit, "Efficiencies Without Economists: The Early Years of Resale Price Maintenance," Working Paper No. 193, Bureau of Economics, Federal Trade Commission, April 1992, p. 22.

How could the Packard Company (or any modern automaker, for that matter) motivate its dealers to comply with these and other detailed requirements concerning how they should conduct the business of selling and servicing cars? Given that "it is absolutely essential . . . that this service should be kept up, that its excellence should be maintained, and that the goodwill that goes with the car should be protected,"[b] why didn't the Packard Company simply integrate forward into retailing and thereby exercise direct control over the sales and repair services offered to its customers? In other words, why choose a network of independently owned and operated dealerships for distributing automobiles rather than a system of wholly company-owned retail outlets? This chapter provides answers to these and a number of related questions.

---

b *Ibid.*

CONTRACTUAL AGREEMENTS CONCERNING PRICE

When buyer and seller transact across the ownership boundaries of firms, each is interested in maximizing his or her own profits. Self-interest-seeking creates divergent incentives with respect to pricing policy. The supplier, on the one hand, establishes a price for its output by setting the marginal revenue associated with its customers' derived input demand equal to the input's marginal production cost. When this price includes a markup and downstream production employs a variable-proportions technology, buyers tend to substitute away from the resource, using fewer units of the input to produce the final product than is optimal from the supplier's point of view. In other words, the supplier's profits would be higher (and, moreover, final product output would be larger and final product price would be lower) if the firm integrated forward into the downstream market and transferred the resource from one division to another at an internal price equal to marginal cost.

The buyer, on the other hand, establishes a price for its output by setting the marginal revenue associated with final product demand equal to the product's marginal production cost; this cost of course includes any markups added to the prices charged by the firm's outside suppliers. When the market-determined price of an input includes a markup over that input's marginal production cost, fewer units of the final product tend to be produced and sold than is optimal from the buyer's point of view. That is, the buyer's profits would be higher (and, moreover, final product output would be larger and final product price would be lower) if the firm integrated backward into the upstream market and likewise transferred resources internally at price equal to marginal cost.

Hence, when buyer and seller transact across ownership boundaries, their interests diverge with respect to price policy. Although each firm maximizes its individual profits by equating marginal revenue with marginal cost, joint profits would be higher if the two firms could find a way to overcome the distortion in input pricing associated with market exchange. Ownership integration, as we have shown, offers one alternative in this regard. Contractual agreements respecting price may have similar purposes and effects.

In the following sections we describe two types of pricing agreements between buyer and seller. These are resale price maintenance and so-called best-price policies.

Resale Price Maintenance

Consider the relationship between a manufacturer of some final product and the retailers who sell the good to its ultimate consumers. The reasons why the manufacturer has an interest in the final sale price should be fairly obvious. Because the retail price determines the quantity of the final product consumers are willing and able to buy, the manufacturer wants the retail price set at the level where consumers' purchases per unit of time equal its own profit-maximizing rate of production.

If the retail price is "too high," sales will be lower than expected, inventories of finished goods will pile up in the distribution system, and the manufacturer will eventually be forced to cut back production. This adjustment will tend to cause short-run average costs to exceed long-run average costs and thereby reduce the manufacturer's profits. On the other hand, if the retail price is "too low," customers' purchases will be greater than expected, shortages will occur, sales will be lost when items are out of stock, and short-run and long-run average production costs will again diverge as the manufacturer increases output to fill backorders and to keep pace with demand. Plainly, the manufacturer has a strong interest in seeing that retail sales dovetail with its own production and inventory plans.

One possible source of insurance in this regard is for the manufacturer to integrate forward into distribution and retailing, and thereby exercise direct control over the price at which the final product is sold to consumers. But there are costs associated with ownership integration. First, the manufacturer will need to acquire new, specialized marketing and retailing information and make decisions based on this information. Ownership integration requires the manufacturer to make decisions about pricing, about the provision of point-of-sale services, about the acceptance of return items, about credit terms, and so on. All of these decisions were formerly delegated to independent retailers.

Second, the daily operations of many company-owned retail outlets in various geographic locations will pose new problems of coordination. In retailing, knowledge of people, knowledge of local conditions, and knowledge of special circumstances are valuable assets that can best be acquired and put to profitable use by the "person on the spot."[1] Something will inevitably be lost in the process of communicating relevant information of this kind up the administrative hierarchy of the vertically integrated company. Moreover,

---

1 Friedrich A. Hayek, "The Use of Knowledge in Society," *American Economic Review* 35 (September 1945), p. 521.

ownership integration requires the manufacturer to learn the peculiarities of the marketing of other manufacturers' products that pass through the same distribution channel. As a result of these and other factors, the total costs of combining the manufacturing and retailing stages may well be greater than the sum of the costs of the two stages operating independently under separate ownership.

Resale price maintenance may offer an economical alternative to ownership integration under these conditions and in similar situations where the interests of buyer and seller diverge with respect to price policy. Resale price maintenance (RPM) describes a contractual provision in which the manufacturer and the retailers that carry its product mutually agree to set a limit on the price charged to the good's final consumers. RPM can involve specifying a *maximum* resale price (see the accompanying case study), but more typically it involves the setting of a *minimum* resale price.

In theory, minimum resale prices can have positive or negative effects on the welfare of consumers, depending on the purpose for which they are employed. The pioneering work in this area is by Lester Telser,[2] who suggested that the use of RPM to establish minimum resale prices might facilitate **collusion** either between manufacturers or between retailers, or that it might increase economic efficiency by reducing "free-rider" problems in the distribution and sale of goods.

Facilitating Collusion. The use of resale price maintenance to establish *minimum* resale prices may be a way for either manufacturers or retailers to limit price competition among themselves, thereby increasing their joint profits at the expense of consumers. Under one scenario, colluding manufacturers agree to use minimum RPM to fix the retail price of a good at the level consistent with the joint-profit-maximizing wholesale price.[3] Adopting this retail pricing policy may help manufacturers enforce their collusive agreement because it reduces their individual incentives to cheat by selectively offering secret wholesale price cuts to dealers.

RPM reduces incentives to cheat because as long as the minimum resale price remains in force, the retailer cannot pass the lower wholesale price on to consumers. And if the retail price cannot be lowered, final sales cannot be increased. The manufacturer accordingly gains nothing from the secret wholesale price cut—the manufacturer has simply given a gift to the retailer who enjoys a higher profit margin on existing sales. Hence, to the extent that RPM aids the members of a manufacturers' cartel in detecting cheating at the wholesale level, it has the potential for facilitating supplier collusion on price.[4]

---

2 Lester G. Telser, "Why Should Manufacturers Want Fair Trade?." *Journal of Law and Economics* 3 (October 1960), pp. 86-105.

3 See Chapter 8 for a discussion of the economic theory of collusion.

4 RPM does not limit cheating on nonprice margins of rivalry, however. Even if the retail price of a good is fixed, one manufacturer can increase its sales (and profits) at the expense of its co-conspirators in a variety of ways, including offering more liberal credit terms to dealers, being more willing to accept the return of defective goods, providing more frequent and more

Maximum Resale Price Maintenance: Read All About It!

Daily newspapers typically reach customers through a network of independent distributors. Some of these distributors deliver newspapers to the owners of newsstands and stock coin-operated newspaper vending machines; others service home delivery routes. The contractual relations between the newspaper's publisher and the distributors who service home delivery routes illustrate the efficiency benefits of specifying a *maximum* resale price.

These distributors are customarily granted exclusive geographic territories by the newspaper's publisher; that is, the publisher agrees not to contract with any other person to deliver its papers in a specified segment of the local home delivery area. Each distributor then purchases papers from the publisher at their wholesale price, sells them to customers at their retail (cover) price, and keeps any profit remaining after paying delivery expenses.

Both publisher and distributor derive advantages from this system of distribution. By contracting with independent distributors and granting them exclusive territories, the publisher avoids the costs of learning the myriad details necessary to efficiently deliver newspapers across a wide geographic area in a timely and predictable manner. These details are left to the distributors who, given the responsibility of serving a subset of the newspaper's entire circulation area, have the opportunity to gather more specific information about the peculiarities of their assigned territories.

Because they have closer daily contact with carriers and with customers, these local distributors can design routes and delivery schedules that best suit local market conditions. Given that the publisher has guaranteed not to locate another distributor in the specified territory, the distributor has a financial incentive to acquire and utilize such information. Any reductions in delivery costs and any cost-effective improvements in service that the distributor discovers and implements will increase his or her own profits. Moreover, the right to keep revenues net of delivery expenses assures that

the distributor will profit directly from local promotional and sales efforts that generate new home delivery customers. These activities also benefit the publisher.

At the same time, however, the discretion delegated to its independent distributors leaves the publisher vulnerable to certain types of opportunistic behavior. In particular, given their more detailed knowledge of local market conditions, some distributors—perhaps those whose assigned territories include high-income neighborhoods—may perceive an opportunity to raise the price of newspapers above the publication's cover price. While such a price increase may increase the profits of the distributor, it may not be consistent with profit maximization from the publisher's point of view.

First, a price increase by some distributors may lead others to follow suit, thereby reducing overall circulation below the level that is optimal in terms of the rates the publisher charges advertisers. (These rates are almost entirely circulation driven—newspapers that reach more customers can demand higher rates from advertisers.) Second, selective price increases by a few distributors may inefficiently divert sales from the home delivery market to newsstands and to vending machines where demand is more unpredictable and where circulation losses are therefore more likely because newspapers remain unsold on some days and are out-of-stock on others. Third, price increases in some home delivery areas provide an incentive for other distributors to poach on the assigned territories of their counterparts who have raised price. Such diversions of sales between exclusive territories can cause the entire distribution system to unravel as distributors scramble to compete with one another city-wide.

For these reasons, newspaper distribution contracts historically contained provisions prohibiting distributors from charging customers more than the publication's cover price. This pricing policy was declared illegal in a case decided by the Supreme Court in 1968, however. The case involved a suit brought by a Mr.

Albrecht, one of 172 authorized distributors of the *Herald* newspaper in the St. Louis metropolitan area.[a]

The *Herald*'s publisher terminated Albrecht's exclusive distributorship after he had repeatedly refused to stop charging his customers more than the newspaper's suggested retail price. The Court held that the *Herald*'s policy of specifying a maximum resale price constituted an unlawful restraint of trade in violation of Section 1 of the Sherman Act, citing with approval an earlier decision's conclusion that agreements to fix maximum prices, "no less than minimum prices, cripple the freedom of traders and thereby restrain their ability to sell in accordance with their own judgment."[b]

It is easy to show that establishing a maximum resale price always improves consumer welfare.[c] Maximum RPM prevents the downstream distributor or retailer from opportunistically raising price and consequently restricting sales below the level consistent with profit maximization at earlier stages of production. And, indeed, a maximum RPM policy generally results in the same price and quantity in the final product market that would exist with ownership integration of the manufacturing (or publishing) and the distribution and retailing functions. Consumers obviously benefit from this development. Price is lower and quantity is larger at retail when a maximum resale price is specified than would be the case otherwise. The *Albrecht* court missed this simple point, however, and laid down a legal rule that arguably interferes with an efficient method of product distribution.

a *Albrecht* v. *Herald Co.*, 390 U. S. 145 (1968).
b *Kiefer-Stewart Co.* v. *Joseph E. Seagram & Sons*, 340 U. S. 211 (1951).
c Roger D. Blair and James M. Fesmire, "Maximum Price Fixing and the Goals of Antitrust," *Syracuse Law Review* 37 (1986), pp. 43-77.

A second RPM collusion theory suggests using minimum resale prices to detect cheating by the members of a retailers' cartel. Here, in an effort to raise dealer profit margins and to limit price cutting among themselves, retailers band together and convince manufacturers to adopt and enforce a minimum RPM policy by threatening as a group to boycott the goods of any supplier that refuses to comply. The difficulty with this theory, however, is that because barriers to entry into retailing are relatively low, any attempt to raise dealer margins in this way is unlikely to succeed. Moreover, because such a retail pricing scheme would tend to reduce profits at earlier stages of the production process, manufacturers would have no incentive to give in to the retailers' demands.

Controlling "Free Riding." Minimum resale price maintenance has alternatively been interpreted as a business practice whose purpose is to reduce **"free rider"** problems among retailers. Retailing typically involves much more than simply transferring a product from manufacturer to consumer. For many goods, the retailer provides prospective customers with important information about performance characteristics, warranty terms, availability, and price. This information is communicated by knowledgeable salespeople who guide purchasers through display areas, point out available models and styles, and perform product demonstrations. These point-of-sale services are

---

reliable delivery schedules, sharing in the cost of local promotional campaigns, and so on. Because successful collusion requires agreement on more than just price, the ability of RPM by itself to enforce a manufacturers' cartel is highly problematic.

in many instances an essential component of the product being purchased and to the extent that customers benefit from such services, manufacturers have a strong interest in seeing that retailers supply them.

It costs something for retailers to provide the point-of-sale services desired by manufacturers, however. Sales personnel must be trained, various models and styles must be kept in stock and displayed in ways that allow comparisons to be made, and so on. Any one retailer may accordingly be tempted to "free ride" on the sales efforts of other dealers. That is, given that other retail outlets continue to provide full service to prospective purchasers, a free rider may be able to increase its own profits in the short run by supplying fewer point-of-sale services and attracting buyers with lower prices. But if consumers can obtain the benefit of retailer-supplied services from one dealer and then purchase the good from a discounter that provides fewer (or no) point-of-sale services, retailers as a group have no incentive to offer the services desired by the manufacturer. Hence, free rider problems at the retail level can adversely affect the manufacturer's sales (and profits) by eliminating the provision of important point-of-sale services.

Retailers as a group also suffer because of this development. Total retail sales are lower in the long run than they would be if point-of-sale services were provided to customers. But while all retailers would gain by supplying such services, each has an incentive to take actions that preclude their provision.

Minimum RPM helps eliminate this free rider problem by preventing opportunistic price discounting. That is, if all retailers who carry a manufacturer's product agree to adhere to a minimum resale price, no one gains an advantage by withdrawing desired point-of-sale services. (If consumers in fact benefit from such services, they will not buy from dealers that do not offer them because those dealers cannot compensate for the lack of services by cutting price.) Put another way, minimum RPM provides retailers with a markup over wholesale price sufficient to induce them to supply point-of-sale service and guarantees that this markup will not be eroded by competition from other dealers who might otherwise free ride on their sales efforts. Minimum RPM helps channel the competition between retailers to the nonprice margins of rivalry both consumers and manufacturers demand.

The automakers and independent dealers who were the subject of the chapter's opening application in fact adopted a minimum RPM policy for precisely this purpose. The Packard Company's representative testified that the sales and service effort required of its dealers would not be forthcoming "without allowing to the dealer and seeing that he gets a margin which . . . is 20 percent above the wholesale price."[5] The underlying economic justification for minimum RPM was described, in language that Telser might have written, by one of Packard's contemporary competitors. According to an executive of the Ford Motor Company,

---

5 Federal Trade Commission, *Conference on Resale Price Maintenance*, p. 673. Quoted in Kleit, "Efficiencies Without Economists," p. 22.

the company's business has been built up to its present proportions by maintaining an organization consisting of dealers in every part of the country—I think about 6,000—who were under contract obligations not only to maintain a garage and a stock of parts for quick repairs, but also to show purchasers how to use and handle and conserve the car, instructing them how to run it, and following and watching every car, remedying the defects, and making it please and satisfy the customer. None of these things is done by the cut-price cutthroat, who has no interest in the car or business. When by his tricky practices he succeeds in taking customers away from their regular dealer the Ford Co. loses its best dealers and salesmen, and the company loses its reputation. The purchasers have troubles with the car that could easily and simply be corrected by any person having knowledge, but there is no one in the vicinity to instruct them. Hence follow dissatisfied customers, loss of the best advertisers—satisfied customers—loss of reputation, loss of sales and loss of business.[6]

Economists have recently begun extending Telser's theory to accommodate other free-ridable margins of retail competition. Howard Marvel and Stephen McCafferty, for example, argue that if the fact that particular retailers carry a manufacturer's product provides a signal to consumers of quality or fashion, minimum RPM can prevent other dealers from free riding on the brand name capital of these reputable sellers. (If Wal-Mart and K-Mart sell Lee jeans at a deep discount, for instance, then the reputational value created in the minds of consumers from having Lee jeans carried by fashionable department stores like Nordstrom's may be greatly diminished.) Similarly, it has been suggested that minimum RPM can play a role in inducing retailers to provide optimal post-sale services and sales efforts, and in insuring them against demand risk.[7]

In sum, by narrowing the divergence of interests between the manufacturer and the dealers that transfer its product to final consumers, minimum resale price maintenance helps promote optimal pricing at retail in situations where ownership integration between these two stages of production would be too costly. And by channeling the rivalry between retailers in the direction of nonprice margins of competition, minimum RPM helps assure that retailers will supply the pre- and post-sale services desired by consumers. RPM is nevertheless illegal where, in the language of the Clayton Act, "it would substantially lessen competition or tend to create a monopoly." Firms should therefore approach its use with caution.

---

6 U. S. House of Representatives, Committee on Interstate and Foreign Commerce, 63rd Congress, "Hearings on H. R. 13305, a Bill to Prevent Discrimination in Price and to Provide for Publicity of Prices to Dealers and the Public," 1915, p. 222. Quoted in Kleit, "Efficiencies Without Economists," p. 23.

7 For a discussion of the pros and cons of resale price maintenance, see Howard P. Marvel and Stephen McCafferty, "The Welfare Effects of Resale Price Maintenance," *Journal of Law and Economics* 28 (May 1985), pp. 363-79.

"Best-Price" Policies

When transactions between successive stages of production take place across ownership boundaries, each party must invest resources in "discovering what the relevant prices are."[8] The objective of economizing on such search and information costs supplies another one of the basic motives for vertical integration between buyer and seller. So-called best-price policies may have similar purposes and effects.

A **best-price policy** consists of two separate contractual guarantees. One of these provisions is a **most-favored-nation** (MFN) or most-favored-customer clause which promises the buyer that during the time a sales contract is in force, the price the buyer pays will be the lowest price at which the seller supplies the same product to any of its other customers. The second contractual provision is a **meet-or-release** (MOR) clause which stipulates that if a rival supplier offers to sell the same product to the buyer at a lower price during the contract period, the seller will either match that lower price or release the customer from its contractual obligations.

Some economists interpret best-price policies, like resale price maintenance, as a practice that facilitates collusion among suppliers. Specifically, because a MFN clause provides that a price discount offered to one customer must be offered to all, sellers may be more hesitant to reduce price than they would be otherwise. This effect of MFN provisions, some argue, helps prevent collusive agreements from unraveling by stabilizing price. MOR provisions are said to reinforce this effect by encouraging customers to report any discount offered to them by one seller in the hope of having their current supplier match it. Customer reporting of price discounts helps the colluding sellers detect the secret price cuts that would otherwise destabilize their cartel. Moreover, MFN provisions discourage such matching because if the seller meets a selective price cut to one customer, the seller must make the same offer of a lower price to all other customers having MFN status.

Some limited empirical evidence suggests that by reducing the incentives of firms to offer selective discounts, MFN provisions may elevate market prices.[9] It is also true, however, that such price guarantees are valuable to customers because they help economize on the costs of switching suppliers. When transactions take place across the ownership boundaries of firms, buyers must invest resources in searching across the various combinations of price, quality, and service offered by rival sellers. Once the buyers have made such investments and have selected a supplier, special arrangements must often be made for credit and billing, delivery, storage, and so on.

Under these conditions, MFN status protects the buyer—especially a small buyer—by assuring that it will receive the benefit of any price concessions secured by other customers from the same supplier during the contract period.

---

8 Ronald H. Coase, "The Nature of the Firm," *Economica* 4 (November 1937), p. 390.

9 David M. Grether and Charles R. Plott, "The Effects of Market Practices in Oligopolistic Markets: An Experimental Examination of the Ethyl Case," *Economic Inquiry* 22 (July 1984), pp. 479-528.

Without such a guarantee, the buyer would be placed at a cost disadvantage relative to any of its competitors in the downstream market that subsequently negotiate a lower price. There would then be an incentive for the customer to breach its existing contract, an action that would both diminish the value of prior investments in search and raise the prospect of costly litigation. In the limit, and depending on the frequency and magnitude of price reductions in the market, long-term contracting—which tends to lessen search and information costs for both buyer and seller—would hardly be an economical alternative to ownership integration.

MOR provisions further protect buyers' prior investments in search by offering assurance that the buyer will have to switch suppliers to take advantage of a lower price offered by another seller only if the current supplier cannot meet that lower price. Moreover, in the event that the current supplier cannot match a rival seller's lower price, a MOR clause guarantees that the buyer will not face a lawsuit for breach of contract if it does in fact switch suppliers.

In these ways, best-price policies help reduce the cost of transacting across the ownership boundaries of firms. MFN and MOR provisions would seem to be particularly valuable to buyers in markets where price changes are frequent and difficult to predict, and where price uncertainty would consequently impede the use of long-term contracting as a method of governing exchange. They are evidently not perfect substitutes for vertical integration, but they may instead represent one element of a set of complementary arrangements adopted by buyers and sellers to solve problems of coordination and divergent incentives across ownership boundaries (see the accompanying case study of the market for lead-based antiknock compounds).

NONPRICE CONTRACTUAL AGREEMENTS

Nonprice competition is a substitute for price competition.[10] A seller can increase sales without lowering the money price of its product by, among other things, providing customers with more frequent or more reliable deliveries, adopting a more liberal policy for accepting the return of goods, lengthening the duration of an existing warranty, offering more favorable credit terms, increasing its promotional activities and sales effort, and improving product quality.

The optimal amount of competition on these and the many other margins of nonprice rivalry depends on two related factors. One is the usual marginal-benefit-marginal-cost calculus which dictates that the seller invest resources in nonprice competition up to the point where the last dollar spent just generates an extra dollar's worth of sales. The marginal benefit of nonprice competition, in turn, depends on the terms at which consumers are willing to trade off the price and nonprice conditions of sale offered by the seller.

---

10 George J. Stigler, "Price and Nonprice Competition," *Journal of Political Economy* 72 (January-February 1968), pp. 149-54.

Getting the Lead In

Lead-based compounds have been used by petroleum refiners since the 1920s.[a] Until recently, refiners routinely added these compounds to gasoline to improve its octane rating and to reduce engine "knock."[b] The lead additives, which are highly volatile and toxic, were supplied to gasoline refineries by a small number of specialized chemical companies. Indeed, the Ethyl Corporation was the sole domestic producer of antiknock compounds until 1948. The strong post-World War II growth in automobile sales (and the corresponding increase in the demand for gasoline) made room for entry by new suppliers, but even so there were only four U.S. producers of antiknock compounds by the middle 1960s: Ethyl, E. I. du Pont de Nemours & Co., PPG Industries, and Nalco Chemical Company.

In 1983, the Federal Trade Commission handed down an opinion that during the years 1974 through 1979, these four producers had independently adopted certain contractual arrangements with their customers that effectively eliminated price competition in the market for antiknock compounds. The FTC challenged in particular the practices of quoting prices only on the basis of delivered price (i.e., inclusive of transportation charges), providing customers with a 30-day advance notice of price changes, and including most-favored-nation (MFN) clauses in their standard-form sales contracts.

As discussed in the text, a MFN clause represents a promise by the seller that during the time the contract is in force, the price the buyer pays will be the lowest price any customer pays for the same product. Ethyl's MFN clause, for example, stated that

> if Ethyl sells a compound of equal quantity and quality at a price lower than that provided for herein to any oil company in the United States, BUYER shall pay such lower price on all shipments of such compounds made hereunder while such lower price is in effect.[c]

Ethyl began including a MFN clause in its standard-form sales contract prior to 1948 when it was the sole domestic producer of lead-based antiknock compounds.

Du Pont followed suit when it entered the industry in that year. But when PPG and Nalco began producing lead additives in the 1960s, they chose not to adopt the industry's practice of offering MFN status to all customers. PPG and Nalco did, however, use such provisions selectively: PPG inserted MFN clauses in two sales contracts written between 1974 and 1979; Nalco granted MFN status to seven customers between 1967 and 1974.

Despite the FTC's allegations, these contractual provisions were apparently altogether ineffective in eliminating vigorous competition among the four sellers. During the six-year period that was the subject of the government's complaint (1974-79), Nalco sold more than 80 percent of its total production of antiknock compounds at discounts off list price. PPG, likewise, discounted between a third and 58 percent of its sales in the corresponding period.[d]

a See *E. I. du Pont de Nemours & Co.* v. *F. T. C.*, 729 F. 2d 128 (2d Cir. 1984) and *Ethyl Corp.* v. *F. T. C.*, 729 F. 2d 128 (2d Cir. 1984), hereinafter cited collectively as *Ethyl*. See also Samson M. Kimenyi, "Antitrust Policy and the Use of Non-Standard Contracts and Practices: The Case of Best-Price Policies," unpublished Ph.D. dissertation, George Mason University, 1986, upon which this case study is based.

b Following passage of the Clean Air Act of 1970, the Environmental Protection Agency promulgated a series of regulations, including placing restrictions on the amount of lead contained in motor fuels and requiring automobile manufacturers to begin installing catalytic converters on all new vehicles, that gradually removed leaded gasoline from the market.

c Kimenyi, "Antitrust Policy," p. 37. Emphasis in original.

d Along with the shrinking market for lead additives resulting from environmental regulations, this sharp price competition caused PPG to operate at a loss in 1979 and to ultimately cease production of antiknock compounds in 1983.

Ethyl and du Pont responded to the competitive pressures in other ways. Rather than embracing their rivals' price cutting strategy, they attempted to hold on to their existing customers and to attract new customers through various nonprice methods of competition. These nonprice margins of rivalry included adopting the practices of late billing of deliveries and of "advance buying," the latter being a policy of allowing customers to place additional orders at the existing price during the 30 days prior to the time an announced price increase would become effective. In addition,

> du Pont and Ethyl also provided valuable "free" services, including (1) provision of free equipment, (2) education on how to use the product more efficiently, (3) assistance in building and monitoring facilities for the storage and blending of antiknock compounds, (4) computer programming assistance, (5) training of refiners' employees, (6) payment for consultant services, and (7) favorable credit terms.[e]

For their part, the industry's customers, which the court described as "large, aggressive and sophisticated buyers,"[f] used all available means to obtain their requirements of antiknock compounds. They negotiated the challenged contracts that provided for advance notice of price changes, price quotations on a delivered price basis,[g] and most-favored-nation treatment. These contracts were typically of one year's duration. All of the refineries customarily entered into contracts with at least two suppliers simultaneously and they apparently often terminated the contracts prior to their expiration dates without penalty. In addition to making purchases through contractual arrangements with two or more suppliers, the petroleum refineries also bought antiknock compounds on a spot-market basis. (Indeed, Ethyl and du Pont, the two companies charged by the FTC with the unlawful use of MFN provisions, sold about half of their total output of lead-based gasoline additives on the open market.)

Finally, five of the largest domestic oil refiners jointly owned a Canadian chemical firm, Octel, that produced antiknock compounds. We can therefore assume that these five customers, at least, had fairly detailed and reliable information about the production of antiknock compounds and would have obtained more of their input requirements from Octel had they been dissatisfied with the terms at which supplies were available domestically. The fact that these refiners continued to obtain most of their antiknock compounds from independent domestic suppliers provides strong evidence that market contracting did indeed serve as a cost-effective alternative to ownership integration. Moreover, the MFN clauses in the sales contracts with other, smaller refineries guaranteed that they could buy antiknock compounds at the same price paid by the owners of Octel. This means that the smaller refineries were in essence able to free ride on the superior information possessed by their larger rivals.[h]

In sum, a careful reading of the facts in *Ethyl* suggests that despite the FTC's allegations, the MFN provisions agreed to by petroleum refiners and their suppliers were one element in a rich set of arrangements designed to promote efficient exchange across ownership boundaries. MFN treatment, along with advance notice of price changes, helped buyers economize on search and information costs—the costs of discovering what the relevant prices are—that might otherwise have impeded market transactions in a declining industry. The Second Circuit Court articulated these efficiency benefits when, on hearing the appeals filed by Ethyl and du Pont, it vacated the FTC's order.

e *Ethyl*, pp. 132-33.

f *Ibid.*, p. 131.

g According to the Circuit Court, the refineries demanded delivered pricing because this system of quoting price meant that their suppliers would "retain title to and responsibility for the dangerously volatile compounds during transit to the refiner's plant." See *Ethyl*, p. 133.

h One explanation for MFN provisions, offered by Vernon Smith, is that because these price guarantees represent an explicit promise by the seller not to engage in price discrimination, they are designed to avoid liability under the antitrust laws. See Vernon L. Smith, "Theory, Experiment, and Antitrust Policy," in Steven C. Salop, ed., *Strategy, Predation, and Antitrust Analysis* (Washington, D. C.: Federal Trade Commission, 1981), pp. 579-606.

Consider waiting time prior to delivery, for example. Consumers will tolerate longer waits only if the money price of the good is lowered sufficiently to compensate them for the value of the opportunities foregone by not receiving deliveries sooner.[11]

Many of the nonprice characteristics of goods that serve as dimensions of rivalry between sellers are determined at the manufacturing stage of production (product performance specifications, product reliability, durability, and styling, for instance). However, nonprice competition is also obviously important at the distribution and retailing stages. The manufacturer accordingly has a strong interest in seeing that the downstream industry supplies the pre- and post-sale services demanded by the product's final consumers. As in other cases of jointness and shared responsibilities, controlling free riding is the basic economic problem. If both price and nonprice terms of sale are keys to a manufacturer's success in competition with its rivals in the final product market, it will want to monitor and control the activities of distributors and retailers carefully.

One way of doing so, of course, is to integrate forward into the final product market, thereby governing the nonprice conditions of sale directly and assuring that the supply of these activities is consistent with its profit-maximizing retail price. But as has been emphasized earlier, combining successive stages of production under common ownership entails costs as well as benefits. Market contracting may therefore offer an economical alternative to the integration of manufacturing and retailing functions under certain circumstances. This section considers three nonprice contract provisions that serve to overcome some of the divergences in interests between buyer and seller when transactions occur across the ownership boundaries of firms. These three contractual provisions are exclusive territory arrangements, exclusive dealing arrangements, and tie-in sales.

Exclusive Territories

The assignment of exclusive geographic territories to individual dealers is a prevalent feature of modern distribution and retailing systems. Firms use this strategy in the marketing of a variety of goods and services, including automobiles, newspapers, electronic equipment, "fast food," and professional sports. Under an exclusive territory arrangement, the manufacturer or franchisor promises its authorized retailers that no other dealer will be permitted to distribute the product or sell the service within a specified geographic territory while the contract remains in force.

Territorial limitations of this sort basically insulate the manufacturer's dealers from competition with each other. **Intrabrand competition** decreases insofar as each retailer retains the exclusive right to sell the manufacturer's product within its own designated territory. As will be explained

---

11 See Gary S. Becker, "A Theory of the Allocation of Time," *Economic Journal* 75 (September 1965), pp. 493-517.

below, however, reduced intrabrand competition within a network of exclusive territories can help *promote* competition among dealers in the products of different manufacturers. In other words, reduced intrabrand competition increases **interbrand competition**.

Why should manufacturers want exclusive territories? The basic answer is that territorial limitations are adopted for many of the same reasons that explain the use of resale price maintenance and also provide a motive for forward ownership integration. Manufacturers have an important stake in the activities of the distributors and retailers of their products. The assignment of exclusive territories to these dealers offers a contractual alternative to ownership integration. This alternative, under certain circumstances, will be the low-cost method of assuring that downstream firms operate in the manufacturer's best interest.

Exclusive Territories and the Theory of Vertical Integration. Exclusive territories are somewhat paradoxical in light of the economic theory of vertical integration. As Chapter 12 shows, the upstream supplier of an intermediate input that is sold at a markup over marginal production cost has no interest in restricting the level of sales downstream. This is because the existence of an output restriction in the final product market (and a corresponding markup on final product sales) reduces the derived demand for the intermediate input and thereby lowers the supplier's profits below the level that could be earned with common ownership of successive stages of production. Hence, a double markup generates a motive for vertical integration that leads to an expansion in final product sales and a reduction in final product price.

With exclusive territories, however, the upstream firm purposely limits competition among its authorized dealers, allowing each of them to charge prices in excess of marginal cost. Because this action by itself tends to reduce the manufacturer's sales, it must be the case that territorial restrictions at the retail level create offsetting benefits that increase the supplier's overall profitability.[12]

---

[12] The presumption that exclusive territories tend to promote economic efficiency has not always been accepted by the antitrust authorities and the courts, however. Territorial limitations were declared illegal per se by the Supreme Court in *U. S.* v. *Arnold Schwinn & Co.*, 388 U.S. 365 (1969). (Similar decisions were rendered in *U. S.* v. *Sealy, Inc.*, 388 U.S. 350 [1967], and *FTC* v. *Coors*, 83 F.T.C. 32 [1973]). But in 1977, the Court overturned these precedents and held that Sylvania's exclusive territory system did not violate the antitrust laws. Faced with a declining market share in retail television sales, Sylvania in 1962 phased out its wholesale distribution network and instituted a plan of selling directly to a smaller and more select group of retailers. In the process, Sylvania designated a new San Francisco retailer, Young Brothers, at a location in close proximity to Continental T.V., Inc. which had previously been one of Sylvania's most successful dealers but which was no longer authorized to sell its products. Continental sued, claiming that Sylvania's new territorial restrictions constituted a per se violation of the Sherman Act. The Supreme Court held, however, that Sylvania's actions had no "pernicious effect on competition." Indeed, it was the majority's opinion that such "vertical restrictions promote interbrand competition by allowing the manufacturer to achieve certain efficiencies in the distribution of his products." See *Continental T.V., Inc.* v. *GTE Sylvania, Inc.*, 433 U.S. 36 (1977).

Controlling "Free Riding." Control of free riding and assurance that dealers will maintain some specified standard of performance are desirable properties in any marketing system, no matter what its structure. Exclusive territories help achieve these goals in two ways. One is in choosing the retailers who will be authorized to carry the manufacturer's product. By offering dealers the exclusive right to sell within a specified territory, the manufacturer promises to protect each of them from competition with the others. This commitment guarantees the authorized dealers that profits based on being the exclusive distributor of a product in a given territory will not be eroded by competition from the manufacturer's other distributors. The promise of exclusivity increases the economic value of the territorial rights and makes it more likely that there will be an excess supply of applicants for each dealership.

Having an excess supply of applicants affords the manufacturer the opportunity to screen candidates—examining their financial records, credit histories, prior business experience, and so on—and select the one most apt to maintain the desired level of performance. This selection process is critical because the ultimate value of the manufacturer's product will depend in large part on these designated distributors. The dealers must have the willingness and ability to supply the pre- and post-sales services demanded by customers, to engage in local promotional activities, to employ pleasant and knowledgeable sales personnel, and to maintain an attractive place of business—in short, they must be the manufacturer's agents in the retail marketplace.

Franchise Agreements. The importance of these considerations is even more apparent in the case of franchise contracts which typically contain exclusive territory provisions. While it is true that the franchisor usually invests in market research to select the optimal franchise location, helps finance the construction of the franchise outlet, and provides the franchisee with a tested, standardized business operation plan, the most valuable item that the franchisor supplies to the franchisee is the franchisor's brand name or trademark. Because this trademark serves as a signal of quality to consumers, the franchisor has a critical stake in the performance of its franchisees. Their actions will have a direct impact on the franchisor's reputation and, hence, on the market value of the licensed trademark.

Although all of the parties have an interest in maintaining a reputation for quality, each franchisee has an incentive to cut corners and allow the quality of its own operation to deteriorate. As long as all other franchisees hold their standards at the level consumers expect, one franchisee can increase its profits in the short run by opportunistically reducing its attention to quality and free riding on the reputations of the others. Obviously, if one franchisee has this incentive, they all do. Left unchecked, such free riding will in the long run cause the manufacturer's distribution system to unravel.

For this reason, franchising arrangements typically contain an elaborate system of controls that help narrow the divergence of interests between the franchisor and its franchisees. One of these controls is a requirement that franchisees invest some of their own capital in the business, a portion of which (and perhaps all) represents a lump-sum, nonrefundable fee paid for the right to operate the franchise. If the franchisor can then terminate franchisees for failing to comply with the contractual agreement, the lump-sum payment is in effect a forfeitable bond that the franchisee posts to guarantee performance. Because a portion of his or her own wealth is thereby at risk, the franchisee has a greater incentive to behave in ways that are compatible with the franchisor's interest.[13]

Other contractual provisions in this regard include requirements that the franchisee purchase some of its complementary inputs directly from the franchisor or from a list of authorized suppliers, and royalty arrangements in which the franchisee agrees to pay a fixed percentage of its profits to the franchisor. In the former case, the franchisor gains a degree of control over the quality of the franchisee's product. Royalty payments based on sales or profits provide the franchisor with a direct measure of its franchisee's performance.[14]

Generally speaking, the lump-sum franchise fee, the royalty payments, the wholesale price of the franchisor's product, and the prices of any complementary inputs sold to the franchisee will be structured in such a way that each franchisee earns a normal rate of return on his or her investment. The assignment of exclusive territories is a way for the franchisor to guarantee that this rate of return will in fact be earned. The assignment of exclusive territories provides franchisees with further incentives to behave in ways that benefit themselves (and the franchisor). Exclusivity assures them that they will capture the gains net of royalty payments associated with local promotional efforts and any cost-effective innovations they discover and implement that result in improved customer service and increased sales. The franchisor cannot of course promise to insulate its franchisees from the competition of the franchisees of other franchisors, but it can guarantee not to opportunistically locate another of its own franchisees within the same geographic territory.

---

13 A casual perusal of recent issues of the *Wall Street Journal* suggests that franchisees are required to invest capital in the range of $100,000 to $450,000. Investments of this size raise the cost to franchisees of cutting corners or taking other actions that may lead to termination for nonperformance. The termination of franchisees is also costly for the franchisor not only because sales may be lost and reputations may suffer during the transition period, but because, as the *Sylvania* case illustrates, terminated franchisees have a propensity to sue.

14 Royalty payments based on the franchisee's *profits* will lead the franchisee to select the same rate of output the franchisor would choose if it wholly owned and operated the franchise outlet. Despite this efficiency property, however, franchise royalty payments are typically expressed as a percentage of *sales*. This is because it will be easier for the franchisor to monitor the franchisee's sales than it will be to monitor its profits, which the franchisee can manipulate by reporting higher costs than were actually incurred. To compare and contrast the franchisee's output choices with a royalty payment based on sales versus a royalty payment based on profits, let $R(Q)$ be the franchisee's revenue function and let $C(Q)$ be its total cost function. Then, if β is the royalty rate on sales, the franchisee will select the Q that maximizes $\pi = R(Q)(1 - \beta) - C(Q)$. By contrast, if δ is the royalty rate on profits, the franchisee will select the Q that maximizes $\pi' = [R(Q) - C(Q)](1 - \delta)$. Because the franchisee bears all of the costs but receives only a portion of the revenue in the first case, it will select a Q that is smaller than is optimal from the franchisor's point of view. In the second case, the same Q maximizes pre- and post-royalty payments.

In sum, the purposes and effects of exclusive territories and franchise contracts are not fundamentally different from those associated with vertical ownership integration. Control of free riding and quality assurance explain the territorial limitations agreed to by retailers and their suppliers. As such, territorial assignments increase consumer welfare by making transactions between manufacturers and retailers more economical in situations where ownership integration would be too costly. This conclusion is strengthened by keeping in mind that the relevant margins of competition are among the authorized dealers of a given manufacturer and the dealer networks of the manufacturers of substitutable products and services. Competition does not decrease in any meaningful sense when McDonald's insulates its franchisees from competition with one another. Instead, such limitations increase the ability of McDonald's franchisees to compete with the franchisees of Wendy's, Burger King, Pizza Hut, Taco Bell, and a host of other rivals.

Exclusive Dealing

An **exclusive dealing contract** involves a commitment by a buyer to deal only with a particular seller. A **requirements contract**, in which a buyer commits itself to purchase all of its supplies of a particular good or service from a specified seller, is a closely related type of agreement. Contractual guarantees of this sort have obvious similarities with franchising arrangements and with vertical ownership integration. They therefore have similar purposes and effects.

Consider gasoline retailing. The owner of an independent station typically enters into an agreement with a wholesale supplier to carry only one particular brand of gasoline. The owner also often agrees to purchase all of his or her requirements of ancillary repair and replacement products—tires, tubes, batteries, motor oil, and so on—from the same supplier. Agreements of this sort have sometimes been held to violate the antitrust laws on the theory that competing suppliers are thereby "foreclosed" from dealing with the retailers who have entered into such contracts.[15] But it is also clear that exclusivity arrangements between buyer and seller promote economic efficiency along several important margins.

First, both parties secure a planned product flow that relieves them of the uncertainties and expense of going to the market more often. This tends to reduce the record keeping and inventory holding costs at both stages of production. Second, and more important, contractual provisions of this type result in improved product promotion by both the supplier and the retailer. Compared to a situation in which retailers carry the products of more than one supplier, exclusive dealing provides an incentive for retailers to channel all of their local promotional efforts toward the sale of the product of their sole supplier.

---

15 See *Standard Oil Co. of California* v. *U.S.*, 337 U.S. 293 (1949).

Given assurance that dealers will work only in that supplier's behalf, the supplier is willing to provide its dealers with specialized training and financial assistance that will assist them in improving service and increasing sales. Such aid may be in the form of payments to be used for the repair or remodeling of retailers' places of business, sharing the costs of local advertising campaigns, and training the dealers' employees in the proper handling of its products.[16] Little incentive to do these things would exist if the retailers carried the products of more than one supplier, because any assistance given to the retailer by one of them would also provide benefits to the others.

Exclusive dealing and requirements contracts increase the returns to product promotion at the supplier level as well.[17] A national advertising campaign or similar promotional effort generates customer patronage for all of the local dealers that carry the advertised product or service. If those local dealers also market the products or services of rival suppliers, a portion of the extra sales attributable to the advertising campaign will redound to the benefit of the advertiser's competitors. This would occur if, for example, local dealers opportunistically steer customers who have been enticed by one manufacturer's ads toward other brands that yield them a higher profit margin. Exclusive dealing contracts thus assure the supplier of capturing all of the gains resulting from its own investments in advertising and promotion.

Vertical control by contract enables a supplier to obtain many of the benefits of forward integration into retailing while avoiding some of the costs, including the capital costs of constructing its own network of retail outlets and the administrative costs of taking full responsibility for supervising and coordinating the activities of its dealers. Contracting with independent retailers allows the supplier to shift the burdens of retail pricing decisions and of managing the day-to-day operations of retail outlets to the owners of downstream dealerships who will tend to have a comparative advantage in gathering and utilizing relevant information about local conditions of demand and supply.

These considerations suggest that exclusive dealing contracts might be particularly advantageous (compared with vertical integration) when a supplier is penetrating a retail market that it has not served previously. In any case, exclusive dealing and ownership integration seem to have similar purposes and effects.

Tie-In Sales

A tie-in sale exists when the buyer of one good, called the **tying good**, must as a condition of sale also purchase from the same seller supplies of some other (usually complementary) good, called the **tied good**. A seller might adopt a tying arrangement for a variety of reasons, including reasons of price

---

16 *Ibid.*

17 Howard P. Marvel, "Exclusive Dealing," *Journal of Law and Economics* 25 (April 1982), pp. 1-25.

Mining the Antitrust Laws

In 1961, the Supreme Court considered the legality of a long-term requirements contract between the Tampa Electric Company and the Nashville Coal Company.[a] At issue was an agreement between these two firms stipulating that Nashville would, for a period of 20 years, supply all of Tampa Electric's requirements for coal (1 million tons annually) at a newly constructed power plant. Tampa Electric's purchases under the contract represented less than 1 percent of the total output of coal produced in the eight-state area the Court considered to be the geographic market relevant for analyzing the contract's competitive effects. Therefore, the Court reasoned that the extent to which competing coal suppliers were foreclosed was minimal. The contract was consequently held not to violate the antitrust laws.

What is interesting about the case is that it came before the Court as a result of Nashville Coal's post-contractual opportunistic behavior. After Nashville had agreed to become Tampa Electric's sole supplier, the market price of coal unexpectedly increased. Nashville came to regret the terms of the contract, which specified a price of $6.40 per ton. It accordingly refused to deliver coal, forcing Tampa to seek other suppliers, one of which the utility ultimately paid a price of $8.80 per ton. Tampa Electric then sued Nashville for breach of contract. Nashville claimed in defense that the requirements clause it had agreed to constituted an antitrust violation and, hence, was unenforceable! Although the Court held otherwise,[b] requirements contracts are evidently not a perfect substitute for vertical integration.

a *Tampa Electric Co.* v. *Nashville Coal Co.*, 365 U.S. 320 (1961).
b In a later case, *F. T. C.* v. *Brown Shoe Co.*, 384 U.S. 316 (1966), also involving a 1 percent market share, the Supreme Court decided that a contract between a shoe manufacturer and various independent retailers, in which the manufacturer agreed to supply certain services in exchange for the retailers' cooperation in "concentrating" on the manufacturer's shoes by refraining from carrying the shoe lines of other manufacturers that competed directly with its products, constituted an unlawful "restriction on dealer choice."

---

discrimination, monitoring and controlling input quality, capturing economies of joint production and distribution, and evading government price controls.[18] However, the discussion here focuses on the possibility of viewing such contractual provisions as a method of overcoming input-price distortions.

Controlling Input Substitution. One result of the economic theory of vertical integration is that the supplier of an intermediate input that is sold to downstream customers at a markup over marginal production cost will find it profitable to integrate forward into the final product market when production there uses variable-proportions technology. The intuitive explanation for this conclusion is that, absent integration, the firm's customers will tend to substitute away from its product, using relatively more of other, less expensive productive resources in selecting their cost-minimizing input combinations. The supplier can accordingly produce the final product more cheaply and thereby increase its own profits by integrating forward, transferring the intermediate

---

18 For a discussion of these theories of tie-in sales, see William F. Shughart II, *The Organization of Industry* (Homewood, IL: Richard D. Irwin, 1990), pp. 307-14.

input internally at marginal cost, and restoring the efficient resource combination corresponding to price equal to marginal cost for all inputs.

Roger Blair and David Kaserman asked whether a tying arrangement could also overcome the downstream industry's tendency to substitute against an input sold at a markup over marginal production cost.[19] They considered a simple case in which production of the final good requires two inputs, one bought at a markup, say input A, and the other (input B) purchased at a price equal to marginal cost. As has been shown, forward integration by the supplier of input A would result in the use of the two inputs in the same proportion that would have been employed downstream had both A and B been available at (market) prices equal to marginal cost.

Blair and Kaserman demonstrated that the producer of input A could achieve the same result by instituting a tie-in sale that requires its customers to purchase their supplies of input B from him as a condition of buying input A. The supplier of A simply purchases B in the spot market (at price equal to marginal cost) and resells it to the downstream industry at a markup. It then *lowers* the selling price of A so that the new input-price ratio is equal to the ratio of the marginal products of the two resources.[20] By adjusting relative input prices in this way, the supplier of A induces its customers to employ the same combination of A and B that would be utilized if both stages of production were combined under common ownership.[21]

A tie-in sale is an imperfect substitute for vertical integration in this setting because by adding a markup to the price of an input that by assumption is available on the market at a price equal to marginal cost, the supplier of A creates incentives for its customers to obtain their requirements of B from unauthorized sources. The tying arrangement consequently demands that resources be spent for the purpose of monitoring and preventing these "bootlegging" activities. Expenditures of this kind would of course not be necessary with full ownership integration.

Quality Control. Suppliers have also employed tie-in sales for the purpose of monitoring and controlling the quality of complementary inputs used by

19 Roger D. Blair and David L. Kaserman, "Vertical Integration, Tying, and Antitrust Policy," *American Economic Review* 68 (June 1978), pp. 397-402.

20 If the supplier only raises the price on input B, holding the price of input A constant at its pre-tying level, as a first approximation the derived demand for A downstream will fall (and the supplier's total profits will decline) because the total cost of producing the final product, which requires both A and B by assumption, will have risen. See Richard A. Posner, "The Chicago School of Antitrust Analysis," *University of Pennsylvania Law Review* 127 (April 1979), pp. 925-48.

21 In the Blair-Kaserman model, tying arrangements increase production efficiency in the final product market by overcoming the downstream industry's tendency to substitute away from inputs sold at markups over marginal production cost. If the upstream supplier is in the business of producing a durable good, the opposite tendency (overutilization of the input) exists. For a discussion of the purposes and effects of tying arrangements in this case, see Robert S. Hansen and R. Blaine Roberts, "Metered Tying Arrangements, Allocative Efficiency, and Price Discrimination," *Southern Economic Journal* 47 (July 1980), pp. 73-83.

downstream customers. Such an arrangement may be justified as a way of ensuring that the seller's reputation is not damaged by product failure or by unsatisfactory product performance caused by buyers' use of inferior inputs. For example, the brand name capital of a manufacturer of tabulating machines could be damaged if the use of low-quality punch cards causes its machines to jam. The manufacturer might therefore want to tie the sale of its own punch cards to purchases of tabulating machines.[22] Similarly, a seller may require buyers to use its own installation and maintenance services in order to prevent untrained repair personnel from tampering with its product.[23]

The courts have generally not treated this justification kindly, however, holding that if a less restrictive alternative is available to the seller, then a tie-in sale will not be permitted. Under this standard, the courts have ordered firms to abandon their tying arrangements in favor of specifying the quality standards complementary inputs must meet. This arrangement allows customers to purchase their input requirements from any supplier that produces inputs that measure up to these standards or from a list of approved or authorized suppliers in which the seller has no financial interest.

Although it seems that quality-control considerations do not demand the use of tie-in sales, the less restrictive arrangements insisted on by the courts may entail higher transaction costs. This is because the seller will typically have more information than the buyer about the quality standards complementary inputs must meet to assure that the tying good performs as promised. In cases where communicating these standards to buyers would be difficult, a tying arrangement helps avoid inefficient, duplicative buyer search.

Joint Cost Savings. The final explanation for tie-in sales to be considered here is that they enable the seller of the tying good to realize cost savings from joint production or distribution that would not be available if the two goods were sold separately.[24] Consider photocopy machines and paper and assume for purposes of argument that by distributing the two goods jointly, the seller can provide paper to its customers at a lower cost per unit than can other, independent paper suppliers. These cost savings might materialize because the seller can combine the delivery of paper with its service personnel's routine visits to perform preventive maintenance on the photocopy machines.

If so, the seller can charge a price for its copying machines which reflects, at least in part, its savings in the cost of distributing paper,[25] and "the tie would tend to guarantee that these savings would, in fact, occur."[26] In other

---

22 *International Business Machines Corp.* v. *U.S.*, 298 U.S. 392 (1936).

23 *U.S.* v. *Jerrold Electronics Corp.*, 365 U.S. 567 (1961).

24 See John L. Peterman, "The International Salt Case," *Journal of Law and Economics* 22 (October 1979), pp. 351-64.

25 The opposite strategy of reducing the price of paper would not serve because, assuming that the market price of paper is equal to its marginal production cost, the firm would thereby incur economic losses on paper sales and, moreover, would be flooded by orders for paper from customers who had not purchased its copying machines.

26 Peterman, "International Salt Case," p. 362.

Warranties, Tie-Ins, and Efficient Insurance Contracts

The manufacturers of durable consumer goods like automobiles, kitchen appliances, and stereo equipment often warrant their products against defects for a specified period of time.[a] By offering to repair or replace the item should it fail to perform as promised, the seller reduces the purchaser's risk and provides a signal of quality to prospective buyers. Honoring warranty commitments is costly, however. The seller who makes such a guarantee must maintain an inventory of replacement parts, must hire and train the personnel who will be responsible for evaluating warranty claims and for making the required adjustments, and so on. Under these circumstances, the seller must decide whether to offer a warranty and, if so, what restrictions and exclusions to include in it. This decision requires that the seller balance the marginal value of warranty coverage to consumers (measured in terms of the additional amount they are willing to pay for such coverage) against the expected marginal cost of honoring warranty claims.

One important complicating factor in this decision-making process is that the seller's cost of providing warranty coverage depends in part on the care exercised by the consumer in using the product. Product performance and, hence, the incidence and cost of warranty claims, are affected by whether the purchaser follows the manufacturer's installation and operating instructions, adheres to recommended maintenance and cleaning schedules, and uses proper complementary inputs such as motor oil or laundry detergent. The seller cannot costlessly verify the degree of care exercised by any one consumer and, moreover, warranty coverage, much like any other insurance policy, diminishes the consumer's incentive to exercise appropriate care. This is the familiar problem of **moral hazard**: Because the purchaser does not bear the full cost of product failure resulting from misuse, he or she will rationally be less careful than otherwise.

Suppose there are two types of consumers of a durable good—high-intensity users and low-intensity users. Further suppose that the probability of product failure is directly related to intensity of use; that is,

high-intensity users are more likely to experience breakdowns and therefore more likely to make warranty claims. If the seller knows that these two types of customers exist, but cannot distinguish one type of customer from the other at the time of purchase, the seller will not be able to offer the same warranty terms to all buyers and still cover the expected cost of honoring warranty claims.[b] Other selling strategies such as making warranty coverage optional at an actuarially fair additional cost,[c] or offering warranties that contain deductibles are therefore required.[d]

a This case study is based on Jeffrey A. Eisenach, Richard S. Higgins, and William F. Shughart II, "Warranties, Tie-Ins, and Efficient Insurance Contracts: A Theory and Three Case Studies," in Richard O. Zerbe, Jr., ed., *Research in Law and Economics*, vol. 6 (Greenwich, CT: JAI Press, 1986), pp. 167-85.

b Let π_H and π_L be the product failure rates experienced by high- and low-intensity users ($\pi_H > \pi_L$), and let C represent the seller's cost of honoring an individual warranty claim. When the seller cannot distinguish between these two types of users, all buyers will be charged the same "pooling premium" for warranty coverage equal to $w = \{[H/(H + L)]\pi_H + [L/(H + L)]\pi_L\}C$, where H and L are the numbers of high- and low-intensity customers. Because w reflects the average probability of product failure, it is by definition greater than the expected cost of claims associated with low-intensity users and less than the expected cost of claims associated with high-intensity users. Hence, if the seller includes in the price of the product a premium equal to w, only high-intensity users will make purchases—a problem known as **adverse selection** in the insurance literature. And if only high-intensity users buy the product, the seller's revenues will not be sufficient to cover the cost of warranty claims.

c An actuarially fair insurance premium is one that is set equal to the expected cost of claims. For example, if the seller offers an optional warranty at a premium equal to $\pi_H C$, where π_H is the product failure rate experienced by high-intensity users and C is the cost of honoring a warranty claim, then only high-intensity users will choose warranty coverage at the time of purchase. Optional coverage generates "**self-selection**" by customers—the high-intensity users identify themselves to the seller by choosing warranty protection and the low-intensity users identify themselves to the seller by not choosing it. The low-risk customers are disadvantaged by this strategy, however, because they are not offered warranty coverage at an actuarially fair premium.

d Deductibles shift a portion of the cost of product failure to the user and can therefore assist the seller in distinguishing high- from low-

But the problem of moral hazard still remains. Once a warranted product has been purchased, the user's incentive to exercise care is lessened because he or she does not bear the full cost of misuse. How can the seller mitigate these incentives; that is, how can the consumer be made to bear more of the costs of careless behavior? One possibility is to institute a tie-in sale that requires the purchaser to obtain supplies of nonwarranted replacement parts or other complementary inputs from the durable good's seller. If the purchaser's consumption of these complementary inputs is correlated with intensity of use and if the seller charges a price for them that includes a premium reflecting the higher expected cost of warranty claims associated with greater intensity of use, then high-intensity users will pay more for warranty coverage than low-intensity (and presumably more careful) users.

A tying arrangement of this sort has two desirable properties. On the one hand, it helps separate consumers into high- and low-intensity-of-use categories so that the seller can charge members of each group prices for warranty coverage that more closely approximate their respective individual costs of claims. On the other hand, by requiring purchasers to pay higher prices for the tied goods than they would pay otherwise, the tie-in sale provides incentives for consumers to reduce their intensity of use. This increased care, in turn, reduces the seller's cost of honoring warranty claims.

The use of tie-in sales to "price" warranty coverage more fairly helps explain why Sohmer & Co. required buyers of its pianos to have them tuned only by Sohmer's accredited representatives. People who play their pianos more often presumably need to have them tuned more frequently. Sohmer could charge these customers a price for service calls that reflected in part the higher expected cost of covering warranty claims for intensive users. Requiring its customers to employ only factory-trained representatives for all tuning or servicing of their pianos further helped Sohmer avoid being forced to bear the cost of warranty claims arising from improper servicing or the use of substandard replacement parts—claims that might well cause considerable damage to Sohmer's reputation.

Similar considerations aid in explaining why Harmsco, Inc. stipulated that purchasers of its swimming pool filters use only Harmsco replacement filter cartridges, and why the Coleman Company required owners of its mobile home heating and air conditioning units to use only replacement parts certified by a nationally recognized testing laboratory. Despite the efficiency benefits that such tie-in sales generate, the practice of conditioning warranty coverage on consumers' use of brand-name replacement parts or on their employment of company-authorized service personnel was declared illegal in 1976 by the Magnuson-Moss Warranty/Federal Trade Commission Improvement Act. All three of the companies discussed here reduced or eliminated their warranty coverages as a result.

intensity customers. Using this strategy, the seller offers a full cover warranty at a premium equal to $\pi_H C$, where π_H is again the failure rate experienced by high-intensity users and C is the cost of honoring a warranty claim, and at the same time offers another warranty that requires the purchaser to pay some portion of this cost when a claim is made. The seller's expected cost of claims in the case is $\pi_L(C - D)$ dollars, where π_L is the failure rate experienced by low-intensity users and D is amount of the deductible they are required to pay. If this restricted warranty coverage is offered at the actuarially fair premium, then low-intensity customers will buy it (provided they are risk-averse). High-intensity users will choose full warranty coverage and in the process both types of customers identify themselves to the seller.

words, the seller could not reduce the price of its copying machines without some assurance that its customers would also make the paper purchases that produce the cost savings. A tie-in sale performs the function of preventing customers from buying the copying machines at the lower price made possible by the joint distribution of machines and paper and then obtaining their paper supplies elsewhere.

In sum, nonprice provisions in contracts between buyer and seller have purposes and effects that are similar to those associated with pricing provisions—and vertical ownership integration. They assist in overcoming input-price distortions, informational asymmetries, and opportunistic behavior. But economists are only just beginning to understand that contractual agreements of the kind discussed in this chapter represent part of the rich set of solutions to the problems of coordination and control that are present to varying degrees in all transactions between successive stages of production. Important questions still remain about "why contracts take the forms observed and what are the economic implications of different contractual and pricing arrangements."[27] It is nevertheless no longer possible to ignore the fact that the various contractual relationships that exist across the boundaries of firms often represent a substitute for the ownership relationships within them.

SUMMARY

This chapter has examined the purposes and effects of contractual agreements between buyers and sellers who transact across ownership boundaries. The parties to an exchange can include various price and nonprice provisions in their contract. These provisions can help achieve some of the efficiency benefits of ownership integration without imposing all of the costs associated with bringing their transaction within the governance structure of the firm.

One type of contractual price provision is resale price maintenance (RPM), whereby manufacturers and retailers mutually agree to set a limit on the price charged to consumers of the final product. On the one hand, a policy of specifying a maximum resale price deters retailers from opportunistically raising the final selling price above the level consistent with the manufacturer's profit-maximizing output rate. On the other hand, by guaranteeing a profit margin on final sales, establishing a minimum resale price controls free riding by discount outlets and thereby provides retailers with incentives to supply desirable pre- and post-sale services to consumers. Minimum RPM may also facilitate collusion at either the manufacturing or retailing stage of production in two ways: by reducing the profitability of defecting from the collusive agreement or by lowering the cost of detecting secret price concessions.

KEY TERMS
resale price maintenance
collusion
free rider
best-price policy
most-favored-nation clause
meet-or-release clause
intrabrand competition
interbrand competition
exclusive dealing contract
requirements contract
tying good
tied good
moral hazard
adverse selection
self-selection

---

27 Steven N. S. Cheung, "The Contractual Nature of the Firm," *Journal of Law and Economics* 26 (April 1983), p. 18.

"Best-price" policies represent another type of contractual price provision. A contractual arrangement in which the seller guarantees that the buyer will receive the benefit of a lower price granted to any other customer is a most-favored nation (MFN) clause. An arrangement in which the seller promises to match a lower price proffered by any other supplier is a meet-or-release (MOR) clause. These policies can reduce the buyer's cost of search and economize on the cost of switching suppliers. An alternative hypothesis explains best-price policies as selling practices that aid in the enforcement of collusive agreements.

The chapter has likewise considered agreements between buyer and seller on various nonprice dimensions of their transaction. The assignment of exclusive geographic selling territories provides distributors and retailers with profit incentives to acquire and utilize specialized information about local market conditions. Exclusive territories also help control free riding behavior among retailers and, like minimum resale prices, consequently promote the provision of optimal pre- and post-sale services.

Exclusive dealing arrangements, whereby retailers agree to carry the products of a single manufacturer, encourage the provision of optimal sales effort in the final product market and enable the upstream supplier to capture more of the returns to its own advertising and promotion expenses.

The policy of tie-in sales requires the buyer of one good to also obtain its requirements of some other related good from the same supplier. This strategy can be variously employed to neutralize input-price distortions associated with transacting across ownership boundaries, to monitor and control the quality of complementary inputs used by retailers, or to capture the cost savings associated with the joint production or distribution of two or more products.

Despite the efficiency benefits of contractual substitutes for ownership integration, the antitrust laws remain generally hostile to their use. This hostility derives from the observation that agreements on the price or nonprice conditions of sale either restrict intrabrand competition—competition among the retailers of one manufacturer's product—or, alternatively, "foreclose" some of the market to buyers or sellers who are not party to the contract. At the same time, though, by lowering the cost of transacting across the boundaries of firms, these contractual substitutes for ownership integration tend to promote interbrand competition—competition among the retailers of rival manufacturers. The resulting ambiguity in the application of the law means that managers must adopt a cautious attitude toward vertical contracting.

QUESTIONS

13.1 Breweries often grant their beer distributors exclusive territories. So long as the establishment of exclusive territories does not substantially lessen competition, they are legal. But, given that the courts often have trouble determining whether a particular contractual provision lessens competition or not, the

National Beer Wholesalers Association and the U.S. Brewers Association have lobbied for enactment of the "Malt Beverage Interbrand Competition Act," which would grant antitrust immunity to exclusive beer distribution territories. The proponents of the legislation argue that it would promote competition, pointing out that a similar bill granting antitrust immunity to the soft drink industry was passed in 1981 with no apparent ill effects. Opponents claim that the malt beverage bill would reduce competition among distributors and raise beer prices. Discuss the pros and cons of the proposed policy of granting antitrust immunity to exclusive beer distribution territories.

13.2 Coors used to have exclusive dealing requirements with restaurants and taverns that sold its beer for on-premise consumption. These retailers were required, in return for the right to sell Coors beer on tap, to refrain from selling any other brand of light-colored draft beer. The retailers were free, though, to sell any brand of dark draft beer and any other brand of bottled beer they wanted to. The Federal Trade Commission challenged this practice and obtained a court order stopping Coors from imposing this requirement on retailers. Why did Coors impose this requirement and why did the FTC stop it?

13.3 Franchise contracts typically contain provisions requiring the franchisee to make monthly or quarterly royalty payments to the franchisor. Show that it is more efficient (larger joint profits will be earned) if the franchisor collects a royalty that is expressed as a percentage of the franchisee's profits rather than its sales. Despite what you have just shown, why do you think that most franchisors collect royalties based on sales?

13.4 Mandatory seat belt laws have reduced the number of automobile fatalities. At the same time, the number of nonfatal automobile accidents and the number of automobile accidents involving property damage have increased. Explain.

13.5 Under Major League Baseball's old "reserve clause," a player, unless traded by the team's owner, was bound to the team that drafted him for his entire professional baseball career. The reserve-clause system has now been replaced by "free agency," wherein players may with some restrictions market their skills to the highest bidder. Kenneth Lehn has investigated some of the effects of this rule change. He found that players tended to lose more playing time due to injury under the reserve clause than they now do under free agency. Lehn also found that player injury rates tend to be lower the fewer the number of seasons covered by the contracts they sign with baseball team owners. Explain these empirical results.

13.6 Until the recent introduction of the Discover® card, Sears credit cards could be used only for making purchases from Sears' own retail or catalog outlets. What was Sears attempting to accomplish by adopting this policy? Now that the Discover card is becoming more widely accepted, why do you think that Sears has begun experimenting with honoring the cards issued by other credit card companies like Mastercard, Visa, and American Express?

13.7 Automobile manufacturers long ago abandoned the use of minimum resale price maintenance in the marketing of new cars and trucks. What reasons, aside from possible worries about antitrust liability, can you offer in explanation for this policy change? Given that minimum resale prices had been used to provide automobile dealerships with incentives to supply pre- and post-sale services to car buyers, how can the manufacturers now assure that these services are supplied?

13.8 Newspaper publishers can no longer set maximum resale prices for their distributors. How can they achieve the purposes for which maximum resale prices had been imposed?

13.9 Some contracts between manufacturers and retailers contain explicit sales quotas which require the retailer to sell a certain number of units each month or pay a monetary penalty to the manufacturer. Provide an economic explanation for this policy of "quantity forcing."

The Internal Structure of the Firm

OVERVIEW

The historical development of the modern business firm is traced in Chapter 1. This chapter analyzes the managerial incentive and performance consequences of the firm's internal organizational structure. Two basic organizational types are compared and contrasted. These are the U-form ("unitary-form") firm, which is organized along **functional** lines (e.g., manufacturing, sales, purchasing, and finance), and the M-form ("multidivisional-form") firm, which is organized along product or geographic lines. We also describe two extensions of the **multidivisional** structure: the conglomerate firm and the multinational enterprise.

The chapter highlights the importance of organizational structure in shaping the managerial decision-making process. We consider how structure affects the information available to the firm's managers, the degree of control managers exercise over the activities of the firm, the extent of decentralization in decision making, and the ability of the firm to adapt to changing market conditions.

APPLICATION

Suppose, for purposes of simplicity, that General Motors produces only two brands of automobiles, Buicks and Oldsmobiles. How should GM's top-level managers structure the company's operations? There are two basic options to consider.

One way of structuring the firm is to establish a separate unit for each of the major business functions involved in the production of automobiles. In such a functional organization, there would be a manufacturing division that is responsible for assembling both Buicks and Oldsmobiles, a central purchasing department that buys raw materials, parts, and other supplies and transfers them to the manufacturing division, a personnel department that is responsible for hiring the company's employees, a transportation unit that delivers Buicks and Oldsmobiles to GM's dealers, and so on. Alternatively, GM could create two separate product divisions, with each division being responsible for its own manufacturing, purchasing, personnel, and transportation activities. In this multidivisional organization, the Buick division and the Oldsmobile division would each separately handle all of the business functions involved in the production of its own car models.

This chapter discusses the costs and benefits of each of these two basic organizational types. Although it is certainly true that the functions of the firm are the same no matter how it is organized, the perspective gained by studying alternative organizational structures suggests that they have a powerful influence on the incentives and constraints managers face.

THE ADVANTAGES OF INTERNAL ORGANIZATION

From the outset, we have emphasized repeatedly that the firm and the market are alternative institutions for achieving the efficient allocation of society's scarce productive resources. We have developed the argument that the firm emerges to supersede the market as entrepreneurs strive to economize on certain types of **transaction costs**. Among these transaction costs are search and information costs ("discovering what the relevant prices are"),[1] bargaining and decision costs, and policing and enforcement costs.[2]

This is not to say that such costs can be avoided entirely by shifting transactions from the market to the firm. Transaction-cost considerations play an important role inside the firm as well. But internal organization has distinct advantages that in certain circumstances help conserve resources that might otherwise be wasted in transacting across ownership boundaries. These

---

1   Ronald H. Coase, "The Nature of the Firm," *Economica* 4 (November 1937), p. 390.
2   Carl J. Dahlman, "The Problem of Externality," *Journal of Law and Economics* 22 (April 1979), p. 148.

advantages loom larger—and therefore the balance tips more in favor of internal organization—the more binding are the constraints imposed on market exchange by bounded rationality, asymmetric information, and opportunistic behavior.[3]

Bounded Rationality: Decision-Making under Uncertainty

Bounded rationality, a term coined by Herbert Simon, refers to the limits, both physical and economic, that restrict the problem-solving abilities of human beings. In Simon's words, *"the capacity of the human mind for formulating and solving complex problems is very small compared with the size of the problems whose solution is required for objectively rational behavior in the real world."*[4] There are two aspects to this constraint. One is the physiological limit to the number of solutions the human mind can identify and evaluate when facing a problem-solving situation. Consider the game of chess. At any given stage of the game there are about 30 legal moves available to a player. This means that for any one move and its replies there are approximately 10^3 possibilities to consider. And if the average game contains 40 moves, 10^{120} moves and countermoves must be considered—an impossibly large number.

Even if the human mind could conceive of all possible alternatives, however, rational problem-solving abilities would still be bounded by limits to the amount of information that can be gathered, processed, and utilized effectively. This constraint is again partly physiological and is manifested in the phenomenon of "information overload." A glut of information impedes the human brain's problem-solving capabilities as much as does a lack of it.[5]

There are also economic limits to information collection and utilization. The amount of information available to problem solvers is bounded because the acquisition of information is itself costly.[6] The chief cost of information collection is the opportunity cost of the problem-solver's time. Time invested in gathering new information cannot be spent on other problem-solving tasks, such as identifying alternatives or retrieving and evaluating existing information. It will simply not pay to acquire all of the information that might be relevant to solving the problem at hand. Eventually, the marginal cost of

---

3 The following discussion is based on Oliver E. Williamson, *Markets and Hierarchies: Analysis and Antitrust Implications* (New York: Free Press, 1975), pp. 20-40.

4 Herbert A. Simon, *Models of Man* (New York: John Wiley & Sons, 1957), p. 158. Emphasis in original.

5 For example, information overload is apparently quite common for jet fighter pilots who are faced with a complex and continuous stream of data about air speed, altitude, fuel consumption, mechanical systems, weapons systems, weather, positions of other friendly and unfriendly aircraft, and so on. They sometimes respond by turning off their "heads-up" cockpit displays. See Stephen Coonts, *Flight of the Intruder* (Annapolis, MD: Naval Institute Press, 1986).

6 George J. Stigler, "The Economics of Information," *Journal of Political Economy* 69 (June 1961), pp. 213-25.

collecting additional information will equal the marginal benefit, and an optimal stopping point will be reached.

Language limits are a second aspect of bounded rationality. This constraint refers "to the inability of individuals to articulate their knowledge . . . by the use of words, numbers, or graphics in ways which permit them to be understood by others."[7] Hence, relevant problem-solving information may be unavailable or incomplete because we lose some facts in communicating with the individuals who possess them.

In short, according to Simon, human behavior is "intendedly rational, but only limitedly so."[8] Decision makers are not, as pure economic theory often assumes them to be, lightning-fast calculators who maximize a known objective function over a known number of choices in the presence of a complete set of information. Decision makers make rational choices, but they do so within the constraints imposed by *knowable* alternatives and by limited information.

The notion of bounded rationality has important implications about the assignment of economic activities between the market and the firm. Indeed, for those economic activities that are assigned to the firm, it has important implications about internal organizational structure.

Bounded rationality suggests that all market contracts are incomplete. The future is simply too complex and too uncertain for us to anticipate all possible events affecting contracts. The inability of contracting parties to foresee the future in perfect detail makes it impossible for them to specify every contingency that may arise and to agree ahead of time on permissible adaptations to each of them. The gaps in market contracts that inevitably result from decision making under conditions of bounded rationality leave room for disputes between buyer and seller that may ultimately cause a mutually beneficial transaction to unravel.

Internal organization allows the parties to an exchange to deal with uncertainty and complexity in an adaptive, sequential fashion. Rather than attempting to specify all of the possibilities in advance, "events are permitted to unfold and attention is restricted to only the actual rather than all possible outcomes."[9] This sequential process of dealing with alternatives as they arise conserves greatly on scarce decision-making resources. It is the economic equivalent of "crossing your bridge as you come to it" rather than "crossing all possible bridges you might conceivably come to."[10]

A further advantage of internal organization over market contracting is that it permits firms to decentralize managerial decision making. Decentralization of decision-making authority within an organizational hierarchy makes it possible for individual managers to specialize in solving smaller problems, thereby reducing complexity and streamlining information requirements.

---

7 Williamson, *Markets and Hierarchies*, p. 22.

8 Herbert A. Simon, *Administrative Behavior*, 2E. (New York: Macmillan, 1961), p. xxiv.

9 Williamson, *Markets and Hierarchies*, p. 25.

10 H. Chernoff and L. E. Moses, *Elementary Decision Theory* (New York: John Wiley & Sons, 1959), p. 192.

Finally, internal organization helps overcome language limits. When relevant problem-solving information would otherwise be lost in attempts to communicate across ownership boundaries, bringing the transaction within the firm may allow the parties to adopt other means of communication, such as hands-on demonstrations and learning-by-doing.

Asymmetric Information

This last observation brings us to the problem of asymmetric information. As Friedrich Hayek has so well observed,

> practically every individual has some advantage over all others in that he possesses unique information of which beneficial use might be made, but of which use can be made only if the decisions depending on it are left to him or are made with his active cooperation. We need to remember . . . how valuable an asset in all walks of life is knowledge of people, of local conditions, and of special circumstances.[11]

Asymmetric information exists when one of the parties to a transaction is better informed than the other "and the second party cannot achieve information parity except at great cost—because he cannot rely on the first party to disclose the information in a fully candid manner."[12] This asymmetry leaves one of the parties (typically the buyer) vulnerable to exploitation by the other, who will often use the superior information to his or her own advantage.

Internal organization offers a transaction-cost-reducing alternative to market exchange in the presence of informational asymmetries. When buyer and seller transact across the ownership boundaries of firms, the buyer must invest resources in monitoring and evaluating the characteristics or attributes of the product or service being purchased. The buyer is often at a disadvantage in this monitoring task because the seller usually has more detailed and more accurate information about his or her own product. This specialized information can include knowledge on such critical factors as production costs, performance specifications, quality variation, and the likelihood of supply interruptions. The buyer cannot acquire information on all of these important attributes by simply observing and testing the final product. Some informational asymmetries can be overcome by arms-length arrangements that allow the buyer to inspect the supplier's facilities and accounting records. And, perhaps, the arrangements could go so far as to permit the buyer to place an inspector on-site. But internal organization promises to reduce such costs further by bringing the supplier's specialized knowledge within the firm.

More importantly, shifting from market exchange to internal organization greatly reduces the incentives for using information advantages strategically.

---

11 Friedrich A. Hayek, "The Use of Knowledge in Society," *American Economic Review* 35 (September 1945), pp. 521-22.

12 Williamson, *Markets and Hierarchies*, p. 14.

Bringing the transaction within the firm promotes the communication and exploitation of specialized knowledge in ways that are mutually beneficial (joint profit maximizing). There are several reasons why this is so. First, the parties to an internal exchange are less able to personally appropriate the gains from exploiting information advantages because these gains will come at the expense of the overall organization. Second, exchanges taking place within the firm can be more effectively audited because insiders have access to more and better transaction-specific information than do outsiders. And, third, internal organization has clear advantages over market contracting in resolving disputes when disagreements do arise.

Opportunistic Behavior

Opportunistic behavior, or "self-interest seeking with guile,"[13] imposes a final constraint on market exchange. Opportunistic behavior tends to plague transactions across the ownership boundaries of firms because each party is motivated by the goal of maximizing his or her own profits. Consequently, as just noted, both have incentives to exploit any information advantages in their possession and, moreover, to behave strategically when, by reasons of bounded rationality, unforeseen events occur.

Competitive market forces do impose a powerful check on the incentives of transacting parties to behave opportunistically. As long as each can turn to alternatives without difficulty, the threat of loss of future business provides strong incentives to behave responsibly. Responsible behavior includes making provisions ahead of time for dealing with unforeseen events (such as agreeing to binding arbitration), disclosing specialized information truthfully and non-selectively, and resolving disputes in a mutually satisfactory manner.

Individuals who attempt to secure short-run advantages will be penalized when contracts come up for renewal. However, as considerations of bounded rationality and asymmetric information loom larger, market forces may no longer be adequate for preventing opportunistic behavior. This is because uncertainty, complexity, and informational asymmetries make transactions more idiosyncratic. Fewer options are available or, what is the same thing, it becomes more costly for one party or the other to switch options. The implied threat to terminate the relationship therefore becomes less credible. A "large-numbers" bargaining situation is transformed into a "small-numbers" exchange relationship and the potential gains from behaving strategically thereby increase.

Indeed, a bargain that was initially struck in a large-numbers setting can become a small-numbers exchange during its execution: "Winners of initial contracts acquire, in a learning-by-doing fashion, nontrivial information advantages over nonwinners. Consequently, even though large-numbers competition may have been feasible at the time the initial award was made, parity no longer holds at the contract renewal interval."[14]

---

13 *Ibid.*, p. 9.
14 *Ibid.*, p. 34.

Defense contracts offer a relevant example of this problem. A contract for the construction of a particular type of naval warship, for instance, is awarded to the winner of a competitive bidding process. Each of the participating bidders is pre-certified. Each has the technical and financial resources necessary to produce warships to the Navy's specifications and, in principle, the contract can be awarded to any one of them. Once the contract is let to a particular shipyard, however, parity among bidders no longer holds. In the process of fulfilling the contract, the winner acquires superior information about the warship and the idiosyncrasies of the naval contract officers who supervise production, sea trials, and delivery. As a result, the contractor gains a substantial cost advantage over its rivals. This cost advantage virtually assures the shipyard of winning subsequent contracts should the Navy later want to order additional ships of the same type. Specialized information, which increases the cost of switching suppliers, helps explain why defense contracts are plagued by performance disputes and by cost overruns.

Even though both parties to an exchange have an interest in seeing the transaction through to completion on the initial terms, circumstances may arise in a small-numbers setting that make it rational (wealth-maximizing) for one of them to take advantage of the other. That is, when an opportunity to exploit an informational asymmetry arises or when, by reasons of bounded rationality, gaps in the original contract appear, it is in the interest of each party to seek the most favorable terms possible. This situation encourages opportunistic misrepresentations and self-interest-seeking haggling. By contrast, both parties will be better off if the dispute can be resolved in a way that avoids bargaining costs and the costs that may be imposed on one of them due to the strategic misrepresentations of the other.

Internal organization has distinct advantages over market contracting in this regard for reasons outlined earlier. Incentives for opportunistic behavior decrease when transactions take place within the firm rather than on the market because the parties to an internal transaction are less able to personally appropriate the gains from such behavior, because internal transactions can be more effectively audited, and because disputes can be resolved at lower cost.

In sum, although there should be a bias in favor of market exchange because of the powerful incentives it provides for using resources efficiently and honoring commitments, there are also advantages to organizing transactions within the firm. These advantages become more important the more the complexity and uncertainty of an exchange limit the parties' ability to anticipate and to agree on permissible adaptations to future contingencies, the greater is the disparity in information between buyer and seller, and the larger are the potential gains from behaving opportunistically.

Internal organization offers a transaction-cost reducing alternative to market exchange under these conditions for several reasons. It facilitates adaptive, sequential decision making, it promotes the communication and exploitation of specialized information, and it reduces incentives to engage in opportunistic behavior. However, the promised benefits of internal organization will not materialize automatically when a transaction shifts from the market to the firm. The parties must first design an appropriate internal structure for dealing with the problems created by bounded rationality, asymmetric information, and opportunistic behavior. The following section discusses this issue.

ORGANIZATIONAL TYPES

As stressed above, simply shifting a transaction from the market to the firm does not automatically conserve on the scarce resources that would otherwise be lost due to incomplete contracts and opportunistic behavior. The advantages of internal organization will materialize only if the firm adopts an appropriate organizational structure. By "appropriate" we mean an organizational structure that economizes on bounded rationality, that promotes the utilization of specialized information, and that reduces incentives for engaging in haggling and opportunistic behavior.

In this section, we compare and contrast several basic organizational types. These are the functional firm, the multidivisional firm, and two extensions of the multidivisional firm: the conglomerate enterprise and the multinational corporation. The basic lesson of the discussion is that structure matters. Profit performance is determined less by what functions a firm performs than by how those functions are organized internally. Moreover, some economists argue that the determinants of internal structure are not exclusively (or even mainly) technological in nature. Instead, one of the important goals of economic organization is to minimize the *sum* of production and transaction costs. To see this conclusion in its starkest terms, we describe a hybrid type of organization (the "inside contracting" system) that stands at an intermediate position between pure market exchange and the formal integration of business activities within the ownership structure of the firm.

Simple Hierarchy: The Inside Contracting System

As domestic markets expanded during the late eighteenth and early nineteenth centuries, business firms employed three basic methods to increase the volume of manufactured output.[15] One method, adopted primarily in the crafts industries, was simply to enlarge existing shops and supplement the existing work force. Makers of furniture, tableware, copper, brass, and pewter items, for example, met the increasing demand for these goods by expanding their production facilities and by employing and training more apprentices and journeymen who continued to work in the traditional manner with traditional tools. Hence, some manufacturers increased output volume by replicating small-scale production methods on a larger scale.

---

15 Alfred D. Chandler, Jr., *The Visible Hand: The Managerial Revolution in American Business* (Cambridge, MA: Harvard University Press, 1977), p. 53.

Managerial Hierarchies as Rank-Order Tournaments

The structure of managerial compensation within the firm is a subject of perennial interest. Recently, critics of the corporate business world have charged, using words like "obscene," that the amount of compensation received by the top executives of many major U.S. companies is unjustifiably high. Six-, and indeed, seven-figure incomes are not uncommon for the presidents and chief executive officers (CEOs) of the leading American corporations, as Table 14.1 shows. Moreover, the pay of the firm's CEO is often substantially larger than that received by the senior managers at the next lower level of authority. Is CEO pay in fact "too high?" What explains the size of the gap between the CEO's compensation and that of the managerial team members next in line for the CEO's job?

TABLE 14.1 THE TOP 25 BEST PAID CEOs OF 1990

COMPANY/ CEO	STOCK OWNED[b]	Compensation[a]			
		SALARY + BONUS	OTHER	STOCK GAINS	TOTAL
Time Warner					
Steven J. Ross[c]	—[d]	$3,200[e]	$17,757	$57,156	$78,113
UAL					
Stephen M. Wolf	$12.0	1,150	2,376	14,775	18,301
Apple Computer					
John Sculley	16.2	2,199	—	14,531	16,730
Reebok Int'l					
Paul B. Fireman	217.7	14,822	4	—	14,826
Waste Mgmt.					
Dean L. Buntrock	113.8	1,582	2,777	8,096	12,455
Giant Food					
Israel Cohen	83.9	1,213	37	10,241	11,491
Paramount					
Martin S. Davis	54.9	3,646	7,653	—	11,299
Walt Disney					
Michael D. Eisner	45.0	11,233	—	—	11,233
Genentech					
G. Kirk Raab	.4	675	196	8,308	9,180
Warner-Lambert					
Joseph D. Williams	6.9	1,585	665	6,568	8,818
Sotheby's					
Michael L. Ainslie	10.0	959	—	7,696	8,654

COMPANY/ CEO	STOCK OWNED[b]	SALARY + BONUS	OTHER	STOCK GAINS	TOTAL
National Medical					
Richard K. Eamer	81.4	1,879	6,690	—	8,569
BHC Comm.					
Herbert J. Siegel	—[f]	8,353	18	—	8,371[g]
Reader's Digest					
George V. Grune	10.6	1,193	6,297	—	7,490
ITT					
Rand V. Araskog	22.7	3,888	3,393	—	7,281
Merck					
P. Roy Vagelos	33.3	2,092	5	5,050	7,147
Eli Lilly					
Richard D. Wood	20.5	1,781	971	4,379	7,137
City National					
Bram Goldsmith	71.2	1,026	1,506	4,559	7,091
RJR Nabisco					
Louis V. Gerstner, Jr.	24.9	3,090	4,053	—	7,073
US Surgical					
Leon C. Hirsch	170.3	1,500	5,571	—	7,071
Coca-Cola					
Roberto C. Goizueta	144.5	3,142	1,656	2,190	6,988
Masco					
Richard A. Manoogian	52.0	1,056	2,477	3,391	6,924[h]
Capital Cities/ABC					
Daniel B. Burke	20.1	1,033	116	5,584	6,733
State St. Boston					
William S. Edgerly	11.8	953	1,551	4,013	6,518
Schering-Plough					
Robert P. Luciano	1.2	1,694	1,311	3,482	6,487

Source: "The Best Paid Chief Executives 1990," *Forbes*, May 1991, p. 216. Reprinted by permission of *Forbes* magazine. © Forbes Inc., 1991.

a $ thousands.
b Current market value ($ millions).
c Office held jointly with N.J. Nicholas, Jr.
d Less than $100,000.
e Estimated.
f Indirect ownership through Chris-Craft Industries.
g Salary paid by Chris-Craft Industries.
h Prior year figures.

One explanation for the executive salary structure observed in the large corporation is that the compensation received at each successively higher level of the managerial hierarchy represents one of the prizes in a rank-order tournament.[a] Such tournaments determine winners on the basis of the order in which contestants finish and not on the basis of some absolute measure of performance. That is, the winner of a foot race is the person who crosses the finish line first independent of the actual time he or she posts in running the distance. Hence, prizes in a rank-order tournament are not contingent on the output *level* produced in a particular contest. After all, the prizes are set in advance. Performance incentives are instead set by attempts to win the contest, and winning depends on *relative* effort. The winner of a rank-order tournament is the person who turns in the "best" performance among all contestants competing for the prize.[b]

We can usefully apply these terms to the internal labor market of the firm. At each tier of the managerial hierarchy, managers vie for promotion to the next higher level. However, because there are fewer positions open at higher executive ranks, only some of these managers will actually win promotions. Senior executives will evaluate the credentials and performances of the candidates for promotion and select, perhaps with the advice and consent of the company's board of directors, those among them who have demonstrated the abilities and skills deemed necessary for success at the next higher managerial rank. Hence, the individuals who are chosen for promotion are the ones who are judged to be the most qualified of those considered for advancement. It is therefore an individual manager's performance relative to his or her peers that chiefly determines success in climbing the corporate ladder.[c]

Consequently, each manager has an incentive to invest time and effort in developing the skills and abilities necessary to enhance his or her chances for promotion. He or she will work long hours, prepare well-researched reports on project assignments, monitor the performances of subordinates closely, develop ideas to improve employee productivity, learn the details of the company's business, take writing and public speaking courses to enhance presentation skills, study *Modern Managerial Economics* on weekends, and so forth.

The individual will, of course, consider only the private costs and benefits of these activities. Costs are measured in terms of the value of the opportunities necessarily foregone when an individual's attention is focused on his or her career. Benefits are measured in terms of the increased likelihood of promotion that such investments produce. These private benefits, in turn, depend on the probability that the individual will be selected for advancement (which is a function both of his or her own effort and the effort supplied by the other promotion candidates) and the value of the "prize" awarded to the promotion contest's winners. That is, the expected payoff from advancement is equal to the probability of being selected times the increase in salary that will be earned at the next higher managerial position.

Rational individuals will invest time and effort in qualifying for promotion up to the point where the marginal cost of such effort is equal to the marginal benefit. It should therefore be obvious that greater effort will be forthcoming the more additional effort raises the probability of promotion and the higher is the compensation the winner of the contest will be paid. Two important conclusions follow from this observation. First, to the extent that promotion criteria are based on factors related to broader performance measures, such as the profitability of the operating unit to which the individual is assigned, managers competing for promotion generate spillover benefits for the firm's stockholders in the process of seeking their own personal gain.[d] They improve their own managerial

---

a See Edward P. Lazear and Sherwin Rosen, "Rank-Order Tournaments as Optimum Labor Contracts," *Journal of Political Economy* 89 (October 1981), pp. 841-64.

b Small joke: Two friends, one an economist and the other an engineer, were camping at Yellowstone Park, when, to their surprise, an obviously angry bear came charging through the underbrush. The economist immediately sat down and began putting on a pair of running shoes. Somewhat taken aback, the engineer exclaimed, "Why are you wasting your time changing shoes You'll never be able to outrun the bear!" The economist's answer was, "I don't have to outrun the bear, I only have to outrun you."

c Absolute performance also matters, of course. If none of the firm's own managers is deemed qualified for promotion, the senior executives have the option of outside hiring to fill vacancies in the managerial team.

d Obviously, if the manager's promotion prospects are unrelated to measurable performance outcomes, there is no incentive to act in the firm's best interest. For example, if advancement becomes more likely the more hours a manager spends playing golf with the

skills, they strive to hold costs down, and they work to increase sales. Competition for promotion provides managers with incentives to behave cooperatively rather than opportunistically and to bring their specialized knowledge to bear in ways that benefit the overall organization. In short, managerial rivalry reduces managerial shirking, thereby increasing the wealth of the firm's owners.[e]

Second, the perceived likelihood of advancement to the top management echelons is very low for individuals beginning their business careers. Therefore, the expected benefit of working toward that remote goal will be sufficient to induce the desired effort only if the salary paid to current executive officeholders is very large. Indeed, if the pay received by the CEO and other top executives is large enough, managers at lower ranks may have an incentive to work harder than is justified by their present salaries because the pay they expect to receive later in their careers will more than compensate them for their efforts.

A salary structure in which lower-level managers are paid less than their current value to the firm—and higher-level managers are paid more than their current value—is therefore broadly consistent with stockholder wealth maximization. In fact, under certain conditions, a compensation scheme that rewards rank yields the same efficient resource-allocation outcome that would be obtained with a piece-rate compensation system which ties pay directly to current output.[f] And, given that observing relative effort is less costly than measuring each worker's level of productivity directly, rewarding rank conserves the firm's scarce resources.

The position of chief executive officer is the ultimate prize in a corporate managerial tournament that only a small number of contestants will ever win. Because the probability that any one manager will advance to that rank is small, the salary paid to the ultimate winner must be large enough so that the expected value of the prize is sufficient to make competing in the tournament worthwhile. Such considerations hold even for those managers who are next in line for the CEO's job. The larger the gap between the pay of corporate vice-presidents and that of the CEO, the larger the expected value of the prize received by the individual who is selected for promotion and, hence, the greater the effort it is worth expending in competing for advancement. Better managers are not only paid more because they are better, but because better managers will strive to replace them.

company's president, promotion contests do not redound to the stockholders' benefit.

e Armen A. Alchian and Harold Demsetz, "Production, Information Costs, and Economic Organization," *American Economic Review* 62 (December 1972), pp. 777-95. Also see Chapter 7 of this book.

f Lazear and Rosen, "Rank-Order Tournaments." This result depends on workers being risk-neutral and homogeneous. When risk aversion is introduced, rewarding either rank or actual productivity will be preferred depending on the degree of risk aversion and the cost of measuring output. Worker heterogeneity complicates matters due to the familiar problem of adverse selection. If firms cannot discern employee productivity types ex ante, low-productivity workers will attempt to "contaminate" firms composed of high-quality workers and the benefits of rewarding workers according to rank will break down. However, if it is possible to gather prior information about worker productivity by, for example, offering tryouts or observing the results generated in other contests (say, college), there exists a "handicapping" scheme that allows employees of all productivity types to work in the same firm.

A second method for increasing the volume of manufactured goods involved the adoption or expansion of the **putting-out system**. Under this arrangement, which was used extensively in the manufacture of shoes and clothing, a merchant would purchase the needed materials—leather, cloth, or yarn—and deliver them to workers in their homes. The merchant would later pick up the finished articles (paying to the domestic worker an agreed-upon piece rate for each item meeting the merchant's specifications), and then arrange for the sale of the final product.

A third and fundamentally different strategy for expanding output in manufacturing and processing was through the adoption of the **factory system** of production. This production method relied on specialized, high-volume machinery and other capital equipment. The appearance of the factory system across industries of course depended on the introduction of new manufacturing technologies. Once reliable, high-volume machinery had been invented and perfected, however, it spelled the end of traditional crafts production where all work, whether carried out in shops or at home, was "done by hand, at the individual's own time and pace."[16]

In shoe manufacturing, for example, the invention of heavy, steam-powered cutting and sewing equipment during the 1850s made it impossible for the putting-out system to survive. Workers and machinery had to be at the same site (near a source of water power) in order to take advantage of the unit cost savings associated with mechanized mass production. The equipment was relatively expensive, meaning that capitalists, not workers, financed its purchase. It required routine maintenance to minimize breakdowns and costly downtime. Most importantly, the specialization and division of labor which the machinery promoted required increased supervision and coordination of separate manufacturing stages in order to utilize more fully the greater production capacity made possible by the new technology.

If technology and economies of scale were the only keys to understanding the emergence of factory production, then almost any method for combining labor and capital equipment at the same location would have proved adequate. Put somewhat differently, if the advantages of factory production over, say, the putting-out system, are measured solely in terms of lower transportation expenses and the reduction in unit costs generated when capital and other overhead expenses can be spread over a large volume of output, then the internal structure of the firm would be of little consequence. We can see that this is not so by considering an early—and ultimately unsuccessful—form of business organization, the "inside contracting" system.

Inside contracting was a natural extension of the putting-out system. According to one student of early business history,

> under the system of inside contracting, the management of a firm provided floor space and machinery, supplied raw material and working capital, and arranged for the sale of the finished product. The gap between raw material and finished product, however, was filled not by paid employees arranged in . . . descending hierarchy . . . but by [independent] contractors, to whom the production job was delegated. They hired their own employees, supervised the work process, and received a piece rate from the company for completed goods.[17]

The inside contracting system provided many, perhaps all, of the technological benefits normally associated with factory production. By assembling people and equipment at the same location, the firm avoided the transportation

---

16 *Ibid.*, p. 54.
17 John Buttrick, "The Inside Contract System," *Journal of Economic History* 12 (Summer 1952), pp. 205-6.

expense of the putting-out system and took advantage of the scale economies associated with producing a large volume of output. In addition, supervision and coordination of separate manufacturing stages in the factory were far more efficient than when home workers labored independently at their own paces using traditional tools and traditional methods.

Despite its many technological advantages, the inside contracting system ultimately failed as a method of business organization. Its failure can be traced to numerous difficulties that plagued the relationships between the firm's owner and the independent contractors to whom production jobs were delegated.

Organizing Production Lock, Stock, and Barrel. American firearms manufacturers adopted the inside contracting system early on. Indeed, independent contractors were in charge of production when the Winchester Repeating Arms Company launched operations in 1855. Inside contracting was perhaps a natural development in the firearms industry's history. The pioneering private-sector toolmakers and armorers of New England began by manufacturing guns on a made-to-order basis for local customers. Both they and their counterparts in government arsenals who produced firearms for the Army and Navy customarily contracted work out to the local shops of the master toolmakers they employed to make specific components—locks, stocks, and barrels. But as markets for firearms expanded due to the westward movement of population and the Civil War, these armorers found it increasingly difficult to meet the growing demand for fabricated wood and metal parts without acquiring additional labor and capital. They sought outside financing from capitalists who usually had no specialized knowledge about firearms manufacture.

At the same time, the introduction of new machinery and new manufacturing techniques led to the growing use of standardized, interchangeable gun parts. This development increased the potential gains from combining workers and capital equipment at the same location. Quality standards and work effort could thereby be more closely monitored and the output rates of the various parts manufacturing and assembly operations could be more precisely regulated and coordinated. Large firearms manufacturing plants making use of the interchangeable-parts principle had significant cost advantages over small-scale, made-to-order production.

A contractual relationship between a master gun maker and an outside financier was therefore mutually beneficial. The gun maker obtained a new source of capital to expand output and meet the growing demand for firearms. And by delegating to the capitalist responsibility for selling the final product, the gun maker was freed to concentrate on "the technical problems associated with production, improvement of the manufacturing process, and labor supervision."[18] For his part, the capitalist could take advantage of a new, profitable investment opportunity despite his lack of technical expertise. His involvement in the firm was limited "to negotiating

---

18 *Ibid.,* p. 207.

contracts with inside department heads, inspecting and coordinating the output of the various departments, and taking responsibility for final sales."[19]

Given the widespread use of "outside" contracting in the early history of the firearms industry, it is perhaps not too surprising that contracts continued to serve as the primary basis for securing fabricated gun parts when these manufacturing operations were brought inside the firm to take advantage of scale economies. At the beginning, the company's owner employed only one or two first-level contractors. (These primary contractors, in turn, subcontracted with other craftsmen to manufacture the various components that were to be assembled into the final product.)

But as the market for firearms continued to expand and as standardization promoted greater specialization, the manufacturing process was further subdivided and the number of contractors increased. One contractor made gun barrels while others were responsible for stocks, receivers, small parts, and so on. In fact, by 1880 a separate contractor at Winchester was in charge of each of the operations necessary to manufacture a gun barrel—forging, drilling, machining, filing, sight fitting, and bluing or browning.

This increasing specialization and subdivision of production responsibility required careful regulation and coordination of the flow of gun parts to the final assembly point. Moreover, as separate contractors began performing different operations on the same component, it became necessary for someone to independently inspect the work between production stages. Having neither the technical expertise nor the time, the company's single owner could not personally assume responsibility for all of these supervisory duties. Consequently, Winchester employed full-time company foremen to take charge of the inspection and final assembly departments, the maintenance crew, the power plant, the forge and machine shops, and the model room. They, along with the owner, "managed" an enterprise that comprised two major divisions. One division, for producing guns, contained a dozen large production departments each headed by an independent contractor, and also contained a half-dozen other minor parts fabricating operations, each also under separate contract. The other division, which produced cartridges, worked under a similar inside contracting arrangement.

The Failures of Inside Contracting. It was not the growing scale and complexity of firearms production that spelled the end of the inside contracting system at Winchester and elsewhere. Rather, the divergent—and ultimately incompatible—incentives of the company's owner and the independent contractors to whom production jobs were assigned eventually led to the system's demise.

The typical arrangement between Winchester's owner and one of the inside contractors contained a negotiated piece-rate payment for each part

---

19 Williamson, *Markets and Hierarchies*, p. 96.

the contractor produced that passed inspection by a company foreman. The company agreed to supply the contractor's machinery, tools, and raw materials and the contractor, in turn, took responsibility for hiring, paying, and supervising the workers who performed the manufacturing or assembly operations in his department. The contractor's net income in any period was consequently equal to the difference between his revenue on parts sales to the company and his cost of labor.

Because the only charge the contractor made against his parts sales to the company consisted of the piece-rate compensation he paid to departmental employees, labor costs were the only costs the contractor had an incentive to control. He did not pay for wasted materials, for defective parts, or for ruined tools, patterns, or machinery. He and his workers therefore tended to abuse equipment and neglect its maintenance. If a contractor's employees damaged a part that had passed inspection before it reached his department, the company, not he, bore the cost of spoilage. In short, with the exception of labor, the inside contractors had little motivation to use resources in ways that were compatible with the owner's goal of maximizing overall company profits from the sale of firearms.

A second critical defect in the inside contracting system was that it did not provide the two parties with incentives to disclose and exploit specialized information in mutually beneficial ways. The owner had detailed knowledge about the marketing of firearms; the inside contractors had detailed knowledge about their departmental production costs. Because owner and contractor were interested in maximizing their individual profits, each tended to hoard information and to attempt to use it to his own personal advantage.

Such asymmetric information led to posturing and disputes at contract renewal time. For example, knowing the company's future production plans, the owner might attempt to negotiate a favorable piece rate schedule prior to announcing an increase in parts purchases from the contractors. Contractors, on the other hand, had incentives to manipulate labor cost figures so that departmental profits appeared small and they could plead for higher piece rates. Because production records showed only the finished output delivered to the company, contractors also had incentives to build up private inventories of parts and sell them in future periods to spread apparent profits over time in the most advantageous manner.

Finally, the inside contracting system distorted the contractor's incentives to develop and implement cost-saving innovations. Because the contractor bore only the labor costs of parts production, he had little motivation to search for new manufacturing techniques that conserved materials or capital equipment. Process innovations were consequently biased in favor of those which were labor-saving. Moreover, contractors had incentives to delay the implementation of such improvements if they thought a reduction in the piece rate was imminent.

Because it failed to align the contractors' incentives with those of the firm's owner, the inside contracting system disappeared at the Winchester Company during the early 1900s. While there had been 18 inside contractors in the firearms division in 1904, there were none by 1914. Over this period, the plant superintendent's office gradually took charge of hiring decisions, and all of the independent contractors and workers became full-time company employees. Contractual relationships gave way to employment relationships and the separate profit streams of the formerly independent production departments were combined. This change in structure increased the benefits of organizing the manufacture of firearms within the firm. The various parties to internal transactions were thereby less able to personally appropriate the gains from hoarding specialized information and from behaving opportunistically. This new relationship aligned their individual incentives more closely with the objective of maximizing the company's overall profits.

The important lesson to be drawn from the Winchester Company's experience is that manufacturers can fully exploit the technological advantages of large-scale production only by adopting an organizational structure that provides individuals with incentives to make use of them. Internal structure has important implications about the amount of information available to owners and managers, the degree of control managers exercise over the firm's activities, the extent of decentralization in the decision-making process, the incentives to search for and implement cost-saving innovations, and the ability of the firm to adapt to changing market conditions. The benefits and costs of two modern organizational structures, the functional firm and the multidivisional firm, are described next.

The Functional Firm

The story of the evolution of the modern American business firm in Chapter 1 showed that structural innovations were in the main driven by the necessity of decentralizing managerial decision-making authority. As, first, the railroads and, later, the great industrial giants that emerged in manufacturing and processing expanded both in scale and scope, it became impossible for one individual (or even a small group of individuals) to maintain hands-on, personal contact with all the details of the firm's daily operations and simultaneously find the time and the psychological commitment necessary for appraising, coordinating, and planning the activities of all departments in the interest of the enterprise as a whole.

The structural innovation adopted and then perfected by the railroads was the functional or unitary-form firm which divides managerial authority along functional lines like manufacturing, marketing, and finance. Figure 14.1 shows a simplified organization chart for this type of firm.

FIGURE 14.1
A Simplified
Functional Firm

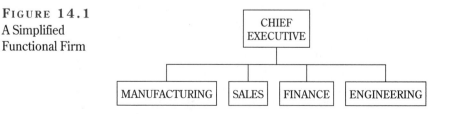

The functional firm was successful for two basic reasons. First, it clearly spelled out the lines of communication and authority between **line** officers, who supervised the firm's major operating departments (manufacturing and sales, for instance), and **staff** officers, who headed units providing ancillary goods or services to other parts of the firm (purchasing, personnel, accounting, and so forth). This decoupling of managerial authority allowed some executives—the operating department heads—to specialize in supervising the day-to-day activities of the firm. And this focus permitted them to acquire and to utilize far more detailed information about their particular areas of responsibility than had been possible previously. At the same time, freed from this burden, the company's top managers in the central office could devote more of their attention to strategic decisions affecting the enterprise as a whole.

Second, the functional type of organization facilitated the exploitation of the economies of scale and scope in each of the major business functions. These economies were not limited to the obvious ones in the manufacturing division.

Consider the personnel department. Many of the costs of hiring and paying employees are start-up costs—advertising vacancies, taking applications, interviewing and screening job candidates, filling out company personnel forms, writing checks, and so on. Therefore, the firm can realize significant cost savings by creating a central office with responsibility for all of the firm's hiring and payroll activities. Rather than asking each department or division to replicate these activities on a smaller scale by handling its own personnel functions, the firm lowers unit costs by spreading these start-up and overhead expenses over the company's entire workforce. Similar economies of scale can be captured with a centralized accounting unit that provides recordkeeping, billing, and disbursement services to the company's other functional divisions, a centralized purchasing department that buys materials and supplies for the entire company, and a centralized sales force that markets the firm's products.

Functional separation also contributed to the specialization and division of managerial skills. Unlike a situation in which one individual or a small group of individuals manages all of the firm's activities, the functional structure enabled some individuals to specialize in supervising production or processing operations, while others specialized in managing the firm's ancillary units. This separation and division of managerial responsibility and authority reduced the information burden on the firm's senior executives by preventing all decisions from being "forced to the top," and it provided management with efficiency benefits similar to those usually associated with specialization and division of labor on the shop floor.

As the great industrial firms of the late nineteenth and early twentieth centuries began diversifying into new products and new markets and began taking on new functions by, for example, integrating backward to acquire more reliable supplies of raw materials and integrating forward into distribution and retailing, some inherent weaknesses in the functional structure became increasingly apparent. One disadvantage was in performance evaluation.

Each of the functional divisions was basically a "cost center," and it was therefore difficult for top-level managers to assess the contribution of individual departments to overall company profitability. This defect became particularly critical as firms sought to more fully utilize their productive capacities by developing new products and penetrating new markets.

What contribution to the total costs of, say, the company's central accounting unit is attributable to product A versus product B? What share of the costs of the company's sales force, which markets the firm's entire product line, should be allocated to each good? Because, in general, there is no objectively correct answer to these questions, top management had no reliable basis for deciding which products and which activities to expand and which to contract or abandon. That is, the flows of cost-based information in the functional firm limited management's ability to allocate the firm's capital to its highest valued internal uses.

In the absence of meaningful criteria for evaluating the performance of the various functional divisions, lower-level managers had weakened incentives to behave in ways that were consistent with the global goal of maximizing overall company profitability. They instead rationally pursued subgoals, such as striving to maximize the sizes or the budgets of their own divisions— goals which were more consistent with their individual self-interests than with the interests of the firm as a whole. The pursuit of these objectives by the functional executives led to growth in managerial bureaucracy, an increasing paperwork burden, and a loss of control by senior managers who thereby became more remote from the company's daily operations.

Finally, the functional firm failed as a method of organization in large-scale, diversified enterprises "when the administrative load on the senior executives increased to such an extent that they were unable to handle their entrepreneurial responsibilities efficiently."[20] **Diseconomies of scale and scope** emerged as top management was forced to oversee a growing number of diverse functions—transportation, sales, finance, research and development, manufacture, wholesaling, retailing, and so on.

In short, the scale economies and efficient division of labor which functional specialization initially made possible were eventually exhausted and unit production costs began to rise. Firms needed organizational innovations to improve internal information flows, to align more closely the interests of the functional executives with those of the enterprise as a whole, and to decouple, again, management's operational decision-making functions from its strategic planning functions.

The Multidivisional Firm

The multidivisional (M-form) firm was the organizational innovation devised by Pierre DuPont and Alfred Sloan in the 1920s to overcome the major defects of the functional structure. As discussed in Chapter 1, "this organizational

---

20 Chandler, *Strategy and Structure*, pp. 382-83.

innovation involved substituting quasi-autonomous operating divisions (organized mainly along product, brand, or geographic lines) for the functional divisions of the U-form structure as the principal basis for dividing up the task and assigning responsibility."[21]

Each of the multidivisional firm's major operating divisions is a "profit center" insofar as it handles all of the functions related to its own product or territory—purchasing, personnel, manufacturing, accounting, marketing, and so on—and is judged on the basis of the profitability of its own operations (see Figure 14.2). Just as importantly, DuPont's and Sloan's innovation transformed the company's central office by adding to the senior executive staff individuals whose sole assignment was to assist the top managers in their strategic decision-making responsibilities.

Taken together, these two structural changes represented an advance over the functional type of organization despite the sacrifice of some of the scale economies and efficient division of labor associated with functional separation. Indeed, the multidivisional structure consciously provided for duplication of functions across operating units. But the additional costs of duplication were more than offset by the multidivisional organization's improved performance evaluation capabilities and its decentralized managerial decision-making structure.

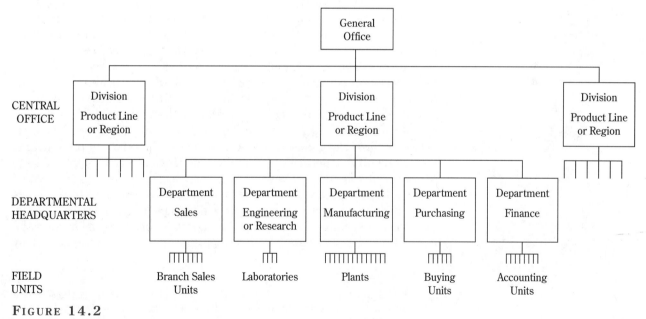

FIGURE 14.2
A Simplified Multidivisional Firm

21 Williamson, *Markets and Hierarchies*, p. 136.

On the one hand, the separate profit figures generated by each operating division provided the firm's top-level managers with a clear basis for appraising the relative performances of individual products, brands, or geographic territories.[22] On the other hand, because lower-level, tactical decision-making responsibilities were delegated to the heads of the semi-autonomous operating units, the top managers in the central office had more of the time and commitment necessary to use the divisional profit information as a guide to strategic planning for the enterprise as a whole.

The multidivisional firm's strategic planning advantages can be described as follows. In consultation with the central office's senior executive staff, the company's top managers allocate budgets to the various operating divisions, making available to each of them the equipment, personnel, and other resources required to carry out their assigned tasks. The heads of the firm's operating units, in turn, take their individual budgets as given and select the particular combination of inputs that yields the maximum possible level of profits from divisional activities. They coordinate and manage "the actual buying, selling, advertising, accounting, manufacturing, engineering, or research" functions necessary to reach this goal.[23]

At the end of the budget period, the company's top managers evaluate the profit performance of each operating division, and then take appropriate action based on whether or not the divisional managers are performing satisfactorily. "By changing or bringing in new physical equipment and supplies, by transferring or shifting the personnel, or by expanding or cutting down available funds,"[24] the top managers penalize poor performance and reward favorable performance, thereby reallocating the firm's resources to their highest valued uses. Overall company profitability is enhanced in the process.

The advantages of the multidivisional structure in this regard illustrate that "efficient production . . . is a result of not having *better* resources but in *knowing more accurately* the relative productive performances of those resources."[25] As such, the multidivisional firm "takes on many of the properties of (and is usefully regarded as) a miniature capital market."[26] To paraphrase Alchian and Demsetz, as a consequence of the flow of profit data to the central office, information about the productive characteristics of a large set of specific inputs was now more cheaply available. Management could more efficiently ascertain better recombinations or new uses of resources under the multidivisional type of organization than under a more centralized, functionally separated structure or by conventional search through the general market.[27] We can see this important point even more clearly by

---

22 Divisional profitability depends in part on the prices at which trades between divisions take place. This transfer pricing problem is discussed in Chapter 9. Also see Chapter 13 for details on the related issue of double marginalization.

23 Chandler, *Strategy and Structure*, p. 8.

24 *Ibid.*

25 Alchian and Demsetz, "Production, Information Costs, and Economic Organization," p. 793 (emphasis in original).

26 Williamson, "Modern Corporation," p. 1556.

27 Alchian and Demsetz, "Production, Information Costs, and Economic Organization." p. 795.

considering two recent extensions of the multidivisional structure: the conglomerate firm and the multinational corporation.

The Conglomerate Enterprise

The expanding scale and scope of business activities that led the large manufacturing enterprises of the 1920s to adopt the multidivisional structure basically involved diversification into new geographic territories and into related product lines. Thus, while the General Electric Company's profit centers grew to number in the hundreds, the firm continued to be a producer mainly of electrical appliances and machinery. Similarly, General Motors diversified by acquiring companies like Frigidaire, a household appliance manufacturer, the Ethyl Corporation, a producer of lead-based gasoline additives, and, later, H. Ross Perot's data processing firm, EDS. But automobile assembly remained its principal focus.

The true conglomerate enterprise, which results from diversification into completely unrelated lines of business, is mostly a post-World War II phenomenon. Indeed, the conglomerate is almost wholly a child of the 1960s and 1970s. Whereas conglomerate acquisitions accounted for just over 10 percent of the total assets acquired through merger between 1948 and 1955, they accounted for 35 percent of U.S. merger activity during 1964-71, and 45 percent of the mergers that took place during 1972-79.[28] There are three hypotheses about the emergence of the conglomerate form of business organization.

The Role of Antitrust Policy. One explanation for the rise of the conglomerate is that it emerged in response to increasingly stringent enforcement of the antitrust laws. Following the passage of the Celler-Kefauver amendment to Section 7 of the Clayton Act in 1950, the Federal Trade Commission and the Justice Department's Antitrust Division took a more hostile approach both to **horizontal mergers** (acquisitions involving firms competing in the same product or geographic market) and to **vertical mergers** (mergers involving the acquisition of an upstream supplier or downstream customer). As a result, firms began to diversify into products or markets that were unrelated to their principal lines of business because such acquisitions raised fewer antitrust concerns. Hence, for example, Beatrice Foods acquired manufacturers of luggage and auto parts, and ITT diversified into insurance, baking, and hotels.

The Potential Competition Issue. A second hypothesis about the conglomerate is that despite the absence of obvious market overlaps, diversification is a way for firms to acquire or to increase their market power. Conglomerate diversification possibly injures competition by providing firms

---

28 Frederic M. Scherer and David Ross, *Industrial Market Structure and Economic Performance*, 3E. (Boston: Houghton-Mifflin, 1990), p. 157.

with the opportunity to eliminate *potential* competitors. This concern has been voiced most strongly in relation to so-called product-line extension mergers whereby two products that do not compete directly but whose marketing channels or production processes are similar are joined under common ownership.

The potential-competition issue arose in the first conglomerate merger case to reach the Supreme Court under amended Section 7, which challenged the Procter & Gamble Company's acquisition of Clorox, the nation's largest producer of liquid bleach.[29] Procter & Gamble, a leading manufacturer of household products including soaps, detergents, and toothpaste, did not itself make bleach and, therefore, its acquisition did not directly lessen competition in that market. Nevertheless, the Federal Trade Commission (FTC) argued that the merger violated the Clayton Act because Procter thereby eliminated itself as a potential competitor of Clorox.

In other words, it was the FTC's view that competitive market forces would be strengthened if Procter entered the bleach market *de novo* by building its own manufacturing facility rather than by acquiring the firm that would have been its chief rival. (Indeed, the FTC produced internal company documents at trial indicating that Procter had previously considered entering the liquid bleach market on its own, but had dropped those plans as being too costly.) The Supreme Court upheld the FTC's opinion and the merger was undone.[30]

Diversification of Risk. Perhaps the most widely accepted, though this is not to say most correct, explanation for the emergence of the conglomerate enterprise is that it has attractive portfolio diversification properties.[31] This hypothesis is based on a well-known result from the modern theory of finance which says that an investor can reduce risk by holding a diverse set of securities having different risk-return characteristics.[32] Specifically, the lower the correlation between the returns generated by the individual securities in an investment portfolio, the lower is the investor's overall exposure to risk.

For example, consider a portfolio comprising two assets, A and B, and let α be the percentage of the individual's wealth invested in asset A. If the individual invests all of his or her wealth in the two assets, the expected return on the portfolio, R_P^e, is equal to the weighted average of the returns expected from the two securities; that is,

$$R_P^e = \alpha R_A^e + (1 - \alpha) R_B^e.$$

---

29 *Federal Trade Commission* v. *Procter & Gamble Co.*, 386 U.S. 568 (1967).

30 Clorox remains an independent company to this day; Procter & Gamble never did enter the liquid bleach market.

31 Morris A. Adelman, "The Antimerger Act, 1950-1960," *American Economic Review Papers and Proceedings* 51 (May 1961), pp. 236-44. Also see Williamson, "Modern Corporation," p. 1558.

32 Harry Markowitz, "Portfolio Selection," *Journal of Finance* 7 (1952), pp. 77-91. See Chapter 15 for a more complete discussion of this topic.

The investor's risk from holding this two-security portfolio is measured by the standard deviation of R_P^e. The standard deviation of R_P^e, denoted by σ_P, is computed as follows:

$$\sigma_P = [\alpha^2 \sigma_A^2 + (1 - \alpha)^2 \sigma_B^2 + 2\alpha(1 - \alpha) r_{AB} \sigma_A \sigma_B]^{1/2},$$

where σ_A^2 and σ_B^2 are the variances of the expected returns of the individual securities and r_{AB} is the correlation coefficient between the returns generated by assets A and B.[33]

The standard deviation of the returns to holding the two-security portfolio is equal to (the square root of) the weighted average of the variances of the returns to the individual securities plus a factor whose sign and magnitude depends on the extent to which the returns to the two assets are correlated with one another. Hence, it is the value of r_{AB} that determines whether or not diversification reduces the investor's exposure to risk. To see this result, suppose that investment A offers a relatively high expected return, say 15 percent (.15), but is also somewhat risky—the standard deviation of the expected returns to A is .10. Investment B, on the other hand, offers a lower but safer expected rate of return. Specifically, $R_B^e = .08$ and $\sigma_B = .05$. Further assume that the individual invests half of his or her wealth in each asset (i.e., $\alpha = .5$).

First consider the case of perfect positive correlation between the returns generated by the two investments. If $r_{AB} = + 1.0$, $\sigma_P = .075$, which is equal to the weighted average of the risks associated with the individual securities. Consequently, diversification offers no advantages when perfectly positively correlated assets are combined in an investment portfolio.

Now suppose that the correlation coefficient between the expected returns is smaller, but still positive. If r_{AB} is equal to, say .2, then $\sigma_P = .0602$. In this case, diversification reduces portfolio risk from 7.5 percent (the weighted average of the risks associated with the individual investments) to just over 6 percent. Finally, consider what happens when the expected returns to the two assets are perfectly negatively correlated; that is, $r_{AB} = -1.0$. Portfolio risk in this case is only 2.5 percent. In fact, when the expected returns to two assets are perfectly negatively correlated, there exists some combination of the securities that completely eliminates the investor's exposure to risk. In the example at hand here, if we construct a portfolio with $\alpha = .33$, $\sigma_P = 0$.[34] That is, with $r_{AB} = -1.0$, if the investor puts one-third of his or her

33 The correlation coefficient provides a statistical measure of the degree to which high (low) values of one variable are associated with high (low) values of some other variable. The correlation coefficient ranges in magnitude from +1.0 for variables that are perfectly positively correlated with one another—high (low) values of one variable are always associated with high (low) values of the other—to −1.0 for variables that are perfectly negatively correlated with one another—high values of one variable are always associated with low values of the other, and vice versa. A correlation coefficient of zero indicates that there is no statistically significant linear relationship between the two variables.

34 More generally, the optimal portfolio is found by choosing the α that minimizes σ_P. This exercise yields $\alpha^* = (\sigma_B^2 - r_{AB}\sigma_A\sigma_B)/(\sigma_A^2 + \sigma_B^2 - 2r_{AB}\sigma_A\sigma_B)$. Only if the two individual assets are subject to the same risk (i.e., $\sigma_A = \sigma_B$) will the minimum variance portfolio have $\alpha^* = .5$.

wealth in asset A and two-thirds in asset B, the diversified portfolio will generate a riskless expected rate of return equal to $R_p^e = .33(.15) + .67(.08) = .1031$.

The implication of the above theory for corporate diversification should be obvious. If a firm expands into several unrelated lines of business (whose expected returns presumably have a low—and, ideally, a negative—correlation with one another), management may be able to reduce shareholders' overall exposure to risk. Hence, the most popular explanation for ITT's diversification into insurance, baking, and hotels is that positive deviations in the expected rates of return generated by investments in some of these industries would help offset negative deviations in the returns from the firm's other lines of business so that investment risk would be lower than otherwise.

However, this explanation for the emergence of the conglomerate enterprise is overly simplistic. Diversification into new product lines or territories where the expected returns to investment have a low correlation with the firm's existing lines of business does reduce risk exposure in the way that portfolio theory suggests. But diversification through ownership integration also entails costs.

Managerial resources are scarce and hence subject to decreasing returns beyond some scale of operation as managers cope with the task of monitoring and controlling an increasingly diverse set of business activities. The daily routine becomes more remote from the top managers as the conglomerate acquires additional products and territories and adds more layers of bureaucracy to its management team. The paperwork burden grows and problems of asymmetric information arise because the conglomerate's central office typically has less product- or territory-specific knowledge than the managers of the formerly independent companies that have been absorbed.

The important point is that firms can achieve all of the risk-reducing benefits of portfolio diversification while, at the same time, avoiding all of the costs associated with ownership integration. Firms do this in the same way that ordinary investors do, namely by purchasing stock in companies whose expected returns have a low correlation with one another. Rather than merging with Continental Baking Company, Hartford Insurance, and Sheraton Hotels, among others, ITT could have reduced its exposure to risk simply by assembling an investment portfolio comprising shares of these firms. Indeed, for the same total outlay ITT could have diversified its portfolio more broadly and, hence, reduced its overall exposure to risk even further, by investing in a mutual fund. In short, corporate diversification offers no advantages in terms of lower risk or lower capital costs: "The firm should evaluate investment projects in the same way that investors evaluate securities."[35]

Corporate diversification does offer one advantage not available to the individual investor. Diversifying into new products and new territories lowers

---

35 Clifford W. Smith, Jr., "'The Theory of Corporate Finance: A Historical Overview," in Clifford W. Smith, Jr., ed., *The Modern Theory of Corporate Finance*, 2E. (New York: McGraw-Hill, 1990), p. 6.

the variance of projected net cash flows. In this way the firm may be able to reduce the probability of default on its outstanding debt obligations and, hence, lessen the expected costs of bankruptcy. However, evidence suggests that the direct costs of bankruptcy, which consist of lawyers' and accountants' fees and the value of managerial time spent in supervising the sale of assets and resolving disputes between various claimants, do not seem to be important. One estimate suggests that these costs amount to only about one percent of the market value of the firm prior to bankruptcy.[36] Moreover, there is nothing in the historical record to indicate that bankruptcy costs rose sharply during the 1960s when the conglomerate enterprise first emerged as an important form of business organization.[37]

The Advantages of Conglomerate Organization. Rather than being viewed as a portfolio diversification strategy or as a method of reducing expected bankruptcy costs, the conglomerate form of business organization is more usefully thought of as a logical extension of the multidivisional firm.[38] To reiterate, the multidivisional structure is distinguished by its performance-evaluation and resource-allocation advantages. By reorganizing in this way, the firm enhances its overall profitability "because cash flows no longer return automatically to their origins but instead revert to the center, thereafter to be allocated among competing uses in accordance with prospective yields."[39] For strategic planning purposes alone, it makes little difference whether the organization's profit centers are in similar lines of business or are completely unrelated to one another.

Viewed as an extension of the multidivisional firm, the conglomerate is a miniature capital market in the sense that management's resource-allocation decisions replace those that would otherwise be made by external investors.[40] The conglomerate's top managers in essence become the agents of the stockholders and lenders who supplied capital to the enterprise's formerly independent constituent parts. These capitalists delegate to the conglomerate's central office authority to supply resources to, and to monitor the performance of, the managers in charge of the firm's various operating divisions.

Internal monitoring of resource-allocation decisions by the conglomerate's management has two main advantages over external monitoring by stockholders and other capitalists. First, internal monitors arguably have access to more and better information about resource productivities and

---

36 Jerold B. Warner, "Bankruptcy Costs: Some Evidence," *Journal of Finance* 32 (May 1977), pp. 337-48. Other, indirect costs of bankruptcy, including lost sales, lost profits, subsequent restrictions on the firm's ability to obtain credit or issue stock, the costs of non-value-maximizing decisions by court-appointed trustees, and the higher compensation demanded by managers and employees because of higher probabilities of unemployment, may not be so trivial, however.

37 Williamson, "Modern Corporation," p. 1558.

38 *Ibid.*

39 *Ibid.*, p. 1559.

40 *Ibid.*

performance than do external monitors. Audits of operating division records by the conglomerate's senior executives can be more wide-ranging, more frequent, and more thorough than those conducted by outsiders. Access to superior information allows the conglomerate's central office to make more profitable use of divisional resources than would have been made had the operating unit remained an independently owned firm.

Second, when performance failures are detected, the conglomerate's top managers can more readily alter the composition of the operating division's management team and more quickly implement other changes necessary to improve divisional profitability than could the unit's former owners. The central office can trim budgets and reassign or fire managers without the costly proxy fights or other margins of discipline to which external monitors must resort.[41]

Some limited (but unfortunately dated) evidence exists which suggests that the conglomerate does indeed have efficiency advantages over other forms of business organization. Weston and Mansinghka compared the performances of large conglomerates with those of other large firms between 1958 and 1968.[42] They found that the conglomerates exhibited significantly higher growth rates in total assets, sales, net income, earnings per share, and market value over this period than the other companies in their sample. Moreover, although the conglomerates had earnings records that were inferior to those of the other large firms in 1958, they were doing at least as well as—and in some cases better than—the other companies on this performance measure by 1968. The authors concluded from this evidence that "an important economic function of conglomerate firms has been raising the profitability of firms with depressed earnings to the average for the industry generally."[43]

In short, the conglomerate form of business organization facilitates the allocation of productive resources across competing uses. Far from being a novel innovation designed to limit stockholders' exposure to risk, conglomerates emerged as a natural extension of the multidivisional type of internal organizational structure. The conglomerate enterprise differs from the more traditional M-form firm only in the diversity of sources from which cash flows are centralized and redirected to high yield uses.[44]

The Multinational Corporation

Although the operations of any company that sells goods or services to foreign buyers are "multinational" in some sense, for present purposes the distinguishing feature of the modern multinational corporation (MNC) is that the enterprise owns or controls production or service facilities overseas.

---

41 *Ibid.*
42 J. Fred Weston and S. K. Mansinghka, "Tests of the Efficiency Performance of Conglomerate Firms," *Journal of Finance* 26 (September 1971), pp. 919-36.
43 *Ibid.*, p. 934.
44 Williamson, "Modern Corporation," p. 1558.

Such ownership or control is accomplished through **direct foreign investment**. The domestic firm establishes a physical presence in another country either by acquiring an ownership interest in an existing foreign producer or by building its own overseas facility from scratch.

Like its conglomerate cousin, the multinational corporation emerged in the post-World War II era. Table 14.2 shows international investment figures for the 12-year period ending in 1989, the most recent year for which these data are available. The table indicates that while U.S. private direct investment abroad exhibits considerable year-to-year variation, it is sizeable. Overseas investments by domestic firms are typically something on the order of 20 to 25 percent of their outlays on plant and equipment at home (see the column labeled "net nonresidential fixed domestic investment").

It is also apparent that foreign direct investment in the United States has grown at significantly higher rates than U.S. private direct investment abroad during the 1980s. Indeed, the rate of increase in foreign direct investments has been large enough during recent years that by 1989, the accumulated stock of foreign-owned capital in the United States exceeded for the first time in history the accumulated value of U.S. direct investments abroad. Still, while foreign direct investment has been heavy during the 1980s, the overall pattern of international investments is not substantially different from historical trends. In 1989, the accumulated stock of foreign-owned capital in

TABLE 14.2   NET NONRESIDENTIAL FIXED DOMESTIC INVESTMENT AND INTERNATIONAL INVESTMENT POSITION OF THE UNITED STATES, 1978-89 (BILLIONS OF DOLLARS)

YEAR	NET NONRESIDENTIAL FIXED DOMESTIC INVESTMENT[a]	U.S. PRIVATE DIRECT INVESTMENT ABROAD[b]	FOREIGN DIRECT INVESTMENT IN THE U.S.[c]
1978	82.2	16.7	7.9
1979	98.9	25.2	12.0
1980	88.9	27.5	18.5
1981	98.6	12.9	25.7
1982	65.5	− 6.5	16.0
1983	45.8	5.2	12.4
1984	91.1	6.4	22.5
1985	102.1	18.8	20.0
1986	75.3	29.5	35.8
1987	65.8	54.5	51.4
1988	88.6	19.2	57.1
1989	84.0	39.9	71.9

Source: Council of Economic Advisers, *Economic Report of the President* (Washington, D.C.: USGPO, 1986), p. 371; and Council of Economic Advisers, *Economic Report of the President* (Washington, D.C.: USGPO, 1991), pp. 304 and 401.

a Nonresidential structures and producers' durable equipment.

b The accumulated stock of U.S. private direct investment abroad was $146.0 billion in 1977; it was $373.4 billion in 1989.

c The accumulated stock of foreign direct investment in the United States was $34.6 billion in 1977; it was $400.8 billion in 1989.

the United States stood in essentially the same relationship to U.S. GNP (about 8 percent) as it did in 1914.[45]

What does distinguish the post-World War II pattern of international trade and capital flows is the extent to which multinational corporations have come to dominate it. Depending on one's definition, there are about 250 to 750 of these firms, about half of which are based in the United States. The largest of these enterprises are gigantic by almost any measure. According to one observer, over 20 percent of the total GNP of the noncommunist world is now produced by MNCs. And about 25 percent of world trade consists of trade between subsidiaries and branches of multinational corporations.[46]

As might be expected, the largest of the multinationals are producers of motor vehicles and petroleum products. Table 14.3 lists the ten largest U.S.-based MNCs as of 1988, ranked by export sales. Foreign producers in these same industries dominate the list of the ten largest MNCs based outside the United States (see Table 14.4). (A breakdown of the domestic and export sales of the foreign-based multinationals is unfortunately not available.) But, again, the sheer size of these enterprises is impressive. The total annual sales recorded by the largest MNCs compare favorably with the GNPs of many smaller western nations. In 1988, for example, General Motors' sales were only slightly less than Austria's total GNP of $126.7 billion; GM's 1988 sales were greater than the GNPs of half the members of the Organization for Economic Cooperation and Development. The total sales of the tenth-ranked foreign-based multinational, Volkswagen, exceeded the GNP of Ireland ($27.6 billion) in the same year.[47]

TABLE 14.3 THE LARGEST U.S.-BASED MULTINATIONALS

Rank by Export Sales					Exports as percent of Sales	
1988	1987	COMPANY	EXPORT SALES[a]	TOTAL SALES[a]	PERCENT	RANK
1	1	General Motors	9.4	121.1	7.8	41
2	2	Ford Motor Company	8.8	92.4	9.5	35
3	3	Boeing	7.8	17.0	46.3	1
4	4	General Electric	5.7	49.4	11.6	29
5	5	IBM	5.0	59.7	8.3	39
6	8	Chrysler	4.3	35.5	12.2	28
7	6	E.I. du Pont de Nemours	4.2	32.5	12.9	26
8	7	McDonnell Douglas	3.5	15.1	23.0	5
9	10	Caterpillar	2.9	10.4	28.1	4
10	11	United Technologies	2.8	18.1	15.8	20

Source: Edward Prewitt, "America's Biggest Exporters," *Fortune*, 17 July 1989, p. 51.

a Billions of dollars.

45 Wilfred Ethier, *Modern International Economics* (New York: Norton, 1983), p. 270.
46 Ibid., p. 267.
47 U. S. Department of Commerce, Bureau of the Census, *Statistical Abstract of the United States 1990* (Washington, D. C.: USGPO, 1990), p. 841.

TABLE 14.4 THE LARGEST FOREIGN-BASED MULTINATIONALS

Rank by Total
Sales

1988	1987	COMPANY	COUNTRY	TOTAL SALES[a]	TOTAL PROFITS[a]
1	1	Royal Dutch/Shell	Britain/Neth.	78.4	5.3
2	3	Toyota	Japan	50.8	2.3
3	2	British Petroleum	Britain	46.2	2.2
4	4	IRI	Italy	45.5	.9
5	5	Daimler-Benz	Germany	41.8	1.0
6	7	Hitachi	Japan	41.3	1.0
7	9	Siemens	Germany	34.1	.8
8	8	Fiat	Italy	34.1	2.3
9	10	Matsushita	Japan	33.9	1.2
10	6	Volkswagen	Germany	33.7	.4

Source: "The International 500," *Fortune*, 31 July 1989, p. 291.

a Billions of dollars.

What explains the growing importance of multinational corporations in international trade and capital movements? Modern advances in communication and information processing have certainly played a key role.[48] So has trade protectionism. Japanese automobile manufacturers, for example, have invested heavily in production facilities in the United States in part to overcome "voluntary" restrictions on the number of vehicles they are permitted to export to the U.S. market. Automobiles assembled in the United States are not counted against these export limits.

But the growing integration of world markets made possible by improved communication does not by itself explain why the ownership of firms should also be integrated internationally. Neither do the trade barriers that shape international investment patterns in some industries. After all, businesses that wish to sell in foreign markets can do so in two ways. They can export goods from domestic production sites. Or, if foreign production is more attractive because of trade barriers or because of locational advantages such as lower labor or transportation costs, they can license a foreign firm to produce the product in the foreign market.

The multinational corporation, like the conglomerate enterprise, is best understood as a natural extension of the multidivisional type of organizational structure. We could illustrate a stylized conglomerate enterprise by marking the various operating divisions (profit centers) on a M-form firm's organizational chart with labels indicating diverse lines of business. Similarly, the MNC's operating divisions are divided along areas of global market responsibility—the domestic operating division, the European division, and the Far East division, for example. In other words, "the conglomerate uses the M-form

---

48 The Singer Sewing Machine company opened the first American manufacturing plant in Europe during the 1860s soon after the first transatlantic telephone cable was laid. See Ethier, *Modern International Economics*, p. 269.

structure to extend asset management from specialized to diversified lines of commerce. The [multinational enterprise] counterpart is the use of the M-form structure to extend asset management from a domestic base to include foreign operations."[49]

Of course, the multinational variant of the multidivisional firm did not emerge full-blown as U.S. companies began establishing an overseas presence in the post-war period. The more usual pattern was for domestic corporations to begin penetrating foreign markets simply by shipping products there and, later, establishing sales organizations abroad. But once international markets had expanded sufficiently to make foreign production economical, it became necessary to choose between the two basic alternatives mentioned above. One option was to enter into licensing agreements granting foreign firms the right to manufacture products in overseas markets. The other was direct foreign investment, whereby domestic firms either acquired ownership interests in established foreign producers or built their own manufacturing facilities from scratch.

Initial foreign investments, whether undertaken *de novo* or through merger or acquisition, were in fact usually organized initially as subsidiaries of parent U.S. corporations. These subsidiaries then invariably gained divisional status within M-form structures as the scale and scope of foreign operations later became more complex. For obvious reasons, this transformation in structure typically followed the reorganization of domestic operations along multidivisional lines. It is worth noting that because the multidivisional structure emerged earlier in the United States than in Europe or elsewhere, U.S. firms had a comparative advantage in managing direct investments abroad. This organizational head start may help explain why foreign direct investment in the United States lagged behind U.S. firms' overseas investments until very recently.[50]

The performance-evaluation and resource-allocation advantages of the multidivisional structure for managing the foreign operations of multinational corporations should be obvious and do not need to be belabored here. Delegating operational decision-making responsibilities to the heads of the firm's overseas units offers clear benefits in a global setting where local market conditions vary widely. Knowledge about local customs, local resources, and local political and legal environments can best be acquired and utilized by the person on the spot. At the same time, arranging for the net cash flows generated by the various foreign operating divisions to return to the company's headquarters for redistribution to high yield uses serves a monitoring and control function. This centralization of net cash flows helps assure that managerial decision making in overseas subsidiaries remains consistent with the overall goal of maximizing the multinational firm's profitability.

A more interesting question relates to the choice between ownership of foreign subsidiaries versus licensing established foreign firms to manufacture

49 Williamson, "Modern Corporation," p. 1561.
50 *Ibid*. Also see Chandler, *Scale and Scope*.

products in foreign markets. Tables 14.3 and 14.4 (see p. 494–495) supply an important clue to understanding this choice. The largest multinationals listed there all operate in high-technology industries—motor vehicles, chemicals, and computers, to name the most prominent. In fact, the list of the ten largest U.S.-based multinational corporations is almost identical with the list of the six major domestic industry groups that in recent years have accounted for roughly 84 percent of the private sector's total research and development effort.[51] This observation suggests that **technology transfer** plays a critical role in explaining the emergence of the multinational firm as a type of business organization.

Technology Transfer. To produce overseas, a domestic firm must obviously transfer its capital, its production techniques, and its knowhow to the foreign market. The choice between licensing and acquiring an ownership interest in a foreign subsidiary is basically a question of how much reliance to place on the market in effecting this transfer. More fundamentally, which institution—the market or the firm—enables the domestic company to appropriate returns that are sufficient to justify its transfer of technology to foreign markets? The factors that determine which of these alternatives will be optimal in any particular case correspond closely to those that inform the choice between the market and internal organization generally. But technology transfer does raise some distinctive difficulties that help tip the balance in favor of ownership integration (direct foreign investment).

One can imagine simple cases where the disclosure of a blueprint or a chemical formula would enable the foreign producer to duplicate the domestic firm's product or process. In such a situation, the domestic firm can in principle capture the value of the technology it transfers to the foreign producer by negotiating a licensing agreement that contains an appropriately scaled lump-sum fee for the right to use the technology and/or a schedule of royalty payments for units produced and sold in the foreign market. Market contracting is also feasible in more complicated situations where the technology to be transferred is embodied in knowhow accumulated in a learning-by-doing fashion by the domestic firm's managers or employees. The licensing agreement in such a case can provide for the creation of a "consulting team" by the domestic firm to furnish the foreign manufacturer with assistance in gaining familiarity with the idiosyncrasies of the production process.[52]

However, the theoretical usefulness of licensing agreements to govern the transfer of technology to foreign markets quickly breaks down when we

---

51 U.S. Department of Commerce, Bureau of the Census, *Statistical Abstract of the United States 1987* (Washington, D.C.: USGPO, 1987), p. 567. The six industries, in descending order of research and development spending, are aircraft and missiles, electrical equipment, machinery, chemicals and allied products, motor vehicles and transportation equipment, and professional and scientific instruments.

52 Williamson, "Modern Corporation," p. 1563.

consider the transaction-cost limits to these contracts. Informational asymmetries and asset specialization will place considerable strain on the negotiation and execution of technology transfers across ownership boundaries. In particular, the domestic firm will have superior knowledge about its own product or production process. And the foreign producer will have superior knowledge about local market conditions.

Given separate ownership, each will have an incentive to use its specialized knowledge to its own benefit. This can lead to resource-wasting posturing and to strategic misrepresentations during negotiation of the license fee that will determine each firm's share in the profits generated by the technology transfer. Moreover, technology transfers are by definition highly specialized transactions. Once a licensing agreement is negotiated and the technology is transferred, the domestic firm becomes vulnerable to exploitation by the foreign producer who can opportunistically threaten to terminate the agreement unless more favorable terms are conceded. Such a threat is made credible by the fact that once the technology has been disclosed, the domestic firm may be unable to prevent its licensee from using it even if compensation is no longer forthcoming.

The risk of disclosure is in fact the main impediment to the use of market contracting for effecting technology transfers. This risk derives from the fact that new technology is something of a **public good**. Once one firm has made a discovery, usable information becomes available to others at little or no cost unless the discoverer can maintain secrecy. And one firm's use of the knowledge underlying the discovery does not inhibit its use by other firms. The existence of such external effects, along with the characteristics of nonrivalry and nonexcludability in consumption, raises the problem of free riding: firms can enjoy the benefits of new technology without investing in the research and development efforts that made it possible. Consequently, all firms stand prepared to use the fruits of research and development. But no firm would be willing, without compensation, to finance the capital investment necessary to produce new technology.

The patent laws do of course offer protection to innovators, but enforcement of patent rights is often uncertain and costly.[53] Moreover, factors for which the courts offer less protection, such as secrecy, lead time over imitators, and learning-by-doing effects, are perceived to be more effective than patents as means of appropriating the returns to research and development in many industries.[54] In transferring technology across ownership boundaries, the domestic firm therefore runs the risk that licensees will opportunistically

---

53 For an extended discussion of the law and economics of the patent system, see William F. Shughart II, *The Organization of Industry* (Homewood, IL: Richard D. Irwin, 1990), pp. 357-82.

54 Richard D. Levin, Alvin K. Klevorick, Richard R. Nelson, and Sidney G. Winter, "Appropriating the Returns from Industrial Research and Development," *Brookings Papers on Economic Activity* (1987), pp. 783-820. In only one of the industries surveyed—drugs—did the respondents consider patents to be strictly more effective than other means of appropriation.

confiscate proprietary information about its product or production process. Direct foreign investment reduces this risk because the acquisition of an ownership interest in the foreign producer provides the subsidiary's managers and employees with stronger incentives to maintain secrecy and to use the domestic firm's technology in ways that are jointly profit-maximizing.

In sum, the multinational corporation emerged as an institution designed to cope with the problems of transferring technology to foreign markets. This is a function that promises to increase in importance as the pace of technological change hastens and as world markets continue to become more integrated throughout the remainder of the 1990s and into the 21st century. As these events unfold and as international enterprises grow in number and in size, the perspective gained by studying the internal organization of the firm will undoubtedly become more valuable.

SUMMARY

This chapter has discussed the managerial incentive and performance consequences of the internal organizational structure of the firm. It is certainly true that the functions of the firm are basically the same no matter how it is organized. But structure has a powerful influence on the amount and type of information available to the firm's managers, the degree of control managers exercise over the activities of the firm, the extent of decentralization in managerial decision making, and the ability of the firm to adapt to changing market conditions.

We have compared two basic organizational types: the unitary-form enterprise, which is divided along functional lines, and the multidivisional-form firm, which is divided along product or geographical lines. These successful structural innovations have at least two characteristics in common.

First, they streamline information flows within the firm. Decentralized decision making initially helped the functional organization take advantage of economies of scale and later evolved into the multidivisional structure to exploit economies of scope. These developments reduced the information load on top executives and thereby promoted an efficient division of labor within the managerial hierarchy. The delegation of tactical decision-making responsibilities to functional managers or to the managers of operating divisions allowed senior executives to specialize in the performance-evaluation and strategic-planning activities that were critical to the success of the enterprise as a whole.

Second, successful structural innovations provided individuals with incentives to use resources efficiently and to avoid behaving opportunistically. Firms met these objectives in two ways. On the one hand, they brought transactions involving specialized assets within the firm under common ownership. And, on the other hand, they organized their activities in such a way that managers would have access to the information necessary to monitor and control the performance of the firm's constituent parts. The use of organizational structure to facilitate internal resource allocation decisions

KEY TERMS
functional structure
multidivisional structure
transaction costs
bounded rationality
asymmetric information
opportunistic behavior
putting-out system
factory system
inside contracting
line officers
staff officers
diseconomies of scale
diseconomies of scope
horizontal merger
vertical merger
direct foreign investment
technology transfer
public good

furnished managers with the opportunity to observe divisional profit performance and the authority to reallocate cash flows to their highest valued uses. These factors played a critical role in explaining the emergence of the conglomerate enterprise and the multinational corporation in the post-World War II era.

Technology played a role in this story, but it was of secondary importance. The lesson of the inside contracting system was that a type of organization with all of the technical advantages of modern mass production methods failed to survive because it had none of the attributes of successful internal structure. The explanation for the emergence of the firm as an economic entity is thus not solely (or even mainly) technological in nature. Nor is the structure of the firm merely a shell having no important economic consequences. On the contrary, internal organization has a profound impact on the performance, adaptation, and growth of business enterprise.

QUESTIONS

14.1 In Japan, the typical CEO is paid an annual salary roughly 16 times that of the lowest-paid worker. In the United States, the CEO's annual salary may be as much as 60 times that of the lowest-paid worker. Apart from "cultural" differences, why do you think this is so? Is your answer influenced by learning that Japanese corporations tend to be much more tightly held than their counterparts in the United States? (In particular, perhaps only 25 percent of the equity of the average Japanese corporation is publicly traded; most of the equity is held by investment banks and other financial institutions.) Explain.

14.2 What were the chief defects of the inside contracting system? What lessons does the failure of this type of organization hold for choosing between the market and the firm as ways of governing transactions? Be specific.

14.3 In the functional type of organization, the firm's operating units are regarded as cost centers; in the multidivisional organization, the firm's operating units are regarded as profit centers. In which type of organization do you think divisional headquarters will tend to be more heavily staffed? Why? What implications does this observation have for the firm's overall profitability?

14.4 "New York City is expensive, but it's more expensive to visit than to live there." Explain.

PROBLEMS

14.1 Suppose that an individual has $1,000 to invest in two assets, one of which offers a 12 percent expected annual rate of return and the other of which offers a 20 percent expected annual rate of return. The standard deviation of the expected returns to the first asset is .10 and the standard deviation of the expected returns to the second is .15. If the individual chooses to invest $500 in each asset, what is the expected return to the portfolio and what is the standard deviation of the portfolio's returns if the correlation coefficient between the expected returns of the individual assets is .5? What if the correlation coefficient is −.5? If the correlation coefficient is −.5, how much should the individual invest in each asset to minimize investment risk?

14.2 Suppose that an investor can allocate his or her funds over three assets. The first asset is a riskless U.S. government security that pays a 7 percent annual rate of return with certainty. The second asset generates an expected annual rate of return of 9 percent; the standard deviation of the returns to this asset is .08. The third is another risky asset with an expected annual rate of return of 7 percent and a standard deviation of .1. Suppose further that the expected returns to the two risky assets are statistically independent of one another (their correlation coefficient is zero). Compute the mean and standard deviations of the returns to a portfolio composed of 80% of the riskless asset and 20% of the first risky asset. Compute the mean and standard deviations of the returns to a portfolio composed of 75% of the riskless asset, 15% of the first risky asset, and 10% of the second risky asset. Based on these computations, why does anyone invest in the second risky asset, which has a lower expected return and greater risk than the first? How much should the individual invest in each of the three assets to minimize investment risk?

The Financial Structure of the Firm

OVERVIEW

The goal of this chapter is to provide an overview of topics related to the financing of the firm's operations. We will pay particular attention to capital budgeting problems which involve decisions to invest in projects that are expected to generate a flow of future net cash benefits. The basics of estimating net cash flows, evaluating alternative investment projects, and determining the firm's cost of capital are discussed. And in light of these fundamental concepts, we will consider alternative methods of financing capital projects.

Chapter 15 also covers a number of advanced capital-budgeting issues. These include the impact of the firm's capital structure on stockholder control, managerial incentives, and the firm's vulnerability to bankruptcy and to takeover. Dividend policy is likewise examined through the lens of modern financial economics which increasingly sees the financial structure of the firm as evolving to provide solutions to a wide range of contracting problems. These solutions help to resolve conflicts of interest between the owners (stockholders), managers, and creditors of the firm.

F JS Corporation, a manufacturer of automobile parts, is considering a major investment in robotics. The total cost of the project is calculated to be $500,000, an outlay that is required to expand and remodel the firm's manufacturing facility and to purchase the robots and the computer software program that controls their operations. If management decides to undertake the investment, it will take one year for the project to come on line. Building construction will begin immediately and the robots will be installed and tested later in the year. However, because suppliers indicate that there is currently a six-month order backlog for robots, FJS must commit to purchasing the equipment now to insure timely delivery.

The company's engineers estimate that switching to robotics manufacture will, by conserving on labor and tool requirements, reduce total production costs by $150,000 annually. In addition, the use of robots should lessen the number of production defects and allow FJS to manufacture parts that meet its customers' design tolerances and performance specifications more closely. On this basis, the firm's sales department expects the investment to generate a $125,000 per year increase in revenues.

The firm will depreciate the robots over five years (using the straight-line method), with zero salvage value at the end of their useful lives. The firm faces a marginal corporate income tax rate of 40 percent and its cost of capital is 10 percent.

Should FJS invest in robotics? Questions of this sort plainly rank among the most important of the decision-making problems managers must be prepared to confront. Capital investments require the firm to commit its resources to long-term projects that often cannot be reversed easily if the initial assumptions and forecasts turn out to be overly optimistic. Management must make such decisions in light of the harsh reality that while successful capital projects can rescue the fortunes of a failing enterprise, foolish capital investments can sink an industry leader. This chapter's goal is to provide the tools that can be applied in solving a wide range of capital-budgeting problems, thereby aiding managers in selecting the most desirable investment projects from among the available choices.

THE BASICS OF CAPITAL BUDGETING

Capital budgeting is a straightforward application of the marginal-benefit-equals-marginal-cost rule that we have applied previously in solving a wide range of business decision-making problems. Capital investment decisions differ from other applications of this rule only because the time pattern of benefits and costs must be considered—capital expenditures are defined as outlays that generate a flow of future net cash benefits. Marginal benefit is interpreted in the context of capital budgeting as the expected rates of return on the successive investment opportunities available to the firm. Marginal cost is the cost to the firm of raising an extra dollar's worth of investment capital. The firm should therefore continue to invest in capital projects up to the point where the expected rate of return equals its cost of capital.

In order to identify the investment opportunities that comprise the set of acceptable capital projects, the manager must gather and analyze information that is relevant for evaluating various alternative uses of the firm's capital resources. The problem-solving process consists of four basic steps.

First, of course, proposals for investment projects must be generated. Second, the net cash flows for each of these proposed projects must be estimated. As described below, this step involves forecasting the time pattern of future benefits and costs associated with the alternative investment opportunities. Third, management must evaluate the competing investment proposals in terms of their impacts on the discounted present value of the firm, using this information to identify a set of acceptable projects. The evaluation of investment projects, in turn, requires the adoption of a decision rule for determining which of the competing claims on the capital resources of the firm will be accepted. Finally, the firm must review projects following their implementation. This review process is critical because the decision to abandon an existing capital project is as important as the decision to accept a new one.

Estimating Net Cash Flows

Estimating the future net cash flows that are expected to accrue to each proposed investment opportunity is the first and perhaps the most important step in the capital budgeting process. Proposals for new capital projects arise from a variety of sources. They are sometimes generated by the head of the manufacturing department, who wants to expand the company's production facility and to purchase additional equipment. They sometimes come from the head of the research department, who wants to develop and test market a new product, or from the head of the transportation department, who wants to replace aging vehicles, and so on. In any organization, the manager or department head who lobbies for a particular project will have a natural propensity to overstate the project's expected benefits and to understate its expected costs. Hence, executives having decision-making responsibility with respect to the organization's overall capital budget must review the cash flow estimates for each proposed investment carefully to ensure that they are reasonably free from bias.

Just as importantly, because capital projects by definition commit the firm to outlays that are expected to generate a stream of future benefits and costs, even unbiased cash flow estimates will be subject to uncertainty and, hence, sensitive to changes in the underlying assumptions on which they are based. Moreover, many of the factors on which accurate projections of future benefits and costs depend are beyond the firm's control.

Unanticipated increases in the cost of materials, a shift in consumer spending patterns, changes in government tax and monetary policies, and so on can easily turn an acceptable capital project into an unacceptable one. The firm's top managers must therefore review the cash flow estimates for each proposed investment opportunity under different sets of assumptions concerning relevant future market conditions to ensure that they are reasonably stable under various plausible scenarios.

Assuming that cash flow projections have been checked for possible bias and subjected to sensitivity analysis, certain guidelines should be followed in approaching the evaluation of alternative investments. First and foremost, future cash flows for each capital project should be measured on an *incremental* basis. In other words, the cash flows for each investment opportunity should be measured as the difference between the cash flows that are expected to accrue to the firm if the project is adopted and those that are expected without it. *Only* the additional benefits and costs associated with a proposed project are relevant in estimating cash flows.

Second, in measuring the incremental impact of the proposed investment on the firm's future cash flows, both the *direct and indirect effects* of the project must be considered. For example, in evaluating a proposal to purchase the machinery that enables the firm to manufacture a new product, management must consider the impact of the introduction of the new product on the sales of existing products. Third, future cash flows should be estimated on an *after-tax basis*. Noncash expenses associated with the project—such as depreciation—are excluded from the analysis except to the extent that they affect the firm's after-tax cash flows.

More specifically, for any year during the life of the project, the incremental, after-tax **net cash flows** (*NCF*) are defined as the change in **net income after tax** ($\Delta NIAT$) generated by the investment plus the change in **depreciation** (ΔD); that is,

$$NCF = \Delta NIAT + \Delta D. \tag{15.1}$$

$\Delta NIAT$ is, in turn, equal to the difference in **net income before tax** ($\Delta NIBT$) with and without the project times $(1 - t)$, where t is the marginal tax rate on corporate income:

$$\Delta NIAT = \Delta NIBT(1 - t). \tag{15.2}$$

The **marginal tax rate** on corporate income is relevant for calculating net cash flows because it determines the firm's tax liability on the last dollar in extra income generated by the investment. Depreciation is a noncash item and would not otherwise be included in calculating the project's net cash flows except for its favorable tax treatment which allows the firm to charge depreciation against revenues in computing net income before tax (see below). However, because it is a noncash item, the change in depreciation associated with the investment must also be added back to $\Delta NIAT$ so that only its effect on net after-tax *cash* flows is taken into account when evaluating the proposed investment.

The change in net income before tax ($\Delta NIBT$) is defined as the difference between cash inflows and cash outflows with and without the investment. Cash inflows consist of changes in revenues generated by the project (ΔR). Cash outflows consist of changes in operating costs (ΔC). Because depreciation charges reduce the firm's taxable income, they are subtracted in computing net income before tax. Hence,

$$\Delta NIBT = (\Delta R - \Delta C - \Delta D). \tag{15.3}$$

Substituting equation 15.3 into equation 15.2 yields an expression for the proposed project's impact on net after-tax income:

$$\Delta NIAT = (\Delta R - \Delta C - \Delta D)(1 - t). \tag{15.4}$$

Substituting equation 15.4 into equation 15.1, it follows that the incremental, after-tax net cash flows associated with the investment are:

$$NCF = (\Delta R - \Delta C - \Delta D)(1 - t) + \Delta D. \tag{15.5}$$

To illustrate how equation 15.5 can be applied, consider the capital budgeting problem facing FJS Corporation presented at the beginning of the chapter. Recall that the firm is contemplating an investment in robotics that requires a capital outlay of $500,000 in return for promised improvements in production efficiency and increases in sales. If FJS undertakes the project, there will be a net cash outflow (**net investment**) of $500,000 in the current year in order to expand and remodel the company's manufacturing facility and to cover the cost of purchasing and installing the robots. In each of the next five years there is a net cash inflow of

$$NCF = [\$125,000 - (-\$150,000) - \$100,000](1 - .4) + \$100,000$$
$$= \$205,000.$$

This calculation is based on the assumed projected annual increase in sales of $125,000, the projected yearly *reduction* in operating costs of $150,000, annual depreciation charges of $100,000 (using the straight-line method over the new equipment's five-year life),[1] and a marginal corporate income tax rate of 40 percent. (Table 15.1 shows net cash flow calculations for individual years.)

Estimating an investment's future net cash flows is only the first step in deciding whether or not to undertake the project, however. The capital

---

1 Annual depreciation charges under the straight-line method are equal to the required net investment divided by the equipment's expected useful life. In this example, annual depreciation charges are equal to $500,000/5 = $100,000. For simplicity, depreciation charges associated with the capital outlays necessary to expand and remodel the company's production facility are assumed to have the same useful life as the firm's new manufacturing equipment.

TABLE 15.1 NET CASH FLOWS FOR FJS CORPORATION ($ THOUSANDS)

					Changes in		
YEAR	NET INVEST- MENT	REVENUE (ΔR)	OPERATING COSTS (ΔC)	DEPRE- CIATION (ΔD)[a]	NET INCOME BEFORE TAX ($\Delta NIBT$)	NET INCOME AFTER TAX ($\Delta NIAT$)	NET CASH FLOWS (NCF)
0	–$500	0	0	0	0	0	–$500
1	0	$125	–$150	$100	$175	$105	$205
2	0	$125	_$150	$100	$175	$105	$205
3	0	$125	–$150	$100	$175	$105	$205
4	0	$125	–$150	$100	$175	$105	$205
5	0	$125	–$150	$100	$175	$105	$205

[a]Assuming a five-year useful life and straight-line depreciation.

Notes—$\Delta NIAT = (\Delta R - \Delta C - \Delta D)(1 - t)$, where t is the marginal corporate income tax rate (assumed equal to 40 percent), and $NCF = \Delta NIAT + \Delta D$.

budgeting process also requires the adoption of a rule for ranking investment opportunities in terms of their expected value to the firm. Such a rule is necessary in order to take account of the time shape of the anticipated stream of net cash flows and to compare the project's expected benefits with the costs of raising the funds required to finance it. The following section describes alternative methods for evaluating the investment opportunities available to the firm.

Evaluating Investment Projects

After estimating net cash flows for various investment opportunities, management must evaluate each project to decide which of them will be undertaken. This section discusses a variety of methods for identifying the set of acceptable capital projects. Not all of them are equally valid when judged against the objective of long-run profit maximization. This goal, it will be recalled, is equivalent to maximizing the present value of the firm. The present value of the firm, in turn, is equal to the discounted value of the future stream of profits generated by *all* of the firm's investments; that is,

$$VALUE = \sum_{n=0}^{\infty} \left[\frac{\pi_n}{\left(1 + i_n\right)^n} \right],$$

where π_n is the profit anticipated in period n (total revenue minus total cost), and i_n is the interest rate chosen for discounting the corresponding period's expected future profit.

In principle, and when properly estimated, net cash flows and profits are one and the same. That is, if the net cash flows to a particular capital project are computed on an incremental, after-tax basis with full consideration given to both the direct and indirect effects of the proposed investment on the firm's discounted cash inflows and outflows, then investment decisions consistent with the goal of long-run profit maximization can be made by comparing the present value of the net cash flows accruing to the firm with and without the project.

Such comparisons are quite complicated in practice, however. The indirect effects of proposed investment opportunities are often uncertain and, hence, difficult to quantify because they depend on subtle interactions with the firm's other existing and planned investment activities as well as those of its rivals. The discounted value of the firm at a given point in time is the market's evaluation of the discounted value of the net cash flows accruing to the ensemble of investment projects it has undertaken, is expected to undertake, and should have undertaken, based on all publicly available information relevant to the firm's future prospects.

Cash flow may not in practice be the same as profit, if only for the reason that long-run profitability is the discounted value of the firm's expected future net cash flows in perpetuity whereas the net cash flows to a particular capital project are computed over the project's finite lifetime. The model of the value of the firm nevertheless can—and should—be applied in the evaluation of individual investment projects.

The present value of the firm can be written alternatively as

$$VALUE = \sum_{n=0}^{\infty} \left[\frac{NCF_n}{(1+i_n)^n} \right],$$

where NCF_n is the net cash flow accruing to all of the firm's investment activities anticipated in period n and i_n is the interest rate chosen for discounting the corresponding period's expected future net cash flow. It follows that any project expected to generate net cash flows having a positive discounted value will increase the value of the firm and, hence, should be undertaken.

Net Present Value. The **net present value** (*NPV*) of a proposed investment project equals

$$NPV = \sum_{n=0}^{N} \left[\frac{NCF_n}{(1+i_n)^n} \right].$$

NCF_n is the incremental, after-tax net cash flow anticipated in year n, i_n is the firm's weighted average cost of capital in the corresponding year,[2] and N is the terminal date of the project's expected useful life. Further simplification is possible by assuming that the investment outlays necessary to implement

---

2 The various methods by which the firm's weighted average cost of capital can be estimated are discussed later in the chapter. For present purposes, the value of i is taken as given.

the project all occur in the current period (year 0) and that the firm's cost of capital is constant throughout the project's lifetime. Under these assumptions,

$$NPV = \sum_{n=1}^{N} \left[\frac{NCF_n}{(1+i)^n} \right] - NINV,$$

where $NINV$ is initial net investment in year 0 and the remaining variables are defined as before.

The net present value technique for evaluating investment projects is illustrated in Table 15.2, which shows the relevant calculations for the FJS Corporation. After discounting the expected future yearly net cash flows and summing them over the project's anticipated useful life, the investment's net present value is indeed greater than zero. The NPV rule accordingly dictates that the firm should accept the project because doing so will raise its market value—the discounted value of the expected future benefits more than offsets the expected costs of implementing the investment in robotics. More generally, the NPV rule suggests that the set of acceptable capital projects for the firm includes all proposed investment opportunities having a positive net present value.

Internal Rate of Return. A second measure of the profitability of alternative investment opportunities involves estimating each project's **internal rate of return** (IRR). The IRR rule is perhaps the most familiar criterion for evaluating capital projects. It is seriously defective, however, as the following discussion demonstrates.

TABLE 15.2 NET PRESENT VALUE (AT A 10 PERCENT INTEREST RATE) OF FJS CORPORATION'S PROPOSED CAPITAL PROJECT ($ THOUSANDS)

| | | | Changes in | | | |
| | NET INVESTMENT | DEPRECIATION (ΔD) | NET INCOME BEFORE TAX ($\Delta NIBT$) | NET INCOME AFTER TAX ($\Delta NIAT$) | NET CASH FLOWS (NCF) | DISCOUNTED NET CASH FLOWS |
YEAR						
0	–$500	0	0	0	–$500	–$500
1	0	$100	–$175	$105	$205	$186.36
2	0	$100	$175	$105	$205	$169.42
3	0	$100	–$175	$105	$205	$154.02
4	0	$100	–$175	$105	$205	$140.02
5	0	$100	–$175	$105	$205	$127.29

$NPV = 277.11

Notes.—$NCF = \Delta NIAT + \Delta D$ and $NPV = \sum_{n=0}^{5} [NCF_n / (1 + i)^n]$. Alternatively, $NPV = \sum_{n=1}^{5} [NCF_n / (1 + i)^n] - NINV$, where $NINV$ is the net investment in the current year (year 0).

The *IRR* is defined as the particular discount rate at which the net present value of a proposed capital project is equal to zero. That is, rather than computing the *NPV* of an investment's expected future cash flows using the firm's estimated cost of capital, *i*, the *IRR* rule requires finding some other discount rate, say *r*, at which the investment's *NPV* would be zero.

More specifically, calculating the internal rate of return requires solving

$$NPV = \sum_{n=0}^{N} \left[\frac{NCF_n}{(1+r)^n} \right] = 0$$

for *r*. Alternatively, and again assuming that all investment outlays necessary to implement the project occur in year 0, the internal rate of return is the discount rate at which

$$NPV = \sum_{n=1}^{N} \left[\frac{NCF_n}{(1+r)^n} \right] - NINV = 0.$$

Writing the equation in this way shows that the internal rate of return, *r*, is the interest rate that equates the present value of the project's expected future cash flows with the initial capital outlay required to implement it.

The decision rule implied by the *IRR* technique is that the firm accept all investment projects for which the internal rate of return is greater than or equal to its cost of capital (i.e., $r \geq i$). If the firm adopts this criterion for evaluating investment opportunities, it will generally undertake the same projects that would also be selected under the *NPV* rule described above.

A little thought indicates why this is so. Assume that the net present value of a proposed investment is positive when computed using *i*, the firm's cost of capital. Then the interest rate at which the *NPV* would be zero, *r*, must necessarily be greater than *i*. Consider this in another way. Assume that at the firm's estimated cost of capital, the present value of the stream of future net cash flows generated by an investment project exceeds the initial capital outlays required to implement it. Then a discount rate higher than the firm's cost of capital will be required in order for the present value of the stream of future cash flows to be reduced and made equal to the initial outlay.

Hence, the internal rate of return on the FJS Corporation's proposed investment in robotics must be greater than 10 percent because the project has a positive net present value at that interest rate. Computing the exact value of *r* is not a straightforward exercise, however. This is because the *NPV* equation contains the sums of powers of the discounting factor, $1/(1 + r)$, and one must therefore solve a nonlinear equation to determine the project's internal rate of return.

One solution method is trial and error. (Fortunately, financial calculators are now available to handle the tedious computations.) Table 15.3 shows some representative trial calculations of the net present value of the FJS Corporation's expected future cash flows at selected discount rates. According to the table, the project's internal rate of return is approximately 30 percent,

TABLE 15.3 INTERNAL RATE OF RETURN CALCULATIONS FOR FJS
CORPORATION'S PROPOSED CAPITAL PROJECT
($ THOUSANDS)

	NET CASH FLOWS	Net Present Value at				
YEAR	(NCF)	10%	20%	25%	29%	30%
0	–$500	–$500	–$500	–$500	–$500	–$500
1	$205	$186.36	$170.83	$164.00	$158.91	$157.69
2	$205	$169.42	$142.36	$131.20	$123.19	$121.30
3	$205	$154.02	$118.63	$104.96	$95.50	$93.31
4	$205	$140.02	$98.86	$83.97	$74.03	$71.78
5	$205	$127.29	$82.38	$67.17	$57.39	$55.21
	NPV =	$277.11	$113.06	$51.30	$9.02	–$.71

Notes—The internal rate of return is the discount rate, r, at which $NPV =$
$\sum_{n=0}^{5} [NCF_n / (1 + r)^n] = 0$.

for it is that interest rate which equates the present value of the anticipated
cash inflows with outflows, thereby yielding a zero net present value.

Defects in the IRR rule. The *IRR* rule does have several serious draw-
backs that limit its usefulness, however. First, it provides no information to
the decision maker beyond that provided by the *NPV* rule. As has just been
shown, the internal rate of return for any project having a positive net present
value must be greater than the firm's cost of capital. Consequently, any
investment project that would be acceptable under the *NPV* criterion will
also usually be acceptable using the *IRR* rule.

Second, and more importantly, exclusive reliance on the *IRR* rule can
either lead the firm to reject investment opportunities having a positive net
present value or to accept projects having a negative net present value. This
is because the *NPV* equation may yield either no solution for r or it may yield
multiple solutions. In particular, for the *IRR* equation to have a solution,
there must be at least one algebraic sign reversal in the expected future
stream of net cash flows (i.e., cash *out*flows must occur in at least one period
of the project's useful lifetime.)[3] This requirement is not by itself overly
troublesome for the typical investment project, which is characterized by an
initial capital outlay (cash outflow) followed by a stream of cash inflows.
However, no unique value of the internal rate of return will exist for a project
that promises net cash inflows in every period.

Moreover, if the stream of future net cash flows changes sign more than
once, the *NPV* equation yields multiple internal rates of return. (And, in
general, there will be the same number of internal rates of return as there
are sign changes.) A classic example of this troublesome feature of the *IRR*

3 See Jack Hishleifer, *Investment, Interest and Capital* (Englewood Cliffs, NJ: Prentice-Hall,
1970), p. 51.

rule is known as the oil-pump problem.[4] An oil company must decide whether or not to purchase and install a new high-speed oil pump on an existing well. The pump costs \$1,600 to install and during the first year of operation it is expected to generate an incremental cash inflow of \$10,000. But a cash outflow of \$10,000 is anticipated during the second year because the higher rates of extraction made possible by the pump also deplete the well's oil reserves sooner.

According to the *NPV* rule, the oil company should reject the proposed investment if a 10 percent cost of capital is assumed. Specifically, the net present value calculation yields

$$NPV = -\$1,600 + \frac{\$10,000}{1.1} - \frac{\$10,000}{(1.1)^2} = -\$773.55.$$

But if the *IRR* criterion is used, the project might be undertaken because the two internal rates of return computed by solving

$$-\$1,600 + \frac{\$10,000}{1+r} - \frac{\$10,000}{(1+r)^2} = 0$$

both exceed the firm's cost of capital. Specifically, with some algebraic manipulation,[5] the above expression can be rewritten as

$$\$1,600(1 + r)^2 - \$10,000(1 + r) + \$10,000 = 0,$$

which can be solved using the quadratic formula to obtain r = 25% or r = 400%.[6]

The *IRR* rule is misleading because it assumes that the opportunity cost of the funds invested in a project is equal to the project's implied internal rate of return. This assumption is plainly inconsistent with the goal of long-run value maximization which requires that cash flows be discounted at the market-determined opportunity cost of capital. And, because this requirement is violated, it should not be surprising that exclusive reliance on the *IRR* rule can lead the decision maker to select investment opportunities that not only may fail to maximize the value of the firm, but may in fact reduce it.

The moral of the story is that the internal rate of return criterion should never be used to evaluate proposed investment opportunities. At its best, the *IRR* rule provides no more information to the decision maker than is available

---

4 The example is taken from Thomas E. Copeland and J. Fred Weston, *Financial Theory and Corporate Policy*, 2E. (Reading, MA: Addison-Wesley, 1983), pp. 33-35.

5 Multiply and divide the first term by $(1 + r)^2$, the second term by $(1 + r)$, and collect all three terms over the common denominator $(1 + r)^2$. Multiplying through by $(1 + r)^2$ and moving everything to the opposite side of the equal sign yields the given expression.

6 The equation to be solved for r is of the form $ax^2 + bx + c = 0$, where a = \$1,600, b = -\$10,000, c = \$10,000, and x = $(1 + r)$. The two roots are found by applying the quadratic formula, x = $[-b + (b^2 - 4ac)^{1/2}]/2a$.

with the computationally simpler *NPV* rule. At its worst, the *IRR* rule is thoroughly misleading and can cause the decision maker to implement a capital project that generates a negative rate of return.

Profitability Index. Although the net present value and the internal rate of return criteria are perhaps the two most widely used investment decision-making rules, other techniques for evaluating proposed capital projects exist. One of these is the so-called **profitability index**, which is defined as the ratio of the present value of a project's future net cash flows to the required initial investment outlay. The profitability index, *PI*, can be expressed as follows:

$$PI = \frac{\sum_{n=1}^{n} \left[\dfrac{NCF_n}{(1+i)^n} \right]}{NINV},$$

where *NINV* is the initial net investment, i is the firm's cost of capital, and N is the terminal date of the project's life.

Under this investment decision rule, a proposed capital project should be accepted if its profitability index is greater than or equal to 1.0 and rejected otherwise. Because it uses the same information as the *NPV* rule, the profitability index will generally lead to the same accept-reject decisions. That is, if the calculated *PI* exceeds 1.0, the project will obviously have a positive net present value.

In the FJS Corporation example, for instance, the present value of the expected future cash flows is $777,110 when discounted at the firm's 10 percent cost of capital (see Table 15.2 or 15.3 on p. 509 and p. 511). With a required investment outlay of $500,000, the project's profitability index is

$$PI = \frac{\$777,110}{\$500,000} = 1.55,$$

and the firm should therefore undertake the investment.

The *PI* rule would likewise lead to the rejection of the oil-pump investment which was shown to have a negative net present value. Specifically, the discounted value of that project's expected future net cash flows is

$$\frac{\$10,000}{(1.1)} - \frac{\$10,000}{(1.1)^2} = \$826.45,$$

which when divided by the $1,600 investment required to purchase the pump yields a profitability index of

$$PI = \frac{\$826.45}{\$1,600} = .52.$$

A note of caution must be raised at this point, however. While the profitability index indeed yields the same accept-reject decisions as the *NPV* rule in evaluating independent investment opportunities, a conflict between the two criteria can arise in the case of **mutually exclusive projects**. Mutually exclusive investment opportunities represent cases in which the acceptance of one project necessarily implies the rejection of the other.

For example, two different types of machines that perform the same manufacturing operation may be available and the firm must decide which of them to purchase. Suppose that machine *A* costs $20,000 and is expected to generate future net cash flows having a present value of $25,000 when discounted at the firm's cost of capital. Machine *B*, on the other hand, costs half as much ($10,000) but the discounted value of its future net cash flows is smaller, say $14,000. Machine *A* has a greater net present value and is therefore preferable to machine *B* on this basis. That is, NPV_A = $25,000 − $20,000 = $5,000, while NPV_B = $14,000 − $10,000 = $4,000. But machine *B*'s profitability index (PI_B = $14,000/$10,000 = 1.4) is greater than that of machine *A* (PI_A = $25,000/$20,000 = 1.25). Consequently, if the decision maker chooses the machine that promises the higher net cash flow per dollar of initial investment, he or she will fail to maximize the value of the firm.

Payback Period. The final investment decision-making criterion we consider here is the **payback period**. This very crude rule of thumb suggests that the firm should evaluate proposed capital projects on the basis of the length of time required for summed future benefits (usually undiscounted) to equal summed costs. For example, the payback period for the FJS Corporation's proposed investment is about 2.5 years because the project's cash inflows equal the $500,000 net investment in the middle of the second year.

The payback period rule is normally applied only in the choice between mutually exclusive projects, in which case the rule dictates that the firm select the investment alternative having the shorter payback period. But while the rule can be defended as a rough and ready way of dealing with uncertainty, its shortcomings should be obvious. The payback period method gives credit to future cash inflows only up to the arbitrary date at which they offset the initial investment—and ignores them completely thereafter. Therefore, this method penalizes projects that have relatively high startup costs or whose benefits begin accruing relatively later. The use of such a rule can therefore easily lead to the selection of the investment having the lowest net present value among the choices being considered. And, indeed, the payback period method can persuade the decision maker to select a project having a negative present value.

In sum, while a variety of methods have been proposed for evaluating investment opportunities, the net present value rule is the only one that is reliably consistent with the goal of maximizing the value of the firm. The *NPV* rule includes in the set of acceptable capital projects all investment opportunities having a positive net present value (or, in the case of mutually exclusive investments, dictates that the firm accept the alternative with the largest net present value). This rule is consistent with the goal of value maximization because it requires the decision maker to discount each investment's expected future net cash flows at a rate of interest equal to the firm's opportunity cost of capital. Implementing the rule consequently requires estimating the firm's cost of capital. This topic is presented in the following section.

The Firm's Cost of Capital

The investment projects undertaken by the firm can be financed with funds raised from three principal sources—monies borrowed from outside lenders such as banks and purchasers of the firm's bonds, equity capital obtained from the sale of stock, and retained earnings. An investment opportunity will therefore be profitable only if the project's anticipated future net cash flows cover the cost of raising these funds. That is, the investment must generate enough cash flow to make the interest payments required by creditors, to retire the face amount of any debt, and to pay the dividends expected by shareholders. Put another way, only when expected net cash flows exceed these required payments will the project increase the value of the firm (shareholders' wealth). Discounting an investment's expected future cash flows at the firm's cost of capital is the mathematical counterpart to this statement. A positive net present value is achieved only after allowance is made for the (risk-adjusted) rates of return expected by creditors and shareholders.

In a world without taxes, uncertainty, flotation costs, or risk of bankruptcy, the financing of acceptable investment projects would be guided by the familiar **equi-marginal principle**. A multi-plant firm allocates production among its facilities so that marginal revenue is equal to marginal cost across sites. Likewise, investment capital would be raised—and the optimal debt-equity ratio would be determined—by equating expected benefits with expected costs across sources of funds. At the margin, all sources of funds would then be equally dear and the firm's overall cost of capital would be the same as the cost of any of its components.

In reality, however, because interest payments to creditors are subject to favorable tax treatment and because these same debt holders receive preferential treatment in the event of bankruptcy, the costs of capital differ across sources of funds. At any point in time, then, the firm's cost of capital will be a weighted average of the costs of the various sources of funds that constitute the firm's capital structure. The rate of interest that is appropriate for discounting the future net cash flows expected to be generated by investment opportunities is the firm's **marginal cost of capital**, or the cost of raising the last dollar's worth of new capital. The marginal cost of capital schedule shows how the weighted average cost of capital changes (increases) as more and more capital is raised. The costs of the two principal components of the firm's overall or weighted average cost of capital are discussed in turn below.

Cost of Debt. Although firms, like individuals, can finance investment projects by securing loans from banks or other financial intermediaries, the sale of bonds is a more usual means of borrowing capital for the typical enterprise. A bond represents the firm's promise to repay the amount borrowed (the bond's **face value**, usually $1,000) at some specified future date (the **maturity date**). Bonds may or may not also promise periodic (annual or semiannual) interest payments (**coupons**) to the purchaser.

The before-tax cost of new debt capital is simply the rate of return the owners of the firm must pay to bondholders in order for them to be willing to lend money to the enterprise. The rate of return required by bondholders, in turn, depends on their own market opportunities. That is to say, creditors will be willing to purchase the firm's debt only if the anticipated risk-adjusted rate of return, or **yield**, on the bond issue is at least as great as the rate of return available on their next best investment opportunity.

Consider a simple **zero-coupon bond** which promises no payments to the holder until the stated maturity date. Such debt instruments are sold at a discount from face value and the difference between the bond's market price and the principal that will be repaid at maturity is the implied amount of interest income the holder will earn on his or her investment. Specifically, the present value or market price of a zero-coupon bond is given by the formula

$$PV = \frac{F}{\left(1+k_d\right)^T},$$

where F is the face value of the bond to be repaid in T years and k_d is the rate of return the holder will earn in each of those T years.

For example, suppose that the firm issues a bond with a face value of $1,000 which it promises to repay five years hence. If the rate of return required by investors, k_d, is 10 percent, then the present value of the bond is

$$PV = \frac{\$1,000}{\left(1.1\right)^5} = \$620.92.$$

Alternatively, if we know the bond's market price, its face value, and its maturity date, we can use this same formula to solve for the rate of return required by debtholders. That is,

$$\left(1+k_d\right)^T = \frac{F}{PV},$$

which when solved using the assumed values of F, PV, and T, yields $k_d = 10\%$.

Thinking about the problem in this way illustrates that the rate of return required by investors is the interest rate that equates the present value of all future payments—in this case the single future repayment of principal—with the offering price of the bond. As a first approximation,[7] then, the cost of debt capital to the firm is equal to k_d because this is the rate of interest it must pay for the use of the borrowed funds. Any proposed investment opportunity which the firm considers implementing under these circumstances must promise to yield a rate of return of 10 percent or more, for only then will the project's earnings be sufficient to repay its debt.

The same principles apply to coupon bonds which promise periodic interest payments to creditors in addition to repayment of the face amount at maturity. The present value of a coupon bond is

$$PV = \sum_{n=1}^{T} \left[\frac{C}{\left(1+k_d\right)^T} \right] + \frac{F}{\left(1+k_d\right)^T},$$

where C denotes the annual interest payments in dollars and the other variables are defined as above. That is, the present value of a coupon bond is equal to the discounted value of the stream of anticipated future interest payments plus the discounted value of the principal to be repaid in T years.

As before, k_d is the rate of return required by investors, or the interest rate that equates the discounted value of all expected future receipts—coupon payments plus repayment of principal—with the bond's market price. If PV, C, F, and T are known, we can compute k_d using the method of trial and error or a friendly financial calculator. Notice, though, that if the coupon rate is set equal to the market-determined rate of return required by investors, the firm can sell the bond at par (or close to it, allowance being made for the costs of floating the issue).

For example, consider a *ten* of December 1999 offered in December 1994. This jargon means that the bond's coupon rate is ten percent of face value and that the principal will be repaid at a maturity date five years in the future. If the face value of the security is $1,000 and the purchaser will therefore receive annual interest payments of $100 ($C = .10 \times \$1,000$), the bond's present value or market price is

$$PV = \sum_{n=1}^{5} \left[\frac{\$100}{\left(1.1\right)^n} \right] + \frac{\$1,000}{\left(1.1\right)^5} = \$379.08 + \$620.92 = \$1,000.00.$$

The cost of debt capital to the firm will be less than the coupon rate of k_d, however. This is because interest payments to creditors are a deductible expense for corporate income tax purposes. Hence, the *after-tax* cost of debt capital, k_d', is

$$k_d' = (1 - t)k_d,$$

---

7 Ignoring the tax and risk factors discussed below.

where t is the marginal corporate income tax rate. So if the rate of return required by investors is 10 percent, the after-tax cost of debt capital to a firm in the 40 percent marginal corporate income tax bracket is $k_d' = (1 - .4).1 = .06$ or six percent.

Risk premiums. A complication is introduced by noting that a bond represents a *promise* to pay investors a specified rate of return, and promises cannot always be kept. As long as there is some probability that the firm will default (i.e., be unable to make the promised payments of interest and principal), the rate of return creditors expect to receive will be less than the bond's promised yield.

For example, consider a one-year, 10 percent coupon bond issued at par of $1,000. The security has a promised yield of 10 percent if there is no risk of default. However, if we assume that there is a one in twenty chance that the firm will not be able to meet its obligations to bondholders at the end of the year and that, in the event default occurs, creditors will only be able to recover half of their original investment, the expected future value of the bond is

$$.95 (\$1,100) + .05 (\$500) = \$1,070.$$

In other words, there is a 95 percent chance that the firm will repay the principal plus interest when the bond matures one year hence and a 5 percent chance that creditors will only get $500 when the firm's assets are liquidated at their then-prevailing market price. The expected rate of return is consequently

$$\left(\frac{\$1,070}{\$1,000} \right) - 1 = .07,$$

and so the before-tax cost of issuing the bond at par is 7 percent, not 10 percent.

Of course, if default is a possibility and creditors have an alternative investment opportunity that promises a 10 percent rate of return with no default risk, the firm will not be able to issue its 10 percent coupon bond at par. Given that the rate of return required by investors is 10 percent, the present value or market price of a one-year security with expected proceeds of $1,070 at maturity is

$$PV = \frac{\$1,070}{1.1} = \$972.73.$$

This discount from par can be interpreted as the compensation required for creditors to be indifferent between lending capital to a firm that faces the default risk assumed in the previous paragraph and investing in a risk-free alternative promising a 10 percent rate of return.

The **risk premium** that the firm in the above example must pay can be incorporated explicitly into its cost of debt capital by noting that the one-year bond can still be issued at par, but only if the coupon rate is adjusted upward to reflect the assumed probability of default. That is, in order for investors to be willing to lend capital to an enterprise that may default on its obligations, the firm must promise a coupon payment that is sufficient to compensate them for the additional risk they assume in purchasing the firm's bonds rather than investing in the available risk-free alternative. The required interest payment can be found by solving

$$.95(\$1,000 + C) + .05(\$500) = \$1,100$$

for C, the coupon payment in dollars that yields expected proceeds at maturity equal to \$1,100. The required coupon payment is \$131.58 and the required coupon rate is therefore approximately 13.2 percent.

This risk-adjusted rate of return is the firm's before-tax cost of debt capital. It includes a risk premium of 3.2 percentage points which, when added to the rate of return required by creditors on risk-free investments, just compensates them for the additional risk they assume in lending capital to the hypothetical firm. Despite the complications introduced by considering default risk, it is nevertheless true that the promised yield on a bond serves as a practical measure of the before-tax cost of debt capital to the firm. This conclusion follows because, as has just been shown, the coupon payment will adjust to reflect differences in the perceived risk of default. The after-tax cost of debt capital is then simply the risk-adjusted rate of return times $(1 - t)$, where t is again the relevant marginal corporate income tax rate.

Cost of Equity. Equity is a second source of capital for financing the firm's proposed investment projects. It can be raised externally through the sale of new common stock which gives the purchaser a proportional ownership interest in the enterprise. Or it can be raised internally by earmarking a portion of the firm's retained earnings for investment purposes. As in the case of debt capital, the cost of raising equity capital is equal to the rate of return the firm must pay to shareholders in order for them to be willing to invest in the enterprise.

Dividend-valuation model. The dividend-valuation model offers one way of estimating the firm's cost of equity capital. This model begins by observing that the value of an equity position in a firm equals the present value of the expected future returns to stock ownership discounted at the shareholder's required rate of return, k_e.[8] These expected returns consist of the after-tax cash flows paid out by the firm in the form of dividends and any future change (capital gain or loss) in the market value of the stock.

To the shareholder who intends to hold stock indefinitely, the present value of an ownership position in the firm (shareholder's wealth) is given by the formula

---

8 For simplicity, the fact that dividend payments are taxed at the shareholder's marginal personal income tax rate is ignored.

$$PV = \sum_{n=1}^{\infty} \left[\frac{D_n}{(1+k_e)^n} \right],$$

where D_n is the dollar value of the dividend expected to be received in period n and k_e is the investor's required rate of return. On the other hand, suppose that the shareholder intends to sell the stock after holding it for T periods. The present value of an equity claim under these conditions consists of the discounted value of the expected dividend stream until period T plus the discounted value of proceeds when the stock is sold; that is,

$$PV = \sum_{n=1}^{T} \left[\frac{D_n}{(1+k_e)^n} \right] + \frac{M_T}{(1+k_e)^T},$$

where M_T is the market value of the stock when sold in period T.

But the market value of the stock in period T is equal to the discounted value of the dividend payments expected from that time forward. That is, we can write

$$M_T = \sum_{n=T+1}^{\infty} \left[\frac{D_n}{(1+k_e)^{n-T}} \right].$$

Substituting this expression for M_T into the previous relationship yields

$$PV = \sum_{n=1}^{T} \left[\frac{D_n}{(1+k_e)^n} \right] + \sum_{n=T+1}^{\infty} \left[\frac{D_n}{(1+k_e)^{n-T}} \right]$$

$$= \sum_{n=1}^{\infty} \left[\frac{D_n}{(1+k_e)^n} \right].$$

In other words, the present value of a stock is the same whether the investor holds it forever or for only a finite number of periods. Shareholders' wealth is therefore the present value of the stream of future cash dividend payments in perpetuity, discounted at the rate of return required by the owners of the firm.

Gordon's growth model. The foregoing result implies that the expected growth rate in dividend payments is an important factor in the determination of shareholder's wealth. Myron Gordon has shown that if the dividends paid out by the firm are expected to grow forever at a constant compound rate of g percent per year, then the present value of the firm can be written as

$$PV = \frac{D_1}{\left(k_e - g\right)},$$

where D_1 is the total dividend payment in period 1.[9]

Alternatively, if D_1 is expressed as the dividend payment per share of stock, then PV is the market price per share and the **Gordon growth model** can be rewritten as

$$k_e = \left(\frac{D_1}{PV}\right) + g.$$

This formula provides a convenient method of estimating the rate of return required by shareholders and, hence, the cost of internal equity capital to the firm. (The cost of external equity capital is then k_e plus whatever costs are involved in floating a new stock issue.) Just as in the case of bonds, the rate of return required by shareholders, k_e, is the rate of interest that equates the discounted value of the stream of expected future returns—dividend payments—with the market price of the security.

According to the Gordon growth model, the rate of return required by the owners of the firm is equal to the ratio of this year's dividend payment per share to the market price of the firm's common stock,[10] plus the expected future growth rate in dividend payments. For example, suppose we check the pages of the *Wall Street Journal* and find that the current price for a share of IBM's common stock is $99 and that the annualized dividend based on the most recent quarterly payment is $4.84. Then if IBM's dividend per share is expected to grow perpetually at an annual rate of 4 percent, as a first approximation the firm's cost of equity capital is

$$k_e = \left(\frac{\$4.84}{\$99}\right) + .04 = .089,$$

or 8.9 percent.

Weighted Average Cost of Capital. As mentioned previously, the firm's overall cost of capital is a weighted average of the costs of debt and equity. Specifically, the **weighted average cost of capital**, k_a, is

$$k_a = w_d k_d (1 - t) + w_e k_e,$$

where k_d is the before-tax rate of return required by bondholders, k_e is the rate of return required by shareholders, t is the marginal corporate income tax rate, and w_d and w_e are weights representing the relative proportions of debt and equity in the firm's capital structure, with $0 < w_d, w_e < 1$ and $w_d + w_e = 1$.

---

9 See Myron J. Gordon, *The Investment, Financing and Valuation of the Corporation* (Homewood, IL: Richard D. Irwin, 1962).

10 The ratio of the annualized dividend payment per share to the stock's market price is known as the *yield* and reported as such in the *Wall Street Journal*'s financial pages.

Two basic methods are used for determining the appropriate weights for estimating the firm's overall cost of capital—historical weights and "target" weights. The debate about which of the two methods is more correct has not yet been resolved, because no satisfactory theory of the optimal capital structure of the firm has emerged. However, firms seem to behave as if an optimal debt-equity ratio exists.

Historical weights are based on the firm's existing capital structure. The use of such a weighting scheme rests on the assumption that the firm's present capital structure is optimal and should therefore be maintained in the future. Historical weights are computed by determining the *market* values of the firm's outstanding debt and equity, and then expressing each as a fraction of their total.[11] That is, the market value of debt, B, is simply the number of bonds outstanding times their current market price. (If more than one class of debt has been issued, this valuation procedure is followed for each and the results are then summed.) Similarly, the market value of equity, S, is the number of shares of common stock outstanding times the stock's current market price. The total market value of the firm is then $B + S$, and $w_d = B/(B + S)$ and $w_e = S/(B + S)$ are the percentages of the market value of the firm held by creditors and shareholders, respectively.

Target weights are appropriate if the capital structure considered to be optimal differs from the present structure. For example, suppose that the firm's existing capital structure (market value weights) consists of 25 percent debt and 75 percent equity. If the company intends to raise funds in the future with the goal of increasing the percentage of the market value of the firm owned by creditors to 30 percent, then a weighting scheme consistent with this objective is warranted. The weights for computing the overall cost of capital in this case would be $w_d = .3$ and $w_e = .7$.

Once weights are determined by one of these two methods, the firm's weighted average cost of capital can be computed. To illustrate, suppose that the firm's present (and target) capital structure contains 25 percent debt and 75 percent equity. Further assume that the firm is in the 40 percent marginal corporate income tax bracket, that the before-tax rate of return required by bondholders is 10 percent, and that shareholders require a 9 percent rate of return. Given these assumptions, the company's weighted average cost of capital is

$$k_a = .25(.1)(1 - .4) + .75(.09) = .0825,$$

or 8.25 percent.

At any point in time, the weighted average cost of capital is the appropriate interest rate for discounting the anticipated future net cash flows for *all* of the firm's proposed investment projects, including those that will be

---

11   The use of book or par values to compute historical weights should be avoided because the purpose of calculating the firm's cost of capital is to estimate what the firm *expects* to pay out to bondholders and shareholders for every additional dollar of capital it raises from them. Book values are therefore irrelevant except, perhaps, in the case of short-term debt where market value and book value rarely differ significantly.

financed with only one source of funds. This is because any proposed capital project will be profitable only if it will generate enough cash flow to make interest payments to creditors, to retire the face amount of the debt, and to pay the dividends expected by shareholders.

In other words, the firm may decide to finance an investment entirely by floating a new bond issue which, because of the tax shield provided by interest payments to creditors, may allow capital to be raised at a lower cost than would be incurred in selling an equivalent amount of equity. But the project will not be worthwhile unless its anticipated earnings are sufficient to pay the rate of return required by shareholders as well as the rate of return required by bondholders.[12] Just as the firm cannot evaluate the net cash flows to any proposed capital project in isolation from the cash flows of its other investments, the financing arrangements for any one project cannot be considered in isolation from the firm's overall capital structure.

The Capital Asset Pricing Model

The **capital asset pricing model** (CAPM) offers an alternative method of quantifying the firm's cost of capital. Applied to equity capital, the CAPM is concerned with the tradeoff between the expected returns to stock ownership and risk rather than with the expected growth rate in the firm's dividend payments to shareholders. The theory suggests that the rate of return required by a firm's shareholders is equal to a hypothetical risk-free rate, r_f, plus a premium that compensates them for the risk they assume by investing in that particular company. This risk premium varies from firm to firm and depends on the variability of the expected returns to owning a particular stock. The CAPM estimates the cost of equity capital by measuring the variability in returns to an individual company's stock relative to the variability in returns to holding a broad portfolio of equity investments.

The key to understanding the capital asset pricing model is the idea that the variability in the expected returns to stock ownership can be separated into two components. One component is the variability of returns that is unique to a particular security. In the model's jargon, this is *unsystematic* or **diversifiable risk**. Unsystematic risk is the variability in the expected returns to owning stock in a specific company. It is related to such factors as differential management skills and to events like strikes, natural disasters, or changes in demand that affect the fortunes of that firm only. The second source of variability in the expected returns to stock ownership is the variability of returns that is common to all securities. This is *systematic* or **nondiversifiable risk**. Systematic risk is caused by events like changes in interest rates or economy-wide contractions or expansions that affect all firms equally.

---

12 Hence, the practice of using *marginal weights* in calculating the firm's cost of capital, that is, weighting the costs of debt and equity by the actual dollar amounts of each source of funds to be raised for a given investment project, should be avoided.

For a particular security, systematic risk is the proportion of the total variability in expected returns that can be explained by the variability in expected returns to a well-diversified portfolio of stocks. It is measured by the covariance of the individual security's returns with the returns to some broad market index like the Standard & Poor's 500 or the New York Stock Exchange Index. Unsystematic risk is the proportion of the variation in the individual stock's returns that cannot be explained in this way. Clearly, only the former component of risk is of concern to investors. Systematic risk is, by definition, inescapable. By contrast, unsystematic risk, or the risk that is unique to the particular security, can be diversified away by holding a sufficiently broad investment portfolio.[13] Hence, a security's contribution to systematic (nondiversifiable) risk determines the rate of return investors require to hold it.

Beta. The CAPM estimates the firm's cost of equity capital by calculating the rate of return required by shareholders, k_e, in the following way:

$$k_e = r_f + \beta (r_m - r_f),$$

where r_f is the risk-free rate of return and r_m is the expected rate of return on a well-diversified portfolio of stocks. The coefficient beta (β) is a measure of the security's systematic risk.

Beta is computed by estimating the covariance of the stock's expected returns with the returns to the stock market as a whole.[14] Stocks whose prices vary with the market perfectly have betas equal to 1.0. Put differently, all of the variation in the expected returns to a stock whose beta is 1.0 can be explained by variations in the returns to a well-diversified portfolio of securities. All of the risk of holding such a stock is nondiversifiable, systematic risk. On the other hand, stocks whose prices vary more than the market as a whole have betas greater than 1.0, and stocks whose prices vary less than the market as a whole have betas smaller than 1.0.

The term $(r_m - r_f)$ measures the excess returns received by investing in a well-diversified portfolio of common stocks rather than some riskless alternative asset. The risk-free rate, which is by definition the rate of return on a security having a zero beta, is normally taken to be the annual yield on short-term U.S. government obligations, say three-month U.S. Treasury bills. Therefore, we can think of the amount by which the rate of return on the average common stock exceeds the risk-free rate as the risk premium individuals require on stock market investments. Although the magnitude of this risk premium varies over time, historical figures indicate that the annual rate of return on three-month U.S. Treasury bills averages about 3.5 percent.

---

13 See Chapter 14's discussion of the risk-reducing properties of portfolio diversification in the context of the conglomerate enterprise.

14 More specifically, beta is the estimated slope of the straight line obtained by regressing a particular stock's returns on the corresponding returns for the market as a whole, both variables measured as percentage changes.

By contrast, an individual who invested in a portfolio of securities based on the Standard & Poor's composite index of 500 common stocks and held that portfolio from 1926 to 1988, reinvesting all dividends, would have earned a 12 percent annual rate of return.[15] The historical average market risk premium is consequently $r_m - r_f = 12 - 3.5 = 8.5$ percent.

The average common stock in a well-diversified portfolio has a beta of 1.0. Thus, according to the capital asset pricing model, the rate of return required by investors in that stock is the market rate of return, r_m. That is, substituting the historical figures from the previous paragraph,

$$k_e = .035 + 1(.12 - .035) = .12,$$

or 12 percent. On the other hand, individuals require a rate of return higher than r_m to invest in stocks whose prices vary more than the market as a whole. For example, the required rate of return for a stock with a beta of 1.5 is

$$k_e = .035 + 1.5(.12 - .035) = .1625,$$

or 16.25 percent. And if beta is less than 1.0, the required rate of return will obviously be less than r_m.

The Security Market Line. The CAPM implies that there is a linear relationship between a firm's cost of equity capital (investors' required rate of return) and the systematic risk characteristics of the company's stock. Figure 15.1 illustrates this relationship. The **security market line** (*SML*) shows that the expected return for all stocks in the market is increasing in beta (risk). Its vertical intercept is the risk-free rate of return, r_f, because β = 0 for such an asset. The required rate of return on any particular security will then be greater or less than the market rate of return as the stock's beta is greater or less than 1.0.

It is worth emphasizing that all stocks must lie on the security market line in equilibrium. To see this, consider security A in Figure 15.1 which has a beta less than 1.0 and whose expected rate of return, r_A, is currently greater than the rate of return implied by the capital asset pricing model. The stock is a "bargain" in the sense that it offers a rate of return above that required to compensate investors for the security's contribution to systematic risk. Individuals will accordingly want to take advantage of these supernormal returns by purchasing the stock. In the process, the market price of the stock will be bid up until its expected returns have fallen to the level indicated by the *SML*.

The security market line is an extremely useful concept because it can also be used to evaluate proposed investment projects of differing risk. For

15 See R. G. Ibbotson and R. A. Sinquefield, *Stocks, Bonds, Bills and Inflation* (Charlottesville, VA: Financial Analysts Research Foundation, 1982). Updated in *SBBI Quarterly Market Reports* (Chicago: Ibbotson Associates, various years).

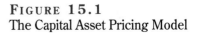

FIGURE 15.1
The Capital Asset Pricing Model

example, suppose that the beta for the firm as a whole is equal to 1.0 so that the company's overall cost of capital is equal to r_m. Further assume that the firm is entirely equity financed so that the cost of debt capital can be ignored. Now let stock A in the previous paragraph be project A—a proposed investment opportunity for the hypothetical firm that is less risky than the company's other investments. Because the project's expected rate of return is less than the firm's overall cost of equity capital, it might be tempting to conclude that the investment proposal is unacceptable. Such a conclusion would be wrong, however. As indicated by the SML, the project's expected rate of return is greater than the rate of return required by the market for an investment of equivalent systematic risk. Hence, the firm should undertake project A. Indeed, for similar reasons, the firm should accept any investment proposal that lies above the security market line (and reject any proposal that lies below it).

ADVANCED TOPICS IN CAPITAL BUDGETING

The previous section has provided an overview of the basics of capital budgeting. To develop a capital budgeting plan consistent with the goal of maximizing shareholder wealth, the firm estimates the incremental, after-tax net cash flows for each alternative investment opportunity, discounting the various streams of anticipated future net cash flows at the firm's weighted average cost of capital, and then identifies the set of proposed investments having a positive net present value. However, it would be misleading to conclude that these steps yield cut-and-dried solutions to the firm's capital budgeting problems. Capital budgeting is complex and the theory on which it is based is still evolving. There is, for example, no generally accepted theory of the optimal capital structure of the firm. Nor do financial economists fully understand why firms pay dividends to shareholders. But the modern theory of finance helps shed light on these puzzles.

Optimal Leverage

Capital budgeting decisions and capital structure decisions are interrelated. When a firm chooses the sources of funds it will tap to finance a proposed investment project, it is implicitly making a decision about the proportions of debt and equity that will comprise its capital structure. The capital structure of the firm, in turn, determines the enterprise's overall cost of capital. Understanding the forces that shape the firm's capital structure is therefore one of the most fundamental objectives of modern financial economies.

Generally speaking, it would seem that the firm is free to choose any capital structure it wants. That is, the value of the firm, V, is normally defined as the sum of the market values of the outstanding debt, B, and equity, S:

$$V = B + S.$$

The proportions in which these claims are issued—the firm's debt-equity ratio—would seem to be of little consequence.

Indeed, one of the seminal contributions to the modern theory of corporate finance suggests that under certain simplifying assumptions the capital structure of the firm is irrelevant. This important proposition, which is due to Nobel laureates Franco Modigliani and Merton Miller,[16] implies that in a world with no taxes, no bankruptcy costs, and "perfect" capital markets, the value of the firm is independent of its capital structure.

The Irrelevance of Capital Structure. Consider two firms that are identical except for differing capital structures. Firm E is entirely equity financed. The market value of this firm's shares is $1,000, which is the same as the market value of its assets (i.e., $V_E = S_E$). Firm L, on the other hand, is leveraged. It has issued $500 worth of debt in addition to common stock whose value is yet to be determined. The total market value of the leveraged firm is $V_L = B_L + S_L$. The Modigliani-Miller proposition requires showing that $V_E = V_L$.

First, suppose that an investor is considering purchasing 10 percent of the equity of firm E. He or she would pay $.10S_E = .10V_E = .10(\$1,000) = \$100$ and in return would expect to receive 10 percent of the firm's anticipated future profits, π^e, where the e superscript denotes the *expected* value of the future stream of uncertain profits. Alternatively, the investor could purchase the same fraction of firm L's equity. Doing so would require an investment of $.10S_L = .10(V_L - B_L)$ dollars. Assuming that the firm's cost of debt capital, k_d, is 10 percent and that its expected profits are the same as those of its unleveraged counterpart, the expected dollar return from this alternative investment strategy is $.10(\pi^e - k_d B_L) = .10(\pi^e - \$5)$, or 10 percent of firm L's expected profits net of interest payments to its bondholders.

These two investments are not directly comparable (investing in the equity of the leveraged company requires a smaller initial outlay, but it also generates a lower expected return). However, there is a third strategy available to the investor that can be shown to be equivalent to the second alternative. This third strategy is for the investor to borrow a portion of the funds necessary to purchase 10 percent of the unleveraged firm's equity.

More specifically, suppose that the investor borrows $.10B_L = \$50$ at an interest rate of $k_d = 10\%$. (The ability of the individual investor to borrow at the same interest rate as the firm is a critical assumption in this example; it is part of what is meant by Modigliani and Miller's assumption of "perfect" capital markets.) The investor then uses the loan proceeds plus $50 of his or her own funds to purchase $.10S_E = .10V_E$. The transaction thus requires a net investment of $.10(V_E - B_L)$ dollars, in return for which the investor expects a return of $.10(\pi^e - k_d B_L)$, or 10 percent of firm E's expected profits net of his

---

[16] Franco Modigliani and Merton H. Miller, "The Cost of Capital, Corporation Finance and the Theory of Investment," *American Economic Review* 48 (June 1958), pp. 261-97.

or her interest payments on the loan. Compared to the first strategy of investing $100 to purchase 10 percent of firm E's equity, this third option requires a smaller initial outlay, but it also generates a lower expected return.

Modigliani and Miller's proposition is demonstrated by noting that the expected dollar returns to the second and third investment strategies are identical. In one case, the investor buys 10 percent of the leveraged firm's equity and receives $.10(\pi^e - k_d B_L)$ in income as a cash dividend. In the other case, the investor purchases 10 percent of the all-equity firm, receives a cash dividend of $.10\pi^e$, and pays out $.10k_d B_L$ in interest. The investor's net income is consequently $.10(\pi^e - k_d B_L)$.

Because the dollar returns on the two investment strategies are the same, it follows that the costs of the two strategies must also be the same; that is,

$$.10(V_L - B_L) = .10(V_E - B_L).$$

This equality holds when $V_L = V_E$, which proves that the market value of the leveraged firm, firm L, is identical to the market value of the all-equity firm, firm E. It must therefore be the case that the unknown value of firm L's equity, S_L, is $500. That is, if $V_L = V_E = S_E = $1,000$ and $B_L = 500, then $S_L = V_L - B_L = $1,000 - $500 = 500.

The Modigliani-Miller capital structure irrelevance proposition is intuitively appealing. As long as individuals can borrow funds at the same interest rate as firms, they can use "homemade leverage" to duplicate the effects of corporate debt, thereby assuring that the market values of otherwise identical firms are independent of the firms' financial structures. Suppose that the proposition did not hold; that is, assume that the market value of a leveraged firm is greater than the market value of an otherwise identical all-equity firm. Rational investors will then simply borrow on their own personal accounts to buy the equity of the unleveraged company. They will do so because they can receive the same dollar return by investing in the all-equity firm as they would by investing in the leveraged firm— and they can obtain this same dollar return at a lower total cost.[17] Such transactions will cause the market value of the unleveraged firm to rise and that of the leveraged firm to fall until the market values of the two firms are equal.

Leverage and Shareholders' Risk. If the market value of the firm is independent of its capital structure, then its overall cost of capital is also unaffected by changing the mix of debt and equity. One way of seeing this result is to consider the impact of leverage on the systematic risk borne by the firm's shareholders. As with any investment portfolio, the beta of the firm is equal to the weighted average of the betas of its outstanding debt and equity. In particular,

---

17 Because $V_L > V_E$ by assumption, the market price of the leveraged firm's shares is higher than the market price of the shares of the unleveraged firm.

$$\beta_{Firm} = \left[\frac{B}{(B+S)}\right]\beta_{Debt} + \left[\frac{S}{(B+S)}\right]\beta_{Equity}.$$

The beta associated with debt is ordinarily very low, however, and, in fact, is commonly assumed to be zero. If this is indeed the case, then

$$\beta_{Firm} = \left[\frac{S}{(B+S)}\right]\beta_{Equity}.$$

Now compare the betas of two firms that differ only in terms of their capital structures. For a leveraged firm, firm L,

$$\beta^L_{Firm} = \left[\frac{S}{(B+S)}\right]\beta^L_{Equity}.$$

where β^L_{Equity} is the systematic risk associated with the equity of the leveraged firm. For its hypothetical all-equity counterpart, firm E,

$$\beta^E_{Firm} = \beta^E_{Equity},$$

where β^E_{Equity} is the systematic risk associated with the unleveraged firm's equity.

If these two firms are otherwise identical, that is, if their expected profits are the same, then their betas must be the same, *viz.*

$$\beta^L_{Firm} = \beta^E_{Firm},$$

which implies that

$$\left[\frac{S}{(B+S)}\right]\beta^L_{Equity} = \beta^E_{Equity}.$$

Given that $[S/(B+S)] < 1$ for the leveraged firm, this equality holds only if $\beta^L_{Equity} > \beta^E_{Equity}$. In other words, the beta of the equity of the leveraged firm must be greater than the beta of the equity of the unleveraged firm.

Leverage increases shareholders' risk. But given that the overall beta of the firm remains constant, the increase in the beta of equity must be proportional to the increase in the fraction of debt in the firm's capital structure. For example, suppose that the betas of an all-equity firm and an otherwise identical leveraged firm are both equal to 1.0. The analysis in the previous paragraph implies that the beta of the unleveraged firm's equity is also equal to 1.0. Consequently, if the leveraged firm's capital structure consists of 50 percent debt and 50 percent equity (i.e., $[S/(B+S)] = .5$), then the beta of the equity of that firm must be 2.0 so that $[S/(B+S)]\beta^L_{Equity} = \beta^E_{Equity}$ continues to hold.

Moreover, because the capital asset pricing model indicates that the firm's cost of equity capital increases with beta, the rate of return required by shareholders rises as the firm issues more debt. Earlier in this chapter, the firm's weighted average cost of capital, k_a, is defined as

$$k_a = \left[\frac{B}{(B+S)}\right]k_d + \left[\frac{B}{(B+S)}\right]k_e,$$

where k_d is the cost of debt capital and k_e is the cost of equity capital.[18] A simple rearrangement of this expression yields

$$k_e = k_a + \left(\frac{B}{S}\right)(k_a - k_d).$$

Because leverage does not affect the value of the firm, the overall cost of capital does not change with changes in the firm's debt-equity ratio, B/S. If $k_a > k_d$ (as it normally would be, given that even unleveraged equity is risky) and if k_d is constant,[19] then k_e rises linearly as the firm's debt-equity ratio rises. The increase in the rate of return required by shareholders (the firm's cost of equity capital) will again be proportional to the increase in the debt-equity ratio so that the firm's overall cost of capital remains constant.

This important implication of the Modigliani-Miller model is illustrated in Figure 15.2, which shows the firm's cost of capital as a function of its capital structure (debt-equity ratio). As the firm issues more debt, each dollar's worth of equity is leveraged with additional borrowings. This increased leverage raises the risk associated with equity and, hence, increases the rate of return required by shareholders. However, because leverage has no impact on the value of the firm, the weighted average cost of capital, k_a, remains constant.

Modigliani and Miller subsequently extended their model to incorporate the effects of corporate taxes on the value of the firm.[20] Using reasoning similar to that outlined above, and continuing to assume perfect capital markets and no bankruptcy costs, they established that

$$V_L = V_E + tB_L.$$

In other words, the values of a hypothetical all-equity firm and an otherwise identical leveraged firm differ by the value of the tax shield afforded by corporate debt, tB_L, where t is the marginal corporate income tax rate and B_L is the market value of the leveraged firm's outstanding debt obligations.

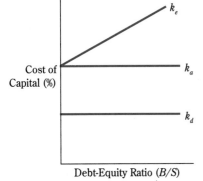

FIGURE 15.2

Capital Structure and the Cost of Capital

18 No distinction is made here between the before- and after-tax cost of debt because the Modigliani-Miller model assumes that corporate income taxes do not exist.

19 The assumption of a constant cost of debt capital is plausible in a world with zero bankruptcy costs because no one firm's borrowings will ever be large enough to affect the market-determined rate of return on debt.

20 Franco Modigliani and Merton H. Miller, "Corporate Income Taxes and the Cost of Capital," *American Economic Review* 53 (June 1963), pp. 433-43.

The intuition here is straightforward. Because interest payments to bondholders are deductible under the corporate income tax code, the after-tax net cash flows of a leveraged firm are higher than the after-tax net cash flows of an otherwise identical all-equity firm. Debt financing consequently raises the expected earnings of the firm's owners (shareholders) and these higher expected earnings, in turn, lead to an increase in the market price of the firm's shares. Because the market value of the leveraged firm's equity increases, the overall value of the firm rises. Given perfect capital markets, the increase in S_L (and V_L) will be exactly equal to tB_L—stockholders will capture the full value of the corporate debt tax shield.

Hence, the deductibility of interest payments to bondholders provided by the corporate income tax code supplies an incentive for the firm to take on more debt than it would otherwise. Indeed, when extended to a world in which corporate income is taxed, the basic Modigliani-Miller result suggests that because the value of the firm increases linearly with leverage, firms should have a capital structure composed almost entirely of debt.

However, both implications of the work of Modigliani and Miller seem inconsistent with observations of the real world. Given the regularities in the debt-equity ratios observed both within and across industries, capital structure does not seem to be random. Nor do most firms choose a financial structure composed almost entirely of debt. Firms, in other words, seem to operate as if there is an optimal capital structure that contains both debt and equity. Two possible explanations for the existence of such an optimal capital structure are discussed below.

Bankruptcy Costs. Bankruptcy costs represent one possible justification for the existence of an optimal capital structure for the firm. As the enterprise takes on more debt, the risk of bankruptcy increases. That is, with higher leverage, scenarios in which the firm's expected net cash flows are insufficient to meet scheduled interest payments to creditors or to retire the face amounts of maturing debt obligations become more likely. Of course, bondholders know that increased leverage increases default risk and, as was demonstrated earlier in the chapter, the rate of return they require rises as the probability of default rises. This increased cost of debt raises the firm's overall cost of capital. But because creditors are thereby compensated for the additional risk they assume, it is not default risk per se that limits the firm's use of debt financing. Instead, limits to the use of debt financing are imposed by the costs that *shareholders* will bear should bankruptcy occur.

The costs of bankruptcy fall into two basic categories. One category consists of the direct costs the bankrupt firm will incur. Trustee fees, legal fees, and other expenses of reorganization or bankruptcy are deducted from the market value of the bankrupt firm's assets and from the proceeds that will be received by bondholders and other creditors. These direct costs of bankruptcy cause the value of the firm in bankruptcy to be less than its value as a going concern.

The indirect costs of bankruptcy further reduce the value of the firm. As the probability of bankruptcy rises, the firm's ability to compete on equal terms with its less-likely-to-fail business rivals may be impaired. For example, sales may be lost if customers fear that the firm will be unable to honor future service commitments. Similarly, firms facing greater chances of bankruptcy must pay higher wages to attract workers away from more secure enterprises, suppliers will demand higher prices and more frequent payments when selling to firms more likely to fail, and so on. These direct and indirect costs of bankruptcy will be reflected in the market price of the firm's equity. And beyond a certain point, further increases in leverage will cause the overall value of the firm to fall.

The observation that bankruptcy costs eventually offset the tax advantages of leverage suggests that the optimal capital structure of the firm will not be composed entirely of debt. In other words, the value of the firm is maximized by choosing a capital structure that contains both debt and equity. Whether or not bankruptcy costs are in fact sizable enough to explain the existence of an optimal capital structure is an empirical question. The jury still seems to be out at this point.

A Principal-Agent Explanation of Capital Structure. We can gain further insights into the optimal capital structure problem by relaxing the assumption of perfect capital markets and by thinking about the financial structure of the firm in terms of the principal-agent relationships that exist between owners (shareholders) and managers on the one hand, and between creditors (bondholders) and shareholders on the other.[21] Suppose, for example, that individuals who supply capital to the firm have no ownership rights. In other words, assume that the firm borrows 100 percent of its capital in the bond market, with the owners of the enterprise investing no funds themselves.

In principle, such a financial structure would be feasible if the owners (and the managers to whom they delegate authority to control the firm's day-to-day operations) could be constrained by the terms of the loan contract to invest the borrowed funds only in the most profitable capital projects and to pay themselves only a specified, "reasonable" rate of compensation until the loan has been repaid. Such restrictions on the uses of borrowed funds are known as **indenture covenants** and are quite common.[22]

In practice, however, it would be impossible (prohibitively costly) to write an "airtight" contract fully protecting bondholders' interests given the superior information available to owners and managers about the firm's

---

21 The basics of principal-agent theory are outlined in Chapter 7. The following discussion is based partly on Henry B. Hansmann, "Ownership of the Firm," *Journal of Law, Economics, and Organization* 4 (Fall 1988), pp. 267-304.

22 Bond convenants do such things as require that all new debt be subordinate to existing debt (i.e., be assigned a lower payoff priority), place limits on dividend payments to shareholders, constrain merger activity, and restrict management's production or investment policies. For concrete examples taken from one firm's experience, see Bryan Burrough and John Heylar, *Barbarians at the Gate: The Fall of RJR Nabisco* (New York: Harper & Row, 1990).

future prospects. The owners and managers of the firm would therefore have a strong incentive to exploit their informational advantage by, for example, paying out large dividends or by undertaking investment projects whose gains accrue disproportionately to themselves and whose losses fall disproportionately on the lenders. Such incentives are magnified in cases where the borrowed funds are secured by highly specialized physical assets. Because they become locked into the creditor relationship to a significant degree, bondholders cannot withdraw their capital if the owners and managers of the firm behave opportunistically.

Such considerations help explain "why the owners of the firm (the residual claimants) are generally also the major capitalists of the firm."[23] Taking an equity position (investing capital) in the enterprise is equivalent to posting a bond that helps assure lenders that the owners will not engage in opportunistic behavior of the sort described in the previous paragraph. In other words, the owners' incentives to undertake actions that lower the value of the firm decrease when a portion of their own wealth is at stake. Merging the interests of owners and capitalists consequently helps reduce a cost of transacting between owners and lenders that would exist if their relationship were instead governed by simple market contracting.

This is not to say that transaction costs will be minimized if the firm's owners are its sole source of capital. It is also true that the owners themselves may not be in the best position to evaluate the investment decisions of management. If the individuals who specialize in lending capital to business enterprises are better able to assess the financial prospects of firms than is the typical stockholder, then some participation in the bond market helps reduce owners' costs of monitoring the performance of their manager-agents. Managers, in turn, have an incentive to borrow funds externally as a *signal* of their willingness to subject themselves to the scrutiny of lenders. Moreover, lenders are more likely to be willing to invest in the enterprise, or to lend on more favorable terms, when its owners provide some guarantee against opportunistic behavior by supplying a portion of the firm's capital themselves.

These considerations suggest that ownership and lending play important, complementary roles that serve to increase the value of the firm by reducing the agency costs that accompany the separation of ownership from control in the modern corporation. Put another way, there is a debt-equity ratio that is optimal (transaction-cost minimizing) for the firm under given circumstances.

Dividend Policy

Dividend payments to shareholders are one of the great puzzles of modern financial economics. Dividends are something of a mystery because if the

---

23 Benjamin Klein, Robert G. Crawford, and Armen A. Alchian, "Vertical Integration, Appropriable Rents, and the Competitive Contracting Process, *Journal of Law and Economics* 21 (October 1978), pp. 297-326.

earnings used to pay them were retained instead, the firm would be able to reduce its reliance on the capital market for financing new investment projects. The key question to be addressed in this section is, why do firms both borrow and pay cash dividends to stockholders? Finding an answer to this question is complicated by the fact that under certain simplifying assumptions, dividend policy has no impact on the value of the firm.[24]

The Irrelevance of Dividends. Recall that the present value of an ownership position in the firm (shareholder's wealth) is given by the formula

$$PV = \sum_{n=1}^{\infty} \left[\frac{D_n}{\left(1+k_e\right)^n} \right],$$

where D_n is the dollar value of the dividend expected to be received in period n and k_e is the investor's required rate of return. Given that the market price of the firm's common stock at any point in time is equal to the present discounted value of the expected future stream of dividend payments from that time forward, we have shown earlier that changes in the market price of equities (capital gains and losses) are incorporated in the above formula. However, it is instructive to consider a simplified two-period case in which dividends and share price changes are treated more explicitly.

Suppose that an all-equity firm will receive a cash inflow of $10,000 this year and next year, after which the company will be dissolved. The firm's managers currently intend to pay out $10,000 in dividends to shareholders in each of the company's two remaining years of operation. But they also want to consider an alternative policy, proposed by the board of directors, of paying an initial dividend of $11,000, followed next year by a liquidating dividend equal to the firm's terminal market value. If the rate of return required by shareholders is 10 percent, the value of the firm under the first scenario is

$$PV = \$10,000 + \frac{\left(\$10,000\right)}{1.1} = \$19,090.91.$$

If 1,000 shares of stock are outstanding, dividends of $10 per share will be paid out and the market price of each share is $19.09. After the first year's dividend is paid, however, the company's stock price will fall immediately. This decline in stock price reflects the fact that any investor who purchases shares after the initial cash dividend is paid can only expect to receive next year's earnings distribution. The post-dividend market value of the firm is accordingly

$$PV = \frac{\left(\$10,000\right)}{1.1} = \$9,090.91,$$

or $9.09 on a per share basis.

---

24 Merton H. Miller and Franco Modigliani, "Dividend Policy, Growth, and the Valuation of Shares," *Journal of Business* 34 (October 1961), pp. 411-33.

Under the alternative dividend policy, the firm will pay a dividend of $11 per share immediately. Because the company's cash inflow this year is only $10,000, an extra $1,000 is required to pay the proposed higher dividend. Suppose that the firm raises the necessary cash by issuing new stock. These new stockholders will not receive this year's dividend, but they will of course require a 10 percent rate of return on their investment. Hence, if $1,000 worth of new stock is issued, $1,100 of next year's cash inflow must be paid out in dividends to them, leaving $8,900 for dividend payments to old stockholders. Under the alternative dividend policy, then, the market value of the firm is

$$PV = \$11,000 + \frac{\$8,900}{(1.1)} = \$19,090.91,$$

or $19.09 on a per share basis. As before, the company's stock price will fall immediately upon the payment of the initial dividend. The new price per share will be equal to $8.09 (= $19.09 − $11) which, not coincidentally, is the market price of the new stock issued for the purpose of raising the cash necessary to pay a higher dividend to current stockholders.[25]

The important point is that the value of the firm is unaffected by its dividend policy under these simplified conditions where taxes (both corporate and personal), flotation costs, and brokerage fees have been ignored and where "perfect" capital markets have been assumed. It is the underlying cash flows of the firm—not the pattern of their distribution to shareholders—that determine market value.

We can demonstrate this conclusion even more forcefully by thinking about how shareholders might react to the announcement of a change in the firm's dividend policy. For example, consider an investor who prefers receiving dividends of $10 per share in each of the company's remaining two years of operation. If management announces a dividend of $11 per share this year, the investor can "undo" the policy change by reinvesting the extra dollar in dividends at the market-determined 10 percent rate of return, thereby creating a "homemade" dividend flow of $10 (= $11 − $1) this year and $10 (= $1.10 + $8.90) next year. Similarly, an investor who prefers receiving $11 per share this year can obtain that dividend even if management announces no change in policy. If the investor sells $1 worth of stock this year, his or her cash inflow is $11 (= $10 + $1). Next year's cash inflow would then be $8.90 (= $10 − $1.10) because each dollar's worth of stock sold this year reduces the investor's dividends by $1.10 in the following year.

---

25 Consequently, 123.61 (= $1,000/$8.09) new shares must be issued to raise $1,000 in extra cash this year. The firm will of course pay out a total of $10,000 in dividends to stockholders when the enterprise is dissolved. Because there will be 1,123.61 shares outstanding at that point, the dividend per share works out to $8.90 (= $10,000/1,123.61). The present value of this expected dividend payment is $8.09 (= $8.90/1.1), which is the market price of the new stock issue and the market price of existing stock after the initial dividend payment is made.

In sum, both managers and shareholders should be indifferent to the firm's dividend policy. Why then do firms pay dividends?

Dividends as Capital-Market Signals. One possibility is that dividend announcements convey information to the capital market. Some empirical evidence has been reported suggesting significant stock price increases for firms that either announced the payment of the initial dividend in their corporate history or resumed dividend payments after an interruption of at least ten years.[26] Managers will rationally announce a new dividend (or raise an existing dividend) only when future earnings are expected to rise enough so that a subsequent cut in the dividend payment is unlikely. Therefore, the implication of this finding is that dividend announcements are a signal of improved earning power (cash flows) that provides new information about the firm's future financial prospects.

Dividends may also provide signals of a different sort.[27] As we observe in the previous section's discussion of the optimal debt-equity ratio, the capital market offers a low-cost mechanism for monitoring the performance of corporate management. Investment bankers and other financial intermediaries who specialize in lending capital to business enterprises are typically better able to assess the financial prospects of firms than is the average stockholder. Because paying dividends requires management to rely more on these lenders as a source of funds than they would otherwise, a policy of distributing earnings to shareholders may provide a signal to the firm's owners of management's willingness to subject its investment plans to the scrutiny of outside financial experts. In this way, the firm can reduce owners' costs of evaluating management's investment decisions.

Two conclusions about dividend policy follow from the preceding analysis. First, because foregoing a positive net present value investment opportunity will cause the market value (stock price) of the firm to fall, management should never bypass such a project to pay a dividend. Second, firms should never issue new stock to pay a dividend. Much more research is needed, though, before the dividend policy of the firm becomes less of a puzzle.

SUMMARY

This chapter has covered the basics of capital budgeting. The fundamentals of estimating expected future net cash flows, evaluating alternative investment opportunities, and determining the firm's cost of capital have been discussed. Among the various methods of establishing an optimal capital budgeting plan, including selecting projects on the basis of their calculated

---

26 Paul Asquith and David W. Mullins, Jr., "The Impact of Initiating Dividend Payments on Shareholders' Wealth," *Journal of Business* 56 (January 1983), pp. 77-96.
27 Frank H. Easterbrook, "Two Agency-Cost Explanations of Dividends," *American Economic Review* 74 (September 1984), pp. 650-59.

internal rates of return, their profitability indexes, or their payback periods, only the net present value technique leads to investment decisions that are consistent with the goal of maximizing shareholder wealth. This decision-making rule requires that the expected future net cash flows accruing to each proposed project be estimated on an incremental, after-tax basis and then discounted at the firm's opportunity cost of capital.

The opportunity cost of capital, in turn, is computed as the weighted average of the after-tax rates of return required by the firm's shareholders and bondholders, where the weights are equal to the proportions of equity and debt in the firm's targeted or optimal capital structure. The set of acceptable capital projects for the firm includes all proposed investments having positive net present values when evaluated in this way.

This chapter has also discussed additional topics related to the financing of the firm's operations. Questions concerning the existence of an optimal capital structure (debt-equity ratio) and the relevance of the firm's dividend policy were raised and debated. It almost goes without saying that the issues in this chapter are among the most complex and challenging of the decision-making problems the manager must learn to solve. And our discussion has only scratched the surface of modern financial economics. The tools provided herein can nonetheless be applied in a wide range of circumstances to assist in selecting the most desirable investment projects from among the available options.

KEY TERMS
profitability index
mutually exclusive projects
payback period
equi-marginal principle
marginal cost of capital
face value
maturity date
coupons
yield
zero-coupon bond
risk premium
Gordon growth model
weighted average cost of capital
historical weights
target weights
capital asset pricing model
diversifiable risk
nondiversifiable risk
beta
security market line
leverage
indenture covenants

QUESTIONS

15.1 A proposed capital project with an expected useful life of 3 years and no salvage value requires an initial cash outlay of $1 million. If the company implements the project, the marketing department estimates, sales will increase by $1 million next year, by $2 million the following year, and by $500,000 during the third year. If the straight-line method of depreciation is used, the marginal corporate income tax rate is 30 percent, and the firm's cost of capital is 6 percent, what is the project's net present value? Should the company undertake the project?

15.2 Using the information in the previous question, calculate the project's internal rate of return. What accept-reject decision would be reached on this basis? Why?

15.3 Data relating to three investment projects are given in the following table:

	A	B	C
NET INVESTMENT	$30,000	$20,000	$50,000
USEFUL LIFE	10 YRS.	4 YRS.	20 YRS.
ANNUAL CASH SAVINGS	$6,207	$7,725	$9,341

Supposing that the firm can implement only one of the projects and ignoring depreciation and corporate income taxes, which of them, if any, should be undertaken using the net present value rule, assuming a 14 percent cost of capital? Which of them would the company implement if it used the internal rate of return criterion?

15.4 A bottling company is considering replacing one of its bottling machines with a new one that is expected to increase sales revenue from $25,000 to $31,000 per year and reduce the firm's annual operating costs from $12,000 to $10,000. The new machine costs $48,000 and has an anticipated useful life of 10 years. The firm uses straight-line depreciation and is subject to a 46 percent marginal corporate income tax rate. The old machine that will be replaced is fully depreciated and has no salvage value. Using the net present value method and assuming a 8 percent cost of capital, should the firm purchase the new machine?

15.5 Assume that there is a 5-year bond with a 10 percent coupon, paying interest annually and having a face value of $1,000. If investors have a required rate of return of 12 percent, what is the market price of the bond when issued? Why doesn't the bond sell at par?

15.6 Assume that there is a 1-year bond with a face value of $1,000. If the firm has a 1 in 10 chance of going bankrupt and investors require a 10 percent rate of return, what coupon payment must the firm promise if it wants to sell the bond at par?

15.7 The estimated beta for a proposed investment project is 1.5. Assuming that the market return is 12 percent and that the risk-free rate is 6 percent, what is the firm's cost of capital (required rate of return) on the project?

15.8 Assume that the current market price of a firm's common stock is $40 per share. A $4 dividend per share is to be paid at the end of the coming year and is expected to grow at a constant annual rate of 6 percent. What is the firm's cost of equity capital?

15.9 Explain the logic behind this chapter's assertion that a firm should never issue new stock to pay a dividend. Similarly, why should the firm never bypass a profitable capital project to pay a dividend? Should the firm suspend a dividend to finance a profitable capital project? Explain.

15.10 According to the Gordon growth model, the market price of a share of stock is equal to the present value of the anticipated future dividends payable to owners of the stock. How, then, can a firm's dividend policy be irrelevant?

CHAPTER

16

Managing the Non-Traditional Firm

OVERVIEW

This chapter addresses the special problems associated with managing the not-for-profit and the employee-owned firm. Publicly owned enterprises, religious and charitable organizations, labor-managed and other non-traditional firms play important roles in many market-based economies. They account for even larger shares of total national output in more socialistic economies. The list of state-owned enterprises in Europe and elsewhere includes some of the most important industrial sectors, such as aerospace, steel, aluminum, shipbuilding, and automobiles. In the United States, public non-profit enterprises dominate the supply of education, water and power, local public transportation, police and fire protection, mail delivery, and other social services. Non-profits operate in many other industries, including the arts, banking, insurance, and health care, often in direct competition with traditional, for-profit enterprises.

Moreover, in some quarters employee ownership is seen as a way of addressing concerns about declining labor productivity and the international competitiveness of American business. Although far from being the dominant form of organization in any domestic industry, greater ownership participation by employees has emerged in a number of important U.S. firms, including a steel maker, a rental-car company, and a commercial airline.

Not-for-profit status and a greater ownership role for the firm's employees have important impacts on the rules of the game under which managerial decision makers must operate. This chapter extends and applies the theory of property rights to discuss the roles played by non-profit and employee-owned enterprises in a market economy. The presentation highlights the incentive and performance differences that arise in situations where ownership rights are weak and where the output of the firm is costly to measure and to price.

APPLICATION

In an important study of the impact of ownership rights on the performance of business enterprise, Anthony Boardman and Aidan Vining examined the track records of the 500 largest non-U.S. industrial firms.[a] Included in their sample were 419 privately owned firms, 58 wholly state-owned enterprises, and 23 companies in which ownership rights were "mixed" (i.e., firms in which a portion of the equity is held by government and the remainder is owned by private parties). The authors compared the 1983 performances of these firms on a number of dimensions, including profitability (measured in several ways: rate of return on equity, rate of return on assets, rate of return on sales, and net income), and cost efficiency—sales generated per employee, sales generated per dollar of assets, and assets per employee.

The results of the study are summarized in Table 16.1, which displays the means of the performance measures classified by ownership

TABLE 16.1 COMPARATIVE PERFORMANCE OF PRIVATE, MIXED, AND STATE-OWNED ENTERPRISES: 1983

PERFORMANCE MEASURE	PRIVATE CORPORATIONS	MIXED ENTERPRISES	STATE-OWNED ENTERPRISES
Return on Equity[a]	4.343	−14.095	−10.195
Return on Assets[a]	1.784	−2.665	−1.184
Return on Sales[a]	1.484	−2.523	−1.732
Net Income[b]	56.553	−16.800	−27.676
Sales/Employee	$201,164	$137,744	$204,649
Sales/Assets	1.472	1.168	1.157
Assets/Employee	$144,728	$132,094	$189,517
Sales[b]	3,199.3	7,054.4	4,843.7
Assets[b]	2,619.9	6,113.7	4,852.8
Employees	32,780	52,007	50,332

a Percent.
b $ millions.
Source: Anthony E. Boardman and Aidan R. Vining, "Ownership and Performance in Competitive Environments: A Comparison of the Performance of Private, Mixed, and State-Owned Enterprises," *Journal of Law and Economics* 32 (April 1989), p. 14.

---

a Anthony E. Boardman and Aidan R. Vining, "Ownership and Performance in Competitive Environments: A Comparison of the Performance of Private, Mixed, and State-Owned Enterprises," *Journal of Law and Economics* 32 (April 1989), pp. 1-33.

type. These measures show that the private corporations generally out-performed their publicly owned counterparts in terms of profitability. The average rate of return on equity is 4.3 percent for the privately owned firms; it is –10.2 percent for state-owned enterprises, and –14.1 percent for mixed enterprises. Similar conclusions can be drawn from the other rate of return measures, which are uniformly negative for the state-owned and mixed enterprises because they lost money in 1983: While the average privately owned corporation earned $57 million, the average mixed enterprise lost nearly $17 million, and the average state-owned enterprise lost nearly $28 million.

Turning to the efficiency indicators, it is apparent that privately owned corporations have the highest average dollar volume of sales per dollar of invested assets, but that there is little difference between the mixed and state-owned enterprises on this basis. In terms of sales per employee, state-owned enterprises rank slightly higher than private corporations which, in turn, rank considerably higher than mixed enterprises. On average, mixed enterprises and state-owned enterprises tend to be larger than their privately owned counterparts, whether size is measured by total assets, total sales, or total employment.

What explains the generally superior track records of the private-ly owned, for-profit corporations? This chapter discusses the rela-tionship between ownership structure and the business performance in the context of the property rights theory of the firm. The special object of the chapter is to highlight the unique prob-lems that confront the manager of the not-for-profit and the employee-owned enterprise.

THE DIMENSIONS OF THE NON-TRADITIONAL BUSINESS SECTOR

The non-traditional business sector includes privately owned, not-for-profit enterprises, publicly owned corporations, and so-called labor-managed firms. In much of the western world, at least, these firms have remained islands in a sea of classical capitalism characterized by private ownership of property and the pursuit of profits. But these islands have expanded in size during the past two or three decades. For example,

> as recently as 1970 not a single manufacturing industry in which state-owned firms held an important share of industrial output could be found in Western Europe. That has now changed radically. In a number of industries, state-owned firms have gained a dominant, or significant, position in European markets. . . . Today, state-owned firms can be found in virtually all industries in Europe. New state firms in the 1970's were created or nationalized in phar-maceuticals, electronics, computers, office equipment, oil, microelectronics,

chemicals, petrochemicals, pulp and paper, and telecommunications. Each year more firms are drawn into the state-owned sector.[1]

Europe has also led the way in adopting partial government participation in the ownership of important private business firms—examples include British Petroleum, Volkswagen, Fiat, and Airbus Industrie—as well as in promoting alternatives to traditional business ownership arrangements. France, for instance, has a relatively well-developed "cooperative" sector in which firms are owned by their employees, by their suppliers, or by their customers.

The United States has not been immune to these trends. We can gain some appreciation for the size and growing importance of the non-traditional business sector by considering Table 16.2, which shows the numbers of non-profit organizations granted tax-exempt status by the Internal Revenue Service in 1977 and 1985. These organizations, which include colleges and

TABLE 16.2 NUMBER OF ACTIVE TAX-EXEMPT ORGANIZATIONS

TAX CODE NUMBER	TYPE OF ORGANIZATION	1977	1985
501(c)(1)	Corporations organized under act of Congress	1,072	24
501(c)(2)	Title-holding companies	5,223	5,758
501(c)(3)	Religious, charitable, etc.	276,455	366,071
501(c)(4)	Social welfare	129,496	131,250
501(c)(5)	Labor, agricultural organizations	87,656	75,632
501(c)(6)	Business leagues	44,100	54,217
501(c)(7)	Social and recreational clubs	50,031	57,343
501(c)(8)	Fraternal beneficiary societies	141,138	94,435
501(c)(9)	Voluntary employees' societies	6,486	10,668
501(c)(10)	Domestic fraternal beneficiary societies	12,410	15,924
501(c)(11)	Teachers' retirement funds	13	11
501(c)(12)	Benevolent life insurance associations	4,801	5,244
501(c)(13)	Cemetery companies	5,264	7,239
501(c)(14)	Credit unions	5,074	6,032
501(c)(15)	Mutual insurance companies	1,450	967
501(c)(16)	Corporations to finance crop operations	31	18
501(c)(17)	Supplemental unemployment benefit trusts	800	726
501(c)(18)	Employee-funded pension trusts	4	3
501(c)(19)	War veterans' organizations	14,305	23,062
501(c)(20)	Legal services organizations	—	167
501(c)(21)	Black lung trusts	—	15
501(d)	Religious and apostolic organizations	63	82
501(e)	Cooperative hospital service organizations	—	82
501(f)	Cooperative service organizations for operating educational organizations	—	—
521	Farmers' cooperatives	3,794	2,542
	TOTAL	789,666	857,512

Source: Virginia Ann Hodgkinson and Murray S. Weitzman, *Dimensions of the Independent Sector: A Statistical Profile,* 2E (Washington, D.C.: Independent Sector, 1986), p.17.

---

1 R. Joseph Monsen and Kenneth D. Walters, *Nationalized Companies: A Threat to American Business* (New York: McGraw-Hill, 1983), p. 1, quoted in Anthony E. Boardman and Aidan R.

universities, hospitals and other health care facilities, mutual insurance companies, agricultural cooperatives, and so on, may collectively account for somewhere between 5 and 6 percent of total U.S. GNP. Because nonprofits are concentrated in labor-intensive service industries, they account for an even larger share of total employment.[2]

Nonprofit Enterprises

Henry Hansmann has usefully classified nonprofit enterprises into four categories on the basis of the source of their funding and of the manner in which they are controlled.[3] A not-for-profit organization, it is important to note, is not prohibited from earning accounting profits, which many of them in fact do. Rather it is barred from distributing those profits to individuals who exercise control over the organization's activities, such as members, directors, officers or trustees. Nonprofit status essentially requires that any earnings in excess of costs, which costs include the payment of "reasonable" compensation to individuals who supply labor or capital to the enterprise, must be retained and dedicated entirely to financing the production of the good or service the organization was established to provide.

Sources of Funding. Religious and charitable organizations, which compose an important segment of the not-for-profit sector, rely almost entirely on voluntary contributions to fund their operations. Organizations such as the Red Cross, the Salvation Army, CARE, and the March of Dimes are obvious examples of what Hansmann calls donative nonprofits. It is also true, however, that many nonprofits finance their activities by charging fees for the services they provide. Not-for-profit nursing homes and hospitals certainly fall into this category of commercial nonprofits—a category that also includes country clubs, fraternal organizations, and labor unions, which fund their activities through membership dues and other fees.

Of course not all nonprofits fall neatly into either the donative or the commercial funding category. Colleges and universities, for example, generate income by charging tuition and fees, selling books, clothing, supplies, and tickets to athletic contests, as well as by soliciting donations from alumni. And many nonprofit organizations that relied heavily in the past on voluntary contributions have, because of cutbacks in government grants and rising competition for donations, turned increasingly to commercial ventures as sources of income. The Boy Scouts sell Christmas trees; museums market books, clothing, jewelry, and many other items through gift shops and catalogs; fraternal organizations offer travel packages, rental-car discounts, and

Vining, "Ownership and Performance in Competitive Environments: A Comparison of the Performance of Private, Mixed, and State-Owned Enterprises," *Journal of Law and Economics* 32 (April 1989), p. 2.

2 James T. Bennett and Thomas J. DiLorenzo, *Unfair Competition: The Profits of NonProfits* (Lanham, MD: Hamilton Press, 1989), pp. 16-17.

3 Henry B. Hansmann, "The Role of Nonprofit Enterprise," *Yale Law Journal* 89 (April 1980), pp. 835-901.

group life insurance policies to their members; and so on. The income generated by the commercial activities of nonprofits is impressive. In 1985, for instance, the Smithsonian Institution's gift shops, restaurants, and mail order catalogs produced $27 million in sales revenue.[4]

Methods of Governance. Nonprofit organizations can also be distinguished in terms of their methods of governance. The activities of mutual nonprofits, like country clubs, fraternal associations, and professional societies, are controlled by their members who select the organization's board of directors and the officers to whom they delegate day-to-day decision-making responsibility. Entrepreneurial nonprofits, by contrast, are overseen by self-perpetuating boards of directors that are largely free of oversight by the members, contributors, or customers who constitute the organization's primary source of income. Most not-for-profit hospitals and nursing homes fall into the entrepreneurial category, a category that also includes charities like the Red Cross and the United Way—organizations over which donors and volunteers exercise little or no direct control.

Table 16.3 summarizes the foregoing discussion. Examples of each of the four categories of not-for-profit organizations are provided to illustrate the polar cases.

Cooperatives

The non-traditional business sector also encompasses a related but distinct type of entity which also operates under a profit constraint. **Cooperatives**

TABLE 16.3 NONPROFIT ENTERPRISES: SOURCES OF FUNDING AND METHODS OF CONTROL

	MUTUAL	ENTREPRENEURIAL
DONATIVE	Common Cause National Audubon Society	CARE March of Dimes art museums
COMMERCIAL	American Automobile Association Consumers Union[b] country clubs	National Geographic Society[a] Educational Testing Service hospitals and nursing homes

[a]Publisher of *National Geographic*.
[b]Publisher of *Consumer Reports*.
Source: Adapted from Henry B. Hansmann, "The Role of Nonprofit Enterprise," *Yale Law Journal* 89 (April 1980), p. 842.

---

4 Bennett and DiLorenzo, *Unfair Competition,* p. 20.

are limited-profit enterprises in the sense that the state laws under which they are organized typically place restrictions on the distribution of earnings to investors. Agricultural and rural electric cooperatives, consumer co-ops, mutual insurance companies, and mutual savings and loan associations resemble the nonprofit organizations discussed above. Laws limit suppliers of capital to earning some maximum rate of return on their investment, and some of these organizations are granted tax-exempt status. The fact that many cooperatives are "mutual" organizations reinforces this resemblance. Their members, depositors, or policyholders are the owners of the firm and typically exercise proximate control over the selection of its board of directors.

Cooperatives are typically commercial enterprises which generate the bulk of their income from pricing the goods and services they were organized to supply. Mutual insurance companies like Northwestern Mutual Life and Mutual of New York, for example, collect premiums from the sale of life, health, fire, and automobile insurance policies. Rural electric cooperatives sell power to their customer-members. And agricultural cooperatives earn income by assessing fees on growers for the marketing and advertising services they provide on their members' behalf. Cooperative enterprises are distinct from nonprofits, however, because their members may receive unlimited profit distributions. (These profit distributions are often required to be proportional to the individual member's financial participation in the organization, though.)

Other Non-Traditional Firms

Government regulations also impose profit limitations on many other privately owned firms. A large number of public utilities, for example, are organized as private, profit-seeking firms but are subject to governmentally imposed price controls that limit indirectly the rate of return earned by investors to some specified maximum. There is no direct constraint on profit distributions to suppliers of capital, however, and in this sense investor-owned utilities have much in common with other for-profit enterprises. They issue securities, pay dividends, and the owners exercise formal control over the firm. But **rate-of-return regulation** imposes some upper limit on their profitability. This limit distinguishes these businesses from the more traditional capitalist enterprise.

Public enterprises constitute a final major segment of the non-traditional business sector. Government agencies and bureaus produce and sell electric power; supply urban mass transit, fire, police, and garbage collection services; operate airports, hospitals, educational institutions, museums, symphonies, and parks; provide disaster relief, charity, and a variety of other social services; manage pension funds; and so on.[5] The dollar value of

---

5 The public enterprise roll also includes a small number of agencies that are organized as public corporations and which operate off the public budget. These public corporations, which include the U.S. Postal Service, the Pension Benefit Guarantee Corporation, Amtrak, the Commodity Credit Corporation, and the Federal Deposit Insurance Corporation, differ from

the public sector's activities is immense. The federal government alone spends in excess of $1 trillion annually, or approximately 20 percent of the total value of goods and services produced in the United States. Expenditures by state and local governments account for another five percent of GNP.

Public enterprises are nonprofit firms which are distinguished by the absence of well-defined ownership rights. Their "owners"—the taxpayers—do not receive profit distributions and have no financial claims which can be sold or otherwise transferred. Moreover, any control that taxpayers may exercise over the appointment of directors or managers of public enterprises must be expressed through political processes. These organizations consequently tend to be entrepreneurial rather than mutual.

In sum, the non-traditional business sector is both large and growing. It has two distinguishing features. Limitations imposed on profit distributions represent one important characteristic of the non-traditional firm. These profit limitations may be explicit and direct, as they are for proprietary organizations established as tax-exempt nonprofits under the Internal Revenue Code and government bureaus. Or the profit constraints may be indirect, as they are in the case of firms subject to rate-of-return regulation. Whether these constraints are direct or indirect, however, their existence fundamentally alters the relationship between the owners and the managers of the enterprise.

A second distinguishing feature of the non-traditional firm is that the rights associated with ownership are attenuated. That is, laws that limit the profit distributions owners may receive also change the nature of the control the owners exercise. Indeed, in the cases of most nonprofits and all public enterprises, ownership rights do not exist in any meaningful sense. Weakened or ill-defined ownership rights further alter the incentives and constraints faced by management. The following section explores the causes and consequences of these distinguishing features of the non-traditional firm.

PROPERTY RIGHTS AND MANAGERIAL INCENTIVES

The discussion in Chapter 7 focuses on several modern theories that shed light on the nature of the firm. One of these theories highlights the shirking-information problem associated with team production.[6] In brief, this theory suggests that the firm emerged as an economic entity in order to capture the additional output made possible when separately owned resources are combined under the direction of an entrepreneur. At the same time, however, because the marginal productivity of the team is greater than the sum of the

---

more traditional government bureaus in that they price the services they were established to provide and are, at least in theory, self-financing. They do, however, have access to the Treasury to meet any operating losses they may sustain.

6 Armen A. Alchian and Harold Demsetz, "Production, Information Costs, and Economic Organization," *American Economic Review* 62 (December 1972), pp. 777-95.

marginal products of the individual team members, it becomes more difficult to measure and reward individual contributions to the team's effort. This metering problem, in turn, creates opportunities for **shirking**. That is, because each team member bears only a portion of the total cost of his or her increased consumption of leisure on the job, individuals have incentives to reduce their effort. In the limit, the additional output attributable to team production will be lost.

The firm emerges in the team production framework because of the entrepreneur's opportunity to acquire specialized knowledge about the productivities of the resources under his or her command. This information becomes accessible to the entrepreneur through daily monitoring of the activities of the team members over whom he or she exercises proximate control. Because the entrepreneur gains more knowledge about team inputs, opportunities for the profitable employment of productive resources are available at lower cost within the firm than on the market. Superior knowledge about the productivities of individual team members, in turn, both aids in the policing of shirking and allows rewards to be more precisely scaled to effort. Still, an important question of motivation remains: What incentives exist for the entrepreneur to gather and utilize specialized information of this sort?

Property Rights in the Classical Capitalist Firm

The problem of motivation is overcome in the classical capitalist firm through a property rights assignment that establishes the entrepreneur's claim on the **residual** associated with team production activities. In other words, the entrepreneur-monitor hires the productive resources that will constitute the team, contracting with the owner of each of them to supply materials or equipment of specified grade and quantity, or to perform specific tasks with a stipulated level of effort. In exchange, the entrepreneur agrees to pay each resource owner compensation equal to that resource's expected contribution to the value of the output produced by the team.

Residual Claims. The entrepreneur-monitor thus becomes a residual claimant—he or she owns the right to keep whatever residual (profit or loss) remains after the output of the team has been sold and the team members have been paid their agreed-upon compensation. Obviously, the greater the value of the team's output (the less the shirking), the larger will be the entrepreneur-monitor's residual. Consequently, the classical capitalist firm provides the entrepreneur-monitor with a profit motive to acquire and utilize the specialized information about resource productivities that aid in holding shirking to its cost-effective minimum.

The existence of a monitor with a claim to the residual generated by team production is one component of the bundle of rights associated with ownership of the classical capitalist firm. In order to play the role of residual claimant effectively, the entrepreneur-monitor must also (1) be the central party to all input contracts; (2) have the right to observe input behavior, which includes the duties of assigning tasks, establishing rewards, and metering performance; (3) be able to alter the membership of the team unilaterally; and (4) have the right to sell the residual claim. The last of these rights is perhaps the most critical. An alienable (saleable) ownership right enables the entrepreneur-monitor to capture in the selling price of the residual claim the discounted present value of any organizational improvements he or she discovers. This ability to personally appropriate the value of organizational innovations, in turn, provides an economic incentive for implementing them.

The existence of alienable residual claims means that the costs of any resource-allocation decision or choice are fully borne by the entrepreneur-monitor.[7] The owners of private firms consequently have strong motives to ensure the efficient use of productive resources. Failure to do so reduces the size of their residual and therefore causes the market value of their claims on it to decline. In the modern corporation, however, ownership is separated from control. Nonexpert owners delegate decision-making authority to managers who themselves are either not residual claimants at all or who own only a trifle of the company's outstanding shares. Moreover, because the stockholders of corporations are numerous and dispersed, rarely does any one of them own enough shares to justify taking an active interest in the day-to-day operations of the firm. Managers accordingly have a great deal of discretion which they may use to further their own self-interests rather than those of the owners. "Corporate plundering" by managers who fail to maximize stockholder wealth is a possibility.[8]

The capital-raising advantages of the corporate form of business organization are well known. One may well ask, then, why do millions of stockholders willingly turn over a portion of their wealth to a small group of individuals who may have little regard for their welfare?[9] One answer is that the divergence of interests between the owners of the firm and its managers is limited by the **market for corporate control** and by the managerial labor market. A profit can be made by taking over a poorly run enterprise and replacing incumbent management with individuals willing to take steps that increase stockholder wealth.[10] Moreover, managers who consistently direct the resources of the firm in ways that reduce its market value will in the long run command lower salaries as they compete for jobs against individuals more skilled at managing business enterprises.[11]

---

7 Armen A. Alchian, "Some Economics of Property Rights, " *Il Politico* 30 (1965), pp. 816-29.

8 Adolf A. Berle and Gardiner C. Means, *The Modern Corporation and Private Property* (New York: Macmillan, 1932), p. 355. Berle and Means' basic criticism of the corporate form of business organization was restated recently in Gardiner C. Means, "Corporate Power in the Marketplace, " *Journal of Law and Economics* 26 (June 1983), pp. 467-85.

9 Armen A. Alchian, "Corporate Management and Property Rights," in Henry G. Manne, ed., *Economic Policy and the Regulation of Corporate Securities* (Washington, D.C.: American Enterprise Institute, 1969), p. 337.

10 See Henry G. Manne, "Mergers and the Market for Corporate Control," *Journal of Political Economy* 73 (April 1965), pp. 110-20.

11 Eugene F. Fama, "Agency Problems and the Theory of the Firm," *Journal of Political Economy* 88 (April 1980), pp. 228-307.

Alienable Rights. These margins of control are available to the owners of nearly all types of for-profit business organizations, however. More important to the stockholders of corporations is the alienability of their residual claims. Share transferability limits the extent to which managers can take actions that benefit themselves at the expense of stockholders. That is because individual owners are free to sell their residual claims if the gap between management's decisions and those that would maximize their own welfare becomes too wide. Moreover, stockholders can sell their residual claims without consulting the other owners of the firm.

Share transferability promotes economically efficient specialization by owners and managers. Managers, whose comparative advantage lies in coordinating, supervising, and evaluating the performance of productive teams, can specialize in business decision-making. The owners of the firm, on the other hand, can specialize in risk-taking. They need only monitor the market price of their residual claims to determine whether or not management is acting in their best interest. Hence, share transferability—along with an active stock market—provides a monitoring function that disciplines managerial decision making, thereby limiting the losses owners would otherwise bear due to the separation of ownership from control in the modern corporation.

The Impact of Weakened Property Rights

The foregoing discussion suggests that restrictions either on the distribution of profits to owners or on owners' rights to sell their residual claims will tend to short-circuit the market's discipline of managerial decision making. Limited profit distributions, on the one hand, lessen the extent to which owners can personally appropriate the benefits of management's resource-allocation decisions. This limitation, in turn, reduces owners' incentives to invest resources in becoming informed about and in controlling the behavior of their manager-agents. Restrictions on the alienability of residual claims, on the other hand, limit owners' ability to avoid having costs imposed on them by managers who use their discretion to guide the resources of the firm in ways that selectively benefit themselves at the owners' expense. Managerial shirking will therefore have freer rein both in profit-constrained firms and in organizations having ill-defined ownership rights or, what is the same thing, limitations on the right to sell residual claims.

Consider the case of partnerships, for example. In such business organizations, the firm's active partners jointly share the ownership and management functions. An individual partner cannot sell his or her ownership interest without the approval of all the other partners. Indeed, a partnership must dissolve if any co-owner wants to withdraw from the firm. This means that if one partner fails to make managerial decisions that maximize the welfare of the partnership as a whole, the other partners can replace this person only by terminating the entire enterprise and reorganizing it under a new partnership agreement. The limitation on the right to sell residual claims makes it more costly for the owners to discipline managerial shirking. Other things being the same, one would therefore expect the resources of partnerships to be used less efficiently than those of other for-profit enterprises whose ownership rights are more freely transferable.[12]

Similar considerations apply to labor-managed firms whose employees are the principal residual claimants. Workers who become dissatisfied with management must both quit their jobs and transfer their residual claims to new employees, whose hiring must be approved by the remaining worker-owners, in order to withdraw from the enterprise. This restriction on the right to sell residual claims again raises the cost of disciplining managerial decision making and therefore reduces management's incentives to pay more attention to owners' interests than to their own.

Profit constraints also tend to widen the divergence of interests between owners and managers. The consequences of restrictions on the distribution of the firm's profits are most apparent in the cases of non-profit organizations and publicly owned enterprises for which, by definition, no residual claimants exist. Indeed, one hypothesis about nonprofits is that they emerged as a type of business organization precisely because the reduction in economic efficiency that predictably follows from prohibiting the distribution of profits to owners may be desirable in some cases.

Private, Not-For-Profit Organizations. Why should reduced economic efficiency be desired in the supply of certain goods and services and, hence, lead to the emergence of not-for-profit enterprises as a type of business organization? One possible answer to this question involves the idea that consumers cannot always costlessly observe or evaluate the benefits they hope they are buying.[13] Shipping food to drought-stricken areas of the Third World, providing emergency relief to the victims of earthquakes and other natural disasters, and offering shelter to the homeless are obvious examples. Contributors to these and other causes are often not in a position to verify whether the services they pay for are actually delivered.

Under these circumstances, a for-profit charitable organization might pocket all donations and produce no benefits at all: "If CARE were organized for profit, it would have a strong incentive to skimp on the services it promises,

---

12 This observation helps explain why the partners of law firms and other professional organizations are often required to serve lengthy apprenticeships before being elevated to partner status. These apprenticeships provide the firm's existing partners with an opportunity to observe and evaluate their associates' abilities to do legal research, to prepare legal documents and to write legal briefs, to argue cases in court, to bring in business to the firm, and so on, in order to select the most promising candidates for promotion. This selection process is made critical by the fact that once an associate becomes a part owner of the firm, replacement will be costly if his or her performance fails to meet expectations.

13 David Easley and Maureen O'Hara, "The Economic Role of the Nonprofit Firm," *Bell Journal of Economics* 14 (Autumn 1983), pp. 531-38. Also see Martin Ricketts, *The New Industrial Economics: An Introduction to Modern Theories of the Firm* (New York: St. Martin's Press, 1987), pp. 261-62.

or even neglect them entirely, and, instead, divert most or all of its revenue to its owners."[14] This conclusion follows from the observation that for-profit enterprises do not operate under any immediate constraints regarding the compensation of managers or the distribution of profits to owners. Coupled with the assumption that contributors cannot easily monitor the charitable organization's output, the absence of any limitation on profit distributions creates clear incentives to produce no output at all.

By contrast, as discussed earlier, state laws typically prohibit nonprofit firms from distributing profits to their operators. These laws also generally stipulate that a nonprofit enterprise's operating costs, including managerial compensation, must be "reasonable."[15] To the extent that such constraints are binding, charitable organizations and other donative nonprofits have incentives to use the contributions they receive above and beyond their "reasonable" operating costs to supply the services expected by donors. These services will of course not be supplied in an economically efficient manner, because nonprofits are not subject to the full discipline of market forces. But contributors thereby have some assurance that not all of their donations will end up in the operator's personal bank account.

In fact, legal constraints on the reasonableness of operating costs and on the distribution of profits may not be required to assure this result. Some evidence of performance will be necessary for donative nonprofits to attract a continuing supply of voluntary contributions. The operators of charitable organizations therefore have a private interest in communicating information to existing and prospective donors about their activities in behalf of the group targeted for aid, their efforts to hold operating costs down, and so on.

The managerial labor market imposes additional discipline on the performances of nonprofits. Individuals who do better jobs of managing nonprofit enterprises will in the long run command higher salaries. The important point is that the nonprofit form of business organization "can be at least partially described by the solution to an optimal contracting problem."[16] In other words, reduced economic efficiency is desirable in some circumstances in the sense that adopting an alternative (for-profit) form of organization to supply costly-to-observe goods and services more efficiently runs the risk that no output will be produced at all.

The costs of observing output are not the only explanation for the existence of nonprofit enterprises—many goods and services that consumers find difficult to evaluate (automobile repairs and medical and psychiatric care, for example) are supplied quite successfully by for-profit firms. This

14 Hansmann, "Role of Nonprofit Enterprise," p. 847.
15 Easley and O'Hara, "Economic Role of the Nonprofit Firm," p. 532.
16 *Ibid.*, p. 538. It is not a perfect solution, however. In early 1992, the national director of the United Way was forced to resign his post in disgrace after it was disclosed that he had been receiving an annual salary of nearly half a million dollars and had spent donations lavishly on personal travel and other perquisites of office.

theory also does not explain the existence of nonprofits that engage in activities where donations play no role, such as country clubs.[17]

An alternative explanation for nonprofits, particularly commercial nonprofits, focuses on the noneconomic or social goals these organizations often pursue. Hence, nonprofit hospitals, for instance, are said to exist for the purpose of providing medical care to indigent patients who would not have access to treatment if all health care facilities operated on a for-profit basis. The absence of a profit motive, it is argued, allows commercial nonprofits to charge for services supplied to those who can afford to pay for them and then use the revenue received from paying customers to subsidize the provision of benefits to individuals who would not otherwise be served. Such cross-subsidization would be less likely to occur if the organization operated for-profit and therefore provided services only when marginal revenue was at least as great as marginal cost.

Although no one has developed a general explanation for the role of nonprofit enterprises in a market economy, the performance consequences of this form of business organization are clear. The profit motive encourages economic efficiency. The owners and managers of profit-seeking firms have strong incentives to choose the least costly means of producing a given good or service. Because of the absence of a profit motive, the managers of nonprofits might therefore be less vigilant in eliminating unnecessary expenses and therefore more likely to incur higher costs of production than their counterparts who manage for-profit enterprises. This is not to say that the managers of nonprofits have *no* incentives to hold costs down, but rather that these incentives are *weaker* than they would be in the absence of constraints on the distribution of profits. Some empirical evidence does indeed suggest that in the health care industry at least, nonprofit hospitals are managed less efficiently than for-profits.[18]

Public Enterprises. Publicly owned enterprises constitute a special case of the profit-constrained firm. They are similar to the nonprofits just discussed in the sense that public enterprises lack well-defined and saleable ownership rights. For the reasons outlined above, we expect public enterprises to compare unfavorably with privately owned firms—to have higher operating costs, to be less attuned to consumers' wants, and to be less responsive to changing market conditions. In short, we expect them to be

17 Eugene F. Fama and Michael C. Jensen, in "Agency Problems and Residual Claims," *Journal of Law and Economics* 26 (June 1983), pp. 327-49, argue that nonprofits may exist because the absence of alienable ownership rights avoids expropriation of (all of) the unrestricted donations contributed by individuals who want to subsidize particular activities (those of churches and universities, for example) but do not want to invest additional resources in monitoring the performance of such organizations.

18 Kenneth W. Clarkson, "Some Implications of Property Rights in Hospital Management," *Journal of Law and Economics* 15 (October 1972), pp. 363-84.

less efficient.[19] The greater room for discretionary behavior on the part of managers which the absence of alienable residual claims implies is reinforced in the public enterprise by the fact that the funding required to finance its operations is coerced from taxpayers and, moreover, these taxpayers are both numerous and dispersed. Any one taxpayer bears so small a share of the cost of financing the goods or services supplied by any one public enterprise that the incentive to monitor the uses to which his or her tax dollars are put is essentially nil.

The weak property rights associated with the publicly owned firm have predictable economic consequences. Without well-defined and saleable residual claims, no one directly bears the costs of error or garners the profits of success. Little motivation to use resources efficiently therefore exists. Management, in particular, cannot personally appropriate the value of any improvements in economic efficiency because the salaries and other pecuniary rewards of government employees are typically subject to statutory ceilings and their promotion opportunities are often tied more closely to longevity than to performance.

Moreover, it is costly for taxpayers to monitor the acquisition of nonpecuniary benefits by these employees. Therefore, the managers of publicly owned firms will have increased incentives to take advantage of job-related rewards derived from nonmonetary sources.[20] This includes allocating resources to enhance their job security,[21] and adopting policies that will ease their workloads and make their jobs more pleasant.[22] Hence, the managers of public enterprises are expected to consume more on-the-job amenities than their private-sector counterparts, that is, to spend more on travel, entertainment, and other perquisites of office; to engage in more racial and sexual discrimination in hiring so that their subordinates have more of the personal characteristics they prefer;[23] and to work to reduce job-related frictions by appeasing vocal employees or customers. As a result of these activities, publicly owned firms will tend to have higher production costs than privately owned firms and will be less efficient by market standards.

There is a substantial amount of empirical evidence supporting this conclusion. In the electric utility industry, for example, studies that have compared the performance of municipal (publicly owned) electric companies with that of their investor-owned counterparts have found that the pricing

---

19 Alchian and Demsetz, "Production, Information Costs, and Economic Organization," and Louis De Alessi, "On the Nature and Consequences of Private and Public Enterprises," *Minnesota Law Review* 67 (October 1982), pp. 191-209.

20 Armen A. Alchian and Reuben A. Kessel, "Competition, Monopoly, and the Pursuit of Pecuniary Gain," in *Aspects of Labor Economics*, Universities—National Bureau of Economic Research Conference Series No. 14 (New York: Arno Press, 1962), pp. 157-75.

21 De Alessi, "Private and Public Enterprises," p. 206.

22 *Ibid.* Also see William A. Niskanen, *Bureaucracy and Representative Government* (Chicago: Aldine, 1971).

23 George J. Borjas, "Discrimination in HEW: Is the Doctor Sick or are the Patients Healthy?," *Journal of Law and Economics* 21 (April 1978), pp. 97-110.

policies of municipal enterprises tend to favor special interest groups. Moreover, publicly owned electric companies tend to have greater power generating capacities and higher operating costs, maintain managers in office longer, and exhibit larger variation in their rates of return. The weight of the evidence from other industries points in the same direction. Publicly owned firms have been found to be less efficient than privately owned firms in supplying a variety of goods and services, including water, urban mass transit, banking, air transportation, fire fighting, garbage collection, and hospital care. Studies reaching the opposite conclusion are in a distinct minority.[24]

The performance consequences of public ownership are well illustrated in this chapter's opening application. Across the wide range of industries and countries studied, which includes the production of machinery, fabricated metal products, chemicals, wood and paper products, rubber, transportation equipment, textiles, and petroleum in Italy, France, Canada, Germany, Britain, and Japan,[25] the typical state-owned enterprise fails to cover its costs. Some of the underlying reasons for the relative inefficiency of public enterprises are illustrated in the accompanying case study of garbage collection.

Given that publicly owned enterprises tend to be less efficient by market standards than privately owned firms, the natural question is, why are some business activities carried out under government ownership while other business activities remain in the private sector? The reasons for this dichotomy are not well understood. Especially puzzling is the fact that in many instances public and private enterprises supply the same goods and services, often in direct competition with one another. In some localities across the United States, for example, electricity is supplied by municipal power companies, while in others it is supplied by private, investor-owned utilities. Similarly, in many cities private, for-profit hospitals coexist with publicly owned health care facilities, private elementary and secondary schools operate alongside public educational institutions, and so on.

The task of explaining government enterprise is further complicated by the observation that public *provision* of goods and services does not necessarily call for public *ownership* of the means of producing the desired output. That is, governments can in principle avoid the well-known inefficiencies of public production by contracting with private firms to supply goods or services and then imposing taxes, paying subsidies, or using regulatory authority to assure that the contractors deliver the required output.

Most of the conventional rationales for government ownership fail when we consider the above point. The standard theories about public enterprises are similar to those advanced to explain the existence of other not-for-profit

24 Many of these studies are cited and summarized in Boardman and Vining, "Ownership and Performance in Competitive Environments." See also Aidan R. Vining and Anthony E. Boardman, "Ownership versus Competition: Efficiency in Public Enterprise," *Public Choice* 73 (March 1992), pp. 205-39.

25 Boardman and Vining, "Ownership and Performance in Competitive Environments," pp. 15-16.

Public versus Private Provision of a "Collective" Good

Local governments have adopted a variety of arrangements for providing household trash collection services for their citizens. In some cities, garbage is collected by a public monopoly. New York City's trash, for example, is collected by a government agency managed and staffed by full-time government employees who schedule and operate collection trucks and other equipment owned by the city. In other localities like Boston, government uses competitive bidding arrangements to contract with private firms that are granted exclusive rights to collect trash within the city's limits. The city pays these private monopolies to remove and dispose of household garbage on an agreed-upon schedule. But the firms are usually free to determine the types and mix of inputs—labor, equipment, and so on—that they will use to provide those services. Still other cities allow unregulated private firms to compete with one another for trash removal business.

Monopoly in the provision of trash removal services is typically justified on the basis of economies of scale. That is, if the unit costs of collecting refuse continue to decline as additional households are served, then a single firm that services the entire market will in principle be more cost-effective than two or more firms each of which services only a part of it. This observation raises two important questions: First, is there evidence of scale economies in the collection of household garbage? Second, if scale economies exist, which ownership arrangement—public or private monopoly—does a better job of exploiting the potential cost savings?

The answers to these questions were explored in a study that examined the performances of public and private trash removal services in 340 U.S. cities.[a] The author assembled cost data from the individual trash collection firms and compared their cost-effectiveness, controlling for service levels provided and relevant local market characteristics. Her findings show that scale economies are indeed important in the removal and disposal of household trash. Across all of the cities included in the author's sample, competitive arrangements for collecting trash were from 26 percent to 48 percent more costly than private monopoly arrangements. This evidence suggests that when rival trash removal services compete for customers in the same market area, the absence of exclusivity leads to firms that are inefficiently small, implying unnecessary duplication of trucks and collection personnel, billing arrangements, and so on.

More importantly, perhaps, the empirical evidence shows that for equivalent levels of service, both public monopoly and the competitive arrangement had costs that were 27 percent to 37 percent higher than private monopoly. Lower labor productivity was one reason for the cost disadvantages experienced by the public monopolies. The typical municipal trash removal service used a crew of 3.26 people to operate each of its collection vehicles, while the privately owned monopolies used an average crew of 2.15 people per vehicle. (Moreover, this labor productivity gap increased with city size.)

Second, the public monopolies also tended to employ capital less productively in the sense that they operated vehicles with smaller collection capacities. The capacities of the trucks used by the public monopolies averaged 20.63 cubic yards, while those of the private monopolies averaged 27.14 cubic yards. Taken together, these figures indicate that in order to collect the same amount of trash, the public monopolies operated more vehicles, made more trips, and used more labor than their privately owned monopoly counterparts. This lower productivity translates directly into higher operating costs. Failure to adopt least-cost production methods accounts for the bulk of the inefficiencies associated with public ownership arrangements in the collection of household garbage.

a Barbara J. Stevens, "Scale, Market Structure, and the Cost of Refuse Collection," *Review of Economics and Statistics* 60 (1978), pp. 438-48.

organizations, namely the costliness of monitoring and evaluating the provision of certain goods and services such as welfare payments and disaster relief, the inability of private firms to supply so-called public goods like lighthouses and national defense,[26] and the unseemliness of profiting from the sale of basic necessities like medical care.[27]

In sum, the reasons for the existence of non-traditional business enterprises represent a relatively unexplored area of research. It seems reasonable to conclude, however, that the ultimate explanations for the roles played by not-for-profit and publicly owned enterprises in a market economy will be based on the fundamental differences in the rights associated with the ownership of for-profit and profit-constrained firms. With limits on the distribution of profits to owners and without well-defined and saleable residual claims in place, the managers and employees of non-traditional business organizations have weaker incentives to use resources efficiently than do their counterparts in the private sector. As a result, the performances of not-for-profit and publicly owned enterprises differ systematically and predictably from those of private, for-profit firms. Systematic differences in performance ought to provide a basis for identifying a systematic explanation for the origins of the non-traditional enterprise.

THE LABOR-MANAGED FIRM

As noted at this chapter's outset, in recent years there has been renewed interest in establishing mechanisms that provide employees with greater opportunities to participate in the ownership and management of the firm. This approach is an alternative to the classical capitalist type of business organization in which owners, managers, and workers compose largely distinct groups. These participatory mechanisms exist in a variety of forms, including the appointment of labor representatives to the company's board of directors, the establishment of labor-management "quality circles" in which small teams of workers and managers combine to develop and implement new ideas that will reduce costs and improve product quality, the adoption of more formal strategies of "codetermination" that provide employees with a voice in managerial decision making, and the creation of **employee stock ownership plans** (ESOPs) that give workers an ownership interest in their employer. Such increased participation, some argue, serves to align employees' incentives more closely with the overall goals of the organization and helps promote the improvements in labor productivity that are necessary if American business is to remain competitive in an increasingly integrated global marketplace.

---

26 Public goods are defined and discussed in Chapter 17.

27 Hansmann, "Role of Nonprofit Enterprise." As Hansmann points out, however, the most basic of life's necessities, food and shelter, are supplied mainly by private, for-profit enterprises throughout most of the Western world.

Although stock market investments by pension fund managers have long made workers major capitalists in the United States, direct participation by employees in the ownership and management of their own firms is a relatively recent development. It has typically emerged as a last resort. Faced with sinking fortunes that have put the firm on the road to bankruptcy or with a hostile takeover that threatens plant closings or mass layoffs, purchase of the company's assets through an ESOP is undertaken as a last ditch attempt to save the workers' jobs. The precise terms on which employees become owners vary considerably from case to case. Employees may acquire a majority of the firm's outstanding shares or they may represent only a minority of the company's shareholders.[28] All stock owned by employees may carry full voting rights, or perhaps only "large" employee-owners will have the opportunity to buy voting shares.[29] All employees may become shareholders or only some of them may purchase stock.[30]

As it has evolved in the United States, the labor-managed firm thus differs significantly from the traditional model of the socialistic enterprise of Eastern Europe. In the former Yugoslavia, for example, where labor-managed firms have been studied extensively, employees collectively "own" the entire enterprise.[31] The ownership rights held by the workers are neither divisible nor saleable. This absence of alienable residual claims makes the analysis of the socialistic labor-managed firm more akin to that of the not-for-profit public enterprise or government bureau than to the capitalist for-profit firm.

The "mixed" nature of the ownership rights in the American labor-managed firm provides important margins of discipline not available to owners of the socialistic enterprise. The existence of outside shareholders—residual claimants who are neither managers nor employees of the firm—helps assure that internal resource allocation decisions will be guided by the objective of maximizing shareholder wealth. The maximization of shareholder wealth is promoted by the ability of outside stockholders to sell their residual claims if internal-to-the-firm decision making fails to serve their interests. In addition, and especially in cases where employees represent only a minority of the shareholders, the market for corporate control constrains the resource

---

28 In the three employee-owned firms studied by Donna Sockell, for example, in no case did workers control more than 45 percent of the outstanding shares. See Donna Sockell, "Attitudes, Behavior, and Employee Ownership: Some Preliminary Data," *Industrial Relations* 24 (Winter 1985), pp. 130-38.

29 *Ibid.* In one of the firms studied by Sockell, voting shares were only offered to employees able to purchase 2,500 or more shares—a $25,000 investment at the then-prevailing market price per share.

30 *Ibid.* The percentages of employees who became shareholders in the three ESOPs studied by Sockell were 30 percent, 66 percent, and 85 percent.

31 See, for example, Eirik G. Furubotn and Svetozar Pejovich, "Property Rights and the Behavior of the Firm in a Socialist State: The Example of Yugoslavia," *Zeitschrift für Nationalökonomie* 30 (1970), pp. 431-54, and Eirik G. Furubotn, "The Long-Run Analysis of the Labor-Managed Firm: An Alternative Interpretation," *American Economic Review* 66 (March 1976), pp. 104-23.

allocation decisions of the labor-managed firm. Failure to maximize shareholder wealth will make the firm vulnerable to takeover by outsiders who perceive opportunities for employing the company's resources more efficiently.

There are nevertheless important differences between the labor-managed firm and the more traditional capitalist enterprise. In principle, it should not matter whether capital hires labor or labor hires capital. But the ownership structure of the firm can have a potentially critical impact on incentives and, hence, performance. These differences arise most particularly in terms of the length of the planning horizon over which the firm evaluates capital investment decisions and in the nature of the firm's responses to changing market conditions in the short run. To see these differences most clearly, it will be helpful to consider a "pure" or idealized labor-managed firm in which employees control 100 percent of the firm's equity and, moreover, all of the firm's employees are shareholders. The differences identified in this case carry over to settings where labor ownership is less complete but perhaps will exist in lesser degrees.

Before discussing specific incentive and performance consequences of employee ownership, we must recognize an important point. Owning stock provides workers with greater incentives to perform their jobs to the best of their abilities and to see that investment decisions are consistent with the maximization of the firm's discounted net cash flows than they would have otherwise. But their own personal interests will still not dovetail perfectly with those of the organization as a whole. This is because while having an ownership interest in the firm increases the cost of shirking to the individual employee, he or she will still not bear the full consequences of such behavior.

The larger is the number of employee-owners, the smaller is the ownership share of each and the more the cost of shirking to the individual owner diverges from the cost of shirking to the owners as a group. With N employee-owners, for example, each employee controls $1/N$ of the firm's shares. When any one owner shirks (reduces the level of effort he or she supplies to the organization and consumes additional leisure on the job) that owner captures all of the benefits associated with this activity, but bears only $1/N$ of the cost. The decline in the market value of equity claims attributable to any one employee-owner's shirking is shared by all. Because of this, each employee-owner will tend to consume more leisure than is consistent with the objective of maximizing the overall value of the firm.

Having a stake in the firm's profitability provides workers with greater incentives to share and exploit specialized information in mutually beneficial ways, to cooperate more fully with other employees and "management," and to supervise each other's effort. These factors may partially offset the increased incentive to shirk. But as the number of employee-owners increases, the ability of each owner to monitor and to police the performance of the others declines. Hence, beyond some point, losses from owner shirking may more than offset the gains otherwise associated with employee ownership of the firm.

Similar considerations apply to the incentives of individual employee-owners to search for and implement cost-saving innovations. Because the benefits of such innovations will be shared by all, a species of free-rider problem may arise in which, due to the fact that no one employee-owner can capture returns sufficient to offset the cost of the time and resources invested in such activities, innovations remain undiscovered or unexploited.

A final general point about employee ownership is that the market value of individual employee-owner's shares can be affected by many events that are both unrelated to individual effort and outside of the individual employee's control. Unanticipated supply interruptions, general trends in the macroeconomy, changes in government policy, and so forth interject "noise" into the relationship between an employee's own performance and the market value of his or her ownership position in the firm. The weaker is this link, the less favorable will be the impact of employee ownership on productivity and performance. All of this goes toward saying that employee ownership is not a panacea for declining labor productivity and failing fortunes. Worker-owners certainly face a different reward structure than is faced by the employees of the traditional, capitalist firm whose compensation is solely in the form of wages or salaries. But if employees' ownership shares are "small," the differences in the reward structure may not lead to dramatic differences in performance outcomes.

Horizon Problems

In the previous chapter, we determined the value of the classical capitalist firm at any point in time by calculating the present value of the future net cash flows expected to accrue to the firm's investments. Guided by the objective of maximizing the firm's market value (shareholders' wealth), managers have an incentive to undertake all proposed investment projects having a positive net present value. This result is independent of the time shape of a particular project's anticipated cash inflows and cash outflows. That is, a proposed investment with a computed positive net present value is acceptable even if its benefits are not realized until far in the future. And a proposed investment having a negative net present value is unacceptable even if its costs do not show up until a much later date. In other words, given that the owners of the firm are interested in maximizing the value of their equity claims, management will tend—allowance being made for agency costs—to adopt a long-term perspective when making investment decisions for the firm.

Do the same considerations apply to the labor-managed firm? That is, when the firm's employees are also its owners and are thereby responsible for managerial decision making,[32] will investment choices still be guided by

---

32 The precise mechanism by which employee-owners manage the labor-managed firm is itself an important topic, but one that is beyond the scope of this text. In principle, managerial decision-making authority can be delegated to a subset of the workers or managerial decisions can be made collectively under an agreed-upon voting rule. The particular voting rule adopted must balance the costs of decision making—the more inclusive the voting rule, the more time and resources will be needed to reach agreement—against the *external* costs of

long-term profit considerations? Or, instead, will labor-managed firms operate within a time horizon that is foreshortened?

Early models of the labor-managed firm adopted the assumption that managerial decisions are guided by the objective of maximizing net revenue (income) per worker. Such an assumption leads inevitably to the conclusion that labor-managed firms are significantly impaired in their ability to make efficient (value-maximizing) investment choices. There are two reasons for this. First, regardless of its impact on the value of the firm, worker-managers will rationally hesitate to implement any proposed capital project that will lead to an increase in output. Such growth would require an expansion of the firm's labor force and, hence, a dilution both in the managerial authority of the current employees and of their pro rata shares in the firm's revenues.

Second, workers with diverse time horizons will disagree over investment plans. This is because while all of the firm's current employees will be required to finance capital projects by reinvesting their earnings, only some of them will remain with the firm long enough to receive their full share of the benefits. Workers who leave the firm before the purchased assets are fully depreciated will be forced to forfeit the remaining undepreciated portion of their original investment.[33] Hence, older employees will tend to adopt a shorter time horizon for investment decisions than is optimal from the viewpoint of younger employees.

Internal Capital Accounts. The time horizon problem described in the previous paragraph implies that the labor-managed firm may undertake investment projects that would be unacceptable when evaluated on the basis of the net present value rule. One possible solution to the defective investment incentives associated with employees' diverse time horizons is to establish a set of formal **internal capital accounts** that provide individual workers with a claim on the firm's future net cash flows.[34] Such a system of internal capital accounts was introduced in the 1950s by the Mondragon group of worker cooperatives in the Basque region of northern Spain. Massachusetts enacted a special incorporation statute permitting the establishment of internal capital accounts in 1982, and similar statutes have since been adopted in Maine, Connecticut, New York, and Vermont.

---

collective decision making which are measured in terms of the welfare losses the winning coalition may potentially impose on the members of the losing coalition. These external costs of collective decision making will be zero only under a rule of unanimity where any one employee-owner can veto a group decision that reduces his or her own welfare. Obviously, however, decision-making costs will be at their maximum if unanimous agreement is required. These ideas are discussed extensively in the context of political markets in James M. Buchanan and Gordon Tullock, *The Calculus of Consent: Logical Foundations of Constitutional Democracy* (Ann Arbor: University of Michigan Press, 1962).

33 David P. Ellerman, "Horizon Problems and Property Rights in Labor-Managed Firms," *Journal of Comparative Economics* 10 (1986), p. 63.

34 *Ibid.*, pp. 63–65. The following discussion relies on Ellerman's description of internal capital accounts as a solution to the horizon problem of the labor-managed firm.

In a labor-managed firm with a set of internal capital accounts, there is one interest-bearing capital account for each current employee. The accounts are established so that their sum equals the market value of the equity on the balance sheet of the firm. Then, in every subsequent fiscal year after interest payments are made, the firm allocates its remaining retained net income (which may be positive or negative) among the capital accounts in accordance with a predetermined formula that is based on employees' labor contributions during the accounting period. Hence, the internal capital account balances are automatically adjusted upwards or downwards so that their sum remains equal to the market value of the firm's equity.

The internal capital accounts help solve the horizon problem that would otherwise plague the labor-managed firm. These accounts furnish each employee with a type of residual claim on the company's future net cash flows. This residual claim, in turn, supplies employee-owners with an incentive to undertake investment projects that raise expected future earnings—and to bypass projects that reduce them—because investment decisions have a direct impact on the market value of the firm's equity and, hence, on the balances in individual workers' capital accounts. Alternatively, the internal capital accounts serve as a "commitment mechanism" that helps guard against opportunistic behavior on the part of individual employees. A worker's capital account balance is equivalent to a bond whose worth will be reduced by actions that lower the value of the firm.

It is true that with a system of internal capital accounts a worker's claim on future net cash flows is partly or wholly contingent on working in the firm.[35] But this more general horizon problem can be handled by closing out an employee's capital account when his or her association with the firm ends and paying the departing worker's balance in the form of **consols**—a type of bond that pays interest in perpetuity.[36] The worker (or the worker's estate) can then choose either to hold the bonds and collect these interest payments or cash out the capital account by selling the securities in the bond market. The firm itself has the option of retiring the debt by repurchasing the bonds. In any of these cases, departing workers have a claim on the present discounted value of their pro rata shares in the value of the firm's equity. Because of this, they have an incentive to support only value-maximizing investments during the time of their active association with the firm.

In sum, the time horizon problem of the labor-managed firm can in principle be overcome by establishing a system of internal capital accounts that furnishes individual employees with a residual claim on future net cash flows. It is important to note, however, that the theory of internal capital accounts requires that the value of the firm's equity and, hence, employees' capital

---

35 Michael Jensen and William Meckling, "Rights and Production Functions: An Application to Labor-Managed Firms and Codetermination," *Journal of Business* 52 (October 1979), pp. 469-506.

36 The market value of a consol at any point in time is equal to F/r, where F is the face value of the bond and r is the market rate of interest.

account balances be determined by economic principles rather than by accounting principles. In this way the balance sheet net worth of the firm equals the *market* value of assets minus liabilities. Obviously, if the firm's assets are carried on the balance sheet at book value (acquisition cost) rather than market value, no adjustment of capital account balances to reflect changes in the value of the firm as a going concern will be possible. But while complicated in practice, "marking to market" (i.e., applying economic principles to value the firm's assets) is conceptually feasible. This implies that a properly structured set of internal capital accounts can be utilized so as to induce the labor-managed firm to more closely mimic the value-maximizing investment decisions of the more traditional capital-managed firm.

A potentially far more serious problem for the labor-managed enterprise is that, unlike the classical capitalist firm, it cannot hire workers in the customary sense. The inability to employ labor without also giving the new workers a voice in management and a share in ownership severely constrains the firm's responses to changing market conditions. The following section discusses the impact of this constraint on managerial decision making.

Flexibility Problems

The ability to adapt to changing market conditions—to adjust output rates and input usage optimally in response to increases or decreases in demand or to increases or decreases in the costs of production—is a hallmark of the classical capitalist firm. Acting as the agents of the firm's owners and guided by the objective of profit (shareholders' wealth) maximization, managers hire capital, labor, raw materials, and other inputs in least-cost combinations to produce the optimal quantity of output. Just as importantly, managers rearrange these input combinations to maintain equality between marginal revenue product and marginal factor cost across all inputs whenever such adjustments are dictated by changes in demand or supply conditions.

The ability of the labor-managed enterprise to replicate the flexible behavior of the more traditional entrepreneurial firm has been the subject of much debate in the economics literature. The crux of the matter is this: "[A]n adequate theory of the self-managed firm must consider the preferences and wealth-increasing opportunities of those individuals *actually making economic decisions*. At any moment of time, particular individuals are members of the working collective, and it is this constituency that must decide the firm's actions in the next time frame."[37]

Put differently, in the labor-managed firm employee-owners have decision-making responsibility with respect to production plans and input usage. Because these decisions have a direct impact on their own personal wealth and welfare, there will be a decision-making bias in favor of labor's interests. In the entrepreneurial firm, by contrast, managers make input decisions on

---

37 Furubotn, "Long-Run Analysis of the Labor-Managed Firm," p. 104. Emphasis in original.

behalf of the suppliers of capital. Because these capitalists own the firm, decision-making will tend to be biased in favor of enhancing the value of the entire enterprise.

A Simple Mathematical Model of the Labor-Managed Firm. The differences in the decision-making biases of the labor-managed and the capital-managed firm lead to sharp differences in their responses to changing market conditions, at least in the short run. Consider two price-taking firms each of which employs two variable inputs, labor and other resources, to produce the same output. One of these enterprises is organized as a traditional profit-maximizing firm (PMF); the other is a labor-managed firm (LMF) which the employees own and manage collectively and which strives to maximize income per worker.[38]

The simple production function utilized by both firms can be written as

$$Q = f(L, X),$$

where Q is the number of units of output supplied per time period, L is the number of workers employed, and X stands for all other variable inputs. There is also a fixed cost of production, k, which can be interpreted as a capital depreciation charge.

The objective of the PMF is to maximize absolute profit, π. The firm attains this objective by selecting the quantity of labor and other inputs that maximize the difference between total revenue and total cost,

$$\pi = PQ - (wL + p_X X + k),$$

where P is the market price of the firm's product, w is the wage rate of labor, and p_X is the unit price of the other variable inputs.

The PMF's maximization problem is solved by partially differentiating the above profit function with respect to L and with respect to X, and then setting the resulting expressions equal to zero. This exercise yields the familiar marginal equations

$$\frac{\partial \pi}{\partial L} = 0 \rightarrow PQ_L = w$$

$$\frac{\partial \pi}{\partial X} = 0 \rightarrow PQ_X = p_X,$$

where Q_L and Q_X are the partial derivatives of Q with respect to L and X. These partial derivatives are interpreted as the respective marginal productivities of labor and the other variable inputs.

---

38 The following analysis is based on B. Horvat, "Labour-Managed Economies, " in John Eatwell, Murray Milgate, and Peter Newman, eds., *The New Palgrave: A Dictionary of Economics,* vol. 3 (London: Macmillan, 1987), pp. 80-81.

The two necessary conditions for a profit maximum stated in the previous paragraph require that the PMF hire labor and other inputs up to the point where the values of their marginal products, PQ_L and PQ_X, are equal to the inputs' respective unit prices. These two conditions can be used to explore how the PMF will respond to changes in the various parameters that enter into its decision-making calculus.

In particular, suppose that there is an increase in the demand for the firm's product which is expected to be permanent. Other things being the same, an increase in P will lead the firm to hire both more labor and more of the other inputs. This result can be seen by noting that with input prices w and p_X assumed to be constant, Q_L and Q_X must *decline* if the two conditions necessary for a profit maximum are to continue to hold. Because the marginal products of labor and other inputs fall with an increase in their usage, it follows that an increase in product price leads the firm to increase employment as well as its purchases of other variable inputs. Furthermore, given that the marginal productivities of all inputs are positive, total output increases as the firm employs more labor and other resources.

A similar analysis of the conditions necessary for a profit maximum establishes that the PMF will respond to an increase in either w or p_X by reducing total output and its usage of the input whose price has risen. Moreover, a change in fixed cost has no impact on the input decisions of the PMF because k does not appear in the marginal equations.

Now consider the responses of the labor-managed firm to the same changes in market conditions. If the objective function of the LMF is to maximize income per worker, y, the firm's problem is to select L and X to maximize

$$y = \frac{PQ - (p_X X + k)}{L}.$$

Note that wages do not exist in this model. Labor's entire compensation is in the form of proportional shares of the firm's sales revenue net of payments to other resources and capital depreciation charges.

The maximization problem is again solved by partially differentiating the above equation for y with respect to L and with respect to X, and then setting the resulting expressions equal to zero. Taking these derivatives yields

$$\frac{\partial y}{\partial L} = 0 \rightarrow PQ_L = \frac{PQ - (p_X X + k)}{L} = y$$

$$\frac{\partial y}{\partial X} = 0 \rightarrow PQ_X = p_X.$$

Although the LMF treats the other variable inputs, X, in the same way as the PMF, employing them up to the point where the value of their marginal product is equal to price, it is also apparent that labor inputs are treated differently. A necessary condition for income per worker to be at a maximum is that the value of labor's marginal product be equal to income per head. That such a condition can lead to perverse behavior by the LMF can be seen more clearly by rewriting the first equation in the following form:

$$Q - Q_L L = \frac{k + p_X X}{P}.$$

Again suppose that there is an increase in the demand for the firm's product which is expected to be permanent. Other things being the same, an increase in P will lead the firm to curtail employment and reduce output. We can see this result by noting that with other input prices, p_X, other input usage, X, and capital charges, k, assumed to be constant, a higher output price causes the right-hand side of the above expression to fall. The left-hand side must therefore also be reduced if the equality is to continue to hold. Because the derivative of the left-hand side with respect to L is positive (i.e., $\partial[Q - Q_L L]/\partial L = -Q_{LL} L > 0$),[39] it follows that labor usage and, hence, output must be reduced in response to an increase in demand in order to continue to maximize income per worker.

Similar reasoning implies that the LMF will increase output and employment in response to a decline in demand and that its decision-making calculus will be affected by changes in fixed cost. In particular, an increase in fixed cost will raise output and employment and a reduction in fixed cost will have the opposite effects.

Additional comparisons between the behavior of the LMF and the PMF follow from observing that $y > w$; that is, income per worker in the labor-managed firm exceeds the wage rate paid to the employees of the profit-maximizing firm. Faced with the same output price, $y > w$ implies that the marginal productivity of labor will be higher in the LMF than in the PMF.[40] The LMF consequently employs fewer workers and produces less output than its profit-maximizing counterpart. For the same reason, the LMF uses a relatively more capital-intensive production process than the PMF. Lower employment and higher capital intensity in turn imply, for a given interest rate, a lower growth rate in output over time for the LMF.

The perverse nature of the LMF's responses to changing market conditions is a result of the assumption that employee-owners seek to maximize income per worker. When demand increases, for example, each unit of output can be sold at a higher price. Higher revenue per unit sold, in turn, affords the opportunity to earn, at a lower level of output, the same total income that had been earned at the previous price-output combination. And if output is reduced, the firm's usage of other variable inputs can be curtailed. Finally, if the firm lays off some of its employees, the net income share received by each of the remaining workers rises.

---

39 The requirement that $Q_{LL} < 0$ is imposed by the second-order conditions for a maximum.

40 In equilibrium, $w = PQ_L$ for the PMF and $y = PQ_L$ for the LMF. At the same output price, $y > w$ implies Q_L (LMF) $> Q_L$ (PMF).

Workers' Attitudes Toward Risk. Some authors have questioned whether this assumption, and the behavioral perversities implied by it, adequately describes the actual workings of the labor-managed firm. One challenge to the empirical relevance of the assumption of the maximization of income per worker asks whether profit-sharing is in fact superior to traditional wage contracts for the typical worker.[41] In the profit-maximizing firm, labor receives a fixed and certain wage rate. Whether or not this wage will in fact be received in any period is uncertain, however, because employees may be laid off if demand unexpectedly declines.[42] In the labor-managed firm, by contrast, labor income is more variable and the probability of unemployment is no less variable. Because workers are subject to more risk in the labor-managed firm, one cannot conclude automatically that profit-sharing is preferable to wage contracts. The answer ultimately depends on employees' attitudes toward risk.

An alternative approach to the problem explicitly takes account of a choice faced by a representative employee-owner when the demand for the labor-managed firm's product rises. This decision is "whether to vote for a dividend-maximizing policy that would cause employment to shrink and thereby jeopardize his own membership in the firm or for a policy of maintaining employment without striving to attain the highest possible dividend."[43] It can be easily shown that, faced with this choice, a risk-neutral, utility-maximizing worker would rationally opt for the latter policy. That is, the worker would accept a smaller increase in income per head in return for the certainty of not being furloughed when demand increases. This response would occur as long as the dividend received at the old, lower price for the firm's product is greater than or equal to the compensation available in the worker's next best alternative employment opportunity outside the LMF.

Such a conclusion is strengthened if workers are risk averse. The upshot is that employment in labor-managed firms will tend to be stable in the face of short-run increases in demand, with adjustments to the new, higher price achieved in the long run "through normal retirements and other forms of voluntary attrition."[44] Similarly, the LMF will respond to a reduction in demand by increasing employment and output if the decline in price is expected to be permanent. But a rational, utility-maximizing worker might be reluctant to opt for expansion if higher product prices are expected to recur in the future. This is because expansion during a downturn in demand would lock into place a larger workforce that would no longer be optimal for the higher price.

---

41 D. M. Nuti, "Codetermination and Profit-Sharing," in Eatwell, Milgate, and Newman, eds., *New Palgrave*, vol. 1, pp. 465-69.

42 It is worth noting in this regard that the theory of compensating wage differentials implies that profit-maximizing firms in which workers face a higher probability of being laid off must pay higher wages to attract labor away from other firms where employment is more certain. See Chapter 17 for a discussion of compensating wage differentials.

43 J. Michael Montias, "On the Labor-Managed Firm in a Competitive Environment," *Journal of Comparative Economics* 10 (1986), p. 3

44 *Ibid.*, p. 4.

In short, explicit consideration of the options available to employee-owners implies that employment will be relatively inflexible in the face of short-run fluctuations in the demand for the firm's product. Such behavior appears to be consistent with empirical observations suggesting that labor-managed firms tend to be characterized by "chronic overemployment,"[45] and are slow to adjust to changes in the prices of non-labor inputs.[46]

The foregoing discussion of the labor-managed firm assumes that the enterprise is wholly owned by its employees. If this assumption is relaxed—that is, if workers are only minority shareholders, for example—then the outside owners will impose a margin of discipline on the labor-managed firm that will tend to limit its perverse behavior. Moreover, if not all employees are residual claimants, so that some of the firm's workers can be hired (and fired!) in the spot market under a standard wage contract, then wayward adjustments to changing market conditions will be dampened.[47]

It is nevertheless true, however, that because the labor-managed firm treats labor differently from its other inputs, impaired economic efficiency is to be expected. Hence, in an economy composed of both labor-managed firms and profit-maximizing firms, the long-term survival of the former is doubtful in the absence of favorable treatment (such as special tax breaks or subsidies) at the hands of public policy makers.

Codetermination and Gain-Sharing

Full employee ownership has not been an option chosen frequently in the United States. But in many firms, concerns with lagging labor productivity and with deteriorating output quality have led to the adoption of group-incentive policies giving workers the opportunity to participate directly in managerial decision making or to share in the gains generated by their own contributions to improved performance.

Codetermination, a process by which workers and management jointly set goals and make decisions affecting productivity, represents one type of group-incentive policy. "Quality circles" supply a relevant example. These circles bring together workers and their supervisors in regularly scheduled meetings to discuss production targets, set quality goals, communicate cost-saving ideas, and so on, for the purpose of discovering and implementing new ways of enhancing the group's performance.

Quality circles and other codetermination strategies are based on the premise that workers acquire in a learning-by-doing fashion a substantial amount of specialized knowledge about their assigned tasks. They

---

45 Horvat, "Labour-Managed Economies," p. 81.

46 John P. Burkett, "Search, Selection, and Shortage in an Industry Composed of Labor-Managed Firms," *Journal of Comparative Economics* 10 (1986), pp. 26-40.

47 See Avner Ben-Ner, "On the Stability of the Cooperative Type of Organization," *Journal of Comparative Economics* 3 (September 1984), pp. 247-60, and Hajime Miyazaki, "On the Success and Dissolution of the Labor-Managed Firm in the Capitalist Economy," *Journal of Political Economy* 92 (December 1984), pp. 909-31.

encounter production problems and identify solutions that, if shared with other members of the team, would result in improved productivity, lower costs, or higher quality from which all would benefit. Quality circles provide a forum in which the routine details of the production process can be discussed and debated in ways that foster a "team spirit". This cooperation cultivates greater job satisfaction by giving employees more of a say in determining the rules and operations of the workplace.

Motivation is the key to the success of any group-incentive policy, of course. While team spirit and enhanced job satisfaction are surely valuable commodities, they may not always provide adequate incentives for individual team members to share the benefits of their specialized knowledge. **Gain-sharing plans** offer explicit monetary rewards to the team for achieving pre-determined group objectives. Under these plans, when a group of workers meets or exceeds a preset goal, all of the members of the group receive a pro-rata bonus tied to the extent to which the goals are surpassed.

For example, the Nucor Corporation, a steelmaker, pays its workers a weekly bonus over and above their base pay determined by the number of tons of steel produced that meet the company's quality standards. Similarly, the Carrier Corporation, a leading manufacturer of air-conditioning and heating equipment, uses a gain-sharing plan that returns to employees half the labor-cost savings achieved by increasing the number of acceptable units produced over and above the number produced in an earlier base year.[48]

As in all other cases of shared responsibility and shared reward, free-riding is the principal economic problem. When the firm rewards collective performance, each member of the group has an incentive to shirk, that is, to behave self-interestedly with the object of receiving his or her share of the group's bonus without bearing his or her share of the cost of producing the gains on which the bonus is based. If one individual has such an incentive, they all do. And while the group as a whole would be better off (receive a larger bonus) if each member contributed diligently to meeting the predetermined objective, shirking can cause group-incentive schemes to unravel. This observation suggests that gain-sharing plans are more likely to be successful when applied to small teams whose members can more easily monitor the contributions of others. In this situation, peer pressure can more effectively keep individual effort in line with the group's objectives.

Gain-sharing can also be effective in situations where it is costly for the employer to determine and reward the contributions of individual employees to team output. How, for example, can the employer measure the contribution of a single member of the research department to the development of a new product? How can the contribution of one member of a design team be determined and rewarded? In such cases, the team members themselves are likely to have more and better information about their individual contributions than the employer is able to acquire. Group incentives may then

---

48 Nancy L. Perry, "Here Come Richer, Riskier Pay Plans," *Fortune* (19 December 1988), pp. 50-58.

motivate the employees to monitor one another's contributions and take steps that encourage individual effort, foster the disclosure of specialized knowledge, and promote cooperative behavior in behalf of the team.

Like all other aspects of economic life, codetermination and gain-sharing strategies involve a trade-off. The manager who considers adopting a group-incentive scheme must therefore weigh the expected increase in productivity against the extra cost of monitoring and controlling shirking behavior.

SUMMARY

This chapter has explored the special problems associated with managing the not-for-profit and the employee-owned firm. The main lesson of the chapter is that not-for-profit status and a greater role for employees in the ownership and management of the firm have important effects on the rules of the game under which managerial decision makers operate. On the one hand, with limits on the distribution of profits to owners and without well-defined and saleable residual claims in place, the managers and employees of not-for-profit organizations, public enterprises, and other profit-constrained firms have weaker incentives to use resources efficiently than their counterparts in traditional, for-profit firms. On the other hand, participation by workers in the ownership of the firm may lead to perverse behavior due to the fact that employee-owners will rationally treat their own labor differently from other inputs.

The practical implication of the theoretical ideas laid out in this chapter is that the manager of the non-traditional firm must devote more time and invest more resources in supervising, coordinating, and monitoring the performances of the productive resources under his or her command than the manager of the classical capitalist enterprise. Failure to do so gives freer rein to the disabilities associated with these alternative organizational forms.

KEY TERMS
donative nonprofits
commercial nonprofits
mutual nonprofits
entrepreneurial nonprofits
cooperatives
rate-of-return regulation
public enterprises
shirking
residual
residual claimant
market for corporate control
employee stock ownership plan
internal capital accounts
consols
codetermination
gain-sharing plans

QUESTIONS

16.1 As far as capital investment decisions are concerned, the managers of public enterprises and the managers of private, not-for-profit organizations have much shorter time horizons than the managers of private, for-profit firms. True, false, or uncertain? Explain.

16.2 As the Russian Republic of the former Soviet Union moves toward a market economy, it has adopted a policy of raising substantially the prices of consumer goods, all of which under socialism had been produced by state-owned enterprises and sold at heavily subsidized prices. Only after consumers have adjusted to these higher prices will steps be taken permitting Russian property, including the government enterprises, to be privately owned. Why can this policy sequence be described as "all pain, no gain?" In other words, explain why private property ownership should have preceded the announcement of major price increases. Given your answer, why do you think that price increases came first?

16.3 The University of Mississippi's School of Business Administration contains two academic departments: the Department of Management & Marketing (M&M) and the Department of Economics & Finance (E&F). In one of the departments (E&F), faculty members are allocated individual research budgets at the beginning of the year which they use to pay for their own business expenses, including travel, long-distance telephone calls, and photocopying. In M&M, such expenses are paid out of the centralized departmental operating budget. The department head periodically reviews the telephone and photocopy accounts to guard against abuse and personally preapproves all travel requests. In which department do faculty make more long-distance telephone calls? Why?

16.4 Which of the following natural resources do you expect the world to run out of first: crude oil or whale oil? Explain.

16.5 The average state spends about $4,000 per year educating a public school student in grades K through 12. The average per pupil cost of a private school education is about $2,000 per year. Explain.

16.6 In the "softer" business courses, groups of students are often required to cooperate in preparing class presentations. A term paper is required of each student in other courses. Write a paragraph explaining why the papers prepared by individual students are "better" (more thoroughly researched, fewer grammatical and typographical errors, and so on) than those prepared by groups of students. Now write a paragraph explaining why the group projects are better.

16.7 There is a perennial debate on college campuses about how much weight should be given to teaching and research in faculty promotion and tenure decisions. Why, given the apparent importance of student evaluations of faculty teaching, is it rational for faculty members to be lousy teachers?

16.8 One explanation for the relatively poor performance of public enterprises focuses on competition rather than ownership. That is, public enterprises tend to have higher costs than private enterprises not because they are publicly owned per se but because they lack the discipline of competitive market forces. A corollary to this theory is that if forced to compete for customers, publicly owned enterprises would produce as efficiently as privately owned firms. Evaluate this argument.

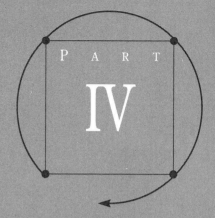

Government and Business

Private Markets and Public Policy

OVERVIEW

Part IV focuses on public policies toward business. Government has a pervasive influence on the private business sector. Antitrust and regulation are among the most important of the public policies that constrain business decision making and thereby influence the allocation of the economy's scarce productive resources. Managers at all levels of the organizational hierarchy must be prepared to deal with the legal and political environments in which their firms operate.

Chapter 17 lays the groundwork for understanding the purposes and effects of public policies toward business. It differs significantly from the standard textbook treatments of these issues which typically assume that governmental policies are formulated and implemented solely with the objective of promoting a freely functioning competitive marketplace. The standard analysis of public policy presupposes that government can and will costlessly intervene in the private economy to restrain the self-interested, profit-seeking behavior of business enterprise in ways that foster social responsibility and advance the public's interest.

This chapter shows instead how legislative and policy decisions in a representative democracy are shaped not by some ideal conception of the public interest, but rather by the interaction between private interest groups seeking protection from the forces of competition and government officials and policymakers seeking to maximize their own political self-interests.

The theoretical justification for government intervention into the economy is based on the concept of "market failure." This rationale suggests that the unfettered private marketplace may fail to produce the socially optimal quantities of some goods. We discuss three examples of market failure. These examples of market failure are "externality," the "tragedy of the commons," and "monopoly." The remainder of Part IV then describes how specific antitrust and regulatory policies themselves often fail to achieve their stated purposes.

APPLICATION

Consider a factory whose smoke emissions damage the laundry hung outdoors by five nearby residents.[a] Assume that, in the absence of any corrective action, each resident suffers $75 worth of damages so that the total social costs of air pollution amount to $375 (= 5 x $75). Further assume that the economic harm caused by the factory's smoke can be eliminated in one of two ways. On the one hand, for $150 a smoke "scrubber" can be installed on the factory's chimney which will cleanse the smoke emissions, thereby removing the harmful pollutants at their source. On the other hand, each of the factory's neighbors can purchase an electric clothes dryer so that they no longer need to hang their laundry outdoors. Electric clothes dryers can be obtained at a price of $50 each.

Assuming that the alternatives are equally effective in eliminating the social costs of air pollution, which of the two possible solutions is the more efficient? Under what conditions will this efficient outcome emerge? That is, consider whether the efficient solution will be adopted if the factory's neighbors have the right to clean air or if the factory instead has the right to pollute. Will the private market fail to correct this environmental externality under either—or both—of these property rights regimes? If so, what role can public policy play in promoting the socially desirable outcome?

a This example is taken from A. Mitchell Polinsky, An Introduction to Law and Economics, 2E. (Boston: Little, Brown, 1989), pp. 11-13.

MARKET FAILURE AND GOVERNMENT FAILURE

The assertion of market failure is perhaps the most important justification for government intervention into the private economy. **Market failure** refers to circumstances in which private market institutions "fail to sustain 'desirable' activities or to estop 'undesirable' activities."[1] Such situations

1 Francis M. Bator, "The Anatomy of Market Failure," *Quarterly Journal of Economics* 72 (August 1958), p. 351.

arise when the benefits or costs of an activity at the level of the individual decision maker diverge from the corresponding benefits or costs of that activity at the level of society. In other words, the private market may fail when the relevant economic agents do not bear the full social costs—or cannot capture the full social benefits—of their resource-allocation decisions.

A market characterized by "externalities" of this sort may supply less than the socially optimal quantity of some goods, such as education, workplace safety, charity, and inoculation against communicable diseases. More than the socially optimal quantity of some "bads," like litter, polluted water, smog, and acid rain, may likewise be produced. Indeed, private markets may be completely unable to provide certain "public goods"—national defense, for example—that once produced are freely available to all, including individuals who have not paid for them.

In an older way of thinking, dealing with market failure was simply a matter of recommending that government levy the appropriate tax or pay the appropriate subsidy necessary to induce private decision makers to take account of the full social costs and benefits of their actions. Modern approaches to the market failure problem raise doubts about the empirical importance of externalities and public goods,[2] and, moreover, emphasize that even where such phenomena exist, the knowledge limitations of public policy makers and the costs of government intervention must be recognized when corrective action is being considered.

These cautionary notes about the efficacy of government intervention for correcting market failure have been raised because economists have come to more fully appreciate the incentives of private parties to resolve disputes involving property rights in a manner that is mutually beneficial and, hence, improves the efficiency with which society's scarce productive resources are allocated. Just as importantly, economists have come to more fully appreciate the limitations inherent in public policy solutions to market failure problems.

Government is not perfect and it, like markets, can fail to achieve ideal outcomes. When government intervenes it necessarily acts on the basis of limited information and must balance the demands of the various special-interest groups that will be affected by its policy decisions. Given these factors, along with the costs of the resources used in the execution of public policy and the inevitable time lags involved in the political process, government intervention can be—and often is—ineffective or perverse. Appropriate solutions to market failure problems in the economy therefore almost always involve a choice among imperfect alternatives—among private solutions that are not perfect and public policy solutions that are not perfect. The costs and benefits of each must accordingly be examined carefully on a case-by-case basis.

---

2 The archetypal public good—the lighthouse—was in fact provided quite successfully by private firms in Great Britain until the early 19th century. See Ronald H. Coase, "The Lighthouse in Economics," *Journal of Law and Economics* 17 (October 1974), pp. 357-76. Also see Harold Demsetz, "The Private Production of Public Goods," *Journal of Law and Economics* 13 (October 1970), pp. 293-306.

Externality

Externalities represent an important example of market failure. As mentioned previously, externalities arise in cases where the benefits or costs of an activity at the level of an individual decision maker diverge from the corresponding benefits or costs of the activity at the level of society. Put another way, persons not directly party to a private market transaction either receive benefits from or are harmed by the resource-allocation decisions of the market participants.

Externalities can either be positive (social benefits exceed private benefits) or negative (social costs exceed private costs). Because the analysis of these two cases proceeds symmetrically, the following discussion focuses on an example of negative externality like the hypothetical air pollution problem described in the chapter's opening application.

Figure 17.1 depicts the relevant cost and benefit schedules for analyzing a negative externality. A factory employs a production process for manufacturing some good that generates an environmentally harmful byproduct. The factory discharges toxic pollutants into the surrounding air or water, for example. These pollutants find their way downwind or downstream, causing injury to wildlife and to innocent third parties who are neither employed by the factory's owner nor purchase the factory's product.[3] These emissions may impair the health of those individuals who live near the factory, threaten their livelihoods by reducing fish and game populations, cause their houses to need repainting more often, and so on.

The important point, however, is that the factory's owner will not take these social costs into account when making decisions about how much to produce. After all, no one owns the air or the water and no fee must be paid for disposing of the factory's waste. Consequently, only the private benefits and costs of the factory's production activities enter into the owner's profit-maximizing calculus. The private benefits of production consist of the revenue earned from selling the manufactured good to consumers. For simplicity, it is assumed that the factory's owner is a price-taker and can therefore sell any quantity of output the plant produces for a price of P dollars per unit.

The horizontal line labeled MB in Figure 17.1 accordingly shows the marginal private benefits of production—each additional unit produced and sold generates P dollars in extra revenue for the factory's owner. The curve labeled MC_P represents the corresponding private marginal costs of producing various possible levels of output. These private costs include the factory owner's outlays on labor, materials, and capital as well as the opportunity costs of the resources used in the production process. The private marginal costs of production are rising, indicating that these resources must be attracted away from increasingly valuable alternative uses as output is expanded.

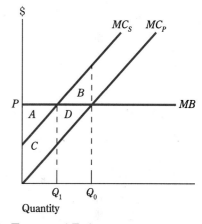

Figure 17.1
Negative Externality

---

3 The possible harmful effects of these pollutants on the factory's employees are analyzed separately in Chapter 18. As shall be demonstrated there, no externality exists in this case because workers will be compensated in the form of higher wages for any additional health risks they bear by taking jobs in this factory rather than choosing safer occupations.

In the absence of any other consideration, the factory's owner will rationally choose to produce Q_0 units of output. An output rate of Q_0 units is optimal from the producer's point of view because at that rate marginal private benefits are equal to marginal private costs ($MB = MC_P$). The producer's *total* revenue at the point of optimal production is represented by the area of the rectangle defined by P times Q_0; *total* costs are represented by the area of the triangle underneath MC_P at Q_0. The net private benefit of production—**producer surplus**—consequently amounts to the difference between these two areas (total revenue minus total cost), or the sum of the areas in the diagram labeled A, C, and D.

The quantity of output chosen by the producer is not optimal from society's point of view, however. This is because the injury sustained by the factory's neighbors also represents a cost of production. The curve labeled MC_S includes the dollar value of these external costs. Put another way, the vertical distance between MC_S and MC_P measures the additional costs borne by third parties exposed to the factory's toxic wastes.

For simplicity, these external costs are assumed to be constant over the range of the factory owner's output choices. They may take the form of outlays on medical treatments for ailments resulting from breathing polluted air or drinking polluted water, reductions in income associated with lost work time or with smaller wildlife populations, decreases in homeowners' property values, and so forth. When these external costs are taken into account, optimal production is Q_1 units, for this is the point at which the producer's marginal private benefits are equal to the marginal social costs of production ($MB = MC_S$).

The total external costs associated with the factory's pollution emissions are determined by multiplying the cost borne by third parties per unit of output produced ($MC_S - MC_P$) times Q_0, the privately optimal level of output. This total is represented in the diagram by the summation of the areas labeled B, C, and D. Hence, when Q_0 units of output are produced, the factory owner's total gains are equal to $A + C + D$ and society's total external costs are equal to $B + C + D$. The *net* social gain or loss is accordingly the difference between these two amounts, or $(A + C + D) - (B + C + D) = A - B$.

If $B > A$, the external costs borne by third parties exceed the producer's gains. The market has "failed" in the sense that it has not stopped an undesirable activity. If $B < A$, on the other hand, no market failure can be said to exist because the producer gains more than third parties lose. "Society," which includes the owner of the factory, is better off on balance than it would be if the good were not produced at all.

Pigou Taxes. When external costs exceed the producer's gains ($B > A$), the socially optimal level of production can be restored, in principle, by levying a tax on the good's producer. This is known as a **Pigou tax** after the British economist who first analyzed the social welfare consequences of externalities.[4]

---

4 Arthur C. Pigou, *The Economics of Welfare* (London: Macmillan, 1932).

Such a tax forces the firm's owner to take account of the impact of the factory's production activities on third parties.

For the case at hand, the optimal Pigou tax, T, is equal to $(MC_S - MC_P)$ dollars per unit of output produced. If the producer is required to pay this tax on every unit of output produced, the social costs of the firm's production activities are transformed into a private cost of production. This cost will then be incorporated into the owner's marginal-revenue-equals-marginal-cost decision calculus. Production will therefore be cut back to Q_1 units, at which point $MB = MC_P + T = MC_S$. The externality is internalized into private production decisions and the socially optimal level of output is consequently chosen.

The Pigou tax, of course, does not completely eliminate the production of pollution emissions. When Q_1 units of output are produced, third parties suffer injuries totalling $(MC_S - MC_P)$ times Q_1. These total external costs are represented by the area labelled C in the diagram. However, because $T = MC_S - MC_P$, government collects C dollars in tax revenue from the producer. If this tax revenue is redistributed in payments to third parties as compensation for the injuries they sustain on account of being exposed to the factory's pollutants, there is a net social gain of A dollars from intervening to correct the market failure.

The Coase Theorem. Before inquiring into the empirical relevance of the Pigou model, it is also important to consider the incentives of private parties to resolve disputes involving externalities. The central idea which underlies the modern analysis of property rights and externalities was laid out in a much cited article published by Nobel laureate Ronald Coase in 1960.[5] This idea, which has since become known as the **Coase Theorem**, can be stated formally as follows: In the absence of transaction costs, the allocation of resources is independent of the initial assignment of property rights.

The Coase Theorem can best be illustrated with reference to this chapter's opening application. Recall that the application involves smoke damage to the laundry hung outdoors by five of a polluting factory's neighbors. The total pollution damages, which amounted to $375 (damages of $75 borne by each of the nearby residents), could be eliminated either by the installation of a smoke scrubber costing $150 or by providing each neighbor with an electric clothes dryer at a cost of $50. The efficient solution is obviously for the factory's owners to install the smoke scrubber because it will eliminate total damages of $375 for an outlay of $150, whereas it would cost society $250 to purchase five clothes dryers.

Coase asked whether the efficient outcome would emerge if the factory's neighbors have the right to clean air or if, instead, the factory has the right to pollute. The answer he gave is that the efficient solution will be chosen in both cases.

5 Ronald H. Coase, "The Problem of Social Cost," *Journal of Law and Economics* 3 (October 1960), pp. 1-44. Also see Ronald H. Coase, "The Federal Communications Commission," *Journal of Law and Economics* 2 (October 1959), pp. 1-40.

To see this important result, suppose first that the factory's neighbors have a right to clean air. The owners of the factory then have three options. They can pay out damages of $375 thereby fully compensating the injured third parties for the costs they bear; they can purchase five clothes dryers for the nearby residents at a cost of $250; or they can install a smoke scrubber for an outlay of $150. The factory's owners will rationally install the scrubber because it represents the least-cost alternative for eliminating the injury caused by pollution emissions.

On the other hand, suppose that the factory has the right to pollute. The nearby residents who are harmed by smoke discharges themselves have three options. They can choose to suffer their collective damages of $375, they can each purchase an electric clothes dryer for a total outlay of $250, or they can purchase a smoke scrubber for the factory's chimney at a cost of $150. Clearly, the factory's neighbors will also choose to purchase the smoke scrubber because they can thereby eliminate $375 worth of injury for $150, yielding a net benefit for themselves of $225.

Note that while the initial assignment of property rights does not affect the outcome, it does affect the distribution of wealth between the parties to the dispute. If those injured by the factory smoke have the right to clean air, the factory's owners bear the cost of eliminating the externality. By contrast, if the factory has the right to pollute, the injured parties bear the cost of eliminating the damages they suffer. The important point, however, is that the efficient solution emerges independently of initial property rights assignments. Private market arrangements internalize the externality in the most cost-effective manner available.

The Coase Theorem does contain an important proviso, namely that efficient solutions to externality problems can be expected to emerge in private markets only in the absence of transaction costs. **Transaction costs** include the costs of acquiring information about the impact of an externality on personal wealth and of identifying other individuals who have common interests on the issue. Obviously, if the injury suffered is "small" or not easily discovered, it will not pay to bear the costs of becoming informed.

Organization costs represent an additional barrier to collective action. Even after a community of interests has been identified, the individuals who join together to resolve an externality dispute must agree on a common course of action. They must then marshal their resources in support of their bargaining efforts and overcome free rider problems—the propensity of individual group members to shirk in the hope of receiving their pro rata share of the group's expected gains without supplying their pro rata share of the effort required to secure those gains. Hence, collective action is worthwhile only if the anticipated benefits exceed the associated costs.[6]

To see the impact of transaction costs on the resolution of externality disputes, suppose that it would cost each of the factory's neighbors $60 to join

6 See, generally, Mancur Olson, *The Logic of Collective Action: Public Goods and the Theory of Groups* (Cambridge, MA: Harvard University Press, 1971).

together in common cause to deal with their smoke pollution problem. (This figure could represent the opportunity cost of a resident's time spent meeting with the factory's owners to negotiate a mutually satisfactory settlement.) Now if the right to pollute is assigned to the producer, the efficient solution will not emerge. This is because by collectively spending $250 to purchase five electric clothes dryers, the factory's neighbors can avoid the $300 in transaction costs necessary to organize and reach agreement on purchasing a $150 smoke scrubber for the factory's chimney.

On the other hand, if the residents have the right to clean air, the smoke scrubber will still be installed because the injured parties' costs of organizing do not enter into the factory owners' decision-making calculus. Hence, not every legal rule for assigning property rights yields the efficient solution to an externality problem in the presence of positive transaction costs.

Although the simple version of the Coase Theorem makes an unrealistic assumption about transaction costs, it nevertheless provides a fruitful way of thinking about property rights assignments and externalities because it identifies the incentives and constraints that shape collective action in this area. In particular, Coase's insight suggests that where transaction costs are low, private markets can be expected to internalize externalities efficiently no matter how entitlements to resources are initially distributed. On the other hand, while positive transaction costs can impede the attainment of the efficient solution to an externality problem, the Coase Theorem implies that direct government intervention may still not be warranted.

Coase versus Pigou. The Coase Theorem has an important implication for public policy solutions to externality problems. Simply asserting that markets have failed does not make it so. Those supporting the need for government intervention to reduce the production of goods generating external costs and to increase the production of goods generating external benefits must therefore bear the burden of showing that transaction costs are high enough to impede the attainment of efficient, private solutions that internalize the externality. And, moreover, they must prove that the value of the resources government will consume in intervening is smaller than the value of the benefits anticipated from such intervention.

This is a difficult case to make for at least two reasons. First, while the textbook derivation of the optimal Pigou tax (or subsidy) is a simple matter of drawing hypothetical marginal benefit and marginal cost schedules and measuring the distance between private costs and social costs (or between private benefits and social benefits), it is unlikely that a government agency will have access to the detailed revenue and cost data required to set the tax or subsidy rate at the optimal level. Critics of the model of profit maximization often claim that it is unrealistic to assume that firms have accurate information about their own cost and revenue schedules. But it is even more unrealistic to assume that such information will be available to outside observers of the firm.

Moreover, firms facing the prospect of taxation will have an incentive to misrepresent their costs in the hope of gaining a lower tax rate. Third parties who bear external costs or who enjoy external benefits will likewise have incentives to overstate either the extent of their injuries or the magnitude of their gains in the hope of receiving greater compensation or larger subsidies. Hence, the knowledge limitations of public policy makers reduce the expected benefits of intervention by erecting barriers to the determination of the socially optimal level of production and the computation of the optimal tax or subsidy rate that will lead to that outcome.

Second, and perhaps in part due to the knowledge limitations faced by government agencies, the tax and subsidy tools recommended by the Pigovian model to induce private decision makers to internalize externalities are rarely, if ever, employed in practice. Instead, government intervention to correct perceived sources of market failure in the private economy normally proceeds through the adoption of arguably less efficient (more costly) "command-and-control" regulations.

Rather than charging effluent fees for the production of toxic wastes, for example, environmental regulators mandate that firms use specific technologies for reducing their polluting byproducts. Rather than levying gasoline taxes to reduce harmful automobile emissions, government imposes fuel economy standards on automobile manufacturers. Rather than providing direct subsidies to the consumers of education, public ownership of the means of producing these services is embraced. Government's failure to adopt cost-effective solutions to perceived market failure problems suggests that objectives other than economic efficiency drive public policy in this area. It is the special purpose of the public

---

● STUDIES IN MANAGERIAL ECONOMICS ●

The Fable of the Bees

The Coase Theorem is rich in empirical content. It shows that a number of popular examples of market failure used to illustrate the need for corrective government intervention are simply not consistent with the facts. Perhaps the most famous of these market-failure examples is the case of apple growing and bee keeping.[a] There are substantial *positive* external benefits associated with the joint production of apples and a honey. On the one hand, the apple blossoms provide a ready source of nectar for the bees, thereby increasing the yield of honey. And, on the other hand, the bees pollinate the apple blossoms in their search for nectar, thereby increasing the apple crop.

Because apple orchards and bee colonies typically operate under separate ownership, it would not seem feasible for scores of independent producers dispersed over a wide geographic area to take account of these reciprocal benefits. Market failure would then exist in the sense that fewer resources are invested in the production of apples and honey than is optimal from society's point of view. That is, more apple trees would

a Steven N. S. Cheung, "The Fable of the Bees: An Economic Investigation," *Journal of Law and Economics* 16 (April 1973), pp. 11-33.

be planted if bee keepers compensated apple growers for the contribution made by their blossoms to the production of honey, and more bee hives would be kept if apple growers compensated bee keepers for the contribution made by their bees to the apple crop. Consequently, Pigovians have often reached the conclusion that "subsidies and taxes must be imposed" by government to achieve the socially efficient outcome.[b]

A careful examination of the bee keeping and apple growing industries, however, reveals that the reciprocal external benefits associated with the joint production of apples and honey are in fact internalized without government intervention. In Washington State, a leading apple producing region, there is a long history of both implicit and explicit contractual arrangements between apple growers and bee keepers. These arrangements establish a system of compensation accounting both for the additional honey production made possible by the ready availability of nectar and for the pollination services furnished by bees.[c]

The externalities are internalized through a complex network of contracts in which individual apple growers lease bee hives from keepers who in turn agree to place their hives strategically in the grower's orchards during the relevant part of the apple growing season. Indeed, bee keepers enter into similar contractual arrangements with the growers of a wide variety of flowering plants, including blueberries, cherries, cranberries, almonds, alfalfa, clover, cabbage, and mint. Each contract specifies a rental payment per hive that explicitly takes account of the substantial variation across crops in the relative values of the pollination services of bees versus the expected additional honey production made possible by giving the bees access to nectar. The rental rate received by a bee keeper may be paid by the grower in terms of honey, money, or a combination of both. In fact, if the value of the excess honey production enjoyed by the bee keeper from locating hives in a particular field or orchard is sufficiently large, the bee keeper will pay a rental fee to the grower.

The contractual arrangements are sophisticated enough to also account for the possible bee loss associated with neighboring growers' use of pesticides (bee keepers receive additional fees to compensate for this risk). Moreover, the growers themselves customarily make (in-kind) payments to one another that reflect the value of pollination services rendered when the bees leased by one grower "spill over" to nearby fields or orchards.

This complex network of contracts results in a well functioning and mutually beneficial system in which bee keepers are kept constantly employed from early spring to late summer, moving their hives from farm to farm, rendering pollination services and extracting honey. In the State of Washington alone, about 60 bee keepers each own 100 colonies or more; at the peak growing season, there is a grand total of about 90,000 colonies under lease. And because each hive is rotated through at least two—and sometimes as many as four—crops per year, the bee keepers deal with a substantial number of growers located throughout Washington State and within the almond growing regions of California. The transaction costs associated with negotiating and enforcing contracts among such a large number of independent producers over such an extensive geographic area seem formidable. Private market arrangements to internalize an externality emerged nonetheless. Careful investigation thus reveals that a popular example of market failure has no empirical support.

b James E. Meade, "External Economies and Diseconomies in a Competitive Situation," *Economic Journal* 52 (1952), p. 58. Also see Bator, "Anatomy of Market Failure."
c Joint ownership of apple orchards and bee colonies would also permit the efficient exploitation of the reciprocal benefits associated with these two productive activities. The fact that such ownership integration is not observed in practice suggests that market contracting is the transaction-cost minimizing solution to this particular externality problem.

Tradeable Pollution Permits

In a departure from traditional regulatory practices, the Clean Air Act of 1990 gave polluters the right to meet sulfur emissions standards by buying and selling pollution permits allotted by the Environmental Protection Agency to individual electric power generating plants.[a] This market-based approach to environmental regulation is designed to provide the owners and managers of coal-fired electric utilities with economic incentives for reducing the sulfur dioxide emissions thought to be a major contributor to "acid rain."

If enough permits are made available and enough firms have the right to buy and sell them, a competitive market for the pollution permits will emerge.[b] The market equilibrium price of pollution rights will then be equal to the marginal cost of pollution abatement and the level of sulfur emissions produced will be the level chosen by the government. Moreover, utilities will be free to select the technology they will use to reduce sulfur emissions. The government's pollution standard will therefore be attained by the most cost-effective method available.

Figure 17.2 illustrates a stylized market for pollution permits. The curves labeled MCA_1 and MCA_2 show the marginal costs of pollution abatement for two hypothetical electric power generating plants. MCA_1 and MCA_2 specify the additional expenditures required to reduce each plant's sulfur dioxide emissions below 14 tons per day, the level of pollution produced if no environmental precautions are taken. By assumption, firm 2's marginal costs of abatement are lower than those of firm 1. This cost difference supplies the economic motivation for buying and selling permits.

One possible approach to environmental regulation is to levy an *emissions fee* on polluting firms. Suppose, for example, that government wants to cut sulfur dioxide pollution in half, that is, to reduce total sulfur emissions from 28 tons per day to 14 tons per day. Such an objective can be attained if electric utilities are required to pay $300 per ton of sulfur dioxide produced.

Each plant has an incentive to reduce its sulfur emissions in order to avoid paying the fee, and it will obviously pay to lessen emissions up to the point where the extra cost of doing so is just equal to the fee. With a fee of $300 per ton, firm 1 will cut back its sulfur emissions to eight tons per day and firm 2 will cut back the pollution it generates to six tons per day. Even though all firms are required to pay the same fee, this regulatory policy has the desirable property of creating incentives for those firms having the lowest costs of pollution abatement to reduce their emissions the most. The total cost of achieving the mandated pollution standard is consequently minimized.

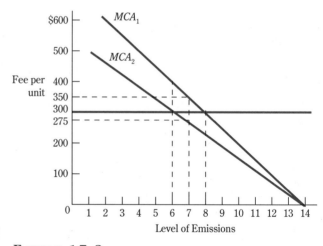

FIGURE 17.2
A Market for
Pollution Permits

a Peter Passell, "A New Commodity to be Traded: Government Permits for Pollution," *New York Times*, 17 July 1991, p. A1.
b *Ibid*. The Chicago Board of Trade voted in July 1991 to begin trading sulfur dioxide emission permits.

Perhaps because establishing the appropriate emissions fee requires detailed information about the private costs of abatement (and the social benefits of reducing emissions), traditional regulatory practices in the United States have relied on pollution standards rather than fees. An *emissions standard* is simply a legal limit on how much pollution a firm can emit. Monetary penalties are then assessed if the firm exceeds that limit.

Suppose that the electric utilities in Figure 17.2 are each required to reduce their emissions to seven tons of sulfur dioxide per day or face substantial monetary fines. Like the emissions fee described above, this standard achieves the goal of cutting pollution in half. But it also imposes a differentially higher cost burden on firm 1 which must pay $350 to eliminate the last ton of daily sulfur emissions necessary to comply with the mandated pollution standard. Firm 2 can achieve the same level of compliance at a marginal cost of $275. Hence, when firms differ in the efficiency with which they are able to achieve reductions in pollution emissions, applying the same environmental standard to all places some at a significant disadvantage.

Some of the disadvantages of emissions standards can be avoided by introducing marketable pollution permits. To see how this works, suppose that government again wants to reduce total daily sulfur dioxide emissions to 14 tons. This goal can be accomplished by allotting to each electric utility seven pollution permits each of which grants its owner the right to discharge one ton of sulfur dioxide per day. Firm 1 would be willing to pay up to $350 for one more of these permits so that emissions can be increased from seven to eight tons per day. The corresponding value of that permit to firm 2 is only $275, however. Firm 2 will therefore have an incentive to sell one of its permits to firm 1 for a price somewhere between $275 and $350.

Both parties are made better off by this transaction. Firm 1 purchases the right to generate one more ton of sulfur dioxide emissions for a price that is less than the cost it would otherwise incur in reducing its daily discharges from eight to seven tons. Firm 2, on the other hand, receives a payment from firm 1 that defrays most (and perhaps all) of the additional cost necessary to reduce its own sulfur emissions to six tons per day. The result is the same total reduction in emissions (8 + 6 = 14 tons of sulfur dioxide are discharged). Moreover, because the firm with the lower cost of abatement reduces its emissions to a greater extent, the total cost of achieving the given environmental standard is minimized.

---

choice model outlined later in this chapter to breathe political life into the Pigovian approach to the analysis of externalities.

The Tragedy of the Commons

The tragedy of the commons represents a second type of market failure. The "commons" refers to property—a natural resource, for instance—that is set aside for collective use and to which all have equal access. Meaningful ownership rights do not exist in the sense that the gains from utilizing the resource do not accrue to any one individual. And, moreover, no member of the collective may sell to some other party his or her pro rata stake in the common gains. The "tragedy" refers to the tendency of common property to be over-utilized. This over-utilization occurs because the absence of well-defined ownership rights means that conservation efforts go unrewarded. The value of common property consequently tends to dissipate much more rapidly and to a much greater extent than is optimal from society's point of view.

Consider Figure 17.3, which relates whaling effort to the value of the whale harvest.[7] The world's whale population is a common pool resource that no one owns and to which the whaling fleets of all nations have access. Although in recent years the harvesting of whales has been restricted somewhat by international agreement and by the efforts of Greenpeace and other environmental organizations, whaling is nevertheless an archetypal common property problem.

The downward-sloping curve labeled AB denotes the average benefit of whaling measured in terms of the number of whales harvested per season. MB is the corresponding marginal benefit schedule and MC represents the private marginal cost of whaling effort. Marginal cost is assumed to be constant throughout the relevant range of harvesting decisions; for simplicity, cost is denominated in terms of whales rather than dollars. Specifically, it is assumed that the cost of putting one more whaling vessel to sea is equal to the value four whales fetch on the market. Put differently, a vessel's owner must harvest four whales per season to cover the opportunity cost of the resources employed in whaling.

The number of whales harvested in any given season depends on the number of whaling vessels that put to sea in search of whale herds. As the size of the whaling fleet increases, the number of whales that any one vessel can harvest declines. This decline in average productivity simply reflects the fact that each vessel's captain will tend to select the most promising harvesting location available. Subsequent arrivals will therefore be forced to take up less and less favorable stations relative to the herd. In Figure 17.3, for example, 11 whales can be harvested in a season if one whaling vessel puts to sea; if two vessels put to sea, each can only harvest 10 whales; and so on.

FIGURE 17.3
The Tragedy of
the Commons

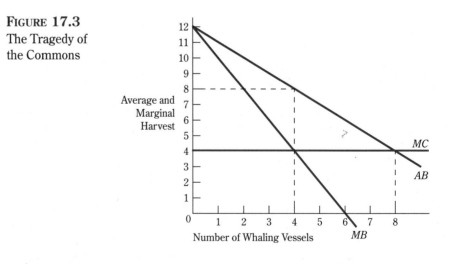

7 The diagrammatic exposition is based on the analysis in Terry Anderson and Peter J. Hill, "Privatizing the Commons: An Improvement?," *Southern Economic Journal* 50 (October 1983), pp. 438-50.

In deciding whether or not to put to sea, each vessel's owner compares the private benefits of whaling with its private costs. If three vessels are actively engaged in whale harvesting, for example, the fourth vessel's owner can expect to catch eight whales. Because the value of the anticipated catch exceeds the opportunity cost of the whaling effort—an economic profit of four whales can be earned—it is rational for the fourth vessel's owner to put to sea. The fact that putting to sea reduces the expected catch of the other three vessels from nine whales to eight is irrelevant to the fourth vessel's owner.

The fifth vessel's owner makes a similar decision. If that vessel puts to sea, the average catch declines to seven whales, but this number still exceeds the private costs of whaling and so it is rational for the fifth vessel to participate in the harvest. Indeed, because there are by assumption no exclusive rights to exploit the whale population, entry by whaling vessels will continue until the average private benefits of whaling equal the private costs. In the limit, eight whaling vessels will participate in the season's harvest. A total of 32 whales will be caught and each vessel's owner will, by harvesting four whales, earn a normal return (zero economic profit) on his or her investment.

This outcome is wasteful from society's point of view, however. When eight vessels participate in the whale harvest, the marginal social benefit of whaling is less than the opportunity cost of the resources devoted to this activity. In fact, the marginal benefit of whaling is negative at this point—the decisions by the owners of the seventh and eighth vessels cause the total whale harvest to decline. Too many of society's scarce economic resources are invested in whale harvesting in the sense that the same number of whales (32) could be caught if access to the common pool could somehow be restricted to four vessels, each of which would then expect to catch eight whales. The resources thus freed from whale harvesting could then be redeployed to produce more highly valued goods, thereby increasing the welfare of consumers.

The socially optimal number of whaling vessels is four because at that number, the marginal increase in the total whale harvest is just equal to the marginal cost of whaling effort (marginal benefit equals marginal cost). But the private, self-interested resource-allocation decisions of the market participants fail to sustain this desirable result.

One solution to the common pool problem is to bring public authority to bear in restricting access to the whale population. Government might issue whaling licenses that confer on their owners the exclusive right to participate in the whale harvest. By restricting entry to four licensed vessels, socially wasteful private resource-allocation decisions can in principle be avoided. Whether or not such a policy actually improves society's welfare depends on how the licenses are allocated among vessel owners.

An alternate solution is to privatize the commons, that is, to allow private individuals to own the rights to exploit the whale population. Such an owner or group of owners would have a strong economic motive to restrict access to the resource. A profit can be made by charging vessel owners a fee for the right to participate in the harvest. The owners would establish the profit-maximizing fee, as always, by equating marginal benefit with marginal cost.

For the example at hand, the optimal fee is the dollar value equivalent of four whales. If this fee is charged, four vessels will put to sea, each of which will then earn a normal economic return. (The value of the eight whales each expects to catch just offsets the private cost of the whaling, which consists of the opportunity cost of the whaling effort plus the fee paid to the resource's owner.) While the notion of ownership is somewhat fanciful in the case of whale herds, it is not such an unrealistic solution for overcrowded national parks, overcut national forest lands, or deteriorating national highways. The important point is that profit-seeking behavior by private resource owners leads unintentionally to socially optimal resource-allocation decisions.

Monopoly

It has been assumed throughout *Modern Managerial Economics* that the demand curve facing the firm and its managerial decision makers is downward sloping. This assumption was made because virtually all firms in the real world conduct business in markets characterized by product differentiation. Due to differences in quality, reputation, location, and so on, each seller's product or service has unique attributes that distinguish it in the minds of consumers from the products or services offered by rivals. The demand schedule confronting the firm slopes downward under these conditions, indicating that the seller must be prepared to reduce price in order to attract consumers away from the sellers of rival products and to increase its own sales.

Product differentiation does, however, lead to a type of market failure that is of great concern to public policies toward business, particularly regulatory policy and antitrust policy. This type of market failure is known as the market failure due to "monopoly."

In the textbook model of pure monopoly, the industry is *assumed* to consist of a single firm that produces and sells a product having no close substitutes. By definition, the demand curve confronting the monopolist is the industry demand curve which, because of the assumption that no other firm produces a closely substitutable product, is downward sloping. This again implies that the firm must reduce price in order to sell more output. But it also means that the firm can raise price without losing all of its sales. The monopolist is therefore said to possess "market power." Rather than taking market price as given, the firm *searches* for the price that maximizes its profits.[8]

Firms that produce and sell differentiated products also enjoy some degree of market power in the aforementioned sense. They, too, are price searchers. But the "monopoly power" or "market power" that most firms in the real world possess exists only by way of comparison with another textbook model of the firm—the price-taker model of "perfect competition." In this model, all rivalry between firms is again assumed away.

Competition is perfect in the model of perfect competition because the market is assumed to be populated by such a large number of sellers that

---

8 See Chapter 8 for a more complete description of the price-searcher model.

no one of them can, acting on its own, influence market price. The absence of market power in the model of perfect competition is further assured by assuming that the product or service produced and sold by each firm in the industry is identical to that offered by every other seller, that there are no barriers to the movement of resources into or out of the industry, and that information about prices and costs is freely available to all market participants.

Because the existence of economic profits will immediately attract new sellers into the industry under these assumptions, no firm can charge a price above marginal production costs in the long run. Price equal to marginal cost is associated with an optimal allocation of society's scarce productive resources (**allocative efficiency**). In addition, market price is equal to minimum long-run average cost. **Production efficiency** is maximized in the model of perfect competition because the industry's output is produced by the socially optimal number of firms, each of which employs its own production capacity at the efficient (cost-minimizing) rate.

The Welfare Costs of Monopoly. Public policy makers have adopted this combination of allocative efficiency and production efficiency as a benchmark for evaluating the performance of firms operating in the real world. The failure of most firms to achieve the standards set by the textbook model of perfect competition has been used to justify government intervention into the private economy in a variety of forms, including regulation of the prices firms may charge and the selling methods they may employ. Figure 17.4 shows the basic market failure model on which these rationales for government intervention are based and contrasts the twin benchmarks of perfect competition and monopoly.

A perfectly competitive industry facing market demand schedule D and, for simplicity, constant long-run average and marginal production costs C maximizes profits by supplying Q_C units of output per time period. This optimal level of sales is determined by noting that with constant marginal production costs assumed, the curve labelled C is also the competitive industry's supply schedule. Point E in the diagram thus represents the intersection of industry supply with market demand, and so provides the usual criterion for establishing market equilibrium. Each unit of output is sold at a price of p_C dollars, which is equal to the industry's marginal production costs, C.

With constant marginal production costs assumed, marginal cost is equal to average cost throughout the range of the industry's output choices. Because p_C is in turn equal to average cost, the perfectly competitive industry earns no economic profit. All of the welfare gains from production are consequently enjoyed by consumers. These welfare gains (**consumer surplus**) are measured by the difference between the total amount consumers would have been willing to pay to purchase Q_C units of output and the amount they are in fact required to pay for this quantity. For each unit of output purchased, consumer surplus is represented by the vertical distance between the point on the demand schedule corresponding to that unit and p_C, the market equilibrium price. (Consumer surplus on the Q_Mth unit, for

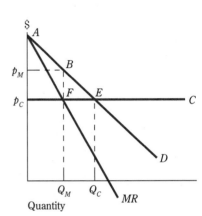

FIGURE 17.4
The "Market Failure" Due to "Monopoly"

example, is equal to the distance B minus F). If we sum the welfare gains determined in this way up to the Q_Cth unit, consumer surplus equals the area of the triangle AEp_C.

Alternatively, suppose that a monopolist produces the same good. Facing the same demand and cost conditions, the monopolist restricts output to Q_M units (determined by equating marginal revenue, MR, with marginal cost, C) and raises price to p_M dollars per unit. The monopoly output restriction reduces consumer welfare by an amount equal to the area of the trapezoid $p_M BEp_C$. (The triangle ABp_M represents the surplus consumers continue to enjoy with monopoly.) Part of this total welfare loss—the area of the rectangle $p_M BFp_C$—is redistributed to the monopolist in the form of pure economic profit. (This redistribution, by itself, has no impact on *social* welfare because the producer's gains exactly offset the losses of consumers.) The remainder—the area of the triangle BEF—represents a "deadweight" welfare loss because its value is transferred away from consumers but not captured by the producer.

Monopoly thus fails to achieve desirable results in the sense that fewer units of output are produced (and fewer resources are therefore allocated to the production of the monopolized good) than is optimal from the viewpoint of the standard set by the model of perfect competition. The monopolist fails to meet the benchmark of allocative efficiency because p_M exceeds marginal cost. The value that consumers place on the last unit of output supplied by the monopolist is greater than the value of the resources used in producing that last unit. Moreover, although the monopolist achieves production efficiency under constant-cost conditions, only by coincidence will the monopolist produce where average costs are at their minimum with more usual U-shaped cost curves.

The market failure due to monopoly could be thought of as a transaction-cost problem because there are unexploited gains from trade between the monopolist and the consumers of its product. Given that total consumer welfare losses exceed the monopolist's total gains from restricting output below the perfectly competitive level, consumers could in principle bribe the monopolist to expand output and reduce price. That is, they could offer to pay the monopolist an amount greater than $p_M BFp_C$ but less than $p_M BEp_C$ under the condition that the monopolist produce Q_C units and not Q_M. In this way, consumers could reduce their aggregate welfare loss below the level otherwise imposed on them by the monopolist's price and output choices. If in fact such private solutions to the monopoly problem are not observed in practice, this suggests that even though exchange would make both parties better off, the costs faced by consumers of organizing to reduce their welfare losses exceed the benefits they expect from collective action.

In any case, allocative inefficiency and the associated deadweight welfare loss provide a theoretical basis for government intervention against monopoly. The presumption is that appropriate public policies can and will correct the market failure due to monopoly by moving price and output toward the perfectly competitive ideal. Society would experience a net gain from such intervention if the cost of implementing procompetitive policies is less than the resulting improvement in consumer welfare.

As mentioned at the outset of this chapter, most textbook discussions of the public policy process assume that public policies toward business are formulated and executed by somewhat imperfect but basically well-intentioned public servants. Government intervention to correct sources of market failure in the private economy is still widely believed to operate in the public interest. By "public interest" is meant the pursuit of the goal of maximizing social welfare (the sum of producer and consumer surplus).

The conventional wisdom is that the purposes of most public policies toward business are beyond dispute. Were it not for environmental regulation, profit-seeking firms would plunder the nation's natural resources, clear-cutting forests and fouling the air and water. Were it not for the antitrust laws, unchecked monopoly power would foreclose markets, raise prices, and stifle innovation. Were it not for consumer product safety standards, firms would sell shoddy and dangerous goods that maim their purchasers. Were it not for advertising regulation, firms would mislead consumers into buying products they don't want at prices they cannot afford. Were it not for occupational health and safety regulation, firms would expose their employees to unacceptable workplace hazards. And so on.

Thus, whenever public policies toward business fail to achieve their stated goals (as they do quite often by many accounts), the failures are attributed to one or more of a number of correctable errors. The critics accordingly prescribe reforms that urge the enforcement agencies to do a better job, recommend that legislators and government officials learn economic principles, call for the replacement of incumbent policy makers with people better able to serve the public interest, or endorse higher levels of funding for the relevant bureau.

The conventional approach to the analysis of public policies toward business thus suggests that market failure and market power arise from the activities of individuals and firms seeking only their private gains. On the other hand, government intervention into the economy is viewed as being undertaken by public-spirited public servants seeking only to promote the general welfare. In James Buchanan's words, this is not a closed behavioral system.[9] In one setting, individuals are assumed to be selfish; in another, they are assumed to be selfless. The analyst cannot have it both ways. A decision about how individuals behave in general must be made.

Closing the behavioral system is a simple matter of recognizing that the same rational, self-interest-seeking motives that stimulate human action in ordinary markets guide decision making in the public sector as well. The assumption that *all* individuals pursue their own self-interests is one of the fundamental tenets of public choice. Just as economic theory assumes that consumers want to maximize their utility and that firms want to maximize

---

9 James M. Buchanan, "Toward Analysis of Closed Behavioral Systems," in James M. Buchanan and Robert D. Tollison, eds., *Theory of Public Choice* (Ann Arbor: University of Michigan Press, 1972), pp. 11-23.

their profits, public choice assumes that public policy makers want to maximize their own welfare.

The generic objective attributed to policy makers and other government officials is the maximization of political support. Depending on the particular policy process being analyzed, the goal of self-interest may take various forms. One is the maximization of the probability of election or of reelection to political office. Another is the maximization of the probability of appointment or of reappointment to a position of public responsibility. And a third is the maximization of personal wealth, which includes the salary and perquisites of public office as well as the income expected from post-government employment.

In short, *homo politicus* and *homo economicus* are one and the same. The critical implication of this assumption of universal self-interest is that the differences in outcomes observed between public choices and private choices emerge not because individuals adopt different behavioral objectives in the two settings, but rather because the constraints on behavior are different.

The private market is a proprietary setting in which individual decision makers capture the full benefits and bear the full costs of their own actions. A firm that introduces a new product sinks or swims on the basis of consumers' reactions to it. An individual who invests in the stock market enjoys a capital gain or suffers a capital loss. A homeowner who remodels captures the value of the improvements when the house is sold. An employee who quits to look for a new job garners a higher salary or better working conditions if the search is successful; he or she bears the consequences if no acceptable opening can be found.

The political market, by contrast, is a nonproprietary setting. The benefits of any decision or choice are less fully captured by public officials—and the associated costs are less fully borne—than if the same action were undertaken in a private market setting.[10] This is because, on the one hand, the compensation payable to public servants is subject to statutory ceilings. These ceilings limit the extent to which officials can personally benefit from improvements in the quality of service their agencies deliver.

On the other hand, the cost of failure is largely borne by the taxpayers who are called upon to finance the provision of public goods and services. Therefore, public decision makers have weaker incentives than private decision makers to use resources efficiently. The looser behavioral constraints facing public officials are magnified by the fact that the "owners" of public bureaus and agencies (the taxpayers) are numerous and dispersed. Each one of them therefore has little to gain from monitoring the performance of his or her politician-agents.

It is the special object of public choice theory to model and derive testable implications about behavior in the nonproprietary institutional setting that characterizes public decision making. In doing so, public choice theory stresses that the proper unit of analysis is the individual, not "society" or

10   Armen A. Alchian, "Some Economics of Property Rights," *Il Politico* 30 (1965), pp. 816-29.

some other vague collective entity. "Society" does not make choices; individuals do. Economic theory studies how the interactions of large numbers of self-interest-seeking producers and consumers in ordinary private markets determine outcomes like prices, quantities, incomes, and profits. Likewise, public choice theory studies how the interactions of large numbers of self-interest-seeking demanders, suppliers, and brokers of wealth transfers determine outcomes like tax rates, income subsidies, and regulatory intervention in political markets.

The deceptively simple insights of public choice theory have been fruitfully exploited by modern scholarship in the areas of public finance, industrial organization, and regulation. These insights move the discussion of public policy away from nonscientific debates about "good" and "bad" law or "good" and "bad" enforcement toward a more hard-nosed analysis of how public institutions actually function. One implication of the public choice approach is that in order to uncover the actual objectives of a particular public policy or program, it is necessary to look behind the stated intentions of the policy's supporters. When we seek to explain why a policy was adopted or why it persists, "the theory tells us to look, as precisely and carefully as we can, at who gains and who loses, and how much...."[11]

If we find evidence, for example, that until the enactment of deregulation in 1978, public regulation of commercial airline fares and routes provided large benefits to the established air carriers while imposing substantial costs on passengers, then—rhetoric about protecting the flying public aside—the conclusion that regulation was intended to benefit the airlines is warranted.[12] Similarly, we may observe that the antitrust law enforcement agencies frequently attack mergers that promise to result in improved economic efficiency (and, consequently, lower costs and prices) rather than deterring anticompetitive mergers that might lead to increased market power. In these cases, despite the concern for consumer welfare expressed by antitrust's proponents, the conclusion seems justified that the law on mergers was intended to protect inefficient rival producers from the increased competition they would thereby face.[13]

Errors can of course be made out of ignorance or failure to foresee all of a policy's "unintended" consequences. "But errors are not what men live by or

---

11 George J. Stigler, "Supplementary Note on Economic Theories of Regulation (1975)," in George J. Stigler, *The Citizen and the State: Essays on Regulation* (Chicago: University of Chicago Press, 1975), p. 140.

12 See, for example, Theodore E. Keeler, "Airline Regulation and Market Performance," *Bell Journal of Economics* 3 (Autumn 1972), pp. 399-424, and George W. Douglas and James C. Miller III, "Quality Competition, Industry Equilibrium, and Efficiency in the Price-Constrained Airline Market," *American Economic Review* 64 (September 1974), pp. 657-69.

13 Studies reporting evidence supporting this conclusion include B. Espen Eckbo, "Horizontal Mergers, Collusion, and Stockholder Wealth," *Journal of Financial Economics* 11 (1983), pp. 241-73; Robert Stillman, "Examining Anti-Trust Policy Towards Horizontal Mergers," *Journal of Financial Economics* 11 (1983), pp. 225-40; and B. Espen Eckbo and Peggy Wier, "Antimerger Policy under the Hart-Scott-Rodino Act: A Reexamination of the Market Power Hypothesis," *Journal of Law and Economics* 28 (April 1985), pp. 119-49.

on.... [A]n explanation of a policy in terms of error or confusion is no explanation at all—anything and everything is compatible with that 'explanation.'"[14] Hence, if "the announced goals of a policy are ... unrelated or perversely related to its actual effects,"[15] and this divergence persists through time, then as a first approximation it seems reasonable to conclude that the actual effects are not only known, but desired. The *truly intended effects* [of a policy] *should be deduced from the actual effects.*"[16]

In short, public choice theory suggests that what the conventional wisdom treats as policy "failures" are in fact the predictable consequences of self-interest-seeking behavior on the part of rational individuals operating under a particular set of institutional constraints. To public choice scholars, economic markets and political markets are one and the same. The individuals who interact in these markets are motivated by similar goals and their behavior can be analyzed with the same set of tools.

RENT SEEKING BY BUSINESS ENTERPRISE

If "majority rules" were in fact a meaningful way of characterizing political outcomes in a representative democracy, there would be no minimum wage law, no agricultural price supports, and no import tariffs and quotas; in short, there would be none of the many and varied government programs and policies that benefit the few at the expense of the many. Yet, such special-interest measures exist—indeed flourish—in the United States and elsewhere. This simple observation about politics raises two important questions. If a large number of public policies generate few discernible benefits for the majority, why are such policies adopted? Given the very real costs, both direct and indirect, borne by the taxpaying majority to support the machinery of wealth redistribution, why do such policies persist?

The Market for Wealth Transfers

The answer to both of these questions is that there is a market for wealth transfers just as there are markets for automobiles, shoes, and thousands of other ordinary goods. The existence of this market for wealth transfers derives from the fact that government's powers to tax and to spend and to compel or to prohibit put it in a position to selectively help or hurt a large number of individuals and firms. The political machinery of the state can be used to secure direct cash payments, relief from tax obligations, control over prices charged and wages paid, restrictions on entry and conditions of employment, and many other similar favors.

---

14 Stigler, "Supplementary Note on Economic Theories of Regulation (1975)", p. 140.
15 *Ibid.*
16 *Ibid.* Emphasis in original.

And because public authority is so enormously valuable, it represents "a blank check on which everyone wants to write."[17] But only certain groups will be successful in using the political process for their own gain, while other groups will bear the costs. The problem is to determine which special interests will tend to receive wealth transfers and which will tend to supply them.

The proposition that private interests—and not the "public interest"—drive policy outcomes was articulated in its modern form by George Stigler.[18] In its simplest construction, what has since become known as the interest-group or "capture" theory of government is usually stated in terms of traditional economic regulation of price and entry. This is because the theory was first applied in explaining the wide divergence observed between the actual and purported effects of this type of government intervention into the private economy. Stigler asked why it is that the application of regulatory controls to industries like trucking and commercial airlines, and the imposition of licensing requirements on occupations like medicine, lawyering, and barbering, rarely seem to benefit consumers. In his effort to answer these questions, he formalized the notion that coalitions of producers will often find it profitable to use the apparatus of public regulation for their own gain.

The interest-group model is much more general, however. It does not consistently pit producers against consumers or "capital" against labor. The model applies to any situation in which political authority can be mobilized to selectively help or hurt various interest groups. Indeed, public policies toward business are often tailored to redistribute wealth between groups of producers.

The Logic of Collective Action. The key to understanding wealth transfer activity in a representative democracy lies simply in the fact that certain information and transaction costs are associated with collective action. Given the existence of these costs, political representatives themselves have incentives to search for specific policies and programs that provide opportunities for trade between demanders and suppliers.

It is often the case that an outsider can only identify the winners and losers *ex post*, after the market has determined who they are. But as a general matter smaller coalitions with a strong community of interests will tend to have a comparative advantage in transfer-seeking activity. Each group member thereby has a larger financial stake in a given political issue insofar as the potential gains (or losses) are divided among fewer hands. These greater financial interests raise the expected rate of return to acquiring information about the wealth effects of transfer activity. At the same time, smaller coalitions face lower costs of reaching agreement on a common course of

---

17 John E. Chubb and Terry M. Moe, *Politics, Markets, and America's Schools* (Washington, D.C.: Brookings Institution, 1990), p. 29.

18 George J. Stigler, "The Theory of Economic Regulation," *Bell Journal of Economics* 2 (Spring 1971), pp. 3-21. Also see Sam Peltzman, "Toward a More General Theory of Regulation," *Journal of Law and Economics* 19 (August 1976), pp. 211-48, and Richard A. Posner, "Theories of Economic Regulation," *Bell Journal of Economics* 5 (Autumn 1974), pp. 335-58.

action and of monitoring and controlling free-riding behavior by individual members.[19] Taken together, these observations help explain why small, cohesive interest groups are often successful in obtaining wealth transfers at the expense of the general "public," whose interests are more diffuse and whose costs of organizing to avoid supplying transfers are relatively high.

In addition, however, it is worth noting that a significant portion of the costs of engaging in transfer-seeking activity are start-up costs. Once they have been borne, the cost of supplying additional collective effort is relatively low. Groups that have already organized for some other purpose therefore have an important advantage in the market for wealth transfers: to the extent that political lobbying is a byproduct of performing some other function, these groups can avoid a large part of the initial costs of transfer seeking. Labor unions, industry trade associations, professional societies, farmer cooperatives, and so on are well situated to act on political issues that affect their wealth precisely because the costs of identifying and organizing a community of interests have already been incurred.

Moreover, to reiterate, politicians themselves have incentives to seek out issues on which the prospective winners are well organized and well informed, while the losers remain rationally ignorant about the wealth effects of transfer activity. "Pork barrel" policies and programs whose benefits are narrowly focused on small, well organized interest groups but whose costs are spread more diffusely across the polity as a whole are politically popular precisely because the expected political payoff to the broker is larger. When the prospective gains will be shared by relatively few individuals, the winners will have a strong incentive to provide the broker with political support (votes, campaign contributions, and the like) in exchange for the benefits conferred on them. On the other hand, when the bulk of the cost of financing these narrow benefits will be borne by taxpayers in general, the losers will not find it worth their while to become informed about the policies and programs and to withdraw their political support in an effort to block the broker's expropriation of their wealth.

This asymmetry in the payoffs facing brokers of wealth transfers is particularly evident in a geographically based representative democracy. A legislator in such a setting can expect a high return from taking positions that provide benefits narrowly tailored to the local (district or state) interests he or she has been elected to represent in the national legislature. But there will be little or no return from taking vague positions in support of the "public interest."

This conclusion follows because nonresidents cannot vote in the legislator's assigned political jurisdiction. Benefits provided to groups located outside the district or state consequently go unrewarded and any costs imposed on these outsiders go unpenalized. A political-support-maximizing legislator will accordingly search for programs and policies that transfer wealth to local interest groups at the expense of taxpayers in general. This is just another

---

19 Olson, *Logic of Collective Action.*

way of stating the obvious point that the political representatives of rural states and districts will tend to promote agricultural interests in the national legislature, that the representatives of jurisdictions where the local work force is heavily unionized will tend to promote labor's interests, and so forth.

The political equilibrium level of wealth transfer activity in a geographically based representative democracy is determined through "logrolling." In this process, individual legislators seeking to further the provincial interests of the citizens they have been elected to represent search for vote-trading bargains that can be struck with the representatives of other political jurisdictions, each of whom likewise wants to promote the interests of his or her own constituents.

In other words, through vote trading and compromise, the legislature attempts to arrive at a level and pattern of wealth redistribution that jointly maximizes the membership's political support. This process of searching for political equilibrium is facilitated by an elaborate system of legislative committees and subcommittees, each of which is charged with the task of becoming informed about and monitoring legislative activity in specific policy areas. Complex legislative rules on such matters as bill introductions, floor action, and voting procedures have similar purposes.

The important implication of the foregoing discussion is that political representatives have much to gain from promoting programs and policies that advance local interests and little or nothing to gain from promoting programs and policies that advance the "public interest." Thus, it is the behavior of rational, self-interest-seeking legislators operating under a particular set of institutional contraints, and not error or ignorance, that explains the wide divergence often observed between the stated objectives of public policies toward business and the actual effects of those policies. It is not that public policies toward business are well meaning but deformed in their execution by fallible human beings. Rather, the failure of government intervention to achieve its announced goals is simply due to the fact that "public interest" does not appear in the objective function being maximized by public policy makers.

Rent Seeking and Profit Seeking

The term **rent** refers to that part of the compensation received by the owner of a resource over and above the resource's opportunity cost. Economic profit is one example of a rent. Rent seeking and profit seeking therefore have much in common. Both refer to the process by which resource owners strive to put themselves in positions to earn incomes in excess of those which their resources would command in any alternative use. But there is also an important distinction between profit seeking and rent seeking.[20] This distinction is

---

[20] This distinction is discussed at length in James M. Buchanan, "Rent Seeking and Profit Seeking," in James M. Buchanan, Robert D. Tollison, and Gordon Tullock, ed., *Toward a Theory of the Rent Seeking Society* (College Station: Texas A&M University Press, 1980), pp. 3-15. Also see Robert D. Tollison, "Rent Seeking: A Survey," *Kyklos* 35 (1982), pp. 575-602.

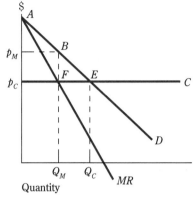

<figure>
FIGURE 17.5
Rent Seeking and Profit Seeking
</figure>

made necessary by the fundamental differences in the welfare implications of rent-seeking activities in the private sector as opposed to the public sector.

Consider once again the welfare-loss model of Figure 17.4, which is reproduced here for convenience as Figure 17.5. The "monopoly" profit rectangle, $p_M BF p_C$, provides a static measure of the value of the rent created by a restriction of output below the perfectly competitive benchmark. (One could also think of the profit rectangle as representing the present value of the stream of returns in excess of opportunity costs associated with the output restriction.)

In a private market setting, the existence of profits (rents) offers an important motivation to resource owners and to entrepreneurs which induces them to shift scarce productive resources from less highly valued to more highly valued uses. The above-cost payments received by entrepreneurs or resource owners attract other profit seekers to enter the industry or closely related industries. And as these resource reallocation decisions are made in response to profit signals, output expands, prices decline, and in the limit rents are competed away. Profit seeking in the private sector is motivated by entrepreneurs' and resource owners' pursuit of personal gain. But this behavior tends to improve the efficiency with which society's scarce productive resources are allocated and to increase consumer welfare by redistributing previously lost surplus back to them.

Suppose, however, that the rectangle of excess returns over costs in Figure 17.5 exists due to an artificial restriction of output created by government. These above-cost payments might be made available through the granting of an exclusive franchise to supply electricity, cable television, or other public utility services in a specified area, by granting inventors the exclusive right to produce and sell their new products or new production technologies for a specified period of time, by imposing tariffs or quotas on the goods of foreign producers who compete with domestic firms, and so forth.

Resource owners and entrepreneurs will again be motivated to reallocate their resources in pursuit of these returns in excess of costs. But rather than investing their resources to discover ways of producing products or services that consumers will value more highly than those being supplied by the established firms, they will spend these resources to influence the public officials who have the authority to award the right to receive the above-cost payments. Bribery of government officials aside, resources will be invested in such ways as contributing to the campaigns of politicians willing to advance a particular cause, the hiring of lawyers and lobbyists to fill out the required government forms and to help sway official decisions, and the designing of advertising campaigns to secure "grass-roots" support for a particular point of view.

Because such resource expenditures do nothing to increase the production of the good or service on which above-cost payments have been made available by government, they do nothing to remove the welfare loss associated with the artificial output restriction. Indeed, the investments made by entrepreneurs or resource owners in the process of competing for the right to receive returns in excess of costs created by the public sector serve to increase the welfare cost of monopoly over and above the simple deadweight loss (the triangle *BEF* in Figure 17.5) associated with output restrictions in the private sector.

Consider Richard Posner's example.[21] Suppose that 10 risk-neutral bidders vie for a monopoly right worth $100,000 that only one will win. These returns in excess of cost may represent the net present value of a local cable TV franchise, for example. If the bidders cannot collude with one another, if the bids are nonrefundable, and if the selection process for awarding the franchise is unbiased, then each bidder would be willing to invest $10,000 for a 10 percent chance of winning the right to earn rents worth $100,000. The successful bidder will enjoy a net private return amounting to $90,000. But at the level of society the total value of the rents associated with the artificial output restriction is exactly dissipated by the resource expenditures made by the rent seekers—$100,000 is spent to capture $100,000.

To avoid confusion, it is important to distinguish these processes from the similarly motivated but fundamentally different profit-seeking activities in the private sector. Therefore, we use the term **rent seeking** in reference to the resource-wasting expenditures made in pursuit of the above-cost payments associated with artificial scarcities created by government.[22] The important implication of rent-seeking theory is that the welfare cost of monopoly in the public sector may be as large as the area of the trapezoid $p_M BE p_C$ in Figure 17.5.[23]

When artificial output restrictions are created, consumers lose the conventional deadweight loss triangle. And, depending on the institutional framework within which rent seeking takes place, resources equal to the value of the rent rectangle may be wasted as well. Moreover, society is made permanently poorer in consequence of these resource-wasting rent-seeking investments. Because the resources spent to secure monopoly rights are by and large sunk (i.e., used to purchase assets with little or no salvage value), little can be gained from a social welfare viewpoint by removing previously created artificial scarcities.[24]

Governments' artificial restrictions on output thus give rise to what Gordon Tullock has called a "transitional gains trap."[25] The promise of above-cost payments motivates interest groups to seek special privileges from the public sector. These gains are subsequently eroded by competitive

21 Richard A. Posner, "The Social Costs of Monopoly and Regulation," *Journal of Political Economy* 83 (August 1975), pp. 807-27.

22 The term rent seeking was coined by Anne Krueger in her study of the value of the excess returns associated with trade protections imposed by the governments of Turkey and India. She estimated that in the mid 1960s roughly 15 percent of Turkish and Indian GNP was consumed in competing for import licenses and other valuable monopoly rights. See Anne O. Krueger, "The Political Economy of the Rent-Seeking Society," *American Economic Review* 64 (June 1974), pp. 291-303.

23 Gordon Tullock, "The Welfare Costs of Tariffs, Monopolies and Theft," *Western Economic Journal* 5 (June 1967), pp. 224-32.

24 Robert E. McCormick, William F. Shughart II, and Robert D. Tollison, "The Disinterest in Deregulation," *American Economic Review* 74 (December 1984), pp. 1075-79.

25 Gordon Tullock, "The Transitional Gains Trap," *Bell Journal of Economics* 6 (Autumn 1975), pp. 671-78.

forces of one sort or another. The capital value of the rents associated with the artificial scarcity is dissipated up front in the pursuit of the monopoly right or, alternatively, is dissipated by competition between the privileged,[26] by newcomers who purchase the right to replace an established producer, and so on. In consequence, incumbent firms earn only a normal return on their rent-seeking investments in the long run. Yet there is no politically acceptable way to abolish a program or policy that is inefficient both from the standpoint of consumers, who pay artificially high prices, and from the standpoint of the privileged, who no longer make exceptional profits.

This is because the current members of the group who were privileged to receive short-run gains would suffer a capital loss if the artificial output restriction were abolished. These capital losses would be smaller than the overall social welfare gains from removing the output restriction. But it will generally not be possible to devise a compensation scheme for getting out of the trap: "Those persons and groups who have established what they consider to be entitlements in the positive gains that have been artificially created will not agree to change, and those persons and groups who suffer [ongoing] losses will not willingly pay off what they consider to be immoral gainers."[27] This observation implies that the optimal policy is to avoid granting special privileges in the first place.

The owners and managers of private business enterprises are by no means the only seekers of rents in the economy. Wherever the public sector holds a policy monopoly, there will be attempts to influence policy makers to use their authority to compel or to prohibit in a way that selectively benefits some individuals or groups at the expense of others. The taxing, spending, and regulatory powers of government represent a valuable resource that can be called upon to help or to hurt a vast array of special interests.

But private business firms are among the most active of rent seekers. This is because producer groups are typically small enough in number and their financial interests are sufficiently concentrated that the potential benefits from organizing and lobbying for monopoly rights will exceed the associated costs. Firms are well situated to engage in rent seeking because the pursuit of political favors can often be a byproduct of the activities of industry trade associations and other producer groups that have organized for other business purposes.

The decision to invest in rent seeking is no different than any other capital-budgeting problem the firm confronts. Faced with a loss of sales to a new or an established rival, for instance, the firm can respond by cutting price, by improving product quality, by increasing its advertising expenditures, or by

---

26 For evidence that the rents made available to the commercial airlines by government regulation of fares and routes were dissipated by nonprice competition between the established carriers, see Douglas and Miller, "Quality Competition, Industry Equilibrium, and Efficiency in the Price-Constrained Airline Market."

27 James M. Buchanan, "Reform in the Rent-Seeking Society," in Buchanan, Tollison, and Tullock, ed., *Toward a Theory of the Rent-Seeking Society*, p. 365. Also see James M. Buchanan and Gordon Tullock, "The 'Dead Hand' of Monopoly," *Antitrust Law and Economic Review* 1 (Summer 1968), pp. 85-96.

Hogging all the Rents

The story of Harley-Davidson supplies a relevant example of how the political process can be used to secure protection from competitive market forces. During the 1950s and 1960s, Harley-Davidson was the leading domestic producer of large, "heavyweight" motorcycles. During the 1970s, however, Japanese manufacturers such as Honda and Suzuki, which had begun operations soon after the end of World War II by installing small surplus military engines on bicycles, started producing larger motorcycles for the export market. Because of their quality and cost advantages, these Japanese producers rapidly made substantial inroads into Harley-Davidson's U.S. sales. Indeed, Harley-Davidson was pushed to the brink of bankruptcy. Its plants were threatened with closure and thousands of jobs were at risk.

Apparently unable or unwilling to cut costs and improve quality, Harley-Davidson's management appealed to government for protection from what they characterized as "unfair" foreign competition. They were joined in their appeal by other special interest groups having a financial stake in Harley-Davidson's survival. State and local public officials in the areas where Harley's manufacturing facilities were located faced the threat of a smaller tax base if plants closed and jobs disappeared. Labor union leaders who represented Harley's production workers faced the prospect of smaller membership rolls. Parts suppliers, local merchants, and motorcycle retailers faced losses in income.

Arrayed against these vocal groups having a strong financial interest in Harley-Davidson's continued existence were the consumers of motorcycles who benefited from the lower prices made possible by competitive market forces and who stood to lose if these forces were short-circuited by trade protectionism. Consumers, however, are not well-organized and they are dispersed geographically. Hence, on the one hand, the demanders of protectionism were well positioned to threaten to withdraw political support from their elected representatives should those politicians not act on their behalf. On the other hand, the cost of protectionism would be spread diffusely across the economy, falling mainly on consumers who resided—and voted—in districts and states where Harley did not operate.

The capture or interest-group theory of government teaches that politicians elected to the national legislature have a strong incentive to respond to demands for protectionism under these conditions. Each member of Congress is obligated to protect and further the provincial interests of the citizens of the jurisdiction he or she has been elected to represent. This is because "the welfare of his constituents may depend disproportionately on a few key industries. The promotion of the industries [consequently] becomes one of his most important duties as a representative of his district... however unimportant those interests may be from a national standpoint."[a] Neglecting this duty will result in a loss of wealth for the politician's state or district and a loss of political support for the politician.

This asymmetric payoff facing the members of Congress who would have been most directly affected by Harley-Davidson's failure provided these politicians with an incentive to trade votes with the representatives of other states and districts in order to secure a majority in favor of enacting favorable legislation. They struck "logrolling" bargains in which they offered to support one side or the other on an issue of less pressing interest to their own constituents in exchange for their colleagues' votes in behalf of Harley-Davidson's interests. These efforts were successful. A bill imposing heavy tariff duties on imported Japanese motorcycles was enacted. The duties, which were instituted in 1983, increased the tariff immediately by 45 percentage points (from 4.4 percent to 49.4 percent), scheduling them to be lowered gradually back to their original level over the next five years.[b]

a Richard A. Posner, "The Federal Trade Commission," *University of Chicago Law Review* 37 (1969), p. 83.

b See "Helping the Hogs: Reagan Hikes a Tariff," *Time*, 11 April 1983; Lester C. Thurow, "The Road to Lemon Socialism," *Newsweek*, 25 April 1983, p. 63; "Tariff Boost: Dubious Aid for Harley-Davidson," *Fortune*, 2 May 1983, p. 7; and Beth Bogart, "Harley Davidson Trades Restrictions for Profits," *Advertising Age*, 10 August 1987, p. S-27.

Figure 17.6 illustrates the impact of the legislation by depicting the world supply and domestic demand for motorcycles. In the absence of trade protectionism, a total of Q_{US} motorcycles would be sold in the U.S. market at a price of p_{US} dollars each. This quantity and price is determined by the intersection of the domestic demand for motorcycles, D_{US}, with the world supply schedule, S_W, which is the horizontal sum of domestic, S_{US}, and Japanese, S_J, production. (The latter supply schedule is not shown, to avoid cluttering the diagram.) With no barriers to international trade, the domestic price, p_{US}, equals the world price, p_W. At that price, domestic producers are willing and able to supply Q_D motorcycles (determined by the intersection of the world price with the domestic supply schedule); the remaining units sold in the U.S. market, $Q_{US} - Q_D$, are imported from abroad.

Now suppose that a tariff bill is enacted that imposes a duty on each Japanese-manufactured motorcycle shipped for sale to the U.S. market. The immediate impact of the tariff is to raise the domestic price of motorcycles above the world price. If the tariff amounts to T dollars per motorcycle, the domestic price rises to $p'_{US} = p_W + T$. As a result of this tariff-induced price rise, domestic consumers reduce the number of motorcycles they purchase from Q_{US} to Q'_{US}. However, the sales of domestic producers *increase* from Q_D to Q'_D at the tariff-ridden price and there is a corresponding reduction in imports to $Q'_{US} - Q'_D$.

Hence, even though total motorcycle sales decline, Harley-Davidson captures a larger share of the domestic market.[c] The changes in prices and quantities caused by the tariff transfer wealth from domestic consumers and foreign producers to the protected U.S. firm. In particular, Harley-Davidson's total revenues increase by the area of the rectangle $p'_{US}ADp_{US}$. This is simply the increase in the domestic price of motorcycles caused by the tariff times the total number of domestically produced motorcycles sold at that price. However, additional resources in the amount indicated by the triangle CAD must be purchased in order to increase the output of Harleys. Harley-Davidson's *net* gain (rent) is therefore equal to the area of the trapezoid $p'_{US}ACp_{US}$.

But consumers' losses are substantially larger than Harley-Davidson's gains. U.S. motorcycle consumers'

welfare is reduced by the area of the trapezoid $p'_{US}BFp_{US}$. Part of this total loss is transferred to Harley-Davidson in the form of the aforementioned rent and part of the total (the rectangle $ABED$) is transferred to the government in the form of tariff revenue collected on imported motorcycles. The remainder of the reduction in consumer welfare (the triangle BEF) represents the deadweight social loss from trade protectionism in the traditional analysis.

However, the prospective private gains to Harley-Davidson from securing protection from Japanese producers supplies it with an incentive to invest real resources in lobbying for favorable treatment at the hands of the Congress. In the limit, Harley's management and other interest groups supporting the firm's demands would have been willing to collectively spend an amount equal to the area of the trapezoid $p'_{US}ACp_{US}$ in order to influence legislative action in their behalf. If they did so, then the total social welfare cost of the tariff would be equal to $p'_{US}ACp_{US}$ plus BEF.

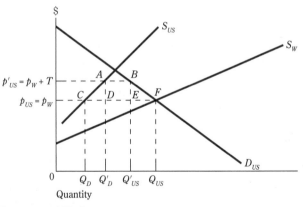

FIGURE 17.6
The Welfare Cost of Trade Protectionism

c Harley's market share had fallen to six percent prior to the tariff hike. By 1986, it had 19.4 percent of the market. See Bogart, "Harley-Davidson Trades Restrictions for Profits."

taking any of a number of other actions, or combination of actions, that normally characterize the workings of a competitive market economy.

Alternatively, the firm can appeal to government for protection. It can lobby for favorable legislation, it can attempt to influence a bureaucratic ruling, or it can instigate an investigation of its rival by supplying information about possible illegal activity—regulatory or antitrust violations, for example—to one of the public law enforcement agencies. In any given circumstance, the firm simply selects the strategy offering the highest expected rate of return.

The basic moral of this discussion is that when the opportunity to earn above-cost payments is available, firms will spend resources to gain access to them. The motivation to seek private gain is independent of the source of returns in excess of cost. But the welfare implications of such self-interest-seeking activities are fundamentally different in two stylized institutional settings. In the private sector, individuals and firms seek profits by searching out ways of serving consumers better; in the public sector, individuals and firms seek rents by searching out ways of influencing the political process. In one setting, the forces of competition enhance consumer welfare by pushing individuals and firms to keep prices in line with costs; in another setting, consumer welfare is reduced as individuals and firms strive for protection from the forces of competition.

An even more basic lesson of the discussion, however, is that political markets and economic markets work in much the same way. Outcomes in both settings are determined by the interaction of large numbers of individual and firms seeking private gain. Outcomes differ in the two settings not because the people interacting in them are motivated differently but simply because the constraints on behavior are different.

SUMMARY

This chapter has provided an overview of the public choice model. The theory of market failure underlies the traditional justification for most public policies toward business. In the cases of externality, common pool resources, and monopoly, government can in principle use its authority to correct private market failures in ways that improve the efficiency with which society's scarce productive resources are allocated, thereby enhancing social welfare.

The traditional arguments supporting the idea that government has a role to play in harnessing the self-interest-seeking behavior of private individuals and firms rest on an unstated assumption. They assume that the behavior of the public officials who are charged with the responsibility of enacting and enforcing policies and programs aimed at correcting perceived market failures cannot be explained by the economic model. The conventional wisdom on public policies toward business assumes that public policy makers are motivated not by their own self-interests, but by the interests of others. It insists that government's power to compel and to prohibit can and will be used with the intention of helping that most diverse and unorganized of interest groups—the "public." Accordingly, whenever and wherever public policies

KEY TERMS
market failure
producer surplus
Pigou tax
Coase Theorem
transaction costs
allocative efficiency
production efficiency
consumer surplus
rent
rent seeking

toward business fail to achieve their stated objectives, or achieve their goals but at a cost that far outweighs any reasonable estimate of their benefits, "better" policies and "better" policy makers are called for.

The public choice model, by contrast, recognizes that the same rational, self-interest-seeking behavior that motivates human action in ordinary markets applies to decision making in the public sector as well. Just as consumers seek to maximize their own satisfaction and firms seek to maximize their own profits, policy makers seek to maximize their own political support. This insight implies that what the conventional wisdom treats as policy failures are in fact the predictable consequences of rational public decision making under a special set of constraints. This process furnishes higher political payoffs to programs and policies that benefit special interests than to programs and policies that serve the "public interest." As such, the public choice model does not entail value judgments about how public policies toward business *should* work. Instead, it draws testable implications about how public policies *do* work, based on applying sound principles of economic theory to the analysis of political markets.

The public choice model is rich in empirical content. The next chapter takes up some applications of it to public policies of immediate concern to management —antitrust, health and safety regulation, and advertising regulation.

QUESTIONS

17.1 The Coase Theorem makes it clear that there is no rationale for government intervention to limit negative externalities—private bargaining will achieve efficient outcomes. True, false, or uncertain? Explain.

17.2 Public choice theorists are often criticized for insisting that individual behavior in political markets is guided by the same self-interested motivations that guide individual behavior in ordinary economic markets. The legislator or bureaucrat who maximizes only his or her own political self-interest is portrayed by the critics of the public choice model as an unrealistic caricature without room for altruistic motives and concern for society's welfare. Write an essay that responds to these critics.

17.3 Majority rule is one of the fundamental principles of democracy. In practice, however, narrow special-interest groups tend to dominate the political process. Why is this so? Can you suggest a change in constitutional rules that would limit the ability of minoritarian interests to obtain political favors from an unwilling majority?

17.4 Use the concept of rent seeking to discuss the welfare costs of monopoly.

17.5 Consider the problem of "acid rain" as discussed in the chapter's "Tradable Pollution Permits" case study.
   a. Explain how sulfur emissions could be analyzed as a common pool resource problem.
   b. Using simple marginal-cost-marginal-benefit analysis, show that the socially optimal quantity of sulfur emissions is not zero, but that in the absence of environmental regulation, more than the socially optimal quantity of these pollutants will be discharged into the atmosphere.
   c. Using Figure 17.2 (see p. 582), explain why the equilibrium price of permits will be $300 if there are a sufficient number of market participants whose marginal costs of abatement can be represented by those of the two firms shown.

17.6 Education is often used as an example of a good that generates significant *positive* externalities (social benefits exceed private benefits). Using simple marginal-benefit-marginal-cost analysis, show that in the absence of government intervention less than the socially optimal quantity of education will be produced. What policy recommendations are implied by your analysis?

17.7 In recent years, public policy makers have embraced the idea of establishing entry fees to limit access to public parks, public museums, and similar public facilities.

    a. Use a diagram to establish the socially optimal entry fee for a public park. Assume that the demand for entry to the park is downward sloping and that the marginal cost of admitting visitors is upward sloping.

    b. Despite your answer to part (a), explain why a self-interested public park manager might have an incentive to establish an entry fee that is "too low" (i.e., less than the socially optimal entry fee).

Antitrust and Regulation

OVERVIEW

This chapter continues the discussion of public policies toward business. Antitrust policy, price and entry regulation, occupational health and safety standards, advertising regulation, and other public programs and policies that place significant constraints on decision making in the private sector are analyzed. The theoretical basis of the discussion is the public choice model presented in Chapter 17.

The chapter's central purpose is to show how the tools of economic theory can be applied in analyzing the public policy process. Viewed in this way, the transfer of wealth to politically well-organized special interest groups often turns out to be an important consequence of government policies. This is *not* to say that wealth redistribution is the *only* factor that motivates policy makers in the design and implementation of public policies toward business. Nor does the emphasis on the wealth transfer characteristics of public policy imply either that policy makers are corrupt or that special interests have subverted the process. Rent seeking through governmental processes is simply a logical expression of rational, self-interest-seeking behavior under a particular set of institutional constraints.

The Utah Pie Company was a moderately sized family-owned and -operated bakery that had been producing and selling fresh pies in the Salt Lake City area for 30 years. In 1957, the company began selling frozen dessert pies locally, a product that until then had only been supplied by leading national firms. Pet, Carnation, and Continental Baking Company shipped their pies to Salt Lake City from plants located in California. When Utah Pie entered the frozen pie segment of the market, it adopted a strategy of selling pies at prices well below those charged by the majors. Its entry was an immediate success and by 1958, Utah Pie accounted for two-thirds of the frozen dessert pies sold in Salt Lake City. The company built a new production facility to keep up with the rapidly growing demand for its new product line.

The national companies countered Utah Pie's expansion by lowering their own prices in Salt Lake City. In many cases the majors sold pies in Salt Lake City at prices below those charged in locations nearer their California plants. Utah Pie responded by suing its three principal rivals. It charged Pet, Carnation, and Continental with violating sections 1 and 2 of the Sherman Act by conspiring to monopolize the frozen pie market in Salt Lake City and with violating Section 2(a) of the Robinson-Patman Act by engaging in illegal price discrimination.

The case was eventually decided by the U.S. Supreme Court in 1967.[a] In reaching their decision, the justices relied on evidence summarized in Tables 18.1 and 18.2. When Utah Pie began marketing frozen pies in Salt Lake City, frozen apple pies were wholesaled in the range of $4 to $5 per dozen. By 1961, the wholesale price per dozen frozen apple pies had fallen by $1.50 or more, and they were being sold for as little as $2.75 per dozen. As a result of these price reductions, the majors took a big slice of Utah Pie's share of local frozen dessert pie sales. Its market share fell from two-thirds to one-third within a year due in large part to the inroads made by Pet. Utah Pie nevertheless accounted for just under half of the market by 1961. Throughout the period in which the conspiracy to monopolize was alleged to have operated, Utah Pie consistently increased its frozen pie sales and continued to make a profit.

How would you have decided this case? Were the major national companies illegally selling frozen pies in Salt Lake City at prices below their own costs? Was the Utah Pie Company the victim of an illegal conspiracy to drive it out of business, or did the company instead use the antitrust laws to shield itself from competitive market forces? In the process did it injure both its rivals and the consumers of frozen pies in Salt Lake City? Chapter 18 addresses these important questions.

a *Utah Pie Co.* v. *Continental Baking Co. et al.*, 386 U.S. 685 (1967).

TABLE 18.1 PRICES AND MARKET SHARES OF FROZEN PIE SALES IN SALT LAKE CITY

Prices per dozen (frozen apple pie)		
	EARLY 1958	1961
Utah Pie	$4.15	$2.75
Pet	4.92	3.46
Carnation	4.82	3.46
Continental	5.00 +	2.85

Market Shares (percent)				
	1958	1959	1960	1961
Utah Pie	67	34	46	45
Pet	16	36	28	29
Carnation	10	9	12	9
Continental	1	3	2	8
Others	6	19	13	8

Source: Utah Pie Co. v. Continental Baking Co. et al., 386 U.S. 685 (1967), pp. 690-92.

TABLE 18.2 SELECTED PERFORMANCE MEASURES FOR UTAH PIE COMPANY

	1958	1959	1960	1961
Sales (thousands of dozens)	38	38	84	103
Sales ($000's)	353	430	504	589
Profits ($000's)	7	12	8	9
Net Worth ($000's)	32	NA	NA	69

Source: Utah Pie Co. v. Continental Baking Co. et al., 386 U.S. 685 (1967), pp. 689 and 691-92.

PUBLIC POLICIES TOWARD BUSINESS

Government has a pervasive influence on resource-allocation decisions in the private economy. This influence may be at a very general level, such as the constitutional and legal rules that establish ownership rights to private property. The influence also involves very specific regulations that are tailored to help or hurt selected special interests. Examples include the restrictions placed on entry into the taxicab business by many local governments and the federal excise tax formerly levied on sales of margarine (but not butter!).

It is impossible in a single chapter to list, let alone describe, all of the public programs and policies that affect private business decisions. After all, the federal government alone spends more than one trillion dollars annually, or roughly 20 percent of the total gross domestic product. State and local governments spend another 5 percent of GDP. And spending is only the tip of the public policy iceberg. Government regulates hours and conditions of work, sets minimum wages and environmental quality standards, requires disclosure of financial information, polices advertisers' claims and the safety of consumer products, controls the prices at which many goods can be sold, and limits entry into a wide range of occupations.

As discussed in Chapter 17, public policies toward business have traditionally been justified as necessary to remedy certain types of market failure. One type of market failure addressed by public policy is the result of monopoly—the power to charge prices above marginal cost. "Natural" monopolies—industries such as electric power or water distribution where scale economies are so large that one firm can serve the market at lower cost than two or more firms—attract government's attention. Government may intervene by regulating the prices charged by the private firm to whom it grants an exclusive franchise. Alternatively, government may replace private production entirely by creating a public enterprise to supply the good or service. Public policy toward monopoly also operates through the enforcement of the antitrust laws. These laws prohibit certain business practices thought to aid private firms in acquiring or exercising the power to raise price above marginal cost to the detriment of consumer welfare.

Second, government intervention may be needed to reduce negative externalities such as air and water pollution and to promote the production of goods generating positive externalities such as public health and public education. In these cases, public policy operates by mandating standards and punishing noncompliance on the one hand, and by subsidizing private producers or by transferring production to the public sector on the other.

Third, government intervention is justified as necessary to redress informational asymmetries in the private marketplace. Some regulations require the disclosure of financial information to investors and others dictate warnings to consumers about the potential safety hazards associated with product use. These rules and regulations rest on the theory that unfettered markets will often fail to provide consumers with accurate and complete information on which to base their purchase decisions.

However, the large volume of research that followed George Stigler's lead in developing the economic theory of regulation has shown that in many instances public policies toward business are ineffective or perverse.[1] Government, too, can fail. Policies and programs have been adopted that either do not achieve their intended objectives or achieve them at a cost far greater than their expected benefits. In what follows, antitrust policy and regulatory policy are analyzed within the interest-group framework laid out in the previous chapter.

---

1 George J. Stigler, "The Theory of Economic Regulation," *Bell Journal of Economics* 2 (Spring 1971), pp. 3-21. For an introduction to this literature, see George J. Stigler, ed., *Chicago Studies in Political Economy* (Chicago: University of Chicago Press, 1988).

Enforcement of the antitrust laws is one of the most important public policy tools available to government. Antitrust policy is based on the belief that private market institutions often cannot be relied on to produce results consistent with the allocative and production efficiency benchmarks established by the theoretical model of perfect competition. The presumption is that by prohibiting certain business practices thought to be either causes or consequences of market power, government can and will use its discretionary authority to intervene in ways that serve consumers' interests.

Antitrust policy differs from alternative public policies toward business in that one of its major provisions—the law concerning merger policy—is preventive in nature, that is, designed to hinder the acquisition of market power. Moreover, antitrust law is a method of intervention that applies not to specific industries, but rather to practices that might arise across a broad range of industries. Finally, antitrust policy is unique in that its main provisions are enforced by two separate federal agencies (the Antitrust Division of the U.S. Department of Justice and the Federal Trade Commission), by the attorneys general of all 50 states, and by private parties who have explicit standing to sue under the antitrust statutes.

The substantive provisions of the U.S. antitrust laws are few and brief. The relevant language is contained in three statutes: the Sherman Act (1890), the Clayton Act (1914), and the Federal Trade Commission Act (1914).[2]

The Sherman Act

Section 1 of the Sherman Act states that "every contract, combination, or conspiracy, in restraint of trade or commerce among the several States, or with foreign nations, is declared to be illegal." It then goes on to specify that

> every person who shall make any contract or engage in any combination or conspiracy hereby declared to be illegal shall be deemed guilty of a felony, and, on conviction thereof shall be punished by fine not exceeding one million dollars if a corporation, or, if any other person, one hundred thousand dollars, or by imprisonment not exceeding three years, or by both said punishments, in the discretion of the court.

Section 2 follows up by declaring that "every person who shall monopolize, or attempt to monopolize, or combine or conspire with any other person or persons, to monopolize any part of the trade or commerce among the several States, or with foreign nations, shall be deemed guilty of a felony." The penalty provisions are the same as those set for Section 1 violations.

In short, the Sherman Act declares illegal existing conspiracies and combinations in restraint of trade (Section 1) and attempts to create them

2 For a discussion of the origins of U.S. antitrust law, see William F. Shughart II, *The Organization of Industry* (Homewood, Il. Richard D. Irwin, 1990), pp. 194-99.

(Section 2). From an early date, however, it became clear to those favoring an activist antitrust policy that the reach of the Sherman Act was limited. Dissatisfaction with the Justice Department's efforts to enforce the new statute was almost immediate. Only 16 antitrust cases were brought in the first decade following its passage. Indeed, the government brought an average of just six antitrust complaints per year through 1914.[3]

If the Justice Department initially lacked zeal in bringing Sherman Act cases, its hesitancy was in part due to the rough going that it met in the courts. For one, the "conspiracy" and "combination" language of the law made it powerless to attack anticompetitive business practices of a single firm acting alone. Second, judicial interpretations of the meaning of several of the act's key terms blunted its application, at least temporarily.[4] Similarly, actions by a firm that injured its competitors were held immune from the Sherman Act if those otherwise illegal actions occurred in a foreign country.[5]

Thus, despite some early successes against price fixing by the powerful trusts that dominated the meat and tobacco industries,[6] there was soon a demand for additional legislation that would define more precisely the boundaries of antitrust policy. The belief that new antitrust laws were needed reached a peak following the Supreme Court's 1911 decision in *Standard Oil*, which held that the Sherman Act did not prohibit all restraints of trade, but only those that were found to be "unreasonable."[7]

The Clayton Act

There were two opposing views about how to remedy the perceived deficiencies of the Sherman Act. In the House of Representatives, the favored course of action was to list specific illegal business practices and make them criminal offenses. By contrast, the Senate wanted to create a new agency, the Federal Trade Commission (FTC), as an expert antitrust law enforcement body granted the flexibility and broad authority to attack undefined "unfair methods of competition." A compromise was eventually reached in which both approaches to reform were adopted.

---

3 Richard A. Posner, "A Statistical Study of Antitrust Law Enforcement, " *Journal of Law and Economics* 13 (October 1970), p. 366.

4 In *U.S.* v. *E. C. Knight Co.*, 156 U.S. 1 (1985), for example, Chief Justice Fuller held that the Sherman Act could not be used against the sugar trust because the defendant firms were engaged in the *manufacture* of sugar and manufacturing was not commerce: "Commerce succeeds to manufacture and is not part of it." This interpretation was overturned three years later when Judge Taft determined that the manufacture of cast iron pipes affected commerce. See *U. S.* v. *Addyston Pipe & Steel Co.*, 85 F. 271 (6th Cir. 1898).

5 *American Banana Co.* v. *United Fruit Co.*, 213 U.S. 347 (1909). The lawsuit charged that agents hired by United Fruit had destroyed property owned by American Banana in Central America to preserve United Fruit's domination of banana exports to the United States.

6 *Swift & Co.* v. *U.S.*, 196 U.S. 375 (1905) and *U.S.* v. *American Tobacco Co.*, 221 U.S. 106 (1911).

7 *Standard Oil Co.* (*N.J.*) v. *U.S.*, 221 U.S. 1 (1911).

The Clayton Act was passed in 1914, declaring illegal several specific business practices, but not subjecting violators of its provisions to criminal penalties. At the same time, the FTC was created and provided with authority to enforce both its own enabling statute and the Clayton Act. The Clayton Act was also made more flexible by the insertion of qualifying language declaring that the specified business practices would be illegal only where their "effect may be to substantially lessen competition or tend to create a monopoly."

The Law on Price Discrimination. Section 2 of the Clayton Act declares price discrimination—the practice of charging different customers different prices for the same good—to be illegal.[8] Permissible defenses required showing either that a price difference was justified by actual differences in the cost of supplying the same good to various categories of buyers or that price discrimination was necessary to meet an equally low price charged by a competitor.

Until the late 1970s, Section 2 was perhaps the most actively enforced provision of the antitrust laws. Indeed, 100 such cases had been prosecuted by the end of 1919.[9] However, during the Roaring Twenties the original language of Section 2 was rendered ineffective by the courts. First, the courts interpreted the law to be concerned mainly with the possible injurious effects of price discrimination on rival sellers, so-called "primary-line" injury. In fact, the original intent of Section 2 was to prevent "financially powerful corporations" from using local price-cutting tactics to impair the competitive positions of their smaller rivals.[10] The "secondary-line" injury suffered by buyers who paid higher prices because of sellers' price discriminating practices did not come within the statute's protection until 1939.[11]

Second, simple quantity discounts were held not to represent an unlawful form of price discrimination under Section 2's original language. Defendants naturally used this loophole frequently.[12] Because of the limits placed by the courts on Section 2, enforcement efforts slowed considerably; only nine price discrimination complaints were issued between 1925 and 1935.[13]

The Robinson-Patman Act. These loopholes were closed when the Robinson-Patman Act amendment to Section 2 was passed in 1936.[14] Sections

8   Chapter 6 discusses the theory of price discrimination in some detail.
9   Posner, "Statistical Study of Antitrust Enforcement," p. 370.
10   Phillip Areeda, *Antitrust Analysis: Problems, Text, Cases*, 3E. (Boston: Little, Brown, 1981), p. 1061.
11   *George Van Camp & Sons Co.* v. *American Can Co.*, 278 U.S. 245 (1929).
12   See, for example, *Goodyear Tire & Rubber Co.* v. *FTC*, 101 F.2d 620 (6th Cir.), cert. denied, 308 U.S. 557 (1939). Although this decision was rendered after passage of the Robinson-Patman Act amendment, the case was initiated under the original language of Section 2 and decided on that basis.
13   Posner, "Statistical Study of Antitrust Enforcement," p. 370.
14   For a discussion of the political origins of Robinson-Patman (the original bill was drafted by an attorney employed by the Wholesale Grocers Association), see Thomas W. Ross, "Winners and Losers under the Robinson-Patman Act," *Journal of Law and Economics* 27 (October 1984), pp. 243-71.

2(a) and 2(f) of the Clayton Act are the basic changes made by Robinson-Patman. Following the original language of Section 2 outlawing price discrimination "where the effect of such discrimination may be to substantially lessen competition or tend to create a monopoly," the amendment adds, "or to injure, destroy, or prevent competition with any person who either grants or knowingly receives the benefit of such discrimination, or with customers of either of them." Robinson-Patman thereby brought both primary- and secondary-line injury explicitly within the Clayton Act's reach. Section 2(f) makes it illegal "knowingly to induce or receive a prohibited discriminatory price."

In addition to these changes, Robinson-Patman inserted new language that lengthened Section 2 significantly. Section 2(b) put the burden of justifying a price difference on the party charged with violating the law. Section 2(c) prohibited paying or granting, or receiving or accepting,

> anything of value as a commission, brokerage, or other compensation, or any allowance or discount in lieu thereof, except for services rendered in connection with the sale or purchase of goods, wares, or merchandise, either to the other party to such transaction or to an agent, representative, or other intermediary therein where such intermediary is acting in fact for or in behalf, or is subject to the direct or indirect control, of any party to such transaction other than the person by whom such compensation is so granted or paid.

Any payments that a manufacturer or distributor makes for services or facilities furnished by its customers must be made "available on proportionately equal terms to all other customers competing" with that buyer, according to Section 2(d). And, under Section 2(e), it is unlawful for the seller to furnish services or facilities to one customer unless they are made available to all "on proportionately equal terms."

The Robinson-Patman amendment retained both the meeting competition and cost justification defenses provided for in the original language of Section 2. It stated further

> that nothing herein contained shall prevent price changes from time to time where in response to changing conditions affecting the market for or the marketability of the goods concerned, such as but not limited to imminent deterioration of perishable goods, obsolescence of seasonal goods, distress sales under court process, or sales in good faith in discontinuance of business in the goods concerned.

However, Section 2(a) added that even if valid cost justifications were advanced in defense of price differences, the FTC might still set limits on the use of quantity discounts if it determined that these discounts were not available to a sufficient number of buyers.[15]

---

15 See *FTC* v. *Morton Salt Co.*, 334 U.S. 37 (1948), in which the Supreme Court held that Morton Salt's pricing policy violated Section 2 on evidence that only five grocery chains bought sufficient quantities of salt to qualify for the company's lowest discounted price. Noting that

The Robinson-Patman Act invigorated the FTC's enforcement efforts under Section 2. The FTC prosecuted an average of 31 cases each year in the decade following passage of the amendment. The high-water mark of Robinson-Patman enforcement was reached in 1963 when the FTC issued 234 Section 2 complaints.

The commission's Section 2 enforcement efforts slowed during the late 1970s to one or two cases a year. Part of the reason for this decline is simply that the FTC turned its attention to other antitrust matters. It stepped up its merger law enforcement activities, and engaged in more industry wide rule making. It also may be true that the commission has listened to the critics of the Robinson-Patman Act. Most respectable scholarship on price discrimination concludes that the law is "mistaken in its assumptions and further deformed in its application."[16] The critics point out that a defense against a charge of illegal price discrimination is "impossible" because of the difficulties of measuring the firm's costs.[17] The law is exceedingly difficult to interpret and the burden of justifying price differences rests with the accused firm. Hence, the Robinson-Patman Act requires business decision makers "to consult their attorneys before making price moves."[18]

The *Utah Pie* case described in the chapter's opening application illustrates just how difficult it is to distinguish between the normal workings of the competitive marketplace and unlawful price cutting designed to injure a competitor. When the Utah Pie Company began baking and selling frozen dessert pies in Salt Lake City, it gained market share by setting its prices below those charged by its major rivals. These rivals, in turn, reduced their own prices below those charged by the aggressive newcomer. When the dust had settled, more frozen pies were being sold to Salt Lake City's consumers at lower prices than had been the case beforehand. Yet, after hearing Utah Pie's complaint, the Supreme Court equated this "drastically declining price structure" with below-cost pricing and predatory intent to injure Utah Pie.

Another interpretation is simply that the Robinson-Patman Act afforded the Utah Pie Company an opportunity to shield itself from the forces of competition.[19] What better victory could there be than to have a judicial decree

---

Morton Salt's price discounts were not *functionally available* to all of its customers, the majority held that "the legislative history of the Robinson-Patman Act makes it abundantly clear that Congress considered it to be an evil that a large buyer could secure a competitive advantage over a small buyer solely because of the large buyer's quantity purchasing ability."

16 Robert H. Bork, *The Antitrust Paradox: A Policy at War with Itself* (New York: Basic Books, 1978), p. 384. Also see Richard A Posner, *The Robinson-Patman Act: Federal Regulation of Price Differences* (Washington, D.C.: American Enterprise Institute, 1976) and American Bar Association, *Report of the American Bar Association Commission to Study the Federal Trade Commission* (Chicago: American Bar Association, 1969).

17 Posner, *Robinson-Patman Act*, p. 30.

18 Frederic M. Scherer, *Industrial Market Structure and Economic Performance*, 2E. (Boston: Houghton-Mifflin, 1980), p. 581.

19 Its success in this regard was short-lived, however. The company went bankrupt in 1972 as a result of mismanagement. Carnation ceased production of frozen dessert pies in 1967, and by 1975 Pet's share of frozen pie sales nationally had fallen to 3 percent. See Kenneth G. Elzinga and Thomas F. Hogarty, "Utah Pie and the Consequences of Robinson-Patman," *Journal of Law and Economics* 21 (October 1978), pp. 427-34.

entered against a rival ordering it to "stop competing, leave your competitors alone, raise your prices?"[20] In short, the law on price discrimination, passed at the request of independent wholesalers and retailers to halt the growth of a more efficient method of product distribution,[21] is perhaps the leading example of the argument that enforcement of the antitrust laws serves private interests, and not the public interest.

The Law on Mergers. Section 7 of the Clayton Act is sometimes called the "holding company" section. It was designed to dismantle the great turn-of-the-century industrial trusts. The trusts had been created by establishing companies that purchased and held stock in several independent enterprises and thereby acquired ownership interests in competing firms within the same industry and, sometimes, across the boundaries of related industries.

At first, Section 7 was eloquently silent on means other than stock purchases by which one firm could gain an ownership interest in another. It soon became clear that mergers carried out through the purchase of physical assets did not violate the Clayton Act, even if stock was also acquired in the transaction.[22] This glaring loophole made section 7 nearly powerless. It was gutted further by court decisions holding that after consummation of a merger, an acquiring firm could not be made to divest the physical assets it had purchased even if the stock acquisition was subsequently found to have been illegal.[23]

It was not until 1950 that Congress moved to strengthen Section 7 by passing the Celler-Kefauver Act. This amendment explicitly prohibited the acquisition of another firm's assets if the effect of the acquisition was to substantially lessen competition. The asset loophole was thereby closed. The Celler-Kefauver Act amended Section 7 to read:

> No person engaged in commerce or in any activity affecting commerce shall acquire, directly or indirectly, the whole or any part of the stock or other share capital and no person subject to the jurisdiction of the Federal Trade Commission shall acquire the whole or any part of the assets of another person engaged also in commerce or in any activity affecting commerce, where in any line of commerce or any section of the country, the effect of such acquisition may be to substantially lessen competition, or tend to create a monopoly.

---

20 James C. Miller III and Paul A. Pautler, "Predation: The Changing View in Economics and the Law," *Journal of Law and Economics* 28 (May 1985), p. 498.

21 These efforts continue, but at a much slower pace than during the heady days of Robinson-Patman enforcement. In December 1988, the FTC issued a Section 2 complaint against six major book publishers, charging them with offering discriminatory discounts to several large retail bookstore chains. See Monica Langley, "FTC Charges Six Publishers with Price Bias," *Wall Street Journal*, 23 December 1988, p. B4.

22 A representative case is *U.S.* v. *Celanese Corp. of America*, 61 F. Supp. 14 (S.D.N.Y. 1950).

23 *Swift & Co.* v. *F.T.C.*, 272 U.S. 554 (1926).

The amendment was quite effective in strengthening antimerger law enforcement. Until the late 1960s, the federal government rarely lost a case it brought under Section 7.

Premerger notification. In 1976, the Hart-Scott-Rodino Antitrust Improvement Act further strengthened the ability of the antitrust enforcement agencies to attack mergers. This law, which established a premerger notification process, was designed to provide the Justice Department and the FTC adequate time to assess the competitive effects of proposed acquisitions before their consummation. Before the amendment to Section 7 was passed, the two federal antitrust agencies learned about prospective merger activity only by indirect means. They relied on announcements in specialized business publications and the popular press, company news releases, and other publicly available sources to discover merger plans in the economy.

Moreover, there was no assurance that the law enforcement bureaus could act quickly enough to prevent a questionable acquisition from proceeding. The government had no authority to require that a merger be postponed while an investigation was pending. And, while the antitrust laws have no statute of limitations as far as federal enforcement efforts are concerned, the inability to delay events meant that many unlawful mergers could only be challenged *ex post*. The authorities were required to seek divestiture of illegally acquired assets or attempt by some other means to undo acquisitions already completed.

The Hart-Scott-Rodino Act imposes premerger notification requirements when the acquiring firm has total assets of at least $100 million or annual sales of at least $10 million and the acquired firm has at least $10 million in assets or annual sales. The law covers any transaction meeting these criteria if the acquiring firm will thereby gain control of more than $15 million worth (or 15 percent) of the acquired firm's stock or assets.

In broad outline, the Hart-Scott-Rodino Act establishes the following premerger notification timetable. The acquiring firm first files premerger notification forms simultaneously with the FTC and the Department of Justice announcing its intention to acquire an ownership interest in another enterprise. These forms provide preliminary information about the parties involved in the transaction—their identities, their locations of operation, their ownership structures, their products, and so on.

The two enforcement agencies then have 30 days (15 days if the transaction is in the form of cash only) to decide which of them will have jurisdiction and whether or not to seek supplementary information from the prospective merger or acquisition partners.[24] If neither agency requests

---

24 The decision as to whether the Justice Department or the FTC will have jurisdiction over the merger is handled through an elaborate liaison agreement in which one agency grants "clearance" to the other. The liaison procedure was worked out in the wake of the Supreme Court's decision in *FTC* v. *Cement Institute*, 333 U.S. 683 (1948), which held that the FTC could bring Sherman Act antitrust cases under Section 5 of the FTC Act. For an analysis of the impact of the liaison agreement on agency budgets and case-bringing activities, see Richard S. Higgins, William F. Shughart II, and Robert D. Tollison, "Dual Enforcement of

additional information, the merger may proceed at the end of the relevant waiting period. If one of the agencies seeks more information about the transaction, however, a second decision point is reached after the firms have complied with the agency's request. If the government decides to challenge the merger or acquisition, it must seek a preliminary injunction in federal court within a specified time limit (10 days for a cash transaction and 20 days if the acquisition involves the purchase of stock). Otherwise, the merger can go forward when the extended waiting period has elapsed.

In practice, the Hart-Scott-Rodino timetable gets lengthened considerably because the clock does not start until the agency having jurisdiction certifies that the firms have fully complied with its request for information. This is especially likely when the merger or acquisition involves one of the leading firms in an industry. The burden placed on firms in responding to "second requests" can be immense. For example, in responding to the FTC's subpoena concerning Kohlberg Kravis Roberts (KKR) & Company's proposed acquisition of RJR Nabisco, KKR's attorneys amassed 680 cartons of company documents. In order to meet the FTC's submission deadline for these materials, which required the services of 150 lawyers and paralegals to assemble, the law firm "discovered that the cheapest way to get everything there was to rent a DC-9."[25]

Merger guidelines. The mandate of Section 7 requires the federal antitrust authorities and the courts to identify and to prohibit those mergers and acquisitions that "may substantially lessen competition or tend to create a monopoly." Doing so requires first defining a "line of commerce" and a "section of the country"—relevant product and geographic markets—within which the merger's effects on competition are to be analyzed. Once the antitrust market has been defined, Section 7 then asks: does the merger or acquisition create a firm with such a large share of total sales that it could profitably raise price? Alternatively, does the disappearance of a former competitor increase the expected gains or reduce the expected costs of collusion among the remaining firms so price could be profitably increased? The answers to both of these questions—and, therefore, the decision about whether to challenge a proposed transaction—follow directly from the market definition adopted in that particular case.

As it has evolved in the decisions of the courts, market definition has basically become a question of market concentration and market shares.[26] That

---

the Antitrust Laws," in Robert J. Mackay, James C. Miller III, and Bruce Yandle, eds., *Public Choice and Regulation: A View from Inside the Federal Trade Commission* (Stanford, CA: Hoover Institution Press, 1987), pp. 154-80.

25 "For Further Details, See Carton No. 587," *Wall Street Journal*, 15 March 1988. p. B1.

26 The leading precedents are *U.S.* v. *Columbia Steel Co.*, 334 U.S. 495 (1948), a pre-1950 Section 7 case that set "percentage command of the market" as a critical element of merger analysis; *U.S.* v. *E. I. du Pont de Nemours & Co.*, 351 U.S. 377 (1966), which created a "reasonable interchangeability" standard for defining relevant antitrust markets that stressed the availability of substitutes to buyers; and *Brown Shoe Co.* v. *U.S.*, 370 U.S. 294 (1962), which listed "practical indicia," like the product's peculiar characteristics and uses, unique production facilities, distinct customers, and distinct prices, for defining the boundaries of relevant antitrust markets.

is, whether or not a particular merger violates Section 7 depends mainly on the degree to which sales in the relevant market are concentrated in the hands of a few firms (both pre- and post-merger). This judgment, in turn, depends on how narrowly or broadly the market boundaries are drawn. Most merger cases are therefore decided when the judge accepts one side of the argument between the plaintiff, who supports narrow boundaries, and the defendant, who seeks a broad definition, about which products and geographic areas are "in" the market and which are "out."

Market definition in antitrust analysis consists of the task of identifying the products and firms that do—or could—offer reasonable alternatives to buyers if they face a price increase following the merger of two former rivals. But instead of using Section 7 to organize and summarize the information relevant for analyzing the likely competitive effects of mergers and acquisitions, the government has made market definition the principal issue in these cases.

Under the current merger guidelines, a relevant market is defined as

> a product or group of products and a geographic area in which it is sold such that a hypothetical, profit-maximizing firm, not subject to price regulation, that was the only present and future seller of those products in the area would impose a "small but significant and nontransitory" increase in price above prevailing or likely future levels.

Thus, the Department of Justice defines the relevant market by identifying the smallest group of firms that could, if they acted in concert, profitably raise price above its current level and sustain that price increase.

As a practical matter, a 5 to 10 percent price increase is considered to be "small but significant" and a year or more is considered to be "nontransitory." The likelihood of a post-merger price increase is then gauged on the basis of the number and size distribution of the firms included in the defined market. Price increases are considered to be more likely if the market contains only a few large firms than if the market contains many small firms.

More precisely, the degree of market concentration is measured by calculating a **Herfindahl-Hirschman Index** (*HHI*). The *HHI* is computed by determining the percentage share of total market sales of each firm included in the defined antitrust market, and then summing the squares of these individual market shares. For example, if the relevant market contains one firm that accounts for 100 percent of the total sales, then $HHI = 100^2 = 10,000$; if there are two firms each accounting for 50 percent of the market, then $HHI = 50^2 + 50^2 = 5,000$; and so on.

Numerical concentration measures are computed both pre- and post-merger. The merger guidelines set threshold *HHI* values that make legal challenges to the transaction more or less likely. The guidelines state that no merger in a market with a post-acquisition *HHI* of less than 1,000 is apt to violate Section 7. On the other hand, a merger that raises the *HHI* by 50 points or more is likely to meet with opposition if the post-merger concentration index calculated for the relevant market exceeds 1,800. Acquisitions that cause the market's post-merger *HHI* to fall in the range between 1,000 and 1,800 may or may not be challenged. (A challenge is more likely if the transaction causes the market concentration index to rise by 100 points or more.)

The politics of merger law enforcement. The market share and market concentration standards laid out in the merger guidelines are fairly precise. But it is nevertheless true that the decision to challenge the legality of a proposed merger or acquisition basically depends on which products and which geographic areas are included in the numerical calculations. Narrow market boundaries increase the chance that the antitrust authorities will object to any given merger or acquisition and, moreover, make it more likely that the objection will be upheld in the courts.

The frequency with which the enforcement agencies draw arbitrarily narrow market boundaries encourages the strategic use of Section 7 by the competitors of the firms that seek government's permission to merge. Consider the following example. Many mergers and acquisitions result in the closure of outmoded production facilities, the replacement of incumbent management, the combination of duplicative product distribution networks, and other synergistic effects that promise to reduce costs. Increased economic efficiencies of these types will increase the value of the firm targeted for takeover (and the wealth of the target's owners) by allowing the product to be produced and sold more cheaply. Consumers also benefit from improved economic efficiency and lower prices.

At the same time, however, rival sellers face the prospect of increased competitive pressures. These rivals can respond by trying to copy the organizational innovations the merger partners plan to implement or by taking other steps to reduce their own costs and prices. Alternatively, the competitors can complain to the antitrust authorities of a possible violation of Section 7. They will almost surely be joined on the issue by the employees of the target firm who face the prospect of losing their jobs, and by local public officials who face the prospect of plant closings and a smaller local tax base. The members of Congress who represent the interests of the affected districts and states will transmit these demands for protectionism to the law enforcement agencies.[27]

Of course, it is possible that opposition to a proposed merger or acquisition could arise from a public-spirited attempt by competitors to block a transaction they perceive as leading to increased market concentration and higher prices for consumers. After all, business rivals have access to more and better information about relevant market conditions than will the law enforcement agencies as they go about their task of distinguishing between efficiency-enhancing and market-power-increasing merger motives. Even if this is not the case, surely the antitrust authorities could see through and reject competitors' complaints that are nothing more than self-serving attempts to handicap their rivals.

---

27 The interest-group basis of antitrust enforcement is laid out in detail in William F. Shughart II, *Antitrust Policy and Interest-Group Politics* (New York: Quorum Books, 1990).

The GM-Toyota Joint Venture

In 1983, General Motors Corporation announced its intention to enter a joint venture with Toyota for designing and producing a new subcompact automobile in the United States.[a] The plan involved combining GM's idle production facilities in Fremont, California, with Japanese-supplied engines and Toyota's designs and managerial expertise to produce a U.S. version of the Toyota Corolla. GM claimed that the venture would generate significant economic benefits because it would learn from Toyota the secrets that made Japanese automobile manufacturers more efficient than their U.S. counterparts. GM would presumably then be able to apply those secrets in its other plants.[b]

Soon after the agreement was announced, both Chrysler and Ford, the horizontal competitors of GM and Toyota, petitioned the Federal Trade Commission to block the joint venture. Chrysler and Ford argued that the combination of two of the world's largest automobile companies would substantially lessen competition in two ways. First, GM and Toyota proposed to set the selling price of the new vehicle by reference to the average price of specified other subcompact models they produced. Therefore, the exchange of competitive information between the joint venturers would promote collusion. Second, Chrysler and Ford alleged that the joint venture would increase GM's market power over sales of larger automobiles.

This argument was based on results from marketing studies showing a high degree of brand loyalty among car buyers. According to the petitioners, as the incomes of automobile consumers increase over their lifetimes, they tend to "trade-up" to successively more expensive models produced by the same manufacturer. For this reason, it was said to be a common marketing strategy for auto makers to sell subcompact cars at prices below cost with the expectation that these losses would later be recouped on sales of larger vehicles carrying higher profit margins. Chrysler and Ford claimed that sales of the joint-venture vehicle, which was to be sold through GM's franchised dealers, would allow GM to "lock-in" additional customers to its product line, allowing it to eventually capture a larger share of the market for luxury automobiles.

The opposition by Chrysler and Ford to the joint venture illustrates antitrust's potential for subverting the competitive process. If, as claimed by the petitioners, the GM-Toyota agreement would have promoted collusion or increased GM's market power in any segment of the domestic automobile market, then silent acquiescence from rivals would have been expected. This conclusion follows because any attempt on the part of the joint venturers to restrict output and raise price would have presented their horizontal competitors with two profitable options. One alternative would be to raise their prices as well and share in the colluders' profits. The other option would be to maintain their prices at existing levels and thereby gain sales at the colluders' expense. On the other hand, complaints by rivals are predictable if the joint venture would lead to lower costs or improved product quality. In that event, market forces place rivals at a competitive disadvantage; they must "run correspondingly faster in order to stand still."[c]

---

a See William J. Baumol and Janusz A. Ordover, "Use of Antitrust to Subvert Competition," *Journal of Law and Economics* 28 (May 1985), pp. 256-57, and Fisher, "'Horizontal Mergers," pp. 36-37.

b *General Motors Corp. et al., Federal Register* 48 (1983), p. 57246. Toyota's incentives for participating in the joint venture were in large part driven by existing "voluntary export restraints" (VERs) which placed limits on the number of automobiles Japanese companies could export to the United States on an annual basis. An important benefit of the joint venture to Toyota was that the automobiles produced under the agreement were not subject to the VERs.

c Baumol and Ordover, "Use of Antitrust to Subvert Competition," pp. 256-57.

The FTC ultimately approved the GM-Toyota joint venture. In doing so, however, the commission provided Chrysler and Ford with an important victory: It ordered the joint venturers to limit their production of the new vehicle to no more than 250,000 units per year. This output restriction, which is inconsistent with antitrust's stated goal of promoting consumer welfare, possibly prevents GM and Toyota from taking full advantage of economies of scale, resulting in higher average production costs and higher prices than might otherwise have been realized. Such an outcome is, however, consistent with an implication of the interest-group theory of government, namely that special interests play greater roles in shaping public policies toward business than does the public interest.

However, the evidence supports neither of these possibilities. Tests using data from financial markets suggest that the horizontal mergers and acquisitions challenged by the Antitrust Division and the FTC under Section 7 of the Clayton Act have not been anticompetitive, on average. Instead, competitors of the prospective merger partners appear to benefit most from enforcement of the law on mergers.[28]

The Federal Trade Commission Act

As noted earlier, both the Clayton Act and the Federal Trade Commission Act grew out of dissatisfaction with enforcement efforts under—and judicial interpretations of—the Sherman Act. Among those favoring new legislation, one view was that it would be unwise to list specific illegal business practices because any list was bound to be incomplete. The FTC Act was thus passed in 1914 in response to calls for the creation of an expert agency that would have the flexibility and broad enforcement authority to deal with a wide range of present and future antitrust problems.

Section 1 of the FTC Act established a five-member commission, each member to be appointed by the president to a seven-year term, with authority to investigate, prosecute, and adjudicate antitrust violations. (No more than three of the commissioners can at any one time be members of the same political party.) Section 5 laid out the commission's mandate, stating simply that "unfair methods of competition in commerce are hereby declared unlawful." In 1938, the Wheeler-Lea Act amended this language to extend the FTC's authority to consumer protection matters. Section 5 now reads: "Unfair methods of competition in or affecting commerce, and unfair or deceptive acts or practices in or affecting commerce, are hereby declared unlawful."

---

28 See, for example, B. Espen Eckbo, "Horizontal Mergers, Collusion, and Stockholder Wealth," *Journal of Financial Economics* 11 (1983), pp. 241-73; Robert Stillman, "Examining Anti-Trust Policy Towards Horizontal Mergers," *Journal of Financial Economics* 11 (1983), pp. 225-40; and B. Espen Eckbo and Peggy Wier, "Antimerger Policy under the Hart-Scott-Rodino Act: A Reexamination of the Market Power Hypothesis, *Journal of Law and Economics* 28 (April 1985), pp. 119-49.

From the beginning, the FTC was empowered to enforce compliance with Sections 2, 3, 7, and 8 of the Clayton Act. Such authority was specifically vested in the commission by Section 11 of that law. The FTC's authority under the Sherman Act was not clarified until 1948, however, when the Supreme Court held that under Section 5 of the FTC Act the commission could prosecute any business practice that would also violate the Sherman Act.[29] The commission is limited to seeking relief for antitrust violations in the form of orders to "cease and desist" the practices it determines to be unlawful. (The FTC can, however, impose civil penalties— monetary fines—if the guilty party later fails to comply with the order.) Only the Justice Department's Antitrust Division can bring Sherman Act suits involving criminal charges.

The Federal Trade Commission is perhaps the most intensively studied federal agency. With its broad antitrust and consumer protection missions,[30] the commission has attracted considerable attention from scholars interested in evaluating the performance of government bureaus. Research on the FTC has paid particular attention to its ties to the Congress. What is becoming increasingly clear is that the commission, rather than operating as the independent, expert law enforcement body it was conceived as being, has in large part followed policies that are consistent with, and responsive to, the political preferences of its overseers in Congress.

REGULATORY POLICY

The two basic points of view concerning governmental regulatory policy and its effects were discussed in Chapter 17. One of these views holds that public policy makers and regulators can and should intervene to correct a wide variety of perceived market failures in the private economy, including market failures due to externalities, monopoly, and imperfect (and asymmetric) information. The other view holds that government lacks the precise information about the benefits and costs of economic activities necessary to regulate optimally. Moreover, even when such information is available, the asymmetric political payoffs facing self-interest-seeking policy makers and regulators cause them to choose methods of intervention that benefit narrow, private interests rather than the public interest. Thus, regulatory policy itself creates market inefficiencies.

The first clear expression of the legitimacy of government's power to regulate private industry can be traced to a decision by the Supreme Court

---

29 *FTC* v. *Cement Institute*, 333 U.S. 683 (1948).

30 In addition to the Clayton and FTC Acts, the commission enforces a long list of specialized statutes. These include the Truth-in-Lending Act, the Fair Credit Reporting Act, the Fair Debt Collection Act, the Fair Credit Billing Act, the Equal Credit Opportunity Act, the Trademark Act, the Export Trade Act, the Fair Packaging-Labeling Act, the Consumer Leasing Act, the Hobby Protection Act, the Textile Act, the Wool Act, and the Fur Act.

in 1877. The Court held that when private property is "affected with a public interest" government regulation can be justified despite the Fourteenth Amendment's guarantee that "no State shall...deprive any person of life, liberty, or property, without due process of law."[31] In the following years, the courts construed the "public interest" standard strictly, approving state regulation of only a select group of industries, including banks, fire insurance companies, insurance agents, and grain elevators.[32]

But the Supreme Court rejected these narrow interpretations in 1934, declaring that "the phrase 'affected with a public interest' can, in the nature of things, mean no more than that an industry, for adequate reason, is subject to control for the public good." The Court went on to say that "there can be no doubt that on proper occasion and by appropriate measures the state may regulate a business in any of its aspects, including the prices to be charged for its products or the commodities it sells." In effect, the Court held that there was no constitutional distinction between public utilities and other industries. The states were free to regulate any business enterprise within their jurisdictions for any reason that could be justified as promoting the public interest as long as the regulation was "neither arbitrary nor discriminatory."[33]

At the federal level of government, public regulation of industry dates from the Act to Regulate Commerce (1887), which created the Interstate Commerce Commission to ensure that railway rates were "just and reasonable." Today, regulation of industry is pervasive at all levels of government. Table 18.3 lists the major federal regulatory agencies and gives a brief summary of their jurisdictions. In addition, state and local governments actively regulate many business enterprises. Among other things, they issue "certificates of convenience and necessity" to regulate hospital construction; set qualification standards and issue licenses to barbers, physicians, architects, veterinarians, public school teachers, engineers, accountants, and other professionals; enforce building codes to regulate the use of construction materials and enforce zoning laws to regulate the locations of construction projects; license taxicab operators and set taxicab fares; and regulate such public utilities as telephone, water, and electricity suppliers. The list could go on and on. In what follows, a small number of these regulatory policies are described in more detail.

---

31 *Munn* v. *Illinois*, 94 U.S. 113 (1877). Munn and Scott, two grain elevator operators, had challenged a provision of the Illinois constitution designating privately owned grain elevators as "public" warehouses and a law passed by the Illinois legislature in 1871 setting a ceiling on the rates that could be charged for grain storage. The Supreme Court upheld a decision of the Illinois courts finding Munn and Scott guilty of charging higher rates than the statute permitted.

32 Alfred E. Kahn, *The Economics of Regulation: Principles and Institutions*, vol. 1 (New York: Wiley, 1970), p. 3.

33 *Nebbia* v. *New York*, 291 U.S. 502 (1934), pp. 531-32. In its decision, the Court upheld the right of New York's Milk Control Board to regulate the prices at which milk could be sold in the state.

TABLE 18.3 MAJOR FEDERAL REGULATORY AGENCIES

AGENCY	YEAR ESTABLISHED	JURISDICTION
Interstate Commerce Commission	1887	Interstate railroads (1887); trucks (1935); water carriers (1940); telephone (1910-34); oil pipelines (1906-77)
Food and Drug Administration	1906	Safety of food and drugs (1906); cosmetics (1938); effectiveness of drugs and medical devices (1962)
Animal and Plant Health Inspection Service	1907	Meat and poultry packing plants
Federal Reserve Board	1914	Federally chartered commercial banks
Federal Trade Commission	1914	Antitrust; false and deceptive advertising (1938)
Federal Communications Commission	1934	Interstate telephone (1934); broadcasting (1934); cable television (1968)
Securities and Exchange Commission	1934	Public security issues and security exchanges; public utility holding companies (1935)
Federal Power Commission[a]	1935	Interstate wholesale electricity (1935); natural gas pipelines (1938); field price of natural gas (1954); oil pipelines (1977); gas and gas pipelines (1978)
Civil Aeronautics Board[b]	1938	Interstate airline routes and fares (1938-82); airline safety (1938-58)
Atomic Energy Commission[c]	1947	Nuclear materials and power generating plants (1947-75)
National Highway Traffic Safety Administration	1970	Automobile safety (1970); automobile fuel economy (1975)
Occupational Safety and Health Administration	1971	Workplace safety and health
Environmental Protection Agency	1972	Air, water, and noise pollution
Consumer Product Safety Commission	1972	Safety of consumer products
Mine Enforcement Safety Administration[d]	1973	Safety and health in mining

a Superseded by the Federal Energy Regulatory Commission in 1977.
b Airline safety regulation was transferred to the Federal Aviation Administration in 1958.
c Superseded by the Nuclear Regulatory Commission in 1975.
d Superseded by the Mine Safety and Health Administration in 1978.

Price and Entry Regulation

One widely used method of reducing the allocative inefficiency of monopoly is to regulate the prices that monopoly sellers can charge their customers. In the case of interest here, government uses its regulatory authority to establish a *maximum* selling price that is below the level the profit-maximizing firm would choose in the absence of regulation, but that generates revenues sufficient to cover its costs of production.

Price regulation of this type has typically been applied in cases of "natural" monopoly—industries in which scale economies loom so large that one firm can serve the market at lower unit cost than if two or more firms served the market. Most public utilities—firms supplying electricity, water, natural gas, and local telephone services, for example—fall into this category. Production of these goods requires substantial capital investments up front, but once these fixed costs have been incurred, average costs fall sharply as additional customers are served.

Because a monopoly is "natural" under these circumstances, state and local governments frequently grant one firm exclusive service rights in a given geographic area. The governments then regulate the prices the firm may charge to limit the welfare loss that would otherwise be imposed on consumers. Price regulation goes far beyond the case of natural monopoly, however. Among the industries that have been or are currently subject to it are cable television, commercial airlines, retail gasoline, oil pipelines, railway and motor carriers, taxicabs, commercial banks and thrift institutions, stockbrokers, and insurance companies.

Price regulation is almost always accompanied by **entry regulation**. On the theory that it is more efficient for a single firm to serve the entire market, regulated public utilities are granted the exclusive right to supply the regulated good or service in a particular geographic location. However, such entry restrictions provide a telling argument against the theory used to justify them. If it were in fact the case that the entry of new firms would cause market price to fall below average cost so that all suppliers would incur losses, then no explicit entry restrictions would be needed. Knowing that their entry would lead to price below average cost, potential entrants would not enter. Entry restrictions are only called for if prices are higher than they would be after entry, not when they are below what they would be after entry. This observation suggests that the natural monopoly theory of price regulation is invalid and that entry restrictions serve to protect the prices and profits of regulated firms against competitive market forces in ways that diminish the welfare of consumers.[34]

In theory, price regulation is capable of moving price and output toward the perfectly competitive benchmark. Consider the natural monopoly depicted in Figure 18.1. With no regulation in place, the profit-maximizing firm sets output at Q_m units and price at p_m. Two forms of price controls are possible.

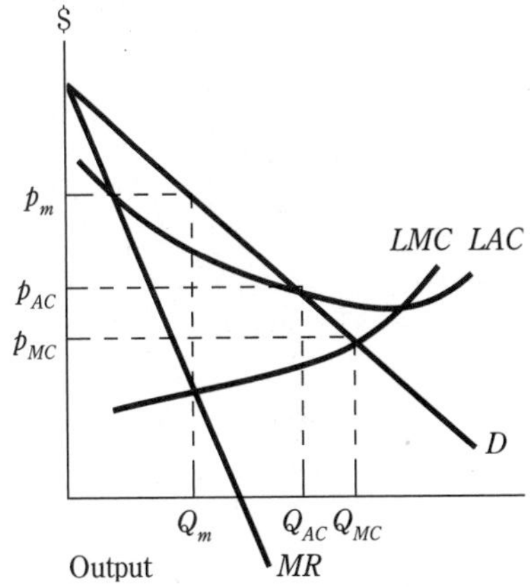

FIGURE 18.1
Two Forms of Price Regulation

34 See Harold Demsetz, "Why Regulate Utilities?," *Journal of Law and Economics* 11 (April 1968), pp. 55-65.

Under an **average-cost pricing** policy, the regulatory agency requires the firm to charge customers a price equal to its long-run average production cost, *LAC*. At such a price, which is shown in the diagram as p_{AC}, the firm's marginal revenue schedule is effectively replaced by the horizontal line at p_{AC} up to its intersection with the demand curve, *D*. Marginal revenue then has a vertical segment that intersects long-run marginal cost, *LMC*, at Q_{AC}. Equating marginal revenue with marginal cost, the firm therefore expands output to Q_{AC}, at which point, because price is just equal to average cost, it earns zero economic profit.

The problem is to determine this optimal average-cost price. To do so, the regulatory agency must have access to very detailed information about the regulated firm's revenue and cost schedules. This is unlikely to be the case and, moreover, regulatory errors can be quite costly. In particular, if the regulated price is set "too low" (i.e., below p_{AC}), the firm's revenues will not cover its costs of production and economic losses will be sustained.

Marginal-cost pricing is an alternative form of price regulation. Under such a policy, the regulatory agency requires the firm to charge a price equal to its long-run marginal cost. This price is represented in Figure 18.1 by p_{MC}. The firm's normal marginal revenue schedule is replaced by the horizontal line at p_{MC}, and marginal revenue now equals marginal cost at the point where *LMC* intersects the demand schedule. The natural monopolist consequently expands output to the "perfectly competitive" level, Q_{MC}.

As shown in the diagram, however, a marginal-cost pricing policy generates economic losses for the regulated firm. These losses are sustained because price is less than average cost at Q_{MC}. Indeed, this relationship between revenue and cost is the hallmark of natural monopoly: The market demand curve cuts the long-run average cost curve while the latter is still declining, and marginal cost lies below average cost when average cost is falling. Thus, it is not feasible for the market to be served by a perfectly competitive industry charging price equal to marginal cost. For marginal-cost pricing to be a viable regulatory policy in the long run, then, the government must pay the regulated firm a subsidy—equal to the difference between average cost and marginal cost on the last unit sold times total output—so that the firm can break even. A successful marginal-cost pricing policy also requires that the regulatory agency gather very detailed information about the regulated firm's revenue and cost schedules in order to determine the optimal marginal-cost price.

The theoretical literature addressing the technical aspects of price regulation is immense.[35] Indeed, a well respected academic journal, the *Bell Journal of Economics and Management Science* (retitled as the *RAND Journal of Economics* since the breakup of the Bell system's long-distance telephone monopoly), was launched in the early 1970s to provide scholars with a forum for debating the efficacy of various price regulation schemes.

---

35 The classic reference is Kahn, *Economics of Regulation*. More recent developments are surveyed in Michael A. Crew, ed., *Regulating Utilities in an Era of Deregulation* (London: Macmillan, 1987).

But while technically demanding, the standard economic theories of price regulation have at least two missing elements. On the one hand, these theories often overlook the fact that the owners and managers of regulated firms are rational economic actors whose responses to the changes in relative prices associated with regulation might cause regulatory initiatives to have "unintended" effects on behavior. And the costs of these effects could more than offset any of regulation's direct benefits.

On the other hand, the traditional analysis of price regulation is set in a political vacuum. Regulatory agencies are typically assumed to have no motivation except to make mechanical attempts to force the regulated firm's price and output toward the perfectly competitive ideal. This assumption ignores the reality that regulators at the local, state, and federal levels of government either stand for election themselves or are appointed and overseen by individuals who hold political office. Both of these omissions serve to focus economists' attention on the announced or intended goals of regulation rather than on the observed effects of the regulatory policies actually adopted.

The failure of traditional economic models of price regulation to consider the motives of the regulators was first revealed in a body of research showing that regulatory policies often do little in the way of achieving their announced goals. A large number of studies reaching similar conclusions raised two important questions: If regulation generates no apparent benefits for consumers, why are regulatory policies adopted? Given the very real costs to taxpayers of supporting the apparatus of public regulation, why do regulatory policies persist?

The answer given to both of these questions in Chapter 17 is that there is a market for regulatory legislation. Certain groups, whose interests are sufficiently concentrated and whose costs of organizing to obtain regulatory favors are relatively low, stand to gain more than other groups from the controls on price imposed by public regulatory agencies. These prospective benefits create incentives for some special interest groups to use the apparatus of public regulation to increase their own wealth at the expense of groups that face relatively high costs of organizing to oppose regulatory controls. The regulators themselves, in turn, serve as brokers of these wealth transfers. Their motivation for doing so also has a basis in self-interest—it is grounded in the political support offered to them by the demanders of public regulation.

Rate-of-Return Regulation

Rate-of-return regulation involves establishing a price for the firm's output that allows the owners of the regulated firm to earn only a "fair" or "reasonable" return on their investment. In other words, the regulatory agency charged with the responsibility of overseeing the distribution of profits to the firm's owners determines a selling price (or schedule of prices) such that the firm can earn no more than some fixed percentage of the value of invested capital in any given year. The value of the firm's capital is called the **rate base**.

The stated purpose of such regulation is to prevent the firm from charging monopoly prices—and the firm's owners from earning monopoly profits—in a market setting where competition is considered to be either infeasible or inefficient. That is, a natural monopoly exists because of sharply declining average production costs. Consequently, the unit costs of supplying the good or service in question will be lower if only one firm serves the entire market than if two or more firms each serve only a part of it.

Moreover, competition may lead to wasteful duplication of production capacity—electrical generators, power lines, telephone switching equipment, and so on. Under these circumstances, governments have adopted one of two approaches for attempting to capture the production efficiency benefits of monopoly while limiting its welfare costs to consumers. In some localities, public utilities are publicly owned. In other jurisdictions, a privately owned firm is granted the exclusive right to serve the market but made subject to rate-of-return regulation.

The Averch-Johnson Effect. In an important paper, Harvey Averch and Leland Johnson demonstrated that rate-of-return regulation can lead to a distortion in the firm's use of inputs.[36] Specifically, the **Averch-Johnson** (A-J) **effect** associated with rate-of-return regulation causes the firm to overinvest in capital.

The A-J effect operates as follows. Suppose that a regulated public utility produces a final product by employing two inputs, labor and capital. Further suppose that the firm purchases these inputs at market-determined unit prices w and r. As stated above, rate-of-return regulation is structured so as to allow the utility's owners to earn only a "fair" return on their invested capital. To do this, the regulatory agency sets a price for the utility's output such that net revenues yield a total return on capital of, say, $z = r + v$, where v is the rate of return allowed above the firm's unit cost of capital. Output price and, hence, v, is presumably chosen so that z is below the rate of return that would be earned if the firm were free to charge a monopoly-profit-maximizing price.

Because the allowed rate of return is fixed at z and is greater than the unit cost of capital, r, the utility has an incentive to purchase relatively more capital than it would in the absence of regulation. This incentive is simply a rational, profit-maximizing response to a regulation-induced decline in the relative price of capital. Even though the utility's profit *rate* is fixed by the regulatory agency, the *level* of the firm's profit is an increasing function of the size of its capital stock under rate-of-return regulation: Each unit of capital purchased adds v—the difference between the allowed rate of return and acquisition cost—to the utility's profits. The utility accordingly expands its capital stock or rate base.

Rate-of-return regulation provides an incentive for the firm to select a capital-labor ratio that is "too high" compared with the efficient (cost-minimizing)

---

36 Harvey Averch and Leland L. Johnson, "Behavior of the Firm under Regulatory Constraint," *American Economic Review* 52 (December 1962), pp. 1052-69.

input combination that would be chosen in the absence of regulation. Averch and Johnson's model thus suggests that the input choices of the firm might be distorted by a type of regulation that is intended to reduce allocative inefficiency in the market served by a natural monopoly.

Figure 18.2 graphically depicts the A-J effect. A public utility produces electricity using two inputs: capital, K, and labor, L. The U-shaped isoquants show the various combinations of these resources that can be employed to produce a particular quantity of output which is measured in, say, kilowatt hours of electrical power generated per month. (Higher, more northeasterly, isoquants correspond to larger output quantities.)

The linear, downward-sloping budget ("isocost") schedules show the various input combinations the firm can employ to produce electricity for a stipulated total expenditure and given input prices. In particular, the solid budget line indicates the quantities of labor and capital available to the firm in the absence of regulation, that is, when the firm purchases these inputs at market-determined unit prices w and r. With labor on the horizontal axis and capital on the vertical axis, the slope of this budget line is $-w/r$. Therefore, the profit-maximizing firm selects the input combination at point A where the marginal product per dollar spent on each input is the same (i.e., $MP_L/w = MP_K/r$). This is the particular input combination that minimizes the cost of producing the indicated quantity of output or, alternatively, maximizes the output that can be produced for a given total expenditure.

Under rate-of-return regulation, however, the cost of capital to the firm is no longer equal to its market-determined price, r. This is because for each additional unit of capital purchased, the regulatory agency allows the firm to earn a profit that it would otherwise forego. This profit is equal to the difference between the market price of capital and the stipulated "fair" rate of return. Rate-of-return regulation consequently reduces the relative price of capital, causing a distortion in relative input prices that is illustrated by the more steeply sloped, dashed budget line in Figure 18.2.

In response, the utility rationally selects the more capital-intensive production process, B, which minimizes the cost of producing electricity *under the constraint imposed on its allowed rate of return*. But the important point is that input combination B is comparatively inefficient. The cost of producing any given quantity of electricity is higher along *expansion path* 2 than it is along *expansion path* 1 which shows the combinations of capital and labor that minimize *market* production costs.[37]

There has been considerable controversy over whether the Averch-Johnson model actually describes the behavior of firms subject to rate-of-return regulation. Empirical evidence on the model's predictions has been mixed. The Averch-Johnson model is nevertheless useful in pointing out that regulatory intervention can create incentives for firms to take actions

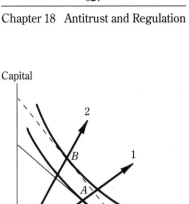

Capital

Labor

FIGURE 18.2
The Averch-Johnson Effect

---

37 As a reminder, the *expansion path* shows how the firm's optimal input combination varies as output varies, holding relative input prices constant.

that are rational under the given constraints, but which are undesirable by market standards.

The Rate-of-Return Constraint. Some additional effects of rate-of-return regulation can be seen by explicitly considering the rate-of-return constraint imposed on the firm. As before, suppose that the regulated firm produces electricity using capital and labor, inputs whose market-determined prices are r and w. The rate of return earned by the owners of this firm is defined as the ratio of the profits generated by electricity sales in any period to the value of the firm's capital stock or rate base, rK. Profit, in turn, is simply gross revenue minus cost or $pQ - wL - rK$, where p is the price charged on electricity sales to consumers, Q is the quantity of electricity sold, wL is total labor expense, and rK is the firm's cost of capital. The rate of return (ROR) on capital is thus

$$ROR = \frac{(pQ - wL - rK)}{rK}.$$

Suppose that the regulatory agency decides to constrain the rate of return earned by the utility's investors to $z = r + v$, where v is the "fair" return allowed over and above the firm's unit cost of capital. The rate-of-return constraint can be written as

$$\frac{(pQ - wL - rK)}{rK} \leq v,$$

or as

$$\frac{(pQ - wL)}{rK} \leq (r + v) = z.$$

That is, rate-of-return regulation requires that revenues remaining after the firm has covered its labor expenses cannot exceed z, the market price of capital plus the stipulated fair rate of return. Hence, if the utility "pads" its rate base by acquiring additional capital, K, the regulatory agency is forced to raise the price of electricity, p, to keep the rate of return from falling below z.

Rate-of-return regulation does not of course guarantee that the firm's owners will actually earn a "fair" rate of return on their invested capital. Precise information about the value of the firm's capital stock (the rate base), its operating costs, and its projected revenues is needed in order for the regulatory agency to determine the price (or schedule of prices) that will yield the allowed rate of return. This information is typically gathered during periodically scheduled rate hearings in which representatives of the utility present evidence on costs to justify requested price increases, consumers and other interested parties present opposing views, and the regulatory agency then approves a rate schedule that will remain in effect until the next formal rate hearing is held.

Because it takes time for the regulatory process to operate, there will necessarily be a lag between changes in the public utility's costs and appropriate regulatory adjustments to the rate schedule. The traditional literature on regulation often cites **regulatory lag** as one of the inherent limitations of public policy toward natural monopoly. On the one hand, the existence of regulatory lag means that the regulatory process may not work quickly enough to reduce earnings that subsequently prove to be "excessive." Indeed, the rates of return actually earned by regulated firms often exceed the stipulated regulatory maximum.

On the other hand, this same slowness to act may provide regulated firms with more of an incentive to hold costs down than they would have otherwise. Regulatory lag supplies utilities with incentives to implement cost-saving measures because they know that any savings realized from the more efficient use of resources will not be penalized immediately with equivalent reductions in rates. After considering these costs and benefits, at least one economist has recommended that regulatory lag be explicitly adopted as a regulatory policy,[38] "thus assuring to companies the rewards and penalties" it provides.[39]

Occupational Health and Safety Regulation

The Occupational Safety and Health Act of 1970 established a formal federal policy toward worker health and safety. Before the law was passed, workers who were injured on the job or whose health was impaired by exposure to workplace hazards could seek redress in the courts under tort law. But the usual legal standard applied in such suits required showing that the harm suffered by the worker resulted from willful negligence on the part of the employer—a case that was often difficult to prove. The Congress responded by creating the Occupational Safety and Health Administration (OSHA), an agency whose broad purpose was "to assure as far as possible every working man and woman in the Nation safe and healthful working conditions." The law provided further that "to the extent feasible," no worker "will suffer material impairment of health."

OSHA has several weapons at its disposal for dealing with threats to worker safety and health. First, the agency requires employers to report information on job-related injuries and illnesses. Second, it oversees a workplace inspection program and has the authority to impose monetary fines on employers who maintain unsafe working conditions. Third, OSHA may promulgate industry-wide rules which require firms to reduce specific workplace hazards. For example, OSHA issued a rather complex standard in the late 1970s designed to limit textile workers' exposure to cotton dust, a hazard

---

38 William J. Baumol, "Reasonable Rules for Rate Regulation: Plausible Policies for an Imperfect World," in Almarin Phillips and Oliver E. Williamson, eds., *Prices: Issues in Theory, Practice, and Public Policy* (Philadelphia: University of Pennsylvania Press, 1967), pp. 108-23.

39 Kahn, *Economics of Regulation*, vol II: *Institutions*, p. 59.

associated with development of a serious respiratory disease known as "brown lung."

Two basic premises underly occupational safety and health regulation. One is that workers are in general relatively uninformed about workplace hazards that may result in injury or illness. Because of the lack of such information, individuals accept jobs at wage rates that would be unacceptable to them if they knew the actual job-related risks. The second premise of occupational safety and health regulation is that in striving to hold costs down in a competitive marketplace, firms will take advantage of workers' ignorance. They will tend to neglect the well-being of their employees and expose them to hazardous working conditions that would be expensive to correct. Hence, public regulation of occupational safety and health is justified as a way of overcoming the private market's failure to supply safe and healthful working conditions.

Both of these premises are open to question, however. Mandating reductions in job-related risks of injury and illness may not be in the best interest of workers because in a competitive labor market wages tend to adjust to reflect differences in the working conditions that distinguish jobs from one another.

The Theory of Compensating Wage Differentials. Employees rationally desire to avoid unpleasant working conditions of all sorts—long commutes, high noise levels, dirty and dangerous workplaces, and so on. Because of this fact, employers hiring individuals to fill less desirable or relatively risky jobs will be forced to pay higher wages than they would if the same jobs were performed under more favorable conditions. The higher wage is paid to the employee to compensate him or her for the "undesirable" job characteristics. This wage premium, known in the economics literature as a **compensating wage differential**, provides an incentive for individuals to be willing to engage in unpleasant work. Put another way, such wage premiums act as a financial penalty for employers who provide unfavorable working conditions.[40]

Compensating wage differentials can be thought of as the "price" at which unpleasant working conditions are sold to employees for comparable work. Similarly, for those individuals who choose more pleasant or less risky jobs, the wage premiums thereby foregone represent the price at which these more agreeable working conditions are purchased. Compensating wage differentials represent the amount paid to individuals who perform jobs under adverse conditions over the wages earned *for comparable work* in more pleasant or less risky workplace environments. It is not appropriate to conclude that employees working under "bad" conditions receive higher wages than those working under "good" conditions.

---

40 Compensating wage differentials have been recognized since at least the time of Adam Smith, who wrote that "the most detestable of all employments, that of public executioner, is, in proportion to the quantity of work done, better paid than any common trade whatever." See Adam Smith, *An Inquiry into the Nature and Causes of the Wealth of Nations* (Edwin Cannan ed.) (New York: Modern Library, 1937), p. 100 (first published in 1776).

Coal mining, for example, is a risky occupation. In the former Soviet Union, despite that economic system's philosophical emphasis on wage equality, coal miners were paid wages roughly double those of comparable factory workers. Moreover, Soviet miners who were assigned to more risky jobs were required to work only a 30-hour week, compared to the 36-hour work weeks required of other miners whose work was less hazardous. And in Siberia, where winters are particularly harsh, wages were between 60 percent and 180 percent higher than those paid to comparable workers in other parts of the Soviet Union.[41]

Economic theory suggests that if labor markets are competitive and that if individuals are sufficiently informed about the relative hazards or unpleasantness of various jobs, wages will adjust upward to compensate workers for any additional risks they assume in choosing one employer over another. Market-determined wage rates will then reflect differences in workers' attitudes toward risk and in employers' willingness to provide safety. A reduction in risk may not be in the best interest of employees under these conditions because some workers may prefer to self-insure against workplace hazards in return for additional compensation.

Consider Figure 18.3 which, for simplicity, considers the risk preferences of one employee and one firm's willingness to provide safety. The employee's preferences are represented by the indifference curves labeled U_1 and U_2. These indifference curves are drawn as upward sloping to reflect the assumption that risk is an economic "bad." Each indifference curve shows the various possible combinations of risk, R, and wages, W, that generate a given level of total utility for the worker. (Higher levels of total utility are shown by higher, more northwesterly indifference curves.)

Comparing any two points on one of these indifference curves indicates that the individual requires a higher wage in compensation for greater risk to remain feeling equally well off. The opposite is also true: If the employee is to continue to enjoy the same level of total satisfaction, a lower wage is acceptable only if there is a compensating reduction in job-related risk. The slope of an indifference curve at any point consequently measures the rate at which the employee is willing to substitute risk for wages while maintaining the same level of total satisfaction.[42]

The tradeoff between wages and risk from the employer's point of view is represented by the upward-sloping "safety-offer curve," O. Reducing the risk of job-related illness or injury is costly to the firm. The firm will therefore

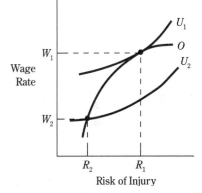
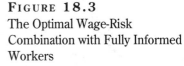

FIGURE 18.3
The Optimal Wage-Risk Combination with Fully Informed Workers

41 Ronald G. Ehrenberg and Robert S. Smith, *Modern Labor Economics*, 3E. (Glenview, IL: Scott Foresman, 1988), p. 252.

42 The assumption that individuals place a monetary value on their health and safety and are therefore willing to accept greater risk in return for additional compensation may be distasteful for some readers. Evidence that workers in fact behave in this way is reported below. At this point, the reader can grapple with the moral issues raised by the discussion by considering the possibility that someone who says, "I wouldn't do that for a million bucks," might well do it for $2 million.

provide a safer working environment only if an offsetting reduction in the wage rate paid to the employee is possible. The slope of the offer curve at any point reflects the rate at which wage rates and risk can be substituted for one another while holding the total value of the employee's compensation package—which consists of a level of job-related risk and a corresponding wage rate—constant.

Equilibrium in this model occurs at the point of tangency between the worker's indifference curve and the firm's safety-offer curve. The tangency yields a risk-wage combination of R_1 and W_1. This particular compensation package maximizes the worker's total satisfaction subject to the constraint imposed by the employer's cost of providing safety. This constraint, it must be stressed, has nothing whatsoever to do with the employer's own preferences. The total cost of the compensation package is the same at every point on the safety-offer curve. Therefore, the employer will provide the level of safety the worker prefers as long as wages can be adjusted (downward) to offset the higher cost of creating less risky working conditions.

Given that the interaction of workers and firms has determined an equilibrium wage and level of risk, a government-mandated reduction in risk to, say R_2 will make the employee worse off. To reduce workplace risk to R_2, the firm must lower its wage offer to W_2. The worker's total level of satisfaction accordingly decreases from U_1 to U_2. At the new risk-wage combination of R_2 and W_2, the worker has an incentive to offer to accept a higher level of risk in return for a higher wage because his or her total utility would thereby be increased.

The low-risk/low-wage compensation package is consequently not consistent with equilibrium unless welfare-improving exchanges between employers and employees are precluded by non-market forces such as government policing of workplace safety requirements. The important point is that as long as workers are informed about occupational hazards, and as long as employers are free to adjust wages and working conditions so as to tailor employee compensation packages in ways that comport with worker's preferences, government intervention to reduce workplace risks may not be in the best interest of employees.

If, on the other hand, workers are poorly informed about job-related hazards, it may be possible for government regulation to improve the well-being of employees. Consider Figure 18.4, which—again for simplicity—depicts the preferences of one worker and one firm's willingness to provide safety. The safety-offer curve of the firm is again labeled O; it shows the employer's cost of reducing risk in terms of the offsetting reduction in wages necessary to hold the total value of the employee's compensation package constant.

Suppose that the worker has accepted a wage rate equal to W_1, which he or she mistakenly believes corresponds to risk level R_1. At the wage-risk combination of W_1 and R_1, the worker thinks that utility level U_1 has been attained (point A in the figure). Thus, the worker has underestimated the risk of illness and injury related to his or her current employment:

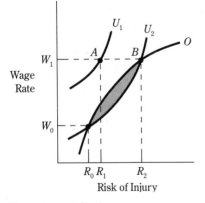

FIGURE 18.4
The Optimal Wage-Risk Combination with Poorly Informed Workers

The actual risk associated with W_1 is R_2. At this latter combination of risk and wage, the worker is at point B and experiences the lower level of satisfaction U_2.

The worker and the firm may be unable to negotiate further trades between wages and risk because, for example, the health effects of long-term exposure to workplace hazards are difficult to establish scientifically. In such a case, it may be possible for the government to mandate a reduction in risk and make the worker better off.[43] To see this result, refer again to Figure 18.4. The shaded area in the diagram represents unexploited gains from trade due to the employee's imperfect information about job-related risks. If the government requires a reduction in risk to some level between R_0 and R_2, the worker's welfare is improved. That is, the worker achieves a higher level of total satisfaction with a safer working environment and a correspondingly lower wage. Mandating a reduction in risk to a level below R_0, however, would cause the employee to be worse off than he or she was initially.

In light of the above discussion, mandatory risk reduction should be approached with caution. When workers are fully informed about workplace hazards, government intervention to improve workplace safety makes workers unambiguously worse off. And even when workers are poorly informed about the risks of illness and injury on the job, occupational safety and health regulations can work against the interests of employees if they are too stringent.

As an illustration, consider the case of mandatory risk reduction in coal mining. The Federal Coal Mine Health and Safety Act requires that all miners be x-rayed annually to detect the presence of so-called black lung disease. If clinical evidence of disease is found, the employer must offer the miner a job in a less risky working environment. In the 1970s, only 10 percent of the miners to whom such offers were made accepted the lower paying and less hazardous jobs. The miners, as indicated by their own behavior, apparently preferred receiving a higher wage in return for the known risk of developing black lung.[44]

The Regulation of Advertising

Whenever it is costly for consumers to verify a seller's claims prior to purchase, there is an incentive for the seller to attempt to mislead prospective buyers with advertising messages that are fraudulent or deceptive. A profit can be made in the short run if false claims cause consumers to buy more of a product (or pay a higher price for it) than they would given more complete (truthful) information. This is not to say that consumers are irrational—they will not continue to purchase a product that fails to meet their expectations.

---

43 As noted above, because the firm is indifferent to trading risk and wages along O, the firm would be made no worse off by a mandated reduction in risk as long as wages can be adjusted appropriately.

44 Ehrenberg and Smith, *Modern Labor Economics*, p. 274.

How Much is a Life Worth?

Do wages and job-related risks actually vary in the way predicted by the economic theory of compensating wage differentials? The theory suggests that workers' employment decisions will reflect the amount they are willing to pay to avoid the risk of job-related illness or injury. If workers in fact behave in this way, the implied "price" of occupational safety and the value of human life can be estimated. Evidence of the existence of such a market for occupational safety and health would support the idea that wage rates adjust to reflect differential risks across jobs and firms. Moreover, this evidence would underscore the notion that employers must bear the costs of the working environments they provide.

Much recent research focuses on estimating the amount workers are willing to pay to reduce the probability of fatal injury on the job. For example, if a typical employee accepts $1,000 less in annual earnings to work in a job where the chance of fatal injury is .001 lower per year, the implied value of life is $1 million (1,000 workers would each give up $1,000 to avoid one job-related death per year). Hence, by examining differences in wage rates for different occupational risks of death, economists can compute the implicit value of life.

Some recent empirical studies estimate the value of life to be between $420,000 and $5,595,000 (in 1979 Canadian dollars).[a] One researcher who surveyed this evidence concluded that "as far as risk of death is concerned, employers who offer jobs with greater risk must bear the cost of this risk in the form of significantly higher wages. Consequently, employers have a financial incentive to reduce this risk."[b] Later research has added to the evidence that wage rates are significantly higher in industries and occupations where workers face a higher probability of fatal injury.[c]

Government agencies implicitly place monetary values on human lives by adopting safety regulations. These values tend to be substantially higher than those determined by studies of compensating wage differentials. Table 18.4 lists the implied values of human life from a sample of government health and safety regulations. The values range from $390,000 to $94 billion per life saved!

TABLE 18.4 REGULATORY VALUES OF LIFE

Regulation	Agency	Annual Deaths per 100,000 of Exposed Population	Cost per Life Saved
Mandatory seat belts	National Highway Traffic Safety Administration	9.1	$390,000
Alcohol and drug use by railroad employees	Federal Railroad Administration	.2	$650,000
Disposal standards for benzene	Environmental Protection Agency	2.1	$4 million
Standards for uranium mine wastes	Environmental Protection Agency	43.0	$69 million
Worker exposure to asbestos	Occupational Safety and Health Administration	6.7	$117 million
Worker exposure to formaldehyde	Occupational Safety and Health Administration	.1	$94 billion

Source: Louis S. Richman, "Bringing Reason to Regulation," *Fortune*, 19 October 1992, p. 96. © 1992 *Time Inc*. All rights reserved.

a Samuel A. Rea, Jr., "Regulating Occupational Health and Safety," in Donald N. Dewees, ed., *The Regulation of Quality: Products, Services, Workplaces, and the Environment* (Toronto: Butterworths, 1983), p. 117.

b *Ibid.*, p. 118.

c See, for example, Charles Brown, "Equalizing Differences in the Labor Market," *Quarterly Journal of Economics* 94 (February 1984), pp. 113-34; William T. Dickens, "Differences Between Risk Premiums in Union and Nonunion Wages for Occupational Safety Regulation," *American Economic Review Papers and Proceedings* 77 (May 1987), pp. 320-23; Alan Dillingham, "The Influence of Risk Variable Definition on Value-of-Life Estimates," *Economic Inquiry* (April 1985), pp. 277-94; and Robert S. Smith, "Compensating Wage Differentials and Public Policy: A Review," *Industrial and Labor Relations Review* 32 (April 1979), pp. 339-52.

Rather, the opportunity for sellers to capture benefits from deceptive advertising arises simply from the fact that consumers cannot costlessly verify the accuracy of the seller's claims.

Indeed, given that resources are scarce, the optimal amount of fraudulent advertising in a market economy is not zero. Although deceptive advertising clearly reduces consumer welfare, society must sacrifice some of its valuable resources to prevent it. Consequently, it is worth investing resources in policing the truthfulness of advertising claims only up to the point where the last dollar spent on enforcement reduces the cost of deception to consumers by one dollar. Thus, as long as advertising regulation is costly, it will never pay to eliminate all deception. It is optimal for society to tolerate some positive amount of fraud by sellers.

In the United States, the Federal Trade Commission has the principal responsibility for policing the content of advertising messages. (A variety of state and local government agencies also play roles in regulating the advertising and promotional activities of sellers.) The FTC's authority in this regard derives from the Wheeler-Lea Act, which in 1938 added language to the FTC Act so that Section 5 would prohibit not only "unfair methods of competition," but "unfair or deceptive acts or practices" as well. Even before the Wheeler-Lea Act expressly made deception a form of unfair competition, however, the courts had held false or deceptive advertising to fall within the commission's jurisdiction. Indeed, fraud and deception have a long history of illegality under the common law.

The Deception Standard. Deceptive advertising cases essentially entail two legal tests. One test is the commission's own interpretation of the claims made in advertising copy; the other involves a determination of the ad's "capability to deceive."[45] In applying these tests, the commission is not required to show that an advertisement has misled anyone in particular. It can determine in its expert capacity that an advertisement has a tendency to deceive.[46] To be deceptive, a claim need not fool a person of even average skepticism. The commission can insist that advertising be clear enough not to mislead even susceptible persons.[47] Deception may occur through omissions as well as through affirmative misrepresentations.[48] It may also involve an ancillary term of sale, such as a promised delivery schedule or an expressed or implied warranty provision, as well as the claims made about the basic product or service itself.[49] The commission may even ban certain types of claims or selling practices on a per se basis if it determines them to be inherently deceptive.[50]

---

45 *Charles of the Ritz Distributors Corp.* v. *FTC*, 143 F.2d 676 (2d Cir. 1944); *American Home Products Corp.* v. *FTC*, 695 F. 2d 681 (2d Cir. 1982).

46 *Chrysler Corp.* v. *FTC*, 561 F. 2d 357 (D.C. Cir. 1977); *In re Jay Norris Corp.*, 91 FTC 751 (1978).

47 *Charles of the Ritz*; also see *FTC* v. *Winstead Hosiery Co.*, 258 U.S. 483 (1922).

48 *P. Lorillard Co.* v. *FTC*, 186 F.2d 52 (4th Cir. 1950).

49 *In re Jay Norris Corp.*

50 *In re Koscot Interplanetary*, 86 FTC 1106 (1975) (establishing a per se ban on so-called pyramid sales schemes).

When a firm is found guilty of making false or deceptive claims about its product or service, failing to disclose material facts, or engaging in some other type of misrepresentation, the commission enters an order to "cease and desist." Failure to comply with the order subjects the violator to civil penalties (monetary fines), which the commission has authority to seek in federal district court. The commission may also order "corrective" advertising to offset the misconceptions created by claims determined to have been deceptive.[51]

To the firm, however, the potential impact of advertising regulation goes far beyond the cost of withdrawing an offending advertisement or of facing the prospect of being fined. Evidence has been reported suggesting that firms whose advertising claims are challenged by the FTC are significantly impaired in their ability to attract first-time buyers and, moreover, that an adverse determination by the FTC may destroy the entire brand name capital of the advertised product.[52]

The regulation of advertising claims raises several critical (and complex) issues, including issues related to constitutional protection accorded to free speech and the nature of the distinction between "commercial speech" and "political speech." As has just been discussed, the development of the unfairness doctrine of Section 5 of the FTC Act basically made the commission's burden one of proving the falsity (capability to deceive) of a questionable advertising claim. Proving the falsity of some claims is a relatively simple matter, as was the case when a manufacturer altered the recipe for its product by substituting one ingredient for another but continued to use its old label and to claim in its ads that it had been selling the "same" product for years.[53]

Proving the falsity of many other claims is much more difficult. A substantial amount of advertising copy today presents consumers with product claims that the seller cannot reasonably be expected to know to be truthful with certainty. This is because the claims are based on statistical analyses of data generated in the firm's quality-control department.

To illustrate, when a manufacturer of light bulbs advertises that its product has a useful life of 750 hours, it does not mean literally that every bulb it sells will burn for that length of time.[54] Rather, the claim is a probability

---

51 See, for example, *Warner Lambert Co.* v. *FTC*, 562 F.2d 749 (D.C. Cir. 1978) (ordering manufacturer to advertise that Listerine mouthwash is not helpful in preventing the common cold); *In re Amstar Corp.*, 83 FTC 659 (1973) (ordering sugar manufacturer to advertise that its Domino brand is not a source of strength, energy, or stamina); *In re Ocean Spray Cranberries*, 80 FTC 973 (1972) (ordering producer cooperative to advertise that Ocean Spray cranberry juice does not contain more vitamins and minerals than tomato or orange juice); and *In re ITT-Continental Baking Corp.*, 79 FTC 248 (1971) (ordering baking company to advertise that its Profile brand bread is not effective in promoting weight loss).

52 Sam Peltzman, "The Effects of FTC Advertising Regulation," *Journal of Law and Economics* 24 (December 1981), pp. 403-48.

53 *Royal Baking Powder Co.* v. *FTC*, 281 F. 744 (2d Cir. 1922).

54 Disclosure of this information has in fact been required since 1981. See *In re Incandescent Lamp Industry*, C.F.R. §409.1 (1981) (ordering light bulb manufacturers to state "average laboratory life" expressed in hours).

statement, made subject to some margin of error, about the product's average expected useful life. The margin of error, in turn, depends on the sample size taken for testing from a particular production run, the accuracy of the devices used to measure and record the performance data, and so on.

The point is that even truthful claims of this sort will be false in the sense that some consumers who take the manufacturer's claim at face value will be misled into purchasing light bulbs that have an actual useful life of, say, only 725 hours. On the other hand, if the manufacturer advertises a useful life that is less than the statistical average, some consumers will suffer welfare losses by mistakenly failing to buy bulbs that would in fact have burned for 750 hours or more.

Thus, when it is costly for sellers to acquire information about the performance characteristics of their own products, which they then choose either to lie or not lie about, the very concept of truth or falsity is at bottom the solution to a complicated statistical decision problem. It will accordingly be difficult for regulatory agencies to verify the truthfulness of advertising claims. Partly in recognition of this difficulty, in the early 1970s the FTC abandoned its traditional approach of challenging advertisements as deceptive by reason of falsity. Instead, the agency announced a law enforcement doctrine that shifted the burden of proving truthfulness to the seller making the claim.

The Ad Substantiation Doctrine. Pfizer, Inc., a major pharmaceuticals manufacturer, had introduced a new sunburn lotion, Unburn®, which it advertised would "actually anesthetize" the nerve endings in sunburned skin.[55] The commission moved to challenge this claim as deceptive, not because the claim was false, but because Pfizer was alleged to have relied on inadequate evidence of its truth.

That is, the FTC charged that Pfizer's claim was *unsubstantiated*, regardless of whether it was true at the time made or whether it could be proven to be true *ex post*. Lack of substantiation was asserted to be deceptive on the theory that when a seller makes an affirmative statement about its product, a factual basis for the statement is implied. In addition, the commission argued that making unsubstantiated claims was an unfair method of competition within the meaning of Section 5 because such a practice impaired "a consumer's ability to make an economically rational product choice, and a competitor's ability to compete on the basis of price, quality, service, or convenience."[56] Pfizer was found guilty, and consented to cease and desist making its unsubstantiated claim. The federal courts have since ruled that the lack of substantiation for an advertising claim is both unfair and deceptive within the meaning of Section 5 of the FTC Act.[57]

---

55 Neil W. Averitt, "Meaning of 'Unfair Acts or Practices' in Section 5 of the Federal Trade Commission Act." *Georgetown Law Journal* 70 (October 1981), pp. 242-43.

56 *In re Pfizer, Inc.*, 81 F.T.C. 23 (1972), p. 62.

57 See, for example, *In re National Dynamics Corp.*, 82 F.T.C. 488 (1973), aff'd 492 F.2d. 1333 (2d Cir. 1976), cert. denied 419 U.S. 993 (1976).

Pfizer established a program of **ad substantiation**, which now represents the principal focus of the FTC's advertising regulation activities. In the years since the program was announced, the commission has conducted a number of ad substantiation "sweeps" or "rounds." Without necessarily having received complaints of widespread deception or having had reason to believe that consumers were being misled by any particular advertising campaign, it has issued letters to a sample of advertisers demanding documentation for their claims. Staff attorneys and expert consultants have then reviewed the submissions and initiated legal action against the firms (and, usually, the advertising agencies they had retained) whose claims appeared to lack substantiation. By the middle 1980s, this enforcement program had generated more than a dozen litigated matters and over 100 orders in which advertisers consented to cease and desist making unsubstantiated claims.[58]

The ad substantiation program has clearly reduced the FTC's cost of regulating advertising by shifting the burden of proof to advertisers. But the underlying theory of the enforcement program is incomplete in the sense that it focuses on only one of the costs of deception to consumers. Put another way, the ad substantiation program overlooks the fact that advertising regulation itself has costs as well as potential benefits. In particular, the commission, operating on the premise that advertising is, with certainty, either true or not true, places the bulk of its concern on the cost to a consumer of making a "false positive" purchase decision—a *Type I error* in the jargon of statistics. Such an error occurs whenever a customer relies on an advertising claim to purchase a product or service that fails to perform as expected. Requiring greater (more accurate) substantiation of advertising claims would presumably reduce the likelihood of Type I errors being made and, if so, this would tend to increase consumer welfare.

At the same time, however, the seller's information about product performance is imperfect. Hence, it can supply additional substantiation of advertising claims only by incurring additional costs—by expanding the sample size from which performance measurements are taken, by increasing the precision of those measurements, and so on. As a result of the higher costs of achieving the level of accuracy demanded by the FTC, the factual content of ads will decline as advertisers limit themselves to making claims that can be substantiated at low cost or the supply prices of advertised products will rise, or both. These cutbacks in the factual content of ads (or increases in price) will, of course, tend to reduce consumer welfare. Ideally, then, efficient enforcement of truth in advertising would require additional accuracy of advertising claims up to the point at which the marginal increase in consumer welfare attributable to the reduction in Type I errors is just matched by the corresponding marginal increase in the cost of substantiation.

---

58 Richard S. Higgins and Fred S. McChesney, "Truth and Consequences: The Federal Trade Commission's Ad Substantiation Program," *International Review of Law and Economics* 6 (1986), p. 153.

As a practical matter, however, the commission does not balance the costs and benefits of requiring the substantiation of advertising claims before the claims are made. When the cost of Type I error to individual consumers is thought to be large, as it might be, for example, in the case of health care products, substantiation is demanded without regard to the number of buyers who are potentially placed at risk. But even if the FTC did make this tradeoff explicitly, there is still another cost of advertising regulation to consider. *Type II* ("false negative") *errors* occur whenever a consumer fails to purchase a product that would, in fact, have performed satisfactorily. Other things being the same, a reduction in the likelihood of Type I error *increases* the likelihood of Type II error.

To illustrate this tradeoff, recall the example in which it was assumed that a light bulb manufacturer advertised its product to have an expected useful life of 750 hours. Assume further that actual performance outcomes are uniformly distributed around this mean, and range from a minimum of 700 hours to a maximum of 800 hours. As it has been defined, a Type I error occurs when a customer purchases a light bulb that was expected to last for 750 hours but actually burns, say, only 725 hours.

Now suppose that in response to the demand for substantiation, which is equivalent to requiring a lower probability of Type I error, the manufacturer revises its claims and begins to advertise an expected life of 725 hours. Obviously, fewer consumers will make false positive purchase decisions as a result: The probability of buying a light bulb that burns for less than 725 hours is smaller than the probability of buying one that burns for less than 750 hours. It should be equally obvious, however, that fewer consumers who are in the market for 750-hour light bulbs will make their purchases from this manufacturer. Although the light bulbs offered for sale still have a useful life of 750 hours, on average, the revised advertising claims have the effect of changing (lowering) consumers' expectations about product performance. As a result, the probability increases that some buyers will mistakenly reject a product that would have been acceptable. Thus, while errors of one kind (Type I) have been reduced, errors of another kind (Type II) have been increased.[59]

If factual advertising claims were either true or false in some absolute sense, and information about the performance characteristics of products were freely available to advertisers, then deterring false and deceptive claims by requiring substantiation would not impose costs on consumers of the sort discussed above. However, truth is a matter of degree, and advertisers can acquire information about performance only at a cost. Therefore, substantiation of advertising claims becomes an economic problem concerning the optimal level of accuracy. Greater accuracy in representations about performance benefits consumers by

---

59 A *known* change in policy will have no impact on consumers' expectations if they have prior information about the actual distribution of product performance outcomes. In this case, however, manufacturers have no incentive to make unsubstantiated advertising claims in the first place; nor will the policy change improve consumers' welfare.

reducing the likelihood of false positive purchase decisions, but it also entails additional costs. These costs take the form of higher supply prices for advertised products (or reductions in the factual content of ads) and of increases in the probability of making false negative purchase decisions.

Summary

This chapter has examined a number of public policies toward business in detail—antitrust policy, occupational safety and health regulation, and the regulation of advertising. These policies were chosen from the long list of public policies and programs that constrain business decision making to illustrate a simple point. In short, when government intervenes in the private economy to correct perceived sources of market failure, it often does so in ways that selectively benefit some firms and interest groups at the expense of others. The prospective gains to the benefiting parties, in turn, provide incentives for using governmental policy processes to their own advantage.

Private business firms are often, but not always, the seekers of rents that are made available through government's power to prohibit or to compel. Firms can secure competitive advantages over rivals by influencing a bureaucratic ruling, by lobbying for favorable legislation, or by instigating an antitrust lawsuit. At the same time, however, firms can be the targets of rent-seeking activities by other groups—labor, consumerists, and so on—who also have incentives to use public policy processes strategically to secure wealth transfers in their own favor.

The bottom line is that an understanding of the political environment in which business operates is every bit as important as an understanding of the economic environment. Private interests play a role in shaping public policies toward business. An appreciation of this role should help dispel the naive view that government intervention is designed and implemented with the goal of protecting that most diverse and unorganized of interest groups, consumers. And managers should prepare for dealing with the market for wealth transfers as well as with more ordinary markets for goods and services.

Questions

18.1 The Corporate Average Fuel Economy (CAFE) standard was enacted by Congress in the mid 1970s with the stated purpose of improving automobile gasoline efficiency, thereby providing environmental benefits and reducing the U.S. economy's reliance on imported oil. CAFE required each producer of automobiles sold in the United States to achieve by 1985 a sales-weighted average fuel-economy rating of at least 27.5 miles per gallon. (The deadline for meeting the goal was later extended to 1990.) The regulation further required each automobile manufacturer to meet the fuel economy standard for its domestically produced and imported cars separately—imports could not be used to offset less fuel-efficient domestic models.

a. Use simple economic analysis to explain why the CAFE standard (*i*) in all likelihood increased total gasoline consumption, (*ii*) increased highway fatalities, and (*iii*) provided Japanese automakers with an opportunity to increase their sales of powerful luxury car models.

b. Given your answers above, can you explain why the CAFE standard was chosen over the alternative and arguably more efficient policy of raising the federal excise tax on gasoline?

18.2 In 1982, after nearly ten years of staff investigation and public hearings, the Federal Trade Commission promulgated an industry-wide "Funeral Rule." This rule required, among other things, that funeral homes stop their customary practice of selling funerals as single-price packages and instead provide consumers with itemized price lists from which they can select only those elements of the funeral package they want to buy.

a. What theory of market failure do you think the FTC relied on in justifying the need for the Funeral Rule? Explain.

b. Since the rule went into effect, spending on the average funeral has *increased* by about nine percent. Use simple economic analysis to explain this "unintended" consequence.

18.3 In the so-called coffee case, *In re General Foods Corp.*, 103 F.T.C. 204 (1984), a case first filed in 1976, the FTC alleged that General Foods had attempted to block the entry of Procter & Gamble's Folger® brand into markets east of the Mississippi River during the mid 1970s by selectively and sharply cutting the price of its own brand of coffee, Maxwell House®. The FTC also charged that General Foods had introduced a new television advertising campaign featuring a pleasant, elderly lady named "Cora" (who, by the way, was portrayed by the woman who had starred as the wicked witch of the East in *The Wizard of Oz*) for the purpose of "neutralizing" the impact of Folger's TV ads featuring "Mrs. Olson," a kindly Swedish lady.

a. Critically evaluate the FTC's charges in the coffee case.

b. Bonus: Name the actress who portrayed "Cora."

18.4 In recent years, many state and local governments have enacted policies that severely limit and in some cases completely ban smoking in the workplace.

a. What does economic theory imply about the optimal amount of environmental tobacco smoke (ETS) in the workplace if nonsmoking employees are fully informed about the possible health risks of exposure to ETS? What public policy response is recommended if this is the case? What if nonsmoking workers are poorly informed about the risks of exposure to ETS? Which situation is more likely; that is, do you think that nonsmoking workers tend to overestimate, underestimate, or correctly estimate the risks attributed to ETS? Explain.

b. Suppose that nonsmoking employees are fully informed about the possible risks associated with exposure to ETS. What explanation for public antismoking laws can you offer if this assumption is valid?

c. Does the Coase Theorem (see Chapter 17) have a role to play in the resolution of disputes concerning smoking in the workplace? Explain.

18.5 Suppose that an industry has ten firms with the following market share percentages: 25, 15, 12, 10, 10, 8, 7, 5, 5, and 3.

a. Calculate the Herfindahl-Hirschman concentration index for the industry.

b. Is it likely that a proposed merger between the top two firms would be challenged under the Justice Department's Merger Guidelines? Why or why not? What about a merger between the fifth and sixth largest firms?

18.6 In the landmark Alcoa case, *U.S.* v. *Aluminum Co. of America et al.*, 148 F.2d 416 (2d Cir. 1945), Alcoa was or was not a monopolist in the production of raw aluminum ingots depending largely on whether scrap aluminum was included in the relevant antitrust market definition. What rationales can you put forward for either including or excluding scrap aluminum from the antitrust market? Which side of the argument do you think the government took? Explain.

18.7 The Urban Mass Transit Administration, a bureau within the U.S. Department of Transportation, pays subsidies to local public transit agencies to help defray their costs of operation not covered by passenger fares. (For the typical urban mass transit system, fares cover only about 38 percent of operating costs.) Given that operating costs but not capital costs are eligible for these subsidies, use a diagram to describe how the subsidies might affect the transit system manager's choice of inputs for producing urban mass transit services. For simplicity, assume that the only inputs used in the production process are busses and bus operators.

18.8 So-called price cap regulation is increasingly being seen as a viable alternative to traditional rate-of-return regulation. Under price cap regulation, a public utility subject to rate-of-return regulation is permitted to earn a rate of return that exceeds the usual regulated rate in exchange for agreeing not to raise price above a predetermined level. Allowable price increases are determined by a formula that only partially offsets increases in the rate of inflation. For example, the allowable price increase might be equal to the rate of increase in the Consumer Price Index less 4.5 percent. This means that the firm can raise its prices only if the rate of inflation is 4.5 percent or more, and then only to the extent that the actual rate of inflation exceeds that figure. What incentives does price cap regulation create that are not created by traditional rate-of-return regulation? What problems, if any, do you foresee in implementing price cap regulation?

Glossary

Ad substantiation: a Federal Trade Commission doctrine requiring documentation supporting advertising claims, prior to making them.

Adverse selection: a situation in which those on the informed side of the market self-select in a way that harms the uninformed side of the market.

Agency costs: the sum of monitoring costs, bonding costs, and the principal's residual loss.

Agent: a person who performs work or provides a service on behalf of another person, the principal.

Alchian and Allen hypothesis: a hypothesis, developed by Armen Alchian and William Allen, which shows how fixed costs can affect the relative prices of low- and high-quality products.

Alienability: transferability of ownership.

All-or-none offer: a pricing strategy which requires consumers to purchase multiple units of a product at a stated price per unit if they want to buy the product at all.

Allocative efficiency: the condition that exists when firms produce the output that is most preferred by consumers; an industry is operating with allocative efficiency when the marginal cost of each good just equals the marginal benefit that consumers derive from that good.

Arbitrage: one customer buying a product at a discount price and reselling the product to customers who would otherwise pay a higher price.

Arc elasticity of demand: elasticity of demand as calculated based on the average values of price and quantity over the relevant range of the demand function.

Asymmetric information: an inequality in the information known by each party to a transaction; or, a situation in which one side of the market has more reliable information than does the other side.

Average fixed cost: total fixed cost divided by output.

Average product of labor: a measure of labor productivity, calculated by dividing total output by total labor input.

Average total cost: total cost per unit of output. Average total cost is equal to total cost divided by quantity of output and is also equal to average fixed cost plus average variable cost.

Average variable cost: variable cost per unit of output. Average variable cost is equal to total variable cost divided by level of output.

Average-cost pricing: charging customers a price equal to long-run average production cost.

Averch-Johnson effect: the tendency of a regulated public utility to select a capital-labor ratio higher than the cost-minimizing ratio in order to increase its rate base and profits.

Barriers to entry: any impediments that prevent new firms from competing on an equal basis with existing firms in an industry.

Best-price policy: a supplier's contractual agreement with a customer, consisting of two guarantees: a most-favored nation clause and a meet-or-release clause.

Beta: a measure of a security's systematic risk, computed by estimating the covariance of the stock's expected returns with the returns to the stock market as a whole.

Bilateral governance: an agreement between buyer and seller specifying permissible adaptations to various contingencies.

Bonding costs: resources invested by an agent for the purpose of guaranteeing his or her performance to the principal.

Bounded rationality: the notion that there is a limit on the amount of information an economic agent, such as a manager, can comprehend.

Break-even analysis: a method whereby a firm can determine the quantity of output that it must sell to just cover its costs, or "break even." Linear break-even analysis assumes that price and average variable cost are constant.

Budget constraint: a spending limit determined by the amount of money available and relative prices.

Capital asset pricing model: a method of quantifying a firm's cost of capital, suggesting that the rate of return required by shareholders is equal to a hypothetical risk-free rate plus a premium that compensates for their investment risk.

Capital requirements: resources needed to enter an industry or continue an established business.

Cartel: a group of firms that have joined together to make agreements on pricing and market strategy.

Ceteris paribus: Latin for "all other things held constant."

Change in demand: a shift in the demand curve for a good or service caused by a change in some variable other than the price of the given good or service.

Change in quantity demanded: a change in the amount of a good or service that consumers are willing to purchase over some time period, which is caused by a change in the price of the good or service.

Classical capitalist firm: a firm employing team production in which a monitor contracts with each team member to perform specific tasks with a stipulated level of effort. The monitor gets to keep the difference between the value of the team's output and the agreed-upon compensation.

Closed market: a market with substantial barriers to entry and exit.

Coase conjecture: Ronald Coase's suggestion that as far as the seller is concerned, producing a perfectly durable good is the same as producing a nondurable good having no resale value.

Coase Theorem: the theory that as long as bargaining costs are small, an efficient solution to the problem of externalities will be achieved independent of initial property rights assignments.

Cobb-Douglas production function: a production function of the form $Q = aK^{b_1}L^{b_2}$. This function is used in many empirical studies of production functions because it has many of the properties predicted by the economic theory of production.

Codetermination: a process by which workers and management jointly set goals and make decisions affecting productivity.

Collusion: a secret agreement for a wrongful purpose (for example, price fixing among manufacturers).

Commercial nonprofits: nonprofit organizations which fund their activities through membership dues and other fees.

Committed costs: future obligations that must be met regardless of the firm's alternative courses of action.

Compensated demand curve: a curve which shows only the pure substitution effect of a change in price of a product on the quantity demanded by the consumer.

Compensating wage differential: a wage premium paid to an employee to compensate for undesirable job characteristics.

Complements: products or services that are usually used together with one another and have a negative cross-price elasticity of demand.

Conglomerate: a firm which operates multiple unrelated production facilities.

Consistent statements: same as **transitive statements**.

Consols: bonds which pay interest in perpetuity.

Constant price elasticity of demand: the type of demand that exists when price elasticity is the same everywhere along the curve; the elasticity value is constant.

Constant returns to scale: a production characteristic in which a given percentage increase in the usage of all inputs causes output to increase by the same percentage.

Consumer surplus: the difference between the maximum amount that a consumer is willing to pay for a given quantity of a good and what the consumer actually pays.

Contestable market: a market in which potential entrants can serve the same market and have access to the same technology as the existing firm.

Contribution margin: the difference between price and average variable cost.

Cooperatives: limited-profit enterprises with restrictions on the distribution of earnings to investors.

Coupons: in reference to a bond, periodic interest payments.

Credence goods: products whose quality is difficult to evaluate both before and after purchase.

Cross-price elasticity of demand: The cross-price elasticity of demand for Product X with respect to the price of Product Y is a measure of the relative responsiveness of quantity demanded of X to changes in the price of Y.

Decreasing returns to scale: a production characteristic in which a given percentage increase in the usage of all inputs causes output to increase by less than the given percentage.

Degree of operating leverage: the percentage change in profits relative to the percentage change in sales.

Demand: a relation showing how much of a good consumers are willing and able to buy at each possible price during a given period of time, other things constant.

Demand function: a mathematical statement which relates the quantities of a product that consumers will purchase during some specific period to the variables that influence their decisions to buy or not to buy the good or service. Examples of such variables include the price of the good or service, prices of related goods or services, and income of potential consumers.

Demand independence: an assumption made about demand when a firm's manufacturing division and marketing division are both selling the same product to outside customers, and neither division's sales affect the demand for the other division's product.

Dependent variable: a variable whose value is affected by the value(s) of some other variable(s).

Depreciation: the value of capital stock used up during a year in producing a product or service.

Derived demand: in a vertically integrated firm, demand for an input constructed by subtracting from the final product's price the cost incurred by the downstream industry in transforming a unit of input into a unit of output.

Direct cost: a cost directly associated with the project or activity.

Direct foreign investment: acquisition of an ownership interest in a foreign firm, or construction of a facility in a foreign country.

Diseconomies of scale: technological and organizational disadvantages that accrue to the firm as it increases output in the long run. Diseconomies of scale increase long-run average costs.

Diseconomies of scope: increases in average production costs as a result of producing two or more closely related products.

Diversifiable risk (or **unsystematic risk**): the variability in the expected returns to owning stock in a specific company.

Donative nonprofits: nonprofit organizations which rely almost entirely on voluntary contributions to fund their operations.

Duopoly: an industry composed of two firms who recognize their mutual interdependence.

Durable good: a good whose consumption generates a flow of services into the future, including utility, maintenance and repair, and potential resale.

Economic efficiency: a production goal of producing a given quantity of output at the lowest possible cost.

Economies of scale: technological and organizational advantages that the firm encounters as it increases output in the long run. Economies of scale reduce long-run average costs.

Economies of scope: forces that make it cheaper for a firm to produce two or more different products than just one.

Efficient-markets hypothesis: a hypothesis which contends that stock prices adjust quickly in response to relevant publicly available information about a firm's expected future net cash flows.

Elastic Demand: a demand characteristic in which a change in price has a relatively large effect on quantity demanded; the percentage change in quantity demanded exceeds the percentage change in price.

Employee-owned firm: a firm in which employees own a majority of shares.

Employee stock ownership plan: a mechanism that gives workers an ownership interest in their employer.

Entrepreneurial nonprofits: nonprofit organizations which appoint self-perpetuating boards of directors that are largely free of oversight by members, contributors, or customers.

Entry regulation: the granting by government of the right to supply a regulated good or service.

Equi-marginal principle: an extension of the marginal-cost-equals-marginal-revenue rule for determining optimal quantities across two or more products, markets, or activities.

Ex ante: planned.

Exclusive dealing contract: a contract wherein a firm buying or leasing the goods of one firm agrees not to deal with competing suppliers.

Expansion path: the line connecting all of the least-cost combinations of inputs for a particular ratio of input prices.

Experience curve: same as **learning curve**.

Experience goods: products whose quality consumers can judge only after use.

Face value: in reference to a bond, the principal or amount borrowed.

Factory system: a production system relying upon specialized, high-volume machinery.

First-degree price discrimination: selling each unit of output at a different price, the price charged for each unit being the maximum amount the consumer is willing and able to pay for that unit.

First-mover advantages: benefits of being one of the first firms to enter a market.

Fixed proportions production technology: technology which offers only one combination of inputs that can produce a specified quantity of output.

Free entry and exit: ability to enter and exit a market freely, with no artificial barriers to the movement of productive resources into or out of the industry.

Free rider: an individual who attempts to capture his or her share of the benefits of group action without bearing his or her share of the cost of producing the benefits.

Full price: the sum of a product's money price and the value (opportunity cost) of the time devoted to search.

Functional firm (or **unitary firm**): a firm whose authority is divided along business activity lines (e.g., purchasing, manufacturing, and sales).

Gain-sharing plans: group incentive policies that offer monetary rewards to production teams for achieving predetermined group objectives.

Gordon growth model: a formula, developed by Myron Gordon, that estimates future rates of return required by shareholders, and, hence, the cost of internal equity capital to the firm.

Herfindahl-Hirschman Index: a measurement of the degree of market concentration, computed by determining the percentage share of total market sales of each firm included in the defined market and summing the squares of these individual market shares.

Historical weights: weighted averages used in estimating a firm's overall cost of capital based on the assumption that the firm's present capital structure is optimal and should therefore be maintained in the future.

Homogeneous product: a product indistinguishable from the same product offered by every other firm.

Horizontal integration: operation of multiple production facilities at the same stage of the production process.

Horizontal merger: a merger in which one firm combines with another firm that produces the same product.

Imperfect substitutes: a case in which the ability to substitute one input for the other depends on the relative quantities of the two inputs in use.

Income effect: a change in consumers' real income caused by change in the price of a good.

Income-inferior goods: goods for which the income effect moves the consumer's purchases in the direction opposite to the substitution effect.

Income-normal goods: goods for which the impact of a price change on the consumer's real income (the income effect) reinforces the substitution effect.

Increasing returns to scale: a production characteristic in which a given percentage increase in the usage of all inputs causes output to increase by more than the same percentage.

Incremental analysis: a generalization of marginal analysis based on the changes in revenue and cost associated with alternative courses of action other than one-unit changes in output. Used for evaluating large changes in a firm's operations.

Indenture covenants: restrictions on the uses of borrowed funds.

Independent variable: a variable whose value affects, but is not affected by, the value(s) of some other variable(s).

Industry supply curve (or **market supply curve**): in the short run, the horizontal summation of all the price-taker firms' supply curves.

Inelastic Demand: demand such that a change in price has relatively little effect on quantity demanded; demand is inelastic when the percentage change in quantity demanded is less than the percentage change in price.

Inferior goods: see **income-inferior goods**.

Inside contracting: a manufacturing system in which a firm supplies space, machinery, raw materials, and capital to independent contractors who then receive a piece rate for production.

Interbrand competition: competition among retailers of two or more manufacturers' products.

Internal capital accounts: accounts established by labor-managed firms to provide individual workers with a property right in the firm's future net cash flows.

Internal rate of return: the net annual percentage yield of a project, obtained by solving for the discount rate that will cause the net present value of a project to be equal to zero.

Intrabrand competition: competition among retailers of one manufacturer's product.

Inventory: producer's stock of finished or in-process goods.

Isocost line: a line which gives all combinations of two inputs that can be utilized for a given dollar cost to the firm, assuming given and fixed input prices.

Isoquant: a curve which indicates the various combinations of two inputs that would enable a firm to produce a particular level of output.

Isorevenue lines: plotted lines showing all of the joint product combinations that generate the same amount of total sales revenue.

Joint complements: same as **joint products**.

Joint costs: costs of services supplied by a central office to several operating divisions or to several product lines.

Joint products (or **joint complements**): products that are interdependent in the production process.

Joint substitutes: goods which consumers view as substitutes for one another and which can be produced using similar processes and resources.

Lagrange multiplier: a variable (represented by λ) used in solving cost-minimization problems.

Law of demand: The quantity of a good demanded is inversely related to its price, other things constant.

Law of diminishing marginal returns: When more and more of a variable resource is added to a given amount of a fixed resource, the resulting increases in output will eventually diminish.

Learning curve (or **experience curve**): a curve which shows how a firm's unit costs of production vary over time with accumulated production experience.

Learning-by-doing: increasing proficiency gained by experience.

Lemons market: a market in which low-quality goods drive out high-quality goods as a consequence of imperfect information.

Leverage: the use of debt financing.

Line officers: in a functional firm, managers who supervise major operating departments.

Line-and-staff: a functional organizational concept which separates operational ("line") and support ("staff") functions.

Linear break-even analysis: a method of gauging the sensitivity of profits to sales which assumes that price and average variable cost remain constant across various possible output levels.

Liquidating dividend: a dividend paid to shareholders when a firm dissolves, equal to the firm's terminal market value.

Long run: a time period sufficiently long that all inputs are variable.

Long-run equilibrium: a tendency for market price and quantity to remain the same until changed by some external economic force.

Long-run marginal cost: the rate of change of long-run total cost as the level of output changes.

Long-run production function: a function used to analyze the technological relationship between input usage and output based on all possible plant sizes.

Long-run supply schedule: a graph indicating an industry's supply capabilities over the long term.

Macroeconomics: the study of the economy as a whole.

Managerial economics: the study of the behavior of a single firm within an industry.

Marginal: a term meaning "incremental" or "decremental," used to describe a change in an economic variable.

Marginal benefit: in the context of capital budgeting, the expected rates of return on the successive investment opportunities available to the firm.

Marginal cost: the rate of change of total cost with respect to changes in level of output.

Marginal cost of capital: the discount rate that represents the marginal cost of investment funds to the firm. Calculated as a weighted average of the after-tax cost of funds from each source.

Marginal product of capital: the change in total output associated with a small change in capital input.

Marginal product of labor: the change in total output associated with a small change in labor input.

Marginal rate of technical substitution: the rate at which two inputs can be substituted for each other while a constant level of production is maintained. The marginal rate of technical substitution is equal to the ratio of the two inputs' marginal products.

Marginal revenue: the rate of change of total revenue with respect to quantity sold. Marginal revenue indicates to a firm how total revenue will change if there is a change in the quantity sold of a firm's product.

Marginal tax rate: rate which determines a firm's tax liability on the last dollar in extra income earned.

Marginal-cost pricing: charging customers a price equal to long-run marginal cost.

Market failure: a condition that arises when unrestrained operation of markets yields socially undesirable results.

Market for corporate control: opportunities to make a profit by taking over a poorly run firm and replacing ineffective managers with competent ones, thereby limiting the divergence of interests between owners and managers.

Market supply curve (or **industry supply curve**): in the short run, the horizontal summation of all the price-taker firms' supply curves.

Markup pricing: a pricing technique whereby a certain percentage of cost of goods sold or of price is added to cost of goods sold, in order to obtain the selling price.

Maturity date: in reference to a bond, the date on which the principal or amount borrowed will be repaid.

Maximin strategy: a strategy designed to maximize the minimum expected payoff from a given action.

Meet-or-release clause: a supplier's contractual agreement that if a rival supplier offers to sell the same product to the buyer at a lower price during the contract period, the seller will either match that lower price or release the customer from its contractual obligations.

Microeconomics: the study of the economic behavior of individual decision makers–consumers and firms–and the markets in which they interact.

Minimum efficient scale: the lowest rate of output at which minimum long-run average costs are achieved.

Money income: income defined in current dollars or purchasing power.

Monitor: in team production, a person assigned to observe and meter the effort of each team member.

Monitoring costs: resources invested in observing and controlling the behavior of an agent or a production team.

Monopolistic competition: a market structure characterized by the existence of many firms in the industry (but with an element of product differentiation so that each firm has some control over price) and by free entry into and exit from the industry.

Moral hazard: a situation in which one party to a contract has an incentive after the contract is made to alter behavior in a way that harms the other party to the contract.

Most-favored-nation clause: a supplier's contractual guarantee that the price a buyer pays will be the lowest price at which the seller supplies the same product to any of its other customers.

Multi-part pricing: a pricing strategy involving multiple or variable prices for a product.

Multi-plant firms: firms which operate at various locations within a country and around the world as divisions of multinational enterprises.

Multidivisional firm (or **M-form firm**): a firm in which a central office allocates resources and coordinates the activities of two or more semi-independent operating divisions.

Mutual nonprofits: nonprofit organizations controlled by their members, who select the board of directors and officers.

Mutually exclusive projects: projects whose relationship is such that the acceptance of one necessarily implies the rejection of the other.

Net cash flow: any increase in revenues brought about by the project less any increase in operating expenses and depreciation, multiplied by $(1-t)$, where t is the firm's marginal income tax rate. The incremental depreciation associated with the project is then added to the preceding sum.

Net income after tax: income remaining after deducting all relevant expenses and paying all required taxes.

Net income before tax: income remaining after deducting all relevant expenses but before paying taxes.

Net investment: in capital budgeting, the current year outlays required to implement the project.

Net present value: the present value of the net cash inflows minus the present value of the cost outflows of an investment. An investment project is acceptable if its net present value is greater than or equal to zero.

Nondiversifiable risk (or **systematic risk**): the variability in the expected returns to stock ownership that is common to all securities.

Normal goods: products or services with positive income elasticities of demand.

Oligopoly: a market structure characterized by the existence of a few dominant firms in an industry (each of which recognizes their mutual interdependence) and by substantial barriers to entry into the industry.

Open market: a market which allows the free entry and exit of resources; a market with low barriers to entry and exit.

Operating leverage: the relative mix of fixed and variable inputs in the production process.

Opportunistic behavior: taking advantage of opportunities with little or no regard for the well-being of others; self-interest seeking with guile.

Opportunity cost: the benefit expected from the best alternative forgone when an item or activity is chosen.

Order backlog: orders in excess of inventory and current production rates.

Ordinary demand functions: demand curves derived from observations of consumer behavior, reflecting substitution effects and income effects.

Ownership integration: the merging of two or more firms into a single economic entity.

Partnership: a firm with multiple owners who share the firm's profits and who each bear unlimited liability for the firm's debts.

Payback period: the length of time required for summed future benefits of an investment to equal summed costs.

Payoff matrix: a table showing the expected benefits from various possible courses of action.

Perfect factor mobility: ability to reallocate resources readily among various uses both within and across firms.

Perfect knowledge: free accessibility to all relevant information in a market, for all buyers and sellers.

Perfect substitutes: two different inputs with identical production characteristics.

Pigou tax: (named after British economist Arthur Pigou) a tax on a producer, designed to maintain a socially optimal level of production when external (third party) costs exceed the producer's gains.

Plant capacity: the rate of output at which the plant's per unit costs of production are as low as possible.

Point elasticity of demand: the elasticity of demand at a particular point on the demand curve.

Predatory pricing: pricing tactics employed by a dominant firm to drive competitors out of business, such as temporarily selling below cost and dropping the price only in certain markets.

Price discrimination: charging consumers in different markets different prices for the same product (based on the price elasticity of demand in each market).

Price elasticity of demand: a measure of the relative responsiveness of quantity demanded of a product to a change in its price. The price elasticity of demand indicates how the seller's total revenue will change as a result of a change in price.

Price skimming: introduction of a product at a relatively high price followed by successive price reductions over time, to take advantage of the willingness of some consumers to pay higher prices than others.

Price-searcher: a firm that has some control over the price it charges because its demand curve slopes downward.

Price-taker: a firm that faces a given market price for its output and whose actions have no effect on the market price.

Principal: a person who enters into a contractual agreement with an agent in the expectation that the agent will act on behalf of the principal.

Prisoners' dilemma: a situation in which there are mutual gains from cooperation, but greater individual benefits from undetected noncooperative behavior.

Producer surplus: the difference between the minimum amount a producer must receive to supply a unit of output and what the producer actually receives.

Product bundling: selling two or more products together at a price that is less than the sum of the prices that would be charged if the products were sold separately.

Production efficiency (or **technical efficiency**): within an industry, production of output by the optimal number of firms, each of which employs its production capacity at the efficient (cost-minimizing) rate. Or, generally, production of the maximum possible quantity of output from a given set of inputs.

Production function: a mathematical statement of the way that the quantity of output of a product depends on the quantities used of various inputs or resources.

Profit maximization: making the difference between total revenue and total cost as large as possible.

Profit-sharing firm: a firm which gives workers a share of its net profits.

Profitability index: the ratio of the present value of a project's future net cash flows to the required initial investment outlay.

Property rights: rights associated with resource ownership.

Public enterprises: nonprofit government firms.

Public good: a good that once produced is available for all to consume, regardless of who pays and who does not, and which is also characterized by nonrivalry in consumption: the amount consumed by one individual does not reduce the amount available for others to consume.

Pure monopoly: a closed price-searcher market in which a single firm sells a product having no close substitutes.

Putting-out system: a manufacturing arrangement in which a merchant or artisan contracts with other individuals to supply parts or components of the final product.

Quality attribute: a product characteristic rated by actual performance or value to the consumer. Represented as quantity multiplied by quality grade.

Quality grade: a standardized rating for the quality of a product.

Quantity demanded: the quantity demanded of a good as affected by changes in the price of that good, holding all other variables constant.

Quasi-rent: for the owner of a resource, revenue minus operating costs minus salvage value.

Ratchet effect: in pricing, an irreversible change in sales volume as a result of a price change.

Rate base: the value of a regulated firm's capital.

Rate-of-return regulation: a government regulation which sets an output price that allows the owners of the regulated firm to earn only a "fair" return on their investment.

Real income: income measured in terms of the goods and services it can buy.

Regulatory lag: in rate-of-return regulation, the time elapsed between changes in a public utility's costs and adjustments to the rate schedule.

Rent: the payment resource owners receive over and above the resource's value in its next best alternative use.

Rent seeking: activities undertaken by individuals or firms to influence public policy in a way that will directly or indirectly redistribute income to themselves; any effort by individuals or firms to obtain favorable treatment from government.

Requirements contract: a commitment by a buyer to purchase all of its supplies of a particular good or service from a specified seller.

Resale price maintenance: a contractual provision in which the manufacturer and the retailers that carry its product mutually agree to set a limit on the price charged to the good's final consumers.

Reservation price: the highest price a buyer is willing to offer, or the lowest price a seller is willing to accept.

Residual: in the classical capitalist firm, profit or loss remaining after team production output has been sold and the team members have been paid.

Residual claimant: in team production with a classical capitalist firm, a monitor who has the right to keep all of the income generated by the team's productive activities not owed by contract to the team members.

Residual loss: in a principal-agent relationship, any reduction in welfare suffered by the principal due to the agent's failure to maximize the principal's wealth.

Returns to scale: changes in output when all inputs are increased by the same multiple (e.g., doubled or tripled).

Ridge lines: the lines connecting the points where the marginal product of an input is equal to zero (one line for each input) in the isoquant map and forming the boundary for the economic region of production.

Risk premium: an upward adjustment of a bond coupon rate to compensate for probability of default.

Satisficing: a cautious management approach involving the pursuit of multiple goals consistent with the long-run survival of the firm.

Search goods: products whose quality consumers can judge at the time of purchase.

Second-degree price discrimination: separating customers into two or more groups and charging the same price to all buyers in a given group.

Security market line: a graphed line representing the relationship between a firm's cost of equity capital and the systematic risk characteristics of the company's stock.

Self-selection: the tendency of consumers to identify themselves to the seller as high- or low-intensity users by their choice or refusal of insurance or warranty protection.

Share transferability: the right of stockholders to sell their shares without consulting the other owners of the firm.

Shirk: to evade responsibilities, neglect details, and reduce work effort.

Short run: a time period sufficiently short that at least one input is fixed.

Short-run production function: a function used to analyze the technological relationship between input usage and output based on a single plant size.

Signal: use a proxy measure to communicate information about unobservable characteristics.

Slope: a measure of the steepness of a line, expressed as the ratio of the change in the value measured along the vertical axis to the change in the value measured along the horizontal axis.

Socialist firm: a firm wholly owned and managed by its workers, the state, or some other collective entity.

Sole proprietorship: a firm with a single owner who has the right to all profits and who bears unlimited liability for the firm's debts.

Staff officers: in a functional firm, managers who head units providing ancillary goods or services to other parts of the firm.

Strategic decision: a decision affecting the future direction of an entire enterprise.

Substitutes: products or services that can be substituted for one another and that have a positive cross-price elasticity of demand.

Substitution effect: When the price of a good falls, consumers will substitute it for other goods, which are now relatively more expensive.

Sunk costs: costs that cannot be recovered and that are therefore irrelevant when an economic choice is being made.

Superior goods: goods exhibiting an income elasticity of demand greater than 1.

Systematic risk (or **nondiversifiable risk**): the variability in the expected returns to stock ownership that is common to all securities.

Tactical decision: a decision involving matters of relatively short-term consequence.

Target weights: weighted averages used in estimating a firm's overall cost of capital based on the assumption that the optimal capital structure differs from the present structure.

Team production: production in which several different resources are employed, the final product is greater than the sum of the separate parts, and not all of the resources used in the production process are owned by the same individual.

Technical efficiency (or **production efficiency**): production of the maximum possible quantity of output from a given set of inputs.

Technological independence: within a multidivisional firm, interdivisional independence such that the operating costs of one division are not affected by the level of operations carried out in another division.

Technology transfer: movement of capital, production techniques, and knowhow to a foreign market.

Third-degree price discrimination: separating customers into two or more subgroups based on differences in their elasticities of demand, and charging a higher price to the group whose demand is less elastic.

Tied good: a good whose purchase is required, as a condition of sale, in conjunction with the purchase of another product from the same seller.

Total product curve: the curve that represents the relation between labor input and output.

Total variable cost: total dollar amount of costs that vary with the level of output.

Transaction: an exchange within the firm or on the market.

Transaction costs: the costs of time and information required to carry out an exchange.

Transfer pricing: pricing of goods and services that a firm exchanges internally among its divisions or units.

Transitive statements: statements involving consistent relationships when comparisons are made among three or more entities (for example, if A > B and B > C, then A > C).

Trilateral governance: an agreement between buyer and seller to accept third-party assistance in the resolution of disputes.

Two-part tariff: the combination of an entry fee plus a per-unit charge for specific services or products.

Tying good: a good whose purchase, as a condition of sale, requires the purchase from the same seller of some other good.

Unit cost time line: same as **learning curve**.

Unit elastic: the type of demand that exists when a percentage change in price causes an equal percentage change in quantity demanded; the elasticity value is one.

Unsystematic risk (or **diversifiable risk**): the variability in the expected returns to owning stock in a specific company.

Utility: the amount of pleasure or satisfaction an individual derives from consuming a particular bundle of goods and services.

Variable proportions technology: technology which can produce the same quantity of output with different combinations of inputs.

Vertical integration: the expansion of a firm into stages of production earlier or later than those in which it has specialized.

Vertical merger: a merger in which one firm combines with another from which it purchases inputs or to which it sells output.

Weighted average cost of capital: a firm's overall cost of capital as influenced by the before-tax rate of return required by bondholders, the rate of return required by shareholders, the marginal corporate income tax rate, and the relative proportions of debt and equity in the firm's capital structure.

Yield: in reference to a bond, the anticipated risk-adjusted rate of return.

Zero-coupon bond: a bond which promises no payments to the holder until the stated maturity date.

Index